"COMBINING SERVICE AND LEARNING is an essential resource for all those interested in establishing their own community service programs. This comprehensive book successfully blends some of the most thoughtful perspectives on service to date, with practical advice from those in the field. A 'must' for those who wish to connect learning to life." — *Ernest Boyer, President, Carnegie Foundation for the Advancement of Teaching*

"This is a useful distillation of the lessons learned in the last two decades about programs that combine service, citizenship, and education. Practical examples and the principles that seem essential for success are highlighted. As the nation seeks opportunities to provide this kind of experience to more of our people, this is a valuable resource." — *David Broder, National Political Correspondent and Columnist, THE WASHINGTON POST*

"COMBINING SERVICE AND LEARNING is an excellent resource for both teachers and community persons interested in expanding students' awareness of social concerns. Of special interest to me are the sections on successful and unsuccessful programs, and what factors contributed to their success or failure. We as educators must encourage young people to become more involved in meaningful activities that will break down pre-conceived cultural prejudices." — *Ninon H. Cheek, 1989 Wake County Teacher of the Year and 7th Grade Language Arts Teacher in Raleigh, North Carolina*

"COMBINING SERVICE AND LEARNING is an impressive, comprehensive book on service programs. The massive task of assembling this reference work will pay real dividends as Americans recognize the benefits which accompany programs for service and learning." — *Bill Clinton, Governor of Arkansas*

"This is a valuable and important book — one much needed at this time, when community service is becoming more and more a part of the lives of so many young people." — *Robert Coles, Professor of Psychiatry and Medical Humanities, Harvard University, and Pulitzer Prize winning author, CHILDREN IN CRISIS and THE MORAL LIFE OF CHILDREN*

"At a time when many in our country doubt our ability to tackle our social ills, these volumes appear and give us example after example of how we can take charge and build a more productive and humane society. These volumes reflect the rich diversity of creative community leadership. Seldom does one see combined in one work such an array of best practices *and* scholarly analysis of the dynamics behind such successful cases."

— *David DeVries, Executive Vice President*
Center for Creative Leadership

"This extraordinary book looks at service-learning from all the angles that matter. It shows how our democracy might become better when students are properly prepared to take civic action. It shows how our colleges and universities might engage more fully in learning — and in life!"

— *Zelda Gamson, Professor of Sociology,*
University of Massachusetts at Boston;
Author, LIBERATING EDUCATION; and
Director, New England Resource Center
for Higher Education

"Instilling good citizenship is fundamental to a high-quality education. COMBINING SERVICE AND LEARNING offers a thorough and thoughtful roadmap for those who seek to enrich students' understanding of the communities and nation in which they live."

— *Senator Nancy Kassebaum (R-Kansas)*

"Community service deserves to become part of the education of every student in America, from kindergarten through college. In COMBINING SERVICE AND LEARNING, the field's leading experts explain why — and how to make it work effectively in every community. This essential handbook can help educators bring the concept of community service to life for millions of students across the country."

— *Senator Edward Kennedy (D-Massachusetts)*

"COMBINING SERVICE AND LEARNING breaks new ground by offering the most comprehensive rationale and in-depth presentation yet for service-learning. Rather than extending broadly and sometimes superficially, as have many recent publications, this three-volume set reaches deeply to the roots of service-learning, demonstrating its well-developed theory and wide-ranging practice. It gathers from among the liveliest and best informed writers, making the exercise of reading this ambitious collection an enjoyable task.

The entire set is a 'must' for those who are serious about the integration of this important method into the mainstream of education." — *James Kielsmeier, President*
National Youth Leadership Council

"An important, impressive, and inclusive compilation of information about programs at all levels of education that use experience in serving our communities and fellow citizens as a basis for learning. This comprehensive handbook is an essential reference and guide for all who seek to actively engage young and old to learn through service. I can't think of a better way for people in a democracy to learn." — *Ed Meade, Chief Program Officer (retired)*
Ford Foundation

"An excellent resource for the research and practice of education. This collection provides a wealth of information for creating effective service-learning programs at all levels. NSIEE has done a yeoman's task in compiling what will be an invaluable tool to everyone interested in teaching and learning."
— *Suzanne Morse, Director of Programs*
Kettering Foundation

"COMBINING SERVICE AND LEARNING is an important and unique contribution to the community service efforts taking place in schools and colleges across the entire country. I hope it will be used extensively in colleges and schools because these volumes represent the most comprehensive collection of information on the educational value of community service."
— *Frank Newman, President,*
Education Commission of the States, and
Co-Founder, Campus Compact

"The spirit of young people and the practical examples and ideas in this book will make community service a trademark of future generations." — *Brian O'Connell, President, Independent Sector*

"The student community service movement of the '90s truly stands on the shoulders of giants. You will find no other collection of essays like this one where service-learning leaders speak out critically, historically, and with deep conviction. COOL is proud to be a collaborating organization for this vital text."
— *Julia Scatliff, Executive Director*
Campus Outreach Opportunity League

COMBINING SERVICE AND LEARNING

A Resource Book for Community and Public Service

Volume I

by Jane C. Kendall and Associates

A publication of the
National Society for Internships and Experiential Education

in partnership with the
**Mary Reynolds Babcock Foundation
and the Charles F. Kettering Foundation**

and in collaboration with
91 national and regional organizations

 **National Society for Internships
and Experiential Education**

Jane C. Kendall and Associates, *Combining Service and Learning:*
A Resource Book for Community and Public Service,
Raleigh, North Carolina: National Society for Internships
and Experiential Education

International Standard Book Number (ISBN): 0-937883-08-5
Library of Congress Catalog Number: 90-060427

Cover design by Tracy Wang, Sabine Moore, and Carol Majors
Production by Publications Unlimited
Printed in the United States of America

Table of Contents for Volume I

Intellectual Development

Cross-Cultural Learning

Leadership Development

Moral and Ethical Development

Strategies for Institutional Change

PART V: HISTORY AND FUTURE OF THE SERVICE-LEARNING MOVEMENT

Important: See the Other Two Volumes!

This volume is only part of a three-volume resource book on combining service and learning. All three volumes are intended to go together as a coherent whole. Volume I contains essential principles, theories, rationales, research, institutional and public policy issues and guides, and the history and future of service-learning. Volume II contains practical issues and ideas for programs and courses that combine service and learning, as well as case studies of programs in diverse settings. Volume III is an annotated bibliography of the literature in the field.

Preface

COMBINING SERVICE AND LEARNING is a treasure trove of practical guidance for addressing the national crisis of public disengagement. The 1980s' celebration of individual gratification robbed our young people of a vision of the rewards of active citizenship. As we enter the 1990s, all Americans concerned about our future are asking how we can prepare today's youth to meet the unprecedented challenges of the 21st century. COMBINING SERVICE AND LEARNING is a major contribution to answering this question. It offers both inspiration and concrete lessons for re-engaging young people.

COMBINING SERVICE AND LEARNING pulls no punches. It does not romanticize learning through community experience. It clearly poses the toughest questions. Leaders in the field ask what is necessary to turn a community service activity into a practice that builds the capacities and ongoing commitments of all involved.

In one place, COMBINING SERVICE AND LEARNING is the collected wisdom of decades of experience and reflection. It can well serve to spur a national dialogue on the meaning of democracy itself. As a people we simply can no longer afford to teach our youth that being a good citizen means not causing trouble and that democracy is merely a set of fixed institutions we have inherited. This impressive work can go far in helping to redefine democracy as the problem-solving practices of active citizens, and schools as places where citizens learn the rewarding arts of democracy.

— *Frances Moore Lappé*
Author, DIET FOR A SMALL PLANET
Director, Institute for Food and Development Policy
and Project Public Life

Cooperating Organizations

Combining Service and Learning: A Resource Book for Community and Public Service is a publication of the National Society for Internships and Experiential Education (NSIEE). This massive, three-year project was done in partnership with the Mary Reynolds Babcock Foundation in Winston-Salem, North Carolina, and the Charles F. Kettering Foundation in Dayton, Ohio. NSIEE and the users of this resource book are also grateful to the following organizations which graciously cooperated with NSIEE in this project:

ACCESS: Networking in the Public Interest
American Association for Higher Education
American Association of State Colleges and Universities
American Association of University Women
American Council on Education
American Institute for Public Service
American Political Science Association
American Sociological Association
American Youth Foundation
Association for Community-Based Education
Association for Experiential Education
Association for Volunteer Administration
Association of American Colleges
Association of Episcopal Colleges
Association of Voluntary Action Scholars
Campus Compact
Campus Outreach Opportunity League
Carnegie Foundation for the Advancement of Teaching
Center for Creative Community
Center for Creative Leadership
Center for Global Education, Augsburg College
Center for Youth Development and Research, University of Minnesota
Commission on Voluntary Service and Action
Community Service Volunteers, United Kingdom
Constitutional Rights Foundation
Cooperative Education Association
Council for Adult and Experiential Learning
Council for the Advancement of Citizenship
Council of Chief State School Officers
Council of Independent Colleges
Council on Social Work Education
Education Commission of the States
Educators for Social Responsibility
Executive High School Internship Association
Facing History and Ourselves National Foundation
Fund for the Improvement of Postsecondary Education, U.S. Department of
    Education
Great Lakes Colleges Association, The Philadelphia Center
Higher Education Consortium for Urban Affairs
Independent Sector

Institute for Food and Development Policy
Intercultural Development Research Association
International Christian Youth Exchange
The Johnson Foundation
Maryland Student Service Alliance, Maryland Department of Education
Michigan Campus Compact
Minnesota Association for Field Experience Learning
Minnesota Campus Service Initiative
Minnesota Youth Service Association
National Association for Equal Opportunity in Higher Education
National Association of Independent Schools
National Association of Partners in Education
National Association of Schools of Public Affairs and Administration
National Association of Secondary School Principals
National Association of Service and Conservation Corps
National Association of State Boards of Education
National Association of Student Employment Administrators
National Association of Student YMCAs
National Center for Effective Schools, University of Wisconsin
National Civic League
National Coalition of Alternative Community Schools
National Commission on Resources for Youth/Institute for Responsive Education
National Commission on the Public Service
National Community Education Association
National Conference on Governors' Schools
National Crime Prevention Council
National Governors' Association
National Institute for Work and Learning, Academy for Educational Development
National Service Secretariat
National Youth Leadership Council
New York State Cooperative and Experiential Education Association
North Carolina Youth Advocacy and Involvement Office
Operation Civic Serve
Overseas Development Network
Partnership for Service-Learning
PennServe
Project Service Leadership
SerVermont
Society for Intercultural Education, Training and Research
Society for Values in Higher Education
Southern Regional Education Board
Thomas Jefferson Forum
United Negro College Fund
VISTA/Community Service, ACTION
VOLUNTEER: The National Center
The Washington Center
YMCA of the USA
Youth and America's Future: The William T. Grant Foundation Commission on
   Work, Family, and Citizenship
Youth Policy Institute
Youth Service America

About the
The National Society for Internships and Experiential Education

THE NATIONAL SOCIETY FOR INTERNSHIPS AND EXPERIENTIAL EDUCATION is a national resource center and professional association that supports the use of *learning through experience* for civic and social responsibility, intellectual development, cross-cultural awareness, moral/ethical development, career exploration, and personal growth.

NSIEE's mission: As a community of individuals, institutions, and organizations, NSIEE is committed to fostering the effective use of experience as an integral part of education, in order to empower learners and promote the common good.

NSIEE's goals are:

- to advocate for the effective use of experiential learning throughout the educational system and the larger community;
- to disseminate information on principles of good practice and on innovations in the field;
- to enhance professional growth and leadership development in the field;
- to encourage the development and dissemination of related research and theory.

Experiential education includes community and public service when combined with learning, internships, field studies, intercultural programs, leadership development, cooperative education, experiential learning in the classroom, outdoor education, and all forms of active learning.

NSIEE's services include conferences, workshops, publications, newsletters, the National Resource Center on Service and Learning, professional network services, and in-depth consulting for program and institutional planning. See pages 485-495 for membership information and a publications list.

NSIEE was founded in 1971 as the National Center for Public Service Internship Programs and the Society for Field Experience Education. NSIEE's national office is in Raleigh, North Carolina.

To Ran

*for a lifetime of combining
service and learning*

Combining Service and Learning: An Introduction

Jane C. Kendall

This chapter explains who the intended readers for this three-volume resource book are, how history makes this a particularly important time for such a resource, the purposes of the resource book, how it was developed, and the language used in it. The last section provides a quick walk through each of the three volumes.

Who Is This Book For?

THIS THREE-VOLUME RESOURCE BOOK is for anyone who wants to start, strengthen, or support a program or course that combines community or public service with learning. It is also for anyone who is in a position to make decisions about funding or policies that create or affect such efforts. And finally, it is for those who want to explore the philosophical, historical, conceptual, and cultural contexts of their efforts related to integrating service and learning.

The chapters are geared toward those with different levels of experience. Newcomers will find essential principles and practical tips about where to start. Veterans will find plenty of substance with which to struggle and debate. This three-volume book is written for educators, students, policymakers, legislators, program directors, foundation staffs and trustees, corporate executives, parents, and citizens.

This book covers policies, issues, and programs in **colleges and universities, K-12 schools, community-based organizations, public agencies at all levels, youth agencies,** and others that combine community and public service with learning. All three volumes contain sections of interest to people in all these settings. Because many readers will be interested in the chapters written from the perspective of those in similar roles or settings, some of these perspectives and the particular sections or authors that present

them are pointed out below. You can also use the authors' affiliations listed in the Table of Contents to identify the chapters written
by your closest counterparts. *Please do not limit yourself to this narrow
approach, however, because one of the primary purposes for this resource
book is to give you quick access to the valuable lessons in different settings
that can be applied in your own context.*

Educators and Students. This resource book is for educators
interested in educating students for social and civic responsibility.
It is written for those who are concerned about their students'
intellectual development, their awareness of other cultures, their
moral and ethical development, their ability to provide effective
leadership, their capacity for civic judgment and participation, their
career development, and their personal growth. The first chapter of
Volume I, "Principles of Good Practice in Combining Service and
Learning," is the place for educators to start. Although written from
very different perspectives, most of the chapters in Volume I are
intended for educators at all levels. The program profiles in Volume
II provide case studies of courses and programs at the elementary,
middle school, high school, undergraduate, and graduate levels.
Volume III provides an annotated bibliography of other resources
available.

College and University Educators. This resource book is writ-
ten for those in a variety of positions at colleges and universities.
Neale Berte, Don Kennedy, William O'Connell, John Stephenson,
Neil Thorburn, David Warren, and Clyde Williams share their per-
spectives as *presidents* of institutions. Barry Heerman, Warren
Martin, Sharon Rubin, Robert Sexton, Ormond Smythe, and Urban
Whitaker write from an academic administrator's point of view.

Articles for and by *faculty* are a significant part of each section of
the book. Dwight Giles, Glen Gish, Edmund Gleazer, Barbara
Hursh, Louis Iozzi, David Moore, Ed O'Neil, Virgil Peterson, and
Michele Whitham are among those who write here from a faculty
perspective. Harvard's Robert Coles suggests in a lively interview
with *Change* editor Art Levine that public service begins in faculty
members' *own* experiences, and Urban Whitaker lists basic principles faculty can use to assess the learning derived from community service experiences. *Student affairs* perspectives are voiced
eloquently by Jim Case, William Ramsay, and several others. *Directors and staff members of programs* that combine service and learning
speak through the chapters by Richard Couto, John Duley, Barbara
Hofer, Jane Permaul, Steve Schultz, Tim Stanton, and others.

John Farr describes a student-initiated seminar at Stanford. Jamille Freed, Tom Gerth, Kim Gross, Rosemary Klie, Gary Steele, and Jane Zimmermann also give voice to *students'* perspectives. And finally, *researchers'* findings and views are presented by Diane Hedin, Nancy Gansneder and Paul Kingston, Fred Newmann, Rick Williams, and by Marc Ventresca and Anna Waring with Jeanne Wahl Halleck.

K-12 Educators. Authors in all three volumes of this resource book include K-12 school superintendents, principals, teachers, counselors, program directors, school board members, educational association representatives, researchers, and others. In addition to the "Principles of Good Practice" in the first chapter, "A Nation at Risk: Another View" is essential reading. So are the Part II chapters by Diane Hedin and Dan Conrad, Ernest Boyer, Shelley Berman, Ralph Tyler, James Kielsmeier and Rich Willits, Rob Shumer, and Fred Newmann. Alonzo Crim and William Cirone write from a superintendent's perspective. If you are from a private school, see Lee Levison's chapters. Read Cheryl Keen's if you are interested in Governors' Schools.

Most of Part III in Volume I focuses on public policy issues related to K-12 education. David Hornbeck provides a provocative view, and policy statements from the National Association of State Boards of Education, the Council of Chief State School Officers, and others offer useful guidelines.

In Part IV, see *Foxfire's* Eliot Wigginton's comments, Dan Conrad's funny and persuasive "Arguments for Educators," and the pro/con views on required versus voluntary community service (Levison, Klie, Steele). Conrad, Cathryn Berger Kaye, and NSIEE offer excellent practical advice for gaining support from teachers and administrators.

Volume II is full of specific ideas and advice. See the chapters from Michael Goldstein, Diane Hedin and Dan Conrad, John Duley, Barry Fenstermacher, Urban Whitaker, and ACTION. And see Kate McPherson's ideas for finding class time for service! Part III in Volume II provides 55 pages of short, meaty case studies of specific programs and courses in both public and private schools, from first grade through twelfth. See the annotated bibliography in Volume III for further references.

Community-Based and Agency-Based Leaders. For those in community or government organizations, youth-serving agencies, or other nonprofits, the "Principles of Good Practice" at the beginning of Volume I are the first stop. In Part II, Robert Sigmon's chapters on principles and on the use of these principles in the workplace are also excellent. Howard Berry, Nadinne Cruz, and Ivan Illich offer valuable international perspectives. Rick Jackson and Keith Morton provide ideas useful for youth programs. In Part III, James Kielsmeier and Rich Willits outline approaches used in Minnesota that could be adapted in any state. In Part V, the chapters by Alec Dickson, James Case, and Robert Sigmon raise stirring ideas for organizations and communities everywhere.

Volume II begins with a list of specific project ideas for students and other service-learners — ideas that might help out on your organization's staff load. Michael Goldstein addresses the legal questions that managers often ask about hosting students. Diane Hedin and Dan Conrad outline models plus practical tips for re- cruitment, transportation, and evaluation in youth programs. Wil- liam Ramsay provides wise counsel about supervision and the rela- tionships between schools and the organizations that host their students. Marilyn Mecham and I suggest ways to utilize students effectively in your organization. In Part II, Irene Pinkau gives an international perspective. Part IV contains 55 pages of valuable case studies of specific programs that are working, including firsthand advice from those who coordinate them — in a migrant farmwork- ers' center, a public interest group, an intergenerational program, several state and city governments, a federal agency, three founda- tions, a botanical garden, and with the Cherokee Nation. Volume III provides references for other resources available.

Public Policy Leaders. For public policymakers and their staffs, the first chapter of Volume I, "Principles of Good Practice," is the place to start. Part II of Volume I offers plenty of ammunition for proposing policies that combine community and public service with learning. The chapter entitled "A Nation at Risk: Another View" is a good short one. The chapters by Rick Williams, Dan Conrad, and Diane Hedin provide useful research data. See Tim Stanton's two chapters and the one by Shelley Berman if you are interested in higher education's role in developing students' citizenship and leadership skills. Cheryl Keen's chapter is about the New Jersey Governor's School on Public Issues and the Future.

All of Part III focuses on public policy issues, mostly related to youth and young adults. Start with the chapter from the Grant Commission. If you are interested in state policy, see the National Governors' Association chapter, the summaries of state initiatives, and Jim Kielsmeier's chapter on Minnesota. For education policy at the state or local levels, also see the chapters by David Hornbeck and Claire Cunningham and the policy statement from the National Association of State Boards of Education.

Part IV is for those interested in the challenges faced by local institutions; some have implications for public policy. The chapters by Lee Levison, Rosemary Klie, and Gary Steele discuss the pros and cons in the "mandatory versus voluntary service" debate. Part V lists the federal programs related to community service and offers a useful historical perspective and a glimpse at the future.

Volume II provides examples of how policies might look in practice — and some of the problems they might create on the local and state levels. Michael Goldstein's chapter in Part I covers legal issues related to service-learning programs. In Part II, Irene Pinkau compares policies and programs in several countries. Part IV describes the California Human Corps legislation, provides case studies of several government-sponsored programs, and outlines creative approaches related to migrant farmworkers, older persons, and the environment. Volume III is a useful annotated bibliography for further research by policy analysts and committee staffs. All three volumes can help in responding to constituents' requests.

Foundation Executives and Trustees. The most important chapter for foundation executives and trustees is the first chapter of Volume I, "Principles of Good Practice in Combining Service and Learning," because it provides an important *checklist for evaluating grant proposals.*

Part II provides many useful ideas for those refining or rethinking your foundation's priorities; see the Table of Contents for the chapters most relevant to your concerns. Those who lean toward philosophical questions will enjoy Parker Palmer's fine chapter. "A Nation at Risk: Another View" and Tim Stanton's chapter on socially responsible education are good reading for foundation leaders concerned about the future of education. Separate sections on social and civic responsibility, intellectual development (see Hedin and Conrad), cross-cultural learning (Berry, Cruz), leadership (Gardner, Stanton, Berman, Jackson, Morton), moral and ethical development, and career exploration make it easy to find the parts related to your interests. Part III of Volume I is for funders of public policy research and development.

See Part IV if you are interested in the important issues in gaining support for community and public service within colleges, universities, and K-12 schools. You can read *many* funding needs between the lines in this section. The strategies for organizational change discussed here may also be useful for your grantees in a variety of settings. Part V provides a useful historical perspective; the last five chapters raise stimulating questions for the future.

Volume II is full of program examples and tips valuable for foundation staffs and trustees evaluating proposals *and* for grantees and applicants. The Table of Contents and Index can help you find the chapters that fit your particular program interests, whether they relate to the effective design, administration, and evaluation of programs combining service and learning; the relationship between schools and their communities; or particular social issues — cultural diversity, hunger, the environment, literacy, dropouts, health, aging, consumer rights, drugs, the needs of persons with disabilities, and others. Volume III lists other resources available.

Corporate Executives. Thoughtful corporate executives interested in community affairs, socially responsible corporate leadership, and the future of education will find several parts of this resource book useful. Start with the first chapter of Volume I, "Principles of Good Practice in Combining Service and Learning." "A Nation at Risk: Another View" also provides good, quick reading. The chapters by Boyer, Conrad and Hedin, Stanton, Schultz, Morse, Newmann, Cirone, Rubin, Berry, Cruz, Gardner, Berman, Jackson and Morton, Iozzi, Gansneder and Kingston, the Grant Commission, Wigginton, and Dickson may be of particular interest in Volume I. Robert Sigmon's chapter in Part II explores how the principles in this resource book relate to the workplace. The sections in Part II on leadership and on education for social/civic responsibility are important for the development of socially responsible corporate leaders. James Case's provocative statement in Part V calls for acknowledgment of a significant role for business in the service-learning movement.

Volume II's chapters for supervisors in community agencies (Goldstein, Ramsay, Kendall, Mecham) will be helpful to your employees who supervise student interns. See Parts II, III, and IV for specific program ideas that might involve your employees and community in creative ways. See Volume III for further references.

Parents and Public-Spirited People. While most of this book is geared toward those directly involved in programs, courses, policies, or funding, it will also be of interest to public-spirited individuals and parents interested in how community and public service can be combined effectively with learning. All three volumes can provide fuel for the citizen's imagination and for public debate.

Why This Resource Book Now?

In the last half of the 1980s and the start of the 1990s, the surge of interest in involving young people and adults in public and community service experiences has been tremendous. Through the Overseas Development Network, University YMCAs, the Campus Outreach Opportunity League, and other groups, students have organized themselves to initiate programs. College and university presidents have formed a "Campus Compact" to call for an increased commitment of their institutions to public service. Tutoring programs have sprung up in communities across the country to try to address the problem of illiteracy. Community agencies have had to wrestle with how to involve hoards of volunteers in soup kitchens and shelters for homeless persons. Through the Independent Sector, leaders in the nonprofit sector have urged adults and youth to contribute five percent of their time and their income to the causes they support. While Eastern Europe struggles with democratic reforms, report after report has called for increasing the civic awareness and commitment of our young people through public service in our own democracy. With interest growing in legislation to foster youth community service, lawmakers are debating several proposed bills in this session of Congress.

This is an exciting time. Hands-on experiences in the community are essential for educating the next generation about human needs and for building among young and old a commitment to social responsibility in their careers and in their lives as active citizens. As Confucius' wisdom reminds us, "I read and I forget, I see and I remember, I *do* and I understand."

The Community Service Movement of the 1960s and 1970s. The current surge of interest and programs will be short-lived, however, if we fall into the same pitfalls that truncated a similar wave of interest in community and public service in the late 1960s and the early 1970s. In the early 1970s, students from campuses across the country were working in their communities through the national University Year for ACTION program. Volunteer and social action programs sprouted everywhere. Large urban corps programs developed in cities across the country to channel the energies and commitment of young people to help with the problems of the inner cities. Many young people and adults in diverse fields saw firsthand the tremendous potential for service and for learning that can be unleashed through direct involvement in the community.

But the student community service movement of the 1960s and 1970s did not last. Why? There were some very common — and in retrospect, predictable — pitfalls that brought about the demise of many of the programs that involved young people in public service. *And* we can learn some very important lessons and principles from this experience.

Lessons Learned. There are three primary lessons from the community service movement of the 1960s and 1970s that are important for us to build on today.

1. Most of the programs were not integrated into the central mission and goals of the schools and agencies where they were based. They generally remained separate both administratively and budgetarily. Thus, when money later ran tight, they were marginal to the institutions whose support they needed. Those based in colleges and high schools did not build service experience into the core curriculum, which is the main expression of what the institution believes is important for students to learn. As early as 1968, the American Council on Education had already identified the need for "institutional support for the service curriculum" as a major issue.[1] Faculty members participated out of their hip pockets and their hearts, but this participation was not taken into account in their course loads, and certainly not in their tenure decisions. As one political scientist at a major research university expressed it, "The university was very supportive of my teaching students about public service and public issues as long I did not ask for money, secretarial assistance, tenure, a blurb in the catalogue, or time at faculty meetings."

The same valuable lesson also came from the experiences of those who participated in the federal University Year for ACTION program (UYA), which from 1971 to 1979 involved more than 10,000 college students from 100 colleges and universities in community service projects. The UYA programs surviving today — for example, at the Universities of Rhode Island and Virginia — are those that built service-learning into the missions and curricula of their academic institutions. Most that did not have not survived. Roger Henry, now at Brevard Community College, lamented about his work in the 1970s with Kent State University's former UYA program, for example, with this comment: "We focused on getting students involved and did not pay enough attention to faculty. That was our downfall."[2] In addition, many campus programs were initiated by student affairs staff who lacked the clout to gain support in the coin of the academic realm — classes, full-time-equivalent students, and published research.

On the community side, organizations and agencies also did not structure the supervision of students into their regular staff workloads in a significant way. As with the colleges and high schools, most of the programs were "nice, but extras." In both cases, when the enthusiastic advocate left or the supportive faculty member moved on, there was no institutional base. There was no toehold in administrative structures and policies that helped to guarantee a continuing institutional commitment. Thus, many experienced the painful lesson of what happens when programs are not built into the fabric of the institutions and agencies where they are based.

2. *Those in the community service movement learned several important programmatic lessons about the balance of power and the pitfalls of "helping others" or "doing good."* As an undergraduate tutor of farm children outside Chapel Hill, North Carolina, from 1969 to 1971, I learned that universities and well-intentioned students cannot decide what "the community needs." When the superintendent invited us to "go back to the campus where you belong" and reminded us that he "didn't invite [us] to come teach [his] fifth graders how to do calculus anyway," I was given the vivid, firsthand lesson that people must decide what their own needs are and how those needs will be met.

In 1974, after working with some of the initiators of the service-learning movement in the Southeast, I went to my first conference of the Society for Field Experience Education and the National Center for Public Service Internship Programs, both founded in 1971. (These two merged in 1978 to form the National Society for Internships and Experiential Education.) There I found out that people involved in similar efforts across the country were learning the same painful lessons. We were learning that balancing and respecting the needs of the community organization, the community residents whom the programs were intended to serve, the student (most of that movement did involve students), and the school was more difficult than one would think. We were learning that without clear expectations, continuing mechanisms for negotiation, and respect for the differing goals and needs of each of these parties, programs eventually lose the support of the multiple parties whose full participation is necessary for continuation.

We were learning that without an emphasis on the relationship between the server and "those served" as a reciprocal exchange between equals, that relationship can easily break down. As Debbie Cotton observed in her work at the Volunteer Clearinghouse of the District of Columbia, "It is easy for the 'service' to become patronizing charity." Paternalism, unequal relationships between the parties involved, and a tendency to focus only on charity — "doing for" or "helping" others — rather than on supporting others to meet their own needs all became gaping pitfalls for program after well-intentioned program.

3. *We learned that while it sounds great to help young people learn through service experiences in the community, the service experience alone does not ensure that either significant learning or effective service will occur.* Learning from service experiences is not automatic or easy to facilitate. Critical reflection by the student on what is being learned in the service experience is essential, but developing program structures that support this is difficult. As I completed graduate school and began working with several programs for undergraduate and graduate students, I learned that just putting students into service projects was not enough, that it was also essential to help them prepare for the service experience and the learning, to monitor and support both their learning and their service performance during the experience, and to help them debrief, assimilate, and analyze what they learned after the experience. As Jim Keith, an official of Guilford College in Greensboro, North Carolina, says, "There's a real difference between just putting young people out into the community, which is relatively easy to do, and establishing thoughtful programs that foster real learning by young people and by those being served, which is hard to do."

A sign of the growing recognition of the importance of this reflective learning in conjunction with the service experience came in 1979 when the National Student Volunteer Program, begun in 1969 in the U.S. Office of Economic Opportunity, decided to change its name to the National Center for Service-Learning (NCSL). NCSL's strong staff, in touch with grassroots programs across the country, recognized that "volunteerism" and "service" alone were not enough. They saw that community service and learning are intricately interwoven. (NCSL was a major partner in the development of the service-learning concept in the 1970s and early 1980s. Since NCSL ended with political changes in the mid-80s, its considerable written resources have been distributed by the National Society for Internships and Experiential Education; selected parts of them are reprinted in this resource book.) And finally, we learned that the combination of service and learning, when done well, carries even more potential for individual and community development than anyone might have imagined.

The "Transition Team." A number of educators, community leaders, and students who saw or experienced the tremendous potential of such programs continued throughout the "me genera-tion" of the late 1970s and the 1980s to build on the lessons of this movement and to identify the factors that can help programs be *sustained* over time. A small, but committed group of people also struggled quietly with the question of what worked and what did not work in the early 1970s, as we tried to identify the elements that need to be incorporated into new programs that involve young people — and adults — in their communities in meaningful ways. It became clear to those of us involved in these "service-learning" ef-forts that there are several underlying principles of good practice that are essential, but difficult for effective programs. Some of the key principles are the need for critical reflection on experience, re-ciprocity of learning, a careful balance of power among all parties involved, and sustained support in the hearts and budgets of the institutions and organizations where the programs are based. Through experimentation and the exchange of ideas throughout the late 1970s and the 1980s, this "transition team" developed and refined several program models across the country that reflect these important principles.

Potential and Pitfalls of the Current Efforts. Imagine the joy to these torchbearers of "service-learning" to see a renewed interest in community and public service begin to catch fire in the late 1980s! The repeated calls for student and youth service and for educating students for social and civic responsibility are music to the ears of those who struggled to keep service-learning alive for a decade or two. We want this surge of interest to last, to be institutionalized in education's values and practices — rather than be just another ex-citing, but short-lived wave.

And imagine the pain of watching many of the current programs repeat the same mistakes of the 1960s and 1970s — the paternalism, the unequal relationships between the parties involved, the lack of emphasis on integrating learning with the service experience, the lack of attention to long-term institutional support, the emphasis on charity over social justice. Most of the new programs are unaware of the deep well of experience about specific models and approaches which could help them avoid those predictable pitfalls. For ex-ample, one school superintendent recently pointed out the problem of insufficient community input when he commented about college students volunteering to be tutors in his schools, "We don't want any more university students showing up on our doorstep saying 'We are here to help whether you want us or not.' We have had all of this type of help we can stand." When I heard a program director report that superintendent's comment, I understood what Yogi Berra meant when he said "It was *déjà vu* all over again!"

A Critical Juncture Now. The current surge of interest in community and public service is at a critical juncture now. Waves of interest only have a few years to become institutionalized — or they recede with the tide to the next idea wave that comes along. As new programs begun in the late 1980s enter their third, fourth, or even fifth year, they are bumping into the same problems that programs in the 1970s confronted: How do you involve the residents of a community in defining the service tasks? How do you balance and respect the differing goals of agencies, students, schools, and the individuals or groups whom these three have decided to "serve"? How do you gain the institutional support required for a strong, continuing program? How can schools and colleges assess what students learn through community and public service? What types of public and institutional policies create a climate of sustained support for combining service and learning? There is a growing realization of the need — and complexity — of combining service with learning, of integrating action in the community with reflection on the experience and with analysis of the issues addressed. As Bobby Hackett, former Co-Director of the student-run Campus Outreach Opportunity League and now a business student, remarked recently, "Now I see that the service experience needs to be carefully linked with the learning [process] in order to provide good service. We don't really know how to do that."[3]

In addition, many of the key actors — college and university presidents, school principals, young people, faculty, students, community leaders, program coordinators, lawmakers, foundations — are currently struggling to clarify what constitutes good practice and what their respective roles should be. The college presidents are acknowledging that faculty are the key to the long-term capacity of their institutions to commit to public service and to meaningful learning in the community. Most of the presidents know that the ownership and leadership for this initiative must come from within the ranks of respected faculty. In a five-year longitudinal study completed in 1989, the National Society for Internships and Experiential Education found there are two primary barriers to the full utilization of community-based learning in the 487 colleges and universities studied: (1) a lack of adequate faculty involvement and faculty skills in helping students integrate what they learn in the community and in the classroom, and (2) top-level administrative support.[4] A separate study completed in 1989 by Stanford University with Campus Compact's 150 schools found the same results.[5] And the ACE study identified the same barriers in 1968![6]

At the same time, public schools are struggling with how to educate students for civic participation in the midst of persistent calls for basic math and reading skills. *Will schools be able to make the case for civic literacy in this "back to basics" climate?* But then how basic is *civic literacy* for their students' future and for our own?

For educational institutions at all levels, the hard work of integrating public and community service experiences into the curriculum — when some liken the difficulty of curriculum change to that of moving a graveyard — is clearly the task at hand. As Sharon Rubin, Dean of the Fulton School of Liberal Arts at Salisbury State University, says, "The people who will make the biggest difference in the long-term viability of community service-learning programs are the faculty, administrators, and community leaders who are in a position to support the programs on a continuing basis. These key people need to be aware of the principles of good practice. They need to know what other schools and communities are doing so they don't waste precious time and money starting from scratch. Many are not aware of the resources they could draw upon."

As the students who sparked the recent interest on college campuses now graduate, they are realizing the difficulty of sustaining programs with transient student leadership. At the same time, community organizations are experiencing the challenge of incorporating large number of well-meaning, untrained, short-term, and sometimes self-righteous young people into their work and their organizations. Some of the foundations and corporations that funded the "early" programs of the mid-1980s are moving on to other interests, and some of them see the depth of the challenges that will have to be addressed for long-term institutionalization of these programs. And Congress is debating legislation that could have tremendous impact — or very little impact — on the future of these efforts. All these developments suggest that this is a time of tremendous opportunity — or quick death — for the current service-learning movement.

Other Contributing Trends. A number of other changes are afoot that make this a critical point in history and a time of great opportunity for efforts to combine service and learning. I will mention only two here. First, in addition to the increasing public expectation about the role of education in teaching the next generation to be responsible, productive citizens, the **undergraduate curriculum reform** efforts of the past decade continue to simmer. In 1987, Tim Stanton of Stanford University linked the two efforts when he wrote, "When effectively structured, facilitated, related to discipline-based theories and knowledge, and assessed ... service-based learning is the means to link the initiative to develop [students'] social responsibility ... with the efforts to improve undergraduate education. This evolving pedagogy of experience is key to ensuring the development of graduates who will participate in society actively, ethically and with an informed, critical habit of mind."[7] Parallel to curriculum reform are the disillusionment and frustration of many faculty which are being expressed both internally and externally — concern about the increasing specialization and isolation of the disciplines and the emptiness of the publish-or-perish race for tenure and promotion. And there is more public discussion about the high cost of college tuition coupled with the difficulty many graduates have with basic writing and multiplying.

Second, the movement for the **use of experience-based education** gained ground in academic institutions and K-12 schools in the 1980s. This is important for two reasons:

1. The *methods* of experiential education are the same as those needed for the effective combination of service and learning. These methods were better refined and articulated in the 1980s, thus offering a deeper body of knowledge — and greater potential for success — to the current community service advocates than was available to their counterparts in the 1960s and 1970s. There is more expertise about how to facilitate and assess the learning that is derived from experience, and there are now more courses that use field components. While the use of direct experience has always been a significant part of preparation for most professional and technical fields, more liberal arts faculty are now doing what the American Association of Colleges recommended in a 1988 report — building into their courses the active engagement of students in the subject matter.[8] In 1987, the very widely distributed "Seven Principles for Good Practice in Undergraduate Education" by Arthur Chickering and Zelda Gamson also acknowledged the importance of "active learning."[9]

2. A number of institutions now have more experience in dealing with the *institutional* issues that off-campus education raises. This growing sophistication increases the likelihood that more colleges and schools will be able to institutionalize service-learning as an integral part of their missions because they now have more administrative and curricular models for supporting the use of experience-based learning than they had in the 1970s.

Since 1983, for example, almost 500 institutions have participated in the National Project to Strengthen Experiential Education Within U.S. Colleges and Universities. Begun with two grants from the Fund for the Improvement of Postsecondary Education to the National Society for Internships and Experiential Education, this continuing NSIEE program now offers a cadre of experienced consultants who can help educators with the *internal*, institutional issues raised by the combination of service and learning.

Most campuses and schoolhouses still have a long way to go to offer the level of institutional support needed for full integration of community and public service experiences into their curriculum. But the increased acceptance and sophistication in some schools for the use of experiential learning approaches over the past decade create a potentially promising and timely climate for the current service-learning efforts.

The Purpose of This Resource Book. The purpose of this resource book is thus to pass on some of the lessons learned through the work of thousands of people over the past two decades — wise lessons that can support and sustain the current wave of interest in combining community and public service experiences with reflective learning and critical analysis. We have tried to do this in four ways through this book:

1. by articulating and discussing principles of good practice for effectively combining service and learning;
2. by making the best writing from the past two decades easily accessible to thoughtful advocates, practitioners, and policymakers;
3. by giving current thinkers, practitioners, and leaders from many arenas a forum in which to reflect on the issues and opportunities in the current movement; and
4. by involving in the development and dissemination of this resource book 91 key national and regional organizations which offer very diverse perspectives.

On a more personal note, doing this book ties together my own journey in the service-learning movement — as a student, as a coordinator of local, regional, and national programs, and finally as a student again of the philosophical, theoretical, and institutional issues behind this transforming social movement.

How Did This Resource Book Come About?

When the *National Society for Internships and Experiential Education (NSIEE)* observed the needs described above, we began talking in 1986 about ways to help those involved in the current movement to be more aware of the vast reservoir of experience and expertise that was developed during the 1960s and 1970s. We talked about how to get the best pieces from our rich collection of materials — many of them heavily used by practitioners and educators across the country but never published — into the public debate and into the hands of new and renewed practitioners. We wanted to help new programs and efforts avoid reinventing the wheel, pass on the lessons learned, and help the new movement both *deepen* (from "service" to "service-learning" approaches) and *last.* Several steps led from those concerns to this three-volume resource book.

First, to document the existing literature and make it accessible, the *NSIEE Service-Learning Special Interest Group* began work early in 1987 on an annotated bibliography of the existing published and unpublished literature, which was completed in 1988. Janet Luce and Tim Stanton of Stanford University, Jenny Anderson of UC-Santa Cruz, Jane Permaul and Rob Shumer of UCLA, and Sally Migliore of NSIEE worked for a year to identify, review, and summarize the best articles, books, and papers. They polled the leading thinkers and practitioners in the country to comb their files and review materials to be considered for inclusion. The result is Volume III of this resource book, entitled *Service-Learning: An Annotated Bibliography. Campus Compact,* a project of the Education Commission of the States representing a coalition of supportive college and university presidents, cooperated with NSIEE in this project.

Second, the *Charles F. Kettering Foundation* of Dayton, Ohio, worked in partnership with NSIEE to commission and publish four new papers for the fall 1987 NSIEE National Conference in Smugglers' Notch, Vermont. These papers, which formed the initial set of chapters for this book, explored several issues related to community and public service — the evolution of higher education's role in public service, the relationship of service experiences to education for civic and social responsibility, the role of the community, and the relationship of service-learning to traditional education.

Third, in 1987 NSIEE also began intensive work on articulating the principles of good practice that are important for the effective combination of community and public service with critical reflection and learning. The 30-month evolution of those principles from several early drafts to a widely distributed set of ten "Principles of

Good Practice in Combining Service and Learning" is described at the beginning of the first chapter of Volume I. This evolution was possible because of (1) the gracious participation of 77 other national and regional organizations that responded to NSIEE's invitation for input and debate, and (2) *The Johnson Foundation's* timely sponsorship of a May 1989 Wingspread Conference in Racine, Wisconsin, to write the final version. Hal Woods of the University of Vermont calls these principles of good practice "the most valuable resource in the field in twenty years." Allison Smith of the Volunteer Center of Marin County says, "This is what I've been waiting for — just what I need for our volunteer coordinators." The first 50,000 copies, printed in an attractive fold-out format by The Johnson Foundation, were gone within three months of their release in October 1989. Now deans are requesting copies for their faculty, national groups are sending them to their members, teachers are giving them to their principals, citizens are sending them to their Senators (and vice versa), and consultants to nonprofit groups are giving them to their clients. These ten principles are the cornerstone of this book and appear at the front of Volumes I and II.

Fourth, late in 1987, we decided after talking with practitioners across the country that what was really needed was a very broad-based resource book that reflected the diversity and breadth of the emerging field. This resource needed to incorporate a variety of terms, perspectives, service settings, and participant age levels. We invited 35 sister organizations with some expressed interest in the topic to cooperate with us to try to create the breadth of perspectives needed. All but three agreed readily and began to send in their best published or unpublished manuscripts for consideration.

I took a corner of our dining room table at home for what I envisioned to be a six-month project resulting in a 250-page book. Soon, the list of participating national organizations grew to 50, and manuscripts poured in from their members and from other practitioners across the country — classics from the past and new chapters written especially for this book. The corner of the dining table grew. It became clear that there was something very significant going on. People in the field wanted to take the time to write and reflect on their own experiences in developing programs and courses that combine service and learning. People were hungry to share the worn file copies of their most useful pieces they had used lovingly for a year, a decade, or more.

In the fall of 1988, we began the research for the program profiles which form the backbone of the second half of Volume II. People in the field spent days completing the long surveys and responding thoughtfully to NSIEE's endless questions. The *Mary*

Reynolds Babcock Foundation in Winston-Salem, North Carolina, provided timely financial support. Throughout 1988 and 1989, the leaders of the Cooperating Organizations reviewed drafts, sent more manuscripts that were bubbling up from their constituents' programs, and helped us think through how the book could be made most useful to their members. By the summer of 1989, 85 national and regional organizations were participating actively.

By now, invitations to friends to come over for dinner had ceased. The piles had taken over our whole dining room table, my office floor, the kitchen table, the kitchen counter, and the weekends. I read 150,000 pages of materials and skimmed that many more (not bad for a field that some claim does not have a literature base!). People from the NSIEE Service-Learning Special Interest Group, the NSIEE Board of Directors, and the Cooperating Organizations helped. The resource book grew to two volumes. When the printers said these were too thick to print easily, we decided to keep the bibliography as a separate volume.

In the spring of 1990, we finally gave birth to this three-volume, 1300-page resource book. There are two primary reasons it is so long. First, a total of *91 other national and regional groups worked with NSIEE as Cooperating Organizations* on this massive effort. Each group has a different and valuable perspective to add — and multiple perspectives take space. Second, the book is written for a variety of audiences interested in community and public service, and we wanted to give serious coverage to each audience's interests (see ""Who Is This Book For?"). To make such a large reference book easy to use, we added indices and subheadings.

The Importance of the Language Used

Over the past 20 years, I have participated in hundreds of debates about the language used in combining service and learning — debates that will probably rage forever. Part of the challenge in doing this book has been to make sense of the diversity of terms used to describe programs and courses that combine service and learning in an intentional way. The debates are understandable. As Benjamin Whorf says, "We dissect nature along the lines laid down by our native language ... Language is not simply a reporting device for experience but a defining framework for it."[10]

Diversity of Language. Among the 147 terms used in the literature I reviewed are the following examples of the breadth and complexity of the existing options for terminology: action research, altruism, citizen involvement, citizenship, civic awareness, civic literacy, collaborative learning, community-based education, community education, community service, cooperative education, cross-cultural learning, education for social responsibility, experiential education, field experiences, field studies, global awareness, intergenerational development, international experiences, internships, leadership, national service, public service, reciprocal learning, service-learning, servant leadership, social action, study-service, voluntary action, volunteerism, youth involvement, youth participation, youth service. The list of Cooperating Organizations at the front of this resource book also suggests a host of other terms.

From broad-based, fundamental truths. What is important about this diversity of language — and the resulting strong feelings and inevitable debates about what terminology to use — is the broad range of settings and traditions that have come somewhat independently to the same conclusion: *that there is something uniquely powerful about the combination of service and learning, that there is something fundamentally more dynamic in the integration of the two than in either alone.* Each of those settings and traditions has its own history and culture — and therefore its own language. Whether it is the settlement houses of the early 1900s, the concerns about social relevance in the 1960s, the youth participation movement of the 1960s and early 1970s, the volunteerism movement of the 1980s, curricular reform in general education and the liberal arts, K-12 school reform, the 4-H Clubs in agricultural communities, university YMCAs, urban community development, experiential education, or citizenship, the theme of integrating community and public service with reflective learning is the same.

At different points in history, in different countries, for different age groups, and for different social issues, the same universal truth emerges. The combination of service and learning touches something very fundamental about the human spirit and its relationship to other human beings and to the surrounding culture. This combination integrates humankind's head and heart, and our unique capacity for both action and reflection. The raging debate about language is a sign that this broad-based participation continues across time and traditions. Let it rage on. It is a sign that we are on to something.

"Service-Learning." Even in a debate that lasts for decades, one has to choose some words in order to communicate. In this resource book, the various authors use the potpourri of terms listed at the beginning of this section. In the abstracts and in the general concept of the book, I have chosen "service-learning" as the primary term that most closely expresses what this work is about. There are actually two levels of meaning for "service-learning": (1) as a type of program, (2) as an overall philosophy of education that reflects a particular epistemology and set of values. The richness of these two levels is what has kept the term "service-learning" coming back to center stage in the debate over language for the past 25 years.

Service-learning as a type of program. Service-learning programs emphasize the accomplishment of tasks which meet human needs in combination with conscious educational growth (a useful 1969 definition from the Southern Regional Education Board).[11] They combine needed tasks in the community with intentional learning goals and with conscious reflection and critical analysis. "Tasks which meet human needs" and "needed tasks in the community" are not limited to direct services to people in need, such as through soup kitchens, tutoring, and shelters for homeless persons. These tasks can also include policy-level work on environmental issues, economic development, housing policy, international relations, or other issues that relate to the quality of human life and the social and political structures which can enhance it.

There are two factors that distinguish service-learning programs from other community service programs. First, service-learning programs explicitly include features which foster participants' **learning** about the larger social issues behind the human needs to which they are responding. This includes understanding the historical, sociological, cultural, and political contexts of the need or issue being addressed. Service-learning programs may have several types of learning goals in this reflective component — intellectual, civic, ethical, moral, cross-cultural, career, personal. Different programs emphasize different combinations of these types of learning.

A good service-learning program helps participants see their questions in the larger context of issues of social justice and social policy — rather than in the context of charity. A program for "charity" focuses on "doing for" other people without asking Robert Greenleaf's important question: "Are those being served better able to serve and be served by their own actions?"[12] Of course, responding to critical human and environmental needs is important, but doing this only in the form of direct service without a parallel concern about the societal policies or cultural habits that *create* these needs may actually perpetuate the underlying problems and foster further dependence. Programs that combine service and learning must assist participants to see the larger contexts behind the needs they help address.

A service-learning program might encourage participants working in a local soup kitchen, for example, to ask why people are hungry, what policies in our country do or do not contribute to this problem, and what economic, cultural and logistical factors result in hunger in a world that already knows how to grow enough food to feed everyone. Participants in a program that focuses on primarily on charity, on the other hand, might serve food in the same soup kitchen, but they would not be encouraged and supported to ask these types of questions. After a direct service experience related to local hunger, a young person might then be ready to explore the issue of hunger more deeply through work in a government agency, a citizens' group, or a public policy research project. An international service-learning experience might then help the young person see the issues from a global perspective. These later steps in the service-learning process are especially helpful for developing the skills and awareness needed for responsible global citizenship. "The community" in the definition of service-learning programs can thus refer to the local neighborhood as well as the state, national, or international community.

Just as programs in soup kitchens might ask why people are hungry, stream clean-ups might ask what regulations do and do not keep pollutants out of our water. Literacy programs might ask why our country apparently lacks the will to teach our population to read at the same level as a majority of the other industrialized nations. To incorporate this element of probing in service-learning, Barbara Baker includes in her definition of service-learning programs the goals of helping participants "better understand the causes of social injustice ... and to take actions to eliminate the causes and effects of social injustice."[13] Michele Whitham uses the continuum of "serving to enabling to empowering"[14] to describe the shift of emphasis from a goal of "doing for" people in need — to that of supporting people to address their own needs. This view is very consistent with the principle of service-learning that Robert Sigmon derives from Robert Greenleaf's concept of servant leadership.[15]

Service-learning programs thus build in structures — pre-service preparation, seminars, group discussions, journals, readings, debriefing, or others — that actively support participants to learn from their service experiences. Howard Berry of the Partnership for Service-Learning, for example, defines service-learning as "the union of public and community service with structured and intentional learning."[16]

The second factor that distinguishes service-learning from other community service programs is an emphasis on **reciprocity**. Reciprocity is the exchange of both giving and receiving between the "server" and the person or group "being served." All parties in service-learning are learners and help determine what is to be learned. Both the server and those served teach, and both learn. Such a service-learning exchange avoids the traditionally paternalistic, one-way approach to service in which one person or group has resources which they share "charitably" or "voluntarily" with a person or group that lacks resources. In service-learning, those being served control the service provided; the needs of the community determine what the service tasks will be. It is this reciprocity that creates a sense of mutual responsibility and respect between individuals in the service-learning exchange, what Howard Berry calls "parity of esteem."[17] This service-learning exchange is also an important step toward a commitment of responsibility of the individual participant to the larger community. Building programs on a philosophy of reciprocal learning can thus help to avoid the ever-present pitfall of paternalism disguised under the name of service.

Of course, program names or labels do not necessarily clarify whether they fit the definition of service-learning programs as described here. Many programs labeled community service, volunteer, or youth service also include elements that encourage this critical reflection and reciprocity; those that do so explicitly are also service-learning programs. Many programs for internships, field studies, and experiential education also contain these essential elements. And of course there are some programs labeled "service-learning" that do not reflect the basic principles outlined here. *See the "Principles of Good Practice in Combining Service and Learning" in the first chapter for an important summary of the most important elements of a service-learning program.*

Service-learning as a philosophy of education. The discussion of reciprocity above takes "service-learning" to its second level of meaning as a philosophy of education — one which emphasizes active, engaged learning with the goal of social responsibility. As Tim Stanton points out, "Rather than a discrete [program] type, service learning appears to be an *approach* to experiential learning, an expression of values — service to others, community development and empowerment, reciprocal learning — which determines the purpose, nature and process of *social and educational exchange* between learners and the people they serve, and between experiential education programs and the community organizations with which they work."[18] Richard Couto described this as "the exchange between community abilities and student needs and between community needs and student abilities."[19] Service-learning is thus a philosophy of reciprocal learning, a dynamic and interactive approach which suggests mutuality in learning between the student and the community with whom he or she is actively engaged.

Linda Chisholm of the Association of Episcopal Colleges describes this approach as a *pedagogy of learning through service*, which "establishes a new rhythm of reflection and action, uses new teaching resources, suggests a less passive and more self-directed student who will demand a new relationship of teachers and student, and requires both faculty and student to adopt a new definition of and stance toward 'course material.' The country and culture of those the student serves become the heart of the curriculum.... But the means of learning and the values implied are age-old and honored. Reflection upon experience is, after all, the most fundamental of means to human learning."[20] This is almost identical to the pedagogy of experiential education as described in this resource book and elsewhere (see "A Nation at Risk: Another View" in Volume I).

Service-learning as a philosophy of education is also described well by the literature of the "learning by participation" movement. Bruce Dollar and Val Rust describe this approach to learning as "an integrative process that includes participation in society, critical reflection on that participation, and the relation of experiences to theoretical knowledge, while maximizing the participation of all learners in decisionmaking affecting both the programme as a whole and their own individual activities in the programme."[21]

In his chapter in Volume I of this book, Parker Palmer articulates the world view and way of knowing that characterize service-learning. He talks about an epistemology of "relatedness" or "community." He shows how a relational approach to how we know things and how we learn — when used in creative tension with the traditional objectivist approach of higher education — can transform the learning process for everyone.[22]

Thus, service-learning is a type of program that combines service and learning based on particular principles. It is also a philosophy of human growth and purpose, a social vision, an approach to community, and a way of knowing. In this resource book, service-learning is most often used to refer to a type of program, but there are occasional uses of it at the second level.

Observations on Language. Over almost 20 years in this field, I have observed that both practitioners and programs tend to progress over time from providing direct service to asking systemic and structural questions about the *reasons* that service is needed. Local issues, responsibly explored, eventually are seen in a larger global context. I have also noticed that with time, thoughtful practitioners tend to move from the language of service, volunteerism, and charity to words and concepts that are very different — words like service-learning, reciprocity, mutuality, and exchange; concepts like social justice and global awareness, and parity of esteem. As practitioners and faculty move to this new language, they progress to greater sophistication and scope in the questions *they* ask. Through this progress, they enable the participants in their programs and courses to move to deeper levels of understanding and learning also. More kinds of questions are acceptable. And more creative solutions to the critical issues facing our communities and our globe become possible. *This* is education for civic and social responsibility at its best — education for ourselves *and* for our students and children.

Problems with the Word "Service." The term "service-learning" is not a panacea to solve the raging debate. I have tremendous problems with the word "service." It suggests an inequity between the "servers" and "those served." It suggests that the former have resources and that the latter do not. I do not like the implication that someone does something *to* someone else; this does not suggest the mutuality and reciprocity that make service-learning — when done well — fundamentally different from charity. It does not carry the connotation of social justice that is also an essential component of service-learning. For African Americans and people who have experienced oppression anywhere, "service" can still conjure the images of indentured servitude. And finally, I have heard "service" used many times as a self-righteous, vaguely disguised ticket to salvation for upper and middle class people who feel guilty about their access to resources. This book is not about service; it is about the particular potential for and the critical importance of the *integration* of service and learning.

Choice of Terms. So why is the book called *Combining Service and Learning*, and why is the term "service-learning" used in many of the abstracts if "service" is so problematic? First, because there is no other term that fits what I mean by the integration of meaningful community involvement with reflective learning *and* that is commonly understood by the intended audience for this book. "Reciprocal learning in the community" probably comes closer than anything, but would you have picked up the book with that title? So there is no perfect term. I chose this language because it seems to be the most accessible for the most people at this time. If the debate over language continues, I hope that a new public language will emerge that gives people a way to talk about this powerful combination — or that "service-learning" will gain general acceptance in a way that allows it to shed the current baggage of its component words.

Second, the "Principles of Good Practice" outlined at the front of each volume define what is meant by good practice regardless of the language used. If these principles are respected and *intentionally* and *actively* built into the design of programs and courses, then the pitfalls of the term "service" become much less worrisome.

Other Notes about the Language Used. I decided not to eliminate a piece just because the language used in it is obsolete or limited *if* the chapter offers something of unique value to the field. As a result, the language from chapter to chapter is not consistent. In some cases, you will have to translate or even try to overlook the language as you read.

"Volunteerism" and "Youth Service." "Service-learning" as defined here incorporates the altruism and maturational goals of volunteerism and youth service, but it take these traditions one step further. Service-learning builds on these traditions by emphasizing *critical reflection* on the service experience, *reciprocity* between the providers and acquirers of services, and *learning* as a significant part of the exchange for everyone involved. Many volunteer and youth service programs incorporate these elements intentionally and thoughtfully, but some do not. This book will focus on programs that intentionally support these and the other "Principles of Good Practice" described at the beginning of each volume.

"Community Service" and "Public Service." "Community service" and "public service" are used interchangeably in most of the chapters despite the use of the former by some as an alternative to incarceration and use of the latter to denote government service. While some argue that public service encompasses community service, others argue the opposite. I have opted not to try to solve this debate here.

"Experiential Education" and Service-Learning. The relationship of service-learning to experiential education is an intricate one. The two share both theoretical and methodological bases. Experiential education represents the methods of teaching and learning that are essential for effective service-learning programs. Because they draw on the basic tenets of experiential learning, all service-learning programs can thus be viewed as experiential learning programs. But there are also experiential learning programs that do not have the service emphasis that is a central part of service-learning. The previous discussion about the meaning of "service-learning" explores the concept of reciprocal learning which underlies both. Because of the importance of effective experiential education to

effective service-learning, a number of chapters use the language of experiential education. In several of these, the terms could almost be used interchangeably.

"Students." Some of the authors use the word "student" when referring to the participants in their programs. Please read this as "participant" if those in your program or constituency are not enrolled students. The authors' messages are usually transferrable whether the participants are students, dropouts, independent learners, older adults, or citizens of your state. The premise of this book is that we are all learners and all teachers, so most of what is said applies to all program participants regardless of their relationship to formal educational programs.

"Agencies." Many of the authors use "agency" to refer to any organization that hosts students or other learners in a community setting. Many of the authors do not intend for "agency" to describe only governmental organizations. Similarly, some authors use "community organization," "host organization," "field sponsor," or "sponsoring organization" to refer to the settings where service-learners serve.

A Quick Walk Through This Resource Book

The three volumes of *Combining Service and Learning: A Resource Book for Community and Public Service* are intended as one book. Volume I tells the "why" and the "what," Volume II tells the "how," and Volume III tells the "where else" for other important literature. While each can be used alone, they are intended as a coherent whole. The tables of contents for the other two volumes are provided in the back of each volume.

Volume I. Part I of Volume I lays out essential principles, including the "Ten Principles of Good Practice in Combining Service and Learning" developed in 1989 through a collaborative effort of 77 diverse national and regional groups. Each principle includes an explanation and examples.

Part II discusses why the combination of service and learning is important and powerful at this time in history. It presents multiple perspectives about the value of combining service and learning — for students, for youth and learners of all ages, for communities and the organizations that support them, for educational institutions, for a free society, and for the larger globe. It explores the role of community and public service experiences in developing a sense of social and civic responsibility, for fostering intellectual development at all educational levels, for moral and ethical development, for global awareness and cross-cultural learning, for leadership, and for career exploration. *Provocative chapters by Parker Palmer, Tim Stanton, Nadinne Cruz, and Ivan Illich — and a commentary by John Gardner — are highlights.*

Part III takes the debate to the public policy arena with chapters from the National Governors' Association, the Council of Chief State School Officers, the William T. Grant Foundation Commission on Youth and America's Future, and the National Association of State Boards of Education. Summaries of several state policies provide models for states considering legislation or program initiatives. *With his bold vision for Minnesota, Jim Kielsmeier challenges other states to make a serious commitment to the involvement of young people in the common good.*

Part IV is about the institutional policy issues raised by combining service and learning and how to establish the types of commitment needed for sustained institutional support. This section provides practical suggestions and strategies based on the hands-on experiences of people in different positions and settings — university presidents, students, K-12 and college faculty, administrators, catalysts in national resource organizations, and others. *Sally Migliore summarizes the results of a national study which show how 487 colleges and universities are using a service provided by NSIEE to help them with institutional planning for supporting the effective use of community experiences to meet their educational goals.* A college president and a faculty member suggest how postsecondary institutions might rethink the concept of academic service. Administrators from a state university describe the process they used in integrating an experience-based program into their campus culture and academic structures. And finally, both sides from a 20-year debate have their say on whether participation in programs for service-learning should be required or voluntary. At the end of Part IV, a special section on "Strategies for Institutional Change" offers valuable ideas and examples for both postsecondary and secondary educational settings. *Dan Conrad's funny and sage chapters on "Arguments for Educators" and "The Myth of Sisyphus Revisited" are priceless, as are Kim Grose's tips to other students.*

Part V outlines the history and future of the service-learning movement, tracing its beginnings through a strong network of campus- and community-based leaders developed through the Southern Regional Education Board in the late 1960s and early 1970s. And a short summary of the findings from a 1968 study by the American Council on Education shows that "institutional support for the service curriculum" had already been identified as a major need more than 20 years ago! Another summary provided by the National Governors' Association lists some of the federal antecedents of community service — the Civilian Conservation Corps, Teacher Corps, National Health Service Corps, University Year for ACTION, National Center for Service-Learning, Peace Corps, and VISTA. The results of a Campus Compact study show some ways institutions are supporting student involvement in public service. Finally, Jim Case, Bob Sigmon, and Alec Dickson raise important questions for the future.

Volume II. The second volume contains sections on a variety of practical issues and ideas for programs and courses that combine service and learning. Part I lists project ideas for service-learners of all ages, gives tips on establishing and cultivating school-agency relationships, discusses legal issues and the issue of compensation, outlines program models, and gives practical advice for recruitment. It explores the use of journals, debriefing techniques, and cross-cultural learning methods. One chapter gives a firsthand account of how an interdisciplinary service-learning program was integrated into the liberal arts curriculum.

A special section on "Faculty Issues and Resources" in Part I gives extensive advice and examples for increasing faculty involvement, raises ideas and issues from a faculty member's perspective, discusses teaching methods and ways of finding time for community service, explores approaches for infusing service-learning into the curriculum and into the faculty workload, gives principles for assessing the learning students derive from service experiences, and summarizes the findings of a 1989 study on the faculty's role in integrating the practice of civic participation into the mission and values of postsecondary education. Another special section in Part I focuses on community issues and tips — how to use students effectively in a public or private organization; how to orient, train, and supervise students; and the role of the agency supervisor. Richard Couto discusses how to assess a community setting as a context for learning. A section on evaluation — of programs and of individual student performance — completes Part I.

Parts II, III, and IV contain profiles of specific programs and courses that combine service and learning. This information was gathered through an extensive case study process conducted by the National Society for Internships and Experiential Education. The Cooperating Organizations nominated programs and courses for consideration. An introduction to all the profiles provided just before Part II gives more information about these case studies.

Part II focuses on specific college and university courses and programs. Each case study describes who participates in the program or course, the prerequisites, the most effective means of publicity, the program's history and an overview, goals, philosophy, administrative and staffing structures, how faculty are involved, the annual budget, how service sites are selected, how students prepare for their service experiences, how the community sites are involved, how opportunities for reflection and analysis are built into the program or course design, how learning is facilitated, whether academic credit is given and (if so) how the learning is assessed for credit, how the quality of service is monitored and evaluated, who evaluates what, and whether the various participants (students, faculty, site supervisors and staff) receive any special recognition.

An important part of each profile is the section where practitioners offer open-ended observations and advice. Faculty and program directors discuss how their programs benefit the institution, problems they have addressed and how, the most important lessons they have learned, current challenges, and advice they have to offer the readers of this resource book. Following the case studies are several chapters discussing specific programs in depth — from faculty, student, and international perspectives.

Part III contains the profiles for programs and courses in 29 K-12 schools. The format and topics of the case studies are very similar to those for the college and university programs described above, except that these topics have been added for the K-12 schools: transportation, liability insurance, and contractual arrangements. Included in this section are program descriptions researched and provided for this resource book by the Council of Chief State School Officers. Following the profiles are chapters about a middle school program, an early adolescent helper program, a program for eighth graders, a high school course that includes a consumer action service, and *a program that involves students as young as first graders!*

Part IV provides in-depth profiles for programs in community-based organizations, government, and youth-serving agencies. The type of information included for each entry varies slightly according to the nature of the program and the sponsoring organization. Most profiles include information on who participates and for how long, the most effective means of publicity, the qualifications and responsibilities of the participants, how applicants are screened, the criteria used to determine the roles filled by participants, a program history and overview, the program's goals and philosophy, the administrative and budget structure, number of staff, compensation of participants, agreements used, how participants are oriented and supervised, how their performance and the program are evaluated and by whom, how participants' learning is facilitated and monitored, whether and how academic credit is usually received, what special recognition is given, how the organization benefits from the program, problems they have addressed and how, their current challenges, and other lessons they have learned that might be of assistance to others.

Following the community-based profiles are chapters on the California Human Corps legislation, the Cherokee Nation's approach to leadership, a fifth grade recycling project, and programs that address the needs of migrant farmworkers, older persons, and Hispanic young people.

Volume III. Volume III is *an annotated bibliography* written and edited by the Service-Learning Special Interest Group of the National Society for Internships and Experiential Education. This group realized that the literature of service-learning needed to be pulled together, annotated, and presented — both to give coherence and strength to the current movement, and to call attention to the gaps in our knowledge. Sections of the bibliography include definitions and history, rationales, service-learning in higher education and in secondary education, theoretical and philosophical roots, experiential education, higher education for social responsibility, volunteerism and national service, research, program development/implementation/evaluation, program examples from postsecondary and secondary education, and other print and organizational resources.

Indices. A complete index in each volume — by topic, author, and name of program or organization makes all three volumes accessible for continuing reference.

What Is Not in this Book? This resource book does not cover everything that is important to say about volunteerism, youth service, civic awareness, leadership, public service, or experiential learning. It focuses instead on the aspects of these efforts that relate specifically to the combination of service and learning. It shows how these efforts can be enriched by drawing on the principles and lessons of combining service and learning. This book also does not say much about national service, but I hope that the lessons here are read closely by those who are developing or implementing public policies related to national service.

Differing Perspectives. The effective combination of service and learning is hard. It has inherent dilemmas and contradictions.

One of the main purposes of this book is to present a variety of perspectives for your consideration. As a result, some of the chapters argue with each other. This dialectic is the nature of a human endeavor as rich and complex as combining a service ethic with the dynamics of learning. *I disagree deeply with some of the perspectives presented here, and you will, too.* I have tried to select pieces that are consistent with the principles of good practice in the first chapter. A few violate them unmercifully, but they are included because of a unique perspective they add to the whole.

If You Want More Information. Some readers will want a cookbook to answer the question "How do I run a good community service program?" or "How do I develop a course that incorporates public service?" or "How can my agency use students and volunteers better?" Begin with the "Principles of Good Practice in Combining Service and Learning" in Volume I and the case studies of specific programs in Volume II. But cookbooks are too simplistic for responsible action on local needs and issues, so I hope you will use this entire resource book to probe deeper into the complex issues behind those seemingly simple questions. Keep it on the shelf for future reference, too. The longer you work with such programs, the richer and more rewarding the combination of service and learning will become.

If you need help with how-to's on specific aspects of program or course development that are not covered here — *or if you want more theoretical or research background* — please contact the National Society for Internships and Experiential Education, 3509 Haworth Drive, Suite 207, Raleigh, North Carolina, 27609, (919) 787-3263. Begun in 1971 during the previous surge of interest in service-learning, NSIEE's comprehensive National Resource Center for Service and Learning incorporates the current materials and grass-roots networks of a wide variety of national, regional, and local resource organizations and programs.

Useful in 2000? 2050? The literature of the movement to combine service and learning is still evolving. The chapters of this resource book are selected for their timeless value, so they will still be useful in 10 years or 60. By the year 2000, a few chapters will offer primarily an important historical perspective, but most of them will still go to the heart of the potential and the challenges of combining service and learning — in any decade. I hope this book adds to the likelihood that the thoughtful combination of community and public service with learning will be alive and well in 2000 and 2050. "Alive and well" means being a vital, articulated part of the agenda of the 21st century for schools and colleges and for all our civic and social institutions.

Jane Kendall is Executive Director of the National Society for Internships and Experiential Education. As a Kellogg National Fellow, she is also conducting national and local research about issues in the nonprofit sector. She has served as director of the FIPSE-funded Peer Assistance Network in Experiential Learning and of the Southern Regional Economic Development Intern Program. Before coming to the staff of NSIEE in 1978, she worked with experiential education programs at the University of North Carolina, Chapel Hill.

Footnotes

[1]American Council on Education, Educational Record, Spring 1968, p. 2.

[2]Personal conversation with Roger Henry, April 1986.

[3]Bobby Hackett, panel presentation at the National Conference of the Partnership for Service-Learning, February 19, 1988, Chevy Chase, Maryland.

[4]Sally A. Migliore, "National Study Shows Progress and Needs in Strengthening Institutional Support for Experiential Education," in *Combining Service and Learning: A Resource Book for Community and Public Service*, ed. Jane C. Kendall, National Society for Internships and Experiential Education, Vol. I, 1990, pp. 526-529.

[5]Timothy K. Stanton, "A Survey of Campus Compact Institutions: Major Findings and Recommendations on the Faculty's Role in Integrating the Issues and Practice of Civic Participation with the Mission and Values of Postsecondary Education," Campus Compact, in Kendall, *op. cit.*, Vol. II, pp. 210-216.

[6]American Council on Education, *op. cit.*, p. 2.

[7]Timothy K. Stanton, "Liberal Arts, Experiential Learning and Public Service: Necessary Ingredients for Socially Responsible Undergraduate Education," in Kendall, *op. cit.*, Vol. I, pp. 175-189.

[8]Association of American Colleges, *A New Vitality in General Education: Planning, Teaching, and Supporting Effective Liberal Learning*, Task Group on General Education, Joseph Katz, Chair, 1988, pp. 28-35.

[9]Arthur W. Chickering and Zelda F. Gamson, "Seven Principles for Good Practice in Undergraduate Education," *The Wingspread Journal*, The Johnson Foundation, Special Edition, June 1987.

[10]Benjamin Whorf, "Thinking in Primitive Communities," in *New Directions in the Study of Language*, ed. Hoyer, 1964.

[11]Southern Regional Education Board, *Service-Learning in the South: Higher Education and Public Service 1967-1972*, 1973.

[12]Robert K. Greenleaf, *Servant Leadership*, Paulist Press, 1977, as quoted by Robert L. Sigmon, "Service-Learning: Three Principles," *Synergist*, National Center for Service-Learning, Vol. 8, No. 1, Spring 1979, p. 10.

[13]Barbara E. Baker, "Are We Really Providing a Service? Some Guiding Principles of College-Level Service-Learning Programs," Masters Thesis, University of Michigan, 1983, p. 10.

[14]Michele Whitham, comments at a winter 1986 planning meeting in Washington, D.C., co-sponsored by Campus Compact and the National Society for Internships and Experiential Education.

[15]Sigmon, *op. cit.*, p. 10.

[16]Howard A. Berry, "Service-Learning in International/Intercultural Settings," *Experiential Education*, National Society for Internships and Experiential Education, Vol. 13, No. 3, May-June 1988, p. 3.

[17]Ibid., p. 3.

[18]Timothy K. Stanton, "Service Learning: Groping Toward a Definition," *Experiential Education*, National Society for Internships and Experiential Education, Vol. 12, No. 1, January-February 1987, p. 4.

[19]Richard A. Couto, presentation at 1987 National Conference, National Society for Internships and Experiential Education, Smugglers' Notch, Vermont, October, 1987.

[20]Linda A. Chisholm, "The Intersection of Church and College," *Views & News on Education*, Association of Episcopal Colleges, Vol. 2, No. 1, Fall 1987, p. 3.

[21]Bruce Dollar and Val Rust, "Learning by Participation," in *Learning from Work and Community Experience: Six International Models*, edited by Heather Chisnall on behalf of IMTEC, NFER-Nelson Publishing Company Ltd., 1983, p. 26.

[22]Parker Palmer, "Community, Conflict, and Ways of Knowing," *Change*, Vol. 19, No. 5, September/October 1987, pp. 20-25.

PART I

Essential Principles in Combining Service and Learning

Principles of Good Practice in Combining Service and Learning

IN 1987 THE NATIONAL SOCIETY for Internships and Experiential Education (NSIEE) began a process of articulating and refining principles of good practice for programs that seek to combine service and learning effectively. This was in response to the burgeoning growth of community service programs for youth, students, and adults and the increasing awareness among thoughtful practitioners that effective service and learning do not necessarily happen automatically.

As programs of the 1980s experienced the same challenges about program *quality* that programs of the 1960s and 1970s had also faced, NSIEE began a broad-based process of articulating the principles learned by experienced practitioners. We reviewed the advice of leaders in the community and public service movement of the late 1960s and early 1970s. We asked members of the NSIEE Service-Learning Special Interest Group to reach into their group's 15-year reservoir of experience. We asked more than 75 other national and regional organizations to do the same; the staffs and members of most of the organizations responded by adding their diverse perspectives, experiences, and advice. Nine drafts were circulated over an intense, 12-month period of refinement.

Then in the spring of 1989, the Johnson Foundation generously agreed to host a Wingspread conference to hammer out the final product. Several national organizations co-sponsored the May 10-12, 1989, working session: the American Association for Higher Education, Campus Compact, Constitutional Rights Foundation, Council of Chief State School Officers, National Association of Independent Schools, National Association of Secondary School Principals, National Society for Internships and Experiential Education, and Youth Service America.

The 75 national and regional groups that had participated in the review process also provided examples of the implementation of the ten principles that resulted from the Wingspread working session.

What follows here are the ten principles refined from this two-year collaborative process, an explanation of each, and examples of each one as used in actual programs. Ellen Porter Honnet and Susan J. Poulsen of The Johnson Foundation graciously produced the final copy.

We invite you to use these principles in the context of your particular needs and purposes. You may decide to reject some of them, but we hope this work at least helps you ask some of the right questions about combining service and learning in an effective, sustained way.

— Jane Kendall, NSIEE

Introduction

The level of interest and sense of urgency in community and public service grows greater every day. In every community, programs are being designed for participants from kindergartners to the elderly. Is there a set of guiding principles by which service programs can be designed and by which their effectiveness can be judged? Is there a set of ideas which have the potential for deepening and sustaining the current movements?

The principles described in this section reflect the grassroots experience and the thinking of thousands of people, hundreds of programs, and numerous national organizations over the last two decades. They are offered with the hope that current initiatives to create service programs will benefit from this rich history.

The combination of service and learning is powerful. It creates potential benefits beyond what either service or learning can offer separately. The frequent results of the effective integration of service and learning are that participants:

- develop a habit of critical reflection on their experiences, enabling them to learn more throughout life,
- are more curious and motivated to learn,
- are able to perform better service,
- strengthen their ethic of social and civic responsibility,
- feel more committed to addressing the underlying problems behind social issues,
- understand problems in a more complex way and can imagine alternative solutions,

- demonstrate more sensitivity to how decisions are made and how institutional decisions affect people's lives,
- respect other cultures more and are better able to learn about cultural differences,
- learn how to work more collaboratively with other people on real problems, and
- realize that their lives can make a difference.

The emphasis on learning does not mean these Principles are limited in any way to programs connected to schools. They relate to programs and policies based in all settings — community organizations, K-12 schools, colleges and universities, corporations, government agencies, and research and policy organizations. They relate to people of all ages in all walks of life.

Preamble

We are a nation founded upon active citizenship and participation in community life. We have always believed that individuals can and should serve.

It is crucial that service toward the common good be combined with reflective learning to assure that service programs of high quality can be created and sustained over time, and to help individuals appreciate how service can be a significant and ongoing part of life. Service, combined with learning, adds value to each and transforms both.

Those who serve and those who are served are thus able to develop the informed judgment, imagination and skills that lead to greater capacity to contribute to the common good.

The Principles that follow are statements of what we believe are essential components of good practice. We invite you to use them in the context of your particular needs and purposes.

Principles of Good Practice in Combining Service and Learning

An effective and sustained program:

1. Engages people in responsible and challenging actions for the common good.

2. Provides structured opportunities for people to reflect critically on their service experience.

3. Articulates clear service and learning goals for everyone involved.

4. Allows for those with needs to define those needs.

5. Clarifies the responsibilities of each person and organization involved.

6. Matches service providers and service needs through a process that recognizes changing circumstances.

7. Expects genuine, active, and sustained organizational commitment.

8. Includes training, supervision, monitoring, support, recognition, and evaluation to meet service and learning goals.

9. Insures that the time commitment for service and learning is flexible, appropriate, and in the best interest of all involved.

10. Is committed to program participation by and with diverse populations.

See the following pages for an explanation of each principle and examples of its use.

Principles of Good Practice in Combining Service and Learning

1. An effective program engages people in responsible and challenging actions for the common good. Participants in programs combining service and learning should engage in tasks that they and society recognize as important. These actions require reaching beyond one's range of previous knowledge or experience. Active participation — not merely being a spectator or visitor — requires accountability for one's actions, involves the right to take risks, and gives participants the opportunity to experience the consequences of those actions for others and for themselves.

Some Examples:

College students from the United States helped create a local primary school in Liberia; students in Ecuador work with foster and abandoned children; students in England care for mentally and physically handicapped persons; and in Jamaica, they work at a Human Rights Center and in literacy projects. In each of these cases, students are matched up with professional staff members of local agencies through the Partnership for Service Learning in New York City.

A program of the Anderson YMCA/YWCA in Stockton, California, helped establish a relationship between area university students and the local Cambodian community. This enabled students to help respond to the needs of the Southeast Asian community in the aftermath of a sniper who killed nearly a dozen children. Students acted as translators, attended funeral services, and comforted grieving families.

At Grant High School in Los Angeles, students in the Community Service Leadership class assessed community needs and helped develop projects. Additional students were recruited from the Constitutional Rights Foundation's (CRF) Youth Community Service group on campus. A child care group initiated tutoring in a local elementary school; a group working with the homeless organized collection and distribution of goods, as well as serving food at homeless shelters; an environmental committee worked on community beautification and treeplanting; a senior citizens group "adopted grandparents" at a local convalescent home and led aerobic classes for the elderly.

The Retiree Group of Mellon Volunteer Professionals in Pittsburgh volunteer thousands of hours each year doing mailings, bookkeeping, and conference registration, among other things, for local charities and non-profit organizations.

Youngsters in Addison County, Vermont, know where to turn when they're in trouble, thanks to the efforts of students and teachers at Middlebury Junior High School. Under a SerVermont grant, the students produced a resource guide, "If You're In Trouble, We're Here to Help." A journalist came to the school to help the students learn to interview; computer students taught their peers how to do desk-top publishing, word processing, and graphics; students interviewed local service agencies and published the information in a booklet created especially for area middle school students.

In Chestnut Ridge School District in Pennsylvania, the National Honor Society requires that members earn 20 points per year in public service to remain in the Society. Members may choose from tutoring programs, programs to install emergency road signs, and plotting of emergency call numbers for homes and businesses to assist the local fire department, among other interesting projects.

In the Big Brothers/Big Sisters program of the Golden Triangle in Columbus, Mississippi, high school students learn the value of service by working with children in need of direction. Matched up with needy youngsters, these high school students offer companionship, attitude development, self-esteem, relationship skills, recreational activities, school adjustment, male-female role models, and improvement in family function.

2. An effective program provides structured opportunities for people to reflect critically on their service experience. The service experience alone does not insure that either significant learning or effective service will occur. It is important that programs build in structured opportunities for participants to think about their experience and what they are learning. Through discussions with others and individual reflection on moral questions and relevant issues, participants can develop a better sense of social responsibility, advocacy, and active citizenship. This reflective component allows for intellectual growth and the development of skills in critical thinking. It is most useful when it is intentional and continuous throughout the experience, and when opportunity for feedback is provided. Ideally, feedback will come from those persons being served, as well as from peers and program leaders.

Some Examples:

As part of "Project Motivation" at the YMCA of the University of Minnesota, students are paired with 2nd through 6th graders in need of "Big Buddies." Volunteers attend a retreat at the beginning of the program, and meet bi-weekly throughout the school year. They are assisted by school social workers who help them learn more about issues related to their work and lead them in discussions of problems and successes they are having with their "little buddies."

At San Francisco State's Community Involvement Center, students working with outside agencies keep journals on their community service and meet for two hours a week in support sessions to discuss, evaluate, and solve problems relating to their work. In other high school and college level programs, students compile annual reports of service experiences that reflect different themes and personal growth. City-wide conferences scheduled throughout the year provide opportunities for high school volunteers to exchange ideas, interact with community representatives about pressing issues, and reflect on leadership, philanthropy, and service.

Some school programs link reflection more formally with the curriculum. In Indiana, Goshen College students are required to submit extensive journals reporting on their international service experiences. Project Community at the University of Michigan at Ann Arbor complements field experience with an academic program back on campus that includes readings and writing, as well as a weekly seminar that helps students integrate their experiences with their reading.

As part of the Center for Service-Learning's Vermont Internship Program, students at the University of Vermont participate in one of three courses which provide structured reflection and articulation of learning from the service experience. Students may earn from 1 to 18 credits and participate in weekly or bi-weekly seminars with other students, keep journals and write critical essays on aspects of the service experience. One course, the Field Studies Internship, is portable, in that it provides a service curriculum and reading material which can be taken to a service assignment in a foreign country or other setting outside Vermont.

3. An effective program articulates clear service and learning goals for everyone involved. From the outset of the project, participants and service recipients alike must have a clear sense of: (1) what is to be accomplished and (2) what is to be learned. These service and learning goals must be agreed upon through negotiations with all parties, and in the context of the traditions and cultures of the local community. These goals should reflect the creative and imaginative input of both those providing the service and those receiving it. Attention to this important factor of mutuality in the service-learning exchange can help keep the "service" from becoming patronizing charity.

Some Examples:

Students from Hinesburg, Vermont, in the Champlain Valley Union High School DUO (Do Unto Others) program design a learning program with their school supervisor and the agency in which they'll serve. This is done during the student's interview for the service opportunity. Activities and goals are agreed upon by all parties at that time, and are used in the evaluation process throughout the experience.

At-risk students in two San Antonio school districts are identified as "valued youths" and trained to tutor youngsters at nearby elementary schools. The "valued youths" are given training in communications skills, child development theory, and economic opportunities. Volunteers meet their service goals by tutoring the children; they meet their learning goals by reinforcing their own academic skills as well as those of the younger students. Participants in this program have also been found to be much less likely to drop out of high school, and they cite the development of relationships with the children as a key factor to staying in school. (Valued Youth Partnership Program, Intercultural Development Research Association.)

The University of Minnesota YMCA conducts informational meetings for nearly every program and requires an interview for all program participants. Volunteers in some programs are asked to sign learning contracts.

Stanford University's Ravenswood Tutoring Program, serving a primarily minority and low-income population, stipulates that tutors must make a minimum two-quarter commitment to work with an individual student. Before beginning tutoring, the Stanford student meets with the pupil's teacher to discuss and outline a set of learning goals and objectives for the sessions.

"Project DownEast SERVE" in Lubec, Maine, works with rural community members with low incomes to motivate students who have limited educational and vocational aspirations. The learning goal of the project is to encourage students to complete high school and further education and to move on to satisfying careers. Students volunteer in health care, social services, teaching, day care, and fundraising activities to help local agencies as part of their service.

4. An effective program allows for those with needs to define those needs. The actual recipients of service, as well as the community groups and constituencies to which they belong, must have the primary role in defining their own service needs. Community service programs, government agencies, and private organizations can also be helpful in defining what service tasks are needed and when and how these tasks should be performed. This collaboration to define needs will help insure that service by participants will: (1) not take jobs from the local community, (2) involve tasks that will otherwise go undone, and (3) focus their efforts on the tasks and approaches that the *recipients* define as useful.

Some Examples:

In a successful student-generated community service project sponsored by SerVermont in Chester, Vermont, senior citizens were included as "SerVermont Seniors." Students were required to include a senior citizen and a teacher on each planning team.

The Murray State University YMCA in Murray, Kentucky, held a college day for sixth graders. After a full day of participating in classes, recreation, and meals, the sixth grade guests were given a needs assessment to identify what they felt to be critical needs and issues of their peers. Together with college students, they developed a plan for several program activities.

Employee volunteers in one corporation's "Public Affairs Action Committee" invite speakers from local agencies to make presentations during monthly lunch meetings to learn about service opportunities and find innovative ways in which employees can be involved in service work.

College students at Virginia Tech, through their YMCA, responded to a call for assistance in the small community of Ivanhoe. During their spring break, students helped renovate a community center. Community members provided potluck meals, home stays, and evening social activities for the students. Students continue to travel the 40 miles to Ivanhoe on weekends and school holidays to be of further help. A community organizer from Ivanhoe now teaches a course in community development at Virginia Tech.

The Atherton YMCA in Honolulu includes both students and the developmentally delayed teens they work with in the process of planning events and activities.

5. An effective program clarifies the responsibilities of each person and organization involved. Several parties are potentially involved in any service and learning program: participants (students and teachers, volunteers of all ages), community leaders, service supervisors, and sponsoring organizations, as well as those individuals and groups receiving the services. It is important to clarify roles and responsibilities of these parties through a careful negotiation process as the program is being developed. This negotiation should include identifying and assigning responsibility for the tasks to be done, while acknowledging the values and principles important to all the parties involved.

Some Examples:

Agencies accepting students in programs coordinated by Operation Civic Serve in San Francisco are given written guidelines on the agencies' responsibilities including the requirement for supervision and evaluation of students. They remind the agencies that students need direct personal contact with clients, and that there should be minimal, if any, clerical and clean-up work. Students, in turn, are given detailed requirements, including number of hours required, the importance of keeping a journal, and the need to attend support sessions.

In programs sponsored by the Partnership for Service Learning, the student, the faculty, and agency personnel work together to achieve the goals of service and learning. Job descriptions and schedules are defined by the agencies. Learning is matched to the individual service experience, and all involved provide evaluation and reflection on the value and achievements of the learning and the service.

The United Negro College Fund (UNCF) and Citicorp in New York City work together to provide a mentorship opportunity each year for one male and one female entering freshman from each UNCF college. The students must have demonstrated outstanding academic and leadership potential, as well as community and school service. A Citicorp executive volunteers as a mentor for each selected student. Mentors are screened and assigned for four years. They help students with academic and personal problems, summer work, and internships.

Many community service agencies have found it useful to have clear job descriptions, not only for staff, but also for board members, student staff, and volunteers. Ideally, the responsibilities and expectations of the volunteers are reviewed during early orientation sessions and periodically throughout the experience.

Some business people and lawyers, in cooperation with a local Chicago youth agency (the Centre, Inc.), helped a group of urban young people follow through on their idea to organize a small store-front office supply business. Clear divisions of responsibilities were set out for all those involved. The business people and lawyers consulted with agency staff and advised the youth, who actually ran the business. The young people gained valuable skills and enhanced their sense of self-worth and alternatives for their futures.

6. An effective program matches service providers and service needs through a process that recognizes changing circumstances. Because people are often changed by the service and learning experience, effective programs must build in opportunities for continuous feedback about the changing service needs and growing service skills of those involved. Ideally, participation in the service-learning partnership affects development in areas such as intellect, ethics, cross-cultural understanding, empathy, leadership and citizenship. In effective service and learning programs, the relationships among groups and individuals are dynamic and often create dilemmas. Such dilemmas may lead to unintended outcomes. They can require recognizing and dealing with differences.

Some Examples:

At the University of California-Berkeley's Student Volunteer Clearinghouse (Cal Corps), a graduate student has developed software that, within two or three minutes, can provide a list of volunteer opportunities based on a student's interests, preferred location, schedule, and need for public transportation.

The Honors College at Michigan State-Kalamazoo works with the local Voluntary Action Center in identifying appropriate sites for students. To help broaden the connections, the College hosted a Volunteer Opportunities Fair involving many area service agencies.

The Literacy Council in Bedford County, Pennsylvania, is one of several programs run by students. The students make most of the decisions, assist trainers, apply for funding, produce television spots, do public relations, and recruit adults to work as tutors. While this is primarily a tutoring project, only a few of the students actually tutor due to the difficulty of daytime scheduling, students' safety concerns, and adult embarrassment in admitting to a high school student that they can't read.

High school students in Los Angeles help match their interests to community service needs through a 60-Minute Community

Search Activity provided by the Constitutional Rights Foundation. The students use the session to go out into their communities, identify resources, assess their own abilities and interests, and connect with agencies and businesses in need of volunteers.

Recognizing that initial matching of the participant to service opportunity is only the beginning, Partnership for Service Learning programs incorporate ongoing evaluations into all service experiences. These are conducted jointly by the student, the coordinating agency, and the recipients of the service as a basis for responding to changes and reshaping the program for subsequent participants.

High school students in the Vermont "DUO" Program establish a clear understanding of talents and skills as well as goals for the service experience through an initial meeting involving a school staff member, agency supervisor, and the student. After the student spends three days at the site, the supervisor is called to check on progress, and a site visit is made by the school staff member. The student keeps a written journal of the experience. Final evaluations are written by the student, the agency supervisor, and the school staff member.

Hospital Auxiliary Aids in a midwestern community conduct a review after the first two weeks of service and monthly thereafter to be certain that the volunteer is comfortable in that position and is meeting the hospital's service expectations. In some cases, participants who have been assigned to emergency room admissions find that they would be more comfortable working in the gift shop; after working with people in the out-patient admissions area for several months, a volunteer may discover a gift for consoling families and may be placed in the hospice program.

7. An effective program expects genuine, active, and sustained organizational commitment. In order for a program to be effective, it must have a strong, ongoing commitment from both the sponsoring and the receiving organizations. Ideally, this commitment will take many forms, including reference to both service and learning in the organization's mission statement. Effective programs must receive administrative support, be an ongoing part of the organization's budget, be allocated appropriate physical space, equipment, and transportation, and allow for scheduled release time for participants and program leaders. In schools and colleges, the most effective service and learning programs are linked to the curriculum and require that the faculty become committed to combining service and learning as a valid part of teaching.

Some Examples:

Corporations across the country commit thousands of hours of employee release time each year in the United Way Loaned Executive program. Employees are given time away from their regular jobs to serve on area campaigns, helping United Way raise funds to support a wide range of community service agencies.

The "DUO" high school program in Vermont has received full funding from its school district for the past 17 years. An office, staff, funds for professional growth, and transportation funds for students are included in the school budget. Teachers, guidance counselors, and administrators encourage students to get involved.

Commitment to student service by the college or university president is critical to the success of service programs on campus. Campus Compact: The Project for Public and Community Service, is a consortium of college and university presidents who provide leadership and visible institutional support for service as a part of the educational experience on their campuses. Campus Compact, headquartered at Brown University, provides coordination and support for service projects and opportunities for students, including literacy programs and mentoring.

COOL (Campus Outreach Opportunity League) promotes the creation of a "green Dean" administrative position on college campuses. Each college or university involved hires an energetic recent graduate to organize community service programs for undergraduates. The positions may be funded for one to two years or, ideally, become permanent staff positions, as they have at Carleton College and Fordham University.

Some colleges and universities integrate service components in the educational structure and curriculum. These programs are not "at risk" to budget constraints; they remain central to the educational mission of the school and are supported by the Faculty. Antioch College in Yellow Springs, Ohio; the University of Massachusetts at Boston (College III especially); Alverno College in Milwaukee; the Fielding Institute in Santa Barbara; Goshen College; and Manchester College in Indiana are good examples.

The National Society for Internships and Experiential Education provides on-site consultants, a handbook, and other services to colleges and universities interested in integrating community and public service experiences into their curricula, their institutional mission, and their approaches to assessing learning.

Other institutions provide resources for volunteer programs. The University of San Francisco provides university-owned vans to bring volunteer tutors to community centers to meet with young members of the Southeast Asian community and help them bring their scholastic achievements up to grade level.

Nearly all college-affiliated YMCAs have at least one full-time staff person who works with student leadership groups and with volunteers. These staff people must be trained in the YMCA Career Development Program or be full-time members of the university staff. The commitment to having a consistent staff person ensures continuity of relationships with students, university, and community. It also allows from programming that goes beyond being a broker for students and the service programs, to addressing the developmental needs of students.

The Community Volunteer Center in Albion, Michigan, provides clerical and computer support, a meeting place, information, technical assistance, and training to meet a wide range of needs for volunteer organizations. Their program helps new volunteer organizations get started, and encourages support and participation within the community for both students and non-student adults.

8. An effective program includes training, supervision, monitoring, support, recognition, and evaluation to meet service and learning goals. The most effective service and learning programs are sensitive to the importance of training, supervision, and monitoring of progress throughout the program. This is a reciprocal responsibility and requires open communication between those offering and those receiving the service. In partnership, sponsoring and receiving organizations may recognize the value of service through appropriate celebrations, awards, and public acknowledgement of individual and group service. Planned, formalized, and ongoing evaluation of service and learning projects should be part of every program and should involve all participants.

Some Examples:

At Stanford University's Ravenswood tutoring project, tutors are required to take a one-day training session. Staff of the Tutoring Program provide students with support and resources to plan effective tutorials. Student Tutor Coordinators act as liaisons between teachers and tutors in each school. Stanford's Education Department offers a 2-4 unit course in tutor training; teachers from the Ravenswood schools lead math and reading workshops throughout the year; on campus there is a Tutor Resource Center and a monthly newsletter called *Tutoring Times.*

The international service programs of the Partnership for Service Learning include pre-program academic and cultural materials, a statement of expectations of behavior and responsibility, a two-week introductory orientation to the culture and what it means to serve, and ongoing monitoring by academic and agency personnel. Evaluation is comprehensive and includes academic grading for demonstrated learning. It also includes service agency reports on the behavior and value of the student to the community.

The United Way of Minneapolis helped to fund a longitudinal study of the impact of the "Big Buddy" program on elementary school children.

Volunteers from Walker Manufacturing Company, Racine, Wisconsin, "pitched in" to help clean up the Root River. In recognition, the company provided personalized tee shirts ("Susan Pitched In") which the employee could then wear to other corporate and voluntary functions. The event was prominently pictured on the back cover of the company magazine, and volunteers were recognized for their ongoing service at an annual banquet hosted by the company president.

Hudson High School in Ohio gives each student who contributes time to the service program a handsome certificate. Many schools recognize service through award ceremonies, banquets, presentations of award pins, or other celebrations.

The "Prompters" organization at SUNY-Purchase in New York involves some 175 community members in the process of linking the campus and its arts programs with others in the community. After an extensive in-service training, community members become "ambassadors" for the arts programs of the college, speaking in schools, and helping expose some 8,000 elementary and secondary school students to the arts.

9. An effective program insures that the time commitment for service and learning is flexible, appropriate, and in the best interests of all involved. In order to be useful to all parties involved, some service activities require longer participation and/or a greater time commitment than others. The length of the experience and the amount of time required are determined by the service tasks involved and should be negotiated by all the parties. Sometimes a program can do more harm than good if a project is abandoned after too short a time or given too little attention. Where appropriate, a carefully planned succession or combination of participants can provide the continuity of service needed.

Some Examples:

Many successful programs arrange projects to accommodate the busy schedules of student and professional participants. A Stanford student, for example, whose heavy schedule made her unable to work during daytime hours, answered calls for a crisis hotline in her dorm room from midnight to 8:00 a.m.

Members of "New York Cares," a group of 600 professionals, can only volunteer on weekends and in the evenings. The coordinator of the group works closely with service agencies to arrange service activities that fall within these time constraints. For example, teams of volunteers plan, fund, and host parties on weekends for children living in hotels for families who are homeless.

Many academic programs that link service to the curriculum design the time commitment based on two factors: what is needed for legitimate recognition of academic credit, and the length of service that agencies and their clients define as necessary. In some cases, this may require the commitment of a semester or even an entire academic year, while others may be as short as a summer or even a couple of weeks.

Many successful programs in high schools and colleges organize activities to keep students involved for the entire school year. They conduct retreats, have weekly or bi-weekly meetings, and use extensive communications to keep track of participants. Others recruit students on a rotating basis. These operate on the philosophy that students should be afforded opportunities to serve whenever they are ready. This gives more flexibility for program entry and exit.

The Mellon Volunteer Professionals (MVP) Retiree Group generally places people in short-term projects without long-term, ongoing commitments to a specific task in order to accommodate participants' travel and lifestyle schedules. Professionals work on events such as intergenerational fairs, special fundraising events, and development campaigns for local non-profit organizations.

10. An effective program is committed to program participation by and with diverse populations. A good service and learning program promotes access and removes disincentives and barriers to participation. Those responsible for participation in a program should make every effort to include and make welcome persons from differing ethnic, racial, and religious backgrounds, as well as varied ages, genders, economic levels, and those with disabilities. Less obvious, but very important, is the need for sensitivity to other barriers, such as lack of transportation, family, work and school responsibilities, concern for personal safety, or uncertainty about one's ability to make a contribution.

Some Examples:

The best school programs are designed specifically to be open to all students. They meet each student at an appropriate place where they can learn, give, and feel of value to the community. Release time from traditional classrooms is provided (often as much as one day a week), and transportation is available for students who do not have access to an automobile. Students may also do projects after school, on weekends, or during the summer.

"City Year," a service corps program in Boston, in its original charter, proposed to include a diverse group of participants and to have specific recruitment efforts to create a balance of participants that reflects the diverse population of Boston.

A group of largely Asian and Latino students in the "Learning Through Service" program in seven San Francisco area high schools perform after-school community service in their own ethnic communities. These students, many of whom were initially reluctant to volunteer, noted at a recent recognition luncheon that they had come to discover, in their own words, "the great rewards of serving."

In many programs in which activities are culturally integrated, students report that stereotypes break down and that they learn to appreciate cultural differences, and find out that they share similar goals and values.

The "Magic Me" program in Baltimore links children with nursing home residents, specifically enlisting students who are not doing well in school. This allows both the youngsters and the elderly to "serve" one another. It also makes it possible for a group of persons confined to a nursing home, who traditionally could not engage in service, to make a difference to society.

Elderly persons are often among those most willing to volunteer, yet least able because of logistical barriers. One successful literacy program provides transportation for senior citizens to the community centers where they help others learn to read and write.

A high school in Steel Valley, Pennsylvania, has adopted the elderly community. Youngsters visit with residents one-on-one at a personal care facility, helping with arts and crafts and performing concerts. One important aspect of the program is that it involves a wide range of students — not only those with high academic achievement.

Contributing Organizations

In addition to the Cooperating Organizations listed in the front of this resource book that participated with the National Society for Internships and Experiential Education (NSIEE) in the development of this book, the following organizations provided assistance with the development of the "Principles of Good Practice in Combining Service and Learning":

ACCESS: Networking in the Public Interest
American Association of State Colleges and Universities
American Sociological Association
Association for Experiential Education
Association of American Colleges
Association of Episcopal Colleges
Campus Compact, Education Commission of the States
Campus Outreach Opportunity League
Center for Creative Community
Constitutional Rights Foundation
Council for Adult and Experiential Learning
Council for the Advancement of Citizenship
Council of Chief State School Officers
Educators for Social Responsibility
Executive High School Internship Association
Facing History and Ourselves National Foundation, Inc.
William T. Grant Foundation Commission on Work, Family and
    Citizenship
Higher Education Consortium for Urban Affairs
Independent Sector
Intercultural Development Research Association
Thomas Jefferson Forum, Inc.
The Johnson Foundation
Charles F. Kettering Foundation
Maryland Student Service Alliance
Michigan Campus Compact
National Association of Secondary School Principals
National Association of Service and Conservation Corps
National Association of Student Employment Administrators
National Civic League
National Coalition of Alternative Community Schools
National Community Education Association
National Crime Prevention Council
National Institute for Work and Learning, Academy for Educational

Development
National Service Secretariat
National Society for Internships and Experiential Education
National Youth Leadership Council
New York State Cooperative and Experiential Education Association
North Carolina State Government Internship Program
Operation Civic Serve
Overseas Development Network
Partnership for Service-Learning
PennSERVE
The Philadelphia Center, Great Lakes Colleges Association
SerVermont
Service-Learning Center, Michigan State University
United Negro College Fund, Inc.
VISTA Student Community Service, ACTION
VOLUNTEER-The National Center
YMCA of the USA
Youth Policy Institute
Youth Service America

Mutual Respect Is Vital

Emphasizing that collaboration is necessary between the university and the community, Catherine Milton [of the Haas Public Service Center at Stanford University] noted that the basis for successful collaboration lies in developing mutual respect for the values, needs and expectations of both groups: "It's time-consuming, but if you skip it, you may have 100,000 volunteers who are doing more harm than good. It can't be a missionary effort with the university coming in and saying it has all the answers. Each group must have the opportunity and take the time to understand and respect the problems and priorities of the others."

Reprinted from "California College Students and Community Service," by Theo Steele, California Coalition on University-Community Services, 1987, p. 3.

Service-Learning: Three Principles

Robert L. Sigmon

A practitioner discusses three fundamental principles of service-learning and several tools for putting them into practice. Reprinted from Synergist, National Center for Service-Learning, ACTION, *Vol. 8, No. 1, Spring 1979, pp. 9-11.*

SERVICE-LEARNING TERMINOLOGY has emerged since the late 1960s, and — as in the case of many traditional Christmas carols — the authors are unknown. The great carols belong to the public, a product of folk traditions at their best. Service-learning represents the coming together of many hearts and minds seeking to express compassion for others and to enable a learning style to grow out of service.

The term service-learning is now used to describe numerous voluntary action and experiential education programs. Federal laws use the phrase. Its diffusion suggests that several meanings now are attributed to service-learning. If we are to establish clear goals and work efficiently to meet them, we need to move toward a precise definition.

The following notes indicate three fundamental principles of service-learning and several tools for practitioners who are involved with service delivery and learning programs.

My first contact with service-learning was in the late 1960s when the Southern Regional Education Board (SREB) — using federal dollars — popularized a service-learning internship model. Service-learning at that time was defined as the integration of the accomplishment of a public task with conscious educational growth.

Voluntary action and experiential education programs have grown steadily in this country during the past decade. Service-learning rarely has been examined carefully as a style and has been overshadowed by more popular program styles. These, in brief, are:

- *Classroom-based experiential education* in the form of simulations, games, programmed instruction, computerized learning packages, group process techniques, and library-based independent study;
- *Career exposure and life-style planning* programs, part of the massive career education movement that has been popularized by the writings of such people as Richard Bolles;
- *Outward Bound* programs and their counterparts using outdoor and wilderness settings for growth and learning;
- *Cooperative education*, placing students primarily in "for profit" settings;
- *Adult self-initiated learning exercises* sustained without the aid of educational institutions or professional teachers;
- *Programs rooted in public need settings*, including voluntary action programs, public service internships, academically based field practica, and some work-study programs.

All six styles have in common an emphasis on individual development. Programs based in public need settings add *service to others* as a major dimension. The service-learning style is best understood in this type of program, for it focuses on both those being served and those serving.

Principles

Based on my work designing, managing, and evaluating programs with service and learning dimensions, and with a spirit of inquiry about how any of us serve well and are served well by our actions, I suggest the following three principles for those in similar positions:

Principle one: Those being served control the service(s) provided.

Principle two: Those being served become better able to serve and be served by their own actions.

Principle three: Those who serve also are learners and have significant control over what is expected to be learned.

Robert Greenleaf, author of *Servant Leadership, A Journey into the Nature of Legitimate Power and Greatness* (see box), defines service as it is used in this service-learning formulation:

One who serves takes care to make sure that other people's highest priority needs are being served. The best test, and

Servant Leadership, by Robert K. Greenleaf, Paulist Press, New York, 1977.

In the 1920s Greenleaf finished college and became a groundman — post-hole digger — for the American Telephone and Telegraph Company. In 1964 he retired as the company's director of management research. Since then he has been active as a management consultant to businesses, educational institutions, and social service groups.

His concept of the servant as leader was developed over the years and crystalized when he read Herman Hesse's *Journey to the East*, a story that shows how a group disintegrates with the disappearance of the servant who had sustained the members with his spirit as well as his menial labor. Greenleaf contends that great leaders are those who are servants first, *i.e.*, who lead because of a desire to serve rather than to gain power or personal gratification.

Greenleaf cites historical examples of servant leaders, including Thomas Jefferson, and predicts that in the next 30 years leaders will come from the "dark skinned and the deprived and the alienated of the world" rather than from elite groups who have not learned to listen and respond to the problems of those to be served.

In his chapter on "Servant Leadership in Education," Greenleaf returns to his theme of the need for secondary and post-secondary schools to prepare the poor "to return to their roots and become leaders among the disadvantaged." He states that the goal of a college education should be to "prepare students to serve, and be served by the current society."

Greenleaf also devotes chapters to "The Institution as Servant," "Trustees as Servants," "Servant Leadership in Business," "Servant Leadership in Foundations," "Servant Leadership in Churches," "Servant Leaders" (profiles of Abraham Joshua Heschel and Donald John Cowling), "Servant Responsibility in a Bureaucratic Society," and "America and World Leadership."

Greenleaf shows a way of putting together two overworked words (service and leadership) into a fresh perspective. In *Servant Leadership* he offers experiential learning managers a holistic framework for understanding the significance of service-centered learning for individuals and institutions.

—*Bob Sigmon*

difficult to administer, is: do those served grow as persons; do they while being served, become healthier, wiser, freer, more autonomous, more likely themselves to become servants? And, what is the effect on the least privileged in society; will they benefit, or, at least, will they not be further deprived?

Learning flows from the service task(s). To serve in the spirit of the Greenleaf definition requires attentive inquiry with those served and careful examination of what is needed in order to serve well. As a result, *learning objectives are formed in the context of what needs to be done to serve others.*

Unfortunately, learning objectives may be superimposed upon rather than derived from the service task even in programs that strive to adopt the service-learning style. In the SREB service-learning internship model of the 1960s, for example, the hyphen between service and learning was highlighted because it illustrated the link between the two. Unfortunately, the nature of the service received limited attention; the focus was on the learning outcomes sought. The proper emphasis in service-learning, in my view, is not on the link between the two, but on the distinctiveness of a service situation as a learning setting.

Exercise for Principles One and Two

An awareness-building exercise for prospective servers helps assure that principles one and two are taken into account. The exercise is a simple process of using guided questions based on a distinction between "acquirers" and "recipients" of services. To be an "acquirer" suggests active involvement in the request for and control of a service. As an "acquirer" an individual or institution is involved in some self-analysis of the situation and is active in selecting the type of service and provider. To be a "recipient" connotes limited, if any, active participation in seeking assistance, treatment, or help.

To understand the distinctions between "acquirers" and "recipients" and to plan activities, students might do the following:

1. Describe one or more situations in which each student has been an "acquirer" of a service;
2. Describe one or more situations in which each has been a "recipient" of a service;
3. Describe one or more situations in which each has been a direct service provider to an individual, organization (Were those served viewed as "acquirers" or "recipients"?);

4. Discuss these experiences with a partner or a small group;
5. List the key themes noted in the descriptions of services;
6. Examine these themes alongside the three service-learning principles, or the Greenleaf definition of service, or within the "acquirer"-"recipient" framework; and
7. Move into various phases of discussion and planning for a service-learning activity.

Constituencies: A Service Task Check List

An analytical tool for looking at four basic constituencies in service delivery situations has been helpful to me. The first constituency is made up of those who acquire services; the second, service providers; the third, technology developers (those who budget, plan, manage, develop curricula, design, monitor and generally run things); and the fourth, those who provide resources, the policy makers.

Service-learning projects can have as the "acquirer" of service any of these four constituencies. The central question is: Does the service being provided make any sense to those expected to benefit from the services delivered? Will they be better able to serve themselves and others because of it? Closely related is the question: Who are the individuals who fill the roles in any service delivery activity, and how do they relate to one another?

The accompanying Service Task Check List is a practical tool for examining program elements and actors in most voluntary action or public service-oriented internships. Seven participants are listed along the horizontal axis, and 10 program functions associated with student projects are listed on the vertical axis.

The Check List can be used in several ways. The list across the top *introduces major categories of actors* in a service-learning activity and their distinctive expectations, roles, and relationship patterns. The questions down the left side relate to the development and implementation of a service project and can be *guides for planning an activity*. Participants should be required to be specific in their responses and encouraged to examine closely the implications of who controls the services to be rendered.

A faculty member, an agency supervisor, and the student involved can use the list to *examine a student's service-learning activity*. Two avenues of analysis are possible: What are the similarities and differences in perspective among the three participants, and who in fact is in control of the services being provided? As a planning tool for individual projects, the Check List can provide a similar overview of *who will be in charge* and how each participant views the control issues in a proposed activity.

In order to review a departmental or institution-wide service-oriented education program either being planned or in existence, different constituencies can complete the check list and then note and *discuss comparisons and contrasts.* These profiles also can be checked out against the Greenleaf service definition or the three principles outlined earlier.

A Service Plan Work Sheet

A project or service plan work sheet is another tool for helping discover responses to "Who is to be served by this activity?" and "How are those to be served involved in stating the issue and carrying out the project?" Proposed categories for a model work sheet are:

1. Summary of the situation to be influenced;
2. Key individuals, organizations, and institutions involved in the situation (the direct providers, technology developers, and policy makers concerned about the dilemma);
3. Proposed specific service objectives;
4. Experiences (activities, resources, settings, methods, and the like) to be used in conducting activity;
5. Criteria for assessing service outcomes; and
6. Specific citizens and/or institutions to be served.

Providing service in situations where "acquirers" speak in other tongues — or don't speak, or speak from cultural perspectives unfamiliar to us — is no easy task. There is a great need for the invention of tools and exercises that help potential servers better engage those to be served. The chief tool for most of us will most likely be one we invent for the unique situations we face.

Principle Three: All Are Learners

Principle three — those who serve are also learners and have significant control over what is expected to be learned — can have many varieties of expression.

Since SREB days, I have viewed *all* the active partners in a service-learning experience as learners — not only the student, but also the faculty counselor, the agency or community supervisor, and those being served. This expectation strongly suggests that mutuality is an important dimension in learning.

In a service-learning activity, the service situation allows ample room for the coordinator to define some learning objectives (*e.g.*, what skills and knowledge does the task require, what skills and knowledge does the student possess, what still needs to be learned for the student to meet some of his or her own learning expectations, for the program sponsoring the activity to have stated learning outcomes, and for the acquirers of service to have attainable learning expectations.) The critical task is making sure the services to be rendered are not overwhelmed by the learning tasks. It is my conviction that once an appropriate service activity is formulated and checked out, the learning potential becomes apparent.

Even in well-planned service-learning programs with clearly defined learning objectives, however, significant unplanned learning will occur. Often it will challenge value assumptions and will require thoughtful reflection and sharing with others.

A major need in service-learning is for educational researchers to examine the distinctive learning outcomes associated with service delivery. Where does service end and learning begin in a service-learning setting? How is service delivery aided or handicapped by learning expectations? Do the service-learning principles stated here make any difference to the quality of service and learning acquired?

Service-learning is called a utopian vision by some and too demanding and impractical by others. Service-learning, as discussed here, is rooted in the belief that all persons are of unique worth, that all persons have gifts for sharing with others, that persons have the right to understand and act on their own situations, and that our mutual survival on the planet depends on the more able and the less able serving one another.

Service-learning as formulated here is a partial corrective to the self-deception many of us service providers practice. We spread around our talents and knowledge because we have it to use and enjoy sharing. We do research in communities to justify our positions or test a promising methodology. We do group-oriented work because we are trained in group processes. We want clients to come to us. We advocate for the poor, young, elderly, and minorities because we want to serve without realizing that they may not be impressed.

As providers, our degree of control over services and service systems is excessive in most instances. If we are to be measured by the Greenleaf criterion of those served growing as persons, becoming healthier, wiser, freer, more autonomous, more likely themselves to become servants, then we are called to invent ways to

Service Task Check List

Place a check in the appropriate box for each question. If more than one answer is valid, rank the answers in order of importance.

	Citizens, the service acquirers	Direct care providers	Policymakers, resource sanctioners Technology developers	Technical staff and faculty advisors	Individual advisors Program coordinator	The service-learner or volunteer	Other
Who initiates the tasks to be addressed?							
Who defines the tasks?							
Who approves the methods used in doing the tasks?							
Who monitors the daily/weekly task activities?							
Who is the server responsible to in the community or agency?							
Who determines when the task is completed satisfactorily?							
Who benefits from the task being done well?							
Who decides that a server doing a task should be withdrawn from the work?							
Who owns the final product of a server's work with the community or agency?							
Other							

engage those to be served, and that primarily has to be on their turf and terms.

My hope for these notes is that they will stimulate dialogue on what service-learning principles say to those using the major experiential education styles mentioned earlier.

A constant challenge those of us who provide learning opportunities for people in service settings face is to be what Greenleaf calls "servant leaders." Servant leaders are people who formulate visions, arrange the structures, and manage the action within the spirit of the service-learning principles. Greenleaf pushes me and, I hope, many others to invent the distinctive ways in which we all can better serve and be served.

Robert Sigmon is Acting Director of the Wake Area Health Education Center in Raleigh, North Carolina. He has helped develop and manage service-learning models in South Carolina, North Carolina, Georgia, and Tennessee. He also helped to found the National Society for Internships and Experiential Education in 1971.

Service Learning: Groping Toward a Definition

Timothy Stanton

Is service learning a type of experiential education program or a philosophy of education? Stanton explores these questions which every service-learning educator eventually confronts. Adapted from Experiential Education, National Society for Internships and Experiential Education, *Vol. 12, No. 1, January-February 1987, pp. 2, 4.*

WHAT IS SERVICE LEARNING, anyway? Administrators and staff of service learning programs have multiple and sometimes conflicting sets of purposes for their programs. These include social action, voluntary service, cognitive and problem-solving skill development, academic knowledge and leadership development, among others. Their practices vary as well. Finding a single, firm, universally acceptable definition of service learning is like navigating through fog. How do we distinguish service learning from cooperative education, internship programs, field study and other forms of experiential education?

A review of the literature on the subject suggests that service learning is more of a *program emphasis*, representative of a set of educational, social and sometimes political values, rather than a discrete *type* of experiential education. In fact, one may encounter forms of service learning in many different types of experiential education programs.

Fine, you say, but how would you recognize service learning if you encountered it? First, you would sense in a program's structures, objectives and processes a profound emphasis on *service to others*. While other forms of experiential education emphasize career development, academic knowledge, skill development or some combination of these objectives, programs described as service learning place primary value on the service performance of students and on the outcomes of their activities for those off campus who are recipients of the service.

Yet service performance is valued in most co-op and internship programs. What else is involved in qualifying a program as "service learning?" Bob Sigmon (1979) asserts three principles which offer some clues:

1) Those being served control the service provided. The needs of the host community, rather than of the academic or career program, come first in defining the work of students placed there; and the community defines those needs.

2) Those being served become better able to serve and be served by their own actions. The aim of the students' service should be the collaborative development and empowerment of those served.

3) Those who serve are also learners, and have significant control over what is learned.

In these principles, Sigmon suggests a philosophy of *reciprocal learning:* all parties in service learning — those serving and those served — are learners and have influence in determining what is to be learned. "The proper emphasis in service-learning . . . is not the link between the two, but on the distinctiveness of a service situation as a learning setting" (1979, p. 10). Students' career goals, developmental needs and intellectual curiosity, while relevant and integrated into their activities, still must be defined and operationalized in the context of their service performance and the needs of those being served.

Is there a means of describing service performance in students' service learning activities by focusing on the recipients of the service and on the types of service provided? The *individual* dimension includes the traditional helping activities such as tutoring, working with persons with disabilities, counseling and so on: those activities often labeled "volunteer work." The *organizational* dimension occurs when an organization (as opposed to individuals) is the primary recipient of service. Activities in this dimension include administrative assistance, policy analysis, special project work, and similar internships. Their third dimension is *interorganizational*, with students involved in generating and/or applying knowledge as field researchers, needs assessors and so on, serving coalitions, associations or networks. The fourth is *locality*, which includes general problem-solving, consulting and action research focusing on issues in a particular locale.

In noting that most service learning programs include a mixture of these dimensions, Giles and Freed demonstrate that the service in service learning is not necessarily restricted to non-profit and government organizations, the traditional hosts of such activities. They suggest that the distinguishing characteristic of service learning is the nature of the *social exchange* between the service learner and those who are being served. That exchange is shaped by the values of the service learning educators, the students, and the institutional and social contexts in which the service learning occurs.

Out of the fog a definition thus begins to emerge. Rather than a discrete type of program, service learning appears to be an *approach* to experiential learning, an *expression of values* — service to others, community development and empowerment, reciprocal learning — which determines the purpose, nature and process of *social and educational exchange* between learners (students) and the people they serve, and between experiential education programs and the community organizations with which they work.

There is much debate on the relationship between the current interest in public service, civic responsibility, civic education and the traditions of service learning. New concepts of service learning may be needed, a language better able to help us define it, discuss it and link it to the new movements in education.

Is service learning a *form* of experiential education which can stand beside internships, field study and cooperative education? Or is it a *philosophy* of experiential education which suggests methods and practices that should inform all programs? Perhaps it is both.

Timothy Stanton is Associate Director of the Public Service Center at Stanford University and former President of the National Society for Internships and Experiential Education.

References

Giles, Dwight and Jamille Freed, "The Service-Learning Dimensions of Field Study: The Cornell Human Ecology Field Study Program," paper presented at the National Conference on Service-Learning, Washington, DC, March 1985. Available from NSIEE.

Sigmon, Robert L., "Service-Learning: Three Principles," *Synergist*, National Center for Service-Learning, ACTION, Vol. 8, No. 1, Spring 1979, pp. 9-11. Available from NSIEE.

Choose Engagement Over Exposure

Lee M. Levison

In this conclusion to his national study of community service programs in independent schools, funded by the Ford Foundation, Levison warns that without careful preparation, reflection, and analysis, community service programs can simply reinforce stereotypes of those "served." He calls for programs that provide engagement *and not just* exposure *for students — programs that reach both their minds and their hearts and allow them to understand the context of the social problems they encounter. This section is reprinted with permission from* Community Service Programs in Independent Schools *by Lee M. Levison, National Association of Independent Schools, 1986, pp. 104-119. For a copy of the full report, write NAIS, 75 Federal Street, Boston, MA 02110.*

Exposure

STUDENTS REPEATEDLY CLAIM that community service expands their horizons. Their assumption appears to be that their horizons, their knowledge of the world and of people who are different, are narrow. But for television news stories, they rarely see the pain, suffering, death, and poverty that effects people across this country and throughout the world. Community service gives them, as one student said, "a sort of reality."

Students speak of being exposed to "real world" issues and of learning to deal with people from many different backgrounds. Community service is a means for students to "see a different slice of life," the lives of people who are "less fortunate." They work with people who are poor, people who have very little schooling, people who are on society's sideline. They work with the elderly, the mentally retarded, and the handicapped. According to students, working with these people helps them put their own lives into perspective. As students' horizons expand, their former concerns are far less important — they appear trivial.

The Limits of Exposure

> How seriously do students and teachers approach the joint endeavor of confronting the subject that brings them together? How much do they really care? How much energy are they willing to expend?

> ... Intensity is the difference between the capacity to perform and the will to perform, between a passive and an active attitude. It signifies desire, sweat, and hard work exerted toward well-understood personal or group objectives. (Powell, Farrar, and Cohen, pp. 70, 96-97)

Exposure is what most students experience during their involvement in community service. The vast majority of programs aim to expose students to people who are less fortunate than they are — people with whom they would not ordinarily come into contact. Yet some programs aspire to go beyond such exposure, to *engage* students. *Engagement* implies intensity. In such programs students take service seriously, they are intellectually engaged, the school's approach is multi-dimensional, and the school genuinely cares about service. Programs that engage students demand not only that students use their hearts (e.g., sympathize or empathize with clients); they also insist that students understand intellectually the "broad social dynamics" underlying the situations of the people they serve (the plight of the elderly, causes of poverty, racism, etc.). Engagement programs require more commitment from their students than just fulfilling the required number of hours.

In 1982 Conrad and Hedin concluded that "... experiential-based educational programs can be highly effective in promoting personal, social, and intellectual development — and can do so more effectively than classroom instruction alone" (p. 75). More recently, Newmann and Rutter found that "community service programs contribute to students' sense of social competence and responsibility to the community beyond school"(1983, p. 40).

Other researchers have concluded that community service is more symbol than substance (Cookson and Persell, 1985). Some school heads and faculty question whether elaborate programs are needed to attain program goals.

To judge from interviews of students, schools with elaborate community service program structures, elegant program mission statements, and full-time staff do not necessarily have better, more effective programs. Some school heads and faculty argue that, in fact, elaborate structures are as symbolic as minimal program structures. They say that less structure is better — the emphasis ought to be on service, not on the program. As one faculty member put it, there is a virtue in having a "quiet commitment to service." Some believe that too much structure makes service less spontaneous, consequently less meaningful for students. One head said, "there is nothing wrong with being intramural instead of varsity. Sometimes intramural play can have more meaning than varsity play. If we get it [the service program] too shined up, it might not have the allure that it has now."

The difference between varsity and "intramural play" is that fewer people care about the outcome. If the caring, intensity, and commitment often associated with "varsity" athletics could be transferred to community service programs, students' service experiences might become as memorable and significant as many of their athletic experiences are. Schools that succeed at engaging their students may disprove Cookson and Persell's claim that community service in independent schools is merely rhetoric.

Engagement versus Exposure

Like most successful athletic programs, *engagement* service programs reflect purpose, preparation, care, effort, and recognition. The objectives in engagement programs are as clear and precise as objectives in athletics (although more complex than simply winning or losing!). Coaches and players expend extraordinary effort in preparing and playing their games. Coordinators and students prepare just as rigorously. In some schools students attend orientation meetings, participate in workshops on working with the elderly, retarded, or chronically ill, and read extensively before going to their placements. Summers are used by coordinators to review the program, work with placements, evaluate courses, and read. Students care about the people they serve and the opportunities they have to grow. Service coordinators and students invest substantial time and effort to insure that their "performances" at the placements are helpful to the client and meaningful for the students themselves. In engagement programs the efforts of students, faculty, parents, and site personnel are honored at celebrations. One school has an annual luncheon to thank all the people who are associated with the program.

Perhaps the most conspicuous difference between engagement and exposure programs lies in program objectives. Engagement programs have detailed, explicit, and comprehensive objectives. Engagement programs move beyond the rhetoric. Their objectives are concrete: to learn about a community need and/or social service agency; to develop skills in organizing activities and solving problems; to understand the principles and practices of helping others in a social service setting; to examine the social implications of certain practices and values in society.

By contrast, the objectives of an *exposure* program might typically be "to allow students an opportunity to serve the community" or "to broaden students' horizons." These are not unworthy goals; they are just not specific, concrete, or ambitious. Elegant statements of purpose without detailed and explicit objectives are, as Cookson and Persell claim, "camouflage." Engagement service programs proceed from reasonable but ambitious, concrete objectives — not from rhetoric.

Engagement programs are intellectually demanding. Students are asked not only to feel, but to think. They are asked to think about social problems, social policies, and personal feelings about helping. Engagement programs conduct reflection sessions for participating students. Students are expected to keep journals, to research issues related to their placements, (mental retardation, aging, child development, poverty). As one coordinator observed, "Students need to understand the broad social dynamics of poverty to really understand people in need. They need something analytic to understand the social dynamics of the poor."

Conclusion. No one of the programs studied fully exhibits all the engagement characteristics described above. Yet engagement programs aim to do more than expose their students to the "real world" or to cultivate in them the service habit. Engagement programs demand that students move beyond "feeling badly" about the people they serve and toward an understanding of the "embedded inequalities of power, privilege, and esteem" in our society (Bellah *et al.*, 1985, p. 204). The habit of service, as cultivated in exposure programs, is insufficient.

As John Dewey wrote in *Democracy and Education*:

Habit means that an individual undergoes a modification through an experience, which modification forms a predisposition to easier and more effective action in a like direction in the future.... But habit, apart from knowledge, does not make allowance for change of conditions, for novelty.

In other words, knowledge is a perception of those connections of an object which determine its applicability in a given situation ... While a habit apart from knowledge supplies us with a single fixed method of attack, knowledge means that selection may be made from a much wider range of habits. (p. 395)

Service without knowledge, without an understanding of the "embedded inequalities" of our society, means, for example, that students are unable to make connections between the plight of the poor and social policies. Going through the motions, just doing service without reflection and without knowledge, undermines the power of people who serve to make changes in institutions, to make things better for people who are in need. Service without engagement prepares students to make things "less bad," and it fails to help them make the connections that will lead to change.

Conclusion to the NAIS Study

There is today a dangerous mismatch between the country's urgent need for civic mindedness and the parochial attitudes of its citizens ... there are clear signs that self-interest is undermining public interest. (Newman, 1985)

If America is to remain viable as a unified nation and as a democracy its young people must have a sense of civic responsibility, a sense of responsibility to and for the whole society. (Chandler, 1985)

Newman and Chandler sense a malaise among today's youth. School heads repeatedly remark that community service aims to mitigate the self-centeredness of today's student generation. Derek Bok, president of Harvard University, said in his 1985 commencement address, "We hear that students have lost interest in the welfare of others and the problems of society. They have abandoned their idealism for a consuming preoccupation with themselves, their security, and their careers." Such claims are supported by survey data from incoming college freshmen: since 1972, students have lost interest in issues such as the environment, racial equality, and community matters (Newman p. 37).

Authoritative voices in schools, in government, and in higher education indicate that community service is an activity that will mitigate the current trend of self-interest among young people. Community service, it is argued, will foster a more active interest in societal problems such as racial equality and poverty. In independent schools, in particular, community service is expected to expose students to a world not often encountered by them or by their families — a world of poverty, pain, suffering, and death. Such "exposure" is important, it is held, because independent schools train society's future leaders.

Among school heads, faculty, and parents, community service is perceived as a panacea for the current student generation's unhealthy preoccupation with self. Yet the quality of this "panacea" varies widely from school to school. *Instrumental* service programs are directly related to the school's mission. In schools with such programs, the school policies support the service program by making time available in the academic schedule for students to engage in service. Committed program coordinators are diligent in their efforts to insure that community service is a worthwhile experience for students. In reflection sessions and academic courses, students are asked to think intellectually and analytically about their service experiences. *Strategic* service programs have a more tenuous philosophical foothold in their schools. Such programs are fueled by the efforts of a single committed adult rather than by institutional purpose. School policies related to the schedule are untouchable, and students rarely have the opportunity to reflect on their service experiences with other students and adults. *Symbolic* programs do not have philosophical roots in their schools. As is the case with strategic programs, individuals drive and sustain symbolic service programs. School policies rarely support symbolic programs and occasionally undermine them, and students almost never talk or think about their service experience as part of the program.

Great expectations surround community service programs in independent schools. According to students, the most important benefit derived from service is that it exposes them to the "real world." Many students express genuine sympathy for the people they serve — some saddened by the treatment of the elderly, some puzzled by the lack of opportunities for inner city blacks and Hispanics, and some frustrated by the marginalization of handicapped people. Students "feel badly" about people who are "less fortunate"; however, their comments rarely reflect a sensitivity to or understanding of the social dynamics of poverty and racism. Students seem to accept such circumstances as a given. Their comments focus on the personal satisfaction they derive from serving, not on underlying issues. Few students articulate a vision of a world without poverty and racism or other social ills.

If the prime benefits of service for students are that it makes them feel good and it exposes them to the "real world," then is it realistic to expect community service to mitigate the alleged self-centeredness and narrowness of the current student generation? Does community service go far enough?

> Schools attempt to teach the duty of ritualistic citizen participation in voting, letter writing or volunteer service, but fail to generate active inquiry about the nature of the public good or commitment to working for it. The dominant rationale for education is individual aggrandizement and personal fulfillment. We see this ideology as leading to cultural degradation and global suicide, because it neglects human needs for communal (as opposed to individual) fulfillment, it minimizes the significance of interdependence in the larger human community, and it abdicates collective moral responsibility for the survival and integrity of human life. (Newmann and Rutter, pp. 3-4)

If community service programs do not address the synergystic relationship between social, political, and economic institutions and the plight of the "less fortunate," will students ever move beyond sympathy, will they ever be motivated to initiate change in order to eradicate such situations?

The risk of not addressing such issues is that community service becomes a stereotype-confirming experience for students. In his study of privileged children, Robert Coles writes, "One can brusquely try to help others, and care little for them, only for the experience of looking down upon the helpless or weak — thereby gaining a sense of personal strength and confirming any number of prejudices about those in need of 'help.'"(1977, p. 493). As one teacher commented, "You can't undo stereotypes by merely sending kids to hospitals or to inner-city schools."

These questions are raised to prompt discussion among school people about a potentially rich and rewarding learning experience for students and faculty. In many schools, community service is a hollow ritual, not a dynamic, challenging, and multi-dimensional learning opportunity for students. Nevertheless, thousands of students make significant contributions to their communities. In some cases, community service has a profound impact on students — their lives are radically changed as a result of engaging in service work. But the goal of community service is not to cultivate people for the service professions. Community service can be a vehicle for promoting understanding which then can lead to change, to improvement, and to making life better for people in this nation and in the world. Our students *see* different people but there is rarely any interpenetration — the world of the "less fortunate" remains separate and mysterious.

Formal, adult-sponsored opportunities for students to learn about, to analyze, and to ponder the circumstances of the people they serve and their personal reactions to those circumstances, may expand the emotional and intellectual understanding students have of their service experiences. Such emotional and intellectual *engagement* may also demystify people who are poor, handicapped, elderly, and in the racial minority. Some programs in this study do strive to transcend mere *exposure*, such programs aim to *engage* the hearts and the minds of students.

Lee Levison is Dean of Students at Noble and Greenough School in Dedham, Massachusetts. He received his doctorate from the Harvard Graduate School of Education, where he did his thesis on student community service.

References

Bellah, Robert W., Richard Madsen, William M. Sullivan, Ann Swidler, and Steven M. Tipton. *Habits of the Heart: Individualism and Commitment in America Life,* University of California Press, 1985.

Bok, Derek, Commencement Address at Harvard University, Cambridge, Massachusetts, June 6, 1985.

Chandler, John W., "Toward The Year 2000: Challenges For The School, Keynote Speech at the Council for Advancement and Support of Education/National Association of Independent Schools Conference, Norfolk, Virginia, December 4, 1985.

Coles, Robert, *Privileged Ones: The Well-Off and The Rich in America,* Little, Brown and Company, 1977.

Conrad, Daniel, and Diane Hedin, eds., *Youth Participation and Experiential Education,* Haworth Press, 1982.

Cookson, Peter W., Jr., and Caroline Hodges Persell, *Preparing for Power: America's Elite Boarding Schools,* Basic Books, Inc., 1985.

Dewey, John, *Democracy and Education,* Macmillan, 1916.

Newman, Frank, *Higher Education and The American Resurgence,* Carnegie Foundation for the Advancement of Teaching, 1985.

Newmann, Fred M., and Robert A. Rutter, "The Effects of High School Community Service Programs on Students' Social Development," Final Report to the National Institute of Education, December 1983.

Reflective Civic Participation

Fred M. Newmann

Arguing that increased social participation alone is not suffi-cient as an objective of civic education, Newmann says that participatory activities ought to be designed to increase student competence to participate as public citizens. The educational benefits of participation are determined largely by the kinds of reflection it stimulates. He suggests five guides for the central questions which drive this reflection. Reprinted with permis-sion from Social Education, *ed. Sam Natoli, October 1989.*

OUR ULTIMATE EDUCATIONAL PURPOSE is not simply to in-crease the rate or amount of social participation, but instead to develop student competence to exercise influence in public affairs according to democratic and ethical principles (Newmann, 1975). To be sure, special forms of community participation are necessary to build this competence, but participation alone is unlikely to offer much educational benefit unless it is accompanied by solid, in-depth study and rigorous reflection. What should students think about as they participate? The participation curriculum we pro-posed (Newmann, 1975; Newmann, Bertocci & Landsness, 1977) provided an initial outline. Thanks to more recent scholarship on the crisis of citizenship in the United States, here we take further steps in building a curriculum framework for reflective civic partici-pation.

Participating as Public Citizen

First we must give students opportunities to participate as and reflect upon the role of the "public citizen." As explained by Aristotle, Jefferson, Dewey, and more recent analysts such as Tuss-man (1982) and Barber (1984), the main task for the democratic public citizen is to deliberate with other citizens about the nature of the public good and how to achieve it. Authentic (rather than academic) occasions for these discussions are characterized by conflict among private interests, but competing notions of the public good, by uncertainty about the actual consequences of policies and actions, and by the necessity of resolving differences through argument, reason, and negotiation, rather than by coercion or appeal to arbitrary authority. Questions of the public good arise in arriving at policies for groups and institutions and in making judgments on the disposition of specific cases. Such deliberations need not be confined to the highest legislative halls or government agencies; they can occur in any situation where, in their attempt to govern, people must consider a common or collective good. Opportunities for public citizenship can, therefore, be found in voluntary associations, businesses, unions, churches, political parties, neighborhoods, and schools (Newmann, 1981).

This special attention to the attributes of public citizenship is necessary in order to reverse a precipitous decline of civic life. Only recently have we come to understand how the dominant conception of citizenship conveyed in media and in the teaching of civics, government and political science acts like a virus that weakens our civic culture. According to the dominant conception, the democratic citizen is a person who learns how to advance one's private interests through rational, critically-minded participation in the choosing of governing elites and who supports the essential democratic procedures and institutions (electoral politics, checks and balances, civil liberties) that presumably permit maximum freedom for others to do the same.

From different perspectives, numerous recent scholars of citizenship (Barber, 1984; Butts, 1980; Ketcham, 1987; Pratte, 1988; Battistoni, 1985; Bellah *et al*, 1985; Janowitz, 1983; Tussman, 1982) have shown that this conception, the one that continues to frame most of our educational efforts — even those aimed toward enhancing student participation — is fatally flawed. Without space to recapitulate their arguments, I think these critics have shown that this view of citizenship fails to deliver the democratic promise of empowerment of the governed, it produces vast inequalities in material opportunity, it deprives humans of critical forms of intercourse and personal growth which only participatory democracy can provide, and it threatens the very survival of the human species and the planet. This critique sends a powerful message to educators: in planning social participation activities, our vision should focus on educational needs of the public citizen working to forge agreement in pursuit of the public good, rather than upon the one who participates primarily to advance private interests.

When educators talk about social participation, they may intend community service, electoral politics, vocational internships, social advocacy, oral history, local surveys on social issues, or mock trials. All of these can extend student contact beyond the school to adults in the community and can have important educational benefits (Conrad & Hedin, 1981; Newmann & Rutter, 1983), but none will *necessarily* involve the student in the kinds of discussions emphasized above. Students will often be preoccupied with other more parochial matters — how to identify one's most loyal supporters to win an election, learning new technical skills to tutor a student with disabilities, mastering the rules to process a student grievance against the school administration, or becoming assertive enough to obtain special information on consumer complaints from adult bureaucrats.

Participation in these roles can contribute to community welfare, to students' sense of efficacy, and most importantly to the empowerment of previously disenfranchised groups. But we should constantly be asking about the potential of these experiences to help us move from the dominant, privatistic view of civic life to a more publicly-minded democracy. Unless students are placed in settings and roles that require them to deliberate about the nature of a public good and to participate in the processes of influence and negotiation to achieve it, students will fail to reap the personal benefits of citizenship, and the civic culture will languish. For this reason, we should try whenever possible to structure participatory roles within schools, community service and social advocacy projects so that students confront the kinds of issues faced by public citizens. With this point in mind, we will consider some issues that students need help in resolving if they are to participate reflectively and productively.

An Agenda for Reflection

Two main intellectual challenges for the active citizen are to formulate a position and to win support for it (Newmann, 1975). These processes are not neatly sequential. They often interact, because the particular policy stand one takes will depend in part upon the kinds of support needed. Simiarly, the process for winning support will depend in part upon the policies to be advocated. For the reflective citizen, personal conclusions are likely to change during the course of formulating a defensible position and in the process of winning support. To nurture students' development as public citizens, students need to study issues in civic participation that go beyond what is conventionally included in the teaching of history and social studies, even beyond the agenda of previously developed curriculum for analysis of public issues (Oliver & Shaver, 1966; Newmann & Oliver, 1970; Engle & Ochoa, 1988) or citizen participation (Newmann *et al*, 1977; Coplin & O'Leary, 1988). The agenda below calls attention to five dimensions: the necessity for decision and action in the face of pervasive uncertainty and ambiguity; the morality of public policy and personal choice; issues of strategy in setting of policy and action goals, clarification of students' personal civic commitments; and finally, how to enable students and teachers to talk with one another honestly and seriously about these issues.

A. Uncertainty, conflict, ambiguity, but the need to act. The public citizen will be engaged in deliberations of profound uncertainty, due to conflicting interests that must be accommodated, the lack of conclusive knowledge on most matters, and the fact that most public problems are never fully resolved. At the same time, the politics of governing requires that choices be made and actions be taken. This work can be frustrating, and for understandable reasons, students and adults alike may prefer to avoid the difficulties that critical discourse entails. The educator's challenge is to prevent the paralysis of commitment that critical inquiry so often entails. That is, our work with students must make both critical inquiry and imperfect action personally rewarding. We have offered some suggestions for how teachers might support students in facing uncertainty and conflict (Newmann, 1975, Newmann *et al*, 1977; Newmann, 1984). More recently, Purpel (1989) made an important curricular proposal by indicating how the student of prophetic literature can provide inspiring historical examples that may help students to understand and cope with this tension.

B. Morality of public policy and personal choice. Moral issues are construed here as disagreements about the ultimate values that justify public and personal actions. Typically these are phrased as values in the "American Creed" (Myrdal, 1944) and the Constitutional tradition; for example, the right to life, liberty, and the pursuit of happiness; equality of opportunity; general welfare; national security; justice and due process of law; consent of the governed. Yet their definitions are often problematic, and they may conflict with one another in specific contexts; for example, does the right to life of a fetus conflict with the liberty of the mother to control her body?

As students participate in community service, social advocacy, electoral politics, or in governing their own schools and organizations, they should have opportunities to articulate the primary values they seek and to reason about value conflicts. Approaches to such discussion have been developed (e.g. Oliver & Shaver, 1966; Newmann & Oliver, 1970; Mosher, 1980; Lockwood & Harris, 1988), but this work needs to be extended. If moral discussion is to respond to real, felt concerns of the public, its language must reach beyond the formal concepts of the American Creed, technical ethical principles, and Constitutional rhetoric. Gilligan (1982), for example, has reminded us that securing justice and the common good is not simply a question of defining duties, rights and obligations, but also of finding opportunities for people to care for and to nurture one another. Barber (1984) has shown that a major function of political discussion is not merely to resolve disputes, but also to *generate* affiliation and commitment to the common good. Butts (1988) and Purpel (1989) have suggested how tensions within American culture related to individual freedom, cultural diversity, and materialism have led to alienation, relativism, and a profound spiritual-moral crisis. Purpel calls upon schools to explicitly abandon the myth of neutrality and instead to involve students in continuous moral discourse that rekindles personal commitment to compassion and the common good. In short, we dare not assume that students come to school with a basic commitment to the common good; our discussions of values must help to promote it.

C. *Strategic issues.* Those interested in improving public life face a number of strategic issues such as the scope and priorities of action. By way of illustration, assume students are considering what ought to be done and what they themselves might do about poverty.

Scope. How ambitious or comprehensive should the policy or action objective be? Limited goals might include volunteer tutoring in a low-income school, or persuading neighbors to vote for a candidate who supports effective job training programs. More ambitious goals might be revising the income tax structure, or developing programs to create new jobs in poverty areas. How much attention should we give to short-term versus long-term goals (e.g., finding shelter for the homeless versus reducing the number of homeless through programs of housing, income maintenance or social services)?

Priorities. In choosing among the many ways to approach the poverty problem, a thoughtful citizen will try to establish priorities; that is, to explain why some actions should come before others, and why some efforts might legitimately deserve a greater investment of resources than others. Asking about the relative costs and benefits of alternative actions, including the costs of *not* doing certain things (opportunity costs), can help to establish priorities. One might, for example, decide to work hard in the campaign of a candidate who is unlikely to win, on the ground that only he/she will raise public awareness of the connection between poverty, education, and the local economy that may need to be developed before appropriate resources would be invested in the education of low-income students.

Strategic thinking helps first of all in deciding whether a proposed course is the best way to advance one's ultimate social objectives (e.g., "If we are successful in increasing the number of shelters for the homeless, to what extent will this reduce the burdens of poverty?"). Strategic reflection is also necessary in choosing steps to maximize achievement of intermediate goals (e.g., "Will our proposed strategies actually produce an increase in the number of shelters?").

D. Personal civic commitment. Family, occupation, friendship, and leisure all compete for energy that we might otherwise invest in civic affairs. If educators are to enhance civic participation, we will have to help students reflect upon their personal civic commitments. In doing so, we must generate excitement about the quest for the public good and try to replace pervasive cynicism about democratic participation with more hopeful moral inspiration. It may help to consider at least three issues that influence students' personal commitments: efficacy, integrity and responsibility.

Efficacy. Here the challenge is to structure participation and conversation to increase efficacy rather than powerlessness. This involves setting goals that seem attainable, but which also carry enough challenge and significance to a problem that their fulfillment brings students a sense of efficacy, rather than only the satisfaction of having finished an easy, routine task. Beyond successful action, efficacy depends also upon cognitive mastery — developing a better understanding of the problem. Students who have tasted the complexity of social issues, need a sense of intellectual mastery at least over limited aspects of a problem, along with relief from the expectation that success consists only in exhaustive understanding.

Integrity. Participation can involve assaults on a citizen's integrity, especially through the trade-offs, negotiations, and compromises that apparently involve co-optation, selling out, or otherwise abandoning basic principles. One may need to deal with people whose motives are suspect and whose interests may actually undermine the public good. In winning support, one may become involved in one-sided advocacy, along with manipulation of opinions and votes, rather than in honest, open discussion of issues. And it may be necessary to take forceful stands with incomplete knowledge of the solutions to a problem. Such threats to integrity can reduce civic commitment, and ways to cope with them should be discussed. The main topic for reflection here is "How does one maintain a sense of personal integrity while participating in the real world of politics?"

Responsibility. Participation in governance or advocacy brings the awesome responsibility of having real influence in peoples' lives, and young people are not alone in shying away from this, especially when the responsibility may bring painful personal consequences. Resolving issues through legislative, executive and judicial action, and through elections, creates winners and losers. Losers usually suffer psychologically and economically. Public decisions on budget and personnel distribute economic resources and the opportunity to serve the public to some, while denying these to others. Conflicts of opinion among peers and the process of building coalitions can jeopardize friendships. Facing such unpleasant consequences of civic participation can be stressful. To minimize the negative effects of such stress on civic commitment, these issues should be acknowledged and discussed in some detail.

E. Building authentic discourse. Barber (1984) discussed several important functions of talk in democracy: the articulation of interests; bargaining and exchange; persuasion; agenda-setting; exploring mutuality; affiliation and affection; maintaining autonomy; witness and self-expression; reformulation and reconceptualization; and community-building as the creation of public interests, common goods, and active citizens. Others (e.g., Oliver & Shaver, 1966; Newmann & Oliver, 1970; Newmann, 1988) have also celebrated discussion as the critical educational medium of citizenship. A persisting problem, however, is how to nurture in schools a culture of conversation in which students can talk honestly and seriously about personal dimensions of civic participation. Authentic discourse is usually suppressed by the belief that the purpose of teaching is to transmit fixed knowledge to students so that they can reproduce it in identical form for the teacher, by rewarding students for playing the game of telling teachers what they want to hear rather than asking and answering questions which students consider important, and by enormous efforts to keep order and control over masses of students. In pursuing the agenda for reflection outlined here, we must work constantly on the problem of building authentic discourse. To assist this effort, we should consider the work of Giroux (1988) and Oliver (in press) who, from different perspectives, explain why it is so important to integrate the students' lived experiences into the talk of school.

Summary

Based on the proposition that increased social participation alone is insufficient as an objective of civic education, I began by stipulating that participatory activities ought to be designed in order to increase student competence to participate as public citizens. The forms of participation to be promoted should take account of the current crisis in civic life caused in part by the society's reliance on a view of citizenship that sees democracy essentially as a set of procedures for the pursuit of private interest. Instead, participation should be informed by a conception of the public citizen. In any case, the educational benefits of participation will be determined largely by the kinds of reflection it stimulates. We need to think more carefully about the intellectual substance or the central questions to drive reflection, and I discussed five main areas to guide this project: the necessity for decision and action in the face of uncertainty and ambiguity; the morality of public policy and personal choice; issues of strategy in setting of policy and action goals; clarification of students' personal civic commitments; and finally, how to enable students and teachers to talk with one another honestly and seriously about these matters. If we can help students to resolve these issues, their civic participation should reduce individual alienation and enhance public life.

Fred Newmann directs the National Center on Effective Secondary Schools and is Professor of Curriculum and Instruction at the University of Wisconsin.

References

Barber, Benjamin R., *Strong Democracy: Participatory Politics for a New Age*, University of California Press, 1984.

Battistoni, Richard M., *Public Schooling and the Education of Democratic Citizens*, University Press of Mississippi, 1985.

Bellah, Robert N., R. Madsen, W. M. Sullivan, A. Swidler, and S. M. Tipton, *Habits of the Heart: Individualism and Commitment in American Life*, University of California Press, 1985.

Butts, R. Freeman, *The Revival of Civic Learning: A Rationale for Citizenship in American Schools*, Phi Delta Kappa, 1980.

Butts, R. Freeman, *The Morality of Democratic Citizenship: Goals for Civic Education in the Republic's Third Century*, Center for Civic Education, Calabasas, California, 1988.

Conrad, Dan and Diane Hedin, *Executive Summary: Experiential Education Evaluation Project*, Center for Youth Development and Research, University of Minnesota, 1981.

Coplin, W. D., M. K. O'Leary, and J. J. Carroll, *Effective Participation in Government: A Guide to Policy Skills*, Policy Studies Associates, 1988.

Engle, S. H. and A. S. Ochoa, *Education for Democratic Citizenship: Decision Making in the Social Studies*, Teachers College Press, 1988.

Gilligan, Carol, *In a Different Voice: Psychological Theory and Women's Development*, Harvard University Press, 1982.

Giroux, Henry A., *Schooling and the Struggle for Public Life: Critical Pedagogy in the Modern Age*, University of Minnesota Press, 1988.

Janowitz, Morris, *The Reconstruction of Patriotism: Education for Civic Consciousness*, University of Chicago Press, 1983.

Ketcham, Ralph, *Individualism and Public Life: A Modern Dilemma*, Basil Blackwell, 1987.

Lockwood, A. L. and D. E. Harris, *Reasoning with Democratic Values: Ethical Problems in United States History*, [Instructor's Manual], Teachers College Press, 1988.

Mosher, R. L., *Moral Education: A First Generation of Research and Development*, Praeger, 1980.

Myrdal, G., *An American Dilemma: The Negro Problem in Modern Democracy*, Harper & Row, 1944.

Newmann, Fred M., *Education for Citizen Action: Challenge for Secondary Curriculum*, McCutchan, 1975.

Newmann, Fred M., "Political Participation: An Analytic Review and Proposal," in D. Heater and J. A. Gillespie, Eds., *Political Education in Flux*, Sage Publications, 1981.

Newmann, Fred M., "The Radical Perspective on Social Studies: A Synthesis and Critique," *Theory and Research in Social Education*, Vol. 13, No. 1, 1984, pp. 1-18.

Newmann, Fred M., *The Assessment of Discourse in Social Studies*, National Center on Effective Secondary Schools, University of Wisconsin, 1988.

Newmann, Fred M., T. A. Bertocci, and R. M. Landsness, *Skills in Citizen Action: An English Social Studies Program for Secondary Schools*, National Textbook Company, 1977.

Newmann, Fred M. and D. W. Oliver, *Clarifying Public Controversy: An Approach to Teaching Social Studies*, Little Brown, 1970.

Newmann Fred M. and Robert A. Rutter, *The Effects of High School Community Service Programs on Students' Social Development*, Wisconsin Center for Education Research, University of Wisconsin, 1983.

Oliver, D. W., *Education, Modernity and Fractured Meaning: Toward a Process Theory of Teaching and Learning*, SUNY Press, in press.

Oliver, D. W. and J. P. Shaver, *Teaching Public Issues in the High School*, Houghton Mifflin, 1966.

Pratte, R., *The Civic Imperative: Examining the Need for Civic Education*, Teachers College Press, 1988.

Purpel, D. E., *The Moral and Spiritual Crisis in Education: A Curriculum for Justice and Compassion in Education*, Bergin & Garvey, 1989.

Tussman, J., *Obligation and the Body Politic*, Oxford, 1982.

Rationales and Theories for Combining Service and Learning

Learning from Service
Experience Is the Best Teacher — Or Is It?

Dan Conrad and Diane Hedin

Reprinted with permission from Youth Service: A Guidebook
for Developing and Operating Effective Programs *by Dan
Conrad and Diane Hedin, Independent Sector, 1987, pp. 39-45.
The term "youth service" as used here includes an emphasis on
combining service and learning.*

*Today I got to the nursing home at 2:00. Talked to some ladies.
Passed out popcorn at the movie. Went home at 4:00.*
    — From a student's journal

THE STUDENT QUOTED above was surrounded by human
drama. On every side were loneliness, love, struggle, joy, death,
dignity, injustice, and concern. There were people with wisdom she
could draw upon, and with pains she could ease. There were more
than a dozen health-related careers to observe. She missed it all.

The same barren sentences were entered in her journal, twice
weekly, for six weeks. She was in a youth service program where
she had chosen her own assignment. She was needed there. She
was engaged in tasks that mattered to others. But she'd seen, felt,
and experienced virtually nothing.

It's not supposed to be that way. People are supposed to learn
from experience. In fact, a central part of the case for youth service
rests on claims for the possibility, even necessity, of learning from
experience.

To say that experience is a good teacher, however, does not
imply that it's easily or automatically so. If it were, we'd all be a lot
wiser than we are. It's true that we can learn from experience. We
may also learn nothing. Or we may, like Mark Twain's cat who
learned from sitting on a hot stove lid never to sit again, learn the

wrong lesson. The key, as Aldous Huxley explained, is that "experience is not what happens to a man; it is what a man does with what happened to him."

Rewards Of Reflection

The purpose of this chapter is to provide practical suggestions for encouraging young people to reflect on their experiences: to think about them, write about them, share them with others, and learn from them.

This is not so easy to accomplish. Serious reflection is seldom the preferred activity of active young people. Its value is not always immediately obvious, and is never guaranteed.

It is important, then, to be able to answer with conviction the question: "Why do it?" Three kinds of benefits are described below: improved academic learning, personal development and program improvement.

Academic Learning

Improved basic skills. Improving reading, writing, and speaking abilities are a deliberate aim of many youth service programs. Writing about and discussing their experiences and reading about their area of service is an engaging way for students to practice these basic skills.

Better learning of subject matter. A major goal of many school-based programs is to enhance learning by giving students the opportunity to apply knowledge and to practice skills learned in the classroom: helping in a day-care center as part of a child development class or interning at city hall as part of a civics class are two obvious examples.

Since the "real world" is, by nature, *not* organized by academic disciplines, a side benefit is that students learn not only about one particular subject, but also about the interrelationships between that subject and many others.

Higher level thinking and problem solving. Being able to analyze problems, generate alternatives, and anticipate consequences are critical skills in any area of life. A national study of 30 school-sponsored youth participation programs revealed that the key factor in stimulating complex thinking and improving the problem-solving ability of students was the existence, regularity, and quality of a reflective component (Conrad & Hedin, 1982).

Learning to learn from experience. Reflection is a skill, more accurately a cluster of skills, involving observation, asking questions, and putting facts, ideas, and experiences together to add new meaning to them all. Learning to learn in this way, and instilling the practice as a habit, can allow program experiences to live on in the students' lives in new experiences and new learning.

Personal Development

Awareness of changes in oneself. Ongoing reflection helps to reveal what personal changes are occurring in self image, skills, ideas about people, and thoughts about a career. Articulating them to others helps make those changes tick.

A sense of community. Meeting with other volunteers provides the opportunity to share successes and failures, to call on the help and advice of others, and to gain support, recognition, and a sense of belonging to some greater effort. It also develops a sense of ownership of the project, and a commitment to its success.

Taking charge of life. Being able to learn from experience gives us the power to influence the meaning and impact of things that we do or that happen to us. It also increases our capacity to influence subsequent experiences. It puts us in charge. It does this by providing a clearer understanding of the world, a heightened sense of who we are and can be, and an increased capacity and inclination to empower others.

Program Improvement

Improved service. A major reason for including time for reflection is to improve the quality of service. Reflection, considered in this light, includes such things as learning specific skills required by the project, problem solving, brainstorming, devising plans and strategies, and working on communication skills. As a general rule, the more practical the sessions and the more obviously related to the service experience, the more important they will seem and the more energetically the volunteers will participate.

Improved program. For a program director, the ongoing feedback from participants on how things are going and discussion of how to make them go better is invaluable.

Times of Reflection

In many cases the real question is not whether to encourage reflection, but where and when to do so. The following approaches commonly are used, often in combination.

Individual conferences. In every program, there is some opportunity for individual discussions between participants and their teachers or adult supervisors. As part of the initial placement interview, for example, a student may be guided to set particular goals. These will serve as groundwork for a journal or other self-monitoring method, as well as for periodic follow-up conferences during the course of the program.

Brief daily meetings. Students may meet together briefly either before or after going to their community placements to get equipment, arrange transportation, file reports, and so forth. These gatherings provide opportunities for exchanging ideas, for reporting on successes or difficulties, or for group problem-solving. On occasion these sessions are extended to allow for more in-depth discussions.

"Being able to learn from experience ... increases our capacity to influence subsequent experiences."

Weekly group meetings. In some cases a group session is built into the program's structure from the beginning. For example, a program involving students in child care might be scheduled for a double period each day, with the students spending three days each week in day-care centers and two days in group meetings. These meetings may be devoted to studying early childhood development or planning activities to be conducted with the children.

Periodic workshops. In some cases, special workshops are scheduled into the overall program. These often are full- or half-day events focusing on such things as the special needs of the people being served and the necessary skills to respond effectively. These sessions may be conducted by the program leader and/or by experts from the community.

Where and How to Reflect

Designing effective seminars or reflection sessions is difficult, paradoxically, because youth are in new roles of importance and respect: being in charge of things, working alongside adults rather than as underlings. The classroom component may seem too much like business-as-usual. To return to the student role can seem like a let-down, as one 16-year old girl wrote in her journal: "... and now it's time to return to school, to change from person back into student."

Making the sessions as little like school as possible by altering both the setting and the format is the key to success. Some leaders have found it possible — and productive — to hold their group meetings in the agencies where the students volunteer, in their own or the students' homes, or even in a conference room at the United Way or Chamber of Commerce. If you must meet within the school, try to find somewhere other than a normal classroom.

Beyond the obvious observation that discussion should be the primary mode of the sessions and that they should include a variety of activities, the format should be that of staff training or staff meetings. This point is not at all trivial, for both setting and format must convey that these sessions are serious, significant, and a continuation of the students' important roles in the community.

The second key to success is that the sessions be directly related to the work being done in the community. This is the most easily accomplished when all the participants are performing similar kinds of service, or are working in the same agency or on one large project. Sometimes the same effect can be achieved by dividing the total volunteer team into two or more subgroups.

When these steps are not possible (and very often they are not), the job of constructing a relevant curriculum is more complicated but not impossible to achieve. The key is to find as many common elements as you can, starting with the unifying factor that all will be providing service to others.

Organizing the Reflective Component

Learning activities can be organized into the three phases of a program which we refer to as the "three P's":

- *Preparation* — Learning activities conducted prior to a student's volunteer work;

- *Processing* — Assisting students during their service placement to understand the setting, their feelings, and to solve problems which arise; and

- *Product* — Activities designed to achieve closure and pull together the strands of experience.

Preparation

There is no formula to determine exactly the right amount of preparation needed prior to the start of volunteer work. A good rule of thumb, however, is that it's usually better to err on the side of too little preparation than too much.

Those who volunteer often do so precisely because they want a new kind of experience. A lengthy orientation period is almost certain to turn them off. In addition, it is nearly impossible to know what actually will be helpful until real issues arise from the work. Even what *we* know is important will not necessarily seem so to young people until they have had a taste of real experience in the field.

A list of topics that could be valuable before the volunteers begin their service experiences follows. We suggest you choose only some of these and leave the rest until later in the project.

1. *Build cohesion within the group.* This is crucial if the group is to function as a source of support and ideas for each volunteer. Members of a cohesive group know and respect each other, and will listen and feel free to talk.

2. *Clarify responsibilities and expectations.*

3. *Explore service options* so each person can make as informed a decision as possible concerning what he or she will be doing. An exploratory visit that does not imply obligation for either the agency or the potential volunteer should be made whenever possible.

4. *Arouse interest in and commitment to the program* and specific service projects. This is as useful and valid for those who participate out of idealism as for those with less lofty motives.

5. *Assess the values, knowledge, and skills* each volunteer brings to the project. The benefits of doing this include building the confidence of the volunteer, learning to share sensitive and important things with the group, and providing a portrait of each person as she begins the program which can be contrasted with what/who she is at the end.

6. *Develop background information* about the people and problems the volunteers will encounter. The goal is more to sensitize and revise preconceptions than to provide detailed information.

7. *Develop and practice skills* that will be used (from using a crosscut saw to listening to a child). This should include practice in the skills needed to learn from service, namely, to be vigilant observers and persistent questioners of experience.

Processing

It is in the day-to-day processing of experience that we realize, or miss, the limitless potential for learning from service. Processing experience always means thinking about it, being *consciously engaged* in it. This conscious engagement will take many forms: observing, thinking, talking, listening, asking questions, writing, reading, creating, and more. The unique value of the result lies in its personal nature: personally discovered knowledge, personally formed ideas, and personally acquired values and beliefs.

A list of topics and techniques to help bring substance and form to this task follows. Some are individual activities: most involve a group.

1. *Writing, especially keeping a journal* may be the most common requirement in youth service programs. This is a mystifying new experience for many young people, and suggestions for what to include in a journal are included at the end of this chapter.

2. *Analyzing and solving problems* is a useful way to think about experience and is necessary for effective action. A most useful approach for identifying and analyzing problems is that of the "Critical Incident." An exercise is found below.

Exercise
Critical Incident

1. Describe an incident or situation that was a critical problem in at least the sense that it was not immediately obvious to you what to do or say.

2. What's the first thing you thought of to do (or say)?

3. List three (3) other actions you might have taken (or things you might have said).

4. Which of the above seems best to you now? Why is it best?

5. What do you think is the real problem in the situation? Why do you think it came up at all?

Its special strength, and that of problem-solving generally, is that it gives meaningful focus to group discussions. Rather than the often awkward "show and tell," it treats the volunteer group as a problem-solving team, a source of ideas on how to deal with one another's real dilemmas.

3. *Learning and practicing skills* probably will be a feature of the everyday service experience, but it also can be given concentrated emphasis through special workshops held during the course of the program.

The skills to emphasize will be dictated by the nature of each program, and may be as specific as how to glaze a window or as general as learning to be assertive.

Some skills, such as assertiveness, could be useful in almost any kind of service experience. The same is true of interpersonal skills such as active listening and effective communication.

Some program leaders have found it useful to focus their seminar sessions or workshops around a cluster of skills that relate to some central theme (such as leadership) or occupation (such as human service professional).

4. *Giving observation exercises and assignments* may help give participants an idea of where to look to find learning opportunities in service. A day-care center can present a scene of mass confusion, or be "just a bunch of little kids playing around" to a person who has no questions, no idea of (or interest in) the wonders that may be discovered by watching the scene more closely. The same scene can be a valuable laboratory to the person looking for answers to specific questions on child development.

5. *Providing background sessions* (such as lectures or films) can be highly useful when sharply focused on the work the students are doing. For example, a description of the operation of small claims court would be extremely helpful to students in a consumer advocacy group who are about to present a claim.

Problems can arise when group members are in a wide variety of placements, however. One solution is to ask the agencies to conduct such sessions for student volunteers and/or to include them in their own staff training or briefing sessions.

6. *Teaching academic subject matter* is the chief focus of reflection in some school-based programs, and can be useful in any program when the application to real experience can be directly shown.

Product

Service programs almost always will be strengthened if participants work toward some product that summarizes and integrates their previous work. The product may center on the achievements of individuals and/or what was gained by the group.

> *"It is in the day-to-day processing of experience that we realize, or miss, the limitless potential of learning from service."*

There should be the opportunity, even the requirement, for individuals to articulate what has been gained. It is in giving expression to what we have learned that learning is solidified, clarified, and incorporated into our being. Some ways to encourage this are listed below.

1. *Have each participant prepare a "tip sheet"* of things he or she has learned to pass on to later volunteers. For example, youths working in nursing homes have prepared sheets outlining "Ten Rules for Working with the Elderly." Young volunteers may even agree to return to "break in" their successors.

2. *Have each participant write an informal essay or structured research paper* to demonstrate the expertise he or she has gained. One approach is to have each participant, at about the midpoint of the program, formulate a list of questions about his or her volunteer work. The final paper is *their* answer to one or more of their own questions, with the information drawn from their own experiences and reflections on those experiences.

3. People often need *help in finding language to express what they have learned* or how they have changed. Sometimes it is helpful to have a list of possibilities to respond to. See "Aims and Outcomes of Service Programs" on pages 517-518 for a list from which one could construct a master list of the "things one might have gained this year."

For the group as a whole, there should be the opportunity to present, proclaim, and preserve what they have accomplished. Some suggestions follow.

The *project itself may culminate in an event* or a product such as a freshly painted house, a newly built playground, or a published booklet on facilities accessible to handicapped persons. Even then, perhaps especially then, there is additional value in documenting the accomplishment.

One way to do this is to produce a lasting document on the project: a photo essay, videotape, booklet, or slide presentation. This should show both the achievements and the process in order to help interested persons attempt a similar project.

Student groups also might make a formal presentation on the project to a school principal or board member, or to an appropriate audience like the city council, school board, cooperative extension agents, service club, or other students. The point is to have the chance to tell *some* outside audience what you have achieved.

Finally, *there ought to be a formal closing to the project* that affirms and celebrates what has been accomplished. This can range from a simple sharing of personal highlights to a full-scale party involving volunteers, agency personnel, funders, and people served.

Dan Conrad directs community involvement programs at Hopkins High School in Minnesota. Diane Hedin is former Director of Community Relations at the Pillsbury Foundation and is now a professor at the Center for Youth Development and Research at the University of Minnesota. Over the past 17 years, Conrad and Hedin have co-directed several research and publications projects in experiential education, youth participation, and service-learning.

Activity
Writing a Daily Journal

Asking each young person to keep a regular journal is one of the most valuable and commonly used reflective activities. In some cases the journals remain the confidential property of their writers; in others, they are shared regularly with an adult leader or peer; sometimes they are discussed by a group.

The point of keeping a journal is to prompt people to notice what is happening, think about experiences and reflect on their meaning and, from that, to grow. At the very least, keeping a journal gives participants a record of what they have done and some ideas to share in group discussions and individual conferences.

The following suggestions will help young people who say: "I don't know what to write!" The whole list could be given out at once with the suggestion of writing on one or two items a day. Alternatively, a smaller number could be selected and given as a guide for a weekly or monthly report.

Suggestions for a Daily Journal

About your work

- What do you do on a typical day at your placement?
- How has this changed since you first began there (different activities, more or less responsibility, etc.)?
- Tell about the best thing that happened this week; something someone said or did, something you said or did, a feeling, an insight, a goal accomplished.
- What's the most difficult part of your work?
- What thing (or things) did you dislike most this week? Why?
- If you were in charge of the place where you volunteer, what would you do to improve it?
- If you were the supervisor, would you have the volunteers do anything different from what you are doing? Would you treat them differently?

—continued

- Tell about a person there whom you find interesting or challenging to be with. Explain why.
- What do you feel is your main contribution?
- If a time warp placed you back at the first day of this program, what would you do differently the second time around?

About you

- How do people see you there? As a staff member? a friend? a student — or what? What do you feel like when you're there?
- What did someone say to you that surprised you? Why?
- What compliments have been given and what did they mean to you? How did you react? What about criticisms and your reaction to them?
- Did you take (or avoid taking) some risk this week? Were there things you wanted to say or do that you didn't say or do?
- What happened that made you feel you would (or would not) like to do this as a career?
- What kind of person does it take to be successful at the kind of work you do (as volunteer, as a career)?
- What did you do this week that made you proud? Why?
- What feeling or idea about yourself seemed especially strong today?
- What insights have you gained into people (what makes them happy or sad, successful or failures, pleasant or unpleasant, healthy or sick, etc.)?
- How similar is your impression of yourself to the impression others seem to have of you?
- Tell about something you learned as a result of a disappointment or even a failure.
- Think back on a moment when you felt especially happy or satisfied. What does that tell you about yourself?

Service:
Linking School to Life

Ernest L. Boyer

The President of the Carnegie Foundation for the Advancement of Teaching summarizes his advice for linking service to school after a survey of 1,100 public and private high schools. Reprinted with permission from the Community Education Journal, *National Community Education Association, Alexandria, Virginia, Vol. XV, No. 1, 1987, pp. 7-9.*

THE CURRENT FOLKLORE has it that teenagers are selfish, lazy, and undisciplined. The image of an apathetic, self-indulgent generation simply does not square with reality. It does, however, mask the real youth problem in this nation. Former U.S. Commissioner of Education Harold Howe II (1981) captured it powerfully when he called American youth an island in our society. The message it receives from the adult world is:

> We have no use in our economic system for you young people between the ages of 12 and 18, and precious little use in our community affairs. So we suggest you sit quietly, behave yourselves, and study hard in the schools we provide as a holding pen until we are ready to accept you into the adult world.

During our study of the nation's high schools (Boyer, 1983), I became convinced that the problems of our schools are inextricably tied to this larger problem — the feeling on the part of many of our youth that they are isolated, unconnected to the larger world outside their classrooms. Again and again during our study, we met young people who saw little, if any, connection between what they were doing and learning in school and the communities in which they lived.

More to the point, perhaps, is that the spirit outside the school shapes powerfully the climate within the school itself. Students do not see formal education as having a consequential relationship to who they are, or even, in a fundamental way, to what they might become. Like the rest of their world, the school is run by adults. Students do not often feel a responsibility to the institution where they spend many of their waking hours, nor are they encouraged to see ways to contribute to the workings of the school. Today it is possible for American teenagers to finish high school without ever being asked to participate responsibly in life in or out of the school — never encouraged to spend time with lonely older people, help a child who has not learned to read, clean up litter on the street, or even do something meaningful at the school itself.

To encourage young people to become more fully involved in the communities of which they are a part, we proposed in *High School* that every student complete a service requirement — a new "Carnegie unit" that would involve them in volunteer work in the community or at school. The Carnegie unit, as historically defined, measures time spent in class — academic contact time. This new unit puts emphasis on time in service, but it is not bound rigidly by calendar or clock. We suggested that a student spend not less than 30 hours a year, a total of 120 hours over four years, in order to qualify for one Carnegie service unit. Students could fulfill this service requirement evenings, weekends, and summers.

I believe such a service program taps an enormous source of talent, lets young people know that they are needed, and helps students see a connection between what they learn and how they live. The goal is to help students see that they are not only autonomous individuals but also members of a larger community to which they are accountable.

Since the Carnegie Foundation proposed the new Carnegie unit, we have been encouraged by the response. School districts from coast to coast have expressed interest in the idea, and new programs have been launched. A survey of 1,100 public and private high schools conducted for the Carnegie Foundation's special report, *Student Service: The New Carnegie Unit* (Harrison, 1987) showed that about one-quarter of the service programs now in existence have been started since 1983. The same survey found that 80 percent of today's students who are engaged in community or in-school service do so not for career orientation but for altruistic reasons.

This humane aspect of volunteer work becomes apparent in talks with students who participate in service programs. A young girl attending Hudson High School in Ohio who helps retarded children, said: "I like to see people gain from what I can do for them. I like myself better for helping them."

A boy whose high school offered a little academic credit and a little scholarship money as part of his service in a nursing home said: "It's too much work for the credit and the money, but I just enjoy it. It's one of the best things I've ever done."

A student who didn't have much self-assurance before becoming a community volunteer said: "I used to wonder what I could do, because I don't think of myself as pretty or popular. Now I realize I have a lot to give. I used to say, 'Just let me lead my life,' but now I look around and see a world that needs me."

A boy who tutors immigrant children in English said: "I don't mind giving up my Saturdays because I'm learning, too. It's a very satisfying experience."

College students, too, have found satisfaction in serving. In our most recent study, *College: The Undergraduate Experience in America* (Boyer, 1986), we learned that a growing minority of today's college students believe they can make a difference and are reaching out to help others. In a national survey of 5,000 undergraduate students 52 percent reported that their high school provided an opportunity for community service. And about half participated in some form of service activity during their college years. We recommend in our report that every student complete a service project — involving work in the community or at the college — as an integral part of his or her undergraduate experience.

Schools and colleges have adopted a variety of service experiences and strategies. Atlanta and Detroit are among the cities that have made the completion of a service project a high school graduation requirement. Several states, including Maryland, are experimenting with the addition of a service component to the curriculum in all their high schools. In a number of other states, legislators, educators, public officials, and business leaders are joining forces to encourage young people on both the high school and college levels to undertake community service.

The success of local school service programs has given added momentum to the drive for initiatives on the federal level. In all, a half-dozen measures related to youth service have been introduced in the House and Senate this year.

In a recent issue of *Phi Delta Kappan,* distinguished education journalist Anne C. Lewis (1987) wrote: "To put substance into a campaign against illiteracy, to help the elderly, to meet the needs of disadvantaged children, to make the environment safer and more pleasant for citizens — all of these are worthy causes that could use the energies and enthusiasm of young people."

*The problems of our
schools are inextricably
tied to the feeling on the
part of many of our youth
that they are isolated,
unconnected to the larger
world outside their
classrooms.*

Principles to Consider

From our own study of school service in local schools, several principles are beginning to emerge that administrators should consider in embarking on a service program.

A service program begins with clearly stated educational objectives. A service program is rooted in the conviction that schooling at its best concerns itself with the humane application of knowledge to life. Service is concerned with helping others, but, above all, it is concerned with improved learning. It is about helping students to discover the value of the curriculum, and to see that, in the end, formal learning must be considered useful not just economically but socially as well.

The point is this: altruism can best be appreciated as an experience rather than an abstraction. Semantic quarrels about the meaning of altruism aside, service will be no less valuable to those who acquire it as a requirement than to those who volunteer for it.

A service program should be carefully introduced and creatively promoted. From our surveys it is clear that thoughtful people differ, not over the notion of service, but over how — or whether — it fits in the program of formal education. Further, there often are procedural barriers to be considered. To move too far too fast may lead only to confusion. A cautious beginning is appropriate. Several key teachers and student leaders might be brought together at first to consider the idea, define the goals, and shape a plan by which a service program could be experimentally introduced.

If a few selected projects are successfully completed, the students involved and those who have been helped might offer testimonials to other students and teachers, describing the program and providing both information and inspiration. Since we have testimonials in schools honoring those who are successful in athletics, is it unthinkable to have special convocations to honor those who have helped their fellow human beings?

Service activity should be directed not just to the community but also toward the school itself. We were reminded time and time again that students see the school as belonging to adults. They are expected to follow rules imposed by principals and teachers, but there is no sense of ownership in the process. Further, high school students remain relatively passive from the beginning to the end of the experience. We urge that the notion of service focus more directly on the school itself, through tutoring, of course, but also through other tasks, so that students begin to discover what it takes to make a school work and accept a more active and responsible role. Teaching is the most effective way to learn, and as students gain knowledge and experience, they should understand the obligation they have to pass on what they have learned.

A service program should be something more than preparation for a career. Students may supervise children in a playground without planning to be physical education teachers or coaches; they may stuff envelopes for a charity mailing without planning to work in an office; and the list goes on. Students who engage in such activities obviously perform useful functions and relieve professionals for duties requiring special training and experience. Students in such settings may derive profound satisfaction from their direct contacts with those who benefit from their help, and from knowing they are participating in something worthwhile. These values are important in life, whether one's service is ultimately related to a career or not.

Students should not only go out to serve; they should also be asked to write about their experience and, if possible, to discuss with others the lessons they have learned. Almost all service experiences cultivate such laudable personal traits as punctuality and reliability, the capacity to see a task through to completion, and the ability to get along well with others. Students, time and time again, speak of personal fulfillment and discovering their own strengths and worth.

Service is not just giving out, it is also gaining insight. There will be joy and satisfaction, and the pain of frustration, too. In any event, if students are to be educationally affected by service, they should be asked to comment on their experience and explore with a mentor and fellow students how the experience is related to what they have been studying in school.

In all of this, the goal is to help students consider the connection between what they learn and how they live. The spirit of student service was captured best, perhaps, by Vachel Lindsay (1964) when he wrote,

> ... It is the world's one crime its babes grow dull ...
> Not that they starve, but starve so dreamlessly,
> Not that they sow, but that they seldom reap,
> Not that they serve, but have no gods to serve,
> Not that they die, but that they die like sheep.

Ernest L. Boyer is President of the Carnegie Foundation for the Advancement of Teaching and Senior Fellow at the Woodrow Wilson School, Princeton University. He was formerly U.S. Commissioner of Education and Chancellor of the State University of New York.

References

Boyer, Ernest L., *High School: A Report on Secondary Education in America*, Harper and Row, 1983.

Boyer, Ernest L., *College: The Undergraduate Experience in America*, Harper and Row, 1986.

Harrison, Charles H., *Student Service: The New Carnegie Unit*, Princeton University Press, 1987.

Howe, Harold II., "The High School: Education's Centerpiece for the 1980s," *College Board Review*, 120, Summer 1981, p. 27.

Lewis, Anne C., "Washington Report," *Phi Delta Kappan*, Vol. 68, No. 8, April 1987, p. 573.

Lindsay, Vachel, "The Leaden Eye," in *Collected Poems*, Macmillan, 1964.

Community, Conflict and Ways of Knowing:
Ways to Deepen Our Educational Agenda

Parker J. Palmer

Parker Palmer presents an epistemology of "relatedness" or "community" that offers a firm underpinning for service-learning as an emerging pedagogy. He shows how a relational *approach to how we know things and how we learn — when used in creative tension with the traditional* objectivist *approach — can transform the learning process for everyone. These ideas were presented in a speech at the 1987 conference of the American Association for Higher Education in Chicago. From* Change, *Vol. 19, No. 5, September/October 1987, pp. 20-25. Reprinted with permission of the Helen Dwight Reid Educational Foundation. Published by Heldref Publications, 4000 Albemarle St. N.W., Washington, D.C. 20016. Copyright © 1987.*

TWELVE YEARS AGO, my own yearning for community in education led me out of the mainstream of higher education to a small place called Pendle Hill, a 55-year-old Quaker living/learning community near Philadelphia. It is a place where everyone — from teachers to cooks to administrators — receives the same base salary as a witness to community. At Pendle Hill, rigorous study of philosophy, nonviolent social change, and other subjects, goes right alongside washing the dishes each day, making decisions by consensus, and taking care of each other, as well as reaching out to the world.

Out of that long, intense experience, what might I share that would somehow be hopeful and encouraging? I learned, of course, that community is vital and important, but is also terribly difficult work for which we are not well prepared; at least I was not. I learned that the degree to which a person yearns for community is directly related to the dimming of memory of his or her last experience of it.

I came up with my own definition of community after a year at Pendle Hill: Community is that place where the person you least want to live with always lives. At the end of my second year, I came up with a corollary: When that person moves away, someone else arises immediately to take his or her place.

But the question I want to address is this: How should we be thinking about the nature of community in the modern college and university? I think that question puts the issue where it belongs. We need a way of thinking about community in higher education that relates it to the central mission of the academy — the generation and transmission of knowledge. The way we think about community in settings of higher learning, in other words, must be different from the way we think about community in other settings, like the civil society, the neighborhood, the church, or the workplace. Within the academy, we need to think about community in ways that deepen the educational agenda.

As I listen to the current conversation about the place of community in the academy, it seems to go something like this. First, there has been a collapse of civic virtue in the society around us, a collapse into expressive and competitive individualism, and a loss of integrated vision. This view was articulated for us most recently by the work of Robert Bellah and his colleagues in *Habits of the Heart*.

Second, the argument runs, higher education can and should respond to this collapse by becoming a model of community in at least two ways. One is to develop new, cooperative social forms for campus life (i.e., in dormitory and classroom life, where cooperative habits can be formed). Second, higher education should reorganize curricula toward a more integrated vision of the world, offer more interdisciplinary studies, and do more ethical and value-oriented work.

There is value in this line of argument, but I think much of it parallels the way we think about renewing the civil society itself, where we argue that we must build structures and teach the content of civic virtue to bind the community together. The argument is valuable, but it does not respond to the unique heart-and-core mission of higher education.

So I would like to press the question of community in education a step further. I want to go beyond altering the social forms of education, as valuable as that may be, go beyond altering the topical content of courses, as valuable as that may be, and try to reach into the underlying nature of our knowledge itself. I want to reach for the relation of community to the very mode of knowing dominant in the academy.

To put it in philosophical terms, I want to try to connect concepts of community to questions of epistemology, which I believe are the central questions for any institution engaged in a mission of knowing, teaching, and learning. How do we know? How do we learn? Under what conditions and with what validity?

I believe that it is here — at the epistemological core of our knowledge and our processes of knowing — that our powers for forming or deforming human consciousness are to be found. I believe it is here, in our modes of knowing, that we shape souls by the shape of our knowledge: It is here that the idea of community must ultimately take root and have impact if it is to reshape the doing of higher education.

My thesis is a very simple one: I do not believe that epistemology is a bloodless abstraction; the *way* we know has powerful implications for the *way* we live. I argue that every epistemology tends to become an ethic, and that every way of knowing tends to become a way of living. I argue that the relation established between the knower and the known, between the student and the subject, tends to become the relation of the living person to the world itself. I argue that every mode of knowing contains its own moral trajectory, its own ethical direction and outcomes.

Let me try to demonstrate this thesis, this link between epistemology and life. The mode of knowing that dominates higher education I call objectivism. It has three traits with which we are all familiar.

The first of these traits is that the academy will be objective. This means that it holds everything it knows at arm's length. It distances the knower from the world for a very specific purpose; that is, to keep its knowledge from contamination by subjective prejudice and bias. But even as it does this distancing, it divorces that knowledge — a part of the world — from our personal life. It creates a world "out there" of which we are only spectators and in which we do not live. That is the first outcome of knowing.

Secondly, objectivism is analytic. Once you have made something into an object (in my own discipline, that something can be a person), you can then chop that object up into pieces to see what makes it tick. You can dissect it, you can cut it apart, you can analyze it, even unto death. And that is the second habit formed by the objectivist mode of knowing.

Third, this mode of knowing is experimental. And I mean this in a broad and metaphoric sense, not laboratory operations *per se*. I mean by experimental that we are now free with these dissected objects to move the pieces around, to reshape the world in an image more pleasing to us, to see what would happen if we did. It is this "power over the world" motif that I am reaching for when I say "experimentalism" in the epistemology called objectivism.

Objective, analytic, experimental. Very quickly this seemingly abstract way of knowing, this seemingly bloodless epistemology, becomes an ethic. It is an ethic of competitive individualism, in the midst of a world fragmented and made exploitable by that very mode of knowing. The mode of knowing itself breeds intellectual habits, indeed spiritual instincts, that destroy community. We make objects of each other and the world to be manipulated for our own private ends.

Remember if you will those students in an earlier Carnegie study, Arthur Levine's *When Dreams and Heroes Died.* These were the students who thought, 80 to 90 percent of them, that the world was going to hell in a handbasket, that its future was dim and grim. But when asked about their own personal futures, 80 to 90 percent of them said, "Oh, no problem. It's rosy. I'm getting a good education, good grades, I'm going to a good school, I'm going to get a good job." A psychoanalyst looking at this data would say, "schizophrenia."

I want to argue that it's a *trained* schizophrenia: It is the way these students have been taught to look at reality through objectivist lenses. They have always been taught about a world out there somewhere apart from them, divorced from their personal lives; they never have been invited to intersect their autobiographies with the life story of the world. And so they can report on a world that is not the one in which they live, one they've been taught about from some objectivist's fantasy.

They have also been formed in the habit of experimental manipulation. These students believe they can take pieces of the world and carve out for themselves a niche of private sanity in the midst of public calamity. That is nothing more than the ethical outcome of the objectivism in which they have been formed, or deformed. It is a failure to recognize their own implication with society's fate.

Objectivism is essentially anticommunal. As long as it remains the dominant epistemology in higher education, I think we will make little progress on communal agendas. I do not believe that any interdisciplinary combining of objectivist courses can overcome this kind of ethical impact: You can't put all the objectivisms together and come up with something new. I don't believe that courses on ethics placed around the perimeters of this objectivism can in any way deflect its moral trajectory, because objectivism is not about neutral facts that can somehow be reshaped by add-on values — it is a kind of knowledge that has its own ethical and moral course.

My definition of community is simple, if partial: I understand community as a capacity for relatedness within individuals — relatedness not only to people but to events in history, to nature, to the world of ideas, and yes, to things of the spirit. We talk a lot in higher education about the information of inward capacities — the capacity to tolerate ambiguity, the capacity for critical thought. I want us to talk more about those ways of knowing that form an inward capacity for relatedness. Objectivism, which destroys this capacity, must be countered if the academy is to make a contribution to the reweaving of community.

On a hopeful note, I believe there are promising movements towards community in the world of intellect today. They are found in the emergence of new epistemologies, which emerge most often in fringe areas of the academy's work. The underlying theme in all of these "fringe" areas is the theme of the relatedness. Let me give examples.

First and most prominent is feminist thought. Feminist thought is not primarily about equal pay for equal work. It is not primarily about equal power and status for women. It is about those things, but it is primarily about another way of seeing and therefore another way of being in the world. It is about an alternative epistemology. It is vital for that reason.

I see an alternative epistemology evolving in black scholarship. If you read a book called *There is a River*, by Vincent Harding, you are reading another kind of history, history that refuses to allow you to divorce your own story from the story being told. It is history told with a passion that draws you in; it will not let you escape. It is factual, it is objective, *and* it is passionate. It refuses to let you off the hook.

Native American studies have much the same quality. Ecological studies are also giving rise to new epistemologies, as are the philosophies of the new physics, the work of people like David Bohm, and the work of someone like geneticist Barbara McClintock. These latter have a "feeling for organism." In all of these places we are learning that the act of knowing itself, if we understand it rightly, is a bond of community between us and that which we know. The act of knowing itself is a way of building and rebuilding community, and it is this we must reach for in our education.

Throughout the literature in the fields I have mentioned, certain words keep popping up — words like organic, bodily, intuitive, reciprocal, passionate, interactive, and communal. These are words of epistemology, long before they are words of ethics. They are words about a way of knowing that then becomes a way of living.

What happens when higher education and its dominant epistemology are challenged by studies such as these, or by virtually any other problem? If the problem will not go away, the strategy is add-a-course. And so we add a course in black studies, or feminist thought, or Native American literature, or in ethics or ecology to try somehow to bleed off the pressure that these new epistemologies put on objectivism.

The strategy misses the point. These studies are a challenge to an outmoded way of knowing, and to an ethic that is essentially destructive to community.

I want to make it clear that these epistemologies do not aim at the overthrow of objectivity, analysis, and experimentation. Indeed, the feminist thinkers that I know use those very tools in their writing. But they want to put those tools within a context of affirming the communal nature of reality itself, the *relational* nature of reality. So in these studies, objectivist modes are used in creative tension with their relational counterparts. For example, the mode of objectivity is held in creative tension with another way of knowing, the way of intimacy, the way of personally implicating yourself with the subject. Virtually every great scholar finds this way of appropriating knowledge, of living and breathing it and bringing it so close to your heart that you and it are almost one. Objectivity and intimacy *can* go hand in hand; that's what the new epistemologies are calling for.

Alongside analysis, the same principle holds. These new epistemologies juxtapose analysis with synthesis, integration, and the creative act. Alongside experimentation — that need we have to manipulate the pieces to see how things might go if it were otherwise — these scholars cultivate the capacity appreciatively to receive the world as it is given as a gift, not as an exploitable playground for our minds.

These paired and paradoxical modes of knowing need to find a more secure and prominent place in higher education if we are to make our unique contribution to community. They help us uncover what Thomas Merton once called the "hidden wholeness" of things. They enhance community by enlarging our capacity for relatedness.

Let me push my argument further by saying that the job cannot be completed on the epistemological level alone. These insights must be carried over into our pedagogies as well. Community must become a central concept in ways we teach and learn.

Many communal experiments in pedagogy have been tried in the history of American higher education, and many have fallen by the wayside. And the reason, I think, is simple: The underlying mode of knowing remained the same. You cannot derive communal ways of teaching and learning from an essentially anticommunal mode of knowing. The pedagogy falls apart if the epistemology isn't there to support and sustain it.

The root fallacy in the pedagogy of most of our institutions is that the individual is the agent of knowing and therefore the focus for teaching and learning. We all know that if we draw the lines of instruction in most classrooms, they run singularly from teacher to each individual student. These lines are there for the convenience of the instructor, not for their corporate reality. They do not reveal a complex web of relationships between teacher and students and subject that would look like true community.

Given this focus on the individual in the classroom, competition between individuals for knowledge becomes inevitable. The competitive individualism of the classroom is not simply the function of a social ethic; it reflects a pedagogy that stresses the individual as the prime agent of knowing. But to say the obvious, knowing and learning are *communal* acts. They require many eyes and ears, many observations and experiences. They require a continual cycle of discussion, disagreement, and consensus over what has been seen and what it all means. This is the essence of the "community of scholars," and it should be the essence of the classroom as well.

At the core of this communal way of knowing is a primary virtue, one too seldom named when we discuss community or set community against competition. This primary virtue is capacity for creative conflict. It troubles me when we frame the issue as community versus competition, because too often we link competition with conflict, as if conflict were what needed to be eliminated. But there is no knowing without conflict.

Community in the classroom is often advocated as an affective or emotional supplement to cognitive education; the debate often poses the "hard" virtues of cognition against the "soft" virtues of community. My point is that there is very little conflict in American classrooms, and the reason is that the soft virtues of community are lacking there. Without the soft virtues of community, the hard virtues of cognitive teaching and learning will be absent as well. Our ability to confront each other critically and honestly over alleged facts, imputed meanings, or personal biases and prejudices — *that* is the ability impaired by the absence of community. The ethos of competitive individualism breeds silent, *sub rosa*, private combat for personal reward — it's all under the table, it never comes out in the open — that's what competitive individualism is all about. Competitive individualism squelches the kind of conflict I am trying to name. Conflict is open, public, and often very noisy. Competition is a secret, zero-sum game played by individuals for private gain. *Communal conflict* is a public encounter in which the whole group can win by growing. Those of you who have participated in consensus decision making know something of what I mean.

A healthy community, while it may exclude this one-up, one-down thing called competition, includes conflict at its very heart, checking and correcting and enlarging the knowledge of individuals by drawing on the knowledge of the group. Healthy conflict is possible only in the context of supportive community. What prevents conflicts in our classrooms is a simple emotion called fear. It is fear that is in the hearts of teachers as well as students. It is fear of exposure, of appearing ignorant, of being ridiculed. And the only antidote to that fear is a hospitable environment created, for example, by a teacher who knows how to use every remark, no matter how mistaken or seemingly stupid, to upbuild both the individual and the group. When people in a classroom begin to learn that every attempt at truth, no matter how off the mark, is a contribution to the larger search for corporate and consensual truth, they are soon emboldened and empowered to say what they need to say, to expose their ignorance, to do, in short, those things without which learning can't happen.

Community is not opposed to conflict. On the contrary, community is precisely that place where an arena for creative conflict is protected by the compassionate fabric of human caring itself.

If you ask what holds community together, what makes this capacity for relatedness possible, the only honest answer I can give brings me to that dangerous realm called the spiritual. The only answer I can give is that what makes community possible is love.

I would like to think that love is not an entirely alien word in the academy today, because I know that in the great tradition of intellectual life it is not. It is a word very much at home in the academy. The kind of community I am calling for is a community that exists at the heart of knowing, of epistemology, of teaching and learning, of pedagogy; that kind of community depends centrally on two ancient and honorable kinds of love.

The first is love of learning itself. The simple ability to take sheer joy in having a new idea, reaffirming or discarding an old one, connecting two or more notions that had hitherto seemed alien to each other, sheer joy of building images of reality with mere words that now suddenly seem more like mirrors of truth — this is love of learning.

And the second kind of love on which this community depends is love of learners, of those we see every day, who stumble and crumble, who wax hot and cold, who sometimes want truth and sometimes evade it at all costs, but who are in our care, and who — for their sake, ours, and the world's — deserve all the love that the community of teaching and learning has to offer.

Parker Palmer has been a teacher, leader, and writer about public life and learning in college, university, community, and foundation settings. He is the author of The Promise of Paradox, The Company of Strangers, *and* To Know As We Are Known. *He now writes in Madison, Wisconsin, and is in demand as a speaker and workshop leader.*

A Nation At Risk: Another View

A joint statement of the Association for
Experiential Education (AEE),
the Council for Adult and Experiential
Learning (CAEL), and
the National Society of Internships and
Experiential Education (NSIEE)

*This joint statement, written in 1983, is a concise rationale for
experience-based learning that is still useful today for K-12,
collegiate, and community educators. Effective service-learning
depends on the effective use of principles of experiential learning.
This statement was published in response to* A Nation at Risk:
The Imperative for Educational Reform *from the National
Commission on Excellence in Education. Readers are invited to
use it freely with this credit: Reprinted with permission from*
Experiential Education, *National Society for Internships and
Experiential Education, Vol. 9, No. 2, March-April 1984, pp. 1, 3.*

1983 WAS THE YEAR TO LOOK AT EXCELLENCE. Thomas J.
Peters and Robert H. Waterman, Jr. wrote about excellence in corporations in *In Search of Excellence.* George Keller wrote about excellence in institutions of higher education in *Academic Strategies.* The
National Commission on Excellence in Education published its recommendations for excellence in the American educational system in
A Nation at Risk: The Imperative for Educational Reform. All three
studies seem to agree on some basic ingredients of a quality institution:
   • a clearly articulated goal,
   • the investment of all of the players in the (shared) goal, and
   • attention to available, relevant research.

We, representatives of AEE, CAEL and NSIEE, are concerned that the National Commission seemingly lost sight of these basic ingredients as it prepared its plan for ensuring quality in American education. The report does not address its original goal of educating to improve quality of life; instead, it focuses more on beating the competition in high technology. It virtually ignores the primary players, the students, as it focuses on teaching rather than learning. Finally, it ignores the large body of research about how and why individuals learn, how they develop cognitively, morally and socially, and how they differ among themselves. Instead, it makes recommendations for more homework and longer days for everyone.

We submit that there is a need to look again at what we are educating for, and to create learning environments which are attentive to students' and teachers' attitudes and which maximize the potential for learning despite individual differences. We believe that a major component of such learning environments must be opportunities for not only abstract but also experiential learning; that is, learning in which the learner is directly in touch with the realities being studied rather than simply reading about, hearing about, or talking about these realities.

A Sound Goal, A Flawed Strategy

The beginning of *A Nation At Risk* clearly articulates a goal for American Education "... that all children by virtue of their own efforts, competently guided, can hope to attain the mature and informed judgment needed to secure gainful employment, and to manage their own lives, thereby serving not only their own interests but also the progress of society itself" (p. 4). We applaud the implications of this statement, namely:
- that equity of educational opportunity be guaranteed,
- that individuals must assume responsibility for their own learning,
- that learning can be guided, facilitated, and
- that education is important not only to fulfilling career goals but also to enhancing the quality of life of individuals and ultimately of society.

We do not believe, however, that these goals will be realized if the strategies for reaching them are limited to more classroom experiences, longer hours in school, and more homework — more of the same types of learning experiences with which many students and teachers are dissatisfied. Current research suggests that excellence in productivity results from close attention to the people in the organization — how they feel about what they are doing and about the organization. *A Nation at Risk* ignores the fact that many of our students do not see their schools' programs as relevant to their lives, and many teachers feel they have no control. Longer days and merit pay will not change these attitudes, will not increase productivity. *The need is to change the environment.*

Changing the educational environment means acknowledging what research has proved: a) that genetic and environmental factors influence learning, b) that not everyone learns everything in the same way, and c) that learning is ultimately self-directed, an individual matter, and occurs best when motivation and interest are internal. A critical task of educational institutions is the design of learning environments and teaching strategies which allow for the differences in learning styles and which build upon the intrinsic interests of the learners.

Toward a Better Strategy

We offer no nostrum for what is patently an enormous and a complex undertaking of the American educational system. But, quality in education is not primarily a matter of such things as time spent in class, of subject matter covered, or of teacher compensation. The most crucial factors in learning are strength of motivation, appropriateness of learning resources to the learning tasks, choice of strategies of inquiry, and the climate of the learning environments. If a genuine, lasting and pervasive change for the better in American schooling is to be achieved, it will have to grow out of more thoughtful attention to these crucial factors.

For many learners, from the youngest to the oldest, the learning of certain concepts is most interesting — and most successful — when it comes through concrete experiences and involvement in practical problems (as confirmed in the work of Jean Piaget, James Coleman and David Kolb). We "experiential educators" therefore advocate a mix of abstract and experiential learning. An environment providing this mix includes the laboratory as well as the classroom, includes occasions in which the teacher is primarily a facilitator rather than an "information-giver" and includes occasions which are student-centered rather than teacher-centered. Sometimes the laboratory is a classroom, more often it is an environment more suited to the learning; e.g., the mountains, the inner city, a museum, a corporation, a government office.

We strongly recommend that a variety of forms of non-classroom, experience-based learning (e.g., internships, cooperative education, practica, clinics, outdoor education, service-learning, work-study) become part of the required curriculum of American schools and colleges. At high schools and colleges across the country the experiential approach is proving successful in motivating students to learn and develop those skills, strategies, and attitudes which will enable them to be productive and responsible adults. There are clear reasons for the success:

The experiential approach is a powerful motivator for learning because it is positive, and meaningful, and real. The learning environment is success-oriented rather than competitive. It offers opportunities for real-life problem solving in which feedback is uncontrived and immediate, and in which results are real-life physical and emotional consequences. Because the learners participate in the design, implementation and management of their own learning, they are invested in the goal, hence internally motivated. That motivation frequently transfers back to the traditional classroom as students recognize the need for more theoretical background, as they try to draw inferences and conclusions from their experiences, or as they find reasons to improve their basic skills. The need to write becomes important when one needs to write a report or proposal for a community organization. The need for theoretical understanding of human relations becomes important if one is helping in a crisis intervention center. Understanding of motivation is important when marketing a new product.

Additionally, by providing for integration of ideas and actions into the large community, experiential learning facilitates the transition to adulthood and develops skills for responsible citizenship. Documented outcomes of experiential learning include concern for fellow human beings; the ability to get things done and work with others; self-motivation to learn, participate and achieve; an improved self-concept, confidence, competence and awareness; responsibility to the group or class; openness to new experiences; and a sense of usefulness to the community.

Finally, experiential education contributes to the preparation of a well-educated and productive workforce. If our goal were merely to beat the Japanese in the high-tech race, we could train our students to be crack technicians through classroom experiences in math, science and computer technology. If our goal is to prepare an enlightened citizenry to lead productive and purposeful lives and to contribute to the growth and development of society, then we must insure that they learn how to learn, how to grow and adjust to change.

Workers of the future need both generalized competence and specific job skills which may not apply to their future job requirements. Future jobs will require different skills, and workers must be prepared to meet the changing needs. We must teach students how to reflect on their experiences, define their learning goals, and independently manage their own learning. These outcomes require an education which combines experiential learning with abstract learning.

120

The Impact of Experiential Education on Youth Development

Diane Hedin and Dan Conrad

*Researchers found that high school experiential learning pro-
grams have a positive impact on the social, psychological and
intellectual development of participating students. The research
included tests of moral reasoning, self-esteem, social and personal responsibility, attitudes towards adults, and others, career
exploration, and empathy/complexity of thought. The authors
found that the most valuable programs include a reflection
component, give students substantial responsibility, last at least
one semester and involve participants in the community four or
five times a week. This research was conducted for the Experiential Education Evaluation Project at the Center for Youth Development and Research at the University of Minnesota. Reprinted
from "Study Proves Hypotheses — And More" in Synergist,
National Center for Service-Learning, ACTION, Vol. 9, No. 1,
Spring 1980, pp. 8-14.*

IN THE 1970S, experiential education became an increasingly
significant feature of the rhetoric and practice of American education. All the major commissions and panels (see References) that
studied secondary education and adolescence recommended that
schools extend the depth and breadth of experience available to
adolescents. For example, a study of high schools by the Carnegie
Council on Policy Studies in Higher Education recommends that
juniors and seniors attend classes three days a week and devote the
other two to education-related work or community service.

While strong endorsements of experience-based education by
leading educators and social scientists abound, relatively little hard
evidence of the impact of such programs on students appears. Little
effort has been made to test systematically the assumptions under-

.ying the endorsements or to investigate empirically which specific forms or formats of experiential programs may be the most effective in realizing the hypothesized benefits.

The Evaluation of Experiential Education Learning Project (EELP) was undertaken to do just that — to assess the impact of experiential education programs on the social, psychological, and intellectual development of secondary school students and to use this data to identify empirically the program variables that are most effective in facilitating such development.

EELP's findings show that experiential education increases students' social, psychological, and intellectual development more than traditional education does. Research also indicates that the most effective programs give students substantial autonomy, include a reflection component, last at least one semester, and involve students in the community for four or five days a week. Furthermore, service-learning programs scored higher than the three other types of experiential programs studied in several important developmental aspects.

Initiated by the Commission on Educational Issues and cosponsored by the National Association of Secondary School Principals, National Association of Independent Schools, and the National Catholic Education Association, EELP evaluated 30 experiential learning programs in independent, public, and parochial schools around the country. The Center for Youth Development and Research, University of Minnesota, conducted the research.

Approximately 4,000 students ranging in age from 12 to 19 participated. They were urban and rural, poor and affluent.

For purposes of the study, experiential programs are defined as "educational programs offered as an integral part of the general school curriculum, but taking place outside of the conventional classroom, where students are in new roles featuring significant tasks with real consequences, and where the emphasis is on learning by doing with associated reflection." The kinds of program activities include volunteer service, political and social action, outdoor adventure, internships in government and business, and research in the community. The study encompasses virtually all forms of what is termed experiential education in secondary education, with the notable exception of work-related or vocational programs and the Experience Based Career Education Program (EBCE), which have been extensively evaluated elsewhere.

At the heart of the project is its panel of practitioners, teachers, and administrators directing programs in 20 diverse school systems from Beverly Hills, California, to Newark, New Jersey. With the assistance of educational evaluators, the panel members were responsible for defining the issues to be studied, for helping select and develop instruments for implementing the design, for helping interpret the data collected — and for keeping the whole study practical, understandable, and applicable to everyday life in schools.

Selecting the Issues

The first step of the research process was to survey the directors of the 30 experiential programs. The survey asked what they most confidently believed to be their programs' actual effects on students, what the directors each had directly experienced, seen, and heard.

The 24 effects that appeared with high regularity formed the basis of a questionnaire administered to all 4,000 students in May 1978. The students were asked which, if any, of the outcomes listed represented what they personally had learned from their program.

In summary, on 14 of the 24 items, all programs had an average agreement level of more than 80 percent. The most positively rated outcomes had to do with self-motivation and initiative, social and personal responsibility, problem solving, self-concept, knowledge of the community, and learning from experience. Each of the other items received from 80 to 100 percent agreement in the programs where they were a deliberate emphasis.

Two schools asked the students' field supervisors and parents to respond to the same list. The only differences between their ratings and those of the students were a slight variation in the order of agreement and a higher incidence of "strongly agree" responses about positive aspects of the students' learning and growth. The high level of agreement elicited by these surveys made it reasonable to conclude that the items did represent the major hypothesized effects of experiential programs.

A winter 1979 report in *Synergist* invited directors of service-learning programs to administer this same questionnaire to their students. Thirteen high school programs completed the survey (see the list at the end of this chapter). In general, the results from the 13 service-learning programs were similar to those in the original experiential education survey group, indicating that experience-based programs have certain generic effects. The only consistent difference was that the service-learning programs, in general, were rated more positively. Specifically, the service programs received substantially higher ratings on the following items: openness to new experiences, learning from direct experience, communication skills, and assuming new tasks in the community and the school. These differences are noteworthy because the experiential programs in this study were selected because of their exemplary features. That a self-selected group of community service programs turns out to be even stronger than some of the most established and most exemplary experiential programs in the country indicates the basic soundness of service-learning education for helping young people learn about themselves, their community, and the basic intellectual skills of learning from direct experience.

With the key issues thus identified, the next task was to translate what were essentially self-reports into research questions suitable for more rigorous examination. The list of outcomes was trimmed to 20 items by including only those in which students and program directors had at least a 70 percent level of agreement. The findings of this preliminary work helped in creating the Experiential Education Questionnaire.

Research Method

Three major considerations guided the selection of instruments for measuring these key outcomes. First, the methods must not rely solely on traditional paper and pencil tools. Second, multiple measures should assess each outcome since previous research offered little guidance regarding which instruments would prove efficacious. Third, whenever possible, standardized instruments should be used so that the outcomes of experiential learning programs could be compared to those of other programs.

Five data-gathering tools and/or approaches were used:

- The Experiential Education Questionnaire, a series of paper and pencil instruments administered at the beginning and end of courses to students in experiential education and to comparison groups in the traditional school program;
- Questionnaires to parents and community supervisors regarding the student's progress in his/her experiential program;
- The qualitative notebook in which the coordinator or teacher systematically collected anecdotal and case study materials;
- Systematic observations and interviews with students and staff conducted by two members of the panel of practitioners;
- A follow-up study of participants in three schools three to four years after they have completed the off-campus program.

This article discusses only the data derived from the several instruments — some designed especially for this study — that form the Experiential Education Questionnaire.

The study was designed to answer two major questions: To what extent do experiential learning programs affect students' social, psychological, and intellectual development, and in what ways do different program forms and formats (length, intensity, program characteristics) affect student growth in these areas? The question of development was broken down into a number of specific questions and instruments were found, adapted, or designed to find the answers.

Experiential programs' impact on students' *level of personal and social responsibility* was measured by scores on the Personal and Social Responsibility Scale (PSRS), an instrument created for this study. The PSRS assesses the extent to which students have responsible attitudes, feel competent to act responsibly, feel a sense of efficacy so that they are willing to take responsibility, and perform responsible acts.

Semantic differential scales measured the students' *attitudes toward adults* in general and the kind of persons with whom they were in primary contact in their field placement, such as elderly or handicapped persons. *Attitudes toward active participation in the community* also were measured by semantic differential scales.

To measure *involvement in career planning and exploration*, EELP used an adaptation of the Career Exploration Scale developed by the Educational Work Program of the Northwest Regional Laboratory, Portland, Oregon. This instrument focuses on actual behaviors in planning and exploring careers.

To check psychological development EELP used two well tested instruments: the Rosenberg Self-Esteem Scale to measure *general self-esteem* and 10 items from the Janis-Field Feelings of Inadequacy Scale to measure *self-esteem in social situations*.

EELP had two new instruments designed to measure intellectual development. The Community Problem Inventory, included as part of the post-test only, examined *knowledge of community issues and resources*. The Problem Solving Inventory tested *ability to analyze and solve problems*. The Inventory was designed as a proximate measure of a person's inclination and ability to perform five tasks that John Dewey deemed central to the process of solving problems involving interpersonal and ethical conflict. The five tasks are: reacting instinctively to a newly perceived problem (approximated by a stimulus story), generating more alternatives, considering the consequences, choosing and evaluating the outcome.

The second major area of investigation was the extent to which different types, forms, and structures of experiential programs affected student growth. The four specific program features selected for analysis were:

- Type of experience — adventure education (patterned after Outward Bound), community service, career internships, or

community study (surveys and historical research)/political action;
- Length (four weeks to nine months) and intensity (an hour a day to full-time);
- Existence of a reflective component (a regularly scheduled class or seminar);
- Characteristics of each student's individual experience.

To measure these dimensions, EELP gathered descriptive information on program features from both the students and staff. Students also rated the overall program on a four-point scale from excellent to terrible and explained their rating. Finally, they were given a list of characteristics of field experiences and asked how often each was a feature in their own situation. Items included such characteristics as "made important decisions," "talked about experience with friends and family," "felt I made a contribution."

In almost all programs, students' participation was voluntary — as is often the case with experiential programs. Therefore, it was not possible to use a true experimental design with random assignment of students to experimental and control groups. The approach taken was to use quasi-experimental designs. Six schools had comparison groups made up of students not involved in an experiential program and who were virtually identical in age, grade, sex, and socioeconomic status to the students in the experiential program. In the other schools, the best obtainable design was the one-group pre- and post-test design. The major use of the results was comparison with other forms of experiential programs, not with more traditional classes.

Psychological Development

An important research finding is that the formal academic curriculum does not automatically lead to personal and psychological growth. In fact, numerous studies have reported negative effects on such variables as self-esteem, interest in learning, and personal autonomy.

Proponents of experiential education have argued that psychological growth is more likely to be achieved through placing the student in direct confrontation with practical problems.

This study corroborated this theory. Students in 24 of the 28 programs increased both *general self-esteem* and *self-esteem in social situations*. The results suggest that the increased interaction with a variety of people, new places, and novel responsibilities tended to give these young people more confidence in themselves in social situations — speaking in front of a class, meeting new people. General perception of self-worth, such as feeling more useful and more able to do things well, also increased.

Social Development

A common view today is that young people are locked in an adolescent ghetto separated from meaningful interaction with adults. The implicit assumption is that separation breeds suspicion, if not hostility, and that greater contact with adults would promote more positive attitudes. The study confirmed this hypothesis. Students in the experiential programs, who were in more collegial relationships with adults, tended to show large, consistent changes on the semantic differential scale toward *more positive attitudes towards adults*. There was a positive change in 22 of the 28 experiential groups, with older students tending to show larger gains that the younger ones. Remaining in a classroom with an adult teacher appears not to raise adolescents' esteem for adults. Six of the seven control groups evaluated adults more negatively at the end of the test period.

The study hypothesized, therefore, that students would develop *more positive feelings toward the kind of persons* (government officials, the elderly, etc.) with whom they were in primary contact in their field placement. A strong rationale for experiential programs is that youth who become involved in responsible tasks on behalf of others in their community develop more positive attitudes toward a variety of people. The data very strongly indicate that the hypothesis is correct.

In the pre-test, students rated the elderly, business persons, and children considerably higher than junior high students, police, and government officials. On the post-test, the ratings of all except business persons increased significantly. That exception is difficult to interpret. One factor could be that the students in business internships tended to be more observers than participators.

In the past decade, the public has shown great concern about teenagers' level of *personal and social responsibility*. Social critics have pointed out the increased narcissism, hedonism, and aimlessness in society, and particularly among adolescents. This apathy becomes overwhelming in regard to social and civic participation, e.g., in 1975, 58 percent of those 18 to 24 did not vote in the presidential election, with percentages rising to 72 percent among black youth and 78 percent among Hispanic youth.

Proponents of action- and service-learning claim that by placing students in responsible roles in which their actions affect others, more responsible attitudes and behaviors will develop.

The findings support these claims. **Students in 21 of the 28 experiential programs changed in a positive direction; in 14, changes were statistically significant. In contrast, students' level of personal and social responsibility in six of the seven comparison groups declined.**

The data also were analyzed by subscales that included a *sense of duty or obligation, social welfare orientation* (degree to which a person feels an obligation to other persons in society), *sense of social efficacy, competence* (assessment of one's capacity to perform responsible acts), and *performance* (actual performance of responsible actions). The strongest gains were recorded on the subscale related to students' sense of competence, duty, and social efficacy, and the most highly significant differences between the two groups were the much greater sense of duty and social welfare orientation evidenced by those in experiential education programs.

Students in service-learning programs had the highest Social and Personal Responsibility Scale pre-test scores, followed by those in community study, career internships, and adventure education. This would indicate that those who volunteer for programs in which helping and serving others is the major task tend to be more responsible than students in other experiential programs.

The other measure used to assess students' *interest in and reaction to community participation* was a semantic differential on "being active in the community." It was hypothesized that direct participation would lead students to value such activity more highly and increase the likelihood of their participation in the future. The results confirmed this hypothesis.

While both students in experiential programs and in the comparison groups started out valuing community participation about equally, by the end of the program the experimental groups had a higher evaluation of it and the comparison groups a lower one.

Perhaps the most commonly cited critique of adolescent socialization is the inability of many youth to make a smooth *transition from school to work*. This is thought to occur because youth lack opportunities to learn about and explore a variety of possible careers; to acquire the basic work habits of orderliness, punctuality, and attention to work; and to develop the desire to be productive in the workplace.

An oft-expressed goal of experiential learning is to increase a young person's knowledge about the myriad of career options. To learn whether this goal was achieved, EELP administered the Career Exploration Scale. Of all the measures of student growth and achievement, this scale showed the most consistent and positive increases, with 27 of the 28 programs increasing, 19 of them significantly so. The comparison groups also showed an increase, but a much smaller one. Analysis of the subscales revealed that greater increase for students in experiential programs was largely because of greater gains on items relating to exploratory activities and not on factual information gathered about careers.

It is also noteworthy that both the community service and community study programs — even though they had almost no organized and explicit focus on careers — produced approximately as much change (a substantial increase) as those whose major goal was career development.

Intellectual Development

Theorists of learning and intellectual development from Aristotle through Dewey to James Coleman have stressed the necessary relation of experience and education. Experience serves both as the source of knowledge and as a process of knowing. Education is of, by, and for experience. The study examined this relation by looking both at academic learning and intellectual development.

Because the programs' academic goals varied widely, it was not practical to test academic learning through any general test of facts or concepts. Instead, EELP asked students how much they felt they had learned in their experiential programs compared to what they had learned in an average class in school. Nearly 80 percent of the students said they had learned more or much more in their experiential program. Only 9 percent reported learning less.

Student responses on the Problem Solving Inventory were scored according to the number of alternatives suggested, the degree to which they took responsibility for solving the dilemma, the degree to which they justified a decision according to its consequences, and the level of empathy and complexity of thought shown in the overall analysis of the problem. None of the programs showed significant changes except in the last category. The Complexity/Empathy Scale, which combined several developmental frameworks into one in a seven-level scale, showed significant upward movement by students in most of the experiential programs and no change in the comparison groups. The movement was from the fourth level (stereotyped thinking, concern for rules, focus on physical needs) to the fifth (emphasis on friendship and belonging, on communication, and concern for emotional as well as physical needs).

The strongest increases were found in those programs where students were in a helping role that related closely to the dilemmas to be solved and were engaged in regular seminars in which they processed their experiences. Both of these elements were critical. Since these were common features of the service-learning programs, most consistent gains on this measure were found in this program type.

Program Variables

The second major focus of the study was to identify the program variables that were most effective in facilitating development in students. The clearest finding is that no single factor or set of factors guarantees effectiveness. Within every program, some students gained a great deal and others did not. Though the analysis is not complete, preliminary conclusions are that the strongest predictor of change proved to be the degree to which students perceived themselves as having the freedom to develop and use their own ideas, make important decisions, explore their own interests, make an important contribution, and assume adult responsibility. *In short, the most powerful experiences were those in which students participated with substantial autonomy in activities that made a difference.*

A corollary finding was that the factors that most influenced growth were not the same as those that influenced how positively students rated a program. For students, the key issues were how interesting they found the experience and whether they felt appreciated. Taken together, these findings reflect Dewey's point that what is "satisfying" is not necessarily "satisfactory." While it is important that an experience be interesting enough to engage students, that is not sufficient. The experience must also challenge them and stretch their capacities.

Among the general program characteristics, the strongest factor influencing change, particularly on social attitudes and complexity of thought, was the existence of a seminar in which students reflected on their experiences.

The most effective programs were those lasting at least a full semester (18 weeks) and involving students in the community four or five days each week.

The overall conclusion of this study, then is that experiential education programs can promote social, psychological, and intellectual development more effectively than classroom-based programs.

Participating Schools

Independent: Dana Hall School, Wellesley, Massachusetts; Francis W. Parker School, Chicago; Packer Collegiate Institute, New York; Duluth (Minnesota) Cathedral High School; St. Benedict's Preparatory School, Newark, New Jersey.

Parochial: Bellarmine High School, Tacoma, Washington; Ward High School, Kansas City, Kansas.

Public: Eisenhower High School, Hopkins, Minnesota; Mitchell High School, Colorado Springs; Minneapolis Public Schools; Allegheny Intermediate Unit, Pittsburgh; Students Serving Students, St. Paul; South Brunswick High School, Monmouth Junction, New Jersey; Rochester (Minnesota) Public Schools; Bartram School of Human Services, Philadelphia; Beverly Hills High School; Ridgewood High School, Norridge, Illinois; Kirkwood (Missouri) High School, North Central High School, Indianapolis.

Diane Hedin and Dan Conrad co-directed the Evaluation of Experiential Learning Project at the Center for Youth Development and Research, University of Minnesota, St. Paul. Hedin now serves as Director of Community Affairs for the Pillsbury Company. Conrad directs the Community Involvement Program at Eisenhower High School, Hopkins, Minnesota.

References

Center for Youth Development and Research, University of Minnesota, "Requirements for Health Development of Adolescent Youth," *Adolescence,* 1973, 8, pp. 291-316.

Frankena, W.K. *Three Historical Philosophies of Education,* Scott, Foresman, and Company, 1965.

Kerr, Clark, *Giving Youth a Better Chance: Options for Education, Work, and Service,* Jossey-Bass, 1979.

National Commission on the Reform of Secondary Education, *The Reform of Secondary of Education,* McGraw-Hill, 1973.

National Panel on High School Education, *The Education of Adolescents: The Final Report and Recommendations,* U.S. Government Printing Office, No. (OE) 76-00004, 1976.

National Association of Secondary School Principals, *American Youth in the Mid-Seventies,* 1972.

Panel on Youth of the President's Science Advisory Committee, *Youth: Transitions to Adulthood,* University of Chicago Press, 1974.

Weinstock, J., ed., *The Greening of the High School,* Institute for Development of Educational Activities, Inc., 1973.

The Impact of Field Education on Student Development: Research Findings

edited by Rick Williams

Rick Williams summarizes the findings from twelve studies of field experience participation by high school, junior high, and college students. Reprinted from The Voices of Volunteers, *edited by Rick Williams, The Korda Project, Sharon, Massachusetts, 1980, pp. 18-50, 56-60.*

IN THE LAST DECADE researchers have conducted studies to measure and to determine the effects of field education on young people. Twelve studies of field education are reviewed here. Nine of the studies involved high school age students. In addition, two studies involved junior high school students and two studies involved college age students. Although the majority of the studies are competent, none is definitive. Nevertheless, the contention here is that, taken as a whole, the studies provide a strong argument for field education. Despite differences in type of program, choice of measure, population, and other significant factors, the results are consistent. The studies strongly confirm the personal observations of field education practitioners. Field education does promote the development of young people and this development is reflected in measures of achievement, self-concept, career maturity, and values and attitudes.

What do students gain from participation in field education programs? In the next section the research studies will be reviewed in some detail. The studies have been grouped into four areas: Personal Development, Career Development, Affective Development, and Academic Achievement. In these four areas the individual studies will be discussed followed by summary comments. Information from various questionnaires will then be presented. Finally, there will be some general observations and recommendations based on the research.

Personal Development

The research on the effects of participation in field education on personal development have utilized instruments to measure change in five areas:

A. Ego Development. Sprinthall found significant movement in ego development on Loevinger's scales. He describes this movement as a shift "from wary, self-protective to more trust and open communication and higher self-respect and complexity. Essentially, this is a shift from other-directedness to the beginnings of a more integrated inner-reliant and less egocentric stage" (1974, p. 19).

B. Self-Concept. Five studies have measured changes in self-concept. Beister (1978) and Usher (1977) both found significant improvement in the self-concept of participants in contrast to non-participants. The University of Pittsburgh (1975) and Urie (1971) both found marked positive trends toward improved self-concept. Robinson (1975) found a positive trend for females but not for males.

The results of Usher's study are the most informative and also summarize the findings of the other studies. Usher's measure was the Self-Concept Scale constructed by Gill and D'Oyley. Of the different scales that compose this measure, the following showed significantly higher scores:

Perceived Acceptance by Peers and Teachers scale: "As a result of the program ... students tended to see themselves as more liked and accepted by their peers than did students in other programs" (p. 74).

Perceived Reaction to School Program scale: The program "resulted in higher positive perceptions as to the school program's ability to help students achieve their general life goals and to allow them to work on their own, and to use their talents" (p. 74).

Perceived Self-Satisfaction scale: "The course resulted in greater self-understanding, greater self-satisfaction, and greater understanding of the individual by most members of his family " (p. 75).

Perceived Concentration Ability scale: The program "resulted in the students perceiving themselves as more patient, less easily distracted, and less inclined to daydreaming than the (non-program) students" (p. 75).

C. *Maturity*. Owens and Fehrenbacker (1975), using the Psychosocial Maturity Scale, found significant gains in the areas of individual and social adequacy and interpersonal communications.

D. *Relations with Others*. Two studies measured changes in psychological orientation toward other people. Usher (1977) found significantly lower scores on the Social Avoidance and Distress Scale. He concluded that participation in the program "resulted in a greater tendency to approach others in social interactions and lower presence of anxiety in social situations" (p. 65). Robinson (1975), however, found no positive effects on the Besag TT Alienation Scale.

E. *Personality Characteristics*. Urie (1971) and Usher (1977) both examined personality characteristics using standardized measures. Urie conducted his study on college students who served as aides for handicapped college students. His pre- and post-test measure was the Minnesota Multiphasic Personality Inventory. The female aides' scores significantly altered on only one scale. This change indicated that female aides were less likely to use a defense mechanism that converted anxiety into physical symptoms. The male aides' scores were significantly lower on eight scales. The results indicate that male aides had: less worry and depression, less somatization, willingness to get involved more emotionally and intimately with other people, less rebelliousness, less tendency to use others, lowered concern for what others think about one, less sensitivity to the feelings of others, a tendency toward greater flexibility and less rigidity, a tendency toward less social introversion, and less dependency or more self-sufficiency (p. 51). Unfortunately, although the male aides demonstrated these changes after participation in the program, the changes cannot be attributed solely to their work as aides since there was no comparison group.

Usher's measure was the Eysenck Personality Inventory. He found significant change on both the Extroversion-Introversion Scale and on the Neuroticism-Stability Scale as compared to a control group. He concludes: "The data indicate that the ... course results in higher out-going, uninhibited, impulsive, and sociable inclinations. In terms of the neuroticism dimension, the data indicate a lower general emotional overresponsiveness and lower liability to neurotic breakdown under stress" (p. 67).

Summary

The research on the effects of participation in field education programs on personal development is strong and positive. Of the ten measures of personal development, seven found significant gains for students. Two others found a positive trend. After participation in field education programs, students appear to have higher self-respect, less anxiety and depression, and more emotional comfort and confidence in social interactions. The research confirms that experience through field education appears to foster maturity, self-respect, and social competence.

Career Development

One of the most popular goals for field education has been career development. These programs have been designed to expose students to the world of work and to provide information for career planning. Seven studies are reported here that looked at two aspects of career development:

A. Career Interests. Usher (1977) and Newton (1975) both used standardized vocational interest surveys in their studies. Usher concluded that the results of pre- and post-testing on the Strong-Campbell Interest Inventory "suggest that the effects of the (program) on vocational orientations ... are not significantly different from effects of (non-program) courses" (p. 76).

Newton, using the Ohio Vocational Interest Survey, found no significant change in vocational interests. However, he did find significant change in the degree of interests. Although program participants did not significantly change their choice of vocational interests, the strength of interest in their choices declined on the post-test significantly more than the control group. In referring to the change in degree of interest, Newton observed: "The distribution of change in degree of interest demonstrated by the experimental group, as opposed to the control group, may be attributed to a work experience program that provided experimental pupils with data and experiences from which to make a more realistic appraisal of job areas as they relate to self" (p. 33).

B. Career Maturity. Six studies have used the same measure, the Career Maturity Inventory (CMI). The CMI is composed of two scales: the Attitude Scale and the Competence Test. "The Attitude Scale ... attempts to measure the maturity of attitudes that are important to realistic career decision making. The dimensions assessed within the context of the Attitude Scale are: involvement in the choice process, orientation toward work, independence in decision making, preference for career choice factors (extent to which an individual bases his choice upon a particular factor), and conceptions of the choice process (extent to which an individual has accurate or inaccurate conceptions about making a career choice)" (Newton, 1975, p. 25).

"The Competence Test attempts to measure the maturity of competencies that are considered critical in career decision making. In contrast to the Attitude Scale, the Competence Test seeks to assess the more cognitive factors involved in occupational selection" (Newton, 1975, p. 27). The Competence Test contains five subtests: Knowing Yourself (Self-Appraisal), Knowing About Jobs (Occupational Information), Choosing a Job (Goal Selection), Looking Ahead (Planning), What Should They Do? (Problem Solving).

Two studies fully used both of the scales of the CMI. Stead (1977) did not find significant differences between the experimental and control groups. However, the experimental group did make more positive gains than the control group on three of the Competence subtests (Goal Selection, Self-Appraisal, and Planning). The Lafayette Parish School Board, LA (1973) also did not find significant differences between the experimental and control groups for their ninth grade sample. The study did find a significant difference in favor of the experimental group for the eighth grade sample.

Newton (1975) used the Attitude Scale and three subtests (Self-Appraisal, Occupational Information, and Goal Selection) of the Competence Test. His sample was a group of students in a middle school. He found no significant differences between the experimental and comparison groups.

Owens (1975) and Carey and Webber (1979) used only the Attitude Scale. Neither found significant differences between their experimental and comparison groups. Owens does maintain that the experimental group in his study had "a positive (and significant) growth for the year ..." while, "neither comparison group made a significant change over the year" (p. 6).

Finally, Beister (1978) used two subtests (Occupational Information and Planning) of the Competence Test. Over a two-year period, the cumulative change in scores for the experimental group was significantly better than for the control group.

Summary

No general or simple conclusions can be drawn from the research on career development. Five of the seven studies reviewed found positive gains for the field education students. But only two of these studies measured significantly greater gains for the field education students in contrast to control students. Since six of these programs were designed to enhance career education, the findings, though positive, are not conclusive.

One critically important issue must be raised in order to assess this research. A consistent finding of researchers is that vocational interests are both formed early, usually by the ninth or tenth grade, and are resistant to change. The research reviewed here seems to support both of these points. Two studies found significant differences between experimental and control students. In the Lafayette Parish School Board study, the researchers did not find significant differences for the ninth grade sample but they did find significant differences for the eighth grade students. Beister did not find significant differences between groups in the first year but did find significant cumulative score differences after two years. Thus, one study demonstrates that career attitudes and interests may be formed at an early age. The other study shows that, once formed, these attitudes and interests may require extensive experience before significant changes are seen.

Given both the research on vocational interests and the research presented here, more attention must be paid to the type of measure utilized in the research on field education. Standardized measures of vocational interests such as the Strong-Campbell and the Ohio Vocational Interest Survey are probably not suitable for detecting subtle, yet important, changes in vocational interests. Also, unless students are placed in the vocational areas of most interest, as indicated by the surveys, the field experience will probably not make a major impact on their interests. The student placed in a work experience dissimilar to his expressed interest will not be exposed to the experience and information necessary to influence his career choice.

One of the most suggestive findings of the research is Newton's observation of a shift in degree of career interests. Young people's exposure to the world of work is generally limited. As a consequence, they tend to have naive or unrealistic expectations both about the world of work and about specific careers in which they are interested. Through such media as television they often see the glamour and fruits of work but rarely see the frustrations and drudgery.

For further research, three suggestions emerge from this review:

1. Research should concentrate on measuring competencies and practical knowledge rather than vocational interests and attitudes.

2. Shifts in career awareness would be expected in the direction of realistic assessments of self and career choice vis-a-vis work.

3. Intensive, long-term field experiences would have more impact than shadowing type programs or short-term experiences.

Affective Development

Educators have come to believe that student attitudes and values critically affect learning and academic performance. A few studies have investigated the effects of field education experiences on values and attitudes. The studies have focused on three areas:

A. Moral Development. Sprinthall (1974) designed a program for high school students that combined coursework in psychology with peer counseling. Using Kohlberg's Test of Moral Maturity, Sprinthall found significant gains in levels of moral reasoning. He comments, "It usually takes teenagers two or three years, to move from stage III to IV and even then a substantial minority never make it past stage III" (p. 19). In contrast, students in Sprinthall's study move to stage IV in considerably less time.

B. Attitudes Toward Others. Urie (1971) studied a program in which college students acted as aides for other disabled college students. The measure used was the scale, Attitudes Toward Disabled College Students. Urie found that over time the aides expressed less positive attitudes toward the disabled students. His comment was:

> This "less favorable" attitude picture can hardly be taken at face value but should probably be interpreted as increased honesty. As the aides became more familiar with persons with physical disabilities as human beings, they were increasingly willing to point out faults and to criticize the handicapped as friends. If this is the case, the less protective attitude [might be] a positive by-product of the project experience (p. 52).

C. Attitudes Toward School and Learning. Four studies have attempted to assess students' attitudes toward school and learning. Carey and Webber (1979) employed Osgood's semantic differential that measures students' perceptions toward education. They found no significant differences between experimental and control students. Usher's (1977) measure, Student Orientations Survey, Form C, yields ten scales. On eight of the scales there was no significant difference between experimental and control groups.

There was a significant difference on the Assignment Learning scale. The program "resulted in higher preferences among the students for a mode of learning which is specific, formal and linear in nature" (p. 70). Results on the Interaction scale were marginally significant.

To measure attitudes toward school, Newton (1975) administered the School Sentiment Index (SSI) to experimental and control groups of middle school students. The SSI measures five aspects of attitude toward school: teachers, learning, school structure and climate, peers, and the notion of school in general. The experimental group had a significantly better attitude toward learning than did the control group. Significant differences were not found on any of the other dimensions nor on the composite index. "However, the mean score of the experimental group for the composite index (comprehensive attitude toward school) and the significance level computed (.15) indicate the group approached having a better comprehensive attitude toward school than did the control group. A higher mean for the experimental group was also computed for the dimensions, 'notion of school in general' and 'attitude toward teachers'" (Newton, 1975, p. 29).

Beister (1978) measured attitudes toward school using the Assessment of Student Attitudes Toward Learning Environments Scale (ASA). The ASA is a Likert scale developed by two of the study's researchers. Subscales include Attitudes Toward Education in General, Attitudes Toward School Curriculum, Attitudes Toward School Resources, Attitudes Toward School Counseling, and Overall Attitudes Toward Learning Environments. During the first year, experimental students made significantly greater gains than control students in attitude toward school curriculum, school counseling, and overall learning environments. During the second year, the experimental group showed significant growth in attitudes toward education in general, school resources, and overall learning environments. Beister's interpretation of this fact was: "... first year growth was clearly illustrated in those areas of learning environments which the intervention of the (program) immediately and most directly affects, namely, school curriculum and school counseling. Attitudes toward more remote factors such as education in general and learning resources remained stable during the first year but significantly increased during the second year of program participation" (p. 9).

Summary

The research in this area must be divided into two groups. The first group is composed of Sprinthall's and Urie's studies. Obviously, there is too little evidence on moral development or attitudes toward others to draw any conclusions.

A cautionary note must be given on Sprinthall's study. His program was unique and intensive and dealt with issues that were, in fact, moral or were secondarily related to moral issues. Most field education experiences are likely to raise moral issues with which participants must cope. But the assumption, based on Sprinthall's study, that field education programs necessarily affect moral development would be rash.

The second group of studies are those that measured attitudes toward learning and school. Of the four studies, one found no significant improvement in attitudes; one found partial improvement; one found a positive trend; and one found significant improvement. Additional information is given by Bloom (1976) in her review of the research on tutoring programs. She reports a number of studies in which students had significant improvement in attitudes toward school.

The research on the effects of field education on attitudes toward school and learning, though not conclusive, is very encouraging. The objective measures indicate that following participation in a field education program, students have a more positive attitude toward school. The subjective reports of teachers, parents, and students on questionnaires agree that students are more interested in school and are more motivated to learn.

An indirect way to assess attitude toward school would be to consider behavior in school (e.g. discipline, truancy, and drop-out rates) and academic achievement. These areas are discussed here in other sections.

Academic Achievement

None of the studies reported here were conducted on field education programs that were specifically designed to improve academic achievement. The programs studied were intended to involve students in community life, provide a needed service (e.g. tutoring), or enhance career education. Nevertheless, many practitioners believe that field education experiences do have a positive effect on achievement. The studies that have measured achievement have been grouped according to the type of measure employed.

A. *Grade Point Average.* Neither the University of Pittsburgh (1975) nor Urie (1971) conducted a statistical analysis of grade point averages. Their purpose for keeping records of grade point average was to be sure that the student participants did not suffer academically from their involvement in the field education programs. In both studies, students did, however, have higher grade point averages at the completion of their participation in the program. Urie's conclusion summarizes the findings for both studies:

> ... the academic data which were obtained in this project indicate that participation in the project did not prevent such students from making significant scholastic progress. Overall, in fact, they exceeded their non-project peers in academic achievement. While there is no evidence to suggest that project participation had any causal relationship to such achievement, we might speculate that some such relationship did exist. We might wonder, for example, if involvement in the project did, in fact, provide a direction or meaning to participants' lives which tended to facilitate rather than retard their academic progress. (pp. 28-30)

B. *Comprehensive Test of Basic Skills.* In three studies the Comprehensive Test of Basic Skills (CTBS) was the measure of achievement. All three programs studied were career education programs.

Carey and Webber (1979) administered subtests 1-5: Vocabulary, Comprehension, Mechanics, Expression, and Spelling. They found that the control group had significantly better post-test scores on the mechanics and expression subtests.

Owens and Fehrenbacker (1975) measured Reading, Language, Arithmetic, and Study Skills on the CTBS. They specifically state that "it was not a goal of (the program) that its students make greater growth in Basic Skills than a random sample of students ... — only that they not make significantly less growth" (p. 4). Although experimental students made significant gains, the experimental students gained no more than the comparison group.

Beister (1978) tested for Reading Comprehension, Arithmetic Applications, and Arithmetic Concepts on the CTBS. Students participated in this program for two years. Students made significant gains on Arithmetic Concepts and Arithmetic Applications during the first year and significant gains on all three subtests during the second year. In the first year, the experimental students' gains were not significantly greater on any of the subtests than the control group. However, in the second year, the experimental students made significantly greater gains than the control group on the reading Comprehension and Arithmetic Applications subtests. Over the two-year period, the experimental students' cumulative gains were significantly greater than the control group on the Arithmetic Concepts and Arithmetic Applications subtests.

C. *The Watson-Glaser Critical Thinking Appraisal.* Stead (1977) administered the Watson-Glaser Critical Thinking Appraisal to student participants in a career education program. The post-test results indicated that the program students improved their cognitive skills. According to Stead, "the participating students gained 6% on the national norm and improved one stanine from pre- to post-test. The degree of their gain on the post-test approaches statistical significance" (p. 48).

In 1976, Dr. Sophie Bloom published a review of research on peer and cross-age tutoring for the National Institute of Education. Bloom reviews the effects on both the tutors and the tutees on three dimensions: achievement, attitudes toward school, and self-concept. She concludes that benefits for tutors include gains in both attitude toward school and self-concept. But she states: "Perhaps the clearest benefits for tutors is that they improve their own learning .... In 66 percent of these studies there were significant gains in school achievement for tutors. These findings were especially true for measures of gains in reading and language arts" (p. 13).

Bloom summarizes the results of 15 studies in which tutors' grades ranged from 4 to 12. Six of the studies involved high school age tutors. Four of these studies found significant gains in achievement for the tutors.

Summary

The research on academic achievement is surprisingly encouraging. Yet one point must be kept in mind in considering this research. None of the programs studied were deliberately and specifically designed to enhance academic achievement. Several of the researchers pointedly state that they did not expect to find significantly greater gains in academic achievement for the experimental students as compared to control groups. The researchers hoped that students would not suffer academically due to participation in field education programs. On this, the research is conclusive.

In only one of the studies reviewed, (Carey and Webber, 1979) and then on only two of five subtests, did experimental students show no gain in achievement or significantly less gain than control students. On the basis of this research, the confident assertion can be made that participation in field education programs is not detrimental to academic achievement. This is interesting, since field education students in many of the studies spent markedly fewer hours in traditional academic courses than control students.

The research is not conclusive on the obverse statement that participation in field education has definite positive effects on academic achievement. However, the research is remarkably supportive. Of the twelve studies reviewed (one college group and 11 high school groups, six reported by Bloom), experimental students made positive gains in four programs and significant gains in five programs on measures of academic achievement.

The research presented here suggests two conclusions. One, field education programs do not hamper academic achievement despite the fact that field education participants may devote less time to traditional educational courses. Two, participation in field education programs may enhance academic achievement.

There is one other more speculative, yet inescapable, conclusion. Even though a field education program does not directly intend to promote academic learning, successful participation may indirectly and positively affect academic achievement. Urie suggests that participation in a field education program gives meaning to students' lives. Bloom reports that in seven studies the researchers concluded "that tutor gains in achievement were primarily true when achievement gains were also made by their tutees" (p. 14). The review of the research of personal development clearly shows gains in self-concept following participation in field education programs. These threads lead to an intriguing hypothesis.

By heightening self-concept and self-confidence, field education experiences may motivate students to have higher academic achievement. As a result of field education experiences, students may have a stronger sense of self-control and more confidence in their abilities to positively affect their environment, including school. As a consequence, they may have a more positive attitude toward school and learning and more motivation to perform well academically. Thus, regardless of the type of field education program, a successful field education experience may lead to higher academic achievement.

Questionnaires

A few of the studies not only used standardized measures but also questionnaires. These questionnaires were intended more for internal program evaluation rather than for objective evaluation. They do, however, provide an indication of the general support for and value of field education programs. The questionnaires were given to parents, students, teachers, and field supervisors.

One question that was asked by most of the researchers was whether the respondent was supportive of the programs. In all cases where this question was asked, students, parents, teachers, and field supervisors were overwhelmingly supportive of the programs.

When field supervisors were asked if they would either continue with the program or recommend it to other "agencies," the responses were: 77% yes (Stead, 1977); 92% yes (Newton, 1975); 93% yes (University of Pittsburgh, 1975); 94.7% yes (Usher, 1977); and 100% yes (Owens and Fehrenbacker, 1975). The percentage of parents, teachers, and students who responded yes to whether the program was beneficial or should be continued was similar — 90% to 100%.

A second question that was frequently asked was what benefits the students gained from participation in the field experience. Again, there was remarkable agreement among teachers, students, and parents. There was also a strong consistency among the studies in response to this question. The benefits most often cited can be divided into three categories: interpersonal or intrapersonal skills, attitudes toward school and learning, and career awareness.

A. Students. When asked what they had learned through participation in the field education programs, students listed the following:

1. Interpersonal and Intrapersonal Skills
   - responsibility
   - working with others
   - self-control
   - patience
   - control of emotions, especially anger
   - independence
   - being on my own and depending on myself
   - that I was somebody
   - gaining self-confidence
   - tolerance
   - the importance of appearance
   - keeping a schedule and being organized
   - that others depend on you
   - "grew up"
   - how to communicate with others

2. Attitudes Toward School and Learning
   - why it is necessary to stay in school
   - more opportunity for general learning
   - increased motivation toward school
   - more positive attitude toward learning

3. Career Awareness
   - career skills actually needed
   - the education required
   - the competition in this career
   - the rewards in this career
   - the regulations imposed in this career field
   - widened knowledge of career possibilities
   - help in choosing a career
   - more positive attitude toward work.

B. Parents. When parents were asked what benefits they perceived that their children had gained from the program, their most frequent responses were:

1. Interpersonal and Intrapersonal Skills
   - responsibility
   - maturity
   - self-confidence
   - patience, especially with family members
   - sympathy
   - thoughtfulness and consideration
   - awareness of their emotions
   - more positive attitude toward self

2. Attitudes Toward School and Learning
   - more interest in school
   - increased motivation toward school

3. Career Awareness
   - more consideration of future occupations
   - more positive attitude toward work
   - better understanding of world of work
   - help in choosing a career
   - more awareness of career opportunities.

C. Teachers. Teachers, when asked what benefits they perceived that their students had gained, responded:

1. Interpersonal and Intrapersonal Skills
   - responsibility
   - confidence
   - improved planning and organizational patterns

2. Attitudes Toward School and Learning
   - more interest in school work
   - general improvement in attitude toward school
   - made school more relevant
   - helped students see a need to remain in school
   - more motivated to learn.

Even a cursory comparison of the lists given by students, parents, and teachers shows their overall agreement. The composite portrait is of students who are more responsible, mature, and self-confident; more open and positive in social relations; more interested in school and motivated to learn; and more generally aware and knowledgeable about the world of work. These are the subjective perceptions of the people involved. But they tally extremely well with the results of the standardized measures reviewed earlier.

General Observations and Recommendations

There are a few observations that deserve comment. The following are cautious speculations based on slim evidence or peripheral remarks in the research reports. Nevertheless, they are worthy of note and, certainly, of further research.

Young people are often considered to be idealistic. Frequently, this is a polite way of saying that they are impractical or have unreasonable expectations. Several of the studies concluded that participants emerged from the field education experiences being more realistic about themselves, others, school, or work. Hypothetically, the field experience provided concrete information about self, others, education, and work. Based on this information, participants could make more accurate assessments of their own abilities, the characteristics of other people, the purpose of education, and the world of work.

Young people's idealism is particularly apparent in their career and related educational goals and in their expectations about their own abilities and achievements. All too often young people have chosen a career goal, yet they have not considered such issues as the cost of education, the training necessary, the competition, or the personal abilities required by the work. As indicated by the questionnaires, this is the kind of information that students acquire through a field experience. They may not alter their career choices, but they are able to fill the gap between the wish and the goal with a realistic plan based on practical information.

Currently, the drop-out rate for high school students is 23 percent. Clearly, this continues to be a serious problem. Field education programs may contribute to a solution of this problem by providing an educational option that attracts and holds students in school. One study found fewer discipline problems among field education program participants. Two studies found lowered truancy rates. And one study claimed fewer drop-outs among the field education students as compared to the general school population. In another, the parents of participants suggested that the field education program offered an alternative that may have prevented students from leaving school. Admittedly, this is slim evidence for making any strong claim. However, the research does show that field education experiences do enhance attitudes toward school. For students who are disaffected with traditional education, field education programs may stimulate the motivation to continue their education.

One of the criticisms of public education is that the system contributes to age segregation in American society. One of the advantages of field education is that students usually have an adult field supervisor and role model who is neither their teacher nor their parent. Ideally, this relationship can evolve into one of mutual respect, particularly if the student is accepted, and expected to function, in an adult role.

In the questionnaire portions of the research, students indicated the importance of their relationship with their supervisors. They turned to their supervisor for guidance, support, and solutions to problems. The students rated this relationship as more important to them than coursework, school personnel, or program seminars or discussion groups. These elements of field education programs were valued by students. But the key ingredient, for them, was the relationship with the supervisor.

The research indicates that after their field experiences, students felt more accepted by their teachers. And parents reported more understanding, positive relations with their children. One might speculate that students who had positive interactions with adult supervisors were more positive in their interactions with other adults. There may also be a Pygmalion effect: students whose supervisors expected them to act as adults may have, in fact, come to behave and think as adults.

*Rick Williams has provided creative leadership in service-learning pro-
grams through Boston University and other settings in the Boston area.
He currently works with the Polaroid Corporation.*

References

Arkell, R. N., "Are Student Helpers Helped?," *Psychology in the Schools*, Vol.
    12, No. 1, January 1975, pp. 113-115.

Beister, Thomas W., Keith Kershner, and Mark W. Blair, "Evaluation of
    Cumulative Effects of RBS Career Education," Paper presented at the
    Annual Meeting of the American Education Research Association,
    Toronto, Ontario, Canada, March 1978.

Blackmer, A. R. and P. Irwin, *Study of Off-Campus Education*, National
    Association of Independent Schools, January 1977.

Bloom, Sophie, *Peer and Cross-Age Tutoring in the Schools*, U. S. Department
    of Health, Education, and Welfare, 1976.

Carey, Marsha A. and Larry J. Webber, "Evaluating an Experience-Based
    Career Education Program;," *The Vocational Guidance Quarterly*, Vol. 27,
    March 1979.

Carnegie Council on Policy Studies in Higher Education, *Giving Youth A
    Better Chance*, Jossey-Bass, 1979.

Coleman, James, "The Children Have Outgrown the Schools," *Psychology
    Today*, February 1972, pp. 72-82.

Coleman, James, "How Do the Young Become Adults?," *Phi Delta Kappan*,
    December 1972, pp. 227-230.

Gibbons, Maurice, *The New Secondary Education: A Phi Delta Kappa Task
    Force Report*, Phi Delta Kappa, Inc., 1976.

Godfrey, Robert, "A Review of Research and Evaluation Literature on
    Outward Bound and Related Education Programs," Paper presented at
    Conference on Experiential Education, Estes Park, Colorado, October
    8-11, 1974.

Graham, Richard, "Youth and Experiential Learning," in R. J. Havighurst
    and P. H. Dreyer, eds., *Youth*, University of Chicago Press, 1975.

Haan, N., "Changes in Young Adults after Peace Corps Experience: Politi-
    cal-Social Views, Moral Reasoning, and Perceptions of Self and
    Parents," *Journal of Youth and Adolescence*, 1974, Vol. 3, No. 3, pp. 177-
    194.

Hedges, Henry, *Extending Volunteer Programs in Schools*, The Ontario Insti-
    tute for Studies in Education, 1973.

National Association of Secondary School Principals, *Action-Learning*, 1974.

National Association of Secondary School Principals, *This We Believe: Secon-
    dary Schools in Changing Society*, 1975.

National Center for Service-Learning (ACTION), *Synergist*, Vol. 8, No. 3,
    Winter 1980, pp. 2-5.

National Commission on the Reform of Secondary Education, *The Reform of Secondary Education*, McGraw-Hill, 1973.

National Panel on High School and Adolescent Education, "The Education of Adolescents: Final Report and Recommendations," Office of Education, U. S. Department of Health, Education, and Welfare, 1976.

Newton, Mark, "An Experimental Study of the Effects of an Alternative Work Experience Program in the Middle School," Western Kentucky University, 1975.

Owens, Thomas R., and H. Fehrenbacker, "Evaluation of the Community Experience for Career Education Program," Northwest Regional Educational Laboratory, 1975.

Panel on Youth of the President's Science Advisory Committee, *Youth: Transition to Adulthood*, Government Printing Office, 1973.

Peterson, Virgil, "Volunteering and Student Value Development: Is There A Correlation?" in *Synergist*, Vol. 3, No. 3, Winter, 1975, pp. 44-51.

Research for Better Schools, "Career Education Program 1974-1975: Final Evaluation Report," Research for Better Schools, 1975.

Robinson, Ann Garrett, "The Effects of a Community Service-Oriented Curriculum on Alienation, Perceived Student Role, and Course Satisfaction in Community College Students," unpublished doctoral dissertation, Nova University, 1975.

Sprinthall, Norman, "Learning Psychology by Doing Psychology: A High School Curriculum in the Psychology of Counseling," Minneapolis Public Schools, 1974.

Stainback, W. C., S. B. Stainback, and F. Lichtward, "The Research Evidence Regarding the Student-to-Student Tutoring Approach to Individualized Instruction," *Educational Technology*, February 1975, pp. 54-56.

Stead, Floyd, Richard A. Hartnett, and Joseph J. Prentiss, "A Third-Party Evaluation of the Appalachian Maryland Experience-Based Career Education Project: 1976-77," West Virginia University, 1977.

University of Pittsburgh, "Evaluation Report for Senior Semester Program 1974-75," 1975.

Urie, Robert *et al.*, "Student Aides for Handicapped College Students: Final Report and Manual," St. Andrews Presbyterian College, 1971.

Usher, Brian R., "Etobicoke Community Involvement Program Evaluation," Ministry of Education, Ontario, Canada, 1977.

Watson, Kathryn J., "The Going Places Classroom: A Community Involvement Program of Action Learning for Elementary Students," University of Florida, 1977.

Service Through Ideas of Value

Warren Bryan Martin

A distinguished educator argues that issues of value are the
essential concerns of the educational enterprise. Academic insti-
tutions have responsibility not only for analyzing major social
issues and ideologies but also for offering opportunities to stu-
dents to experience and involve themselves in them. Martin's
powerful message from 1977 is an enduring one for the 1990s
and beyond. Reprinted with permission from Redefining Service, Research, and Teaching, *ed. Warren Bryan Martin, Jos-*
sey-Bass, New Directions for Higher Education, No. 18, Summer 1977, pp. 1-16.

MANY EDUCATORS THOUGHT that the 1960s brought with them
a series of challenges to colleges and universities that were not only
unparalleled in the history of higher education but were about all
that these institutions could handle without collapsing. The new
youth culture combined with the war in East Asia shook academic
life to its foundations. Attacks on the purposes, organization, and
place of higher education in American culture came both from the
young, some of whom viewed education as the tool of bureaucracy,
the establishment, and the status quo; as well as from the old, some
of whom saw it as the tool of disruption, disrespect, and political
radicalism.

While we may have thought that things could not get worse in
the 1970s than they were in the 1960s, inflation and recession, with
their concomitant effects, now seem to be having an impact that
exceeds all of the trouble that went before. Higher education is
under attack from the political left, which views education as the
tool of capitalism, as well as from the political right, which sees it as
the tool of egalitarian and populist socialism. Things, alas, are
going from bad to worse, and we must brace ourselves for the possibility that they will get still worse than the worst that we have yet
been able to imagine.

Fred Hechinger of the *New York Times* published an article in the *Saturday Review* entitled, "Murder in Academe: The Demise of Education." He began the essay with this paragraph (1976, p. 11): "America is in headlong retreat from its commitment to education. Political confusion and economic uncertainty have shaken the people's faith in education as the key to financial and social success. This retreat ought to be the most pertinent issue in any examination of the country's condition.... At stake is nothing less than the survival of American democracy." Hechinger believes that the present retreat threatens this nation's movement toward universal education and that, should this upward mobility of the masses be stopped, the consequence will be restoration of "a stratified, class-bound society ruled by a self-perpetuating power elite of economic and social privilege. It would be the end of the road that was opened by Thomas Jefferson when he called for a new aristocracy of talent to replace the old aristocracy of inherited power."

The Nature of the Enterprise

What is at issue, fundamentally, is the nature of the educational enterprise. Is this enterprise characterized by its services? Is it, in fact, serving the needs and interests of students, the expectations of parents and benefactors, and the values of the society at large? Are its traditional trinity of functions — teaching, research, and service — while separate and distinct, all recognized as forms of service? The answer to these questions ought to be yes when, in fact, it is no.

Teaching can be a service to the subject matter specialization, to the educational institution that calls itself a center of teaching and learning, to the learners who benefit from what is taught, and to the teacher — who perhaps gains most of all by active involvement in the deed of teaching. But teaching today is called everything but a form of service. It is "the transmission of knowledge and information." It is "human interaction." It is "a symbolic expression of a great tradition." It is a "job," a "way to earn a living." Would not both teacher and student, academic professional and constituency representative, campus personnel and community leaders, all benefit tremendously if teaching's service function were emphasized and if teaching were defined as a service? This is the appropriate rationale for teaching. It has appeal for the public, it has meaning for students, and it has benefit for the profession.

Research, no less than teaching, is a form of service. The field of inquiry is served, as is the guild of specialists. The service of research may be theoretical and abstract; it may be applied and specific; it may apply to evident, even urgent human needs or make its contribution as building blocks to a pyramidal structure of knowledge whose apex is still obscured from view. But here again the services of research have become obstructed by research that serves only additional research. "Serve the people" is a better motto for research than is "serve the researchers" — especially when it is understood that research that serves the people will take many forms.

What stays the same, then, is that teaching and research have always been and remain today a form of service. What is changing is the focal points of their service and increased questions about other services beyond conventional teaching and research.

Before the emergence of the university model at Johns Hopkins University and at Clark University in the last quarter of the nineteenth century, the service of the college was defined as a service to the church and state, service to a very select and limited group of professions that were closely allied with church and state, and service to the young people who were deemed eligible for training in these professions and/or were eligible for the college experience by reason of birth and social station.

In the first half of this century, and until recently, the service of the university was expanded to include service to the emerging new professions, service to science and technology, service to the advancement of new knowledge, service to the guilds of the academic disciplines, and service to students willing to become initiates in the rite of passage into any profession, including the professions of teaching, business, and industry.

Now, and for the foreseeable future, the services provided by colleges and universities are being extended, not only in their number and range but also in the variety of people they serve. This change has its roots in the nineteenth century, especially in the establishment of the land-grant institutions, but it is essentially a development of the post-World War II decades. It is a change that is most dramatically expressed in the emergence of junior and community colleges, as well as in continuing education and extension programs. It is a change consistent with an egalitarian social philosophy as well as with the determination to put education into the service of the goal of social justice.

Ideas of Value

If the liberating arts are defined as those subjects, objects, and activities that help the individual to develop *ideas of value* — ideas that give a basis for living as well as the means by which to live successfully — then the liberating arts become essential to all else and stand first in significance. And education that transmits ideas of value becomes our nation's most important resource, even as it is education's most important service. Human beings must have ideas of value by which to look at, experience, and interpret the world. When we think, we do not just think, we think with ideas. The mind is not a blank; it is actually filled with good or bad ideas or, more likely, good *and* bad ideas. The trick, obviously, is to determine which among these many ideas can be considered ideas of value. Making that determination is so hard, in fact, that most of us have given up on the job of ordering our ideas deliberately, self-consciously, and selectively and have settled for the doctrine of undifferentiated pluralism, by which many ideas, even competing and contradictory ones, are legitimated.

Nevertheless, despite the difficulty and despite our desire to avoid choice, the fact of the matter is that, in our actions, if not in our pronouncements, we show what are for us the prevailing ideas of value. There is no escaping this outcome. We are trained to look for ideas, to choose ideas by which to make the world and our own existence meaningful. The quest for meaning is the basic movement of humanity. And, no matter how hard the task, we finally assign meaning to certain ideas rather than others, and these become our working ideas of value.

Individualism and Communitarianism

As an example of ideas of value, consider the ideologies of "individualism" and "communitarianism" — a pair of presumed opposites that seem to defy reconciliation but that badly need to be reconciled.

In this century, rampant individualism has offered the most dangerous form of totalitarianism — a totalitarianism of self-centeredness. The legitimacy of the individual has been debased into individualism, which is person-centeredness become self-centeredness. This may be the chief abberation of our time. Collectivism has been repudiated as group conformity, while individualism has emerged as the new conformity.

Actually, it is out of concern for the individual that individualism must be transcended. Neither the problems of society nor the problems of the person can be solved by the self or self-centeredness. Therefore, today the search is on for a better way, for an alternative to individualism. And here, as has happened so many times before, higher education seems to be caught with its principles down.

Having for centuries emphasized the collegial nature of the educational enterprise, reminding us, for example, that there are unique advantages for students who live in a learning environment, more recently colleges and universities yielded to almost absolute individualism: Let faculty members teach what they want to teach, study anything they want, consult with anyone who pays them; let students learn what they want to learn, live anywhere they prefer, be responsible for no one but themselves. Much of graduate and professional education and now undergraduate education became isolated, individualistic, and particularistic. Students were guided away from cooperative learning, sharing, formulating common goals, or learning about interdependency. Predictably behind the time, while desperately trying to get with it, college communities have been giving up all claim to collectivity just when our most perceptive thinkers and planners are emphasizing both the inadequacies of individualism and the promise inherent in the creation of new communities. Now, some educators are having second thoughts and, once again, are asking what the college community ought to do as a community of learning.

George C. Lodge, in *The New American Ideology*, argues for the emergence of an ideology in which communitarianism is replacing individualism, the rights of membership are replacing the rights of property, community need is superseding raw competition, holism and integration are replacing specialization and pragmatism, and more government is replacing less government, with the nation-state becoming the master planner.

An outstanding theorist for radical communalism, the historian William Appleman Williams, believes with Frederick Jackson Turner that the source of the special American addiction to individual autonomy was the vast western frontier. But Williams sees the frontier as a curse that contributed toward making Americans into compulsively restless people moving away from social planning and group responsibilities and encouraged unrestrained, wasteful, individualist democracy. In the twentieth century, with the western frontier closed, Americans have turned to international adventure — with disastrous results. Williams believes, as do others, that America must now be drawn away from such false adventurism and turned toward the development of true organic community. What is called for is nothing less than updated secular versions of the medieval Christian commonwealth, the ancient Jewish fellowship, or the Greek city-state.

To this end, higher education deserves to offer more than the sterile civility of the technological bureaucracy or the boarding-house — a community of comradeship more than merely a community of convenience characterized by the spirit of anomie. At a time when our traditional sources of identity and security are crumbling — home, church, the nation-state — collegiate communities can be important, not only in grappling with these issues and ideologies of individualism and communitarianism but also in demonstrating to students and the public at large the function of community itself.

Experience and Application

It is this grappling with issues of value — this determination not simply to reflect the tensions existing in society but instead to provide useful responses to them — that makes college and university teaching and research essential services to the nation. This task, in which ideas of importance are dealt with, criticized, refined, reordered, and brought to the attention of individuals and other institutions, is perhaps the core service of higher education. By and large, most people do not have the time, the inclination, or the expertise to carry out many aspects of this task. In effect, they delegate the responsibility for such investigation to higher education, asking only that this service be carried out with an eye to its social utility.

Beyond the ideas of individualism and communitarianism or equality and quality, the public expects higher education to consider many other issues of value. Most if not all of them are espoused by educators themselves — ideas and ideals such as reason, good judgment, toleration, magnanimity, cooperation, competence, faith, hope, love, the understanding of nature and of human nature, the value of controlled response, the satisfactions of interdependency, and that of service itself. Their reverse includes solipsism, self-indulgence, irrationality, acquisitiveness, waste, gaudiness, display, ineptitude, hopelessness, nihilism, cynicism, hedonism, and despair.

Are not these issues essential concerns of the educational experience? To the extent that colleges and universities help to introduce positive ideas of value in the lives of their students, they perform invaluable services to society. And to realize such values as these, is there any question that students must *experience* these values in their college lives, rather than merely studying about them? Should not college be the one place above all, where students are expected to examine, test out, and practice these values — and witness their practice by faculty members and administrators?

It is a commonplace that choices are determined largely by our experiences. Is it not the case that practice is determined more by what students experience than by principles and abstractions? After studying the lives of graduates of Haverford College, Douglas Heath, professor of psychology at Haverford, has concluded that "Haverford continued to affect the lives of many of its alumni because it provided an ethos that demanded its students become more mature in their character, not just in their intellect.... It was not enough to just open up and discipline a student's mind. He must be goaded to find a meaning to his education and an idealistic purpose for his life." All too often, he suspects, "many liberal arts colleges neither powerfully confront their students with their values nor actually stand for a distinctive vision of the 'good life'" (1976, p. 186). Confronting students with their values and standing for ideas of value are thus essential parts of college education.

In the determination of students' values, educators must not forget that logic, reason, and philosophy play a smaller role than do experience and emotion. To believe that human beings act logically is itself illogical, contrary to the logic of history and human experience. Passion and the human will are more influential than intellect and reason. Reason is usually brought into the service of emotion rather than the reverse. Our "reasons" are often passion's rationalizations, and reasoning is one of passion's favorite modes of expression.

The crucial question for educators is this: If human passions have been the motive force that has brought our world to its present sad state of affairs, and if our needs for the future are different than this state of affairs permits, how can our passions be changed? The answer is "Certainly not by lectures." If not by persuasion and only minimally by coercion, is not the answer to be found in the power of a new affection — by a new passion, that is, by social or ethical commitments held passionately? Educators can fight fire with fire, as the great religious movements of history have always shown; but what is required is something caught, not taught: a new affection producing sacrificial dedication to high purpose.

We cannot, however, contrive education for the analysis and experience of ideas of value to which students will commit themselves passionately by offering them merely assembly line instruction. Passionate activists and societal leaders are seldom Harvard's or Yale's interchangeable lawyers. *Just as creativity requires more than studying examples of creativity, so the practice of judgment, magnanimity, and other ideas requires opportunities for students to practice these virtues. Providing these opportunities deserves the attention of all faculty members and administrators.*

In sum, given the ambivalence of human nature and passions and the constant needs for social criticism and creativity, colleges and universities must be places for independent thinking and for the investigation of alternative ideologies and ideas of value. As such, they must stand somewhat apart from society's center — on the margin, as it were, of social acceptability. But as institutions that society uses to inculcate important values, they cannot neglect ideologies and ideas.

American society is not likely to allow any of its major social institutions — including institutions of higher education and even private colleges, so long as they have a hand in the public till — to determine their purposes and programs in isolation from the public. Social institutions, even at the edge of the establishment, must work within its constraints. Today, the tax-exempt status of the churches is being increasingly challenged, as one case in point. The autonomy of the medical profession is under attack, an another. The military budget has its critics and is subject to civilian review. In short, no profession is exempt from public scrutiny and accountability. This is particularly true of education, which now takes more than 30 percent of state funding allocations. *Colleges and universities can best warrant this scrutiny and overcome the present retreat from educational commitment and attacks from both left and right by emphasizing the services that are uniquely theirs: both the examination and the experience of ideas of value.*

Warren Bryan Martin is Senior Fellow at the Carnegie Foundation for the Advancement of Teaching. He was previously Vice President of the Danforth Foundation and director of the Danforth Graduate Fellowship Program. He has also served as Provost of the School of Arts and Sciences and Professor of History at California State College, Sonoma; as Research Educator at the Center for Research and Development in Higher Education, University of California at Berkeley; and as the founding Provost of Raymond College at the University of the Pacific.

References

Heath, Douglas, "What the Enduring Effects of Higher Education Tell Us About a Liberal Education," *Journal of Higher Education*, March/April 1976, pp. 173-190.

Hechinger, Fred, "Murder in Academe: The Demise of Education," *Saturday Review*, March 20, 1976, pp. 11-12.

Lodge, George C., *The New American Ideology*, Knopf, 1975.

Martin, Warren B., "Equality and Quality," in D. W. Vermilye, ed., *Individualizing the System: Current Issues in Higher Education*, Jossey-Bass, 1976.
Schumacher, E. F., *Small Is Beautiful*, Harper & Row, 1975.
Williams, William A., *The Roots of the Modern American Empire*, Random House, 1969.

The Community Service Tradition of an Historically Black College

W. Clyde Williams

The former President of Miles College in Birmingham, Alabama, describes the role of community service-learning at his institution. Reprinted from Synergist, National Center for Service-Learning, ACTION, Vol. 9, No. 1, Spring 1980, pp. 22-23.

HISTORICALLY, Miles College has been regarded as a community college in that its curricular offerings and supportive programs have been directed in large part by the communities that produce many of its clientele. Because Miles has systematically given attention to these needs, it has consistently contributed to the prosperity of the larger community of which it is a part.

Although it is not the design of the commentary to give a historical accounting of Miles College, it is pertinent that the reader is aware of circumstances that brought about the genesis of Miles.

Briefly, Miles College is a traditionally black, private, four-year liberal arts college located in Fairfield, Alabama, a suburb on the edge of the city of Birmingham and very much a part of the metropolitan Birmingham community. Miles was founded 75 years ago by the members of the Colored Methodist Episcopal Church (changed to Christian Methodist Episcopal Church in 1952). The purpose of the College at that time was to provide equal opportunity and growth for young black people who had been excluded from such opportunities.

Miles still feels the pulse of the community and uses the varied resources of the College to introduce, support, and sponsor programs and activities that assist and build community potential.

For too long colleges and universities have been separated and isolated from the "real" world. Academic institutions can no longer afford to isolate themselves from other learning forces within the community. Inasmuch as education is a process through which all persons must engage themselves throughout their lifetime, all institutional forces must be used in educating all persons in the community. Additionally, widespread demands of public groups that educational institutions be held accountable for their outcomes make it mandatory that colleges and universities analyze their traditional roles. Accountable education cannot be separate from community.

If students within the institutions are to develop skills and competencies to equip them for living in the world beyond the institution, they must come face to face with the social, political, and economic problems that will confront their generation.

Students gain self-confidence through the utilization of their natural talents and skills. Also, the use of staff abilities and skills can accelerate the institution's efforts to be responsive to community needs. Therefore, the student, the staff, and the community benefit when they engage together in community-based experiences.

One of the first and most important steps in facilitating a service-learning program is that community needs are identified and that all planning fulfills these needs. The community's awareness, understanding, and support are most crucial to any service-learning

If students within the institutions are to develop skills and competencies to equip them for living in the world beyond the institution, they must come face to face with the social, political, and economic problems that will confront their generation.

program. The many successes that Miles College has experienced with community programs can be attributed to its willingness to work with the community and to expand and refine programs over the years in response to changing social conditions.

In addition to its involvement in intrainstitutional and interinstitutional programs, Miles College has received both moral and financial support for many tasks and services to the students and to the community.

Many programs that never existed in Birmingham are the result of the College's efforts toward community service and unity. The highly successful Miles College-Eutaw Program, a portable freshman-year program in the black belt of Greene County (Alabama), makes education available where it was virtually nonexistent.

Other programs that Miles has been responsible for introducing into the metropolitan Birmingham area are: Talent Search (The Educational Talent Search Project), an intensive effort to identify and encourage underprivileged young people, mainly dropouts, to go back to school and go on to college; the Emergency School Aid Act (ESAA), a program implemented for the study of language and culture, designed to ease problems of desegregation of schools; and the Liberty National-Miles College Internship, a joint venture to place business major students at Liberty National Life Insurance Company in order to give them firsthand experiences.

Miles College also offers assistance to the community through such projects as Teacher Corps, Adult Basic Education Program, University Year of Action sponsored by the National Conference of Black Mayors, Greene County Voter Education Project, Eutaw Community-Based Arts Education Program, West Alabama Folk Arts Festival, Rural Youth Work Program, and the Basic Skills Tutorial Program for Elementary Children.

Miles College is committed to service-learning. It is one of the better means of reaching and teaching more people. Academicians must bridge the gap between the community and the academic institution. Community education is one effective mechanism for bridging that gap.

W. Clyde Williams served as President of Miles College in Birmingham, Alabama, until 1986. He now lives in Atlanta, Georgia.

Emergence of the Community College as a Center for Service-Learning

Edmund J. Gleazer, Jr.

The former President of the American Association of Community and Junior Colleges notes the advantages of the community college as a center for service-learning. Reprinted from Synergist, *National Center for Service-Learning, ACTION, Vol. 4, No. 1, pp. 10, 14.*

TWO MAJOR MOVEMENTS in education are merging in a manner that can produce change. One of these movements is the remolding of the two-year college into a community-based, performance-oriented, post-secondary educational institution now generally known as the community college. The second is the evolution of the student volunteer movement into the field of service-learning. Either of these movements, alone, could bring about major changes in adult education. Merged and producing a combined thrust, they can provide a direction and force affecting not only education but the whole of society.

While inspired and developed in many different ways, service-learning programs are now in operation on campuses across the country. Many of these are community college campuses. This is so natural for community colleges, so ideal, that the number of service-learning programs in community colleges is destined to multiply rapidly. The reasons for this go back to the community-based characteristics of the community college, its facilities, its faculty, and, most of all, its student body. Note the advantages of the community college as a center for service-learning:

- The community college is a community agency that can and perhaps should act as an umbrella organization for all the social agencies of the area. It is intimately involved with these agencies, and since its purpose is to serve the community, the college is in a position to put equal emphasis on the service and the learning aspects of service-learning. It is an outwardly directed educational institution that serves not only its students but also the community in which it is located.

- The facilities of the community college are supported by public funds and are for the use of the community. As such, they are available as physical resources for projects that serve community needs.

- Faculties of community colleges are active citizens of the community, interested in its well being. They are interested in social change in the community of which they are part, and they are interested in student education, for which they are responsible. Together this adds up to service-learning.

- It is in the students that community colleges have their greatest resource for combining service to the community with learning opportunities for the students themselves. The students are citizens of the community and personally aware of its needs. They come in all ages, sexes, cultures, economic conditions, and colors. They live in a variety of neighborhoods and either work or intend to work in all types of businesses, industry, and social service organizations. These students have no trouble relating to community people and their needs — they *are* the community people.

In the conventional college, the students most often serve in a community not their own, and serve people of different cultures, ages, races, and economic conditions. This can be done, for everyone is aware of the enormous success of thousands of student volunteer programs and service-learning projects on college campuses across the country. But how naturally community service and student learning fit together in the community college. What an opportunity exists for a merger of service with academic education.

With this obvious opportunity, we can expect more and more community colleges to expand their efforts in this direction, and in the immediate future the merger of the community-based college and of service-learning will bring positive change for society.

Edmund Gleazer, President of the American Association of Community and Junior Colleges until 1981, now teaches in the schools of education at George Washington University and the University of Texas.

Using Principles of Experiential Learning and Servant Leadership for Human Services: In the Workplace and in the Academy

Robert Sigmon

Human service educators, as they make judgments about the ends toward which their educational practices are directed and establish experiential education and servant-leadership norms in their programs, are well positioned to become model servant-leaders and enablers of a sense of shared community. Robert Sigmon draws on his 30 years' experience in combining service and learning in multiple settings to challenge human service educators and workplace leaders to transform their way of looking at both service and learning. He outlines the emerging educational roles of the workplace and explores how both educators and practitioners can redefine their relationships to foster growth in individuals, in organizations, and in communities.

WHEN HUMAN SERVICE EDUCATORS, professionals, and students enter a relationship with service acquirers, each group or individual is in one sense contracting to help the other. Service acquirers struggle to tell human service staff what they are trying to live for and what it will take for them to get there. Human service staff, educators, and students struggle to interpret how they can use their talents and connections to help others attain their expectations and gain more control over their destinies.

In my 30 years' involvement in service-based experiential educational programs in community settings, state government, universities and colleges, and a community teaching hospital, I have been privileged to work in a few settings where mutuality and a sense of community were possible. In these instances, human service educators and practitioners tried to hear what the wants and needs of others were. They understood that the community and workplace were rich educational settings for service acquirers, staff and students. They utilized experiential learning methods, allowing the content for much of the learning to grow out of the situation at hand. Servant-leadership principles were practiced. A sense of shared community emerged.

In these notes, I want to explore some notions about experiential learning and servant-leadership, outline a simple view of a service system, and flesh out some avenues for engaging the workplace as a creative setting for human service education. The focus is on the human service workplace because that is the setting from which most human care is mediated today.

Learning through Experience

Service based experiential learning formats are well suited for trainees or student learners where people "acquiring" services and host organizations are more involved in the design and practice of the program.

"Learning through doing" is a generally understood refrain used by experiential educators. Two other ways of viewing experiential education are illustrated in the following observations from Moshe Feldenkrais (1977) and Robert Kegan (1988).

Moshe Feldenkrais speaks about "learning which goes with physical growth. By this ... I mean learning in which quantity grows and changes to a new quality, and not the mere accumulation of knowledge, useful as this may be. Often we do not see this kind of learning at all; it can go on for more or less lengthy periods of time, apparently aimlessly, and then a new form of action appears as if from nowhere. Most truly important things are learned this way. There was no method, no system in our learning to walk, speak, or count, no examinations, no prescribed term in which to complete the learning, no preset ... aim to be attained ...."

When this type of learning is looked at more closely, my own experience confirms that a sense of community, a level of trust with others, a mutuality of human purpose, and commitment to an end result were usually involved.

Bob Kegan draws a pie with three pieces to encourage us to explore where we place our experiential education energies. One wedge represents "what we know we know." Another slice is "what we know we don't know." The third piece is "what we don't know we don't know." When we face options for designing educational programs for human service workers in community settings, we generally favor one of the following:

a. We focus on enlarging the knowledge already known, by stressing that theory learned in classrooms can now be applied in the field.

b. We assist learners with learning new skills, helping them pursue "what they know they don't know."

c. Or, we arrange for others to immerse themselves in new situations, reveal and address their unmet needs, or face new challenges so that "what we don't know we don't know" is touched and new queries are formed.

Option "c" is a congruent option for human service education. Theories and principles can be taught in classrooms. Skills can be developed and improved through simulations, rote drills, or computer assisted instruction. However, opportunities to sense the whole of a situation, to come to terms with personal values and goals, to listen to the dilemmas and dreams of others, to understand cultural and economic perspectives on how people live their lives, to experience how power is used and not used, to experiment with varieties of ways to learn, to gain a feeling for the strength of mutuality and community, and to make judgments about the ends of education, work and life — these are often not as available in the academy as they are in the workplace/community setting.

In service-based experiential education, all the parties have some stake in the process. The workplace mentor is in tune with the immense possibilities for self-discovery and development by students and "acquirers" of services. The faculty is one interpreter of the varieties of experiential learning possible in the work setting environment. Service "acquirers" also teach out of and learn from their experiences. Students learn as well as become bridges which help link needs with resources.

Communities, workplaces, and the special needs of people are a rich context for experiential learning and leadership development for future human service professionals. The educational dimensions of workplaces and communities are often undervalued by both academic and workplace leaders. What does it take within our human service educational programs to place at least equal value on the non-academic settings in which we expect students to serve and learn?

Servant-Leadership Principles

Servant-leadership is a phrase coined by Robert Greenleaf (1979). After retiring from management training leadership roles at AT&T, he began writing about servant-leadership, which he defines by asking: "Do those served grow as persons? Do they while being served, become healthier, wiser, freer, more autonomous and more likely themselves to become servants?"

Servant-leadership is a mind set which implies that individuals seek to serve the interests, needs and goals of a host community — not impose their own agenda or prescriptions based on theory learned somewhere else or values honed out of their own history. When individuals listen to their hosts and seek to hear what *they* say about their reality, situation, problems, and opportunities, then the activity which emerges from the process has the power to transform individuals in fundamental ways in that moment and for the future. The role of considered reflection on these experiences of "serving and being served by" is critical: I cannot stress this enough. For as Feldenkrais reminds us, "Often we do not see this kind of learning at all; it can go on for more or less lengthy periods of time, apparently aimlessly, and then a new form of action appears as if from nowhere." For new forms of action to appear, experiences have to occur and then some form of reflection has to take place. And someone, somewhere had to imagine the possibilities and structure relationships or programs so that the development could occur. Human service educators are well positioned to provide this kind of servant-leadership through the way they work with students, community organizations, and those "acquiring" services.

The Four Communities Within Human Service Systems

In order for experiential learning and servant-leadership principles to function well in human service settings *for those served*, effective connections among four primary communities in the human service system are essential.

Service acquirers are the primary community in a service system. By viewing those who are served as "acquirers" of services, rather than "recipients" or "clients," a fundamental shift in perspective occurs. "Recipients" are "done unto" by experts who assume they know best what others need and want. "Acquirers" are involved in deciding what it is they need and want in order to improve their situations, and they have a voice in how they are served.

Direct care providers, front line people who work with those "acquiring" services, are another community. These providers can be paid staff or volunteers.

Support personnel (technicians, budget officers, receptionists, lab workers, analysts, reimbursement specialists, etc.) constitute the third group of human service workers in the service system.

Policy makers and managers are the final group, playing essential roles in the forming of policy and procedure and making financial resources available to get the other jobs done.

As human service educators explore how their program designs can include the perspectives of "service acquirers" and assist student learners to understand the connections among the four communities of the service system, a better understanding of the educational faces of a workplace can be helpful.

Educational Faces of the Workplace

Learning in a service system workplace is a creative opportunity often unappreciated and untapped, for the variety of patterns utilized are relatively unknown to many academic practitioners. Seven of the learning practices found in human service organizations are discussed below. Within each of these practices, programmatic possibilities for human service educators to consider are suggested.

1. *Informal give and take on-the-job* represents the most typical teaching and learning component in human service organizations. A new staff member seeks out an experienced, competent worker to find out how he/she understands a process, deals with a problem, or manages a piece of equipment. Donald Schon (1982, 1986) writes convincingly about this phenomenon. He suggests that set theories, principles, and standards established by experts and taught in classrooms are not often used to solve problems or fix situations in practice settings in communities. Schon reports that practicing professionals indicate that 80% of the cases with which they deal cannot be assisted by relying on theories, standards, textbooks, or fixed answers.

An emerging, alternative vision and practice assumes that the key challenge is the ability to state problems and to enable others who face those dilemmas to deal with them. In stating problems, value conflicts and uncertainties are prevalent. Seasoned practitioners build up a body of core experiences and make choices based on their accumulated wisdom. Staff associates, people being served, and student learners become colleagues in the development of this core awareness. Structuring human service education programs around this understanding is an intriguing challenge.

2. *Self-directed learning* approaches are increasingly used in many workplaces. One style is rooted in the findings of Allen Tough (1982). Using a modified questionnaire developed by Tough with 120 human service workers over the past five years, I have met only one person who had not intentionally set out to learn something in a self-directed manner during the previous year. Intentional learning follows a general pattern. Once a desire to learn something is articulated, the learner scans back over his/her prior experience for some clues about how to proceed. From that scan of prior experience, a next step for many is to jump right into the situation via a trial-and-error method. As the learnings get clearer or become bogged down, the learner may seek out some expert advise, a book in the library, or a short course.

This style of intentional, self-directed learning lends itself well to some dimensions of human service education for students. If human service professionals and student trainees are self-directing in their own learning and lives, then it is more likely that they will work with "acquirers" of their services in ways which also enable them to be more self-directing and self-sufficient.

3. Many workplaces have in place their own *training staff* to work with individuals and groups on learning tasks initiated within the organization. These staff often know who the key workplace educators are in their organization, and they can be helpful with student training agendas as well. Staff training programs can be rooted in a variety of program philosophies, ranging from heavy paternalism to sustaining a sense of shared community.

4. *Tuition assistance* is provided by employers for employees to pursue academic courses, to attend institutes, and to participate in continuing education programs outside the work setting. Universities and colleges can offer courses, programs, and technical assistance that address community needs in return for those settings accepting student learners.

5. As guilds, *disciplines and professions* (social workers, nurses, psychologists, counselors et al.) develop legislation which requires competencies and standards for entry and continuation in the field. Required courses and training for certification or recertification are provided by these guilds for their members. In some fields, the discipline determines standards for training, including supervised field work. In some instances these standards are at odds with the contentions of this paper that "acquirers" and

workplaces should be involved together with human service educators and students.

6. The vast *training industry* of consultants and training organizations constitutes a heavily used learning resource for human service organizations. Does this group constitute a competitive or cooperative network for human service educators? Do consultants help foster a sense of community within the organization?

7. *Joint ventures* whereby a human services organization links up with an educational institution through affiliation agreements is a promising development in workplace educational services. Teaching hospitals are a well-known example. Now we hear of teaching nursing homes, teaching social service agencies, and teaching voluntary centers. I currently work with the Wake Area Health Education Center (AHEC) in Raleigh, North Carolina, where we arrange for over 1,300 student learner rotations, 500 continuing education events and thousands of small technical assistance services each year (Key, 1988). Wake AHEC serves as one of nine decentralized clinical training, continuing education, and educational technical assistance sites across the state. These sites receive ample state legislative and local support (Mayer, 1988). Faculty in medicine, nursing, pharmacy, and other disciplines are full-time experiential educators on-site in the AHEC human service settings outside the academy. The content for learning in AHECs is centered in the needs of those people who present themselves for educational or medical assistance. A current challenge is how to help learners, faculty, host settings, and service acquirers go beyond medical models (mostly paternalistic) to wholistic models (shared sense of community) which better understand the context and culture of those "acquiring" services. Through five-year contracts and yearly agreements, four university medical science centers and nine community AHECs work out these arrangements in North Carolina.

I mention these seven practices in workplace education to emphasize that there are comprehensive opportunities for teaching and learning outside the academy. Human service educators can work collaboratively within these forms in spite of traditional approaches which tend to separate service and education functions.

Most service organizations do not speak of their educational role nor indicate that they give much attention to it. When they do mention it, their rationales for supporting educational services are: to increase productivity, services, or market share; to control staff through management training; to increase technical expertise; to help insure organizational survival; to develop people; and to serve

well (enable for self-determination) the "acquirers" of the services.
The final two reasons are too often far down the priority listing.
Student training is generally even a lower priority with most human
service organizations except when staffing shortages are noted, as is
the case at present in most communities. In these circumstances,
agencies and institutions are very interested in "recruitment strategies."

In workplace-based experiential learning programs, regardless
of the sophistication level of programs, I have observed a critical
variable — the identification of a coach, a mentor who cares deeply
about what he/she does and who wants to contribute to the growth
of people. A competent mentor is a living model of someone who
seeks the best interests of those he/she is serving, understands
communities, is aware of cultural forces in a situation, and strives to
learn and grow as a person as well. Identifying these mentors is a
critical dimension in the development and management of experiential education programs in human services and other fields. If
this dimension is solid, good learning can occur even in a setting
where institutional values run counter to a supportive community
of learning.

Concluding Observations

As human service educators and student learners become involved in the lives of people who are frail and elderly, poorly
housed, lonely, unemployed, mentally ill, imprisoned, illiterate,
and other "communities of need," what contributions can we make
to enable others to grow, develop, and come to appreciate the
miracle of a shared sense of community? I will respond to this
question with suggested challenges:

• Can we contribute to increasing the practice of asking those
being served what would best serve their interests?
• Can we assist in supporting private and public workplaces
that are humane and caring and that acknowledge and appreciate
their educational roles?
• Can we invent new forms of partnerships which serve "acquirers" of services, service organizations, academic centers, guilds,
and student learners?
• Can we ask fundamental questions about the outcomes of our
educational activities and engage those with whom we work to do
likewise?
• Can we go beyond paternalism and rights to a sense of shared
community?

• Can we promote the principles of both experiential learning and servant leadership in human need settings as a framework for enabling learners (students, "acquirers," and agency staff) and organizations to grow and in turn to develop their own capacity to serve and learn?

I believe human service educators do and can offer creative leadership in forging more humane approaches to serving and learning in communities and institutions. Service-based experiential education and servant-leadership principles, when applied to human service education programs, contribute to the growth and development of people and communities and of the institutions that serve people and communities. [*See the section of this book on principles of good practice in combining service and learning — principles based on the two sets of principles to which Sigmon refers here.*]

Robert Sigmon is Acting Director of the Wake Area Health Education Center at Wake Medical Center in Raleigh, North Carolina. He is one of the earliest advocates of the concept of service-learning in the 1960s and has worked in it from a variety of perspectives.

References

Feldenkrais, Moshe, *The Case of Nora*, Harper and Row, 1977.

Greenleaf, Robert K., *Teacher as Servant, A Parable*, Paulist Press, 1979 (available through R.K. Greenleaf Center, 210 Herrick Rd., Newton Centre, MA 02159).

Kegan, Robert, from lecture presented at Harvard Graduate School of Education in summer, 1988, Cambridge, Massachusetts.

Key, John C., *Wake AHEC Annual Report*, Raleigh, North Carolina, 1988.

Mayer, Eugene, *The North Carolina Area Health Education Centers Program: 1988 Progress Report*, University of North Carolina at Chapel Hill, 1988.

Schon, Donald, *The Reflective Practitioner*, Basic Books, 1982.

Schon, Donald, *Educating the Reflective Practitioner*, Jossey-Bass Publishers, 1986.

Tough, Allen, *Intentional Change*, Follett Publishing Co., 1982.

PART II

Rationales and Theories for Combining Service and Learning:

Education for Civic and Social Responsibility

Liberal Arts, Experiential Learning and Public Service: Necessary Ingredients for Socially Responsible Undergraduate Education

Timothy K. Stanton

The parallel movements for public service, civic literacy, active learning, and educational reform must work together in order for each of these to be sustained and successful. We must clarify where they intersect and what their intersection offers for improving undergraduate education and producing an informed, active citizenry. When effectively structured, facilitated, related to discipline-based knowledge, and assessed, public and community service-based learning is the means for linking the development of student's social responsibility with the improvement of undergraduate education. This evolving pedagogy of "service-learning" is a key to the success of both efforts. This paper was first commissioned by the Kettering Foundation in Dayton, Ohio, for the 16th Annual Conference of the National Society for Internships and Experiential Education held October 1987 in Smuggler's Notch, Vermont.

"Education for democratic citizenship involves human capacities relating to judgment, to choice, and, above all, to action. To be literate as a citizen requires more than knowledge and information; it includes the exercise of personal responsibility, active participation, and personal commitment to a set of values. Democratic literacy is a literacy of doing, not simply of knowing. Knowledge is a necessary, but not sufficient condition of democratic responsibility."

With these words Richard Morrill introduces an essay in *Liberal Education* in which he challenges academicians to take seriously their historical mandate to "educate for democratic values" (1982, p. 365). He suggests that this form of civic education must combine doing with knowing, that it must be both "the empowerment of persons and the cultivation of minds."

This proposition may make common sense to the average citizen. However, in the world of traditional postsecondary education, where participation is normally separate from scholarly inquiry, these are radical comments. One must often look far afield to find a curriculum that requires of students substantive academic inquiry combined with and based upon active participation in socially responsible activity. In the academy, knowledge development lies within the realm of academic departments. Concerns about work, about moral development, and about community participation lie with student affairs or residence staff, religious groups, or other non-academic administrators.

Fortunately, as a response in part to growing dissatisfaction with this fragmentation and in part to larger social movements, there is an opportunity to bridge this gap, to integrate students' community participation with critical reflection and analysis. On the one hand, there is a strong reform movement within higher education, a movement which questions both the content and the passive, didactic process of postsecondary teaching and learning. On the other hand, individuals outside the academy along with non-academic university and college administrators are expressing concern with students' self-centered attitudes. They see a need for the academy to challenge students to lead more socially responsible lives. In this atmosphere there is potential for establishing an education for democratic citizenship, which Morrill so well defines.

In this paper I trace these complementary movements, the calls for reform in undergraduate education and the initiative for civic responsibility, demonstrating that they have mutual concerns and mutual self-interests. Though largely separate from and unknown to each other, their complementarity provides the basis for joint action. By integrating efforts to increase student involvement in public service with liberal arts curricular reforms which promote active learning and critical thinking, we may establish a model of undergraduate education that promotes the development of responsible *and* intelligent citizens.

The Context of Change in Higher Education

The recent period in American higher education has been one of intense self-examination, external criticism, and debate regarding basic goals and purposes. Career-minded students have questioned the relevance and importance of traditional liberal arts education to an increasingly specialized world. Faculty on many campuses have undertaken reviews of curriculum and requirements to determine whether they effectively promote the development of critical thinking and intellectual excellence. A series of national reports calls into question whether curricula meet their defined objectives and suggests a fundamental re-evaluation of the structure and pedagogy of undergraduate education.[1]

Out of this ferment and debate comes renewed attention to "excellence" in the teaching/learning process and a new focus on the importance of active, experience-based learning. The National Institute of Education's Study Group on the Conditions of Excellence in American Higher Education recommended that faculty increase their use of "internships and other forms of carefully monitored experiential learning" (1984). A study undertaken for the National Endowment for the Humanities indicated widespread acceptance and understanding by faculty of internships and field studies as integral parts of liberal arts education (Caston and Heffernan, 1984). The National Society for Internships and Experiential Education (NSIEE) receives requests for assistance every day from liberal arts institutions interested in linking classroom instruction to supervised field experience in the community. With greater acceptance and utilization of internships, field studies, and other forms of off-campus learning within higher education, the issue for advocates of experiential education now is not so much whether faculty will utilize these methods, but rather how to use them, both inside and outside the classroom, and how to assess effectively the learning that results.

During this same period our society is facing a variety of increasingly complex issues that demand of its citizens greater capacity for critical thinking, civic judgment, and flexible involvement than ever before. These issues — peace in the face of growing gaps between rich and poor nations, nuclear proliferation, equal opportunity for and effective integration of minority populations, poverty, and economic instability — are very complex and deeply ingrained in our social fabric. They are strongly influenced by and interdependent with our relations with the international community. They do not appear to be resolvable by experts alone. To many people they do not appear to be resolvable at all.

If we are to respond effectively to these issues, we need a citizenry with a broad understanding of the interdependence of peoples, social institutions, and communities and an enhanced ability both to draw upon and further develop this knowledge as they confront human problems. We need people with a strong commitment to act out ethically and thoughtfully what John Gardner calls the democratic compact: "Freedom and obligation, liberty and duty, that's the deal" (1984).

Yet, in the face of these social problems, educators and social researchers report that students are becoming increasingly isolated and their vision more narrow and self-centered. According to the annual ACE-UCLA surveys of college freshmen, students since 1972 have attached decreasing importance to helping others, promoting racial understanding, cleaning up the environment, participating in community action and keeping up with political affairs. During the same period, the percentage of students placing high priority on "being well off financially" jumped from 40 to 73 percent. The goal of "developing a meaningful quality of life" showed the greatest decline, almost 50 percent (Cooperative Institutional Research Program, 1974-1984). Surveys by the Carnegie Foundation for the Advancement of Teaching (Newman, 1985) and the Independent Sector (1985) show similar trends.

This research suggests that as the problems facing our society increase in severity and complexity, the interest of most college students in these problems and in acting to solve them appears to diminish. This shift in student attitudes may be due in part to students' perception of more limited economic opportunities over the last decade. Or it may be a function of cynicism developed in response to the size, complexity, and seeming insolubility of the problems. Whatever the cause, this sense of student disinterest and disconnection from social involvement has stimulated many people to examine the role of the academy in encouraging students to serve community needs at the local, national, and international levels and in developing citizens with both "civic literacy" and leadership skills infused with civic values.

Frank Newman argues in *Higher Education and the American Resurgence* that "if there is a crisis in education in the United States today, it is less that test scores have declined than it is that we have failed to provide the education for citizenship that is still the most significant responsibility of the nation's schools and colleges" (1985, p. 31). He identified a failure in the structure and the content of our educational system. Structurally, we have not provided a means of linking classroom study with students' direct experience of social problems and issues. In the area of content, we have failed to educate students effectively with both an understanding of these social issues and an awareness of the traditional responsibilities of democratic citizenship. In response to this situation, college presidents, education scholars, politicians, and others have begun to call for integration of the ethic and practice of social involvement, critique and analysis into the mission and values of higher education.[2]

Thus, alongside the national call for renewal and strengthening of undergraduate education, there has been successfully rekindled a debate on one of the academy's traditional goals: the development within students of civic literacy, responsibility and participation. In response, internships and other forms of active learning are being recognized as effective in promoting students' cognitive skill development and acquisition of knowledge (traditional academic goals), as well as personal and career development (normally considered extra-curricular concerns). Universities and colleges are creating public service centers and other structures which enable students to become involved as volunteers, both to provide community service and to develop in students an awareness of public issues and community needs, leadership skills, and a lifelong commitment to social responsibility.

These are considerable accomplishments, and they have resulted in significant movements for change on campuses in a short period of time. However, to date these two movements — undergraduate education reform and the initiative for social responsibility within higher education — have run along largely separate tracks with little contact.

The undergraduate education reform movement has been undertaken largely by academic administrators, researchers, and faculty concerned with improving the structure and process of liberal arts education. While recognizing the important values of public service, they often view it as inherently lacking in academic substance and best pursued apart from the curriculum.

The movement for student social responsibility has been led by university presidents, legislators, social critics, experiential educators, and civic educators on the one hand, and student affairs and community service program staff on the other. This movement has concentrated on stimulating and enabling students to become involved in community service, focusing attention on the virtues of giving service and the resulting personal development of students rather than on facilitation of students' academic learning through critical reflection on their service activity.

Although these movements share a common concern with the basic aims of higher education, they have engaged in little sustained, cross-group dialogue. Neither group has fully considered the explicit relationship between public service and the core, *academic* mission of higher education institutions. Neither has effectively addressed the place of community service and what students learn from it within the curriculum.

Liberal Arts Education and Public and Community Service: Distinct Yet Complementary Traditions

Though they work out of distinct traditions, an examination of recent literature from those concerned with improving liberal arts education and those advocating public and community service reveals a common concern with the purpose and pedagogy of undergraduate learning. Though they have worked along separate tracks, these groups articulate similar objectives for students. Could these separate, but complementary perspectives be integrated? Would such integration serve the goals both of improving liberal arts education and developing committed, involved citizens?

The Liberal Arts Perspective

Liberal arts educators frequently articulate their purpose as the development of a "habit of mind":

> ... [T]he liberal arts mind seeks freedom through creativity, through reshaping and improving on the past in order to give new meaning to the present .... There is an emphasis on the fair judging of evidence, on writing and thinking with clarity. There is a concern with discipline and order and also with flexibility, a tolerance for ambiguity. There is an effort to envision alternative solutions to a single problem, to see every particular as part of a network or series of networks, rather than in splendid — but ultimately false — isolation. (Coburn, 1985, p. 8)

In addition to and perhaps because of the debate about which content areas should comprise the "common learning" or general education of liberal arts students, these educators have begun to focus on cognitive skill outcomes of a liberal education — "abilities that last a lifetime" (Edgerton, 1984). Current research into the undergraduate experience reinforces this thrust, stressing the importance of these skills and the ability to apply one's learning as benchmarks for student assessment:

We contend that acquiring or storing knowledge is not enough. Unless one carries knowledge into acts of application, generalization, and experimentation, one's learning is incomplete. (Loacker *et al*, 1986, p. 47)

Perhaps the most consistent finding that we have discovered is that the amount of knowledge of a content area is generally unrelated to superior performance in an occupation and is often unrelated even to marginally acceptable performance.... In particular it is not the acquisition of knowledge that distinguishes the outstanding performer, but rather the *cognitive skills* that are exercised and developed in the process of knowledge acquisition and use that constitutes our first factor of occupational success.... These skills transcend analysis, which consists of the identification of parts, and are closer in spirit to the ability to synthesize information from a prior analysis through a process of induction. (Klemp, 1977, p. 43)

The recent national reports, while reaffirming liberal arts traditions, criticize the passive and impersonal nature of instructional methodologies. They call for a pedagogy that is more active and involving, that enables learners to take more responsibility for their education, and that engages them in direct contact with the subjects of their study. Instructional research demonstrates that learning activities which require learners to apply knowledge and skills to the solution of problems more often develop the higher cognitive skills than do traditional classroom methods (Cross, 1987). The National Institute of Education's Study Group on the Conditions for Excellence in American Higher Education recommended use of internships and other forms of monitored experiential learning, saying that such "active modes of teaching require that students be inquirers ... creators, as well as receivers, of knowledge" and noting that "students are more apt to learn content if they are engaged with it" (1984). The learning students obtain from such experiential education opportunities is increasingly seen as linking and integrating their intellectual growth with their moral, personal, and career development.

The Public and Community Service Learning Perspective
Advocates of public service and civic education work to promote and support students' involvement as volunteers, interns, and researchers in the affairs of communities outside their campuses. Responding to an awareness that democracy requires civic respon-

sibility as well as individual entrepreneurship, they seek opportunities for students to develop "skills, beliefs, and confidence that will enable them to be committed, compassionate citizens" (Newman, 1986).

Some of the goals of public service advocates, such as providing community service and leadership training, lie outside the academic missions of their institutions. Yet, many articulate objectives for "service learning programs" — programs that emphasize the accomplishment of tasks which meet human needs in combination with conscious educational growth — that are very similar to ones put forth by their liberal arts colleagues. Examples of these objectives include: "learning how to apply, integrate, and evaluate knowledge or the methodology of a discipline"; "developing a firsthand understanding of the political and social action skills required for active citizenship" (Duley, 1981, p. 602); and "developing perspectives and practicing analytical skills necessary for understanding the social ecology of organizations engaged in the delivery of goods and services" (Stanton, 1983).

To ensure that service promotes substantive learning, service learning practitioners seek to connect students' experiences to reflection and analysis provided in the curriculum (Sagen, 1982-83). They point to the importance of contact with complex, contemporary social problems and efforts to solve them as an important element of a complete education (Lynd, 1945). They see service learning, when it *combines* action with critical reflection, conceptualization and abstract experimentation with analysis, as standing very much within the liberal arts tradition.

> As Dewey states, this process at least results in a "reconstruction" of experience (as in the formulation of the Newtonian laws of motion or in Einstein's reformulation), a recodifying of habits (as in overcoming racial bias), and ongoing questioning of old ideas (a habit of learning experientially). Thus experiential learning so pursued transforms the individual, revises and enlarges knowledge, and alters practice. It affects the aesthetic and ethical commitments of individuals and alters their perceptions and their interpretations of the world. (Keeton, 1983)

For service learning practitioners, community service and academic excellence "are not competitive demands to be balanced through discipline and personal sacrifice [by students], but rather ... are interdependent dimensions of good intellectual work" (Wagner, 1986). They see their challenge as "devising ways to connect study and service so that the disciplines illuminate and inform experience and experience lends meaning and energy to the disciplines" (Eskow, 1980, p. 21).

The Opportunity: To Improve Undergraduate Education by Integrating The Complementary Perspectives of Liberal Arts Education and Public and Community Service Learning

Liberal arts educators appear to be searching for active educational experiences for students, experiences which enable and require students to reflect critically on the world around them, to link theory to practice and *vice versa*, and to induce, synthesize, and experiment with new knowledge. Opportunities made available to students through public and community service programs would appear to be a most important means of providing these experiences.

Practitioners of public and community service learning seek opportunities for students to reflect on their service experiences and to relate them to their academic learning. There is growing recognition among these professionals that use of the cognitive skills developed in liberal arts education must be stressed in public service in order for their programs to meet the developmental and civic literacy goals they hold for students, and in order for the service provided to have a desirable impact in the community.

The separation of these two movements is unfortunate, for as Richard Morrill points out, civic literacy "requires more than knowledge and information; it includes the exercise of personal responsibility, active participation, and personal commitment to values" (1982, p. 365). Those who are "liberally educated" are those with the ability to make "an action out of knowledge — using knowledge to think, judge, decide, discover, interact and create" (Loacker et al, 1986, p. 47).

There is a need to bring these movements together to explore how their distinct, yet complementary traditions, and their complementary goals for and positions within the academy can become mutually enhancing in strengthening both students' undergraduate learning and their service to the community. There is a need for agreement upon a rationale for integrating public service within the curriculum, and for a national agenda to ensure that this integration is carried out in a manner that supports the goals of liberal education and that merits the sustained support and involvement of faculty and administrators at liberal arts institutions.

Ironically, because we lack such agreement, students' public service activities remain largely separate from the academic curriculum despite the fact that experience-based learning is becoming more accepted within higher education. And the curriculum, stressing individualized activity isolated from community experiences, issues and values, has become a primary disincentive to students' public service involvement.

This separation of service from learning reflects higher education's traditional distinction between theory and practice and between teaching and research. It inhibits both the effectiveness of students' service efforts and the depth of their learning while they are involved in service. It leaves the development of citizens who are committed to thoughtful, value-oriented participation in public life to be more of an accidental, secondary outcome of higher education rather than an explicit educational objective.

Faculty are the Keys to Linking Service and the Curriculum

If there is potential for convergence between these two distinct, but complementary traditions, then faculty participation and support of students' public and community service becomes integral. Faculty have a central role to play in ensuring that these experiences are continually challenging and educational as well as useful for the community on the receiving end. As interpreters of the college's or university's mission, faculty are in the critical position for supporting students' interest and activities in public and community service. More importantly, they must assist students in reflecting critically about their public service experiences and in relating them both to broader social issues and to liberal arts disciplines. They must develop an "academics of human reality" (Payne, 1987). Why?

1. To ensure that students serve effectively. People perform best when they have opportunities to reflect regularly upon and analyze their experiences, and then practice or try out what they have learned in the next set of experiences. Research into the professions supports this notion, and it is no less true for students. If students are to be of real service to their communities and if they are to gain knowledge and develop skills as a result, they need opportunities to reflect upon what they are doing. The liberal arts, with its tradition of conscious, reflective analysis, is a logical base from which to sponsor this aspect of service-based learning. Faculty representing liberal arts disciplines have the potential to become service learners' best guides.

2. To ensure that students learn and develop as a result of their public service experiences. Students continually comment on the benefits they receive from their community service, but often their learning is haphazard, accidental, and superficial. They speak about "how much I learned" or "how much I got out of my volunteer experience," but they often draw a blank when asked to describe how "what they got" relates to their classroom education.

Higher education is founded at least in part on the premise that learning is deepest when it is sponsored and facilitated by instructors. As advocates and sponsors of student community involvement, these institutions have the unique responsibility to: (1) facilitate, assess, and accredit service-based learning; and (2) relate that learning to our common intellectual, social, political, and multicultural heritage.

3. To reduce the personal and financial disincentives to student participation in public service. When public service is viewed as an activity to be engaged in if students have extra time, money, self-discipline, good time management skills, or an ethic of self-sacrifice — i.e., as an activity that competes for students' attention and energy with the demands of a separate academic life — then it is not something for everyone. Commitment under these circumstances is hard to give and more difficult to keep. The utilization of public and community service-based learning as an effective pedagogical method for student achievement of academic goals makes public service accessible to all students.

4. To place civic education, civic participation, and social responsibility squarely within the academic mission of higher education. If higher education is to take seriously the role of providing students with the knowledge, skills, beliefs, and confidence necessary for becoming committed and compassionate citizens, then contact with contemporary social problems and efforts to solve them must become an important element of a liberal arts education. Public and community service learning is a means both of connecting outcomes of liberal arts education to social action and of exploring profound human problems basic to the humanities and sciences as they arise in situations which have immediate meaning to students. Public and community service learning can affect students' aesthetic and ethical commitments. Grappling with real-life applications of theories learned in classrooms is effective education and an essential part of students' complete intellectual development.

Conclusion

Much is written about the public roles of postsecondary institutions, about the need for civic literacy among students, and about the need for active modes of learning and curricular reform. There is *not* much conceptualized or articulated, however, that combines these overlapping movements. These complementary perspectives must be brought together to ensure that the current interest in public service becomes sustained and integrated with that of curricular reform. We must clarify and articulate the ways in which they intersect and what their intersection offers to the movements to improve undergraduate learning and to produce an informed, active citizenry.

The current climate of debate about the aims and pedagogy of undergraduate education has created an opportunity for such dialogue and exchange. We can draw from and combine what has been learned from:

- effective community service;
- substantive experience-based learning (including the need for preparation and instruction in qualitative methods of data gathering, facilitating reflection on the experience and connections between theory and practice, etc.);
- assessment of liberal learning outcomes (both in terms of the development of cognitive skills such as critical thinking and in mastery of subject matter content); and
- institutionalization of curricular innovations and teaching improvements.

By drawing from what has been learned from these streams of work, we can establish a means of effectively integrating public and community service-based learning into the liberal arts curriculum. We can articulate a coherent set of principles of good practice,[3] and we can assist faculty and staff in building these methods and structures into existing instructional offerings.

When effectively structured, facilitated, related to discipline-based theories and knowledge, and assessed, public and community service-based learning is the means for linking the initiative to develop students' social responsibility with the efforts to improve undergraduate education. This evolving pedagogy of "service learning" is a key to ensuring the development of graduates who will participate in society actively, ethically, and with an informed, critical habit of mind.

I wish to acknowledge with deep gratitude the valuable assistance of Steven Schultz, Jane Kendall, Jon Wagner, Susan Stroud, Catherine Milton, Carolyn Lougee, Donald Kennedy, Catherine Howard, Zelda Gamson, Dwight Giles, Madeline Holzer, Irving Spitzberg, Dick Cone, Ed O'Neil, and Ted Lobman. Their perceptions, suggestions, and criticism have helped shape both the content and the presentation of this paper. — Tim Stanton

Timothy Stanton is Associate Director of the Public Service Center at Stanford University. He has also directed the Field Study Office at Cornell University, coordinated a community-based program for high school students, and served as President of the National Society for Internships and Experiential Education.

Footnotes

[1] See: *Integrity in the College Classroom: A Report to the Academic Community, The Findings and Recommendations of the Project on Redefining the Meaning and Purpose of Baccalaureate Degrees*, Association of American Colleges, 1985; Bennett, William J., *To Reclaim a Legacy: A Report on the Humanities in Higher Education*, National Endowment for the Humanities, 1984; Boyer, Ernest L., *College: The Undergraduate Experience In America*, Harper & Row for the Carnegie Endowment for the Advancement of Teaching, 1987; Gaff, Jerry L., *General Education Today: A Critical Analysis of Controversies, Practices, and Reforms*, Jossey-Bass, 1983; *Involvement in Learning: Realizing the Potential of American Higher Education, Final Report of the Study Group on the Conditions of Excellence in American Higher Education*, National Institute of Education, 1984.

A thoughtful analysis of the findings in these reports is provided by Kimball, Bruce A., "The Historical and Cultural Dimensions of the Recent Reports on Undergraduate Education," 1987 Lecture for the Fund for the Improvement of Postsecondary Education delivered to the Lilly Endowment Workshop on the Liberal Arts, June 1987.

[2] Responding to leadership from the presidents of Stanford, Brown and Georgetown, more than 125 universities and colleges joined together in 1985 in a "Campus Compact" to strengthen the academy's role in promoting civic responsibility and to endorse, develop and strengthen a variety of forms of public service by students.

The National Society for Internships and Experiential Education (NSIEE), with support from the Fund for the Improvement of Postsecondary Education, has assisted 487 colleges and universities in developing pedagogical methods and administrative structures for strengthening and institutionalizing programs of active community-based learning within their curricula. Its Special Interest Group on Public and Community Service Learning has swelled to a membership of 300 staff and faculty. Service-curriculum linkages surfaced as a primary topic at NSIEE's 1986 National Conference, and "Public Service, Civic Education, and Action Learning" was a major theme for the 1987 conference. "Service-Learning" was the focus of a special all-day workshop at the 1988 conference.

Since 1986 the American Association for Higher Education has convened an annual "action community" of faculty and administrators to examine strategies to increase student involvement in community service.

The Council for Liberal Learning of the American Association of Colleges is exploring the importance of combining academic study with structured community experiences in the development of student insight into the nature of public leadership.

The Kettering Foundation has sponsored a series of "Campus Conversations on the Civic Arts."

Responding to a directive from their state legislature, the California State University and University of California systems are implementing a "Human Corps" concept, which strongly encourages all students to engage in community service.

Finally, despite the predominate mood on most campuses, new student leadership has emerged through organizations such as the Campus Outreach Opportunity League (COOL).

[3] The needed principles for practice include: effective preparation for, facilitation and assessment of service-based learning; institutionalization; working sensitively and effectively with community organization partners in such programs. See Timothy Stanton and Catherine Howard, "Principles of Good Practice for Service Learning in Postsecondary Education," in *Synergist*, Vol. 9. No. 3, Winter, 1981. Also see the chapter of this resource book that discusses "Principles of Good Practice."

References

Coburn, Tom, "Nattering Nabobs, Habits of Mind, Persons in Relations: The Future of Liberal Arts Education in a Specialized Society," in *Liberal Education*, Association of American Colleges, Spring, 1985.

Cooperative Institutional Research Program, *The American Freshman: National Norms*, American Council on Education/UCLA, Fall 1974 - 1984.

Cross, K. Patricia, review of *Problem-Based Learning in Education for the Professions*, in *The Journal of Higher Education*, Vol. 58, No. 4, July/August 1987, p. 491.

Duley, John, "Field Experience Education," in *Modern American College*, Arthur W. Chickering, ed., Jossey-Bass, 1981, pp. 600-613.

Edgerton, Russell, "Abilities that Last a Lifetime: Alverno in Perspective," in *AAHE Bulletin*, American Association for Higher Education, February 1984.

Eskow, Seymour, "A Pedagogy of Experience," in *Synergist*, Spring 1980, pp. 20-21.

Gardner, John W., "Step One: Putting Innovation Into Action," keynote address to First Annual "You Can Make A Difference Conference — Entrepreneurs in the Public Interest," Stanford University, February 25, 1984.

Harrison, Charles, *Student Service*, the Carnegie Foundation for the Advancement of Teaching, 1987.

Independent Sector, "Americans Volunteer, 1985," Washington, DC, 1985.

Kaston, Carren O., and James M. Heffernan, *Preparing Humanists for Work: A National Study of Undergraduate Internships in the Humanities*, sponsored by the National Endowment for the Humanities and the Washington Center, 1984. Available from the National Society for Internships and Experiential Education, Raleigh, North Carolina.

Keeton, Morris, *Innovation Abstracts*, University of Texas, 1983.

Klemp, George, Jr., "Three Factors of Success in the World of Work: Implications for Curriculum in Higher Education" in Dyckman W. Vermilye, ed., *Relating Work and Experience*, Jossey-Bass, 1977, p. 43.

Loacker, Georgine, Lucy Cromwell and Kathleen O'Brien, "Assessment in Higher Education: To Serve The Learner" in *Assessment in Higher Education: Issues and Contexts*, Office of Educational Research and Improvement, USOE, William J. Bennett, ed., U.S. Government Printing Office, October 1986.

Lynd, Helen, *Fieldwork In College Education*, Columbia University Press, 1945.

Morrill, Richard L., "Educating for Democratic Values" in *Liberal Education*, Association of American Colleges, Vol. 68, No. 4, 1982.

National Institute of Education, *Involvement in Learning: Realizing the Potential of American Higher Education*, Final Report of the Study Group on the Conditions of Excellence in American Higher Education, 1984, p. 27.

Newman, Frank, "Campus Compact: Urging Students To Serve," in *Wingspread Journal*, The Johnson Foundation, Spring, 1986.

Newman, Frank, *Higher Education and the American Resurgence*, A Carnegie Foundation Special Report, Carnegie Foundation for the Advancement of Teaching, 1985.

Payne, Bruce, Director of the Duke University Leadership Program, used these terms to describe service-based learning at the "COOL Summit Meeting," Durham, North Carolina, August, 1987.

Sagen, H. Bradley, "Liberal Learning and Career Preparation," in *Current Issues in Higher Education: Liberal Learning and Career Preparation*, American Association for Higher Education, 1982-3, No. 2.

Stanton, Timothy K., "Field Study: Information for Faculty," Human Ecology Field Study Office, Cornell University, 1983.

Wagner, Jon, "Academic Excellence and Community Service Through Experiential Learning: Encouraging Students to Teach," keynote presentation to Ninth Annual University of California Conference on Experiential Learning, May, 1986. Available as NSIEE Occasional Paper, National Society for Internships and Experiential Education, Raleigh, North Carolina.

The Liberal Tradition of Civic Education

Edward H. O'Neil

Ed O'Neil traces the loss of a common social and moral vision in the U. S. since the eighteenth century and outlines the historical responsibility of undergraduate education to teach civic participation. He calls on liberal arts educators to reclaim the role of developing students' civic judgment. He argues that service-learning and other forms of direct participation in public life — and the capacity for considered reflection which they foster — are an essential component of sound civic education. This paper was first commissioned by the Kettering Foundation in Dayton, Ohio, for presentation at the 16th Annual Conference of the National Society for Internships and Experiential Education held in October 1987 in Smugglers' Notch, Vermont.

THIS CHAPTER IS CONCERNED WITH the conceptual and practical relationships among the following: undergraduate education, the liberal arts, civic education and experiential education. While I wish to examine a number of different issues related to these ideas, there is an undergirding theme which I seek to advance. This theme is that the essential component of undergraduate education in this country has been what we call liberal education and that liberal education can only be understood as civic education or education in the civic arts. Experiential education as it is widely practiced in undergraduate institutions today is an essential element of civic education and, if the argument holds, an important component of liberal education and the undergraduate experience it in our culture.

Colleges and universities founded in this country from the early seventeenth century through the early nineteenth century, whether religious or secular, were started for social and political purposes. Private institutions founded in the colonial period served, in part, the religious motivations of their founders. But it is important to remember that most of the institutions were started in colonies where religion was well established. The moral and social order was promoted by the education of the citizens of the colony who were also members of the church. The goal of these institutions was to contribute to the secular creation of the city on the hill serving as a model of political organization. Public institutions of higher learning, following Thomas Jefferson's plan for the University of Virginia, were envisioned as great meritocratic institutions which would offer opportunities to provide "virtue and wisdom enough to manage the concerns of society" to all deserving individuals (Jefferson in Koch and Peden, 1944). While individuals certainly benefited in both the secular and sectarian institutions, the motivation for the founding of these colleges and universities was a desire to serve the collective and public purposes of society.

Civic Virtue the Historical Goal of Colleges

The academic programs of the colleges in the first half of the nineteenth century were amazingly uniform in their structure and content. Undergraduates studied classical languages, rhetoric, literature, political economy and a smattering of the natural philosophies or sciences which were emerging as an important force in the world. There was, as well, a shared and unified sense about the moral order of the universe. Influenced strongly by the Scottish common sense school of philosophy and mainstream Protestantism, undergraduates received a dose of moral philosophy in their senior year, which provided them not only an understanding of their intellectual and moral heritage, but a systematic way of projecting themselves upon the world they found beyond the college walls (Smith, 1956). In this regard the vision of the school leaders of the nineteenth century and the institutions which they founded provided a theory of action and a public language for those students who matriculated for study. This theory of action was not dramatically different from the precepts upon which the country had been recently founded and was richly steeped in the traditions of republican virtue, evangelical Protestantism and a burgeoning democratic individualism (Howe, 1979).

This sort of undergraduate education was possible for several important reasons. First, the social world of the first half of the nineteenth century was a homogeneous one for most Americans. Most of the citizens of the country were natives of or descendents of natives of the British Isles. Those who were not were by-and-large Protestants from other northern European countries. American

Indians were excluded from full citizenship. Intellectually, socially, economically, and politically the non-native inhabitants of the new nation shared a heritage with each other. Another factor that made this relatively uniform moral vision of the world possible was the interrelated and interlaced supporting network of institutions in a society which was still able to conduct much of its business in a face-to-face or at least in a small-scale fashion. Family, church, school, voluntary associations, and community participated in the same moral vision of the world, and they all reinforced that vision on individuals in a number of personal, one-to-one interactions (Ryan, 1981). This close knitting of social institutions, sharing in a moral vision, made it possible for colleges and universities to articulate a conceptual moral unity and to pass it on as a coherent — if simplistic — explanation of a social, economic, political and religious world. But this conceptual unity derived its efficacy from the meaning which traditional communities reinforced in the day-to-day lives of individuals. Because parents, merchants, political leaders, and ministers all participated in this moral world in a relatively uncritical fashion, it was possible for college professors to provide a program of study based upon those beliefs and for the educational experience to have meaning in the public lives of graduates.

The education offered to these undergraduates was civic education because it enriched the capacity of students to understand and extend their experience of the small-scale institutions and face-to-face interactions of family, church, school and community into a broader world. It built upon the public competence and reality which was an essential part of each individual's experience in this traditional world. Commenting on his plan for education in the State of Virginia, Jefferson concluded that the liberal study of history would avail citizens "of the experience of other times and other nations; it [would qualify] them as judges of the actions and designs of men ..." (*Life*, p. 265). The language of this education was both civic and liberal; civic because it was in the vernacular of the culture and liberal because it reached backward and forward in time and participated in the moral culture of the day.

Nineteenth Century Changes

By the middle of the nineteenth century, colleges and universities began a slow evolutionary process of changing their curricula in response to the broader currents of change which were reshaping American culture. While an exhaustive discussion of these changes is beyond the scope of this chapter, it is important to have a grasp of some of the changes as a way of putting the undergraduate experience in the context of its traditional role as education for public life.

Industrialization: On the social and economic front, a number of important changes occurred in American society in the second half of the nineteenth century. Technology had already firmly established itself in industrial towns such as Lowell and Poughkeepsie, in the engineering phenomenon of the Erie Canal, and in the extensive networks of railroads that existed by the beginning of the Civil War. America was already transforming itself from an agrarian, small landholder nation to one of factories and mills. While the numbers of people involved in agriculture would remain dominant throughout the century, the power of technology and industrialization was dramatically displayed in the north's overwhelming material advantage over the south by the time of the Civil War (Kasson, 1976).

Corporatization: Related to the industrialization of the American society was a growing trend towards corporatization. While mutual benefit societies and public incorporations had served the nation from the time of the Mayflower compact forward, by mid-century large scale corporate structures were being created in the private and, later, public realm to accommodate the realities of urbanization, industrialization, and the growing population. While family, home, church, and small schools still had their role to play in society, the seeds of the large-scale, privately held company and governmental bureaucracy were beginning to emerge. Much of the history of the nineteenth century is a transition from small and locally controlled institutions to large institutions which were administered some distance from the people whose lives were affected. It was also a transition from a world in which face-to-face interactions marked the important passages of an individual's life to one in which anonymous forces informed decisions about health, education and employment (Wiebe, 1967).

Emergence of professional and academic groups: One aspect of the corporatization of American society was the growing professionalization of the employment sector which occurred at the end of the nineteenth century. It was in the last two decades of this century and the first two decades of the twentieth that professional groups began to organize themselves. The emergence of the American Medical Association, the American Bar Association, and American Dental Association led the way for this professionalization which would eventually reach to engineers, social workers, and nurses and be sought after by every working group as a mark of success. At the same time, the academic disciplines also began to formalize their structures and limit the scope of their own expertise and knowledge. As physicians, attorneys, dentists, engineers and architects were defining their own rules for membership, purview of expertise, and control of entry into their ranks, historians, philosophers, psychologists, chemists, biologists and every other academic discipline were making a similar adjustment. Specialization in the professions and in the academic disciplines brought even more sophisticated layers of analysis of reality and more technological applications of knowledge. It also limited the professions and disciplines to those who adhered to their standards (Bledstein, 1976).

Twentieth Century Challenges

Changes in cultural and moral authority: One additional social change which occurred in the forty-year period around the turn of the century was the disintegration of a homogeneous American culture. While immigrants who differed from the white Anglo-Saxon tradition of the colonial and early national period of the country had been arriving for over half a century, the white Protestant culture had nonetheless remained dominant. With the freeing of the slaves following the Civil War and the immigration of many southern and eastern European Catholics and eastern European Jews, the cultural hegemony of the white Protestant world no longer held. While the traditional culture remained dominant, it no longer served the unquestioned role of cultural and moral authority.

Coupled with these social and economic changes was an intellectual change which needs brief mention here. The beginning of the century had witnessed a coming together of three powerful ideas: classical republicanism, democratic individualism, and evangelical Protestantism. While these ideas had evolved and changed over the nineteenth century, they remained the intellectual foundations upon which a century of relative peace and prosperity had been built. The success of these intellectual and moral precepts in generating such a world drew not just America, but all of western Europe, into the dawning years of the twentieth century believing that civilization was progressing toward a higher state of moral affairs. Not until the chaos and moral disorder of the First World War and, later, the Second World War and Holocaust did these ideas begin to lose much of their intellectual and, certainly, moral efficacy. In the modern and post-modern world of the twentieth century, it no longer seemed appropriate to believe that classical ideals or republican virtues were adequate to the needs of individual meaning and social integration.

Science and technology: All of these changes had their impact on the undergraduate experience in America. Technology and science took on an increasingly important place in the undergraduate program. Not only did these fields of study come to occupy a more prominent place in what we consider the liberal arts curriculum, but entire majors and schools at the undergraduate level began to develop around them. Some of these incorporated the liberal arts as they had traditionally been studied. Others grew up entirely independent of that tradition. The growing importance of technology and science was also expressed in the growth of the Land Grant university and the extension concept of improving society through technical scientific or social scientific means.

Large research universities: In part, the corporatization of American colleges and universities began with the growth of the large state universities in the last two decades of the nineteenth century. But it was not until after the Second World War and the growing importance of research related to science and technology that large-scale bureaucratic institutions of higher education began to emerge. This was fueled by the demographic aberration of the post World War II baby boom which first created demands for more primary and secondary teachers and later expanded institutions of higher education. Presidents of universities became not professors of moral philosophy who imparted the role of society and man's relationship to it, as they had been in the nineteenth century, but managers who were concerned with the technical affairs and support of these large organizations.

Departmentalization of knowledge: Professionalization, particularly professionalization of the academic disciplines, also had its impact on universities. While one of the first academic historians in the country, Henry Adams, may have sought synthesis and meaning in the writing of history, increasingly the academic disciplines, including history, sought scientific validity from analytical, technical capacity and developed professional standards against the intrusion of moral or normative scholarship and teaching. From the turn of the century through the present time, the academic disciplines have prided and promoted themselves by their capacity for greater and greater abstract analysis and distinct separation from other disciplines. The age of science, technology and positivistic social science came to dominate the university and the undergraduate experience. It is not surprising that in such an environment the graduate and research work of the disciplines became far more important than the work of general education at the undergraduate level.

Culturally, colleges and universities in the twentieth century could no longer depend upon students who shared common values, common experiences in small-scale institutions or even common ages as they approached the university for higher education. In part because questions of value were so complex, they became increasingly absent from most institutions of higher education. Considering the pluralistic reality of American society, the democratic commitment to equal access, and the tradition of separation of church and state, colleges and universities became increasingly concerned with only the technical sides of moral questions, the due process considerations, rather than the substantive issues of the nature of society and the individual's role in it.

Loss of a public moral vision: Finally, so as not to be too hard on those who are called to academic careers, there was increasingly less of a moral center or vision for the whole society. It is a long fall back to the nineteenth century educators and their Scottish realist's views, tempered with a fervent brand of Protestantism. Between the modern age and that earlier time, the moral vision of the nation has necessarily reduced itself to the maintenance of fair fights between conflicting claims. It is the logical progression of a society which is both richly pluralistic and strongly democratic. If the contemporary notion of the liberal arts or civic arts turns out to be a jumble of unrelated distribution requirements which provide at best only very narrow technical expertise with little connection to a broader ground of meaning, then it may be that the curriculum reflects the moral order of the surrounding world, just as the senior seminar in moral philosophy did for the students of the nineteenth century. If the academy has lost its capacity for *public* language to be used in liberal and civic education, then this must be, in part, because of the prevalence of *private* language, thought, action and deed which dominate the social world.

Erosion of civic education: These private selves are free in one meaning of that word, but this freedom has ravaged the tradition of civic and liberal education upon which colleges, universities, and all types of schools were founded in the early years of the nation. Replacing this tradition now is a system of undergraduate education that trains dental hygienists in the same fashion as historians. The problem of the educational system is not so much that the training of hygienists and historians is structured and facilitated in much the same way, but the fact that hygienists are as likely to receive as good an understanding of the civic roles and expectations of themselves as individuals and their obligation to society as is the "liberally educated" historian. In neither case is the probability very great that the educational process of undergraduate education will attach either, in any meaningful way, to an understanding of and a capacity for action in their public roles.

Reawakening Civic Learning in Education

Institutions of undergraduate education have forgotten — in their actions but not in their rhetoric — that an essential role of the educative enterprise in a democratic society is civic education. With the narrowly scientific, technological, professional, and technical social scientific programs and disciplines which pass as undergraduate majors, there is little to contribute to the tradition of liberal education and the language of public life. The crush for research for academic success at most universities has made the humanities and arts second class citizens, but willing participants in the same game. Recent attacks on this sad state of affairs have called for a return to the traditions of classical literature as a way of recapturing this civic tradition (Bloom, 1987). While this is an important part of an effort to reaffirm civic education, it is not sufficient. The work involved is a much more challenging undertaking; one which requires greater vision and more risk than the nostalgia of remembering better days.

To advance this work requires a more distinct definition of civic education. John Dewey described it as the way in which a society passes on the characteristic ways of feeling, thinking and acting to its new members. In this regard it is a generic concept having applicability in any society. In the most traditional societies the teaching of those lessons would be uncritical and, perhaps, unconscious as people take on the traditions, myths, patterns of interaction and language of being which have been passed down from generation to generation. In our modern society the task of education is a much more conscious undertaking involving systems of schools and professionals such as teachers acting as agents for the family, church and state. Such a modern world requires clarity about the public lessons which are to be passed on.

Civic education is also normative relative to particular cultures and times. The characteristics of democracy form the content and process of civic education in this country, making it distinct from other forms of education. "A democracy is more than a form of government; it is primarily a mode of associated living, of conjoint communicated experience" (Dewey, 1966). For this culture to work it must provide a civic education which engenders a full and rich capacity for participating in the various aspects of all things which have to do with the public. This quality is passed along by providing the individual the opportunity for practice of the language, action and habits of being which cultivate the public characteristics of the culture. Being social animals, we are drawn to this practice because we are, in part, fulfilled by the use of these distinctive species characteristics of language and association.

Capacity for considered reflection on experience: In the traditional world this practice of public life was learned first in what Edmund Burke called the "little platoons" of democracy — family, church, community. The lessons began with face-to-face instructions attaching the individual emotionally to the practice of public life. This emotional attachment of individual ego was later extended intellectually over time and space, connecting it to a broader and more diverse ground of meaning and application to individuals unmet and unborn. In this fashion intellectual and emotional properties were brought together to foster in the individual the virtue of public or civic judgment. This practical virtue is the capacity for considered reflection on experience which connects the individual to a historical ground of public meaning and projects the individual into future actions which are consonant with that tradition. As such, it is not sufficient to understand the rules of tradition in order to achieve civic virtue. The individual must also emotionally participate in the verities of public life through direct experience.

Promoting the cultivation of the intellectual side of civic virtue without the experiential component is a futile task — just as experience in isolation from considered reflection is myopic. In the biomedical sciences clinicians are trained with exposure to both, but the final proof of their skills as practitioners is how they bring the intellectual and the applied together in the exercise of clinical judgment. Too much emphasis on one to the denigration of the other jeopardizes their ability for meaningful action. The proper balance not only affords the opportunity for good practice to take place, but it also creates an environment in which judgment is improved upon throughout life as the practitioner is open to each new experience, yet mindful of its relationship to the traditions of the biomedical disciplines. In this tradition schools and teachers are judged by how well they afford their students a place to bring the clinical and the intellectual together. Practitioners are judged by how they have maintained that balance since the time they were licensed to practice.

Practice of civic judgment: Undergraduate liberal education is one of the arenas in which this culture promotes civic judgment. As such it must afford a place for civic judgment to be exercised. The practice of civic judgment is not necessarily conducted in a seminar on Aristotle's *Ethics* or Plato's *Republic*. The study of such works does not provide sufficient opportunity to open most students to the practical dimension of civic judgment. This can only take place when individuals are brought together and engaged in public and community life. These engagements are characterized by several qualities. The participants must share in an understanding of a common problem or issue. They must have the opportunity to participate face-to-face with each other to address the problem or issue. Finally, in our culture, the experience must be influenced by fairness, openness and a willingness to take risks (MacIntyre, 1981).

Conclusion

Opportunities for students to participate in service-learning internships, action research, and other direct experiences of public life will be an essential component of civic renewal in the U. S. *Service-learning and other forms of experiential education provide vehicles for learning the basic cornerstone of civic judgment — the capacity for considered reflection on experience.* These engagements will be critical in evolving a new language of public life and a new understanding of civic responsibility. Given experiences of this sort, undergraduates may begin to develop a capacity for broadening their civic judgment in the classroom, and more importantly, taking that judgment from the school environment to their daily lives upon graduation.

There seems little doubt that public life and civic judgment have atrophied since Jefferson's time. The loss of a unified and religiously endorsed moral order, the profusion of technical knowledge which produces social and individual wealth, and the emergence of large-scale organizations and institutions have loosened the acquisitive and rapacious side of our individualism, which too often withdraws into the private world of consumption and isolation. This withdrawal leaves the public world less able to respond to those needs of individuals which require a public space and language for action.

To revive the public, and perhaps better, nature of our being will require courage — the courage to ask of ourselves and our schools the commitment to try new ideas, to risk failure and to try again. The language of classical civic virtue will not be sufficient to the creation of a new public language, any more than Athenian democracy would fit our needs for participation in government. Both help inform us, but finally it must be up to us to accept the challenge.

Institutions which provide liberal education at the undergraduate level must begin to recognize civic education as central to their purpose. Civic education is concerned with the best of the liberal traditions and, in fact, only by consciously pursuing civic education can colleges and universities hope to fulfill their commitment to liberal learning. Civic education is education for the virtue of civic judgment and as such requires the opportunity for the practice of the virtue in the public realm. Finding that public realm, nurturing it in a sometimes hostile environment and providing students a chance to participate in it and more fully understand it is, at times, an overwhelming task. But because it pulls us as teachers and facilitators out of our narrow disciplines and private lives, it provides us the opportunity to connect once again to that sphere which provides meaning to our daily work. It gives us connections backward to a ground of meaning and forward to the hope of the future and fulfillment that stretches beyond our sometimes shallow private world, reminding that while the challenge is great, the urge to respond is as noble as the human spirit.

Ed O'Neil is an historian who teaches in the Institute of Policy Sciences and Public Affairs at Duke University. He co-directs the Pew National Dental Education and Veterinary Medicine Projects and serves on the Board of Directors of the National Society for Internships and Experiential Education.

References

Bledstein, Burton, *The Culture of Professionalism*, Norton, 1976, pp. 287-332.

Bloom, Allan, *The Closing of the American Mind*, Simon and Schuster, 1987.

Dewey, John, *Democracy and Education*, Free Press, 1966, p. 87.

Howe, Daniel, *The Political Culture of the American Whigs*, University of Chicago Press, 1979, pp. 1-22.

Jefferson, Thomas, "Letter to John Adams", *The Life and Selected Writing of Thomas Jefferson*, ed. by Adrienne Koch and William Peden, Random House, 1944, p. 633.

Jefferson, Thomas, "Notes on Virginia," *Life*, p. 265.

Kasson, John, *Civilizing the Machine*, Penguin, 1976, pp. 181-234.

MacIntyre, Alasdair, *After Virtue*, University of Notre Dame Press, 1981, p. 181.

Ryan, Mary, *Cradle of the Middle Class*, Cambridge University Press, 1981, pp. 1-31.

Smith, Wilson, *Professors and Public Ethics*, Cornell Press, 1956, pp. 3-25.

Wiebe, Robert, *The Search for Order*, Hill and Wang, 1967, pp. 1-43.

Education for Participation: Implications for School Curriculum and Instruction

Ralph W. Tyler

A leading educator and researcher writes about the relationship between "youth participation" and the central goals of education, with special emphasis on how participation can and should be integrated with the school curriculum. These ideas from the youth participation movement provide a helpful background for those combining service and learning in the 1990s. Reprinted with permission from Youth Participation and Experiential Education, *Daniel Conrad and Diane Hedin, Guest Editors, Haworth Press, Inc., 10 Alice St., Binghamton, NY 13904, Child and Youth Series, Vol. 4, Nos. 3/4, 1982, pp. 21-29.*

THREE QUESTIONS ARE COMMONLY raised when schools are considering developing programs of youth participation: Can participation be successfully integrated within the school curriculum? How can effective integration be assured? Will youth participation programs have the potential to influence students to become participating citizens?

The answer to the first question is clearly "yes." For example, the National Commission on Resources for Youth has in its files more than a thousand such programs. The following illustrations are taken from these files:

Duluth Youth Jury: Groups of 12 to 14 Duluth youth jurors hear cases involving their peers of vandalism, shoplifting, misdemeanor assault, possession of marijuana or alcohol, and hunting violations. The jurors question offenders and decide on sentences that usually combine probation with financial restitution or community service. A group of jurors, selected from all Duluth high schools and two neighborhood schools, meets on a rotating basis once a week for three consecutive weeks. Probation officers rotate weekly in their role as hearing officers.

Chicago Alternative Schools Network Video Project: In this project, 100 young people are exploring the issues and needs of their community and are documenting the cultural life of their environment. After attending video training classes, they become involved in their community in a number of ways. They have developed, produced, and distributed numerous tapes dealing with youth and youth-related issues. They often present the tapes and lead discussions about them in the community. They have written a manual about community video projects and are working on a book about jobs for Latinos in the media.

Barefoot Doctors: This program of the New York City Dewitt Clinton High School involves 60 male high school students who provide health screening and information to their peers and other community members. They run a screening clinic at the high school, where they check for venereal disease symptoms, test urine and blood pressure, measure height and weight, take temperatures, and do dental screening. They also provide training in venereal disease prevention and cures in many school classes and have provided screening and information to community members at a variety of sites. Participants also receive first hand experience in many departments at the North Central Bronx Hospital.

These three examples taken from the descriptions of more than a thousand indicate clearly that schools can arrange for youth participation projects in which students can relate what they are learning in school to many significant situations outside of school, and can learn to take adult responsibilities for many of the things they do.

The other two questions cannot be so easily answered. Successful programs of youth participation require careful planning, as do other components of the curriculum. A primary question in any curriculum development project is whether there are important needs of students that are not now being met and for which an intended curriculum project could make a contribution. It is not necessary to prove here that students have unmet needs or to reiterate that young people who participate with adults gain competence and make substantial progress in their transition from childhood and youth to responsible adult life. The report of the Youth Panel of the President's Science Advisory Committee, of the Commission of United States Office of Education, that of the panel appointed by the Kettering Foundation, and those that have been printed in several other publications all agree that youth are too largely segregated from adult life, are given too few opportunities to serve others, and are permitted too few occasions in which they can take major responsibility for actions that affect others.

However, as youth participation becomes more widely advocated, there is danger that it will become a slogan or a passing fad because the concept will not be understood in a fundamental sense and because superficial efforts will be undertaken that fail to meet the need. Hence, it is time to examine the concept and the programs of implementation with the same criteria that should be employed in developing other significant learning experiences in the curriculum. One essential criterion is the significance of the educational objectives that can guide the development of youth participation activities in the curriculum.

Objectives of Youth Participation

As I have observed programs in various parts of the nation, I have noted several educational objectives to which participation projects can make a substantial contribution:

1. Helping students to understand the reality of social experience, connecting this reality with the concepts and principles that help to make sense of what they are observing and experiencing. Many students do not connect what they read and discuss in school with the reality to which these ideas relate. Hence, they often memorize what they have read and heard but do not have a concrete notion of the meaning. Student participation in the world outside of school can be a basis for understanding.

2. Helping students to understand and appreciate the values and limitations of social institutions in serving individuals and groups in our society. Many students have not examined city governments, police departments, courts, fire departments, churches, health agencies, schools, and other social institutions in terms of the need for their service, the effectiveness of these services, and particularly the extent to which they furnish opportunity for individuals to develop themselves for effective participation in the society and help them to achieve self-fulfillment.

3.   Helping students to develop interest in working with others for a common social purpose. Many students have had little or no experience in working with others, either peers or adults, for a common purpose. Many school activities are seen as self-serving and are more likely to be competitive than cooperative. They have not had the satisfaction of accomplishing a social purpose and seeing what it means to those served. Experiences of this sort can stimulate new interests in young people.

4.   Helping students to develop the social skills that are useful in working effectively with peers and adults. Many students have useful social skills but are not confident in the use of them in work situations with peers or with adults. Participation activities can help to sharpen these skills, stimulate them to develop additional ones, and help them to gain confidence in their social effectiveness.

5.   Helping students to develop the skills and attitudes needed to assume responsibility for important social actions. Most students have not had responsibility for making decisions that significantly involve and affect others. Their actions are often impulsive. Decisions are frequently made without careful consideration of alternatives and the probable consequences of each alternative course of action. Participation projects can be a major arena for developing these skills and attitudes.

6.   Helping students to develop appropriate emotional and cognitive reactions as they enjoy the satisfactions of successful activities and bear the consequences of those that fail. Many students have been protected from feeling responsible for either significant failures or successes that involve others who suffer or benefit from the activities. Projects that students have had a major role in planning and carrying out will usually result either in obvious social benefits or losses, or both. They afford opportunity for young people to observe, to question, and to face the facts of success and failure.

7.   Helping students to discover the satisfactions that are obtained when one shares efforts, ideas, and possessions with others and is able to empathize with others in their different moods. Most students have few occasions in which they share matters of importance with persons other than relatives and close friends. Hence, it is hard for them to appreciate what it means to give as well as to receive in relations with persons of other ages, or of different home and cultural backgrounds. A great many youth participation projects involve students in face-to-face relations with nonschool persons who need help and to whom the students are able to give assistance. These situations can be used to aid students in develop-

ing sensitivity to persons of different backgrounds and to empathize with them in joy and sadness.

8. Helping students to discover the satisfactions that are derived from understanding puzzling social, economic, and political phenomena. Many students find the social world complex, and significant phenomena appear contradictory in their limited perceptions. Participation programs frequently provide a perspective on social situations that help the students to identify the previously hidden factors that are needed to explain the ways persons behave in these complex situations. If they are helped to examine and analyze these experiences, they are excited about the way they can understand matters that were previously confusing.

9. Helping students to discover the different roles they can successfully play in working with others. One of the obstacles to cooperation and teamwork among children and youth is the lack of clear ideas of the different roles played by different members of the group in making an effective team. They need to learn that not all team members can be quarterbacks and that a team without linebackers and other roles would be a sorry spectacle. And, as in any good team, they all get satisfaction from the success of the team itself. Many participation projects involve the students in interdependent roles, all of which contribute to the success of the project.

Matching Students to Projects

Objectives like these represent a considerable educational task. It may require many years for most students to obtain them adequately. No one project is likely to furnish the educational experiences necessary to contribute to all of these objectives, but many can be devised that will provide experiences likely to help the students progress toward several of them. Before impulsively selecting or developing participation projects and assessing or encouraging students to undertake particular tasks, however, careful planning is necessary.

In this planning, one must remember that both school populations and individual students differ widely in the opportunities they have had to experience in the real world. Hence a needs assessment is important; that is, as far as possible one needs to appraise each student's present development in each major objective and ascertain the significant and relevant experiences he or she has had. This will help to identify for each student his or her need for further development. This assessment of previous experiences can be made through such techniques as group discussions, questionnaires, individual conversations, student biographies, reports from parents, and reports from previous teachers of the student.

When the needs for further experiences have been identified, one can search out opportunities that can contribute to meeting some of these needs. In judging the potential of a project, one can ask such questions as: Will students in this project have actual responsibility? Will they be interacting with adults in a significant way? Will their activities in this project make a difference to others? Will they be experiencing the results of successful efforts and errors of judgment, and the consequences of poor work habits? Will the activities of the project require the use of present knowledge and skills and stimulate their further development?

When a project has been selected, individual assignments can be worked out that will provide opportunities for the desired learning. As time goes on, a list of types of projects and other useful resources can be built up and classified in terms of their helpfulness for particular kinds of student development. In this review and selection of projects, the students themselves should be major participants so that they become increasingly conscious of the purposes of participation projects and the values that they are expected to have.

Reflection: The Key to Learning from Participation

For the students to gain understanding and appreciation of their out-of-school experiences, it is important to arrange for seminars or other sessions in which students are stimulated to reflect upon their experiences, to become more observant, and to perceive the relationship between what they observe and the school curriculum. Experience in the "real world" can be chaotic and confusing because events often occur rapidly and follow each other in an apparently disorganized fashion. The concepts and principles of school subjects plus the more ordered vicarious experiences provided by novels, short stories, and drama can help students to sort out their experiences and interpret them in terms of organized ideas.

It is often helpful during sessions of reflection on student experiences to raise questions that can guide observation and recall and can stimulate efforts at interpretation. For example, One can ask such questions as: What is the function of the organization with which you worked? What objectives does it appear to have? What were the roles and the tasks of the different people in the organization? How were these tasks viewed by those who carried them out? What seemed to be the motives, attitudes, and social skills of the different persons you worked with and of the persons you served?

How were the persons treated who worked in the organization, and how were the clients treated?

Questions like these are not only helpful for students in observing and recalling their experiences, but they can lead to their looking up relevant material in appropriate references. Thus, the reflective sessions can serve as the primary means for integrating out-of-school experiences and the school curriculum.

In spite of careful planning, some projects may not prove to contribute substantially to the students' development. Hence, one should develop an evaluation plan that will provide for a record of what each student did, both on the project and in the reflection sessions, that can be checked against specific purposes of the assignment. One can ask, for example, what he or she appeared to gain in understanding, skills, interests, attitudes, or appreciations. This evaluation can be used to develop the plan for the student's next participation activity. One cannot always target goals for each individual student and evaluate his or her progress toward these goals because of the time and effort required to obtain the needed information and the appropriate projects. However, if students and relevant adults are involved in the planning and appraisal of projects, their heightened consciousness can help to guide them — students and project personnel — in developing effective projects.

Guidelines for Successful Youth Participation Projects

My experience with out-of-school projects goes back to the Eight-Year Study of the 1930s, in which many of the 30 schools developed youth participation activities. We learned a number of things in that study. Among the most important were:

1. Effective programs must be worked out at the local school level — where the students are, the teachers are, the parents are, and the out-of-school experiences will need to be. District administrators, can encourage projects and furnish technical assistance where needed, but the local schools and their communities vary, so that a simple plan is not likely to work. Furthermore, since those who operate projects — teachers and community members — must understand them, appreciate their potential, have the requisite skills, and be confident that they can do what is required of them, the best assurance is their active participation in planning and developing projects. The parents and community members are

particularly helpful in identifying student needs, suggesting project opportunities, appraising their potential, and furnishing some of the needed resources.

2.   Some teachers lack the skills and attitudes required to carry on effective youth participation projects. In the Eight-Year Study, summer workshops were developed to enable teachers to acquire these skills, to become knowledgeable about projects, and to cultivate appropriate interests and attitudes by working with teachers from other schools in considering ideas and developing plans.

3.   When participation projects are new to a school, the initial experiences should be made available in one or two pilot programs rather than establishing a large-scale effort. We found that the teachers and students learned a good deal from the pilot projects, which in most cases required some revision of plans and activities when unexpected difficulties were encountered. After experimenting with the pilot projects, the large-scale efforts produced fewer failures.

4.   The development of successful participation programs required more time than was anticipated when decisions were made to establish them. In most cases, four to five years were necessary to develop programs, overcome initial difficulties, enable teachers to acquire necessary skills, and allow students to perceive their roles as educationally important. When such programs are undertaken, the allocation of sufficient time for sound development is very important.

These four things that we learned in conducting the Eight-Year Study are probably useful guides today. Although 40 years have passed since then, human problems and social institutions are not greatly different today. New and vital educational programs can be developed and conducted successfully when the persons involved are interested, help to develop them, and have opportunities to learn the new roles that may be required.

The preceding discussion is a response to the second question raised in the introduction to this paper: How can effective integration be assured? The third question, whether youth participation programs will have the potential to influence students to become participating citizens, cannot be answered so clearly in the affirmative.

Does Youth Participation Lead to Adult Participation?

A number of investigations of the relationship of student development in school and college to their performance as adults indicate the complexity of the factors that influence human behavior at different periods in the life cycle. For example, studies of the graduates of Bennington College, Vassar College, and the high school students in Project Talent who were questioned and interviewed 15 years later, all show that the interests, know-how, skills, and attitudes developed in adolescence strongly influence adult behavior when there is a concurrent supportive environment. Yet a considerable portion of these graduates modified their behavior when the social environment was in conflict with their earlier beliefs, skills, and practices. Many of those who learned to participate effectively in the social and political activities of their community discontinued their participation when most of their friends and close associates did not participate. There were exceptions. A portion of them continued the activities developed in their youth in spite of the unfavorable environment, and some were able to influence their nonparticipating associates to join them in various participating activities.

One cannot expect all the young people who have participated in significant out-of-school projects to continue social and political activities during their adult lives. However, as more significant youth participation programs are provided by the schools, there should be fewer adult environments that are unfavorable to responsible social and political participation.

Ralph W. Tyler is Director Emeritus, Center for Advanced Study in the Behavioral Sciences.

Learning by Heart: The Role of Action in Civic Education

Steven K. Schultz

Steven Schultz outlines the weaknesses of an approach to civic education and renewal that is either wholly classical or wholly experiential. He argues for the necessity of integrating these two approaches and building on the complementary strengths of each tradition. For educators, the beginning point for this integration is the modeling of constructive civic participation within the academy itself and between the academy and the larger community. This paper was first commissioned by the Kettering Foundation in Dayton, Ohio, for presentation at the 16th Annual Conference of the National Society for Internships and Experiential Education in October 1987 in Smugglers' Notch, Vermont.

Learning by Heart: 1) Memorization of a text, often of the classical tradition, in order to retain its timeless wisdom; 2) Becoming skilled at an activity, so that it can be performed effortlessly; 3) A process which recognizes an affective dimension to the acquisition of knowledge.

Introduction

This chapter begins with the assumption that an essential role of education in a democracy is to help students become thoughtful, active, and caring citizens. The growing movement to renew the civic purposes of American education indicates that this view is widely shared. At the same time, there is debate about how these civic purposes can best be achieved.

The purpose of this chapter is to propose an alternative approach to civic education. I begin with a brief account of some criticisms of American education from the recent national reports which have a bearing on this discussion. Following this, two contending approaches to the civic role of education are described. For the sake of brevity, I will call them the "classical" and the "experiential" models. Each is essential to the civic purposes of education, but both have suffered from a one-sidedness that reduces their power. I will describe some of the difficulties produced by this one-sidedness. Finally, I will propose a synthetic approach to the dilemma: that to fulfill its civic purposes, education must bring together both the classical and the experiential modes of learning, and do this through the development of civic community among those who call themselves teachers.

The movement for civic literacy takes place in the midst of a period of self-doubt and re-examination of purposes for American education. During the 1980s, various national studies have pointed to confusion about educational aims, ineffective methods, fragmentation among the disciplines, declining standardized test scores and other signs of malaise (Boyer, 1987; Boyer and Hechinger, 1981; Katz, *et al*, 1988; Newman, 1985).

Some of the shared conclusions of these reports have direct implications for a renewal of the civic role of education. These conclusions include the following: 1) That present educational structures have promoted passivity in students, rather than encouraging active involvement in the learning process. Many of our methods treat students as submissive consumers of knowledge. 2) That current educational practices reinforce tendencies within the larger culture towards a narrow pursuit of individual interests, to the exclusion of community involvement and awareness. In addition, these practices reinforce the belief that there are no connections between the quality of personal life and the quality of life within the larger community. There is a broad consensus that our schools have lost a sense of civic purpose and no longer prepare students to be effective participants in public life. 3) That the education we provide has become increasingly technical and instrumental, in the sense that we focus on the *means* for doing all sorts of things (including moral decision-making) without examining the *ends* to which our actions are directed. Discussion of normative values has been avoided in deference to procedural questions. The result is a growing ignorance of our common cultural heritage and a loss of any sense of shared normative values that govern our common life.

Two Contrasting Approaches to Civic Education

These dilemmas of passivity, individualism, and instrumentalism form the backdrop for two rival approaches to civic education.

The first has always been a part of the mainstream of American education and, while temporarily in eclipse, is now enjoying a revival. This traditional position has been termed by some the "classical" view. What I describe here as classical might more accurately be called a kind of contemporary distortion of the classical view, which often placed a high value upon virtue, character and application to life as the goals of education. Following the Enlightenment, abstract reason took on a more and more central role, to the exclusion of other dimensions of knowledge and learning (Murchland, 1976). For ease of discussion, I will use the term "classical" to label the first approach to civic education. It is an approach which focuses on classical texts (the orthodox "canon" varies) and the ideas presented therein, and views the careful study of these as the essential core of a liberal education.

In response to the problems mentioned above, the classical view proposes a return to the teaching of the great books, a passionate engagement with the best thinkers of the Western tradition. It proposes that student passivity can be overcome by engagement with great ideas. Consideration of concepts such as justice and civic community through history will draw the student away from individualism and into an appreciation of the value of democracy. An exposure to the great texts and ideas will also help the student to develop sturdy value commitments and reject a relativistic or instrumental view of life. Looking broadly at the classical perspective, the focus for the renewal of the civic role of education is to modify the content of what is taught, with less concern about the form.

The other tradition is newer and has mostly found itself outside the mainstream. This "experiential" approach places some form of active community service and civic participation at the center of a vital civic education. The experiential model places the student in the role of participant in public life, with the goal of teaching him or her to function effectively as a citizen and to develop values of cooperation, service, and caring for others. This method of civic education speaks to the problem of student passivity by actively engaging the student with his or her society. Experience and, very importantly, critical reflection on that experience are seen as the best means for bringing the student out of individualism and into public life. While one learns how to do things through community service, one also learns directly the meaning of concepts such as justice, freedom, democracy, and social responsibility. This approach to civic education places more emphasis on the form of education, and less on the content.

These two approaches to civic education have tended to ignore one another, and have been seen by some as mutually exclusive alternatives. One either soars with the classics or gets one's hands dirty with community service, but some feel that one cannot do both. The result is an impoverished civic education which tries to fulfill its task with only part of the educational resources available. Some of the problems which develop from a limited approach to civic learning are outlined below.

The Classical View and its Problems

The "classical" approach to civic education has certain elements which can become problematic. When taken in its narrowest sense, the cultivation of reason becomes its sole purpose — reason is abstracted from any context in actual life. Such an education can fail to engage the student as a whole person. It does not cultivate other qualities such as empathy, and in particular, it may allow the student to leave the rarefied concepts of justice, freedom, and democracy back in the classroom without taking them out into public life.

The classical approach is a view of knowledge and of how we know which gives supreme reign to the rational intellect, and ignores other understandings of knowledge. Pursuit of theoretical truth and the development of the human capacity for reason become the ultimate educational task. For the education of citizens, the goal is to develop the rational capacities as fully as possible, so that people might exercise their democratic responsibilities intelligently. As David Mathews describes this approach, "the development of the mind, and the capacity to reason, is the best guarantor of any competence, civic or otherwise" (1985, p. 679).

In the ethical realm, reason is seen as the necessary and sufficient condition for moral action. As Kohlberg stated, "Virtue is knowledge of the good. He (she) who knows the good chooses the good" (1970, p. 58). Teach students about the good society, and they will seek it.

Such arguments are appealing to the hope that all of us share that our teaching will make an impact, but they do not ring true. They ignore the human reality that thought and action are not always coherent. Morally elevated thought does not of necessity result in moral action. To ignore this truth is to present a partial view of what it means to be human.

There are a growing number of voices from different sources which have begun to question this limited description of human knowing. Feminist scholarship has provided some of the most provocative challenges to the emphasis upon rationality to the exclusion of other qualities. Carol Gilligan writes of the conclusions of her work on the contrast between men's and women's development:

> "The inclusion of women's experience brings to developmental understanding a new perspective on relationships that changes the basic constructs of interpretation. The concept of identity expands to include the experience of interconnection. The moral domain is similarly enlarged by the inclusion of responsibility and care in relationships. And the underlying epistemology correspondingly shifts from the Greek ideal of knowledge as a correspondence between mind and form to the Biblical conception of knowing as a process of human relationship." (1982, p. 173)

The implications of this new understanding of "connected knowing" (Belenky *et al*, 1986, pp. 100-130) for civic education seem clear. The values of heart — concern for the common good, a sense of compassion, courage to seek justice, devotion to one's community — all require a sense of connection to others which a completely abstract education cannot provide. I would suggest that these values and this kind of knowing are best nurtured and developed in an educational environment which provides the opportunity for engagement with others through service or in other kinds of action in the community.

A second potential problem with the classical approach to civic education has to do with the difficult question of the authority of tradition. If one defines a particular collection of texts as the classical "canon," one risks disregarding those points of view which are incongruent with the core tradition. One also risks the possibility of communicating to students that there are "right" answers to each question that have been decided by some external authority (the teacher, the historical thinker). In this process, the tradition shapes what we come to understand as the "objective" frame for interpreting the world and analyzing problems. Efforts to bring in other voices which have not been heard, through ethnic and feminist studies for example, are seen as faddish and contributing to the intellectual impoverishment of students (Bloom, 1987). Even non-Western views are ignored.

Civic life in a democracy survives on the basis of respect for opposing points of view:

> "It is no exaggeration to say that democratic society is founded on a kind of faith: on the complete conviction that

each citizen is capable of, and assumes, complete political responsibility. Each one not only broadly understands the problems of government but is willing and ready to take part in their solution.... There must be a completely free exchange of ideas. Minority opinions, even opinions which may appear to be dangerous, must be given a hearing, clearly understood and seriously evaluated on their own merits, not merely suppressed." (Merton, 1968, p. 100)

To consider the classical books as the repository of all necessary and objective human knowledge is to ignore the interests in history that shaped the development of the tradition in a particular direction. Such an approach invites the risk that the openness of mind required by democratic citizens will wither.

Another feminist scholar has written compellingly on this question of excluded knowledge, and describes an alternative approach:

"To date there has been a nearly consistent tendency for feminist ethicists to take as their starting points reflection upon very concrete situations. This procedure is one way, and a main way, in which dominant ideology is unmasked. In this procedure, there is commonality or at least a basis for commonality with those who articulate ethical reflections from other oppressed groups. For until the dominant ideology of a social structure can be exposed as manufactured instead of natural, the terms of an ethical problem will tend to reflect assumptions which support a dominant ideology. For this reason the act of defining a problem is a political act; it is an exercise of power to have accepted one's terms of a problem." (Robb, 1985, p. 213)

The danger of an overly restrictive emphasis on the classical "canon" is that it limits the content and the frame of discussion. Study which proceeds in the opposite direction from the classical model, as described by Robb, could open fruitful possibilities for furthering the goals of civic learning. Engagement with particular people and their needs in "very concrete situations" could promote an appreciation of the range of alternative viewpoints on an issue of social importance, a generosity of spirit, and a knowledge of the importance of being able to think clearly enough to shape one's own position in the midst of contending views.

A third important problem found in the classical approach is that education abstracted from life fails to give students the skills necessary to participate effectively; they are unable to make the link between classical notions of freedom and justice and the situations they encounter in public life. This critique is analogous to the first point regarding the problem of abstraction, with the focus in this case upon skills and effectiveness, rather than on motivation and the affective and ethical dimensions.

The assumption of the classical position is that efforts at application dilute the pure purposes of education. Application and the development of skills is something to be pursued by the vocational schools or by liberal studies students only after they have left the academy. To attempt to make education "useful" is to demote it to the status of a means, rather than an end. Brann writes:

> "Now, if the desire for knowledge is really an aspect and even the essential aspect of human nature, then utilitarian education is a contradiction in terms, a perverse enterprise. Learning is naturally done for love, not for use; it is itself a mode of living, and not a mere means." (1979, p. 59)

The problem with this view in relation to civic education, which Brann goes on to point out, is that:

> "A republic has a genuine public business, which is to provide for the possibility and protection of a good life in the worldly sense. Therefore, it has the responsibility of training its citizens for this purpose...." (*ibid*)

If one of the important goals of our educational process is to educate students for participation in democracy, such a goal must be modeled and practiced within the school and not left as something that the student will do "on her own" when she completes her education. Without engagement in the process during school, the student will probably lack the confidence and skill to enter it later, and her knowledge will remain only at the level of theory. The result for our society is a situation in which more and more of the important decisions about public life are turned over to experts, who focus on the narrowly technical aspects of a problem rather than seeing it in a larger context.

The notion of the hidden curriculum is a helpful one here. The unspoken practices of our educational institutions, along with the ways we treat one another and work together, may be a more powerful educative force than all of our carefully designed course outlines, lectures and reading lists. An abstract classical curriculum, disengaged from the community and focused upon the development of "reasonable men," implies to students that learning the skills of practice in a democracy is unnecessary. Students learn by example that the individual, private pursuit of knowledge "for its own sake" is sufficient. The structure and practices of our institutions cultivate in students the illusion that they are not part of society and are not citizens, and this illusion tends to persist after school is over (Bellah *et al*, 1982).

Donald Schon (1982, 1987) has developed an instructive alternative to the historical division between theory and practice in his study of professional practice and education. Schon describes what he calls the "positivist epistemology of practice" which:

"... holds that practitioners are instrumental problem solvers who select technical means best suited to particular purposes. Rigorous professional practitioners solve well-formed instrumental problems by applying theory and technique derived from systematic, preferably scientific knowledge." (1987, pp. 3,4)

The difficulty with this model is that it does not take into account the dilemmas of practice in the world:

"As we have come to see with increasing clarity over the last twenty or so years, the problems of real-world practice do not present themselves to practitioners as well-formed structures. Indeed, they tend not to present themselves as problems at all but as messy, indeterminate situations. Civil engineers, for example, know how to build roads suited to the conditions of particular sites and specifications. They draw on their knowledge of soil conditions, materials, and construction technologies to define grades, surfaces and dimensions. When they must decide what road to build, however, or whether to build it at all, their problem is not solvable by the application of technical knowledge, not even by the sophisticated techniques of decision theory. They face a complex and ill-defined melange of topographical, financial, economic, environmental, and political factors. If they are to get a well-formed problem matched to their familiar theories and techniques, they must construct it from the materials of a situation that is, to use John Dewey's term, 'problematic.' And the problem of problem setting is not well formed." (1987, p. 4)

Schon's example of a "public works" project to illustrate the complexity of connecting theoretical knowledge with practice is appropriate here. Our students need to be exposed to the "messiness" that Schon describes if they are not to be overwhelmed by either confusion or disillusionment when they seek to engage with their own communities. Democracy is an inherently messy process, and the current cynicism within our country about government and about public life in general makes exposure to these realities during the school years all the more important.

I have attempted to present a brief sketch of some of the most important contradictions in a strictly classical and abstract approach to civic education, along with some suggestions for their remedy. In fairness, I must now do the same with the experiential approach.

The Experiential Model and its Weaknesses

The first and most obvious danger of an exclusively experiential approach to civic education is that it easily lapses into a kind of instrumental "emptiness." At worst, means and methods become the central focus, and a reflective consideration of ends is dismissed as unimportant. In this potential concern with form over substance,

> "… method, process, manner, are preponderant over purposes and contents. Rationalization of means, standardization of form become centrally interesting. In making decisions, the mechanism matters more than the determination…. Not the content but the manner of the judgment matters: sincerity reigns. Similarly also in morals, the intention and the background of a deed, how it came about, is more regarded than the deed itself." (Brann, 1979, p. 139)

In a highly technical society such as our own, it is tempting to adopt such an approach.

With the instrumental approach as their modus operandi, students launch out into the community, ready to right various wrongs. Whether the problems be social injustice, environmental pollution, or the need for basic services, students may try to pursue their action without having done the hard work to understand the history and broader context of the issue they are pursuing: sincerity reigns. Like Don Quixote, they may dash headlong across the countryside, lunging at whatever windmills come into view.

There are obvious parallels here between the problem of instrumentalism and the nearly unanimous criticism of moral education as it has been practiced in recent years. These criticisms fault the current moral education as being almost entirely procedural and without any normative value content, limited to an exclusively individual and non-communal focus, and emphasizing abstract reason. When combined with an instrumental approach to practice, such a moral framework makes the landscape of public discussion about civic purposes an arid one indeed.

In a sense, this initial problem of instrumentalism is at the center of all of the subsequent criticisms of the experiential model of civic education. Thus the second critique of an exclusively experiential approach is that one simply presents things "as they are", accepting present arrangements as "fact" without questioning whether things might be different. The corrective that is required is not simply reflection on the situation at hand. What is needed is something both "higher" and "deeper" that links community service or efforts at social change on the one hand, with the important debates about what it means to be a person in community on the other — debates that began in the West with the birth of the Judaeo-Christian tradition and the writings of the Greek philosophers.

Without an imaginative vision of what we can be as a people and how we might live together in ways which are more just, more free, and more vital, we will continue to attack problems in a piecemeal fashion. Too often today, students feel hopeless about the prospects for their world, and remain passive in the face of this hopelessness. Vital action which is linked to the values which are brought to view in the classical texts would be a powerful antidote to this sense of hopelessness among students.

Here it seems important to state that the classical texts need to be allowed some space to stand on their own in order to fulfill this role, rather than becoming simply a means to serve the ends of particular social problems. R. S. Peters criticizes John Dewey for:

> "... admitting the importance of making the student aware of his cultural heritage, but only on the condition that he should be introduced to it in a way which stressed its relevance to present practical and social problems. This is understandable as said against unimaginative rote learning of classical textbooks, but, if taken seriously, is a good recipe for failing to understand what we have inherited. For it fails to take account of the degree of autonomy which some traditions of inquiry have from contemporary practical problems." (1981, pp. 80, 81)

We risk losing some of the wisdom available in a classical text if we attempt to make overly hasty or simplistic application of its themes to concrete situations.

A third danger of the experiential model is the loss of perspective which is possible in a narrowly focused action approach. One can become so intent upon the problems at hand that one loses awareness of the larger historical and contemporary forces which are acting upon the situation. This can lead to inappropriate action in the present and an inability on the part of the student to generalize from the present experience to subsequent ones.

A study of history can provide the perspective necessary for students to see that the contemporary events often share much in common with the experiences of those in other times and other places. Knowledge of past human reflection and activity within community helps the student to act more intelligently in the present. One of the weaknesses of the political activity of the 1960s was a lack of historical perspective, a kind of disconnection from what had gone before. When the splendid new society that activists envisioned did not appear quickly, many of the participants in the movement for change became easily disillusioned.

This lack of perspective can also take the form of a lack of self-awareness. While experience in public life can be both broadening and liberating, it can also play the role of reinforcing pre-existing prejudices and narrowness. Action alone has no special virtue, unless it is accompanied by the kind of "stepping back" from oneself that carefully guided reflection on the human dilemma might provide.

Addressing the Dilemma

What can be done to counter the limitations of either of these approaches to education when they are used alone? I would submit that civic education, the education of students to become critical and sensitive participants in public life, can be effectively accomplished only through a marriage of these two disparate traditions. Not only must academic learning be complemented by action, but active learning within the public sphere must be connected to an exploration of the concepts and traditions that underlie democracy. In this case, the dichotomy often presented between a "classical" and a "relevant" education is false. Classical texts and their concepts of freedom, rights, justice and community are illuminated for the student by the vividness of concrete experiences. Experience which is grounded in tradition and enriched by its wisdom can have a more significant impact.

The diagnosis presented here requires a more specific proposal for treatment. I suggest that the first step toward the renewal of our commitment to civic education is the renewal of civic community within the academy. If civic education has taken place in disconnected pieces, it becomes clear that those pieces must be brought together through the reconstruction of civic community within the academy. Given the battles over turf that are common in many institutions today, this may seem like a hopelessly idealistic proposal. And yet, as mentioned earlier, the hidden curriculum of institutional culture may speak more loudly than all of the methods and great ideas we present to students about the theme of civic participation.

Those of us who work in educational institutions are subject to the same forces that have withered civic community in the larger society, and we will have to exert a concentrated effort to overcome these barriers. These efforts must take place across three areas in which our educational institutions are presently divided.

First, civic community must be nurtured across the disciplines. Human society is multi-dimensional, and an overly narrow disciplinary focus requires that one look at society from a very limited perspective. This prevents us from having a coherent sense of the "big picture." Thus the fragmentation of the disciplines works against efforts to examine or become involved in public life. Effective civic learning will require creative integration of the disciplines, beyond "inter-disciplinary" courses in which the subject areas are taught alongside one another, and towards courses which seek to present public life in all of its complexity.

Second, civic community must be nurtured between educators who pursue the "classical" and those who follow the "experiential" model. As I have already stated, the development of connections between these groups presents rich possibilities for civic education. At the same time, forming such a community may be one of the most difficult challenges. Our differing philosophies and styles have kept us in separate worlds, and we must each begin to learn the language of the others, as well as to seek out the common goals that we share.

Third, civic community must be nurtured between these two groups of educators and the resource people in the larger community who can contribute to students' learning. We need to make use of the knowledge of community members who care about civic education and who can help students understand the practical realities of public life. Again there can be a process of mutual enrichment: faculty and students can provide the fresh view of those outside the system, as well as infusing public life with debate about foundational ideas.

Such changes are more easily prescribed than undertaken. They will require a movement on the part of all involved — faculty, campus community service staff, and people in the community — towards cooperation with those groups with whom they have not ordinarily joined forces. This also means a willingness to recognize our mutual dependence in order to achieve the shared goal of helping students to become caring and reflective participants in public life. In strengthening these relationships, our institutions might in a small way provide a model for what we hope to encourage in our students.

William Sullivan (1982) has written eloquently about the need for a renewal of civic philosophy in our country. His words describe both the importance of the experience of civic participation, as well as the necessity of reflection on that experience. In this he provides a fitting conclusion to this discussion:

> Awareness of the interdependency of citizens and groups is basic to the civic vision because it enlightens and challenges these disparate parties about their mutual relations. The citizen comes to know who he is by understanding the web of social relations surrounding him. This realization is not only cognitive, it requires experience, finding one's way about and thus coming to know, in practice, who one is.
>
> However, it is important to see that the civic tradition does not simply romanticize public participation. The dangers of misguided, fanatical, and irresponsible civic involvement have been well documented, and some of the most eloquent warnings of those dangers have come from the classical theorists of citizenship. The point, rather, is that the notion of involved concern within an interdependent community provides the image for a collective enterprise in self-transformation. The civic ideal is thus alluring and disquieting, at once delicately fragile and morally consuming in the responsibility it demands. (pp. 158-159)

Steve Schultz is Director of Westmont College's Urban Program in San Francisco. He chairs the publications committee of the National Society for Internships and Experiential Education and serves on the Board of Directors.

References

Andolsen, Barbara Hilkert, *et al*, eds., *Women's Consciousness, Women's Conscience: A Reader in Feminist Ethics*, Winston Press, 1985.

Battistoni, Richard M., *Public Schooling and the Education of Democratic Citizens*, University Press of Mississippi, 1985.

Belenky, Mary Field, Blythe McVicker Clinchy, Nancy Rule Goldberger, and Jill Mattuck Tarule, *Women's Ways of Knowing: The Development of Self, Voice, and Mind*, Basic Books, Inc., 1986.

Bloom, Alan, *The Closing of the American Mind: How Higher Education Has Failed Democracy and Impoverished the Souls of Today's Students*, Simon and Schuster, 1987.

Boyer, Ernest, and Fred Hechinger, *Higher Learning in the Nation's Service*, Carnegie Foundation for the Advancement of Teaching, 1981.

Boyer, Ernest, *College: The Undergraduate Experience in America*, Harper and Row, 1987.

Brann, Eva, *Paradoxes of Education in a Republic*, University of Chicago Press, 1979.

Butts, R. Freeman, *The Revival of Civic Learning: A Rationale for Citizenship Education in American Schools*, Phi Delta Kappa Educational Foundation, 1980.

Cooper, David E., ed., *Education, Values and Mind: Essays for R. S. Peters*, Routledge and Kegan Paul (London), 1986.

Dewey, John, *Democracy and Education*, Macmillan, 1957.

Dewey, John, *Experience and Education*, Macmillan, 1974.

Dewey, John, *The Public and Its Problems*, The Swallow Press, Inc., 1954.

Dewey, John, *The Quest for Certainty: A Study of the Relation Between Knowledge and Action*, G. P. Putnam's Sons, 1929.

Education for Responsible Citizenship: The Report of the National Task Force on Citizenship Education, McGraw-Hill, 1977.

Gilligan, Carol, *In a Different Voice: Psychological Theory and Women's Development*, Harvard University Press, 1982.

Giroux, Henry, *Theory and Resistance in Education: A Pedagogy for the Opposition*, Bergin and Garvey Publishers, Inc., 1983.

Ignatieff, Michael, *The Needs of Strangers: An Essay on Privacy, Solidarity, and the Politics of Being Human*, Viking Penguin Inc., 1985.

Janowitz, Morris, *The Reconstruction of Patriotism: Education for Civic Consciousness*, University of Chicago Press, 1983.

Katz, Joseph, *et al*, *A New Vitality in General Education: Planning, Teaching, and Supporting Effective Liberal Learning*, Association of American Colleges, Washington, D.C. 1988.

Keller, Evelyn Fox, *Reflections on Gender and Science*, Yale University Press, 1985.

Ketcham, Ralph, *Individualism and Public Life: A Modern Dilemma*, Basil Blackwell Limited, 1987.

Mathews, David, "Civic Intelligence," *Social Education*, Vol. 48, November-December 1985, pp. 678-681.

Merton, Thomas, *Conjectures of a Guilty Bystander*, Doubleday, Inc., 1968.

Morrill, Richard, "Educating for Democratic Values," *Liberal Education*, Vol. 68, 1982, pp. 365-376.

Murchland, Bernard, "The Eclipse of the Liberal Arts," *Change*, Vol. 8, November 1976, pp. 22-26.

Noddings, Nell, *Caring: A Feminine Approach to Ethics and Moral Education*, University of California Press, 1984.

Newman, Frank, *Higher Learning and the American Resurgence*, Carnegie Foundation for the Advancement of Teaching, 1985.

O'Hare, Padraic, ed., *Education for Peace and Justice*, Harper and Row, 1983.

On the Uses of the Humanities: Vision and Application, The Hastings Center, New York, 1984.

Palmer, Parker J., *The Company of Strangers: Christians and the Renewal of America's Public Life*, Crossroad, 1981.

Palmer, Parker J., *To Know As We Are Known: A Spirituality of Education*, Harper and Row, 1983.

Palmer, Parker J., "Community, Conflict, and Ways of Knowing," *Change*, Vol. 19, September/October 1987, pp. 20-25.

Peters, R. S., ed., *John Dewey Reconsidered*, Routledge and Kegan Paul (London), 1977.

Peters, R. S., *Essays on Educators*, George Allen and Unwin, Limited, 1981.

Robb, Carol S., "A Framework for Feminist Ethics" in *Women's Consciousness, Women's Conscience: A Reader in Feminist Ethics*, Barbara Hilkert Andolsen, *et al*, eds., Winston Press, 1985.

Schon, Donald, *Educating the Reflective Practitioner*, Jossey-Bass, Inc., 1987.

Schon, Donald, *The Reflective Practitioner: How Professionals Think in Action*, Basic Books, 1983.

Shor, Ira, *Critical Teaching and Everyday Life*, South End Press, 1980.

Sloan, Douglas, ed., *Education and Values*, Teacher's College Press, 1980.

Soltis, Jonas F., ed., *Philosophy and Education: Eightieth Yearbook of the National Society for the Study of Education*, University of Chicago Press, 1981.

Sullivan, William M., *Reconstructing Public Philosophy*, University of California Press, 1982.

Whitehead, Alfred North, *The Aims of Education*, The Macmillan Company, 1929.

Developing a Capacity for Civic Judgment

Suzanne W. Morse

Suzanne Morse explores the critical role of civic judgment in our society and how the capacity for civic judgment can be developed. Civic judgment goes beyond good, sound thinking. It requires the ability to view the same problem from another's perspective through imagination, the ability to reflect on one's experiences and actions, the courage to act, respect for diversity and plurality, and "practical wisdom." All of these require active engagement in issues and problems in concert with others. The challenge for educators, both inside and outside the classroom, has never been greater — or more essential for our very survival.

RECENT POLITICAL ACTIONS have highlighted the topic of judgment in the public arena. When the news revealed that Oliver North participated in and ignored the law in the Iran-Contra deal, his judgment was questioned by some. The revelation that Lloyd Bentsen shared his political knowledge in exchange for pricey breakfasts cast doubt on his ability to judge the appropriateness of a situation despite its legality. When George Bush selected the less experienced Dan Quayle from the list of potential running mates, some debated his judgment in the selection. These most recent headline situations illustrate the importance we place on a leader's ability to judge a particular situation given a general set of rules or criteria.

Interest in judgment, especially public judgment and the ways in which that judgment can be exercised for the collective good, took on new dimensions after World War II. As the knowledge of the massacre of six million Jews became public, the horrified world questioned how the Holocaust could have happened. The Adolph Eichmann war crimes trial, which the philosopher Hannah Arendt reported and the world watched, exemplified in a clear, but shocking way the outer limits of a lack of judgment. Eichmann followed the orders and planned the strategy that killed millions of Jews and recognized no moral responsibility to judge on his own. Unfortunately, the orders handed to Eichmann were inhumane, immoral, and savage; yet he did not exercise thinking or judgment on that particular human situation beyond the instructions he was given. At his trial, Eichmann admitted that he had been a part of one of the worst crimes against humanity in history, yet he said had he not obeyed the orders, his conscience would have bothered him.

Having the ability to judge and act on our common circumstances is fundamental to a healthy republic. With the issues facing society becoming more complex technically as well as socially — and with a growing need for the American public to act responsibly on critical national and international issues — it is important to revisit this necessary political skill of judgment and determine how an individual citizen comes to have it and exercise it.

Oscar Wilde's comment that "radical politics takes too many evenings" may speak also to the waning interest in taking the time to participate actively in civic life. The proposition that citizens can develop a public sense by osmosis, course sequences, or just by living day to day is not enough. As educators, it is important to consider ways that the total college, university, or school community might address this lack of emphasis, the growing concern about the alienation of the next generation of citizen leaders, and the development of civic skills, like judgment, that are so essential to democratic life.

The very real possibility that students might excel in completing high school and college but still lack the ability to judge issues or situations in the larger civic sense raises concern. The primary question for this discussion is this: How is civic judgment developed? The experiential education and service learning movement has added new opportunities and access for students to develop the skills needed for productive civic lives and to reflect on their experiences in meaningful ways. If Kant was correct that judgment can be practiced only and not taught, then it is important to consider those situations and structures that would allow the *praxis*.

Defining Judgment

Judgment is generally thought of as a decision based on certain data or rules. Actually, the term is much more complex. Judgment may have an end — to act or not to act — but it is also a process that can be used when there are no hard or fast rules that point to clear-cut solutions to a problem. It is the ability to think about the particular situation with consideration to all affected parties.

Judgment has sometimes been regarded as something private, only possessed by individuals for their own use: "He has good judgment." However, individuals cannot have it alone even in very personal matters. The judging process requires that others are recognized and considered in the process of thought and action; exercising judgment is not a solo activity. Hannah Arendt said that the kind of thinking that leads to judging allows individuals to lessen their deference to rules and regulations and permits the judging of a particular situation from anticipated conversation with others: "We must have the capacity to accept the human condition of plurality .... judgment (or taste) decides not only how the world will look, but who belongs together in it."[1] Judgment then is the capacity to think with others about collective lives and actions. It goes beyond individual needs toward consideration of common goals. It requires the ability to view particular situations from many perspectives. In his *Critique of Judgment*, Immanuel Kant asserted that there is a need for a different way of thinking; we must "think in the place of everybody else." He called this the "enlarged mentality" (*eine erweiterte Denkungsart.*)[2] Hannah Arendt called this a prerequisite for judging and adapts Kant's view of it.[3]

It can be said that Adolph Eichmann lacked humane judgment because of his primary role in the deaths, but also because of the manner in which he made his decisions. Eichmann acted out of personal ambition, thought of self, and blind complicity. He lacked the capacity to think and thus to judge. Arendt called Eichmann thoughtless. She contended that thinking is one of the conditions that causes people to abstain from evil. Arendt held "that a person's ability to say 'this is right' or 'this is wrong' in the world presupposes that he has stopped to think, felt the 'wind of thought'!" Thoughtlessness is the absence of an internal dialogue. In Arendt's view, a thoughtless person who commits evil is different from a wicked person. To be wicked means overcoming the "thinking" partner, silencing all objections. Thoughtlessness means hearing no internal objection.[4] In a situation where "everyone is swept away unthinkingly by what everybody else says and believes in, a thinking person, who may otherwise be inconspicuous, is conspicuous as a non-participant or resister."[5] This is not to say that Eichmann had no judgment in other realms of his life, but rather that he could not identify those particulars that would be evident to any normal, civilized, morally sighted, judging person. He had a "blindness to the human dimension of things."[6]

In reporting the Eichmann trial, Hannah Arendt shocked many with her term "banality of evil." She interpreted Eichmann and others like him as thoughtless individuals without the capacity to reflect on the awesomeness of their deeds, not human monsters. This impression was reinforced by an editorial writer for *Commonweal* who wrote:

> Eichmann did not have, we must recognize, a queer or esoteric set of values, some fantastic, deranged view of the universe. He seems to have lived, like the rest of us, on clichés and popular pieties: that one must be loyal to one's superiors, that patriotism excuses many excesses, that only a few men are responsible for the crimes of many, that the individual can do very little.[7]

Many critics of Arendt's reporting wanted the assurance that Eichmann was a monster and that his actions went beyond complicity to an evil core that was inconceivable to most other humans. The magnitude of Eichmann's crimes overshadowed the discussion of how he thought or acted and how much of those same methods others may share.

While the Eichmann example is the extreme of what not to do, there are thousands of cases that are positive examples of the process. Two recent books on the World War II period, *The Altruistic Personality* by Samuel P. Oliner and Pearl M. Oliner and *The Rescue of the Danish Jews*, edited by Leo Goldberger, chronicle the efforts of non-Jews who risked their own lives to aid in the escape of their Jewish neighbors. It is estimated that as many as 500,000 Jewish lives were saved through the efforts of these people — the same period in history, but very different responses. In literature, Shakespeare's King John shows the judging process with very different results. While trying to maintain control of his kingdom in England, *King John* decides the heir apparent, his young nephew, Arthur, must die. He orders his loyal servant, Hubert, to perform the fatal deed. Hubert accepts the assignment with honor and obedience: "Anything, my Lord." But as Hubert "thinks" about the task and is in conversation with the young Arthur, he realizes that he cannot perform the inhumane order set before him. He exercises judgment and disobeys his King.

Judgment is exercised on the specifics of a particular situation. It requires a thinking process which embraces plurality and allows the individual to imagine not only the consequences of actions and thoughts, but also the views of others through internal dialogue. Arendt suggested that the lesson drawn may be that in extreme situations, it is the questioners that are the most valuable to society:

the thinkers rather than those who adhere to conventional moral norms.[8]

Developing Civic Judgment

A democratic society is built on its ability to act collectively. Public judgment is required because politics is about the uncertainties that surround public issues. Because judgment implies that what we can know together as citizens we cannot know alone, it is imperative that educators emphasize and expose students to the values of diversity, pluralism, and the need to find common interests. But judgment is more than good, sound thinking. Arendt provided a helpful distinction between what she called "judging insight and speculative thought." Insight, she contended, is based on common sense. "This 'good sense' discloses to us the nature of the world insofar as it is a common world .... Judging is one, if not the most important, activity in which this sharing-the-world-with-others comes to pass."[9]

Civic judgment requires creativity and imagination. Michael Denneny observed that judgment, in Arendt's view, is the ability to view the same problem from another's perspective through imagination: "We are able to put ourselves in the other's position and see, not as he sees, but how it looks to us from his point of view."[10] Arendt said that "While reason requires that I be together with myself in the conscious dialogue called thinking and the will requires that I be identical to myself, only judgment requires that I be together with my fellow man."[11] Thus, for the capacity for judgment to be learned, the use of the imagination is needed.

While the thinking process does not determine or prevent action in and of itself, it too is a necessary prerequisite for judgment and is therefore indirectly related to the morality of actions. When developing the capacity for judgment, the capacity for thinking and reflection on the thinking must be included.[12] Arendt made an important distinction between the deeds of the thinker and the non-thinker. She said the non-thinkers can live with themselves as murderers, whereas the thinker will not be able to. Because thoughtlessness is defined as lack of internal dialogue, the non-thinker or evil-doer is distinct from a wicked person insofar as there are not objections raised because there is no internal dialogue. The wicked person must overcome the objections raised in internal dialogue.

The evolution of thinking and judging is the courage to act. Elizabeth Minnich contends that judgment is necessary "when we cannot have certainty because we are bridging realms that cannot be reduced to each other."[13] Because of this uncertainty, judgment requires courage. This kind of courage was exemplified in the autobiography of Anne Moody, a young, poor, Black student at Tougaloo College in the 1960s. Despite her parents' fears and the fact that prejudice and oppression were a part of life in Jackson, Mississippi, Moody decided to assume her human rights. She participated in the first sit-in in a Jackson Woolworth's store. When refused service at a lunch counter, Moody and her companions refused to leave until served. Though they were threatened, harassed, and beaten, still they refused to leave. Moody could not have known that her action would be one of the first of many in a successful cause, and that is why her action required judgment and courage. In the crisis in South Africa, names like Nelson Mandela, Bishop Tutu, and Alan Paton remind us of those with judgment *and* the courage to act. Aristotle wrote that the ultimate human virtue, *phronesis*, combined judgment and good practice or *praxis*. *Phronesis* becomes judgment that is embodied in action. "If I see what the situation requires but am unable to bring myself to act in a manner befitting my understanding, I possess judgment, but not *phronesis*."[14]

In order to develop the capacity to judge, a person must exercise the faculties necessary for judgment. These include thinking, tolerance of plurality, imagination, practical wisdom, and good practice. These must be learned in concert with others, though according to Kant, a stand-in (if not a substitute) for experience is examples. Use of examples involves two considerations according to Ruel Tyson: "First, examples render the consequence of judgment in action; second, examples themselves, as Kant suggests, are schools for judgment."[15]

Actual experience and examples can be promoted on campus through cooperative work/education programs, campus government, service-learning programs, and community forums. These experiences can teach students about new ways to think about politics: shared interests *not* special interests. They can promote the important civic skills of talk and dialogue and show students how to work with others to move from discussion to action. Students can learn about ways to understand different points of view and values. In addition, the campus can be a microcosm of civic life where students, faculty, and administration work in community toward common goals. Classrooms, faculty meetings, and interaction between "town and gown" can be used to foster these civic skills. The practice, however, must have an epistemological grounding to allow students to reflect on what they have seen and experienced. Reflections on their experiences, on teaching methods, and on subject matter begin to take students beyond rote learning to the integration of learning and life.

Conclusion

The increasing pressures on today's society demand that citizens understand and respect the importance of diversity and choice. Citizens are too often relied on for "opinions" about a particular public issue or piece of legislation and not asked to think or judge beyond a special or personal interest. The process of thinking together with fellow citizens on difficult political problems is key to a healthy civic life. However, understanding the importance of judgment in developing civic responsibility is a process, not an end. Judgment is necessary for a fruitful civic journey, but it has limitations that students and others should consider.

First, judgments can be wrong, given the complexity of issues, range of options, and lack of knowledge. Minnich and others contend that "new knowledge" has an impact on judgments. The reluctant acceptance of women's or cultural scholarship in some areas illustrates how judgments of what is "good," "right," and "academic" are based on a wide array of values, preconceived notions of "what is," and, frightfully, individual prejudices. New knowledge makes available more particulars on which to judge, and it also can redefine the framework by challenging the value systems that were thought firmly in place.[16] Individuals insulate (and limit) themselves because of preconceived notions. Knowledge, even expert knowledge, is not enough. According to Pitkin and Shumer:

> Knowledge alone is never enough. The political question is what we are to do; knowledge can only tell us how things are, how they work, while a political resolution always depends on what we, as a community, want and think right. And those questions have no technical answer; they require collective deliberation and decision.[17]

Second, public decisions which reflect the plurality and diversity which Arendt and others called necessary could bring us to the lowest common denominator. Unless choices reflect the judgment that comes from citizen interaction and deliberation, then decisions could be reduced to a series of trade-offs between special interests, with everybody getting a small slice of the pie.

Third, the notion of dealing with particulars may lead us to have no absolutes. One could argue that laws and policies of government are the anchors for society and that dealing with "particulars" leads to inequities, immoral exceptions, etc. This, too, misses the point because judgment is predicated on enlarged thinking that includes others — and that allows for judgment that is governed by, but not dominated by, general principles.

Finally, political or civic judgment does not mean political agreement. Arendt said that while rational beings together can develop political judgment, there is nothing that would lead us to think that this would result in a single truth.[18] Margaret Canovan said, in interpreting Arendt, that she insisted that action occurs always among individuals who are diverse, whose ideas and endeavors collide and become entangled with one another.[19] Politics are about uncertainty. There should be differences in thought. Arendt might have agreed with political scientist Benjamin Barber when he said that we must "inform the discretion and enlarge the political experience of an active citizenry ... a citizenry in action, capable of thinking as a 'we' in the name of public good."[20]

The challenge for educators is great. Students are enrolled for a relatively short time. They come to institutions from diverse backgrounds with all kinds of values, insights, and expectations. John Dewey said "democracy has to be born anew every generation, and education is the midwife."[21] Creating a working model both in and out of the classroom that allows students to confront choices, differences, new environments, and new perspectives is the first step in the process. Learning in and out of the classroom can be the judging laboratory for students to learn about plurality, shared values, the costs of choices and necessary trade-offs, and the empowerment of thinking and acting for the higher good in concert with their fellow citizens.

Suzanne W. Morse is Director of Programs at the Kettering Foundation in Dayton, Ohio.

Footnotes

[1] Hannah Arendt, *Between Past and Future*, The Viking Press, 1968, p. 223.

[2] Ibid., p. 220.

[3] George Kateb, *Hannah Arendt: Politics, Conscience, Evil*, Rowman and Allenheld, 1983, p. 38.

[4] Elisabeth Young-Bruehl, "Reflections on Hannah Arendt's *The Life of the Mind*," *Political Theory*, Vol. 10, No. 2, May 1982, pp. 279-80.

[5] Hannah Arendt, *The Life of the Mind*, p. 192.

[6] Ronald Beiner, *Political Judgment*, University of Chicago Press, 1983, p. 156.

[7] *The Commonweal*, Vol. LXXVI, No. 12, June 15, 1962.

[8] Beiner, pp. 161-164.

[9] Michael Denneny, "The Privilege of Ourselves: Hannah Arendt on Judgment" in *Hannah Arendt: The Recovery of the Public World*, edited by Melvyn A. Hill, St. Martin's Press, 1979, p. 264.

[10] Ibid., p. 264.

[11] Ibid., pp. 251-2.

[12] Young-Bruehl, p. 292.

[13] Elizabeth Minnich, "New Knowledge," Address at Association of American Colleges meeting, January 1987.

[14] Beiner, p. 72.

[15] Ruel W. Tyson, Jr., "Teaching Political Education," *The Civic Arts Review*, Vol. 1, No. 1, Summer 1988, p. 12.

[16] Minnich, op. cit.

[17] Hannah F. Pitkin and Sara H. Shumer, "On Participation," *Democracy*, Vol. 2, Fall 1982, p. 52.

[18] Beiner, p. 139.

[19] Margaret Canavon, "Arendt, Rousseau, and Human Plurality in Politics," *The Journal of Politics*, Vol. 45, No. 2, May 1983.

[20] Benjamin Barber, "The Politics of Judgment," *Puritan*, Fall 1985, p. 135.

[21] Merle Curti, *The Social Ideas of American Educators*, New and Revised Edition, No. 105, 1965.

Learning Citizenship Through Practice

Fred M. Newmann

Noted researcher Fred Newmann summarizes the current needs in citizenship education and concludes that direct practice through experiential learning opportunities is an essential component. Reprinted with permission from National Civic Review, *National Civic League, Vol. 76, No. 4, pp. 286-287.*

INFORMED OBSERVERS WHO RUN the gamut of the political spectrum from the Right to the Left, think citizen education needs reform. Why all the fuss?

Functionally speaking, and in spite of disappointment with the civic understanding and participation displayed by youth and adults, the U.S. system of democratic governance works remarkably well. Institutions carry on with their work; citizens generally pay taxes and obey the laws; political leadership changes without violence or social instability; and, compared to many other nations, due process of law and civil liberties are respected.

This is not to endorse all outcomes of the U.S. political and economic system. Public life is scarred by indignities and injustices, particularly the oppression of minorities and the poor, destruction of the natural environment, drug dependency, crime, and public officials who violate the public trust. Whether such problems can be attributed to deficiencies in *citizen education*, however, and whether their solution rests with improved citizen education *in schools*, is an open question.... and the possibilities of new, more meaningful expressions of consent of the governed need to be studied.

Learning Citizenship Through Practice. Disciplined study of citizenship issues is badly needed, but this must be informed by efforts to *practice* citizenship. Direct participation is necessary not only to motivate students and to maximize retention and transfer, but to gain valuable knowledge of the subject of citizenship as well. Because we have little authoritative knowledge on how to participate productively in self-governance, dispute resolution, and the formation of public policy, we need to study the experiences of students and others. Citizenship should become a laboratory subject where mastery is built in part through formal study of previously accumulated knowledge but also by reflecting upon actual interaction with the issues and people of civic life.

Successful models of citizen participation have been developed. Community service programs offer opportunities to assist others in nursing homes, hospitals, day care centers, schools, and other service agencies. Mock trials, the model United Nations, and other simulations provide training in dispute resolution, political compromise, and complex decisionmaking. Student governments give students real opportunity to exercise power in conjunction with faculty and the school administration and offer legislative, executive, and judicial experience, as well as public responsibility for collective decisions. Student involvement in political campaigns and social advocacy in the community beyond the school nurture skills of adult interaction and coping with the satisfactions and frustrations of working toward the public good. To succeed in these activities, students must often learn about specific issues and institutions, communicate effectively orally and in writing, and accept personal responsibility for their actions.

The feasibility and success of these model programs has been documented. They have empowered and educated students at minimal cost and without major negative consequences. Although concerns that such programs detract from basic skills education and present insurmountable logistical obstacles have been addressed, few schools have adopted new models. The persuasive rationale for these programs and their records of success lead one to conclude that the schools' reluctance is probably grounded in a more fundamental objection to education for active citizenship. Experiential learning alone is insufficient but without it, other efforts to revive civic learning will at best waste the time of students and teachers; at worst, they increase cynicism and disinterest in public life.

In Conclusion. This analysis began with the claim that citizenship education in schools has failed to empower most of us to participate productively in civic life and that reforms such as newly required civics courses or standardized exams on the Constitution offer no solution. Instead, substantial rethinking of the concept of citizenship education is needed. The first step is to identify fundamental issues of citizenship in the modern United States that are neglected in educational programs. We need more explicit deliberation of three competing perspectives: cultural induction, emancipation, and cynical realism. Whatever content may be included in the curriculum, we must concentrate more on the central issues of pluralism, distributive justice, individual interests and collective responsibility, and meaningful participation. Finally, the study of citizenship must rely significantly upon laboratory experience and direct practice. The approaches outlined here build on previous work in the field, but they are only a beginning and will lead to improved practice only if teachers receive support to struggle with these issues and to generate commitment to programs that they devise.

_____

Fred M. Newmann is director of the National Center on Effective Secondary Schools and professor of curriculum and instruction at the University of Wisconsin.

Community Service and Civic Literacy

William J. Cirone

A school superintendent calls on schools to use community service experiences to help students develop the skills they need to participate in a democratic society. Reprinted with permission from "Community Service: A Bridge to Learning," special issue of the Community Education Journal *edited by John Formy-Duval and Ellen Voland, National Community Education Association, Alexandria, Virginia, Vol. XV, No. 1, October 1987, pp. 18-19.*

IN A SPEECH urging students at Stanford University to get involved in community service, John W. Gardner, former Secretary of Health, Education and Welfare and author of *Self-Renewal*, asked, "Why bother?"

"For two reasons," he replied to his own question. "To give your life meaning and to discharge your obligation to society."

The notion that the citizen has an obligation to reach beyond himself is ingrained in the American value system. As an educator, I believe that our schools not only can, but must, provide opportunities for young people to derive the benefits that come from service to the community. The concept of community service is integral to the notion of civic literacy. Simply stated, civic literacy encompasses the knowledge, skills, and values necessary for participation in a democratic society. And high school community service provides incomparable hands-on teaching opportunities in civic literacy.

"Meism" is an alarming phenomenon in the light of the complex social, economic, technical, moral, and political issues today's students will face tomorrow: the control of nuclear weapons, protection of our environment, integration of a growing minority population, control of genetic engineering, and a changing world economy. If ever there was a time for an informed and involved public, that time is now. It seems to me that educational institutions have no choice but to refocus their energies on developing civic literacy in the young.

Education, in its fullest sense, must include the development of ethical behavior, a sense of civic responsibility, and concern for others. Education can no longer attempt to be value-neutral; it must teach those values that are held in common by our citizens, and that are a part of the foundation of our democratic way of life.

There is a growing consensus, across the political spectrum, about this. Norman Lear, president of People for the American Way; Terrel Bell, former U. S. Secretary of Education; Bill Honig, California Superintendent of Education; Floretta Dukes McKenzie, Washington, D. C., Superintendent of Schools; and Jeane Kirkpatrick, former UN ambassador — to name just a few — have all called upon schools to rededicate themselves to the teaching of civic virtues. The question, really, is how?

Civic education can be improved in at least three ways:

1.   By providing students with the basic knowledge they need about civics and history.

2.   By teaching students commonly agreed-upon civic values and developing in them a sense of civic-mindedness.

3.   By helping students develop the skills they need to participate in a democratic society.

Basic knowledge about civics and history is a prerequisite to developing a set of civic values. Knowledge must go hand-in-hand with, and be the foundation for, those values we can surely agree upon: justice, freedom, equality, truth, authority, respect for persons and property, and personal responsibility for the common good.

But knowledge and values are not enough. We must also teach our young people the skills they need to participate in a democracy. They need critical-thinking skills, so they can process, analyze, evaluate, interpret, and apply the mass of information available to them; consensus-building and bargaining skills; and conflict-management and citizen-participation skills. All of these can be taught.

One way of learning is through voluntary service, which is in the best American tradition. In 1984, California State Senator Gary Hart introduced state legislation that would have established a High School Community Service Program. Under the proposed program, the state would provide funding to help high schools establish voluntary community service programs; students would work a prescribed number of supervised hours serving the community and would receive high school credit for it. In the words of Senator Hart's bill, "Providing service in the community is an effective way for all pupils to acquire a sense of usefulness and contribution to society, as well as the opportunity to develop and utilize citizenship skills ... and to acquire the experience necessary to make effective career, education, and character choices while also responding to the needs of others."

The bill passed both houses of the California legislature but, unfortunately, was vetoed by the governor. Whether the legislation is revived in a subsequent legislative session or not, I think we will have to, as a nation, find some way to encourage community service, since it is, in my opinion, the best possible training for responsible citizenship. The need for teaching civic literacy and incorporating community service into the curriculum is clear, and the opportunities are available. What a splendid way to help our young people, in John Gardner's words, give their lives meaning and discharge their obligations to society.

Bill Cirone, a community educator and long-time advocate of service learning, is Superintendent of Schools for Santa Barbara County in California.

The Obligation of Citizenship

Alonzo A. Crim

Atlanta's former School Superintendent describes Atlanta Pub-lic Schools' required service program, designed to enhance stu-dents' understanding of the obligations of a good citizen. Re-printed with permission from "Community Service: A Bridge to Learning," special issue of the Community Education Journal *edited by John Formy-Duval and Ellen Voland, National Com-munity Education Association, Alexandria, Virginia, Vol. XV, No. 1, October 1987, pp. 18-19.*

THE ATLANTA SCHOOL SYSTEM is committed to three goals for students: (1) preparation for lifelong learning; (2) preparation for gainful employment; and (3) education for citizenship.

Our students have made tremendous gains in basic skills achievement. The Atlanta Partnership of Business and Education, our vocational education programs, and other initiatives have re-sulted in meaningful job opportunities for students, both before and after graduation. And citizenship education has been woven into the fabric of instruction across several disciplines.

In an effort to enhance students' understanding of the obliga-tions of a good citizen, the Atlanta Board of Education approved a course, "Duties to the Community," as a requisite for graduation beginning with the class of 1988. Incoming ninth grade students will be expected to contribute 75 hours of unpaid volunteer service in approved agencies under the supervision of school staff. These hours may be accumulated in grades 9, 10, or 11. Additionally, an acceptable essay or journal must be written and accepted by the Language Arts Department. Once the 75 hours have been com-pleted and the essay or journal accepted, the student receives one semester of credit for the Duties to the Community course.

Our community service requirement emphasizes what a stu-dent can do to help others. It provides students with opportunities for responsible, productive, supervised volunteer service. Service agencies such as character-building organizations, hospitals, churches, child care centers, and schools are potential learning laboratories. Under the direction of school staff, students and parents are thoroughly informed of the requirements. Students bring to this assignment their concern, motivation, and enormous energy. Our challenge is to channel these assets into well-organized volunteer programs that are mutually beneficial to students and the community.

In addition to academic credit, students gain first-hand experience in seeing their actions count. They have the opportunity to get to know and relate to the needs of people of various ages and backgrounds. Volunteer service also gives them a first-hand look at how their community works. They learn how problems arise, what steps can realistically be taken toward their solution, and their own roles in solving them. Volunteering gives them opportunities to test and extend their interests, skills, and talents. Their education becomes more relevant, their contributions validated, and their sense of citizenship enhanced.

Some students combine volunteer service with exploration of career interests. One young man, interested in working in a youth service organization, served as a counselor in a Boys Club. Students who are interested in education have served as tutors in church-sponsored enrichment programs or assisted in media centers in their own schools.

Students learn skills and attitudes that stand them in good stead when they accept paid employment.

Asa Hilliard, Callaway Professor of Urban Education at Georgia State University, says of high school community service: "Schools that have the most meaning are those that realize they are unable to function without being in touch with their communities."

Alonzo A. Crim was Superintendent of Atlanta Public Schools from 1973 to 1988. He is now the Benjamin E. Mays Professor of Urban Educational Leadership at Georgia State University.

Part II

Rationales and Theories for Combining Service and Learning:

Intellectual Development

Service: A Pathway to Knowledge

Diane Hedin and Dan Conrad

A corporate executive and a high school teacher outline the educational benefits of high school community service programs and the elements necessary for these benefits to be realized. Words from young people tell the story. Reprinted with permission from "Community Service: A Bridge to Learning," a special issue of the Community Education Journal *edited by John Formy-Duval and Ellen Voland, National Community Education Association, Alexandria, Virginia, Vol. XV, No. 1, October 1987, pp. 10-14.*

THE MOST IMPORTANT question for anyone planning to start a high school community service program is: what is the student likely to get out of it, or how will he or she be different as a result of having been a volunteer?

We should note, at the outset, that we are advocates of youth community service. Our enthusiasm is based on more than 15 years of experience in running service programs, doing research and evaluating their impact, and teaching courses and conducting workshops on experiential education for teachers, principals, and youth workers.

It is alternately amusing and irksome to see touted as "new" an education idea that has had a respected place in American educational theory and practice at least since the turn of the century. We needn't recount its history here except to note that it *has* a history and a body of research; claims about its efficacy are grounded on more than speculation or wishful thinking. What community service can accomplish is solidly established. The real issue is whether schools want to achieve what service programs can deliver.

What students will get from a community service program depends, of course, on its quality. A good program can be defined very simply as one in which the student plays a significant role in working with others to perform tasks that both the young person and the community regard as worthwhile and needed. Further, a good program supports the service activities with a clear and explicit curriculum that challenges students to think about and reflect on the meaning of their volunteer experiences.

Both elements are critical, but the foundation is the experience itself, what the students actually do. There is a vast array of volunteer tasks that can provide a stimulus for learning. The examples that follow illustrate the kinds of things young people in community services are doing every day (Conrad and Hedin, 1987).

At 7:00 a.m., on his way to school, Jeremy stops at the senior citizen highrise to put drops in the eyes of an elderly woman who suffers from glaucoma. She needs the drop daily but cannot administer them because of her arthritis. Jeremy's friend Ashley will perform the same service on her way home from school this afternoon.

Two high school students, Beki and Paul, are walking around a 4th-grade classroom monitoring the children's mock emergency calls on 911. They're called BATmen by the children, because they are instructors in the Red Cross Basic Aid Training (BAT) program, a six-session course in basic home survival skills for kids who often find themselves alone after school. It was precisely this lesson in getting emergency help that enabled one nine-year-old to save his grandfather's life after a heart attack last fall.

Troy and Angela sit in a corner of the Resource Center with Chao and Thanh-no, who are not long removed from refugee camps near the Cambodian border. Troy and Angela are peer tutors in the English as a Second Language (ESL) program at the school. They come here every day during fifth period. Each ESL student who desires it (100 percent this year) is assigned a peer tutor, who invariably also becomes an advocate and friend.

Three young men in the woodshop are building and drastically modifying skateboards. On a class visit to a day school for severely handicapped children, they noted the children's restricted possibilities for independent movement and autonomous play. An avid skateboarder among the visitors wondered whether any of the kids could move their arms enough to propel themselves along the floor while lying on a low board with wheels. It seemed possible to the staff. The young men put out an urgent call for broken or dust-gathering boards and are now dismantling them and adding width, padding, chin rests, and straps.

Right after school, high school students, some members of Camp Fire, others from Boys Club, take their regular weekly turn as phone counselors at a bank of telephones of the Phone-a-Friend program. This is a service geared to children who find themselves home alone in the hours after school. The teenagers talk to the youngsters, who call on every topic imaginable, from fears of an abusive neighbor to help with a math problem.

These examples demonstrate that there are many settings and organizations in which young people can take on significant tasks and play responsible roles. While many argue for community service as a way to enhance or remediate young people's lagging sense of responsibility, caring, and empathy, the examples above show that these activities can do far more. They can — and to be meaningful, they must — benefit the *larger community* by providing the person-power to work on community problems that could not be as effectively addressed without such a cadre of young volunteers.

They also benefit the *school or youth agency* from which the student volunteers come. Service activities increase the range of meaningful curricular options offered to students and give the organization a new and more positive image as a resource to the community. Most importantly, the *students* gain more personally and intellectually from their experiences than from other classes — even, and not at all infrequently, from *all* of their other high school classes combined. This remarkable assertion occurs with such regularity in formal evaluations of community service programs and in student journals and papers, we have finally come to believe that it ought to be taken seriously as a legitimate finding.

While "learning more" is a clear fact, its actual meaning is not so obvious. In analyzing data from service programs, we have concluded that the "more" attested to is not so much a reference to *amount* as to *significance*, not so much to more information but to more important insights, wisdom, and knowledge. How does this happen, and why?

A simple story that comes, not from an American high school student in the 1980s, but from India many centuries ago, may serve to illustrate what we have come to see as the dynamics of how students "learn more" from direct encounters with significant human problems.

A young prince stirred restlessly under the benevolent prescription of the king that his son be shielded from knowing the pain and ugliness of the world by restricting him to the sumptuous confines of the palace and the life of the royal court. One night the prince slipped away and set out on a journey on his own. On this journey he encountered, in turn, an old man, a dead man, and a mendicant. These encounters shattered his narrow and comfortable view of the world and led him to devote the rest of his life to the search for Truth: about life, the world, himself. The prince never returned to the palace and never became a king. He became, instead, the Buddha.

The basic elements of the Buddha's story parallel closely, if more dramatically, the journey of awakening described by young people in the course of their service to others. Their own words describe the process vividly and authentically.

In Their Own Words . . .

In acting as the providers of service, young people shed the limiting definitions of themselves as immature teenagers and passive, dependent students.

As I walked through the hallway [of the elementary school on her first day of leading children in theatre experiences] ... I realized what I had gotten myself into ... a challenge. But as I step through the door I transform from student to person.... The first day went extremely well, but I'm glad I don't have to go through it again. Now I return to school and become student again.

They assume roles of significance —

What's kind of neat is that I'm treated as a teacher. That's something that's kind of weird to me because I've always been the kid and then suddenly I'm put in someone else's shoes ... It's not like I'm working under the teacher because I AM the teacher!

and affirm this new role through meaningful interactions with others.

I felt I talked to certain residents on an adult level, rather than adult and "teenage" level.

They enter new settings, encounter unfamiliar people from whom they gain new information and understanding.

I feel bad when they're called bums. They realize what they are, they're street people. I kinda understand why they're there. People end up on the streets because of depression mostly. They have a divorce, or they lose the right to see their kids, and they get depressed and end up on the streets. Or they lose their job or their housing, and they get depressed.

National Society for Internships and Experiential Education

One guy I regularly talked to a lot said suddenly one day, "I don't want to talk to you — you're a kid." I was hurt. But I found out his wife had just denied him the right to see his kids. He was lashing out at me as a kid and as a woman.

They broaden their world, increase the range of places and people they know about and with whom they feel a connection.

I have come a *long* way though. I remember my first few days at Oak Terrace. I was scared to touch people, or the doorknobs even. And I used to wash my hands after I left there *every single day!* Can you believe it? Now, I go and get big hugs and kisses from everyone. Get this — I even eat there! That's a horror story for some people.

They not only serve others but gain insight —

Maggie knows just what to say. She really picks me up. We came here to volunteer Maggie, but she volunteers us!

and affirmation.

I used to make jokes about retarded people when I was younger, and now they make *me* feel important.

For the person giving service, responsibility is more than obedience to external rules. It becomes a personally felt obligation to fulfill commitments to others, as the following student discovered after missing a day at her placement.

As I entered St. D's it was my joy to see Adam wearing a smock covered with paint washing his hands at the sink. "Hi," I said.

"Did you go to school yesterday?" he replied shortly.

"Yes," I said guiltily.

"Why didn't you come?" he demanded.

"I didn't have a ride to get back from here," I explained, thinking as fast as I could. When I started to touch his shoulder he jerked away and said, "Don't!" So I left him alone ... I felt like a criminal.

And learning is not merely answering a teacher's questions to get a grade, but asking

---

Different Ways to Learn

"The average student completing the 12th grade has spent nearly 15,000 hours sitting in classrooms. Somewhere in there the law of diminishing returns comes into play. For instruction to remain vital, effective, and relevant, we need to vary the settings and styles in which it is delivered."

—*Youth Service: A Guidebook for Developing and Operating Effective Programs* your own questions to understand and to know what to do.

[After describing another crisis:]

When a little one panics like that I have to wonder what goes on inside their heads? What sparks the fear? What makes them so terrified? How come only a few children ... react this way? It makes me wonder about their home life....

And when learning is from real life, and the consequences are real, you may have to question the surface appearance, the easy answer, and grapple with the deeper complexities of life and relationships.

Paul [a severely and multi-handicapped child] is like any other 3 or 4 year old. He is full of energy and always wants to play. I began recalling the warm feeling he gave me when he hugged me on Monday [an event reported earlier as a great triumph]. Today, for a time, he rejected me. His behavior wasn't rational and I rationalized that he rejected me for no sound reason. I then realized that his Monday hug may have been just as irrational. I felt as though that little "retard" had tricked me and I was confused.

Acts of service often allow — even demand — that individuals act on parts of themselves previously underutilized, perhaps even barely recognized by themselves or others, but affirmed and strengthened through practice.

[A young man on choosing to work with infants:]

I didn't think they would give the job to a guy. Society has always thought that men were too tough to handle children and that they didn't know how to handle them correctly, or wouldn't want to. Well, I was out to prove them wrong.

The first day I started I was a little nervous, since Jodi said that I was the first male to join the staff at New Horizon Daycare in their 17 years of service. And it wasn't that great at first. I had to change diapers, wipe noses, bottle feed them and, most of all, put up with their bloody whining and crying. I started to think that maybe I bit off more than I could chew. But after a week or two I got used to it and it was no bit deal....

All I can say is that I really love these kids. Can you believe that? Enjoying being with babies? Well, they've really affected my life and I'll miss them.

[A suburban cheerleader on venturing into the heart of a city slum to minister to street people:]

This was my senior year and I wanted to do something out of the ordinary. There's a stereotype of cheerleaders as being air-headed, sweet, nice, pure, petite, pretty. Well, I'm completely the opposite.

Affirming these hidden parts of the self can be perplexing to peers —

When I tell friends that I work with children they say, "How can you stand them?" or, "They're just brats, couldn't you have found something better to do?"

and may be met with disbelief.

[A hockey player with the league record for most penalty minutes in a season also worked with Down's syndrome children. His peers reacted.]

You can't mean Gilly? Have you ever seen him play hockey? He's the meanest dude in the league!

It may even bring derision.

Oh, I hear it all the time. Just about every day people ask me, "Don't you hate going there with all of those old people?" Darryl Reuben always gives me a classic one: "Going to work with the old farts again, huh?" I can only ignore these remarks....

The result may be a subtle distancing — a leaving behind of one's peers and one's former, more limited self.

I have learned so much about myself and life and God from going to Oak Terrace. I hate to think what my life would have been like if I'd never been working there. I'd probably be a prejudiced a the rest of the people....

People die there, of course. Everybody dies, so what makes one human greater than another? We are all the same. Old people at Oak Terrace are the same as me, I am no better than them. Maybe that's the whole meaning for me going there. I just wish I could explain to others what I mean, make them understand. If they only knew.

In giving service to others, one travels on a road that brings one into contact with life's ultimate situations.

[On seeing death for the first time:]

On October 19th, I was asked to help out a woman. Her name was Mabel. I had to help her eat and drink because she was paralyzed from the neck down. She was in a wheelchair because of her disabilities. I tried to feed her, but she refused the food. She drank some milk, but she didn't seem to swallow well. She didn't mumble, she didn't moan. She was just quiet and happy. After trying to feed her I was asked to do somebody's fingernails. About a half hour later, I went back to Mabel's room to see how she was doing, and she had passed away. I didn't know quite what to do. I proceeded to close her eyelids — like in the movies — and got a nurse.

[On responding to the loneliness of another's fears:]

One day I was thinking about Jeff [an 8th grader in a gym class where this high school male volunteered] and I remembered I hadn't seen him since they started swimming. I looked for two days to find Jeff and the hall monitor helped me and I told him to get Jeff tomorrow, bring him to the detention room and keep him there until I got there. Well, that worked out great. When I got there I took him down to a room in the locker room. He wanted to be alone and didn't want anyone to see him. So many people have picked on Jeff that he likes to be alone and away from other kids ... they laugh when he can't tie his own shoes. Well, now Jeff and I have our own gym class. I'm the teacher. We work in the weight room, or the upper gym playing basketball and sometimes we even run laps.

Jeff is feeling better and better about himself. We caught the one kid that has been really picking on him and took care of that and no one has been picking on him since.

[On being needed:]

Kids really notice when you've been gone a few days. When I walked in the door they went totally wild and started yelling. "Susan's back! Susan's back!" and jumped all over me. I thought they were going to smother me and I had a time calming them down. But Laura [her special charge] just sat there. I went right over there and asked what was wrong. She didn't even look at me. I didn't say a thing. I just hugged her. She had tears, and so did I.

[NOTE: The above accounts take on added poignancy with the additional knowledge that the first writer was a "loner" himself in junior high and in perpetual trouble in senior high, and that the second writer's having been "gone a few days" was the result of hospitalization from an attempted suicide.]

Seeing life more wholly, and more of it, may cast a different and more intense light on one's own life —

I cannot even begin to count the number of days that I trudge into Glen Lake, thinking about all the "huge" problems in my life I was facing: Homework, fights with my sister, money for college, the right guy not calling my house, gaining too much weight, missing a party ... and the list goes on. I cannot think

---

The Transition to Adulthood

"[B]y providing for integration of ideas and actions into the large community, experiential [experience-based] learning facilitates the transition to adulthood and develops skills for responsible citizenship. Documented outcomes of experiential learning include concern for fellow human beings; the ability to get things done and work with others; self-motivation to learn, participate and achieve; improved self-concept, confidence, competence, and awareness; responsibility to the group or class; openness to new experiences; and a sense of usefulness to the community."

— From *A Nation at Risk: Another View, Joint Statement of the Association for Experiential Education, the Council for Adult and Experiential Learning, and the National Society for Internships and Experiential Education,* March 1984.

---

of a single time where I came out after class not feeling 100% better about life, and also feeling guilty about only thinking negatively about things that are so trivial in my life.

and the institutions of society.

[From a day care center:]

First of all, the children were all put into groups depending solely on their age, it was kind of like being put into army squads. Another thing that bothered me was when Mrs. ... told me I wasn't to get too close to the children, that I was there as a volunteer to help watch the kids. I thought day care consisted of someone caring for another person's child ... not just sitting around watching so they don't get into things they are not supposed to be in.

These people don't put their emotions into what they do, and they're really not there for the kids, they are there physically but they need more than that. They need a friend, not a circus tamer. They have a lot to give, but who takes? Here it's jam 'em in and take their money!

Service provides a new perspective from which to analyze critically their own world, to notice hitherto hidden peculiarities within the more familiar.

My kids have so much loving, touching, caring affection towards me and one another. It's amazing how much better you feel about yourself after getting all of this loving affection at-

mosphere. It makes me wonder where, and when, we lost all
that loving and affection? You never see it in high school. In
what grade does all this stop? Why does it stop? Does it have to
stop? Does our society put such pressure on us that if boys hold
hands in elementary school they will be laughed at and get the
image of fags? Do parents, teachers stop this relationship? or is
it the whole environment in which we live?

**The path of service, as a journey of awakening, opens one to truths
both joyful and disheartening. It may reveal beauty where ugliness was expected, friendship where there was fear. But it may
also reveal superficiality in what had been meaningful and add
confusion to what had been easily understood before. It may
underscore sadness, injustice, and pain.**

[A young woman reflects in her journal on the loss of innocence
in store for a child with whom she is working.]

"I don't want you," he stated defiantly. I just shrugged my
shoulders and told him I liked his shoes. I said they were "cool"
and that they "looked good." So we discussed his shoes. Somehow the subject changed to Scooby-doo. "I used to watch that a
lot!" I exclaimed. Adam told me Scooby fell down into a tree
while being chased by some man who was mad.

This is the important stuff. Talking to a tiny person about
Scooby Doo. It beats all the death in El Salvador. It puts El
Salvador worlds away. Of course, you don't want to tell this kid
that he's going to grow up in a sick world with a demented
society where people die for nothing. Kids don't understand.
Adults don't either. Why mention the fact that as he gets older
he will be confused, judged by others; no, they aren't God but
still it's their self-appointed task to judge you; or worse, you
may become an asshole. The worst thing about assholes is that
they don't realize that they are assholes. It's sad. So you talk to
this tiny person and the world can stop or pass you by and it just
doesn't matter.

Sorry, I got off on a tangent. Anyway, Adam the brat became
my friend.

**The greatest power of service is that it reveals that one is not
powerless, that a contribution can be given, a difference can be
made: "I can do something, I am significant."**

I never knew that a person could give so much to another by just
plain being there. Those people needed me, I've never totally
been wanted like this before. I can tell by their daily hugs and
smiles that spread over their faces ...

Before, I used to want to go into business, but now I'm thinking of going into physical therapy. It always interested me, but I never thought that I could do it. After this semester I really found out what I can and can't do. And, I think I can do it!

Conclusion

Learning from service is, like any real learning, highly personal and idiosyncratic, reflecting both the potentialities in the learning environment and in the learners themselves. Not every service experience is a roaring success. Some placements are barren, and some students don't respond to even the richest opportunities.

But the comments above are not anomalies, special cases, or rarities. Adolescents are curious; they are seeking, wondering about themselves and their world. The power of service as a path to learning is that it places young people in a context in which the learning is real, alive, and has clear consequences for others and for themselves. It does not reach everybody, but it reaches a far higher percentage, more deeply, than any other method we have tried.

Is this education? Is this appropriate for schools? In the ebb and flow of educational fads and fancies, a prominent catch-phrase of our time is that we ought to be stimulating "higher-level thinking." Often, those enamored of this idea don't say what this higher-level thinking should be about. When the question arises, the answers range from the best thinking and writing of our culture to more sophisticated understanding of mathematical and scientific principles. But higher-level thinking must also engage people in questions about themselves and their world. For adolescents, the fundamental questions are: who am I? where am I going? is there any point to it all? The fundamental issues are those of relationship, significance, connection, suffering, meaning, hope, love, and attachment.

Are these not also what education is really about? The purpose of education cannot be merely to pass tests, accumulate facts, get decent grades, get into college. These are means, at best, the end of which must be to arrive, by oneself, at some truth about oneself, and about one's relationship to the world.

To opt for service as a part of the curriculum involves a commitment to the idea that what is most important in the lives of adolescents is also what is most important in their education.

Diane Hedin is Director of Community Relations at the Pillsbury Foundation and a former professor at the Center for Youth Development and Research at the University of Minnesota. Dan Conrad directs community involvement programs at Hopkins High School in Minnesota. Over the past 17 years, Conrad and Hedin have co-directed several research and publications projects in experiential education, youth participation, and service-learning.

Reference

Conrad, Daniel, and Diane Hedin. *Youth Service: A Guidebook for Developing and Operating Effective Programs*, Independent Sector, 1987, pp. 9-12.

Dewey's Theory of Experience: Implications for Service-Learning

Dwight E. Giles, Jr.

Cornell's Dwight Giles relates John Dewey's concepts about education and experience to service-learning. Giles suggests a dialectical interaction between service and learning, which has implications for ensuring quality in service-learning programs and for defining service-learning as a philosophy *rather than as a* type *of program.* Reprinted from Experiential Education, National Society for Internships and Experiential Education, *Vol. 13, No. 5, November-December 1988, pp. 3, 10.*

IT IS DIFFICULT TO DO A brief analysis of John Dewey's educational philosophy in regard to any one of the many dimensions of his theory, and it may also be somewhat speculative to attempt a brief analysis of the implications of Dewey's central theory for an area of education about which he did not write. However, as an earlier discussion of these ideas illustrated,[1] the importance of Dewey's theory of experience is critical for informing our current efforts to develop further the theoretical bases of service-learning and experiential education in general. What I have attempted here, then, is a limited exposition of Dewey's theory of experience, drawn mainly from his later work, especially *Experience and Education* (1938), and then a brief analysis of what the implications are for the theory and practice of service-learning.

Primacy of the Concept of Experience

Central to Dewey's early writings on children's learning during the period of his work at the Laboratory School of the University of Chicago (1896-1916) and to his later and revised thinking about education in a broader context is the *primacy of the concept of experi-*

ence. The fundamental characteristic of this central element of Dewey's educational (and social) philosophy was the "...organic connection between education and personal experience" (p. 25). This connection was not a simple or direct one, as his critics often charged. Rather, Dewey postulated that while "all genuine education comes about through experience (this) does not mean that all experiences are genuinely or equally educative" (p. 25). This conviction that many experiences were mis-educative led Dewey to develop criteria for defining the educative quality of experience. Dewey elaborated on these criteria as the two fundamental principles of experience which are described below. They are derived from the dialectical stance that shaped his entire philosophy. As this dialectic had earlier linked school and society, the child and the curriculum, democracy and education, it now linked experience and education by two other sets of linkages. Dewey called these linkages the Principle of Continuity (also called the experiential continuum) and the Principle of Interaction.

The Principles of Continuity and Interaction

The Principle of Continuity provides the first criterion by which the quality of experience can be assessed for its educative value. This assessment goes beyond the present quality of the experience in order to determine its effect on growth and development, the value of future experiences, and the direction in which the experience is leading. According to Dewey, the task of the educator is to determine the effects of the present experience upon future experiences and to ensure that experiences will be educative by specifying the direction of growth.

The Principle of Interaction provides the second criterion by which the quality of experience can be assessed. Dewey said it is necessary for the internal or subjective elements of experience to be balanced with the external or objective aspects. Application of this principle interprets the educational value of an experience by considering both elements of experience and by demanding that there be a goodness of fit or a "transaction" between the two. This interaction forms what Dewey called a "situation" which is a given of experience and which is also the result of the educator ensuring that both the internal and external aspects of experience are attended to in the educational task. Because the interaction is part of the situation, the concept is a dynamic one. It leads to the corollary that the determination of the quality of an experience involves the interaction between the subject and the environment.

The power of Dewey's theory of experience is that these two principles operate in interaction with each other, taking into consideration the temporal dimension in both the internal and external aspects of experience. The pedagogical task that results from this theory involves a large and complicated set of factors that needed to be identified and structured for both the individual and for society if experience is to be truly educative.

Implications for Service-Learning

Several implications seem readily apparent for service-learning, the first of which is a dialectical and multi-dimensional conceptualization. Indeed, a Deweyian conceptualization would be expressed as "service *and* learning" in order to reflect the dialectical interaction between the two. This conceptualization would move beyond the "Either-Or" educational philosophy that Dewey found so unproductive and that has hindered our own theoretical and practical efforts in service-learning. Furthermore, this conceptualization calls for additional development of the model that Sinclair Goodlad has proposed for service-learning where the dimensions of theory and practice, and of individual and society, are held in tension in curriculum development (Goodlad, 1988).[2]

A second implication, or set of implications, is derived from the application of Dewey's two principles to service-learning programs as a means of ensuring quality. Specifically, this means that attention must be given to the interaction between the server and the served, between past and present experiences, and to the service-learning transactions that are part of the learning. A true situational learning approach helps to ensure the quality of the service (Sigmon, 1979, 1987) and also helps to ensure rigor for the learning derived from the experience of service. Understanding and acting upon the situation in its micro, macro, and interactive components leads to a broad, ecological approach to service and learning.

A third implication, and perhaps the most fundamental one, is for the very definition of service-learning. The question of the definition and location of service-learning within the broader educational endeavor has been posed by Stanton as "Is service-learning a *form* of experiential education which can stand beside internships, field study and cooperative education? Or, is it a *philosophy* of experiential education which suggests methods and practices that should inform all programs?" (1987, p. 4). The answer from Dewey's theory of experience — with its understanding that experience is ultimately social and communal and that education is interactive and reciprocal — suggests the latter view of service-learning as a philosophy of experiential education rather than the former and more restrictive definition.

Dwight E. Giles, Ph.D., is a Senior Lecturer in the Field and International Studies Program of the College of Human Ecology at Cornell University.

Footnotes

[1] This article is based on remarks prepared for the panel "Developing a Common Language for Community Service Programs" presented at the 16th annual conference of the National Society for Internships and Experiential Education, Smugglers Notch, Vermont. October 15, 1987. I am indebted to the panel moderator, Dick Couto, for encouraging me to develop these thoughts and to Debbie Cotton and Bob Sigmon, my fellow panelists, for helping me refine my thinking.

[2] For another multi-dimensional model that reflects the Deweyian dialectic, see Richard A. Couto's illustration of the tensions and relationships between community service and education (1987).

References

Couto, Richard A., "Public Service and Education: Assessing a Community Setting as a Learning Context," presented at the 16th Annual Conference of the National Society for Internships and Experiential Education, Smugglers Notch, VT, 1987. See reprint in this resource book.

Dewey, John, *Experience and Education*, Collier Books, 1938.

Goodlad, Sinclair, "Where Might This Take Us?" presented at the Annual Conference of the Partnership for Service-Learning, Chevy Chase, MD, 1988. Published in conference proceedings, *Service and Learning: Mapping the Crossroads*.

Sigmon, Robert L., "Service-Learning: Three Principles," *Synergist*, National Center for Service-Learning, ACTION, Vol. 8, No. 1, Spring 1979, pp. 9-11. Available from NSIEE, 3509 Haworth Drive, Suite 207, Raleigh, NC 27609.

Sigmon, Robert, ed., *Community Service, Civic Arts, Voluntary Action and Service-Learning*, Occasional Paper #8, National Society for Internships and Experiential Education, 1987.

Stanton, Timothy, "Service-Learning: Groping Toward a Definition," *Experiential Education*, National Society for Internships and Experiential Education, Vol. 12, No. 1, January-February, 1987, pp. 2, 4.

Donald Schon's "Reflective Artistry"

Sharon Rubin

Sharon Rubin summarizes Donald Schon's concept of reflection-in-action, a valuable one for service-learning. Reprinted from Experiential Education, *National Society for Internships and Experiential Education, Vol. 11, No. 4, September-October 1987, p. 4.*

DONALD A. SCHON, A PROFESSOR of urban planning at MIT and a long-time partner with Chris Argyris in organizational and interpersonal consulting, is not so much a theorist of experiential learning as an analyst. In his most recent book, *Educating the Reflective Practitioner* (Jossey-Bass, 1987), he critically examines the model of professional education in ascendency in the United States. By micro-analysis of what he calls "deviant learning environments," he attempts to sort out what actually occurs during student-teacher interactions in architecture design studios, master classes in musical performance, supervision in psychoanalytic practice, and counseling practica. From these analyses, he attempts to provide not only a much-needed terminology for experiential learning, but alternative models for professional education. His ideas are useful for anyone interested in service-learning as well.

The duality he sees in professional education (and that many of us also see in undergraduate education), between relevance and rigor, between the practical skills needed for professional competence and the technical rationality that is "the schools' prevailing epistemology of practice," challenges Schon to try to understand and to articulate a new model, of reflection-in-action, which he distinguishes from knowledge-in-action. People know-in-action when they use prior knowledge, rules, and strategies to deal with expected situations. However, when our routine responses produce an unexpected outcome, or when we meet a situation that doesn't fit our prior knowledge, we use a very different process of reflection.

We not only question the assumptions of our knowledge, but we "restructure strategies of action, understanding of phenomena, or ways of framing problems .... Reflection gives rise to on-the-spot experiment" (p. 28).

Schon is, of course, clear that the actuality of reflection-in-action is not as neat or distinctive as his descriptions. However, he believes that a student can learn to be reflective in action, and that the artistry that results from the capacity to be reflective while doing leads to a very different kind of competency than that of the typically passive professional training.

By trying to understand the practicum as it is used in certain professional fields, by analyzing the minutiae of conversations and activities, Schon is able to distinguish clearly between such coaching functions as demonstrating, advising, questioning, and criticizing. He also defines how coaches shift stance, and how they combine telling/listening with demonstrating/imitating. He brings to our attention the underlying parts of the process of reflection-in-action such as bringing past experience to bear on a unique situation and bringing rigor to on-the-spot experiment by such varying techniques as exploration, move-testing, hypothesis testing, and making explicit what is tacit.

Most of us, if we analyze at all, do it at the macro-level. Schon, by trying to generalize from very detailed, specific cases, and by giving clear terminology to what many of us know intuitively, makes us all more aware of ourselves as teachers and learners and more able to articulate our vision of experiential education to others.

Sharon Rubin is Dean of the School of Liberal Arts at Salisbury State University and President of the National Society for Internships and Experiential Education.

Intellectual Passion

Thomas C. Little

Polanyi's philosophy of epistemology shows why doing is essential to knowing and how service-learning evokes a passionate search for answers. Tom Little uses the writings of Michael Polanyi (1891-1976) to describe an epistemology for service-learning. Trained as a physical chemist, Polanyi pursued a career sequentially as a crystallographer, atomic physicist, labor economist, science historian, and philosopher. From his works in these diverse disciplines, each embracing a different method for knowing, Polanyi came to see that the paths to knowledge are diverse, and that life has greater possibility if this diversity is recognized. Reprinted from Synergist, National Center for Service-Learning, ACTION, *Vol. 8, No. 1, Spring 1979, pp. 45-48.*

IN THE LAST FEW YEARS the terms experiential education and service-learning have gained some acceptance for denoting a variety of educational activities in which experience is the basis of knowledge. Many practitioners and proponents of service-learning embrace a number of assumptions about how learning is effected. These assumptions are not individually distinct; they blend into each other, some assumptions being corollaries of others. Among these assumptions are:

- Knowing requires that the individual interact with the environment;
- Useful knowledge derives from understanding the total relationship rather than the parts of a whole, *i.e.,* the whole is not just the sum of its parts;
- Real knowledge rests on the world as it is commonly perceived and not on intellectualizations of it;
- Knowledge of the whole comes prior to knowledge of its parts;
- Learning is bringing to consciousness something already known;

- Tacit knowledge is sufficient for the individual to function, but explicit knowledge is needed to understand the total relationship of the parts of the whole;
- Each person is unique, so knowledge is ultimately personal.

It is surprising how little attention those in the knowing business — be they researchers or teachers — give to the processes through which knowledge is attained. Epistemology, defined as the study of the methods and grounds of knowledge, gets a quick brush in philosophy of education courses. College professors who teach by the Golden Rule (doing unto others what was done to them) focus their attention almost exclusively on the content of knowledge organized in their academic discipline and show little concern for how this knowledge comes to be.

This lack of interest in the knowing process is not indicative of a lack of consensus as to how knowing occurs. It is a general consensus in the current culture of higher education that knowledge comes through the exercise of the scientific method, *i.e.*, cause-effect relationships of separate entities or events are established inductively.

The learner in the inductive process gradually eliminates factors that are not cause-effect related in order to develop a general theory so future predictions can be made about similar relationships. In the inductive process two conditions are seen as paramount: The knower participates only as a record keeper, with the factors themselves suggesting the direction of the investigative process. The factors and their characteristics are considered to have been identified only if they can be symbolically described in either words or mathematical notations.

This quick description of the scientific method does not describe how students in service-learning programs report how they learn. From his own life of scientific research and study of the history of scientific discoveries, Polanyi — an imminent British scientist — recognized that the scientific method explanation is not accurate. He suggests a number of alternative explanations which, when

---

Useful knowledge derives from understanding the total relationship rather than the parts of a whole.

---

taken together, are a rich resource for developing an epistemology for experiential education and service-learning.

This discussion is a beginning effort to construct an epistemology for experiential education from Polanyi's thought. Just as philosophy must be rooted in reality, an epistemology for experiential learning must explain the same common occurrences in experiential education.

- How can we know without being able to describe in detail what we know?
- Why is action critical to knowing?
- How can we act effectively without being able to define the informational basis for our actions?
- Why are experiential education outcomes hard to generalize?
- Why is it that only experiential learners can direct their own learning?
- Why are experiential learners more motivated both to learn and apply what is learned?
- How can students have different learning outcomes from the same experience?

Polanyi's Language of Epistemology

Epistemology — the study of how we know what we know

Tactic knowledge — recognition of the whole without identification of its parts

Explicit knowledge — identification of the parts without recognition of their purpose in the whole

Focal awareness — perception of an object as a distinct entity

Subsidiary awareness — perception of an object in terms of its purpose

Certainty — accuracy; something demonstrated by repeated occurrences; a criterion for significance

Systematic relevancy — judgment of the significance of the parts of the whole; a criterion for significance

Intrinsic interest — hierarchy of values influenced by a time and social order; the most important criterion for significance

*Proponents of experiential
learning attribute importance
to doing as a basis of knowledge
and invariably testify to the truth
of an old Chinese proverb: "I hear
and I forget, I see and I remember,
I do and I understand."*

A brief look at elements of Polanyi's philosophy may help to provide a context for exploring these dilemmas.

How can we know without being able to describe in detail what we know? A common experience — and one most exasperating for academicians — is that experiential learners, while evaluating their learning most positively ("I learned more in 10 weeks than in all the courses I have taken."), are unable to describe with much specificity what has been learned. Educators question how something can be known if one cannot describe what is known.

Polanyi's explanation is in terms of tacit knowledge as opposed to explicit knowledge. Tacit knowledge, simply put, means knowing something without specifying the component elements of what is known. Polanyi gives numerous examples of this phenomenon. The recognition of another's face is an obvious example. We can recognize a face from among a thousand faces even after years of separation. Yet we have great difficulty saying how we know that face. We cannot, with any specificity, describe the parts which comprise the whole — the eye color, the shape of the mouth, the angles that the nose and ears have with the head.

Similarly, students in service-learning programs in correctional institutions report the ability to detect changes in the atmosphere or mood from day to day. Yet they are unable to articulate the particulars or specify the conditions and the changes in those conditions that form the context of atmosphere or mood. Their understanding of changes in mood within the institution is derived from tacit knowledge (their understanding of the whole from their own direct experience of that whole) rather than from an inductive examination of the individual elements comprising that whole.

Why is action critical to knowing? Proponents of experiential learning attribute importance to doing as a basis of knowledge and invariably testify to the truth of an old Chinese proverb: "I hear and I forget, I see and I remember, I do and I understand."

Polanyi explains this phenomenon — the importance of doing or of being in an active relationship for learning to occur — by employing the concepts of focal and subsidiary awareness. Focal awareness is the awareness of an object separated from other objects, *e.g.*, we can be aware of a hammer and of a nail as distinct entities. Subsidiary awareness, on the other hand, is the awareness of an object in terms of its purposeful value to us, *e.g.*, the character of the hammer and the nail becomes known to us in a purposeful, active relationship. When we strike the nail with the hammer, the handle of the hammer is not only a piece of wood but also a means of directing our action, and in directing this action the important characteristics of both the hammer and nail are known — size of the head, length of the handle, the tensile strength of the handle.

How can we act effectively without being able to define the informational basis for our action? Subsidiary awareness, knowing something for its effect and relationship to us, is the basis for tacit knowledge. Our ability to know things and their relationships without being able to specify their component elements is a common occurrence in what we do. Subsidiary awareness helps explain why service-learners often know how to perform an action competently, yet do not know how they do it and are not able to tell another person how to do it. In this light, the actions involved in organizing a community and in swimming or riding a bicycle become comparable:

> If I know how to ride a bicycle or swim, this does not mean that I can tell how I manage to keep my balance on a bicycle or keep afloat when swimming. I may not have the slightest idea of how I do this or even an entirely wrong or grossly imperfect idea of it, and yet go on cycling or swimming merrily.   — *Knowing and Being* (p. 141)

In an epistemology for experiential education, it is important to explain the role of the individual in the knowing process. The ground of Polanyi's epistemology is his belief that there is an active concern by each individual to understand and control the environment. Polanyi names this concern *intellectual passion, intellectual* to denote distinction from and superiority to sensory activity and *passion* to stress an active and engrossing enterprise.

According to Polanyi, intellectual passion has selective, heuristic or empowering, and persuasive functions. Selectivity is necessary to establish the cognitive content of new knowledge. Selectivity is a necessity. Information about the world is plentiful but information is not informative. Information in itself does not signify; significance is established by satisfaction of criteria independent of the fact content of information. These three criteria are certainty understood as accuracy, systematic relevancy, and intrinsic interest. Certainty is the measure or judgment made that "what is" is and can be demonstrated by repeated occurrences, occurrence to more than one person, or approximation to an independent standard of measurement.

Systematic relevancy is a judgment of the significance of particulars in the context of accepted understandings of the way things are. Just as certainty is a judgment that something is not false, systematic relevancy is a measure that "what is" is not trivial. Intrinsic interest is the condition that some things are deemed of greater value than others, *e.g.*, the living more than the non-living, animals more than plants, the land more than the sea, the present more than the past. These values are socially determined, can change, and can vary from society to society. Within a particular social order at a particular time, they strongly influence what individuals accept as "what is."

These three criteria do not operate individually, nor are they of equal importance. They act summarily and in concert, with intrinsic interest being the most compelling and certainty being the least compelling.

The quick acceptance of Freudianism is a good example of the relative importance of the individual criteria. Freudianism's claims to certainty are hardly convincing. It is now known that many occurrences on which Freudian psychology is based were not real events but were Freud's creations. The client subjects of many of Freud's cases, particularly those which demonstrated Oedipal behavior, were archetypal fabrications. Yet when this became known in the 1960s, there was no rush to deny Freudianism; the intrinsic interest in psychology was sufficiently compelling for Freudianism to retain much of its standing.

Why are experiential learning outcomes hard to generalize? The criterion of intrinsic interest for establishing the validity of knowledge has significant implications for experiential learning, particularly service-learning. Typically students in service-learning programs are involved in a highly intensive way in a restricted environment for a short time. Operating in this environment without a broad perspective, a student can easily come to a knowledge position different from that more generally held. This situation is particularly likely when the student is in a service relationship to a client in a structured service delivery system. In such a situation, if the student is to make a case for a knowledge position contrary to the intrinsic interest of the greater society, he or she must do so by the criteria of accuracy and systematic relevancy. In a service-learning situation where human factors are dominant, these criteria are most difficult to satisfy.

Why can only experiential learners direct their own learning? Lest it be thought that the socially prescribed criterion of intrinsic interest places individuals in a position of being unable to exercise their own imagination and creativity in the knowing process, Polanyi stresses the personal dimension, and thereby brings into focus the empowering or heuristic functions implicit in intellectual passion. It is in his attention to the personal dimension that Polanyi makes a unique contribution to epistemology. It is this aspect of his thought that has the greatest significance for experiential learning.

Knowing has a personal and empowering dimension for Polanyi because each individual seeks knowledge in the context of an overarching "vision of reality." It is the individual, personal vision of what is real that determines both the direction in which the learner seeks knowledge and what he or she accepts as true.

The rejection of witchcraft as an explanation of causation in the sixteenth and seventeenth centuries is an example given by Polanyi for the power of a vision of reality. Witchcraft satisfied the criteria of certainty, systematic relevancy, and intrinsic interest better than any other explanation. Yet it was rejected, for it was in conflict with a vision of a capsulated world populated by human beings and not by spirits.

The power and tasks of an overarching vision are obvious in this Polanyi statement:

> Scientific discovery reveals new knowledge, but the new vision which accompanies it is not knowledge. It is less than knowledge, for it is a guess; but it is more than knowledge, for it is a foreknowledge of things yet unknown and at present inconceivable .... Our vision of reality, to which our sense of scientific beauty responds, must suggest to us the kind of questions that it should be reasonable and interesting to explore. It should recommend the kind of conceptions and empirical relations that are intrinsically plausible and which should therefore be upheld, even when some evidence seems to contradict them, and tell us also, on the other hand, what empirical connections to reject as specious, even though there is evidence for them — evidence that we may as yet be unable to account for on any other assumptions. — *Personal Knowledge* (p. 135)

A vision of reality not only exercises a selective function through suggesting appropriate questions and interpretative frameworks but also provides the emotional energy by which the vision is realized. To talk of emotional energy in the knowing process is to cross the Rubicon, epistemologically speaking. The focus is no longer on the rules which guide the search. The concern is with the emotional bases which empower the search. Rules are the after-the-event abstractions put forth to explain the course of the search; they are not what empowered the search.

The vision of what might be has anticipatory and self-fulfilling powers. In discussing this phenomenon, Polanyi finds evidence in Johann Kepler's discovery of elliptical orbits.

> When I prophesied two-and-twenty years ago, as soon as I discovered the five solids among the heavenly orbits — what I firmly believed long before I had seen Ptolemy's *Harmonics* — what I had promised my friends in the title of this fifth book, which I named before I was sure of my discovery — what sixteen years ago I urged to be sought — that for which I have devoted the best part of my life to astronomical contemplation, at last I have brought to light, and recognized its truth beyond all my hopes.
>
> — *Personal Knowledge* (p. 7)

Kepler's vision was based on a false assumption. In essence, it was a false vision. There is not a simple relationship between the size of the planets and their solar distances. Yet the vision was close enough to direct his search along a path that resulted in an understanding of planetary motion more comprehensive than he had ever dreamed. The dream more than fulfilled itself.

Why are experiential learners more motivated both to learn and apply what is learned? The ideas of Polanyi that knowledge comes from a vision of possibilities, however poorly seen, and that it is awareness of these that provides the persistent energy whereby the possibilities are actualized, explain two common conditions of those learning through direct experience. James Coleman (1977), in an essay comparing the relative worth of classroom (symbolic) and experiential learning, says that experiential learners seem more motivated to learn and retain more of what is learned. From my observation, other descriptions of the same phenomenon are that experiential learners are more enthusiastic to learn and more impelled to action from what they learn. In short, experiential learning is learning that makes a difference for the individual.

It is not mere coincidence that the rise of experiential learning coincided with the student movement of the 1960s. A very specific issue of the movement was the students' demand that learning be mixed with social action and that it be intentionally a base for social action. In many instances, students could not accurately describe the world they wanted, but the vision of a better world did empower action that painfully and slowly moved us toward a more just social order. Polanyi's conception of the power of an overarching vision in the knowing process could not be better demonstrated.

How can students have different learning outcomes from the same experience? The third function of intellectual passion is the persuasive function. Persuasion is a strong word in epistemology. Typically, knowledge is considered to be true if the rules of the knowing process have been followed; validity is through rule-keeping. Polanyi does not agree. Validation for Polanyi is, in the final analysis, persuading another of the rightness of one's position. The condition is not a lack of agreement on the facts of the case. On this there may be agreement. The difficulty is that of different interpretations of meaning. Persuasion is by conversion (Polanyi's term) and not by logical demonstration.

The reason for different interpretations of the same facts is attributed by Polanyi to indwelling. This is the process whereby reference points unique for each individual place a particular interpretation on a given set of facts. In effect, in the final analysis it is what the knower brings to the knowing event that determines what is known. Indwelling whereby an interpretation provides the basis for a jump across a logical gap explains another condition of experiential learners, particularly in service-learning programs where value differences can be significant. Two students in a service-learning program walk through a prison. One from his history sees just another example of a racist society; the other from his history sees sick men whom society must incarcerate for its own safety.

The beauty of service-learning and its potential is that often it is exercised in a logical gap of conflicting interpretations. In this situation, Polanyi's epistemology is instructive. Polanyi says "not to wait until all the facts are in." This will never be, particularly when the question is one that matters. Instead, with a vision of what is desired driving our effort, we act to realize the possibilities, letting our own values come into play in saying what the possibilities really are.

Tom Little, whose own academic training is in chemistry, social ethics, higher education, and philosophy, founded the Virginia Program, a state-

wide experiential education program in Virginia colleges. He has worked with programs for student community service, experiential learning, and appropriate technology around the world for 20 years.

References

Coleman, James S., "Differences Between Experiential and Classroom Learning" in *Experiential Learning: Rationale, Characteristics, and Assessment*, ed. by Morris T. Keeton, Jossey-Bass, 1977, pp. 49-61.

Polanyi, Michael, *Knowing and Being*, University of Chicago Press, 1969.

Polanyi, Michael, *Personal Knowledge*, Harper Torch Books, 1958.

Polanyi, Michael, *The Tacit Dimension*, Doubleday Anchor, 1966.

Experiential Education as Critical Discourse

David Thornton Moore

David Moore argues that experiential educators [and service-learning educators] may represent one of the few paths to creating a critical pedagogy — a form of discourse in which teachers and students conduct an unfettered investigation of social institutions, power relations and value commitments. Moore uses the generic term "experiential education" in this chapter; this term includes service-learning and other approaches to education that combine community or public service with reflective learning.

EXPERIENTIAL LEARNING PROGRAMS have been around for a long time in higher education; cooperative education, for one, started at the University of Cincinnati soon after the turn of the century. After a long period of relative obscurity, they seem to be spreading into more and more schools, and more and more students are getting involved.[1]

Despite this growing popularity, experiential educators [and service-learning educators] still have only an intuitive understanding of what is going on when students engage in non-classroom activities. Traditional conceptions of the process of learning from experience,[2] by and large, focus on two kinds of learning: the "application" of classroom-derived knowledge, and "personal development" in such forms as changed self-concept, enhanced interactional skills, and more effective career planning.

In this chapter, I will sketch the beginnings of a new approach to understanding and conducting experiential education. My view builds on "post-structuralist" conceptions of knowledge-use, ideas proposed by such writers as Michel Foucault, Jacques Derrida and Jurgen Habermas.[3]

Now, a reader familiar with these authors might be tempted to ditch this article right away: These are the people who write about "interpretive analytics," "discourse-practices," "deconstruction," and other blights on the landscape of language. But I beg you to stick with me because I think they have something crucial to say to experiential educators — in fact, to anyone concerned about innovations in higher education.

Conceptions of School-Based Knowledge

The conception of experiential learning that I will propose stands against traditionalist definitions of knowledge stretching from as far back as Plato through St. Augustine and reaching its pinnacle in the positivism of the early twentieth century. More recently, the position has been championed by such writers as Allan Bloom and E.D. Hirsch.

The fundamental premise of this epistemology is that there are persistent "things" in the world and that we can discover the "truth" about them. The world is knowable if we follow appropriate procedures and heed acknowledged authorities.

This positivism had its institutional correlate in the structure of the university as it developed in Europe and the United States. The assumption underlying the university is that (a) knowledge about the world is possible, the "truth" can be found; (b) faculty have mastered that knowledge, discovered that truth; and (c) the function of the faculty's interaction with students is to transmit that stable meaning to the initiates.

In recent years, the debate about higher education has centered on the question of what is worth knowing. Bloom decries the relativism that has distracted us from our search for "the meaning of life," implying that the "classics" can guide us in that odyssey.[4] Hirsch, in arguing for a common cultural base for public discourse, boldly ventures a list of "what every American needs to know."[5] In its most extreme form, the list becomes a fact-a-day calendar explaining "Aida" on April 2 and "Hannibal" on May 15.

In each case, knowledge is treated as stable, masterable, essentially unproblematic. Once it is discovered, it can be passed on to the willing and able. College-level pedagogy, in the main, aims to transmit well-developed and validated units of knowledge to the initiates, and then to reward their competent display of those units. While this portrait of university epistemology is clearly a caricature (plenty of professors would argue with it), it does seem fundamental to the social order of the institution: to classes, exams, degrees, ranks, departments and rituals.

Experiential Education and Epistemology

Field-based education, in which students are thought to learn through experience in "real-world" settings, tends to vacillate in its conception of knowledge. The classic definition of experiential education refers to "learning activities that engage the learner directly in the phenomena being studied."[6] Many programs build the "application of theory" into the student's experience.

One published set of exercises for field-study students,[7] for instance, defines the concept of "organizational culture" and asks the student to apply that idea to her placement site. Another example can be found in the essential practices of cooperative education,[8] which juxtapose the classroom-based learning of theory and method with the workplace-based application of that knowledge. Co-op educators take for granted that the knowledge bases of the two environments are fundamentally consistent.

Experiential educators sense strongly the limits of this positivist epistemology. Indeed, their argument that academic theory needs to be "tested" against experience suggests a nagging feeling that knowledge somehow works differently outside the walls of the classroom.

One element of experiential epistemology that stands out against the traditional background of college studies is its focus on personal development, affective growth and social interaction. Another is that field-based educators contextualize knowledge: They put it in appropriate everyday settings rather than only in the rarefied world of abstractions. And they humanize it: They insist on its relationship to feelings, values and personalities.[9]

Post-Structuralism in Education

My perspective on the possibility of a more powerful conception of experiential learning draws in part on critiques of traditional education variously called "critical," "post-liberal" and "post-structuralist."[10] It arrives at an image of meaning as situated and fragile; of knowledge as negotiated and interactional; and of learning as dialectical and active.

Cherryholmes characterizes the dominant approach to theory and practice in education today as "structuralist." Structural analysis, following Saussure,[11] looks for relationships among the elements of a system, focusing on the parts only as they constitute a whole. As Cherryholmes points out, structuralism:

... promises order, organization and certainty. Structuralism in education promises accountability, efficiency, and
control.... [It] is consistent with teaching for objectives,
standardized educational assessment, quantitative empirical research, systematic instruction, rationalized bureaucra-
cies and scientific management.[12]

Key examples of the structuralist approach include Bloom's taxonomy of educational objectives and Tyler's model of curriculum
development.[13]

The alternative approach, which Cherryholmes calls post-structuralist, draws on the writings of Foucault, Derrida and Habermas,
among others. While they differ from one another in some profound ways, their work suggests a telling critique of dominant
forms of educational thought.

It takes a new reader a while to get used to a central feature of
post-structural criticism: It asks very different questions from more
traditional approaches. Foucault, for instance, in a famous debate
with Noam Chomsky, sidestepped the moderator's abstract question "Does human nature exist?" and posed his own query: "How
has the concept of human nature functioned in our society?"[14]

Foucault was interested not so much in the "truth" of a particular proposition as in its historical evolution and its function in a
society characterized by asymmetrical power relations. He focused
directly not on natural or social phenomena but on "discourses" or
"what is said and written and passes for more or less orderly
thought and exchange of ideas," and on "practices" or "activities
performed on a regular basis, although [with] variation."[15]

Foucault is interested in the political production of truth.
How are discourses constituted? How do discourses constitute institutions? How do institutions constitute and regu-
late discourses? He tries to account for how texts came to be
what they are, not explain or interpret them or say what
they really meant.[16]

All discourses-practices are shaped by underlying rules and by
socio-political arrangements among the participants. Foucault
wanted to uncover and critique these rules and arrangements
underlying particular ways of talking about the world.

Jacques Derrida focuses on written texts, but his criticism applies as well to acted texts, to social life. His basic argument is that
meaning is not centered or fixed, that "structures of meaning are no
more than illusions."[17] When participants in a discourse (or readers
of a text) settle on meanings, their foundations are situational and

pragmatic. There is no "transcendental signified," no single meaning for a word or concept. Rather, people work out meanings as
they go, based on their commitments, values and relationships.

Derrida also shows that many texts make rhetorical claims that
contradict their own logic.[18] Cherryholmes illustrates the process of
"deconstruction" by critiquing Ralph Tyler's famous rationale for
curriculum development.[19] Tyler's whole approach rests on an
"objective" reading of a particular educational situation. Cherryholmes shows that, given the implicit value commitments and
power arrangements of any social setting, including a school, such a
reading is impossible. Thus, the scheme "deconstructs."

Implications for Experiential Education

So what does this arcane, densely written discussion have to do
with experiential education? I want to argue that post-structural-
ism provides a handle on at least three elements of experiential
education: (a) what is actually going on when students are in the
workplace supposedly learning from experience; (b) the place of
experiential learning programs in traditional academic institutions,
and the politics of their survival; and (c) approaches to teaching in
these programs.

The Learning Process

First, what's going on in the internship or service site? Structu-
ralists make claims about students' "applying theory" derived from
classroom learning and "acquiring facts and skills" in the
workplace. Cooperative educators, as an example, teach engineering students the basic principles of physics governing the weight-
bearing capacities of various structures; then they send the students
out to engineering firms to use those principles in the design of a
bridge. At the same time, the student presumably learns something
about the way such a firm operates.

In the single most frequently quoted treatise on experiential
education, David Kolb proposes two concepts that clearly fit the
structuralist mold.[20] First, he suggests that learning proceeds
through a cycle, moving from concrete experience (CE) to reflective
observation (RO), then to abstract conceptualization (AC) and finally to active experimentation (AE).[21] Experiential educators sometimes try to identify the stage a student has reached in the cycle.

The second element of Kolb's theory is really more about learners than about learning. He suggests that different people tend to

favor different aspects of the learning process: CE or AC on the dimension he calls "prehension" (the grasping of experience); RO or AE on the "transformation" dimension (the operations one performs on experience). This two-dimensional structure yields four distinct "learning styles": "divergent" (CE/RO); "assimilative" (AC/RO); "convergent" (AC/AE); and "accommodative" (CE/AE).[22] For a variety of purposes, experiential educators often administer Kolb's Learning Styles Inventory to their students.

The post-structuralist conception of the learning process differs substantially in some ways from these popular visions. First, it takes as problematic (that is, neither assumes nor denies, but inquires into) the transferability of academic concepts into work settings. The problem is that discourses-practices are very different in those two arenas. The same term (e.g., "organizational culture") may mean one thing to sociology professors and quite another to management consultants. The former, for instance, may treat the concept as a clear-cut analytic tool for identifying features of an organization, while the latter may regard it as a tool for enhancing management's control over workers. Part of the learning process, then, entails the student's confronting those shifting systems of meaning.

But the post-structuralist critic will see that confrontation as more than an individual's struggle to compare ideas. Rather, as Foucault would argue, it must be seen as embedded in the histories of the respective institutions, and in the power arrangements underlying the definition and use of terms. So the learning process engages the student as a participant (generally with relatively little power) in an ongoing negotiation of meanings and their uses. That is, contrary to Kolb's image of a particular type of learner encountering a more or less given environment, the post-structuralist sees the interaction as dialectical, emergent, situated and political.[23]

The Politics of Experiential Education

How do experiential programs "fit" in the university? The dominant forms of discourse and practice in academia are clearly what Cherryholmes would call structuralist. Both the history of the institution and the allocation of power across faculty and students confirm the premise that some people have knowledge and others do not, and that the former can both instruct and certify the latter. Moreover, academics, especially those in the liberal arts, tend to value abstract knowledge, ideas which may (or may not) refer to the "real world," but clearly exist on a different cognitive and moral plane. And finally, knowledge is conceived as being divided into identifiable categories called "disciplines," each with its own problems, methods and customs. The departmental structure of the university reflects that division of realms of knowledge.

Traditionally, experiential learning has occupied a marginal place in the university curriculum. Mainstream scholars looked down their noses at it, considering it vocational, soft-headed and escapist. A professor who tolerated a student's urge to do an internship "for the experience" may have vigorously resisted the notion that what is learned from such work merits academic credit. Where experiential programs have taken root, they are often justified on grounds only tangentially related to the primary mission of the university: applying classroom-based knowledge; exploring careers; developing social, emotional and ethical skills. Often, in fact, the appeal of such programs to the faculty is their appeal to students: retention is serious business.

But when experiential educators think seriously about the nature of the learning they encourage, when they examine the epistemological premises of their work, they threaten the essential discourses and practices of the university. They claim that learning should be student-centered rather than discipline-centered. They maintain that faculty members do not always know everything worth learning, and that students can create knowledge as well as receive it. Their methods appear to strip teachers of their hard-won control over the learning process: interns, after all, are usually out of sight, and tests of their accumulated knowledge are next to impossible. Finally, the kinds of problems interns learn about in the field never seem to fit neatly into disciplinary categories, so faculty members feel out of their elements, bordering on incompetent.

All this means, from a post-structuralist perspective, that experiential education potentially constitutes a fundamental challenge to the traditional definitions of knowledge and the historical arrangements of power on which the university operates. That revolutionary character can be muffled or even subverted by experientialists' attempts to abide by the terms of traditional academic discourse (a Foucauldian critic could have a field day with much of the discourse in experiential education these days), but it cannot be destroyed completely.

Teaching for Experience

Finally, what about pedagogy for field-based learning? A structuralist curriculum for an internship program could look very Tylerian: Describe the factual situation in the workplace, state the

Experiential learning offers as good an opportunity as we have in higher education to create a critical pedagogy, a form of discourse in which teachers and students conduct an unfettered investigation of social institutions, power relations and value commitments.

values and objectives to be pursued, select a course of action calculated to achieve those objectives.[24] In fact, as experiential educators refine their practice, they sometimes move in that direction.

Some field study programs require students to participate in a seminar to prepare for, examine or reflect on their experiences.[25] Others do not. The issue here is this: How can we "teach" about experience? What is it that we are teaching?

The structuralist lays out (relatively) clear-cut objectives: The student will learn about child-protection laws, about the operations of the family court, about related social service agencies; she will acquire skills in research and the organization of information on available resources. In the concurrent seminar, the teacher introduces concepts like organizational structure, communications channels and bureaucratic relations; and asks the students to investigate their placements through those terms. The teacher does not consider this agenda exhaustive; she expects serendipitous learning — but she tries to structure the process.

The post-structuralist might start out with many of the same methods, but would use them as a stepping-off point for a process Habermas calls "critical discourse"[26]: the recursive examination of experience in which students learn to "read" their workplaces as "texts," as "discourses-practices." The skillful post-structuralist instructor engages in what several writers have called "critical pedagogy."[27] Habermas claims that critical discourse requires certain conditions: It must be symmetrical and non-dominated, and all participants must be able to initiate comments, challenge assertions and question theories.[28] The teacher in this model does not provide authoritative meanings, facts or answers, but rather establishes the conditions within which everyone can examine and penetrate the histories, power arrangements and values underlying their work organizations. Participants "criticize" their experiences, trying to discover the full range of interpretations through which their worlds might be understood.

Conclusions

Of course, describing this pedagogy in abstract terms is far easier than doing it. In schools, where relations between teachers and students are historically shaped and clearly hierarchical, the conditions for critical discourse may be impossible to meet. But the effort is worthwhile.

The title of this chapter suggests that experiential education can be regarded as a form of critical discourse. I have tried to show that the term fits in several ways:

1. The student intern almost inevitably engages in a crude form of critical discourse because of the differences between the discourses-practices of the school and those of the workplace or service site. Caught between two potentially contradictory roles (the "student" as by definition ignorant, the "worker" as putatively competent), the intern can hardly avoid questions about the meanings of certain terms and relations. Even without intervention, the field experience stimulates some kinds of learning.

2. In the context of higher education, experiential learning necessarily threatens the dominant forms of discourse and practice. Even when experientialists try to describe their programs in terms acceptable to the traditionalists, basic tensions sneak through. Their conversations, therefore, although they cannot meet the condition of symmetry, reveal some crucial insights about the nature of the institution and of the learning process.

3. *Finally, experiential learning offers as good an opportunity as we have in higher education to create a critical pedagogy, a form of discourse in which teachers and students conduct an unfettered investigation of social institutions, power relations and value commitments.*

Much more remains to be done to elaborate this critical analysis of experiential education. I still do not understand half the work these writers publish. But I am convinced that we are on to something.

David Thornton Moore is Director of Social Science Programs in the Gallatin Division of New York University. He is a Kellogg National Fellow and former editor of Experiential Education, *a publication of the National Society for Internships and Experiential Education.*

Footnotes

[1] Jane C. Kendall, John S. Duley, Thomas C. Little, Jane S. Permaul and Sharon Rubin, *Strengthening Experiential Education in Your Institution*, National Society for Internships and Experiential Education, 1987.

[2] See Morris Keeton and Associates. *Experiential Learning: History, Rationale, Assessment*, Jossey-Bass, 1976.

[3] I draw heavily throughout on the interpretations of this work by Cleo Cherryholmes, in *Power and Criticism: Poststructural Investigations in Education*, Teachers College Press, 1988.

[4] Allan Bloom, *The Closing of the American Mind*, Simon and Schuster, 1987.

[5] E. D. Hirsch, Jr., *Cultural Literacy*, Houghton Mifflin, 1987.

[6] Kendall *et al.*, cf. Lenore Borzak, *Field Study*, Sage, 1981, p. 9.

[7] See Tim Stanton, "Field Study Exercises," in *Field Study: A Sourcebook for Experiential Learning*, ed. Lenore Borzak, Sage, 1981.

[8] See Kenneth G. Ryder, James W. Wilson and Associates, *Cooperative Education in a Modern Era*, Jossey-Bass, 1988.

[9] See Keeton and Associates, 1976; and Borzak, 1981.

[10] Cf. Henry A. Giroux, *Theory and Resistance in Education*, Bergin and Garvey, 1983; C. A. Bowers, *Elements of a Post-Liberal Theory of Education*, Teachers College Press, 1987; Cherryholmes, Power and Criticism.

[11] Ferdinand deSaussure, *Course in General Linguistics*, McGraw-Hill, 1966, originally published 1916.

[12] Cherryholmes, p. 30.

[13] Benjamin S. Bloom, *et al.*, *Taxonomy of Educational Objectives*, David McKay, 1956; Ralph W. Tyler, *Basic Principles of Curriculum and Instruction*, University of Chicago Press, 1949.

[14] Paul Rabinow, "Introduction," in *The Foucault Reader*, ed. Paul Rabinow, Pantheon Books, 1984.

[15] Cherryholmes, pp. 2-3.

[16] *Ibid.*, p. 33.

[17] *Ibid.*, p. 36.

[18] Jacques Derrida, *Positions*, University of Chicago Press, 1981.

[19] Tyler, *Basic Principles*.

[20] David A. Kolb, *Experiential Learning*, Prentice-Hall, 1984.

[21] *Ibid.*, p. 42.

[22] *Ibid.*

[23] Cf. Jean Lave, *Cognition in Practice*, Cambridge University Press, 1988.

[24] Cherryholmes, p. 40.

[25] Pat Hutchings and Allen Wutzdorff, ed., *Knowing and Doing: Learning through Experience*, Jossey-Bass, 1988; Ted Theodorou, "The Internship Seminar at LaGuardia: A Curricular Bridge between Classroom and Work," *Experiential Education*, National Society for Internships and Experiential Education, Vol. 12, No. 5, November-December 1987, pp. 4, 12.

[26] Jurgen Habermas, *Communication and the Evolution of Society*, Beacon Press, 1979.

[27] Cf. Ira Shor, *Critical Teaching and Everyday Life*, University of Chicago Press, 1987; David W. Livingstone, ed., *Critical Pedagogy and Cultural Power*, Bergin and Garvey, 1987; Giroux, *Theory and Resistance*; Roger I. Simon, "Critical Pedagogy," in *The International Encyclopedia of Education*, T. Husen and N. Postlethwaite, eds., Pergamon Press, 1985.

[28] Cherryholmes, p. 89.

Enriching the Liberal Arts
Integrating Experiential Learning throughout a Liberal Arts College

Neil Thorburn

A dean and college president describes how a liberal arts college's chief academic officer can encourage faculty to be responsive to student enthusiasm for experiential learning. The generic terms of "fieldwork," "internship" and "field experience" are all used here to refer to experience-based learning opportunities. Experiential education is the method used to teach learners who are engaged in active, direct involvement with the phenomena they are studying. Because service-learning draws on experiential education methods, this chapter is useful for chief academic officers who want to encourage public and community service. Service-learning is often one of several forms of experiential education for which faculty develop academic supports and policies. Reprinted with permission from Enriching the Liberal Arts through Experiential Learning, *Stevens E. Brooks and James E. Althof, eds., Jossey-Bass and Council for Adult and Experiential Learning, New Directions for Experiential Learning, No. 6, 1979, pp. 13-21.*

COLLEGE STUDENTS INSTINCTIVELY RECOGNIZE the value of experiential education, but it is not so readily appreciated by faculty members who are accustomed to the more traditional modes of instruction in the liberal arts college. The challenge for an institution's chief academic officer is to understand why students are so rewarded by their field experiences and then to familiarize reluctant faculty members with the concept of experiential learning, drawing initially on the support of those teachers already committed. These people will communicate their enthusiasm to their more hesitant colleagues.

My purpose here is to outline some of the ways in which we have been successful at Albion College in developing a variety of experiential programs and gaining faculty support for them. Every institution is different, but some of the approaches we tried may be worth emulating on other college campuses. If the administrator is unwilling to support experiential learning, the members of the faculty can easily capitalize on their traditional attitudes toward teaching and learning, not all of which are exciting to students.

Most of the conventional assumptions about liberal learning and the nature of a liberal arts college continue to have great value, as anyone who has ever taught in such an environment will testify. Experiential learning does not contradict any of those assumptions; in fact, thoughtful analysis reveals that it actually reinforces them. Most teachers take it for granted that their students see relevance in what they teach, so they make little effort at application. "Too much material to cover in too short a time," so the argument runs, or, "How will I ever complete the course by the end of the semester?" The study of history, to borrow an example from my own discipline, can be either germane to the problems of the modern world, inspiring students to seek careers in law or public policy, or an intellectual exercise attracting only the most committed of scholars. Rewarding yes, but unlikely to attract a large following among this generation of students. This is deplorable perhaps, but if the ends of liberal learning have intrinsic value, why not pay more attention to the means?

Alongside the traditional study of history lies a conviction that learning takes place only in the classroom or in the library. One learns by reading books, hearing lectures, and writing papers. Fieldwork is rarely undertaken, and then usually in the form of research in another library. But the surge of interest in experiential learning has touched even this most traditional of disciplines, however.

Facilitating Experiential Programs

If historians on the campus of one traditional liberal arts college can recognize the importance of experiential learning, it must be possible for similar faculties to do the same. What does a college's chief academic officer do to facilitate the process? He or she must first recognize that field experience is a part of the curriculum, carries credit, requires faculty advisement and supervision, and involves units that might otherwise be taken in a conventional classroom situation. Faculty members must, therefore, make the basic policy decisions about what kind of field experience, where, and for how long, much as they would in approving a cluster of new courses or reviewing the structure of a general education requirement.

At Albion College we have developed a variety of experiential programs in recent years. The foundation has been laid by the faculty members themselves in the academic policy committee, in ad hoc groups, and in their own departments. We have learned that policies affecting experiential learning are academic policies, and that such decisions must be made within the institution's accepted governance procedures.

Common and readily accepted experiences need to be cited frequently as precedents. Everyone knows that students in education are required to practice teach; they received credit for it long before the terms *internship* or *experiential education* crept into the vocabulary of higher education. Albion students have long participated in a variety of programs sponsored by the Great Lakes College Association (GLCA) to study in foreign countries — experiential learning in the truest sense but exceedingly compatible with time-honored standards for language instruction. Since 1968, our students have also had excellent opportunities in the GLCA Philadelphia Urban Semester [now the Philadelphia Center] and the New York Arts program. Such programs take them away from the campus for a semester, but they come back with a new vitality. This also affects other students in the classroom, and the benefits become apparent even to the most traditional instructor. All teachers appreciate responsive students, and more ambitious experiential learning can follow from such traditional activities as practice teaching and study abroad. Programs that begin in a small way will grow.

Another factor that helps to gain support for experiential learning is in itself a commentary on the value of the education at a liberal arts college like Albion. The classes are small and academic advising is handled more thoughtfully than on many campuses. Faculty members know their advisees well and are often influenced by them. Many of our students come from a secure socio-economic background; their parents are successful professional people or corporation executives whose offspring are acutely aware of the practical consequences of an education. "How will I get into medical school? What do I take that will make me a strong contender for one of the top-rated M.B.A. programs? What will a prospective employer look for on my transcript?" they repeatedly ask.

Faculty advisors are also aware that approximately 60 percent of each graduating class goes directly to work. An academic plan aimed at the study of British literature in graduate school differs little from the plan of any English major directed at employment in the management training program of a large corporation. Academicians know from experience that English majors are prepared to do things other than go to graduate school. But the students may not know that. Too many of them choose a different field when they would have enjoyed literature — to follow that example — because they thought they could not get a job when they graduated. It may sound expedient, but why not let the English major try some things alongside his or her traditional major that make a vocational outcome more likely? "Don't give me a lecture about the value of the liberal arts," the mother of a recently enrolled freshman told me. "We chose Albion because it is a liberal arts college. Tell us what else you can do, because my son will be a better student if he feels confident he can get a job some day."

Our faculty has devised programs — we call them "concentrations" — that are a collection of courses to supplement one of the traditional liberal arts majors. The concentration in professional management, for example, requires a major in economics and management and includes two semester-length internships. The Gerald R. Ford Institute concentration in public service also includes a two-unit internship (eight semester hours), generally to be taken either in a state agency in Lansing or as a legislative intern there or in Washington. The importance of such concentrations is obvious: the student not only has a major but something more. Administrators have given the Ford Institute strong encouragement, and careful consultation with key faculty leaders plus the appointment of a faculty-student advisory committee has brought the program crucial faculty support. "Here is a practical way for our majors to get some experience," they now argue, and "students now take our courses in political science, history, and sociology, when they may not have done so before."

Administrative Support

Administrative support is essential. For both the Ford Institute and the professional management programs, we provide a director who is primarily an administrator, although each also teaches one course a semester. A primary responsibility of these program directors is public relations. The admissions office regularly uses their help in recruiting students, and, of course, internship opportunities must be solicited before students can be placed in them. Such sponsors are not hard to find; often they become warm friends of the college. Encouraged to visit the campus, many do so. The professional management program began with the help of a generous

grant from the Lilly Endowment, but its success has convinced us
that the services provided by the director more than justify his
salary, which was initially provided by the grant but since paid by
the college. Faculty members seem to agree. Other concentrations,
such as a program in human services and another in mass communications, do not have an administrator in charge. They are coordinated by a faculty member who chairs an advisory committee.

Students who graduate with one of these structured concentrations often find themselves with excellent job offers — and success
breeds experimentation. All faculty members like to teach satisfied
students, and the fact that they do well after graduation is a source
of considerable pride to faculty, and of reassurance to underclass-
men. In recognition of this, Albion faculty members have moved
departmentally to develop experiential opportunities for their majors. In each case the spade work is done by the faculty members
themselves, encouraged by administrators who recognize that such
work is time-consuming and requires a modest amount of financial
support. There is no more effective way to spark faculty initiative
than to grant small financial requests. It helps morale. While fiscal
constraints always exist, departments should be encouraged to re-
imburse faculty members for the expenses involved. One example
is the psychology department's practicum — actual clinical experience in a public or private social service agency — which requires an
unusual amount of faculty supervision. Since the services of more
than one person are often required, these duties are shared by two
people with an appropriate adjustment in their teaching loads. To
allow a faculty member to include a practicum as a course underscores its value as an integral part of the curriculum and ensures
careful attention to the project. Load reduction is almost as good for
morale as money is. If such a load adjustment for an experiential
learning program seems unjustified, just compare the number of
students involved and the objectives they attain through it with
other courses regularly offered that may enroll no more than six to
ten students.

Some programs will require special arrangements and unusual
expenses. Albion's biology department sponsors a premedical internship for a group of 14-16 premed students, usually in the summer between their sophomore and junior years. The students are
carefully screened and then placed with a medical doctor for a
substantial part of the summer paying summer college tuition for
one unit of credit. The doctors are selected by two members of the
biology department, who visit them to discuss the program before
they agree to become sponsors. The students are called on twice

during the summer internship by the faculty advisors. The time and travel for the faculty members involved is considerable. They enjoy it, yet we feel that they should be paid for their efforts at the same rate they would be paid if it were a regular course. Travel expenses are also covered. Not surprisingly, among the most willing medical sponsors are Albion alumni. The opportunity to observe a doctor in his or her daily work for several weeks is a marvelous opportunity for premedical students to see where they are headed if they plan a career in medicine. Nearly all our previous summer interns have been successful medical school applicants. Among the few who were not are several who decided, as a result of their field experience, that the practice of medicine was not for them.

We also have a similar program sponsored by the religious studies department, which during the academic year provides an internship with a clergyman, a hospital chaplain, or a professional religious education worker, with much the same objective in mind. "Do I want to go to divinity school and become a clergyman? What does the ministry require anyway? I know what a clergyman does on Sunday morning," a student will ask, "but what are the other obligations?"

Integrating Experiential Learning into a Curriculum

The most difficult challenge for colleges to meet is the student demand for miscellaneous field experiences. "I just want to do an internship," so the statement runs. "I don't know in what or where." An internship committee was organized at Albion, its assigned task being to develop some criteria and a set of guidelines for internships. They would apply to the student rummaging in the dusty basement files of the local historical association as well as to an ambitious communications major working at a radio station. The committee deliberated and devised a document that met with the formal approval of the faculty when it was presented to them. Important distinctions were made between internships involving observation and those which required actual work or service. A cooperative education experience is an internship with a salary; in reality, it is a full-time job. A student-initiated internship may amount to no more than a promise from someone that he may hang around for a few hours a week, hoping to pick up something in the process. The committee insisted that mere observation should not earn the same credit as a formal internship unless it included an elaborate report.

Just as important are the grading criteria. If this is an academic experience, does a person in the field evaluate the work performance or does the faculty advisor? The former is awkward — only faculty gives grades — and interns are often difficult to assess objectively. I participated in some of these discussions, often recalling my own frustration in grading student interns in the offices of New York state legislators. Unless it is fully talked out among faculty, the grading problem can generate opposition to experiential learning. But this dilemma can be resolved. We opted for requiring that internship credit be assigned on the basis of a report written by the student evaluating his or her experience. The faculty decided experiential learning would be subject to the same evaluation process as any other course.

The guidelines also specify that placement be made carefully and only after the student selects the advisor best equipped to provide the supervision. Not only the method of evaluation but also what is to be evaluated is set forth in advance, whether it be a detailed report, as is required of all professional management interns, or a portfolio of articles written by a newspaper intern. Curiosity itself cannot be the only qualification; a student must be prepared for the experience. For example, a student interested in journalism would have taken a course in it or at least had some successful work in expository writing before being recommended to the editor of a newspaper as a candidate for a reporting internship.

Administrative Coordination

Experiential education requires coordination. Our off-campus programs, such as study abroad, are given administrative oversight by a faculty member who receives released time and additional compensation. The directors of the concentrations in professional management and the Ford Institute have already been mentioned. The faculty wanted similar supervision for all other experiential learning, particularly individual internships. Someone has to collect the data on the opportunities available, counsel students, answer innumerable questions, or put a student in touch with a knowledgeable faculty member. This is a time-consuming assignment when all the record keeping is included. We tried it twice with a faculty member released from a course each semester for the purpose. Both did commendable jobs, but both reported the same problems: too little visibility with the majority of students and too much time taken away from regular teaching and advising responsibilities, at least more time than the load reduction warranted.

We then tried another tack, which has proved remarkably successful. The career planning and placement office is well organized to perform its traditional role and headed by a capable director who is greatly respected by the faculty and has at her disposal a variety of information about opportunities. She knows how to get students exploring alternatives. She was given part-time assistance to pick up some of the placement duties in her office, and she took on the responsibility of coordinating the internship program. The student who proposes a field experience outside one of our concentrations, with its own internship arrangement, checks first with the internship coordinator. She must approve the idea and see that an appropriate faculty adviser has been chosen and that the student's own adviser, if it is a different person, knows of the project.

One anticipated fringe benefit of this administrative arrangement has turned out to be far more important than we realized. The correlation of experiential learning with the career planning and placement function encourages students to use field opportunities as a chance to explore potential careers. It is worth repeating that students working in the offices of a law firm, for example, have a chance to see if the law is what they really want; they learn from experienced people what law school was like and what a practicing attorney actually does. Similar benefits accrue to students considering careers or even citizen roles in areas related to community and public service. And to restate the obvious: students and faculty members are often embarrassingly uninformed about what people outside academia do in their jobs. In a generation when students may face more than one career change, they gain firsthand appreciation for the lasting value of liberal learning.

Faculty supervisors of student internships will candidly report that the students' internships are a learning experience for them as well. Many college professors went from baccalaureate straight through doctoral degrees with very little, if any, practical experience outside a college or university. A professor may be superb at the analysis of federal fiscal policy but have little insight into the variety of employment available in budgeting for nonprofit organizations. Through their students' experiences, the professors themselves acquire information that they can then pass on to future students. Consciously or unconsciously, faculty members become more effective career counselors. Some of these people will themselves seek opportunities to use sabbatical leaves or faculty development support to spend a summer or a semester trying an internship. We encourage this and see it as a viable sabbatical proposal.

In more ways than this, a field experience program is a boon to a college's public relations. Successful and accomplished students are automatic ambassadors, enhancing the reputation of their institution. Frequently we find that this benefits the admissions office.

Albion's application pool has increased in the past several years, and it is clear from the remarks of many supporters, that the good impressions made by our students increase respect for Albion College. People are far more apt to give cheerfully to successful colleges.

Institutional Benefits

In the final analysis, what are the most important things for a chief academic officer to encourage in developing experiential learning opportunities within a traditional liberal arts framework? The following seem particularly worth stressing.

Field experiences complement the traditional liberal arts curriculum; they are not a substitute for it. Every effort must be made to see that the field experience is a coherent part of a student's academic plan rather than an isolated episode.

Experiential education may require prerequisites. Much as one studies a foreign language before undertaking study abroad, so one also prepares for an internship in a state legislator's office by some work in economics, political science, and history. To understand the process in which one is to be involved is to be an even more effective participant.

Faculty formulation of the policies guiding experiential learning needs to be encouraged, keeping these policies as close as possible to the standards set for all other educational experiences.

Administrators have to recognize that field experience programs do cost money. The number of student units thus generated in a semester is never as large as opponents predict during the planning process, but it will affect faculty loads somewhat, whether credit is given for the supervision of independent study or not. If this presents a problem, internships and off-campus study may be encouraged during the fall term when enrollment is likely to be higher than during the rest of the year. Departmental budgets must

---

Experiential learning is incompatible with more traditional learning only if the academy is incompatible with the society of which it is a part.

---

be supplemented to provide some support for travel and related expenses for those faculty members who will seek out opportunities for their students and then later need to observe them at work. In some departments internship supervision reaches the equivalent of a course. Such a prospect is less threatening when set alongside the list of courses offered in which only a few students are enrolled, each justified by its indispensability to the liberal arts. The argument that certain courses must be made available for liberal learning can also be used for field experience.

Experiential learning programs gain support from alumni and trustees, as they do from students. Albion trustees inquire regularly into what we are doing in the field and often offer internships themselves. One of Albion's strengths is the loyalty of its friends and alumni, many of whom articulate the values of liberal learning more effectively than any professor in the classroom. With their support, opportunities for our students multiply.

Experiential learning is incompatible with more traditional learning only if the academy is incompatible with the society of which it is a part. In a day when people need to be ever more conscious of the world and its troubles, when events are daily brought to our attention by the media, who is to say that field experience can other than strengthen the mission of liberal learning, which is ultimately to educate for life?

Neil Thorburn is President of Wilmington College in Ohio. He has taught American history at several colleges and was Dean of the Faculty at Albion College in Michigan. His own experiential learning includes a year spent at Union College in Schenectady, New York, as an intern in the ACE Fellows Program in Academic Administration.

Practical Experience and the Liberal Arts: A Philosophical Perspective

Ormond Smythe

Philosopher and academic administrator Ormond Smythe explains why practical experience — including community service-learning — can be a potent tool for the revitalization of the liberal arts. Reprinted with permission from Enriching the Liberal Arts Through Experiential Learning, *eds., Stevens E. Brooks and James E. Althof, Jossey-Bass and Council for Adult and Experiential Learning, New Directions for Experiential Learning, No. 6, 1979, pp. 1-12.*

IN VOCATIONAL EDUCATION, experiential learning is generally acknowledged as indispensable. Apprenticeship is the most ancient of educational institutions, after the family, and "experience required" remains an essential prerequisite of employment. It is standard procedure for vocational schools to provide an array of shops, laboratories, and distributive education programs in which students practice their respective trades. Medical education culminates in an internship and residency, and teacher education in supervised practice. Even in law school — probably the most didactic of professional training institutions — students study cases, prepare briefs, and plead in moot court.

Only in the liberal arts has experiential learning yet to establish itself as a fully respectable, universal element of the curriculum. Great progress has been made in recent years, and the problem of integrating experience with liberal education is, as a practical matter, largely solved. In fact it has been solved in a variety of ingenious ways, some of which are reported in this sourcebook.

Theory, however, tends to lag behind practice — a point that experiential learning advocates are fond of emphasizing. If the integration of experience and liberal education has largely been accomplished in the realm of practice, it remains intractable as a conceptual problem. One result is that experiential learning advocates occasionally become defensive in their relations with traditional academics — a dangerous habit, especially at accreditation time. Without denying that experiential learning is a powerful addition to the liberal arts curriculum, we still need to ask why it is so powerful and where it fits into the scheme of things in liberal education. What is the exact nature of the contribution experiential learning can make to liberal education?

The complexity of the question is obvious; the very notion of experiential learning is hard to define precisely. It covers an astonishing range of programs, including cooperative education, field trips, urban semesters, foreign study programs, simulation games, encounter groups, wilderness living experiences, nontraditional adult degree programs and a growing list of others.

And if experiential learning is a difficult notion to pin down, "liberal education" is harder still. Its long and twisted career in the history of ideas has so far led to no uncontroversial resolution of its meaning and content. The clarification of the conceptual link between liberal education and experiential learning is therefore likely to require detailed philosophical analysis of the logic of both notions. That task is by no means hopeless; in fact, work on it has begun (Smythe, 1978) but is too involved to report in detail here. The best that can be offered for the present is a sketch map of the philosophical territory to be explored, with a special focus on the conceptual tensions that have separated liberal education and experiential learning in the past while vocational education has embraced practical experience without hesitation. What is perhaps most fascinating about these tensions is that in recent times they have been steadily breaking down. That process is bound to be critically important, not only for the experiential learning movement but also for the conceptual realignment of liberal education itself.

Liberal Education and the Empirical Spirit

Experiential learning is, of course, an expression of the empirical spirit associated with the rise of modern science. It is no accident that many of the most articulate early advocates of learning by experience were scientific thinkers. Benjamin Franklin, for instance, in his *Proposals Relating to the Education of Youth in Pensilvania* (1749), urged that the practice of gardening and planting be incorporated into the study of natural history. Friedrich Froebel (1890), the early progressive educator who urged greater use of activity in education, was also a passionate student of natural science whose doctrines were shaped in part by the emerging idea of evolution. And John Dewey, whose theory of experience has become the philosophic touchstone of the experiential movement, points to the etymological connections between *experience* and *experiment*. His famous analysis of experience as a two-phase cycle of trying and undergoing owes its form to the model of scientific inquiry: "The nature of experience can be understood only by noting that it includes an active and a passive element peculiarly combined. On the active hand, experience is *trying* — a meaning which is made explicit in the connected term experiment. On the passive, it is *undergoing*. When we experience something we act upon it, we do something to it; then we suffer or undergo the consequence. We do something to the thing and then it does something to us in return. Such is the peculiar combination" ([1916] 1966, p. 139).

Ours is a scientific age, and it is easy to forget how radical Dewey's view was when seen against the background of centuries of educational practice. Science has only recently come into its own in liberal education. At Cambridge University, for example, science was not part of the regular undergraduate curriculum until 1865, even though Cambridge had by then already produced both Newton and Darwin and took pride in having done so even if it could not entirely take the credit. The scientific revolution of the seventeenth century — the work of Galileo, Kepler, Newton, Harvey, and Boyle — occurred almost wholly outside the walls of academe. From the time of its establishment in the Middle Ages, the university was unreceptive to the empirical spirit. Lord Ashby reminds us of the old story "that in the medieval University of Paris the professors were disputing about the number of teeth in a horse's mouth. They agreed that the number could not be a multiple of three, for that would be an offense to the Trinity; nor could it be a multiple of seven, for God created the world in six days and rested on the seventh. Neither the records of Aristotle nor the arguments of Saint Thomas enabled them to solve the problem. Then a shocking thing happened. A student who had been listening to the discussion went out, opened a horse's mouth, and counted the teeth" (1963, p. 37). That anonymous student, says Ashby, gave us far more than the hardy cliché about the trustworthiness of what comes "straight from the horse's mouth"; his brash act also signaled "the beginning of objective inquiry, the revolt against authority, the empirical attitude, the linking of academic study with the facts of life. His act introduced research into the university" (Ashby, 1963, p. 37). We may add that it also introduced experiential learning.

Of course Ashby's picture is overdrawn. Ancient science was responsive to empirical tests, and objective inquiry far antedates the Middle Ages. But it is not without point to observe that during the period when universities were coming into being the primary method of academic study was to consult classical texts and to dispute their interpretation. And that tradition persists into our own time. The very concept of a university is to this day infected with stereotypes and clichés about bookish, absentminded professors who fail to make contact with "real life." The very work *academic*, in some contexts, has come to mean insignificant, without practical import, a dead letter. And the old-fashioned scholastic is by no means an extinct species, as Walter Kaufmann (1977) reminds us.

Liberal education is, of course, part of the scholastic tradition. There are still plenty of academics willing to argue that liberal education consists of the study of the "great books." But this scholastic attitude is losing its hold on the actual practice of liberal education. Even at St. John's College, where the great books are the foundation stones of the curriculum, the students learn their science in a laboratory as well as in a library. In the twentieth century it is hardly likely that the liberal arts could successfully resist the influence of empiricism even if they wanted to.

What remains of the scholastic legacy is the habit of identifying the liberal arts with the humanities more than with the sciences. That habit is, no doubt, a bad one. Twenty years ago C. P. Snow (1959) reminded us that we are just as ill-educated if we are innocent of the Second Law of Thermodynamics as we are if we have never read a Shakespeare play. That reminder, though still a bit jarring, becomes steadily more difficult to deny. Its acceptance signals the breakdown of the old opposition between the sciences and the liberal arts. This same breakdown is helping to improve the climate for experiential learning in liberal arts colleges.

Experiential learning, meanwhile, is softening its own theory and modifying its practice so as to become steadily less preoccupied with the model of science as the only form of learning. John Dewey, especially in the earliest formulations of his theory of experience, saw experiential learning and scientific thought as two aspects of a single attitude of mind, and he was led to advance claims that sound extravagant today.

"It is not experience," he wrote ([1916], 1966, pp. 139-140), "when a child merely sticks his finger into a flame; it is experience when the movement is connected with the pain which he undergoes in consequence. Henceforth the sticking of the finger into flame *means* a burn. Being burned is a mere physical change, like the burning of a stick of wood, if it is not perceived as a consequence of some other action." Surely this is too strong. It requires that *experience*, in order to merit the name experience at all, must involve the making of an intelligent connection between act and consequence. Meaning must be generated; otherwise "it is not experience." The ordinary usage of *experience*, and even of the notion of learn;ing from experience, is far less restricted than that. Most of us would say that the child in Dewey's example experiences the burn just because he feels it. It is of educational interest, of course, that the child should come to understand that the pain results from the act of touching the flame; but that is immaterial to our decision to call his pain an experience. Feeling is enough.

This is no mere theoretical nicety. The insight it represents appears in the practice of experiential education as well. Dewey insists that all experience must have an active phase — that it must involve more than mere undergoing. This active phase he calls "trying," and suggests that it gives experience the structure of an experiment. "Trying" is, of course, a coherent notion only when there is some object one is trying to attain; one cannot try while trying nothing in particular. In short, on Dewey's account, all genuine experience involves purpose; it is all aimed at something.

Contemporary experiential learning practice recognizes that this is not always the case. Not all experience is purposeful or begins with elements analogous to hypothesis and experimental design. Some experiences, including some of our richest learning experiences, have more the nature of lucky accidents. If they begin with any purpose at all, the purpose may initially have nothing to do with learning. Programs that award credit toward liberal arts degrees for students' preenrollment experiential learning are especially committed to the recognition of this characteristic of ordinary experience. What begins as a mere job, taken on solely in order to earn a living, sometimes becomes invaluable educationally — and no one is more surprised than the learner. What begins as a foreign vacation may, in the same way, develop into a wrenching cross-cultural experience with profound learning consequences. Or what begins as a personal emotional crisis may lead to life-transforming episodes of self-evaluation, contributing critically to one's social, affective, or moral education. The early Dewey would not have counted such cases as experiences at all, since they lack the required trying phase, with its implication of purpose and planning. The later Dewey (1934, 1938) softened this stance a bit, and contemporary practice has moved still further away from exclusive reliance on planned, sponsored, experimentally designed experiences. It is now recognized that planning and purpose are not always necessary for fruitful learning experience, and indeed that fussy insistence on detailed planning may actually interfere with learning. As Morris Keeton writes, "The very heart of learning is ... a process in which unexpected things emerge. To define excellence in learning as having the most detailed syllabi describing how learning will occur and what will be learned is the very antithesis of what higher education should be" (1972, p. 147). For Keeton, much of the promise of the experiential movement lies in its capacity "to force us out into the unknown where something genuinely novel can be discovered and where the study of a problem requires the invention of a new approach to its solution" (1972, p. 147). The critical point is that the most important lessons we learn tend to surprise us. Indeed, surprise is fundamental to learning, as a simple matter of logic; hence it is a prime example of what Israel Scheffler calls the "cognitive emotions" (1977, p. 181). Its very existence "testifies that we are not, in principle, beyond acknowledging the predictive failures of our own theories, that we are not debarred by nature from capitalizing on such failures in order to learn from experience" (1977, p. 181).

Dewey himself often took note of this feature of learning, namely, that it depends on the possibility of surprise and that our plans and predictions are apt to go awry whenever we are genuinely learning. This theme appears wherever Dewey discusses aims and purposes in education (1916; 1938). He insists that our "ends-in-view" be tentative to allow for the possibility that what we learn may itself change our purposes as learners. It is that attitude which is perhaps most fundamental of all from the point of view of experiential learning.

In sum, two conceptual developments have been at work in recent years — developments that tend to bring the ideas of experiential learning and of liberal education closer together. First, the notion of liberal education has undergone a metamorphosis such that it is increasingly receptive to empiricism, science, and experience, and less exclusively scholastic and bookish. And second, the experiential learning movement has become more sophisticated in its conception of experience. It has come to see that the rigidly scientific notions of early experimentalism need to be tempered by a receptivity to surprise and serendipity. These simultaneous trends have now progressed to a point where the compatibility, complementarity, and potential for mutual enrichment of liberal education and experiential learning have become apparent.

The Practical Realm and the Classical Tradition

Another tension between experiential learning and the liberal arts that has also begun to break down and resolve itself into a new synthesis of the two is the one created by the historical affinity of experiential learning and vocational training on the one hand and the historical disaffinity of vocational and liberal arts on the other.

Liberal education was originally defined by its exclusive interest in those elements of knowledge which were thought to possess intrinsic, and not just instrumental, value. For Aristotle, instrumental or "mechanical" subjects, explicitly those associated with "all wage-earning occupations," were "illiberal." "They allow the mind no leisure," he said. "They drag it down to a lower level"; whereas "liberal" studies "form part of education solely with a view to the right employment of leisure" (Burnet, 1903, p. 108).

This sharp division between liberal and vocational arts remains influential, though it has been subjected to widespread criticism. It still provides much of the connotative flavor carried by the notion of liberal education. But Aristotle's way of distinguishing the liberal arts from the rest of education is by no means the only way now available. The distinguished University of London philosopher of education, R. S. Peters (1978), believes that there are at least two alternative interpretations of "liberal education" in widespread use today. One of these uses the phrase *liberal education* more or less as an equivalent to *general education*, suggesting that the liberal arts are those which develop the well-rounded person. The other interprets the world *liberal* as suggesting that a curriculum bearing that label should be in some sense liberating. Both these views are familiar enough, and neither is included in the classical conception. Moreover, there are good reasons to doubt the appropriateness of the classical conception and to suspect that one of the more recent views will prove more serviceable for our time. Modern philosophical writers (Beardsley, 1965; Dewey, 1942; Gregory and Woods, 1971) have cast doubt on the clarity of the notion of intrinsic value, upon which Aristotle's concept of the liberal arts depends. But perhaps a more serious deficiency of the classical view is that to modern ears it is disturbingly elitist.

Aristotle distinguished "liberal and illiberal subjects" mostly by reference to their respective utility, as he saw it, for the education of freeman and slaves. His curriculum therefore functioned as a pillar of what we are likely to regard as an unacceptably rigid social class structure. In short, classical liberal education seems itself illiberal by today's standards. If the contemporary liberal arts are regarded as liberal because they are thought to be in some sense liberating, the classical liberal arts were liberal only because they were intended for the already free and at leisure. These days we are less impressed with the value of liberal education as a fringe benefit of membership in the leisure class. We are more attracted by the prospect of using the liberal arts for the enhancement of freedom among those who have too little of it.

Twentieth-century objections to the elitism of the classical view have led to an increasing breakdown of the sharp distinction that, for the Greeks, divided liberal from vocational studies. In *Democracy and Education*, Dewey sought to accelerate the breakdown and to make clear its political implications. "The increased political and economic emancipation of the 'masses' has shown itself in education; it has effected the development of a common school system of education, public and free. It has destroyed the idea that learning is properly a monopoly of the few who are predestined by nature to govern social affairs. But the revolution is still incomplete. The idea still prevails that a truly cultural or liberal education cannot have anything in common, directly at least, with industrial affairs, and that the education which is fit for the masses must be a useful or practical education in a sense which opposes useful and practical to nurture of appreciation and liberation of thought.... Certain studies and methods are retained on the supposition that they have the sanction of peculiar liberality, the chief content of the term liberal being uselessness for practical ends" ([1916] 1966, p. 257). And if Deweyan educational theory denies the vocational-liberal dualism in the realm of philosophy, the institution of the academic major field has effectively undermined it in the realm of practice. The major field, after all, serves both vocational and liberal arts functions at once. On the vocational side it often serves as preparation for a specialized career and almost always serves at least as an early expression of the student's general career direction. But as an element of the liberal arts, the major field provides the student's most intensive engagement with the methods and concepts of a particular discipline, and thus functions as an indispensable complement to the wide sampling of liberal arts that constitutes the general education portion of the curriculum. The major field is liberal education's best insurance against dilettantism.

The conceptual turn of events here is a complex and fascinating one. In its rebellion against the elitism of classical antiquity, contemporary higher education has turned toward experiential learning partly as a device for improving the accessibility of liberal education for populations that until recently were effectively closed off from its advantages, namely, mature adults, working people, women, and members of minority groups. But the experiential turn has been a cause as well as an effect of the democratization of the liberal arts. The inclusion of practical experience in the liberal arts curriculum represents a major conceptual innovation.

One of the key concepts in transformation is the concept of the practical. The term *practical* shows up frequently as a modifier of *experience*, but it is far from clear that it functions as anything more than a redundancy and a decoration. We hear so much about practical experience that we wonder whether there is any other kind. Are some experiences more practical than others? According to the classical account of liberal education, only the least practical experiences would seem to have a place in the liberal arts. But as newer conceptions of liberal education gather momentum, this rule seems less appropriate.

The term *practical* is employed in a multiplicity of ways, some quite rich and others all but incoherent. Sometimes it appears in lieu of the more proper term *practicable* to suggest workability and ease of implementation. It tends to function (like *realistic*) as a euphemistic substitute for *easy*. It also functions as a euphemism in other contexts. When we remind would-be reformers of the realities of practical politics, the realities we have in mind are typically those of the cloakroom, the pork barrel, and the power play. These are the realities of a politics for the most part unilluminated by principles. Aristotle, who regarded all politics as practical simply because of its primary interest in action, would have found this usage of *practical politics* puzzling, but we have grown accustomed to it.

Another corrupt sense of *practical* associates it with urgent utility. A practical mind, in this usage, is thought of as shrewd, down-to-earth, and perhaps not very abstract or reflective. Practical concerns are with the problems of the moment, and the problems of the day after tomorrow are less practical because less pressing. Practical solutions are those which can be patched together hastily out of whatever is at hand, leaving for tomorrow's practical minds the problem of devising a new patchwork to hold for one more day.

It is this usage of *practical* that lies close to the root of the sharp separation between work-related and liberal education. Studies that do not aim at the development of marketable skills are regarded as impractical. A hierarchy of practicality develops, with vocational and professional studies reigning at the top, scientific and technological studies next (since they are thought to be translatable into skills demanded in the marketplace), social sciences next (same reason, lesser degree), and the humanities last. Art, literature, and philosophy, according to the conception of the practical as immediately useful, are pleasant luxuries with which to adorn the curriculum, but they are too impractical to survive hard times and are apt to be pared away early when enrollments begin to decline.

Experiential learning is often assigned a favored place in the hierarchy of the practical as immediately useful, because of its acknowledged role in the training of workers. But this favored place becomes shaky and soon collapses when experiential learning theorists present agendas including not only apprenticeships but also games, encounter groups, wilderness trips, world travel, and the accreditation of adult students' preenrollment learning experience. Experiences that "merely" contribute to personal growth, to the broadening of one's horizons, or to the development of perspectives are not regarded as practical.

Of course the conception of the practical as immediately useful cannot withstand even cursory analysis, for the notion of immediate utility is riddled with defects. Immediacy, for one thing, is relative. One can imagine a "practical" solution assembled hastily today only to blow up tomorrow, raining down horrors far worse than those it was designed to assuage. Such a solution might be immediately useful in some perverse sense, but no one looking back on it tomorrow would concede it that description in the slightly longer run.

Furthermore, the doctrine of the practical as immediately useful employs the notion of utility incoherently. Invariably, the doctrine regards as useful whatever is in demand in the marketplace. But the two notions — utility and market demand — are not at all the same. There is a demonstrable demand for Coca-Cola but the demand implies no need for it; and there is surely a need for vehicles that do not pollute the air, although buyers might not necessarily line up outside the showrooms to purchase them were they available. Neither need nor demand implies the other. In fact the two notions are of different kinds. Demand is a descriptive concept having to do with market conditions as they actually are, while need is a normative concept having to do with things as they ought to be (Dearden, 1972). To proceed from data about the former to conclusions about the latter is therefore to commit the notorious fallacy of moving from premises entirely about what is to conclusions about what ought to be.

An older and more sophisticated notion of the practical allies it with practice and distinguishes it from theory. Practical problems, in this usage, are those which arise in practice rather than theory — that is, in the course of attempts to do rather than to explain. Solutions to practical problems must be adequate "for practical purposes," that is, for the purposes of getting things done; they need not be adequate for purposes of theory spinning or scientific explanation.

When we recognize that a practical solution is one that solves a problem of practice rather than theory, we eliminate at a stroke any impulse to regard it as a more useful solution than some other one, and thus we escape the logical trap of trying to conceive of a useless solution. Practical solutions, in general, are neither more nor less useful than nonpractical (theoretical) ones. They are useful for different purposes.

This way of seeing the practical carries us back to Aristotle — and here he fares better than he did with his view of liberal education. Aristotle distinguishes the practical from the theoretical by noting that the practical is concerned with action and the theoretical with knowledge. There is also a third realm, the productive, which is concerned with making. From this scheme Aristotle derives three varieties of wisdom: practical wisdom disciplines our acts — hence the practical disciplines include ethics and politics, theoretical wisdom disciplines our quest for knowledge — hence the theoretical disciplines are the sciences, and productive wisdom disciplines our efforts to create — hence the productive disciplines are engineering and the arts.

No doubt it is obvious that this typology is not airtight. Ethics and politics require knowing even if they aim in the end at acting; engineering relies on the sciences in fundamental ways; and science, despite its widespread reputation for moral neutrality, expresses moral commitments and requires them. (Free expression, for example, is a fundamental requirement of scientific work.) From the premise that science has moral import, though, it does not follow that the sciences are indistinguishable from the practical disciplines. Science does not aim at action in the same essential way that ethics does. Science in the end is motivated by the impulse to know, and its interest in moral action is instrumental to the satisfaction of that impulse. Ethics is motivated by the impulse to act rightly, and its interest in knowledge is instrumental to the satisfaction of that impulse. The arts are motivated by the creative impulse, to which knowledge and action are instrumentally subordinated. Despite the interplay among Aristotle's three classes of disciplines, their respective aims may still distinguish them, at least provisionally.

Commenting on the contemporary curriculum from the standpoint of Aristotle's scheme, Joseph Schwab writes that "the great educative significance of this organization of the disciplines for us derives from the extent to which our schools have tended to treat all disciplines as if they were theoretical" (1964, p. 21). Literature and the arts are studied through the eyes of critics and art historians. Morals and politics per se are not taught at all but are supplanted by moral philosophy and political science. The neglect of the arts is serious, says Schwab, but the neglect of the practical is worse.

And yet it is understandable. It is well-known that moral and political education must walk a fine line between the twin pitfalls of absolutism and subjectivism. On the one hand there is the risk of indoctrination and on the other hand the risk that nothing will be accomplished beyond an endless, irresolvable bull session.

From the point of view of liberal education, the difficulty of moral and political education represents an extremely serious dilemma. If liberal education is viewed as the passing on of what is best in the culture up to now, then moral and political values are surely part of its content. Or, if liberal education is viewed as "liberating," its moral and political dimension emerges dramatically to a center-stage position. And yet the teaching of virtue is among the oldest of philosophical issues. Socrates and Plato doubted that it could be done — and so do many modern educators.

Whether virtue can be taught depends, of course, as much on what one means by *teaching* as on one's interpretation of *virtue*. If teaching is conceived of as a didactic process akin to telling, it seems clear that there is little hope. In his famous exchange with Meno's slave, Socrates tried to show that neither virtue nor anything else needs to be taught in any such sense. Learning in general, and virtue in particular, are rather to be sought within one's own soul, as a divine gift. The alternative tradition hails from Aristotle, for whom the cultivation of virtue was a matter of the cultivation of good habits — habits formed by practice. Much has been made of the differences between these two views, and this is no place to enter into the controversy. And in any event what the two views share is of more interest to us here. Neither view regards teaching, when virtue is the content to be taught, as a didactic process. For Socrates there is the famous Socratic method, which relies on the asking of questions rather than on the telling of answers; and for Aristotle there is practice. The latter is closer to the spirit of experiential learning, but it is far from clear that the Socratic orientation is incompatible with the experiential movement. At any rate Lawrence Kohlberg, whose "just community" approach to moral education is highly experiential, sees his theory as "a modern restatement of the Platonic view" (Kohlberg, 1970).

If Schwab is right that the moral dimension of the curriculum is its most sadly neglected aspect, then it is clear that experiential learning holds great promise for the revitalization of the liberal arts, since the experiential strategy offers a way of steering clear of both indoctrination and subjectivism. The threat of indoctrination is diminished in experiential education by the presence of real circumstances to balance abstract doctrines and to test them. And the undisciplined quality of bull-session approaches to moral education becomes a less serious hazard also, when real circumstances check the tendency to wander into unrealistic speculation. A student who must live with the actual consequences of acts has a discipline that no bull session can provide and that no program of indoctrination can test and develop. What experiential learning does for moral education is to recognize that in the moral realm it is conduct itself, and not just propositions about conduct, that is the ultimate concern. Experience is "practical" in Aristotle's sense.

Not that moral education should proceed entirely through the "school of hard knocks," as it is appropriately called. Theoretical study and critical thought are essential as sources of form, structure, and discipline. But in the absence of real acts with real consequences, the discipline is incomplete, and the moral aspect of liberal education becomes as abstract and as remote from the practical as is metaphysics. This is where experiential learning may make its most profound contribution to the liberal arts — and this is where the liberal arts most need a healthy dose of real experience.

Ormond Smythe is Dean of Academic Affairs at Fisk University in Nashville, Tennessee. He was a principal developer of the experiential undergraduate programs of Antioch University at Philadelphia. He also previously taught philosophy and in the College of Public and Community Service of the University of Massachusetts at Boston.

References

Ashby, E., "The University Ideal," *The Center Magazine*, 1963, Vol. 6, No. 1, pp. 37-41.

Beardsley, M. G., "Intrinsic Value," *Philosophy and Phenomenological Research*, 1965, Vol. 26, No. 1, pp. 1-17.

Burnet, J., ed. and trans., *Aristotle on Education*, Cambridge University Press, 1903.

Dearden, R. F., "Needs in Education," in R. F. Dearden, P. H. Hirst and R. S. Peters, eds., *Education and the Development of Reason*, Routledge & Kegan Paul, 1972.

Dewey, John, *Art as Experience*, Minton, Balch & Co., 1934.

Dewey, John, *Democracy and Education*, Free Press, 1966.

Dewey, John, *Experience and Education*, Collier, 1963.

Dewey, John, "The Ambiguity of Intrinsic Good," *Journal of Philosophy*, 1942, Vol. 39, pp. 328-330.

Franklin, Benjamin, "Proposals Relating to the Education fo Youth in Pensilvania (1749)," excerpted in R. Ulich, ed., *Three Thousand Years of Educational Wisdom: Selections from the Great Documents*, 2nd edition, Harvard University Press, 1961.

Froebel, Franklin, *Autobiography*, trans. and ed. E. Michaelis and K. Moore, C. W. Bardeen, 1890.

Gregory, I. M. M., and R. G. Woods, "Valuable in Itself," *Educational Philosophy and Theory*, 1971, Vol. 3, No. 2, pp. 51-64.

Kaufmann, Walter, *The Future of the Humanities*, Reader's Digest Press, 1977.

Keeton, Morris T., "Dilemmas in Accrediting Off-Campus Learning," in D. W. Vermilye, ed., *The Expanded Campus: Current Issues in Higher Education*, Jossey-Bass, 1972.

Kohlberg, Lawrence, "Education for Justice: A Modern Statement of the Platonic View," in N. F. Sizer and T. R. Sizer, eds., *Moral Education: Five Lectures*, Harvard University Press, 1970.

Peters, R. S., "Ambiguities in Liberal Education and the Problem of Its Content," in K. A. Strike and K. Egan, eds., *Ethics and Educational Policy*, Routledge & Kegan Paul, 1978.

Scheffler, Israel, "In Praise of the Cognitive Emotions," *Teachers College Record*, 1977, Vol. 79, No. 2, pp. 171-186.

Schwab, Joseph J., "Problems, Topics, and Issues," in S. Elam, ed., *Education and the Structure of Knowledge*, Rand McNally, 1964.

Smythe, Ormond, "Practical Experience and Liberal Education: A Philosophical Analysis," unpublished doctoral dissertation, Harvard University, 1978.

Snow, C. P., *The Two Cultures*, Mentor Books, 1959.

Part II

Rationales and Theories for Combining Service and Learning:

Cross-Cultural Learning

Service-Learning in International and Intercultural Settings

Howard A. Berry

Howard Berry draws the parallels between the practices of service-learning and those of international and intercultural learning. He points out the role of service-learning in teaching intercultural literacy, knowledge, and sensitivity. He presents emerging principles of effective intercultural learning which are very helpful for service-learning. Reprinted with permission from Experiential Education, *National Society for Internships and Experiential Education, Vol. 13, No. 3, May-June 1988.*

SERVICE-LEARNING, the union of public and community service with structured and intentional learning, has recently received increased national attention. People concerned with the relationship between education and society note that it energizes faculty and curriculum; assists in developing student values, identity and critical thinking; and encourages public and social responsibility.

Many in the field have come to see a fourth aspect of service-learning as equal to the others in importance: its capacity to further international and intercultural literacy, knowledge and sensitivity. These benefits can stem not only from experience in other countries, but also from "domestic" service-learning experiences. A student from a Northeastern urban setting serving in rural Appalachia, a middle-class white student working with urban minorities, a young person learning the culture of the elderly: All of these represent the interaction of cultures.

When seen in this way it becomes clear that the intercultural foundation of service-learning is not an "add-on," but instead provides a basic pedagogy and common thread which brings the service and the learning into a synergy regardless of the physical location. The problems encountered and the lessons learned from international and intercultural programming can thus be applicable to all service-learning programs.

Principles of Intercultural Learning

Some of the principles which have emerged from the experience of the Partnership for Service-Learning with international programs, especially in the Third World, may be helpful.

First and foremost, the key to successful intercultural learning is parity of esteem and mutuality on the part of all concerned. Parity of esteem means that all involved believe that both cultures are equally worthy and that each chooses and shapes what it accepts from the other. Mutuality means that each culture has an opportunity to give to the other as well as to receive; both are donors as well as recipients. The culture (community) into which students go should be able to voice its needs and expectations as an equal partner in the design of the experience.

Second, and related to the above, the program design should reflect the active role of all parties in the learning process. Thus, not only students and faculty, but also the agency and the community should be involved in planning and assessing the learning processes and outcomes.

Third, the service and the learning should be closely integrated in an intentional manner. The hyphen in service-learning is not accidental. The learning about the culture (community) should contribute to and enhance the service, and the service should relate to and support the learning. This praxis of action and reflection is at the heart of education and intercultural learning. In its programs, for example, the Partnership uses an integral study termed "Institutions in Society." By doing an intentional and sequenced "profile of an agency," the student views the actual agency and service as a microcosm of the issues and problems confronting the larger society and culture.

Fourth, academic and cultural pre-departure preparation is of great importance, as are ongoing support structures for students while in the other culture. This is true for any service-learning experience, but especially one in the Third World. Many mis-cues can occur when students are simply told to "go forth and learn." These are inevitable in any program dealing with other cultures, but with ongoing support and feedback they can be turned into positive learning. Examples of questions that arise are "Why is the supervisor treating the clients that way?" and "Why can I talk to some people in the culture and not to others?"

Fifth, the program should intentionally and systematically confront the fact that students' values may be different from those of the communities where they are placed. To pretend that these differences do not exist is to miss the core educational potential in intercultural experience.

The final issue is the controversial one of empowerment. The word is often used in two ways: empowerment of the student's identity and worth through the experience of service, and empowerment of the community being served. The former is a desirable (if difficult to measure) consequence of having students encounter the world and other cultures directly. The latter is fraught with cautions which should be taken seriously. It is one thing for students to learn about the political and social issues confronting minority or alienated communities; it is quite another for them to assume an activist or advocacy stance in complex affairs within which they are only temporary sojourners.

The keynote, however, in all ways is care and concern. If we are to advocate international/intercultural service-learning as a means to awaken sensitivity and connectedness in our students, we ourselves must show the same sensitivity in entering and negotiating with other cultures, whether local or international.

Despite the many problems and obstacles, intercultural pedagogies can be a powerful means to effective service-learning. Watching the growth of students placed in an intercultural setting — whether within the U.S. or abroad — brings a reward and excitement which justify the effort.

Howard Berry is Co-Director of the Partnership for Service-Learning and a Co-Chair of the Special Interest Group on International and Cross-Cultural Learning of the National Society for Internships and Experiential Education.

To Hell with
Good Intentions

Ivan Illich

An address by Monsignor Ivan Illich to the Conference on Inter-American Student Projects (CIASP) in Cuernavaca, Mexico, on April 20, 1968. In his usual biting and sometimes sarcastic style, Illich goes to the heart of the deep dangers of paternalism inherent in any voluntary service activity, but especially in any international service "mission." Parts of the speech are outdated and must be viewed in the historical context of 1968 when it was delivered, but the entire speech is retained for the full impact of his point and at Ivan Illich's request. Reprinted with Ivan Illich's permission.

IN THE CONVERSATIONS WHICH I HAVE HAD TODAY, I was impressed by two things, and I want to state them before I launch into my prepared talk.

I was impressed by your insight that the motivation of U.S. volunteers overseas springs mostly from very alienated feelings and concepts. I was equally impressed, by what I interpret as a step forward among would-be volunteers like you: openness to the idea that the only thing you can legitimately volunteer for in Latin America might be voluntary powerlessness, voluntary presence as receivers, as such, as hopefully beloved or adopted ones without any way of returning the gift.

I was equally impressed by the hypocrisy of most of you: by the hypocrisy of the atmosphere prevailing here. I say this as a brother speaking to brothers and sisters. I say it against many resistances within me; but it must be said. Your very insight, your very openness to evaluations of past programs make you hypocrites because you — or at least most of you — have decided to spend this next summer in Mexico, and therefore, you are unwilling to go far enough in your reappraisal of your program. You close your eyes because you want to go ahead and could not do so if you looked at some facts.

It is quite possible that this hypocrisy is unconscious in most of you. Intellectually, you are ready to see that the motivations which could legitimate volunteer action overseas in 1963 cannot be invoked for the same action in 1968. "Mission-vacations" among poor Mexicans were *"the thing"* to do for well-off U.S. students earlier in this decade: sentimental concern for newly-discovered poverty south of the border combined with total blindness to much worse poverty at home justified such benevolent excursions. Intellectual insight into the difficulties of fruitful volunteer action had not sobered the spirit of Peace Corps Papal-and-Self-Styled Volunteers.

Today, the existence of organizations like yours is offensive to Mexico. I wanted to make this statement in order to explain why I feel sick about it all and in order to make you aware that good intentions have not much to do with what we are discussing here. To hell with good intentions. This is a theological statement. You will not help anybody by your good intentions. There is an Irish saying that the road to hell is paved with good intentions; this sums up the same theological insight.

The very frustration which participation in CIASP programs might mean for you, could lead you to new awareness: the awareness that even North Americans can receive the gift of hospitality without the slightest ability to pay for it; the awareness that for some gifts one cannot even say "thank you."

Now to my prepared statement.

Ladies and Gentlemen:

For the past six years I have become known for my increasing opposition to the presence of any and all North American "do-gooders" in Latin America. I am sure you know of my present efforts to obtain the voluntary withdrawal of all North American volunteer armies from Latin America — missionaries, Peace Corps members and groups like yours, a "division" organized for the benevolent invasion of Mexico. You were aware of these things when you invited me — of all people — to be the main speaker at your annual convention. This is amazing! I can only conclude that your invitation means one of at least three things:

Some among you might have reached the conclusion that CIASP should either dissolve altogether, or take the promotion of voluntary aid to the Mexican poor out of its institutional purpose. Therefore you might have invited me here to help others reach this same decision.

You might also have invited me because you want to learn how to deal with people who think the way I do — how to dispute them successfully. It has now become quite common to invite Black Power spokesmen to address Lions Clubs. A "dove" must always be included in a public dispute organized to increase U.S. belligerence.

And finally, you might have invited me here hoping that you would be able to agree with most of what I say, and then go ahead in good faith and work this summer in Mexican villages. This last possibility is only open to those who do not listen, or who cannot understand me.

I did not come here to argue. I am here to tell you, if possible to convince you, and hopefully, to stop you, from pretentiously imposing yourselves on Mexicans.

I do have deep faith in the enormous good will of the U.S. volunteer. However, his good faith can usually be explained only by an abysmal lack of intuitive delicacy. By definition, you cannot help being ultimately vacationing salesmen for the middle-class "American Way of Life," since that is really the only life you know.

A group like this could not have developed unless a mood in the United States had supported it — the belief that any true American must share God's blessings with his poorer fellow men. The idea that every American has something to give, and at all times may, can and should give it, explains why it occurred to students that they could help Mexican peasants "develop" by spending a few months in their villages.

Of course, this surprising conviction was supported by members of a missionary order, who would have no reason to exist unless they had the same conviction — except a much stronger one. It is now high time to cure yourselves of this. You, like the values you carry, are the products of an American society of achievers and consumers, with its two-party system, its universal schooling, and its family-car affluence. You are ultimately — consciously or unconsciously — "salesmen" for a delusive ballet in the ideals of democracy, equal opportunity and free enterprise among people who haven't the possibility of profiting from these.

Next to money and guns, the third largest North American export is the U.S. idealist, who turns up in every theater of the world: the teacher, the volunteer, the missionary, the community organizer, the economic developer, and the vacationing do-gooders. Ideally, these people define their role as service. Actually, they frequently wind up alleviating the damage done by money and weapons, or "seducing" the "underdeveloped" to the benefits of the world of affluence and achievement. Perhaps this is the moment to instead bring home to the people of the U.S. the knowledge that the way of life they have chosen simply is not alive enough to be shared.

National Society for Internships and Experiential Education

By now it should be evident to all America that the U.S. is engaged in a tremendous struggle to survive. The U.S. cannot survive if the rest of the world is not convinced that here we have Heaven-on-Earth. The survival of the U.S. depends on the acceptance by all so-called "free" men that the U.S. middle class has "made it." The U.S. way of life has become a religion which must be accepted by all those who do not want to die by the sword — or napalm. All over the globe the U.S. is fighting to protect and develop at least a minority who consume what the U.S. majority can afford. Such is the purpose of the Alliance for Progress of the middle-classes which the U.S. signed with Latin America some years ago. But increasingly this commercial alliance must be protected by weapons which allow the minority who can "make it" to protect their acquisitions and achievements.

But weapons are not enough to permit minority rule. The marginal masses become rambunctious unless they are given a "Creed," or belief which explains the status quo. This task is given to the U.S. volunteer — whether he be a member of CIASP or a worker in the so-called "Pacification Programs" in Viet Nam.

The United States is currently engaged in a three-front struggle to affirm its ideals of acquisitive and achievement-oriented "Democracy." I say "three" fronts, because three great areas of the world are challenging the validity of a political and social system which makes the rich ever richer, and the poor increasingly marginal to that system.

In Asia, the U.S. is threatened by an established power — China. The U.S. opposes China with three weapons: the tiny Asian elites who could not have it any better than in an alliance with the United States; a huge war machine to stop the Chinese from "taking over" as it is usually put in this country, and; forcible re-education of the so-called "Pacified" peoples. All three of these efforts seem to be failing.

In Chicago, poverty funds, the police force and preachers seem to be no more successful in their efforts to check the unwillingness of the black community to wait for graceful integration into the system.

And finally, in Latin America the Alliance for Progress has been quite successful in increasing the number of people who could not be better off — meaning the tiny, middle-class elites — and has created ideal conditions for military dictatorships. The dictators were formerly at the service of the plantation owners, but now they protect the new industrial complexes. And finally, you come to help the underdog accept his destiny within this process!

All you will do in a Mexican village is create disorder. At best, you can try to convince Mexican girls that they should marry a young man who is self-made, rich, a consumer, and as disrespectful of tradition as one of you. At worst, in your "community development" spirit you might create just enough problems to get someone shot after your vacation ends and you rush back to your middle-class neighborhoods where your friends make jokes about "spics" and "wetbacks."

You start on your task without any training. Even the Peace Corps spends around $10,000 on each corpsmember to help him adapt to his new environment and to guard him against culture shock. How odd that nobody ever thought about spending money to educate poor Mexicans in order to prevent them from the culture shock of meeting you?

In fact, you cannot even meet the majority which you pretend to serve in Latin America — even if you could speak their language, which most of you cannot. You can only dialogue with those like you — Latin American imitations of the North American middle class. There is no way for you to really meet with the underprivileged, since there is no common ground whatsoever for you to meet on.

Let me explain this statement, and also let me explain why most Latin Americans with whom you might be able to communicate would disagree with me.

Suppose you went to a U.S. ghetto this summer and tried to help the poor there "help themselves." Very soon you would be either spit upon or laughed at. People offended by your pretentiousness would hit or spit. People who understand that your own bad consciences push you to this gesture would laugh condescendingly. Soon you would be made aware of your irrelevance among the poor, of your status as middle-class college students on a summer assignment. You would be roundly rejected, no matter if your skin is white — as most of your faces here are — or brown or black, as a few exceptions who got in here somehow.

Your reports about your work in Mexico, which you so kindly sent me, exude self-complacency. Your reports on past summers prove that you are not even capable of understanding that your do-gooding in a Mexican village is even less relevant than it would be in a U.S. ghetto. Not only is there a gulf between what you have and what others have which is much greater than the one existing between you and the poor in your own country, but there is also a gulf between what you feel and what the Mexican people feel that is incomparably greater. This gulf is so great that in a Mexican village you, as White Americans (or cultural white Americans) can imagine yourselves exactly the way a white preacher saw himself when he offered his life preaching to the black slaves on a plantation in Alabama. The fact that you live in huts and eat tortillas for a few weeks renders your well-intentioned group only a bit more picturesque.

The only people with whom you can hope to communicate with are some members of the middle class. And here please remember that I said "some" — by which I mean a tiny elite in Latin America. You come from a country which industrialized early and which succeeded in incorporating the great majority of its citizens into the middle classes. It is no social distinction in the U.S. to have graduated from the second year of college. Indeed, most Americans now do. Anybody in this country who did not finish high school is considered underprivileged.

In Latin America the situation is quite different: 75% of all people drop out of school before they reach the sixth grade. Thus, people who have finished high school are members of a tiny minority. Then, a minority of that minority goes on for university training. It is only among these people that you will find your educational equals.

At the same time, a middle class in the United States is the majority. In Mexico, it is a tiny elite. Seven years ago your country began and financed a so-called "Alliance for Progress." This was an "Alliance" for the "Progress" of the middle class elites. Now, it is among the members of this middle class that you will find a few people who are willing to spend their time with you. And they are overwhelmingly those "nice kids" who would also like to soothe their troubled consciences by "doing something nice for the promotion of the poor Indians." Of course, when you and your middle-class Mexican counterparts meet, you will be told that you are doing something valuable, that you are "sacrificing" to help others.

And it will be the foreign priest who will especially confirm your self-image for you. After all, his livelihood and sense of purpose depends on his firm belief in a year-round mission which is of the same type as your summer vacation-mission.

There exists the argument that some returned volunteers have gained insight into the damage they have done to others — and thus become more mature people. Yet it is less frequently stated that most of them are ridiculously proud of their "summer sacrifices." Perhaps there is also something to the argument that young men should be promiscuous for awhile in order to find out that sexual love is most beautiful in a monogamous relationship. Or that the best way to leave LSD alone is to try it for awhile — or even that the best way of understanding that your help in the ghetto is neither needed nor wanted is to try, and fail. I do not agree with this argument. The damage which volunteers do willy-nilly is too high a price for the belated insight that they shouldn't have been volunteers in the first place.

If you have any sense of responsibility at all, stay with your riots here at home. Work for the coming elections: You will know what you are doing, why you are doing it, and how to communicate with those to whom you speak. And you will know when you fail. If you insist on working with the poor, if this is your vocation, then at least work among the poor who can tell you to go to hell. It is incredibly unfair for you to impose yourselves on a village where you are so linguistically deaf and dumb that you don't even understand what you are doing, or what people think of you. And it is profoundly damaging to yourselves when you define something that you want to do as "good," a "sacrifice" and "help."

I am here to suggest that you voluntarily renounce exercising the power which being an American gives you. I am here to entreat you to freely, consciously and humbly give up the legal right you have to impose your benevolence on Mexico. I am here to challenge you to recognize your inability, your powerlessness and your incapacity to do the "good" which you intended to do.

I am here to entreat you to use your money, your status and your education to travel in Latin America. Come to look, come to climb our mountains, to enjoy our flowers. Come to study. But do not come to help.

Ivan Illich is the author of Deschooling Society *and other provocative books. Thanks to Nick Royal, Tim Stanton, and Steve Babb for helping to find this speech.*

A Challenge to the Notion of Service

Nadinne Cruz

An experienced practitioner speaks frankly about the inherent contradictions and dilemmas in service-learning and in the mission of one organization that advocates it. Even though this position statement begins with a focus on one organization, the ideas presented here are valuable for any program or organization interested in combining service and learning. The author appropriately struggles with the premises of this resource book in a way that the editor and many of the authors struggle with the dilemmas in this dynamic, delicate, and inherently problematic combination of concepts — service and learning. Reprinted with permission from Experiential Education, *National Society for Internships and Experiential Education (NSIEE), Vol. 14, No. 5, November-December 1989, pp. 15, 23.*

"AS A COMMUNITY OF INDIVIDUALS, institutions, and organizations, NSIEE is committed to fostering the effective use of experience as an integral part of education, in order to empower learners and promote the common good."

The magnet that *draws* me towards association with NSIEE are the individual members, many of whom I have come to treasure as colleagues and friends. What *keeps* me in NSIEE company despite competing priorities is its mission. It is, for me, a compelling one that engages me with our thinking and "doing" as NSIEE'ers. So I will probe a bit and assume that, among friends, we can disagree in the spirit of taking seriously the responsibility for continuing to refine our sense of NSIEE's mission.

NSIEE seems to be experiencing "good times." We applaud development of principles for good practice in service learning, which appears to fit beautifully with our mission. We celebrate the current national interest in youth service and the now standard acceptance of internships. We delight in the connections people are making between service learning and cross-cultural/international study. We exult with those who mine opportunities for enjoining all these with civic responsibility and educational reform.

I am pleased with the apparent nationwide popularity of ideas that we in NSIEE have been talking about for years. On the other hand, the current flurry of interest in youth service brings to focus for me the unease I feel about assumptions we seem to make in NSIEE's mission statement and which are similarly reflected in discussions about service. The articulation of a broad normative position is a necessary beginning point, and we have done it. But I fear our celebratory mood might muffle questions we need to wrestle with in order to deepen understanding of our mission, including areas that people like myself might question. The apparent mainstreaming of some of our ideas notwithstanding, we at NSIEE still have lots of leadership work to do through critical reflection on *our* thinking and practice.

For example, I don't think we have talked enough yet about the intractable issues in service learning or youth service (which I don't think, by the way, are one and the same). Even carefully crafted guidelines for practice can do damage if they are not placed in the context of social realities, namely different and competing interests as well as outright conflict, based on, for example, class, race, gender, and even nationality. We simply cannot gloss over, without cost to us, concrete conflict situations and experiences that make difficult the application of concepts like "reciprocal learning." I would argue that the possibility of mutuality of interests and needs implied in the concept of reciprocal learning could be more easily realized if it were *not* tied to any notion of service.

I want us to talk about why, in the context of conflicting interests and the historical dominance of one racial or gender group over another, it is possible that "service," in and of itself, can have racist or sexist outcomes despite good intentions. For example, I resist the notion of service learning for U.S. students in the Philippines, my country of origin, because I think it perpetuates a "colonial mentality" among Filipinos and a kind of "manifest destiny" among U.S. students. To my way of thinking, the results of the history of U.S. dominance in the Philippines is so overwhelming that it is almost impossible for a U.S. student doing what is regarded on both sides as "service" not to deliver a message of superiority.

I challenge us to talk about the possibility that our social realities as well as the history and practice of the notion of service makes it more problematic than its current popularity might suggest. I think that, in the context of a history of dominance of one group over others, there is an incipient racism in the practice of service that cannot be avoided even if the conceptualization of it includes values and ideals we can respect and the virtues of people who practice it are above question. That is different from saying that reciprocal learning is impossible, even when the partners-in-learning are not equal in power and resources. I am suggesting that reciprocal learning may be *more* possible if it is *not* tied to a notion of service. Odd as it may sound, perhaps the common good might be better served in certain situations if we emphasized learning as the primary goal and "service," as we commonly think of it, as not involved at all.

This brings me back to the NSIEE mission statement, which appears to make assumptions about the connections among: a) the effective use of experience as an integral part of education, b) empowerment of learners, and c) promotion of the common good. I think it is possible to empower learners (through service learning) and *not* promote the common good (by reinforcing a sense of inferiority among those "served" or a false sense of power among those who "serve"). It is possible to use experience as an integral part of education and simply duplicate the realities we wish to change. I am getting at the possibility that our mission assumes or implies the nature of connections among goals that may not in fact hold together.

I want us to discuss assumptions in our mission statement, not in the abstract, but apply them to programs and ideas that appear to reflect a "mainstreaming" of NSIEE. Let us hold them up for scrutiny, which I think can be better done by hearing voices that reflect the real diversity in this society and the social realities that are the context for the commitments we make on behalf of learning. There is no short cut for hearing these voices directly and for airing competing perspectives openly. I hope this is the outcome of our national meeting in Santa Fe, which called for "Meeting the Challenges of Diversity." May diversity bring out conflict where it exists; may conflict deepen and develop further our self-understanding and mission as a community of people in a very special NSIEE organization.

Nadinne Cruz is Executive Director of the Higher Education Consortium for Urban Affairs (HECUA) in St. Paul, Minnesota.

Experiential Education: The Neglected Dimension of International/ Intercultural Studies

Howard A. Berry

A basic overview of the value of international and intercultural service-learning to enhance traditional programs for study abroad. Howard Berry describes one consortial model and lists essential principles for effective programs. Reprinted with permission from the International Programs Quarterly, *State University of New York, Spring-Summer 1985, Vol. 1, No. 3-4, pp. 23-27.*

---

*All experience is an arch wherethrough
Gleams that untraveled world.*
— Tennyson, "Ulysses"

MANY YEARS AGO, in the early days of the move to internationalism in education, Harold Taylor wrote a book whose title has taken on its own vitality, *The World as Teacher*. How many of us over the years have unmercifully plagiarized that title, or variations of it, in justification of our belief in the value and need for international/intercultural education? Our rhetoric about the value of students using the world as teacher gave us a rationale and sense of security in our advocacy of study abroad as a vital part of contemporary education. And yet, as Phillips Ruopp put it in his article, "The Educational Uses of the World" (1977), "The rhetoric of education obscures more often than it illuminates the reality of educational practices."

If we were to examine with candor how well traditional study abroad programs fulfill our stated idealistic goals for developing international/intercultural knowledge and understanding, would we find congruence between rhetoric and reality? Or would we admit that, in many cases at least, the program represents a transplanted home campus environment, classroom-based, lecture-oriented, Euro-centered, with little direct and intentional use of the experience of the other country or culture as the curriculum?

The neglected dimension of education in general, and international education in particular, has been what is broadly called experiential education. This may include service, independent field study, or paid employment, but its common and binding thread is the blend of learning and experience, reflection and action, observation and participation.

Traditionalists assert that the outside world should be brought to the campus, that education and the critical intellect are things given to students in the sanctity of the classroom. Others see no inherent contradiction between the theoretical and experiential modes of learning, that indeed the first purpose of experiential education is to foster the critical and creative use of the mind in a variety of situations. Over 2,000 years ago, Aristotle observed, "For the things we have to learn before we can do them, we learn by doing them." More recently, James Coleman (1974) labeled the traditional curriculum "knowledge rich and action poor," and called for more students to be involved in what he terms the "action curriculum."

There is evidence that students agree. Co-op education, internships, community service, "stop out" and other forms of active learning have seen unprecedented growth in the past decade.... And a *New York Times* article, commenting on the "stop out" phenomenon, reports that half of all Stanford undergraduates stop out, thirty to forty percent of Wesleyan students do so, and that a quarter to a third of Haverford students join this move. Many leave to develop particular talents, others to pursue cultural interests or returning to their country of origin. In most cases, however, they must do this outside of, and unconnected to, their educational pursuits.

Service-learning as an aspect of experiential education is an attempt to span this disparity by joining two goals — academic study and service to the world. Through service-learning programs students continue their academic studies, and at the same time work with individuals and communities to deal with human needs. The studies may be in the liberal arts or directly related to technical skills and career goals. The academic validation may be fulfilled through various plans for independent study [or regular seminars], and may be designed for students of diverse levels of ability, background, and maturity. Sites for service may be local or national (intercultural) or abroad (international). The time of study may be as short as a summer or as long as a year.

What do students gain from the experience of international or intercultural study and service? First, their academic study of history, economics, political science, sociology, psychology, languages, literature, or the arts, is enriched by living in the culture. They field test the ideas and theories of the scholars. They are confronted daily with assumptions based on personal experience or academic research, and they learn to look critically at these. Secondly, the union of intellectual growth, skills development, and positive interpersonal relations contributes to their understanding of their own identity, which Erik Erikson (1950) has defined as the developmental task of the young adult: "In youth, ego strength emerges from the mutual confirmation of individual and community, in the sense that society recognizes the young individual as a bearer of fresh energy and that the individual so confirmed recognizes society as a living process...." The experience of service-learning is an ideal vehicle for the "mutual confirmation" as students study and reflect on their own cultural backgrounds in relation to others.

The relationship to international/intercultural studies begins to become clear. By placing students in an international/intercultural setting in a service situation, and by asking them to study and reflect upon that culture and its values in relation to their own, students gain a new and more sophisticated perspective on human and international issues. Experience of another culture by itself, without intentional and informed analysis, allows too easy a dismissal of the culture as unimportant or wrong. Academic study alone, without direct experience, may fail to reveal the depth and complexity of another system of behavior. Service-learning, combining these two dimensions, leads the student to understand more realistically the nature of human institutions, behavior, and culture. As the service makes relevant and immediate the academic study, so the academic learning informs the work. Through this mode of learning the culture, community, and country truly become the curriculum. In this form of learning, the sites and the people living there are of primary importance — the curriculum itself rather than just a geographic location. These sites can be in the traditional European seats of learning or in the developing world, which cries out for understanding on the part of the U.S., and where indeed success or failure in understanding may determine the fate of the world.

To cite specific examples from existing programs: a young pre-law student serves in a probationary hostel in inner London; a psychology major works in a social agency in rural Wiltshire; in Jamaica a nursing student helps at a rehab center for persons with disabilities; an art student tutors at an inner Kingston community center; a secretarial student aids in the operation of a home for severely disabled children; in Ecuador an education major tutors "English as a Second Language" to primary school children.

They cannot help but come back with enhanced understanding of: the social welfare state and the Common Market in England; the racial, cultural, and economic problems faced by a developing Jamaica; the Latin American perspective of its giant neighbor to the north. Their own words reveal the impact of the experience. One young woman writes, "I learned more in four months than in fourteen years of education." Another says, "While here I have met many wonderful and interesting people, and we have learned from each other our different cultures and ideas. Thank you for getting us out to other countries and cultures to educate ourselves. It is truly the best education." We would be remiss in our educational and international objectives if we do not pay serious attention to this.

As students learn, so also do their supervising faculty on the home campus. Service-learning provides opportunities for faculty members to look at their disciplines in a new way and to discover a profound learning resource, stimulating to themselves as well as to their students. In a time of little faculty mobility and reduced budgets for conferences and sabbaticals, faculty seek ways of preventing intellectual stagnation. Service-learning seminars for faculty allow them to visit the sites, research the learning opportunities for students of their disciplines and departments, and meet their counterparts in another country. Perhaps equally exciting for faculty is the encounter with service-agency personnel and the wide body of expert knowledge they possess.

Various models for academic oversight allow faculty to work out with the student the shape his/her studies will take, to determine what work will be offered for credit, and the form and criteria of evaluation. By designing and supervising learning activities which relate their discipline to the work and location of service, faculty find new dimensions and new relevance in their own research and study, and discover the riches of a new pedagogy in experiential education.

Curriculum impact is also apparent from these programs. Solid pre-departure preparation in participant-observer skills, how to learn in an independent context, writing and journal-keeping, and, of course, knowledge of the culture and country the student is to enter, are all needed to an even greater degree than with traditional study abroad programs. All these can enhance the campus-based dimensions of international/intercultural studies.

As mentioned earlier, these points are not speculative but are based on actual experience and existing programs. Rockland Community College, in affiliation with other colleges and organizations, began using this form of international learning over the past five years. From its initial experiences in Africa (Ghana and Kenya), RCC has gone on to establish programs in England and Jamaica, and, in affiliation with Brookdale Community College in New Jersey, in Ecuador....Out of this experience some patterns and recommendations for program design have emerged. The international service-learning experience can be designed and implemented in several ways, but any design requires careful attention to:

1. Orientation of participants to the theory and practice of experiential learning as well as to the culture they will enter;
2. Networking between college(s) and established service agencies and academic groups to provide placement and learning opportunities;
3. Ongoing communication between academic and service personnel to monitor the performance and progress of the participants;
4. Design of the academic surround so as to relate the experience to learning; and
5. Sound validation and evaluation criteria and processes essentially in the hands of the home faculty.

Based on RCC's experience, one suggested model of program design, adjusted, of course, for the particular country and culture, has emerged:

1. A credit-bearing course conducted by academics in the host country, designed to give students an introduction to the history, culture, politics, and economics of that country. This may take place in a block of time before the service experience, or it may be ongoing during the experience. It also involves field trips and experiential components;

2. The service experience itself (20-30 hours per week) with each student assigned a local academic mentor whose function is to help the student, based on some generic learning objectives formulated with the home campus faculty, link the experience to demonstrable learning, often working in conjunction with the agency supervisor; and

3. The accumulation by the student of a portfolio of demonstrated learning, (journal, papers written, reviews of books read, research surveys made, photographic essays, etc.). The portfolio is basic to the principle that credit is granted not for the experience, but for the learning demonstrated. The portfolio, along with a narrative evaluation by the mentor, is brought back to the home campus for validation.

There are a variety of ways faculty may validate the learning which comes from the experience, but for many of these programs the Learning Contract mode has been chosen. Before departure each student arrives at a generic learning contract with home faculty, emphasizing the learning objectives for validation. The function of the mentors in the other country, then, is to refine this contract in relation to the actual placement, designing individual learning activities which bring together the experience of the placement and the learning objective sought. With the supervision of the mentor, each student develops a portfolio of demonstrated learning. To this is added a narrative evaluation by the student's mentor and placement supervisor. The portfolio is brought back and evaluated in discussion with the home campus faculty.

Another important aspect of this program model is affiliation with existing, in-country organizations having experience with placements. These may be secular, church-related, social, or governmental. The same in-country involvement addresses the need to identify academic individuals and organizations capable of helping to link academic study to experience in community-based studies.

Worth mention, especially in less-developed countries, is the need for at least one local person who can act as a "native informant" in introducing the program planner to the local culture — what to say, what not to say, whom to see, and to what degree to affiliate with governmental offices and personnel. This contact can be of immense help in guiding staff through the cultural, educational, and governmental complexities inherent in all societies.

The possibility of service and experiential programs in the so-called Third World raises many interesting and exciting speculations. Much, for example, has been made of the need in these countries for "intermediate technology," e.g., simple water pumps, agricultural tools, building materials. These countries, however, also have human needs, with the young, elderly, and illiterate. Would it be possible to speculate about undergraduate students in service situations as a form of "human intermediate technology?" That is, instead of bringing things and techniques, they could bring the energy of their hands and hearts, serving human and community needs, and learning the realities of the culture, language, and problems of developing nations. The potential contained in this thought is stirring the imagination of many.

The costs of overseas programs are always of concern. Given the individualistic structure of U.S. colleges and universities, the basis of funding support vary by institution. However, a pattern has emerged from the experience of RCC which may be of help to those seeking to initiate programs. Essentially, students pay tuition at their home campuses, and remain registered there for validation and credit purposes. In addition, students pay for transportation, room and board.

However, the colleges affiliated with this program have developed structures and mechanisms which enable some defraying of costs to students. Because the student remains registered at the home campus, financial aid applies to participation in the program. In addition, the instructional costs generated by the student's tuition may be applied against the instructional costs needed for overseas academic supervision, thus keeping the student from paying twice for the academic validation and supervision of his/her work. Through these mechanisms, existing service-learning programs in several countries can be made available to student for little more than they would pay at the home campus, or living at home.

...Those interested in exploring these opportunities for their institutions and students may want to participate in one of the consortial infrastructures which have been developed to enable these programs to be shared among colleges. Through affiliation with the Partnership for Service-Learning, for example, a coalition of two- and four-year colleges, universities, and other organizations, colleges have immediate access to and ownership of the existing programs for their students. Students remain registered at the home campus, and validation is with the home campus faculty; thus, colleges do not "lose" students by encouraging their participation. In addition, the Partnership provides faculty seminars for on-site experience with the programs and help with program and curriculum development.

Amidst the optimism which these developments may generate, some caveats need to be made, particularly in relation to more traditional study abroad programs:

1. Pre-departure preparation, academic and cultural, is very important, as is selection of students for this experience;
2. The personal and academic support elements for students in the other country need to be intentional, firmly in place, and well-defined;
3. Home campus faculty should be a central and integrated part of the process, with pre-departure preparation and post-program evaluation and validation;
4. Perhaps most vital of all, especially with developing countries, the key to successful affiliations are *parity of esteem* and *mutuality* on the part of all concerned. By parity of esteem is meant that all involved believe that both cultures are equally worthy, and that each culture must choose and shape what it accepts from the other. By mutuality is meant that each culture must have an opportunity to give to the other culture as well as to receive, in a way that ensures that neither culture becomes dependent on the other, and that both are donors as well as recipients. These principles are the basis for respect on the part of all concerned.

Given these cautions, the reality is that these opportunities exist, have been tested, and have demonstrated a powerful potential to move international/intercultural education to new levels. This form of education may not be for all; some students may be better served by traditional programs. However, for those to whom opportunity is less a set of problems than an exciting challenge, experiential education in an international/intercultural setting opens important human and educational avenues. To turn again to Ruopp:

... the aim of experiential education is to bring our accumulated cultural resources to bear on the student's encounter with the insistent present. It places the student's situational encounters within the wider context of his knowledge about the human condition. Rather than being imprisoned by his immediate situation, he uses it to understand the larger reality of which it is a part. He orders his experience by developing his power to conceptualize it. He learns how to transform his situational transactions by investing them with meaning. Finally, his personal response to people and events both tests and tempers his character. (p. 110)

Knowing that there are colleges and universities with vision, and students with the openness and sense of adventure to experience the world firsthand, together we might just be able, finally, to ... follow Taylor's trenchant dictum and truly see "the world as teacher."

Howard Berry is Co-Director of The Partnership for Service-Learning and chair of the Special Interest Group on International and Cross-Cultural Experiential Learning, a committee of the National Society for Internships and Experiential Education.

References

Coleman, James S., et al., *Youth: Transition to Adulthood*, Report of the Panel on Youth of the President's Science Advisory Committee, University of Chicago Press, 1974.

Erickson, E. H., *Childhood and Society*, Norton, 1950.

Ruopp, Philips, "The Educational Uses of the World," *Ekistics*, 255, February 1977, pp. 105-110.

Part II

Rationales and Theories for Combining Service and Learning:

Leadership Development

On Leadership:
Experiences for an Untidy World

John W. Gardner

ONE HOPES THAT well-conceived out-of-classroom experiences provide one or more of the following:

- Opportunities for students to experience the shared responsibilities of group action, and to learn the skills required to make a group function effectively.
- Opportunities for students to test their judgment under pressure, in the face of opposition, and in the fluid, swiftly changing circumstances characteristic of action.
- Opportunities for students to test and sharpen their intuitive gifts and to judge their impact on others.
- Exposure to new constituencies.
- Exposure to the untidy world, where decisions must be made on inadequate information and the soundest argument does not always win, where problems rarely get fully solved or, once solved, surface anew in another form.

... The best off-campus ... experiences are linked to some form of instruction or counseling, so that the young person dropped into a strange milieu is helped to comprehend it. For example, internships in a legislature can be profitably linked to a seminar on the legislative process. Experience, thought to be the best teacher, is sometimes a confusing teacher. Robert Benchley said that having a dog teaches a boy fidelity, perseverance, and to turn around three times before lying down.

From On Leadership *by John W. Gardner, 1990, p. 168. Copyright 1990 by John Gardner. Reprinted by permission of The Free Press, a Division of MacMillan, Inc. John Gardner has served as President of the Carnegie Corporation and the Carnegie Foundation for the Advancement of Teaching; as U.S. Secretary of H.E.W.; founder of Common Cause; and co-founder of Independent Sector. His other books include* Excellence, Self-Renewal, No Easy Victories, The Recovery of Confidence, In Common Cause, *and* Morale.

Service Learning and Leadership Development:
Learning to be Effective While Learning What to be Effective About*

Timothy K. Stanton

Tim Stanton assesses the movements for leadership education and for public service in higher education and argues for the critical role of service-learning pedagogy and programs for the success of both. He describes the unique contributions service-learning makes to these attitudes and skills important for leaders: vision, learning how to learn from experience, judgment in action, cognitive initiative, and enabling others to learn and take action. These ideas were first presented at the Educational Leadership Conference sponsored by the Center for Creative Leadership in La Jolla, California, on June 28, 1988.

BEFORE I OFFER YOU my thoughts on the topic of leadership development through public service, or, as I shall argue, through service learning, let me tell you about how I became interested in leadership education and what my biases are about it. Let me also point out that, like most parts of this book, this is a "work in progress." I welcome your questions and suggestions.

I am a child of the 60s and carry that generation's skepticism about the traditional concept of leadership. Though there were many great leaders among us in those activist days, we questioned the hierarchical structure of our universities, of society, and of our own organizations. We came to believe in a collaborative, cooperative, if not anarchistic view of organization and decision-making.

Title adapted from statement by Arthur Morgan, who created Antioch College's cooperative education program for the liberal arts (Guskin, 1987).

One heritage of this period for me is a skepticism about the seemingly unexamined assumptions in much of the recent leadership literature. For example, do leaders always have the best interests of followers in mind when they exercise their power (Barr and Vanderslice, 1984)? Does participative management necessarily decrease power differentials between leaders and followers (Mulder, 1971)? At a minimum, it seems to me that leadership must be spread as widely as possible.

My interests carried me into a career in youth development, experiential education (learning through direct contact with and participation in the subject area of study) and popular or adult education. I have spent my working life around the margins of campuses seeking to build links between universities and communities, trying to integrate the citizen's life with the academy's tradition of critical reflection. I believe that human development, the goal of education, cannot take place in isolation from the development of communities and our nation.

I have been at Stanford helping to establish the Public Service Center for the past three years. The Center was established four years ago by Stanford President Don Kennedy in response to a sense he had that higher education was doing less than it could and should to promote civic responsibility and participation by students. The Center is multi-faceted and somewhat unique in at least two ways. One is that we both house and advise student organizations involved in public service (and we are slowly learning how to both support their autonomy and rein in their occasional bursts of lunacy!), and we administer our own University-sponsored programs. The other is that we try to focus simultaneously on local community service, government and public policy at all levels, and on international service and development.

We organize and manage student volunteer projects that range from a campus-wide day of service in the local community to six-month sojourns with development organizations in Latin America. We administer specialized voluntary internships and what we call action research programs, stipended fellowships in public service for undergraduates and recent graduates, conferences and seminars. One of my central roles has been advocating the pedagogy of service learning with faculty — trying to link students' public service activities with the curriculum. The purposes are both to strengthen the impact of their service efforts in the community and to deepen their reflections on their experience and relate these reflections to theories and concepts presented in the classroom.

What does this have to do with leadership development? A lot, I think. Due to my democratic, populist ambivalence about the concept of leadership, I have been a latecomer to the leadership movement. However, I see now direct connections between our work at the Public Service Center and the growing interest in leadership development. I will suggest here, however, that the linking mechanism between public service and leadership development is the pedagogy of "service learning."

Over the past year I have been reviewing the literature on leadership development in order to determine how we at the Public Service Center might respond. I have looked at the conceptual work of John Gardner (1986-88), Warren Bennis (1985), John Kotter (1988), Robert Greenleaf (1977), James March (1987), as well as at the more practical offerings of Jim Kouzes and Barry Posner (1987), which are aimed primarily at business leaders, and of George Barbour, Tom Fletcher and George Sipel (1985) who have made similar offerings to managers in the public sector. And, I have conducted my own unscientific survey of business, government, and civic leaders to find out their definitions of leadership and concepts of how leadership is developed. In doing so I have been looking for a way to synthesize these folks' varied ideas about effective leadership, to find out what they have in common, and to put their common elements into a framework that is useful to me as a public service-oriented experiential educator. My question has been: If we (meaning the Public Service Center) were to educate people for effective leadership, what would the content of that education be, and how would we go about it?

Let me briefly review my survey findings. I will then suggest how service learning represents not just the application of leadership abilities, but more importantly, a catalyst for their development.

Leadership Attitudes

Probably the most common attitudinal trait of effective leaders, at least as exemplified in recent literature, is a sense of vision. Effective leaders have visions, are able to share them and can persuade others to take them as their own. The sharing and persuading aspects of leadership relate to skill and ability, which we will come to shortly, but these skills are not of much use without some substantive vision. Bennis (1985) talks of this as a concept that creates a focus for what needs to be done. Others describe vision setting as "meaning construction." Jim March in his Stanford leadership class uses George Bernard Shaw's depiction of St. Joan (1924) as an exemplary visionary leader, enabling people to do more than they ever thought they could.

For me, however, as an educator, the most interesting and important questions related to visions are: Where do they come from, how do we form them, and from what morals, values and ideals do they spring?

A second attitudinal trait of effective leaders is cognitive initiative — whether a person habitually thinks in terms of causes and outcomes or whether she sees herself as an ineffective victim of events which have an unknown cause. There is much research that suggests this variable of how one defines oneself as an actor is a key ingredient to superlative performance (Klemp, 1978). How do higher education and public service experience promote this positive self-perception in students?

Leadership Knowledge

There is an array of knowledge-related leadership traits. Knowing the business you are in — your products, relevant technologies, your competition, etc. — is frequently cited. Effective leaders understand the boundaries of their social system, and how their organization's and their individual (self-knowledge; Bennis, 1985) activity fits into it all. Both leadership writers and professionals talk about the need to understand the complex systems and processes by which communities (and organizations) function. Leaders learn enough about their context to "work the system" effectively.

There is another knowledge area that appears to be equally important to effective leadership, that which John Gardner calls the "heart of the matter" — knowing your people and their needs.

Leadership Skills

There are vast lists of leadership skills related to effective communication, group dynamics and interpersonal relationships, with which I am sure you are already familiar.

However, I also found in my review another set of skills — related to learning — which appears to be equally important. John Gardner talks about "judgment in action" (1988). I would describe this as action through judgment. Donald Schon has conceptualized and created the term, "reflection-in-action" (1983). Others speak of a leader's need for good social perceptiveness and intuition that come from learning "to listen first," as Greenleaf suggests (1977), or "eloquently," as Herman Blake has said (1986). It is out of this listening and observing ("seeing") that leaders develop the knowledge which enables them to conceive of a vision and take action to create it in complex, stressful situations.

Warren Bennis observed (1985) that effective leaders see every false step as a learning opportunity, rather than a failure. Robert Greenleaf talks about "knowing experimentally" (1977). It's quite possible, and strongly suggested in research (Klemp, 1978), that this "meta-skill" of learning how to learn is the most critical one for effective performance, whether one is a leader or not.

A final set of skills of effective leaders appears to be those related to effective facilitating of learning and growth in others and to enabling others to take action. Embedded within these are many of the management and consulting skills now widely accepted in industry and promoted by the "excellence" movement. Interestingly, I also found reference to them in public policy literature. Robert Reich, Harvard professor and economic advisor to Mike Dukakis, in his new book *The Power of Public Ideas* (1988), describes and advocates an enabling notion of public leadership, one that stimulates and provides structures that enable communities to set their policy agendas or to make far-reaching policy decisions by working collaboratively and democratically. One example is Secretary Ruckleshaus' successful facilitation of a decision by Washington state residents on regulating toxic waste from a paper processing plant — almost an application of Carl Rogers to politics.

One final common element I find in the leadership literature is that effective leaders, rather than being born, are made and can develop. Their talents or abilities are not innate. That assumption is the reason you are reading this. It also begs the question: How well are we in education doing in developing individuals with these common traits?

Higher Education and Leadership Development

My sense is that we in higher education are not doing this very well. John Gardner has gone so far as to say that higher education snuffs out leadership (1986), and others concur. Knowledge development which focuses on criticism, as opposed to problem solving, provides no incentives for students to test out or exhibit leadership skills. A research and scholarship tradition based on a positivist epistemology focuses only on understanding and analysis and separates the knower from what is known (Palmer, 1987). It tends to keep faculty from becoming involved directly with social problems and issues and effectively removes them from becoming role models of responsible leadership for students. (For example, several faculty at Stanford are organizing a seminar on poverty for the next academic year. In their list of seminar topics there is no focus on solutions, and on their list of guest speakers there is not one person who has experienced poverty, worked directly with poor people, or is working to solve the problem!)

In addition to this situation we have a curriculum fragmented by disciplines which provides no ready home for the study of leadership — an applied, interdisciplinary and therefore suspect — field. Academic achievement is driven by an individualistic, competitive value system that insulates student academic performance from having consequences for anyone other than students themselves (or maybe their parents!).

Frank Newman in his Carnegie Report, *Higher Education and The American Resurgence* (1985, p. 31), argues that "if there is a crisis in education in the United States today, it is less that test scores have declined than it is that we have failed to provide the education for citizenship that is still the most significant responsibility of the nation's schools and colleges." He identified a failure in both the structure and content of our educational system. Structurally we have not provided a means of linking classroom study with students' direct experience of social problems and issues. In the area of content we have failed to educate students with an understanding of these social problems, an awareness of the traditional responsibilities of democratic citizenship, and the skills to participate effectively.

Happily, however, the winds of change are blowing with the stream of national reports on higher education which call for a variety of reforms. Two currents in this stream are relevant to this discussion — the growth in interest and programs related to leadership education and the rekindled debate (by Newman, Kennedy and others) on the academy's traditional role of developing in students a "civic literacy" and the responsibility and ability to participate, or take leadership in society.

Leadership Education

In response to an oft-cited "crisis in leadership" in this country, leadership education has exploded onto the higher education scene. According to Irving Spitzberg, Jr. in a review of the growing number of leadership development programs (1986), they express an emergence of a "social movement." Descriptions of innovative programs appear increasingly in higher education journals. The Center for Creative Leadership has published a *Sourcebook on Leadership Education* (Clark *et al*, 1987) and offers an annual conference on the subject.

Campus leadership programs tend to fall into two distinct categories which reflect higher education's traditional separation of academic learning from other forms of learning and development. The academic programs tend to include courses on the nature of leadership practice from a behavioral science perspective or on leaders as individuals utilizing biographical and historical literature. Some are purely comparative and analytical in their approach. Others take a more philosophical, value-oriented stance, stimulating students to consider their individual experiences as leaders or their observations of leaders in light of leadership theory and history. A few programs provide internships or mentorships with community, business or government leaders. But, in keeping with academic tradition, most concentrate on providing opportunity for the "analysis of the theoretical concepts, issues, and situations involved in the multidisciplinary study of leadership" (Holliday, 1988). Taking action tends to take third place behind understanding of what is known about leaders and exploration of personal values related to leadership.

Co-curricular leadership programs tend to be administered by student affairs personnel and reflect the values and goals of that side of the higher education "house." These range from weekend leadership training retreats for leaders of student organizations to semester or year-long programs for selected students on leadership practice and skill building. Skills addressed range from collaborative management and team building to those of the more basic communication and group dynamic variety.

In his review (1986) Spitzberg laments the academic/co-curricular fragmentation of these efforts. He cites programs at West Point and Duke University for making efforts to connect the two. He advocates addressing the "nexus between the intellectual and the experiential" as central to the effectiveness of leadership education.

The Public Service Initiative

Our Public Service Center at Stanford is part of a national drive which seeks to encourage students to become involved in public affairs. In 1985 Presidents Kennedy of Stanford, Swearer of Brown, and Healy of Georgetown, formed a Campus Compact: The Presidents' Coalition for Public and Community Service, to encourage the development of a sense of public purpose among students and to increase opportunities for them to become involved in public and community service during their college years. They were impressed with Sandy and Lena Astin's ACE-UCLA surveys which showed that in the face of increasingly complex social problems, students' visions were becoming increasingly narrow and self-interested. They were responding to Frank Newman's challenge to higher education to provide effective "education for citizenship" (1985). They concurred with Ernest Boyer (1987), president of the Carnegie Foundation for the Advancement of Teaching, who articulated an "uncomfortable feeling that the most vital issues of life — the nature of society, the roots of social injustice, indeed the very prospects for human survival — are the ones with which the undergraduate college is least equipped to deal."

Campus Compact now numbers 130 institutions. Universities and colleges are creating public service centers and other structures which enable students to become involved as community volunteers. The State of California, through its "Human Corps" legislation, requires each state university campus to plan for involving all students in community service. Other states are contemplating similar moves.

Led by university presidents, social critics, and civic educators and supported by student affairs and community service program staff, this movement has concentrated on stimulating and enabling students to become involved, focusing on the virtues of giving service and the assumed resulting development in students of an ethic of social responsibility. These advocates have tended to shy away from addressing the need to facilitate students' cognitive development and academic learning through their service activity. In addition, little attention has been given to providing the kind of training and support students need in order to learn from their experience and thereby provide effective and useful service. To date, as successful as it has been, this movement has relied more on assumptions and idealism than on hard thinking about and development of structures that enable students to serve and learn well.

Nevertheless, both sets of efforts — those in leadership education and those in public service — must be applauded. They respond to serious deficiencies in our educational system and they have had significant impact on campuses, students, and communities in a short period of time.

However, we must ask whether these movements, alone or connected as Spitzberg might suggest, effectively respond to the need to develop the qualities of leadership I identified earlier. A quick review suggests that they are taking us in the right direction, but they leave a significant gap, the gap that can be filled through programs of service learning.

Starting in the area of attitude, how are we helping young people develop substantive visions, ones that are not only self-motivating but also motivating for others? Surely the study of effective leaders will help evoke this in students. Visions are infectious. Leadership courses which enable students to explore their own ideals, values and expectations in relation to those of effective, revered leaders will help students become aware of the sources of their values and how these fit within larger traditions in our culture. Community service or other forms of internship learning will broaden the experience of students, exposing them to needs and opportunities they might not otherwise come in contact with, at least while in college, and *potentially* stimulating in them passionate reactions to social injustice and a commitment to work for change.

The area of cognitive initiative appears not to be served well by the authoritarian structure of traditional education. Faculty tend to assume that this is developed through experience, dismissing it as a concern of their colleagues in student affairs. Participation in student organizations or even in leadership development workshops can address this developmental need in students. However, youth development research indicates that emotional maturity requires successful engagement with responsible action which has consequences for others than the youth themselves — action which is difficult, if not impossible to simulate in a classroom or campus setting. Community service opportunities or other forms of experiential learning have been shown to develop self-confidence and a sense of self-efficacy, and thus may play an important role here (see Erynast, 1982, and Whitham and Erynast, 1983).

Many of the knowledge areas needed by leaders can be well served by leadership education and community service experience as well. Through leadership courses students can become aware of theoretical frameworks for viewing organizations and/or communities and their development. They can be introduced to human resource issues and practices and through workshop simulations experiment with many of the requisite management, group dynamics, and interpersonal/communication skills related to effective leadership. Through community service they can learn about social problems and efforts to solve these problems. They can learn about leadership and be introduced to, if not practice, leadership skills "by watching" business, government and public leaders through mentorships, fellowships and the like.

In the skill area of leadership development, we seem to be succeeding with some skills and falling short on others. The growth of co-curricular leadership programs appears to be addressing well the need for interpersonal, communication, and management skills for student leaders and others interested in leadership. Many campuses offer students a wide array of opportunities to play leadership roles on campus — through student organizations, as residence or academic advisors and in peer counseling roles.

However, neither leadership education nor community service programs alone effectively address the cognitive learning-to-learn and "judgment in action" skill areas or the aspects of leadership that involve the effective enabling and facilitating of action by others. I find that service learning is particularly well suited, maybe uniquely suited, to helping students acquire these last sets of skills.

Service Learning

Service learning is a twenty-year-old approach to experiential (or internship) education which developed out of concerns expressed in the sixties and seventies for active, experiential learning opportunities related to community service, community development and social change. It is best defined as the union of structured, intentional learning with public and community service (Berry, 1988). In emphasizing the accomplishment of tasks which meet human needs in combination with conscious educational growth, service learning lies at the intersection of theory and practice and self and society (Goodlad, 1988). It expresses an epistemological commitment that sees knowledge developed out of social practice (Rakoff, 1988).

The goals of service learning programs for off-campus communities include community and individual empowerment, community action, social change, and public and community service. For the on-campus community, and particularly for student participants, program goals fall well within the objectives of the traditional, academic curriculum. Service learning program goals include: "to learn how to apply, integrate, and evaluate knowledge or the methodology of a discipline," "to develop a firsthand understanding of the political and social action skills required for effective citizenship," "to develop perspectives and practice analytical skills necessary for understanding the social ecology of organizations engaged in the delivery of goods and services" (Stanton, 1987).

To ensure that service promotes substantive learning, service learning practitioners seek to connect students' experience in the community to reflection and analysis provided in the curriculum. They seek supervised experiences for service learners that provide contact with complex, contemporary social problems and efforts to solve them. They see this learning, when it combines action with critical reflection and analysis, as standing very much within the liberal arts tradition (Couto, 1982).

Service learning is a pedagogy that is characterized by mutuality between theory and practice and between on-campus and off-campus cultures. There is an active role for all parties in the enterprise — instructor, student, off-campus sponsor/supervisor. The commitment is to making learning and service reinforce each other. Robert Sigmon, an early pioneer in the service learning movement, connects the service philosophy in this pedagogy with the work of leadership writer Robert Greenleaf. Greenleaf, a former executive with AT&T, developed the concept of "servant-leader," one who works to see that other peoples' highest priority needs are served through his/her leadership effort. The test of this type of leader, for Greenleaf, is, "Do those served grow as persons; do they, while being served, become healthier, wiser, freer, more autonomous, more likely themselves to become servants?"

With this foundation Sigmon (1979, p. 10) offers these principles related to service learning:

1. *Those being served control the service(s) provided.* The needs of the host community, rather than of the academic program, come first in defining the work of students placed there; and the community defines those needs. This is a very different emphasis than that found in traditional field study or practicum courses, where field placements and the tasks of interns are defined by the academic objectives of the program or by professional certification requirements.

2. *Those being served become better able to serve and be served by their own actions.* The aim of the students' service should be the collaborative development and empowerment of those served.

3. *Those who serve are also learners, and have significant control over what is learned.* Though the needs of the host organization and its clients come first in service learning, unlike volunteer service where the volunteer offers her time and skills to do what needs to be done, the learning needs of the student must be negotiated and well matched with the needs of the host organization.

The productive tension between the service commitment to the community and the learning objectives of service learners creates a reciprocal process of social exchange.

A foundation for the pedagogical process of service learning may be found in David Kolb's theory of a cycle of experiential learning. Kolb (1984) describes learning as successive stages of concrete experience, reflective observation, abstract conceptualization, and active experimentation with these new concepts through application to continuing experience. As Kolb points out, when students consciously reflect on their experience, form generalizations and theories about it (in the context, I would add, of others' theoretical work), and then test out these theories or their implications through continued experience, they can achieve mastery of theoretical knowledge, of its application in practice, and of the ability to induce new knowledge out of experience.

The design of service learning programs is best explained in the context of the following principles of good practice for school- and campus-based programs. Since there are few programs that illustrate fully all of these principles, I will offer examples from several campuses:

1. *The program provides for an ongoing partnership among educators, community members, and students.* The Ravenswood-Stanford Tutoring Program, in which Stanford students tutor elementary school children in a nearby school district and take concurrent training and reflection seminars, was developed collaboratively between the Public Service Center and officials, staff, and board members of the school district. We jointly conceive program policies and activities, and we evaluate the program cooperatively.

2. *The program negotiates with the host organization and clearly defines the roles and responsibilities of the partners: educators, students, and agency staff.* The Great Lakes Colleges Association's Philadelphia Center program uses learning plan contracting through which interns, the program's "learning process consultant," and the host supervisors clarify roles and responsibilities of each prior to the student's undertaking the internship.

3. *The program provides opportunities for students to do real and needed work, which is desired by the host community or agency, and which offers significant educational, professional, and personal development opportunities.* Students from Vanderbilt University's Center for Health Services learn how to carry out soil and water testing for toxic pollution and offer health screening examinations for community groups and organizations in the Appalachian region. Students working through Stiles Hall at the University of California at Berkeley have designed and provide a drug education curriculum to children in the city's schools.

4. *The program matches the interests, abilities, and needs of students with the interests, needs, and program goals of host community or agency programs.* Cornell University's Field and International Study Program has clearly articulated criteria for matching students with participating placement organizations. Placement

organization needs are established and communicated to potential students, who then go through a two-stage application/interview process with program staff to determine the best possible match.

5. *The program prepares students well for their field experiences.* At Cornell an essential aspect of pre-field preparation is the intricate application and selection process described above.   In addition, all students are required to take a semester-long, pre-field preparation seminar which introduces them to the requisite skills and practice of service learning. Students acquire and try out data gathering and problem solving skills in workshops and practice them through a community-sponsored action research project in the local community. The results of the research project are assessed by and provided to sponsoring community groups.

6. *The program has an identified process through which students can reflect on and learn from their service experience.* Most service learning programs offer concurrent seminars and related reading and writing assignments through which students process their internship experiences and integrate them with academic knowledge.

Cornell's curriculum exemplifies a conscious attempt to utilize Kolb's learning cycle to engage students in an inductive process of relating theory and practice. For example, their curriculum helps students to reflect on a weekly basis on one of a series of questions related to their service learning, conceptualize their reflections and compare them with related theory from assigned readings, and draw conclusions which are tested in the ongoing internship.

7. *The program monitors student and project process and provides ongoing feedback to students, instructors, and host community or agency supervisors. The program evaluates what has been accomplished as well as what has been learned, on both the program and individual levels.* To promote self-direction, self-monitoring and self-assessment of service learning on the part of interns, the Cornell curriculum asks them to articulate, monitor and assess their progress toward individual learning and serving objectives, which they must negotiate with their community supervisor. Student journal writing, telephone calls and site visits by the faculty instructor, and comparative conversations about the service experience in the seminar all promote self-reflective dialogue within the individual student, and among fellow students, instructor and community supervisor. This dialogue enables students to see that their individual goals and objectives for the service learning are met, assessed and documented by the end of a semester.

Vanderbilt's Center for Health Services carries out far-reaching evaluations of the impact of their students' work in improving the health conditions of Appalachian residents.

8. *The program provides a continuity of service or action in selected communities or organizations.* Stanford's tutoring program is a school improvement partnership with the Ravenswood School District. We have made a long-term commitment to undertake efforts appropriate to the abilities of undergraduates to improve Ravenswood students' educational achievement. Should it be mutually determined that Stanford students' contributions would be more effective through activities other than tutoring, the program structure will change to reflect newly defined needs.

Conclusion

In a study of how teachers develop, Stanford's Lee Shulman (1987) found that most model their teaching styles on those of instructors they had when they were students. These findings suggest that we learn much of what we know how to do by watching and then unconsciously emulating people we respect. They also remind us of John Dewey's (1938) caution about the potentially "mis-educative" nature of experience, and the need for reflection and critical analysis. They point out that faculty who teach through lectures and other didactic processes do not provide good models for effective leadership behavior.

Certainly public service experiences and mentorship opportunities enable students to observe and take note of the behaviors of effective leaders. However, such experiences leave it to chance whether students will observe, much less experience, the kind of enabling and facilitating skills identified as good leadership traits. And, they rarely provide the kinds of feedback and learning facilitation which enable volunteers to learn from and be critical of what they experience. Service learning programs, on the other hand, with their emphasis on an action-reflection dynamic, have the potential to offer students the opportunity to observe and interact with enabling leaders through their service experience. This pedagogy requires students to experience through their own growth and development the positive effects of continual feedback, critique and dialogue with an instructor who is consciously striving to help them learn and grow from their experience. In this way service learners are exposed to and learn directly from this trait of enabling leadership.

Most importantly, service learning develops in students the ability to be self-directed in their learning and the cognitive, "reflection-in-action" skills necessary for intelligent behavior. John Gardner (1987), in exploring the development of leaders, suggests that "untutored good judgment is not enough." He calls for opportunities for students to test their judgment in fluid events, to exercise responsibility, to sharpen their intuitive gifts while being exposed to new constituencies and "untidy reality," *all* with support, feedback and guidance. He identifies the workplace as the learning laboratory for leadership development, noting the essential role of evaluation and critical feedback. He sees these processes as the antidote to an educational system which increasingly separates students from the rest of the world.

Integrating public service with intentional reflection, supervision, guided facilitation, and assessment helps provide the learning laboratory Gardner desires, enabling students to achieve multiple competencies, all of which are related to successful performance as leaders. Supervised service learning experience enhances affective competencies such as interpersonal skills, sensitivity to others, and active engagement with responsibilities having consequences for others. The reflective process builds social perceptiveness, an ability to listen with an open mind both to the experience one is in and to others' experience. Practice in conceptualizing these reflections requires service learners to build theory from practice by thinking inductively and strengthens analysis and synthesis skills. Finally, the testing of concepts, particularly one's own, helps students become adept at initiating and contributing to an enterprise from a proactive stance — cognitive initiative. In short, service learners learn intelligent behavior. And they do so in the context of activity which expresses the values of service to others, community development and empowerment, and reciprocal learning.

Richard Morrill (1982, p. 365) points out that civic literacy "requires more than knowledge and information; it includes the exercise of personal responsibility, active participation, and personal commitment to a set of values. Democratic literacy is a literacy of doing, not simply of knowing .... The test of civic education involves the empowerment of persons as well as the cultivation of minds." I would think this test applies to leadership education as well. The pedagogy of service learning, by linking responsible participation in our "untidy world" with a complete cycle of self-reflective learning, provides an essential bridge for linking personal empowerment (and community empowerment!) with cognitive growth. As such it has a key role to play in leadership development.

Timothy Stanton is Associate Director of the Public Service Center at Stanford University. He has also directed the Field Study Office at Cornell University, coordinated a community-based program for high school students, and served as President of the National Society for Internships and Experiential Education.

References

Barbour, George P., Jr., Thomas Fletcher, and George Sipel, *Leadership, Excellence and Public Management*, Center for Excellence in Local Government, 1985.

Barr, Donald J., and Virginia S. Vanderslice, "An Alternative View of Leadership: Incorporating The Dark Side of Power," presentation at the Annual Conference of the American Psychological Association, 1984.

Bennis, Warren G., *Leaders*, Harper and Row, 1985.

Berry, Howard, "Service-Learning in International/Intercultural Settings," in *Experiential Education*, National Society for Internships and Experiential Education, Vol. 13, No. 3, May-June 1988, pp. 3, 7.

Blake, Herman, remarks made at the annual "You Can Make A Difference Conference: Private Initiatives and Public Responsibility," Stanford University, 1985.

Boyer, Ernest L., *College: The Undergraduate Experience in America*, Harper & Row for the Carnegie Endowment for the Advancement of Teaching, 1987.

Clark, Miriam B., Frank H. Freeman, and Sara K. Britt, *Leadership Education '87: A Sourcebook*, Center for Creative Leadership, 1987.

Couto, Richard A., *Streams of Idealism and Health Care Innovation: An Assessment of Service-Learning and Community Mobilization*, Teachers College Press, 1982.

Dewey, John, *Experience and Education*, Collier Books, 1938.

Erdynast, Albert, "Field Experience and Stage Theories of Development," NSIEE Occasional Paper #4, National Society for Internships and Experiential Education, 1982.

Gardner, John W., "Leadership Papers," 1-10, Independent Sector, 1986-1989.

Gardner, John W., remarks made at Stanford University, 1986.

Gardner, John W., seminar presentation at Stanford University, 1988.

Goodlad, Sinclair, "Where Might This Take Us?" presentation to the Annual Conference of the Partnership for Service-Learning, "Service and Learning: Mapping the Intersections," February, 1988.

Guskin, Alan E., "On Changing Fundamental Conceptions of the Undergraduate Experience: Experiential Learning and Theories of Intelligence," presentation to the Annual Meeting of the National Commission on Cooperative Education, June 1, 1987.

Greenleaf, Robert K., *Servant Leadership: A Journey into the Nature of Legitimate Power and Greatness*, Paulist Press, 1977.

Holliday, Vivian, "Leadership Programs Should Include Analysis," letter to the editor, *Chronicle for Higher Education*, May 4, 1988.

Klemp, George O., Jr., "Three Factors of Success in the World of Work: Implications for Curriculum in Higher Education," in Dyckman W. Vermilye, ed., *Relating Work and Education* in New Directions for Higher Education, Jossey-Bass, 1978.

Kolb, David A., *Experiential Learning: Experience as a Source of Learning and Development*, Prentice-Hall, 1984.

Kotter, John P., *The Leadership Factor*, Free Press, 1988.

Kouzes, James M., and Barry Posner, *The Leadership Challenge: How To Get Things Done in Organizations*, Jossey-Bass, 1987.

March, James, from lectures given during instruction of Stanford University course, "Organizational Leadership," fall quarter, 1987.

Morrill, Richard L., "Educating for Democratic Values," in *Liberal Education*, Association of American Colleges, Vol. 68, No.4, 1982, p. 365.

Mulder, Mark, "Power Equalization Through Participation?" in *Administrative Science Quarterly*, Cornell University, Vol. 16, No. 1, March 1971, pp. 31-38.

Newman, Frank, *Higher Education and the American Resurgence*, A Carnegie Foundation Special Report, Carnegie Foundation for the Advancement of Teaching, 1985.

Palmer, Parker J., "Community, Conflict and Ways of Knowing: Ways To Deepen Our Educational Agenda," in *Change*, American Association for Higher Education, Vol. 19, No. 5, September/October 1987, pp. 20-25.

Rakoff, Robert M., from response to Campus Compact survey on the faculty's role in the public service initiative, 1988.

Reich, Robert B., *The Power of Public Ideas*, Ballinger, 1988.

Schon, Donald A., *The Reflective Practitioner: How Professionals Think in Action*, Basic Books, 1983.

Shulman, Lee S., "Learning To Teach," in *AAHE Bulletin*, American Association for Higher Education, Vol. 40, No.3, November, 1987.

Sigmon, Robert, "Service-Learning: Three Principles," in *Synergist*, National Center for Service-Learning, ACTION, Spring 1979, Vol. 8, No. 1, pp. 9-11.

Spitzberg, Irving J., Jr., *Campus Programs on Leadership*, Council for Liberal Learning of the Association of American Colleges, 1986.

Stanton, Timothy K., "Liberal Arts, Experiential Learning and Public Service: Necessary Ingredients for Socially Responsible Undergraduate Eduction," paper presented at 16th Annual Conference of the National Society for Internships and Experiential Education, 1987.

Whitham, Michele A., and Albert Erdynast, "Applications of Developmental Theory to the Design and Conduct of Quality Field Experience Programs," PANEL Resource Paper #8, National Society for Internships and Experiential Education, 1984.

"COLLEGE AND POST-GRADUATE programs move young people steadily away from the mainstream of American experience. ...[Those] selected for our more demanding institutions have exceptional skill in the manipulation of verbal and numerical symbols. That is what the tests test and what it takes to get good grades. With each passing year they find themselves with a more and more highly selected group of young people ... who have almost certainly lost touch with most of their less-gifted friends. As they move through university and graduate school, they drift further and further out of touch with those Americans who would rather play Bingo than watch 'Masterpiece Theatre,' who bowl on Thursday nights and elect presidents on the Tuesday after the first Monday in November. It is not good for the students or for the society."

— John W. Gardner
From *On Leadership*
1990, pp. 168-169

John Gardner is former President of the Carnegie Corporation and the Carnegie Foundation for the Advancement of Teaching, U.S. Secretary of H.E.W., founder of Common Cause, and co-founder of Independent Sector. His other books include Excellence, Self-Renewal, No Easy Victories, The Recovery of Confidence, In Common Cause, *and* Morale. *Reprinted by permission of The Free Press, a Division of MacMillan, Inc.*

The Development of Social Consciousness: Nurturing a Positive and Empowered Relationship with Society

Shelley Berman

The President of Educators for Social Responsibility explores the role of schools and colleges in helping students realize both their personal potential and their social potential: What is the nature and potential of their own relationship to the larger society? Reprinted with permission from Forum, Educators for Social Responsibility, *Vol. 6, No. 2, Winter 1987, pp. 3, 5.*

One of the things I value most about our work in Educators for Social Responsibility (ESR) is the fact that we are continually asking questions and refining our understanding of what it means to educate for living in a nuclear age. This dialogue has carried us from our starting point with nuclear issues, through the exploration of concepts of peace and justice, to the skills of citizen participation. Now this thinking process has brought us to another frontier. We are beginning to explore the development of social consciousness.

The issue of social consciousness emerges from some unsettling questions: Why do people respond in such different ways to the undeniable awareness of the world's problems? Why do some people choose to become involved in political and social issues? Why do others, just as aware and just as able, choose not to participate? What are the factors that determine and structure this active participation? How do people's moral judgments translate into social action? And finally, how do people develop a sense of social responsibility — that is, a sense of personal investment in the well-being of others and of their world?

My research over the last two years leads me to believe that each of us develops a relationship to society and to the world. Furthermore, the way we give meaning to this relationship determines the nature of our participation in the world. I've deliberately chosen the term "relationship" because, like a relationship with another person, our relationship with society includes such powerful factors as interconnection, emotion, and influence.

I also use the term "relationship" because it shifts the context of our thinking. Too often, I think, we focus our attention on individual choice and individual responsibility. Most moral education and moral development theory seems directed at the way people make choices, at the way they balance their individual needs with the needs of others. There isn't much attention paid to the social context for these moral decisions. I've found that people don't make moral decisions in isolation, especially not decisions that relate to larger social and political issues. These decisions emerge directly from people's relationship to society — from what they see as the dominant morality in the political culture, and from their sense of their personal ability to influence that culture.

Because it is difficult for many people to describe verbally their relationship to society, I've been exploring a new approach. I've asked people first to *draw* the way they see their own relationship to society before they attempt to describe it. I've now collected such pencil, crayon, or marker drawings from elementary school children, from high school and college students, and from adults who represent a wide range of lifestyles and viewpoints. These drawings usually reveal complex feelings towards society — sometimes a rich mosaic of interconnectedness, sometimes the painful expression of alienation and powerlessness, and sometimes the struggle to reconcile both hope and pain. Although we all exist in relationship to society, I've come to realize that people seldom talk about the nature of this relationship and how they feel in it. I'm realizing that helping students develop a sense of social responsibility means opening a conversation about this relationship — making explicit some of those things they may not have looked at before.

It has also become clearer to me why the many volumes of work in "citizenship" education have failed in their avowed goal of helping students develop an active, participatory relationships with society. First, these efforts in citizenship education simply inform students about our political culture without ever asking them to reflect on how *they* experience and understand this culture. The idealized picture of our society presented by these programs hardly corresponds at all to the experience of society — often centering on feelings of alienation and powerlessness — that most students have internalized. Second, these programs often teach about democracy without encouraging students to experience their own power and influence, either in the classroom or in the larger world. Finally, by simply presenting information about the democratic process, these citizenship education programs often fail to engage students in genuine, thoughtful inquiry about the various ways that an individual can go about establishing an empowered relationship with society.

Why do some people choose to become involved in political and social issues? Why do others, just as aware and just as able, choose not to participate?

One of the most vital lessons we have learned in ESR is that we cannot impose attitudes and understandings. Instead, we must begin a dialogue by listening carefully to our students' ideas and questions. Not only do they need to feel heard and validated in order to grow into meaningful adult roles in society; but we, too, need to learn from them what their real issues are in order to facilitate their growth most effectively. As we engage in this dialogue, we can build our curriculum around the interest and concerns our students express about the nature of their relationship to society.

To nurture this conversation and build a bridge between school and the larger society, there are many other creative things we can explore. We can help students enter into more direct contact with society. We can give them opportunities to learn about the way the world really is as well as to contribute — in ways they find meaningful — to the peace, justice, and safety of the world. As a model for their participation in the larger society, we can provide opportunities for students to create community and democracy in their classrooms and schools. For most educators, this means a significant shift in our own thinking. We need to balance our traditional effort to help students realize their personal potential with a new, parallel effort to help them realize their social potential.

THE DEVELOPMENT OF SOCIAL CONSCIOUSNESS

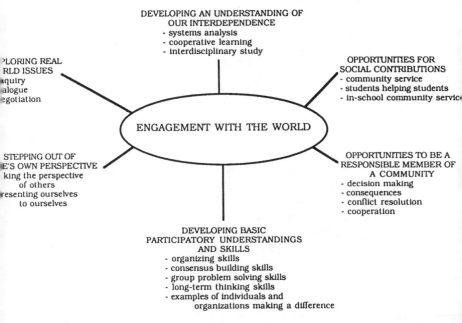

It is important to point out that exploring social consciousness and teaching for social responsibility do not mean enlisting students in adult causes. This kind of teaching is decidedly not about turning out political activists. Although we can nurture their interest in political action, there is an entire range of equally viable ways for young people to express their social responsibility once they leave our classrooms — in their relationships with friends, in their work, in raising children, in their role as consumers, and in many other areas. This kind of teaching, then, is simply about helping young people recognize that their actions create not only their own future but the future of society as well. It is about helping them find *their own* meaningful ways to make a difference.

Shelley Berman is President of Educators for Social Responsibility.

When the knower has to apply knowledge ...

Let us imagine a pilot,
and assume that he had passed every
examination with distinction,
but that he had not as yet been at sea.
Imagine him in a storm;
he knows everything he ought to do,
but he has not known before how terror
grips the seafarer when the stars
are lost in the blackness of night;
he has not known the sense of
impotence that come when the pilot
sees the wheel in his hand
become a plaything for the waves;
he has not known how the blood
rushes into the head when one
tries to make calculations at
such a moment;
in short, he has no conception
of the change that takes
place in the knower
when he has to
apply his knowledge.

— from Kierkegaard, M. S., "Thoughts on Crucial Situations in Human Life," in *Parables of Kierkegaard*, ed. T. C. Oden, Princeton University Press, 1978, p. 38.

Youth Leadership Development

Rick Jackson and Keith Morton

Jackson and Morton outline an approach to youth leadership programs that builds both on leadership theory and on models for the intellectual and moral development of young adults. They describe the University of Minnesota YMCA's program as an example of how the essential elements of both can be incorporated into a powerful youth leadership program. This paper was prepared in August 1988 for Project Leadership-Service, a ten-year-old joint project of Butler University and the Lilly Endowment. Project Leadership-Service challenges high school youth to be servant leaders in their communities following an intensive ten-day leadership experience. The program also structures a cross-age mentoring relationship between the high school students and sixth grade children.

OUR INTENTION in this chapter is to help you build a model of youth leadership that addresses the central issues of youth development. Toward this end we will first describe our understanding of leadership. We will then turn our attention to the intellectual and moral development of young adults. We will conclude by joining leadership and developmental theory in a way that illustrates what we believe are the central challenges that must be answered in building a powerful youth leadership program.

We are working with two assumptions. First, we are assuming a focus on a "servant leader" approach to leadership. Secondly, we are concerned with leadership programs that are appropriate for both high school and college students. The significance of the first assumption is that it raises the question, "Leadership for what?" The significance of the second assumption is that there are developmental differences between high school and college-aged young adults. Each assumption has implications for your leadership development program which will be addressed.

Leadership Examined

Leadership theories, argues Robert Terry, fall generally into one of six categories: power, position, trait, vision, situational, ethical assessment (Terry, 1987). These theories would give us very different descriptions of leaders. Leaders make things happen, regardless of position. Or, leaders inhabit a place in a hierarchy, as in the military. Leaders are born, not made. Leaders articulate direction and meaning for others. Leadership adapts to changing circumstance. Leadership involves ethical reflection and action.

Each of these camps has its advocates. What Terry proposes in his "seventh view" is that leadership is all of these things — and more:

> [Leadership] is grounded in traits, yet the required skills are not exhausted by traits. It is sensitive to shifting situations, yet it recognizes complexity beyond situational theory's reach. It is shaped by roles and position, yet is greater than any organization hierarchy. It is activated by power, yet challenges the primacy of power. It is driven by vision, yet is not satisfied with just any direction. It is ethical, yet tempered by an awareness of existence, ambiguities and unforeseen consequences ... (1987, p. 20)

Clearly, leadership defies easy definition. Terry concludes that it is all of the above, "with more attention to ethical reflection, courage, human ambiguity and dilemmas ... it is a fundamental and profound engagement with the world and human condition" (1987, p. 22).

The challenge for a successful leadership program, then, is to engage participants in activities that coherently and continuously address the skills and worldviews suggested by each camp while engaging with the world and human condition. Participants in a successful leadership program must experience power and position. They must discover their particular strengths and weaknesses. They must learn to confront the "human condition" and to accept ambiguity. They must be introspective as well as active in the world. There must be consequences to their actions. They must be challenged to value, critique and develop vision.

These are characteristics of leadership. It is still fair to ask toward what end leadership should be directed. We believe leaders must serve the common good. Our concern is with the development of a particular type of leadership described by Robert Greenleaf in *The Servant as Leader*:

The servant-leader *is* servant first ... That person is sharply different from someone who is *leader* first, perhaps because of the need to assuage an unusual power drive or to acquire material possessions .... The best test, and most difficult to administer, is: Do those served grow as persons? Do they, *while being served*, become healthier, wiser, freer, more autonomous, more likely themselves to become servants? *And* what is the effect on the least privileged in society; will they benefit, or, at least, not be further deprived? (1970, p. 7 ff.)

Greenleaf's understanding of leadership challenges many commonly held assumptions. In particular, it assumes that the leader is grounded in a community, or in several communities, and that the purpose of leadership is to help articulate and then serve the needs of those communities. In essence, Greenleaf's vision of the leader is that of change-agent. Thus a real task of leadership is grasping the meaning and boundaries of community. At a practical level, this requires that a leader is able to be both a part of a community and stand contemplatively outside it.

That the ability to intellectually move in and out of cultures is a necessary part of leadership is supported as well by the research of George Shapiro (Shapiro, 1988). For the past two years Shapiro has been interviewing ethical leaders designated as such by their peers. For the most part these leaders are positional, and they cut across several professional boundaries. Shapiro believes there are two characteristics that these people share: they are comfortable using power and they believe that the end of power is the common good.

Most importantly, Shapiro points out, two kinds of early life experiences contributed to their growth as leaders. They had *mentors* who modeled good behavior, took them along on attempting worthy tasks, and held great expectations that they would take their gifts seriously. In addition, the leaders pointed to the impact of *one or more significant cross-cultural experiences* which confounded simplistic or prejudicial moral assumptions and affirmed diversity as a positive social reality.

Developmental Concerns

While there is considerable debate regarding the proper description and interpretation of young adult development, there is little question that young adulthood is a difficult and exciting period of change and self-discovery. In essence, young adulthood is a period in which meaning making is of prime concern (Sharon Parks, 1986).

The literature of cognitive and moral development generally adopts a typology of "stages." While these are not always tied to chronological age, their order of succession and the ages at which they occur are generally consistent. Recently there has been instructive discussion of how developmental processes differ between and women and men. As Carol Gilligan has pointed out in her groundbreaking work, *In a Different Voice,* "when women do not conform to the standards of psychological expectation, the conclusion has generally been that something is wrong with the women." The differences may, in fact, result from expectations that male development is the norm (Gilligan, 1982). Nevertheless, a survey of the typologies described by Erikson, Kohlberg, Chickering, Coles and Perry reveals some fairly consistent and useful findings.

In Erikson's schema (1968), the primary tasks of young adulthood are the development of identity (which allows fidelity in relating to others and affirming oneself) and intimacy (overcoming isolation with the ability to be vulnerable and risk love). Similarly, Perry (1970) defines the maturation of young adults as movement from dualism (right and wrong are fixed) to relativism (you do your thing, I'll do mine) and then to committed relativism, where one takes responsibility for one's actions in the world. High school aged young adults often see the world in fixed terms, as do college students in their first year. Over time the surety of this fixed vision is challenged, and the student becomes a relativist — extremely stated, all truth is opinion. At this juncture, there are two choices. Students can retreat to fixed truths, or they can become committed relativists.

For Chickering (1969, 1981), the issue of young adulthood is achieving competence, autonomy, purpose and integrity: becoming a self. The competencies are of three types: physical, intellectual and interpersonal.

Kohlberg describes moral development in terms of movement from pleasing others to acting in accord with social standards to personal integrity which will risk censure in support of strongly believed principles.

Robert Coles (1986), once a student of Erikson, makes what is in many ways the most challenging argument for those concerned with leadership. The "moral trajectory" of an adult, he argues, is determined in youthful experiences. Ideals and values are set largely by early encounters with significant others and cross-cultural experiences. The social, ideological and cultural sources of conscience are shaped by the moral signals a young person receives. Thus, the development of *moral purpose* is the critical task of youth.

Taken together, these developmental theorists suggest that young adulthood is a time when one begins to recognize cultural pluralism; when one struggles with self-identity; when one is challenged to stand on one's own; when one must develop beliefs and values; when one begins to see the "self" as a person *in* the world.

It is important to note several differences between adolescents and young adults. As Erikson (1968) points out, they face different crises: who am I, versus what/who do I love? For adolescents, the self is the object of discovery; for young adults, the self is captured through discovery of the world "out there." Additionally, adolescents are more inclined to be literally minded; they do not trust intuition and they distrust metaphors (Ortony, 1979). Often they are dualists. Even as they challenge social norms, ambiguity and difference are frightening. Young adults, by comparison, are discovering the multiplicity of worldviews that exist in the world. They are being challenged to use their creativity and intuition and can begin to appreciate metaphor. They discover that they must act despite ambiguity. Often they seek communities of support that differ from those into which they were born. They try on a variety of life roles. They seek mates and commitment. They are concerned that their lives have "meaning" and "make sense."

The moral capacity for leadership is rooted in significant ethical objectives which stem from the amount and variety of social experience in youth. Young persons especially, as Coles makes clear, are constantly observing what is just and fair, and rendering their judgments. This process can be acknowledged, nurtured, and respected in leadership programs. Crucial is the opportunity to take a number of roles and to encounter other perspectives. Says Coles: "It is our nature ... to hope against hope. I believe that the active idealism we see in some of our young takes place.... when a beckoning history offers, uncannily, a blend of memory and desire; a chance to struggle for a new situation that holds a large promise, while earning along the way the approval of one's parents, neighbors, friends and, not least, oneself" (1986, p. 35).

The stakes of this development are high. The moral growth a youth achieves, or fails to achieve, is by extension the moral fiber of the communities that make up this nation.

Correspondence of Developmental and Leadership Theory

There is a striking correspondence between the demands of leadership as outlined by Robert Terry and the developmental issues faced by young adults. As Terry notes in his forthcoming book, *Action Leadership*, "Most, if not all development schemes are inherently ethical" (Terry 1988).

Among the parallels between leadership and development theories are:

• The discovery of multiple worldviews, even as one builds and recognizes one's own worldview;

• The discovery of one's competencies or gifts as a leader, and the need for intellectual, physical and interpersonal competency in development;

• The need for vision, as a leader, and the struggle with intuition and metaphor in development;

• The effort to discover who one is, what one loves and what gives meaning to existence; and

• The need for ethical action and integrity if one is to be a leader.

Consider here the proposition that leadership, by definition, opens the way for followers to move to higher developmental stages.

Implications for Youth Development Programs

Our argument, then, is that youth leadership programs should be developmentally grounded. Leadership programming will thus have different meanings depending upon the developmental issues faced by its participants. Specifically, we recommend that you design your youth leadership program to address the developmental needs of participants; that you challenge and stretch the participants to move to the "next" stage; and that you not require participants to skip stages or do what is simply beyond them.

If your program will operate for both high school and college students, it may be necessary to think of it as *two discrete programs working jointly*. Another caution is that it is often difficult for people who are just exiting a developmental stage to work successfully with people just entering that stage. There is the potential for both sides to feel threatened. Thus, there may be some particular challenges in having college freshmen or sophomores work with high school juniors or seniors. Conversely, it can be an enriching experience for someone who has passed a developmental stage to teach, lead, or mentor another person through that same stage.

Ideally, your leadership program would build competencies, affirm the value of the students as individuals, help them discover their gifts and weaknesses, assist them in the transition from dualism to committed relativism, and provide opportunity for students to address the "big," meaning-making questions of life.

Implementation

The task of building a developmentally based leadership program, described in so few words in the previous section, is daunting. The following suggestions are drawn less from the literature on leadership or development than from our personal experiences in running youth leadership programs. What we offer are suggestions that may help you create a context in which leadership development is nurtured.

Our major recommendation is that your leadership program emphasize its action component, one which the participants will know is "real" and necessary. Wayne Meisel, founder of the college-based Campus Outreach Opportunity League, uses strong language in discussing the "structural apathy" of educational institutions which prevents young adults from participating in the work of society. Active participation in *meaningful* work is necessary to the intellectual and moral development of young adults.

Community service offers opportunities for such action, whether in grade school, high school, college or a full-time service corp, and has the potential for several important outcomes: it can place participants in cultures other than their own; the common experience of serving and being served can help build a strong sense of community among participants; it requires and tests commitment and values; it can challenge participants to develop relationships; and it will generate a number of "learning moments" for personal self discovery.

There are, of course, inherent risks in using service as a leadership model. The most significant of these is that the population being served can be left in a worse state than when found. It can be devastating, for example, for a young child in a big-buddy program to feel rejection by a student who drops his or her commitment. Thus, high-quality preparation and support of volunteers is critical. See the chapter of this resource book about other important principles of good practice.

There are, we believe, *four essential dimensions to building a youth leadership program: clear mission, empowerment, program structure, and program resources.* These four dimensions are outlined briefly below along with some of the important issues and program features to be considered in relation to each. Then one program is described as a sample of how these dimensions might be addressed.

Mission: Youth Development

The youth development mission must be foremost, not a by-product, in youth leadership programs. Taking account of the major points mentioned above, this means a clear focus on:

1. *Moral/ethical development* – focus upon growth in personal identity and interpersonal intimacy;

2. *Servant leadership* – affirm hope-filled purpose and active social responsibility as the paths toward making meaning; and

3. *Citizenship* – offer experiences of civic duty in cross-cultural contexts and connected to a global perspective.

Empowerment: Service Learning

Service learning recognizes that the best way to absorb important developmental learnings is to participate actively in the actual work of the community. This means young people:

1. *Youth service* – meet real needs in the community, both short- and long-term;

2. *Mentors* – work alongside role models who hold "great expectations" for our service; and

3. *Peer responsibility* – work together, sharing accountability for tasks and outcomes.

Program Structure: Group Work

Social responsibility cannot be learned alone. Group work remains the primary "classroom" for learning crucial leadership skills necessary for the common good, skills like negotiating, risking, being vulnerable, persevering with faith over time. Good group work is characterized by:

1. *Reference groups* – the group seen as a primary context of identity and learning for the participants, which means that the group involvement must be frequent, intense, and attractive;

2. *Task driven* – the group's tasks are clear, worthy, achievable, and ideally mutually selected and "owned"; and

3. *Community* – the life of the group involves both interpersonal challenge and support, with a balance of time struck between the active "doing" and the reflective "being" needed for relationships to grow and deepen.

Program Resources: Diversity

The best youth leadership development programs actively seek to incorporate diversity into their programs. This means the programs:

1. *Diverse methods* – use multiple curriculums and environments for learning, recognizing persons learn best in different ways;

2. *Mainstreaming* – have an inclusive participant base, which most often means proactive recruitment plans and ample scholarships to assure broad economic and ethnic diversity; and

3. *Commonwealth* – celebrate differences deliberately, demonstrate shared values, and articulate civic duties.

An Example: The University of Minnesota YMCA

Founded in 1887 by University President Cyrus Northrup, the University of Minnesota YMCA (U -Y) has for over a century sought to build "a character for service" in students. The current statement of mission is: (1) *to challenge students to develop commitments to other persons and to issues of social justice;* and (2) *to assist persons in becoming reflective and embracing of views of life that give life meaning.*

The U -Y employs a carefully designed "process programming" model of student work. The goal is first to engage students' interests and energies in challenging tasks, then to gradually increase the focus on personal learning in relationships with other students and program participants. The shorthand for this aspect of the process is "bait and add." This acknowledges the need to identify compelling reasons for students to become involved ("bait" or self-interest) and the subsequent addition of complementary activities which enhance moral/ethical development ("adds" or relational/reflection activities).

This process of programming builds upon what we know from reference group theory and practice. We are social selves, and our attitudes and experiences of self-understanding are clearly linked with those groups with which we most strongly identify. These are our *reference groups* - the select involvements which fundamentally shape our behavior and self-concept.

For a group involvement to be most formative for its members, the following factors must be built into the process:

1. *Definition* - clear understanding of group membership and norms;

2. *Intensity* - considerable intensity of personal involvement;

3. *Length* - longer is most often better;

4.   *Size* - groups small enough for significant personal interaction and a sense of personal acceptance;

5.   *Cohesiveness* - activities which encourage formation of group identity and purpose;

6.   *Great expectations* - high degree of commitment and allegiance to basic group goals insisted upon;

7.   *Visibility* - performance of individual group members and the entire group is recognized as making a difference; and

8.   *Attractiveness* - pride in membership, with a strong sense of personal identification with the group.

Reference groups can be good or bad. Many religious cult groups, for example, employ variations on the reference group methods. Critical differences for a good youth leadership program are the clarity and openness about the group norms at the beginning of involvement, and the practice of "participant democracy" as a teaching and learning methodology throughout the program cycle. In a word, "No surprises."

The "process program" model succeeds or fails on the ability to strike a balance between action and reflection, doing and being. Service activities rendered are critically important, and the "great expectations" motto can generate some extraordinary results from talented and creative students. Still, the service and activity outcomes are the means to an even more important opportunity: the integration of personal learnings and the formulation of initial life commitments. Thus, another motto of process programming is "action precedes commitment."

Action alone does not always produce commitment. Sometimes actions, taken for the wrong reasons (e.g., "This will look great on my resume") can produce contrary outcomes. But action followed by mentored reflection can produce positive results, even when original motivations are not "right" ones. In this regard, several program features are important:

1.   Individual questioning and debriefing of experiences with peers and staff and faculty mentors;

2.   Asking confounding, meaning-seeking questions like, "What did you learn about yourself from this experience?";

3.   Assistance in dealing with painful and conflicting situations such as authority, failure, and value confusion by demonstrated acceptance and intimacy;

4.   Support for exploration of life choices by affirming risk taking and a search for understanding more than control; and

5. Consistent personal feedback to help participants discover their personal authenticity, patience, learning moments, and honest responses.

A belief which undergirds the U -Y program philosophy is that reflection and commitment in life relate to meaning in life. A prerequisite for a sense of meaning is the experience of giving oneself, one's interests, skills and passions to some ethical demand which pushes one's limits in developing compassion for others and for their welfare. This is a process of personal development, and also of the development of ethically sensitive leaders.

Conclusion

Public and higher education are not presently receiving good marks in the area of moral and civic education. Numerous national reports in recent years indicate an alarming lack of preparation for students to exercise civic responsibility. Yet it is unfair to blame students. American society in hundreds of big and small ways teaches them to compete and acquire, not to cooperate and contribute. Too many of our schools and colleges do the same.

The result is that, in spite of record affluence, there exists a failure of moral commitment. Robert Coles (1986) points out this irony in his work when he observes that many of the "culturally deprived" he has studied have a moral sensibility, while many children of wealth and status have the finest education money can buy but lack a moral purpose. Coles urges us to ask great things of our youth, and to expect great service in return. As we do this, we will serve not only the young persons, but ourselves as well.

We believe the best youth leadership programs combine moral and skill development in schemes of active service to the community. The more culturally and socially diverse the participants, the better, since cross-cultural experiences rate high as sources for moral education.

Programs must also have well-trained, stable staffs to maximize role modeling and mentoring relationships over time. Thus designed, leadership programs support the meaning making task of young adults and promote the formation of initial life commitments.

In *The Servant as Leader*, Robert Greenleaf writes: "Many people finding their wholeness through many and varied contributions make a good society" (p. 35). Ultimately, we believe, the value of our educational system will be measured by its success in providing future generations of servant leaders with a challenging and supportive community within which they can both develop as unique persons and lead for the good of all.

Rick Jackson is Vice President of the Minneapolis YMCA and former Executive Director of the University of Minnesota YMCA. He earned a M.A. in ethics from Yale Divinity School, and a M.Div, in theology from United Theological Seminary. He is presently a Kellogg National Fellow.

Keith Morton, Ph.D., is Program Director at the University of Minnesota YMCA. He received his Ph.D. in American Studies from the University of Minnesota in 1986.

References

Bellah, Robert *et.al.*, *Habits of the Heart: Individualism and Commitment in American Life*, University of California Press, 1985. The widely acclaimed critique of modern American professional life and institutions, with a call to rebuild "communities of memory and hope."

Bellah, Robert and William Sullivan, "The Professions and the Common Good: Vocation/Profession/Career" in *Religion & Intellectual Life*, Volume IV, Number 3, Spring 1987. Reasserts the moral imperatives at the center of ethical thought and practice.

Boyte, Harry and Sara Evans, *Free Spaces: The Sources of Democratic Change in America*, Harper & Row, 1986. Identifies the root location of democratic change as the places where small groups of persons share their passions for justice and visions for a better future.

Chickering, Arthur, *Education and Identity*, Jossey Bass, 1969. Describes Chickering's understanding of development and its relation to education.

Chickering, Arthur and Assoc., *The Modern American College*, Jossey Bass, 1981. This master work compiles the major contributors toward young adult development.

Coles, Robert, *The Moral Life of Children*, Houghton Mifflin, 1986. Describes through case studies the moral dilemmas faced by children and the strategies they use to cope with them.

Erikson, Erik H., *Identity Youth and Crisis*, Norton, 1968. Summarizes Erikson's developmental theory.

Flanagan, O., and K. N. Jackson, "Justice, care and gender: The Kohlberg-Gilligan debate revisited," Ethics, Vol. 97, April 1987, pp. 622-37.

Gilligan, Carol, *In a Different Voice: Psychological Theory and Women's Development*, Harvard University Press, 1982. A groundbreaking work that challenges contemporary developmental theory to incorporate the experience of girls and women. Of particular relevance are her discussion of women's concern with person-based, social-situational ethics.

Goodlad, John I., *A Place Called School: Prospects for the Future*, McGraw Hill, 1984. In the author's words, "a discussion of what appears to be the current state of schooling in our country, made real by the illustrative use of data carefully gathered from a small, diverse sample of schools." It is a superb book.

Greenleaf, Robert K., *Servant Leadership: a Journey into the Nature of Legitimate Power and Greatness*, Paulist Press, 1977. Summarizes Greenleaf's ideas regarding leadership and contains a chapter on "Servant Leadership in Education" which is particularly useful.

Greenleaf, Robert K., *The Servant as Leader*, Windy Row Press, 1970.

Janowitz, Morris, *The Reconstruction of Patriotism: Education for Civic Consciousness*, University of Chicago Press, 1983. Reasserts the balance of rights and duties in a free society.

Kohlberg, Lawrence and E. Turiel, "Moral Development and Moral Education," in G.S. Lesser, ed., *Psychology and Educational Practice*, Scott Foresman, 1971.

Lewis, Anne C., *Facts and Faith: a Status Report on Youth Service*, William T. Grant Commission on Youth and America's Future, 1988.

Luce, Janet, *Service-Learning: an Annotated Bibliography for Linking Public Service with the Curriculum*, National Society for Internships and Experiential Education, 1988. The most complete annotated bibliography on linking service with learning and reflection.

Ortony, Andrew, ed., *Metaphor and Thought*, Cambridge University Press, 1979. Contains much of the best writing about the acquisition, use and meaning of metaphor. Relevant to cognitive development, problem-solving skills, vision and cross-cultural experience.

Palmer, Parker, *To Know as We Are Known: A Spirituality of Education*, Harper & Row, 1983. Reasserts the vital connection of mind and heart in the quest for humane knowledge.

Parks, Sharon, *The Critical Years*, Harper & Row, 1986. Explores the connection between personal development and public commitments, and the role "meaning making" (faith) plays.

Perry, William G., *Forms of Intellectual and Ethical Development in the College Years: A Schema*, Holt, Reinhart & Winston, 1970. Summarizes Perry's research on college student development; now a standard among college faculty and staff.

Shapiro, George, "Ethical Leadership," unpublished manuscript, 1988. Summarizes his recent research into the nature of ethical leadership. Information is available from him at the Speech Communication Department, University of Minnesota, Minneapolis.

Terry, Robert, *Action Leadership*, unpublished manuscript, 1988. Summarizes Terry's understanding of leadership based on his work as director of the Hubert H. Humprey Institute's Center for Reflective Leadership. Additional information is available from the Humphrey Institute, University of Minnesota.

Terry, Robert, "The Leading Edge," *Minnesota*, January/February 1987, pp. 17-22.

Part II

Rationales and Theories for Combining Service and Learning:

Moral and Ethical Development

The Perry Model of Development: Ideas for Educators

Mary Jo White

Mary Jo White summarizes the very useful ideas of William Perry and outlines their potential uses for service-learning. She also draws on the work of Lee Knefelkamp and Carole Widick. Reprinted from Experiential Education, *National Society for Internships and Experiential Education, Vol. 13, No. 2, March-April 1988, pp. 3, 9.*

THE MODEL OF COGNITIVE DEVELOPMENT proposed by William G. Perry, Jr., and his associates at Harvard University was first published in his book, *Forms of Intellectual and Ethical Development in the College Years: A Scheme* (1970). It has since become one of the most important theoretical foundations for educators interested in understanding the process of intellectual growth.

All developmental schemes of human learning assume a certain psychological model of change. Individuals progress through a series of stages involving shifts in their patterns of thought from the relatively simple to the more complex. These shifts are caused by conflict or dissonance with familiar cognitive constructs that force an individual to adopt new modes of reasoning. Development, then, occurs as the result of the transition from one stage of thinking to the next.

Four Categories

Perry's model illustrates the course of development in college students' patterns of thought. His scheme describes nine sequential stages or "positions" for the interpretation of meaning, and suggests the kinds of challenges or transitions that precipitate movement from stage to stage. The nine positions are grouped into four categories: dualism, multiplicity, relativism, and commitment. These terms represent the qualitatively different ways in which students view knowledge, the role of the teacher, and their own roles as learners.

Dualism. In the category called Dualism, the student views knowledge and meaning in two realms: good versus bad, right versus wrong, we versus they. The teacher is the authority, the sole source of information. The student's role is to learn the information and demonstrate that the facts have been mastered. Perry describes Positions One and Two in this category as ones in which students have trouble with diversity and multiplicity in learning. They see the world in polar terms and believe there is a single "right" answer for every question.

Multiplicity. The second category, Multiplicity, occurs when the student begins to recognize and accept diversity in the world of knowledge. The student comes to understand the difference between opinion and supported opinion. In Positions Three and Four, the student focuses on *how* to think and comes to appreciate the use of evidence as a method for validating information.

Relativism. In Perry's next category, Relativism, the student comes to view all knowledge as relative and, thus, develops a capacity for objectivity. With Positions Five and Six, the responsibility and initiative that used to be the domain of the teacher as authority become internalized. The focus of control is within. The student sees the potential and necessity for some form of personal commitment and the need to make decisions based on personal values or choices.

Commitment. With the fourth category, Commitment, the student accepts responsibility for establishing a personal identity in a pluralistic world. Through affirmation, choice or decision, the student makes a commitment (to a career, spouse, value, etc.); experiences the implications of the commitment; and affirms his/her identity in realizing the commitment. These steps represent Positions Seven, Eight and Nine.

Perry's scheme represents a purely descriptive formulation of the development of students' thinking. A summary of the scheme and a comprehensive bibliography of works by and about Perry appear in Chapter 3, "Cognitive and Ethical Growth: The Making of Meaning," in Arthur Chickering's *The Modern American College.*

The Challenge for Educators

The challenge for educators is to transform Perry's scheme into programs intended to facilitate students' development.

L. Lee Knefelkamp and Carole C. Widick have perhaps had the most success to date with their process model of instructional design, known as "Developmental Instruction" (Knefelkamp, 1974).

The model assesses student characteristics according to the Perry scheme and allows for the adjustment of four instructional variables: the degree of structure in the learning environment; the degree of diversity in the learning tasks; the type of experiential learning; and the amount of personalism in the learning environment. The purpose of "Developmental Instruction" is to design the learning environment in such a way as to create an optimal balance of challenge and support for students given their level of cognitive complexity.

The work of William Perry and the applications of Knefelkamp, Widick and others offer significant opportunities to service-learning educators. Perry's scheme delineates nine positions or stages of intellectual development and emphasizes the importance of the transitions that move students from stage to stage. Knefelkamp gives us a strategy for creating or stimulating those transitions. She advocates restructuring classroom activity and encouraging a different type of educational experience. She claims that all students can benefit from direct learning opportunities, but students at lower levels of cognitive development tend to *need* such experiences in order to cement their learning. She suggests the use of concrete learning options that can be done outside of the classroom — case studies, interviewing projects, data collection — in order to help students to make a personal connection with the subject matter.

Kneflekamp's demonstration of how teaching and the curriculum can be optimally designed to challenge and support students' development supports arguments for experiential education and gives us an academic rationale for promoting the integration of experiential learning into the curriculum.

Mary Jo White is the Management Assistant to the Chancellor of the University of Colorado in Boulder. She also serves as an NSIEE Consultant on the National Project to Strengthen Experiential Learning in U.S. Colleges and Universities.

References

Knefelkamp, L. Lee, *Developmental Instruction: Fostering Intellectual and Personal Growth of College Students*, doctoral dissertation, University of Minnesota, 1974.

Perry, Jr., William G., *Forms of Intellectual and Ethical Development in the College Years: A Scheme*, Holt, Rinehart and Winston, 1970.

Moral Decision Making in a Scientific Era

Louis A. Iozzi

Louis Iozzi offers a model of decision making that prepares students to solve dilemmas on the basis of social desirability rather than scientific capability. Reprinted from Synergist, *National Center for Service-Learning, ACTION, Vol. 9, No. 3, 1981, pp. 32-37.*

Scenario I

Pete, a high school junior at Washington High School, Mountainville, was telling his class about a disturbing newspaper story he had read. Two men each desperately needed a new kidney soon. The hospital finally located a kidney — only one — and it probably would function equally well in either patient. "So now," Pete reported, "the doctors have to select one of the two patients for the kidney transplant. How can the doctors decide? How can they choose who will live and who will die?"

Mr. Andrews, Pete's teacher, had read the same article. "It seems obvious to me," he said, "that this is a problem we could never resolve here. I guess all of you realize that there really is no correct answer to the problem. I can tell you this, though, a kidney transplant can be very expensive, and you are never really sure if it will work. We still have a long way to go in perfecting transplantation techniques of all kinds." He went on to tell the class about some of the many problems associated with transplanting organs. When the bell rang, a few students, especially those interested in medicine, had gained some understanding of the technical problems associated with transplants. Most of the students forgot the lecture before the next class.

Scenario II

Debbie, also a junior at Washington High School, was in a health class that was part of a service-learning project focusing on medical care delivery. Working in a county hospital, she became acquainted with the kidney patients about whom Pete had read. During class Debbie described the situation and asked, "How should the doctors decide which patient should get the kidney?"

Debbie's teacher, Ms. Cook, responded, "That's a very tough question to answer, Debbie. What do you think?"

"I wouldn't know whom to choose. Both are nice men, always pleasant and cheerful. I met Mr. Harris' wife and children. If they lost him, I don't know what they would do."

Frank joined in, "I've also worked with both men. Mr. Gilbert is a great guy — but Mr. Harris seems to be an old crank. I don't care too much for him."

"Should the doctors give the transplant to the patient they like most?" questioned Tommy.

"Does Mr. Gilbert also have a wife and children?" asked Cathy.

"A wife, no children," said Debbie.

"Why does that matter?" asked Tommy.

"Maybe it does matter," said Cathy. "After all, Mr. Harris has more people depending on him than Mr. Gilbert has."

"Maybe so," said Debbie, "but does that make him less important than Mr. Harris? Your life shouldn't have to hinge on how many children you happen to have."

"What do you think, Billy?" asked Ms. Cook.

"Well, maybe Mr. Gilbert has more responsibilities than Mr. Harris has. I understand that he has helped a lot of kids who have been on drugs."

The dialogue continued throughout the class period. Before class ended, Ms. Cook — who had anticipated the discussion — distributed to each student copies of articles about transplants and the problems involved. She also asked the class to think about what the doctors should do and *why*. In addition, she suggested that her students discuss the dilemma with their parents and those with whom they worked.

"During our next class," she concluded, "we will meet in small groups to discuss what each of you thinks should be done, and why. Debbie, you will be responsible for reporting to us the doctors' decision and the reasons for their decision.

Both teachers seized upon the opportunity to add an issue of contemporary concern and interest to the students, but with different approaches and results.

Mr. Andrews provided information about kidney transplants, focusing almost exclusively on conveying facts that will rapidly become outdated and providing few opportunities for student participation. He was preparing students for the present, at best. Ms. Cook took the opportunity to help her students develop their critical-thinking, problem-solving, and decision making skills. She emphasized initially the affective/moral aspects and then the cognitive aspects of the problem, challenging the students to think, discuss, and learn to use information and knowledge. Ms. Cook provided ample opportunity for student participation. She was preparing students for the present *and*, more importantly, for the future.

Educating for Decision Making

Ms. Cook was integrating students' service experience with socio-scientific reasoning, which is the incorporation of the hypothetico-deductive mode of problem solving with the social and moral/ethical concerns of decision making. The Institute for Science, Technology, Social Science Education at Rutgers has developed a Socio-Scientific Reasoning Model and 14 curriculum modules (but adaptable to many more) for use in grades seven through 12. This model, which is particularly effective when integrated into service-learning programs, is calculated to make education more relevant and to prepare youth for the future.

Educators have professed these goals for centuries. By and large, however, education has fallen short of the mark. Marshall McLuhan, for example, has compared current educational practices to speeding down a superhighway looking in the rearview mirror. In the Fall 1979 *Synergist*, Jean Houston commented, "For the most part — in terms of the incredible complexity and sheer intensity of information and problems of our times — we are being educated for about the year 1825. We use a tiny fraction of our capacities ... less than five percent of our mental capacities."

In view of the accelerating rate of change and rapid growth and accumulation of knowledge in all fields (Toffler, 1970), reliance on traditional programs of instruction and teaching methodologies that emphasize facts and information transfer is, in reality, teaching for obsolescence.

Service-learning programs provide educators with a rare opportunity to make education relevant and to meet community needs. The students gain valuable experience and self-satisfaction while making real contributions to society. Essentially, service-learning both complements and adds another important dimension to schooling.

Service experiences *alone* cannot prepare students for the kinds of problems and situations they will encounter in the future, though these experiences prepare students to deal rather well with the world as it exists now! This is a great improvement over what commonly occurs in schools today, but is it really enough? Are we really optimizing the possibilities offered by service-learning?

Emerging Issues

In addition to making service-learning programs available to secondary school students, what else might schools do to prepare today's youth to function effectively in the world of the future? How can we begin to prepare our most important resource — our students — to deal with problems and conditions that have yet to appear? How can we forecast the types of skills and knowledge needed by problem solvers and decision makers in the future? Several scholars and futurists (Shane, 1977; Schwartz, Teige, and Harmon, 1977) have agreed that the major problems of the next quarter century will be in the areas of food allocation, energy allocation and depletion, biomedical technology, social unrest and conflict, environmental quality and modification, application of existing and emerging technologies, mental health, natural resource use, land use, and science/technology/society conflict.

Of major importance, moreover, will be the impact of science and technology on society. Science and technology will give future generations awesome power. Clearly decision makers we are cultivating today will be required to solve problems and to resolve conflicts that we encounter only in our wildest dreams, or, in some cases, only in our most frightening nightmares.

We are rapidly approaching the day when questions regarding who should get the new kidney will become everyday occurrences. [Are we there now?] Such questions will be among the simpler ones that tomorrow's decision makers would have to resolve. I foresee the following in the not too distant future:

- The question will not be *can* we replace the defective organs in humans after their own have failed, but rather, *should* we?
- The question will not be *can* we colonize outer space or the ocean depths to relieve the pressure of overpopulation, but rather, *should* we?
- The question will not be *can* we modify weather, climate, and other components of our environment, but rather, *should* we?

The basic assumption of the model is that effective problem solving requires simultaneous development in the realms of logical reasoning, social role taking, and moral/ethical reasoning. Purely objective scientific thinking cannot be applied in the resolution of most of the probable future conflicts without regard to the impact of those decisions on human needs and human goals. A technological solution, for example, may be feasible and logically consistent. From a societal perspective, however, one must question whether or not it should be applied. How to best prioritize our needs and evaluate trade-offs with a concern for the needs of future generations involves logical reasoning and critical thinking, but now with an added dimension, a social moral/ethical reasoning dimension.

- The question will not be *can* we harness the almost limitless power of nuclear fusion to provide energy despite its extreme dangers, but rather, *should* we?
- The question will not be *can* we create a Brave New World, but rather, *should* we?

Scientists and engineers can deal effectively with questions of the "can we" variety because such decisions are based on technical facts. Questions of the "should we" type require the consideration of another dimension — a values dimension. Values-based questions must, I maintain, be answered by society. Knowledge about the capabilities of science and technology must be coupled with analysis of their impact and implications on such issues as justice, equity, dignity of life, and individual rights.

These comments should not be interpreted as an attack on science and technology. Quite the contrary. Science and technology will continue to provide society with unique powers and opportunities. The problem, however, will focus on whether society can handle such power in a responsible manner.

Basic Skills for the Future

If schools are to prepare students for their individual and communal future, educators must emphasize the development of another group of basic skills: problem solving, decision making, and analytical and critical thinking. Moreover, a moral/ethical dimension must be included as part of such development if today's students are to deal responsibly and humanely with tomorrow's problems.

Educators, then, must begin to view education as developing those skills necessary for complex problem solving and decision making. More specifically, education should strive to develop in students:

- Increased logical reasoning skills in dealing with problems containing multiple interacting variables;
- Increased decision making/problem solving skills incorporating socio-moral-value considerations and a wider societal perspective;
- Increased knowledge of the broad issues emerging and projected at the interfaces of science-technology/society.

In an attempt to accomplish the aforementioned goals, we at the Institute developed the Socio-Scientific Reasoning Model. This model — which combines the theories of Jean Piaget (logical reasoning/cognitive development), Lawrence Kohlberg (moral/ethical reasoning), and Robert Selman (social role taking) with research conducted by the author — has served as a guide in the development of *Preparing for Tomorrow's World*, a series of educational materials to help junior and senior high school students advance to higher levels of thinking and reasoning capabilities.

While this model has guided our curriculum activities, it is easily generalized and adaptable to nearly all educational settings and programs. That it is *particularly* appropriate for and complementary to service-learning programs — including many on the postsecondary level — will become readily apparent.

While the complexities of the Socio-Scientific Reasoning Model and the theories of Piaget, Kohlberg, and Selman preclude a full discussion of them in this article, an understanding of certain fundamental ideas associated with these theories is helpful.

Logical Reasoning. Piaget (1970; Gruber and Voneche, 1977) views the development of logical reasoning as progression through a series of stages. At each successive stage, the logical reasoning ability of individuals takes on a broader perspective and incorporates the ability to deal with greater numbers of interacting variables of increasing intellectual complexity. Each stage of thinking builds upon the previous one, but takes on a new structural form. Growth in cognition, from this perspective, can be facilitated and nurtured through appropriate educational experience.

In explaining growth in logical reasoning, Piaget refers to the processes of assimilation, accommodation, and equilibration. Assimilation occurs when the learners incorporate new ideas and situations into their existing thought structures. On the other hand, learners also encounter objects and events that do not fit into their existing thought structures. In these contradictory situations, children have essentially two options: They must either enlarge their existing structures or create a new category or structure. Piaget defines this as the process of accommodation.

Intellectual growth, Piaget postulates, occurs when the individual attempts to resolve the tension between the interaction processes of assimilation and accommodation by developing new thoughts and responses that are more suitable or adequate. Equilibrium is re-established when thought structures are altered, producing new accommodations that enable the individual to assimilate the new situations. Intellectual growth, then, occurs through internal self-regulation processes that lead to new, higher levels of equilibration.

Moral/Ethical Reasoning. While there are several approaches to values education, the most encouraging one is the cognitive developmental approach offered by Kohlberg (1976; Gibbs, *et al.*, 1976).

Kohlberg's moral/ethical development theory is an extension of Piaget's cognitive development theory. Kohlberg views moral development as progression through a series of stages (Figure 1). Each stage is characterized by a very different way of perceiving and interpreting one's experiences. At the higher steps (principled), reasoning takes into account concerns for the welfare of others and includes concerns for human dignity, justice, equality — the same principles upon which our Constitution is based. Lower stages, in comparison, consider satisfying personal, self-serving, and less encompassing needs. The needs of others are usually considered only if it is convenient to do so.

Following Piaget, Kohlberg views development as change in thinking capabilities — the structures of thought processes. In the course of development, higher-level thought structures are attained and result in the extension of an individual's social perspective and reasoning capabilities. Applying higher levels of thinking to problems results in problem solutions that have greater consistency and are more generalizable.

Social Role Taking. The research of Robert Selman (1976) indicates that social role taking ability is a developed capacity that also progresses in a series of stages from early childhood through adolescence. Role taking is viewed by Selman in terms of qualitative changes in the manner in which children structure their understanding of the relationship between the perspectives of self and others.

Selman has identified and defined stages 0 through 4. Each of Selman's stages relates closely to and parallels Kohlberg's moral reasoning stages.

The social role taking stages are viewed as a link between Piaget's logical reasoning stages and Kohlberg's moral reasoning stages. Just as Piaget's logical reasoning stages are necessary but not sufficient for attaining the parallel moral reasoning stages, a similar necessary but not sufficient relationship appears to exist between social role taking stages and parallel moral reasoning stages.

As Selman has pointed out, " ... the child's cognitive stage indicates his level of understanding of the nature of social relations, and his moral judgment stage indicates the manner in which he decides how to resolve social conflicts between people with different points of view" (1976, p. 307).

Hence, the Socio-Scientific Model consists of four interacting components: logical reasoning, moral/ethical reasoning, social role taking, and information. Since the content or information component will vary, so too will the concepts of the component. In our curriculum modules — which do not include the invaluable element added by community service — we have concentrated on issues in science/technology/society. Of course, service-learning educators may use the techniques developed in the model to help students think through any dilemma that arises.

Development is both vertical and horizontal. Vertical development is from lower to higher stages; horizontal development relates to the requirements that must be satisfied as one moves from logical reasoning through social role taking to moral reasoning capabilities. The goal, then, is to help each individual achieve more adequate problem solving and decision making capability. "More adequate" refers to the idea that when applied to problem solving, the higher stages of reasoning result in solutions that are more encompassing and generalizable; they enable students to deal with greater complexity and make more equitable judgments.

Disequilibrium and Growth

The application of the Socio-Scientific Reasoning Model centers on identifying those experiences important for assisting students to become more effective and capable decision makers and problem solvers in a highly scientific and technological world. Service-learning provides numerous opportunities for such experiences, and the model can add an essential dimension to processing those experiences.

The main strategy underlying the socio-scientific reasoning approach is based on Piaget's concept of equilibration. By creating cognitive disequilibrium, active restructuring of thought takes place. This active restructuring leads to growth in logical reasoning

Developmental Models	Characteristics of Model Relevant to Secondary School Students	Curriculum Strategy Provides Students Opportunities to:	Curriculum Activities
Piaget: Logical reasoning development in sequential, invariant stepwise stages. Change via restructuring of thought processes through assimilation and accommodation.	Transition from concrete to formal logical thought operations. Reason by hypothesis, ability to deal with logical propositions — probability, implications, correlations, compatibility, thinking about things from the abstract, not limited by concrete relationships.	• Reason hypothetically-deductively • Generate possible alternatives • Distinguish probable and possible events dealing with reality and abstraction • Consider consequences of alternatives • Isolate variables to test validity of proposition, controlling variables • Relate one idea to another • Reflect on own thinking	• Projection of future possibilities • Individualized research of problems/issues • Case studies from wide range and variety of materials • Active experimentation/ systematic analysis • Debates and discussion — developing logical arguments
Selman: Social role taking develops in sequential, invariant, and stepwise stages. Change in perspective taking occurs through social interaction.	Transition from mutual role taking to social and conventional system role taking. Understand nature of social relations in terms of a social system.	• Integrate personal experience into greater social whole "decentration" • Consider perspective of other persons • Partake in variety of social interactions • Recognize role of self and society	• Simulations • Role playing and exchange of roles • Communications in small and large groups • Partake in democratic processes
Kohlberg: Moral/ethical reasoning develops in sequential, invariant stages, and advances to higher stages by resolution of disequilibrium caused by recognition of inadequacy of own reasoning.	Transition from conventional to principle level of reasoning. Decisions based on principles that have validity, consistency, and application apart from authority of groups and individuals, guided by self-chosen ethical principles and concerns for universal social justice and individual rights.	• Interact with peers at more advanced stages of reasoning • Experience diversity of alternative ideas • Consider basis of personal value system and judgment • Evaluation of information, judgments, and opinions • Prioritizing preferences	• Moral dilemma discussions • Role playing • Values clarification and analysis • Student directed activities
Socio-scientific: Integrates the developmental ideas of the above model to promote more effective decision making and problem solving in the realms of science, technology, and society.	Transition from problem solving in a limited context to problem solving encompassing more extensive parameters and multiple interacting variables. Problems are dealt with in a holistic system.	All of the above plus: • Explore problems from perspective of different disciplines • Generate and test hypothesis • Consider short-range and long-range effects and implications of decisions • Explore different problem-solving strategies • Deal with complex interactions of problems	All of the above plus: • Future forecasting methodologies and strategies (prepare scenarios) • Case history investigations and multimedia learning • Creative problem solving/planning/ decision making

and, we contend, growth in social role taking and in moral/ethical reasoning capabilities as well.

Restructuring of existing cognitive structures occurs when the individual feels internal disequilibrium. New experiences and inputs that are not readily comprehensible challenge the individual's existing mode of thought by revealing inadequacies or inconsistencies in that problem solving strategy (Tomlinson-Keasey, 1974). Arrestment at a given stage is partially explained by the developmental theorists as the lack of opportunities that create conflict or dissonance so that the individual needs to assess a particular mode of thinking. Service-learning certainly provides those opportunities.

The cognitive conflict or dissonance so necessary for growth is facilitated when students are exposed to a rich background of diverse experiences. I know of no better way for schools to provide such experiences than through service-learning. Service-learning clearly expands the sphere of learning opportunities from the vicarious and often sterile boundaries of the individual classroom to encompass the rich diversity of experiences of the community, state, nation, and world.

Exposure to a wide variety of community service experiences provides only one — albeit significant — part of the necessary essentials for growth. Such activity serves to trigger the disequilibrium discussed previously. Socio-scientific reasoning and the activities we have identified and will discuss later provide the necessary essential for the re-establishment of equilibrium and synchronous growth in logical reasoning, social role taking, and moral/ethical reasoning. In short, the Socio-Scientific Reasoning Model addresses the learning component of the service-learning experience.

For example, both Pete and Debbie asked about a disturbing incident. Pete learned about the problem by chance while Debbie became personally involved in it through her service-learning experience. The kidney transplant dilemma stimulated interest and concern, and initiated a degree of cognitive dissonance. Mr. Andrews ignored the students' *real* issue of concern and lectured about organ transplants. Ms. Cook, on the other hand, captured the opportunity to explore the fundamental issue through open discussion in a nonthreatening classroom environment.

In attempting to resolve the kidney transplant dilemma, some of Ms. Cook's students experienced increased cognitive conflict because they were exposed to points of view that reflected a higher stage of reasoning than the stage at which they were functioning.

These students experienced dissonance because they could not as-similate the higher stage arguments into their existing thought structures. As the lively classroom dialogue continued, however, these same students began to restructure their thinking (accommo-dation) and, in the process of attempting to re-establish equilibrium, increased their reasoning and decision making/problem solving capabilities. Ms. Cook was employing aspects of the socio-scientific reasoning approach in her service-learning teaching.

Using the Model

What then are some of the strategies utilized in the Socio-Scientific Reasoning Model? How might such strategies be applied in service-learning programs?

The Socio-Scientific Reasoning Model has served as our guide to develop a supplementary educational program that has docu-mented the effectiveness of both the strategies and the materials used in helping to increase cognitive achievement and advance students toward more mature moral reasoning. Each of the 14 curriculum modules comprising the *Preparing for Tomorrow's World* program provides — through a variety of activities — abundant opportunities for students to:

- Encounter a variety of viewpoints in a nonthreatening class-room environment;
- Experience higher level reasoning;
- Take the perspective of others;
- Examine and clarify one's own ideas;
- Examine the consequences and implications of one's decisions;
- Defend one's position;
- Evaluate the range of possible alternatives;
- Consider and recognize the role of the self in society;
- Reflect on one's own value system.

One particularly effective educational activity that incorporates many of these elements is the classroom *dilemma discussion* like the one that took place in Ms. Cook's class. This activity is most commonly associated with the approach employed by Kohlberg and his colleagues and can be readily applied in service-learning programs.

In using the dilemma technique, care must be taken to ensure that the students understand the dilemma and what they are being asked to resolve. Most important, in attempting to resolve the dilemma — a situation with no apparent wrong or right answer — students must express not only what they feel should be done, but *why*. We also have employed such other formats as *role playing, simulations, futures forecasting, and analysis methodologies*. Critical to our approach is a dynamic student-to-student interaction, for each classroom contains a diversity of stage reasoning models. Through discourse, students are exposed to divergent viewpoints and different levels of reasoning. Students taking different positions question and challenge why a particular stance is held. They reflect on their own thinking, clarify their own arguments, and evaluate their own reasoning.

As a result of participating in service-learning programs, students are exposed to a wealth of situations — dilemmas — that can and should be dealt with in the program's classroom phase. Obviously, genuine, unexpected dilemmas that demand immediate consideration may arise in virtually all community service settings. Service-learning educators also may prepare scenarios posing the types of dilemmas that they know their students are likely to encounter. Of course, the dilemmas most likely to develop the basic skills enumerated earlier are those that stem directly from experience.

Although dilemma discussion is only one of many approaches we have employed, it is the one most easily adopted and most highly effective. In using this approach, it is extremely important for the teacher to include a knowledge or information base. Meaningful discussion cannot take place in a vacuum. While general discussion can and should occur during the initial discussion phase, information and/or data — including from articles, library research, films, the agency supervisors — also should be available.

The Socio-Scientific Reasoning Model that has guided our curriculum development efforts is an effective and relevant model for educating youth for today and tomorrow. Emphasizing simultaneous development in the intellectual and moral/ethical realms, this curriculum approach may prepare students for decision making about current issues and issues projected to be of importance during the next quarter century and beyond. Understanding the ways that students structure knowledge at their different thinking levels, we can then develop those instructional materials and service experiences that will help advance their level of thinking.

I am confident that the merger of this model with service-learning will contribute greatly toward promoting one of education's major but elusive goals — to prepare youth to function more effectively and less selfishly in a constantly changing and increasingly complex world.

Modules for the Model

Preparing for Tomorrow's World consists of 14 curriculum modules:
- Energy: Decisions for Today and Tomorrow — grades 7 and 8;
- Coastal Decisions: Difficult Choices — grades 7 and 8;
- Technology and Changing Lifestyles — grades 7 and 8;
- Space Encounters — grades 7 and 8;
- Future Scenarios in Communications — grades 7 and 8;
- Food: A Necessary Resource — grades 8 and 9;
- Perspectives on Transportation — grades 8 and 9;
- People and Environmental Changes — grades 9, 10, and 11;
- Future New Jersey: Public Issues Affecting the Quality of Life — grades 9 and 10;
- Of Animals, Nature, and Man: Societal Dilemmas — grades 10 and 11;
- Environmental Dilemmas: Critical Decisions for Society — grades 10 and 11;
- Dilemmas in Bioethics — grades 11 and 12;
- Beacon City: An Urban Land Use Simulation — grades 11 and 12;
- Technology and Society: A Futuristic Perspective — grades 9 and 10.

The modules are designed to be interdisciplinary. Each can be used in a number of courses. Presentation time is flexible, but teachers generally take 4-6 weeks. Each module includes teaching materials, objectives, activities, and a list of complementary courses. The modules range on a continuum from those that are highly structured sequentially to those that contain discrete, independent activities. Those for the lower grades tend to be more structured, with subsequent activities building upon skills learned in prior activities. A summary description of one module follows.

Energy: Decisions for Today and Tomorrow

Issues surrounding energy production, consumption, and conservation are explored using examples from three energy sources: petroleum, nuclear power, and coal. Problems arising from the utilization of these sources are highlighted in dilemma discussions and role play simulations. Approximate time requirement: 3-4 weeks/flexible.

Materials — teacher's guide, student's guide, student handouts, and transparencies.

Objectives — to develop knowledge about energy and its issues, analysis skills, decision making skills, and awareness of energy concerns and their social, political, and economic interactions.

Student activities — graphing and data analysis, critical reading and analysis of issues, small and large group discussions, and role playing.

Complements — social studies, general science, earth science, and health education.

For more information on the Socio-Scientific Reasonsing Model or Preparing for Tomorrow's World, a Title IV-C validated program, contact Sopris West, 1140 Boston Avenue, Longmont, CO 80502-1809.

Louis A. Iozzi is associate professor of education and chair of the Department of Education at Rutgers — The State University of New Jersey, New Brunswick.

References

Beck, Clive M., *Ethics*, McGraw Hill, 1972.

Gibbs, John, L. Kohlberg, A. Colby, and Betsy Speicher-Dubin, "The Domain and Development of Moral Judgment," *Reflections on Values Education*, Wilfred Laurier University Press, 1976.

Gruberg, Howard E. and J. J. Voneche, *The Essential Piaget. An Interpretative Reference and Guide*, Basic Books, Inc., 1977.

Hersh, R., D. Paolitto, and J. Reimer, *Promoting Moral Growth from Piaget to Kohlberg*, Longman Press, 1979.

Iozzi, Louis A., "Education for the '80's and Beyond — The Socio-Scientific Reasoning Model," in *Needs of Elementary and Secondary Education in the 1980's*, U.S. Government Printing Office, Washington, D.C., 1980.

Lickona, Thomas, ed., Laurence Kohlberg, James Rest, and Robert Selman, *Moral Development and Behavior: Theory, Research, and Social Issues*, Holt, Rinehardt and Winston, 1976.

Piaget, Jean, "Piaget's Theory," in *Charmichael's Manual of Child Psychology*, P. H. Mussen, ed., Wiley, 1970.

Piaget, Jean, *To Understand Is To Invent*, Penguin Books, 1977.

Schwartz, Peter, Peter Teige, and Willis Harmon, "In Search of Tomorrow's Crises," *The Futurist*, Vol. XI, No. 5, October 1977, pp. 269-278.

Shane, Harold G., *Curriculum Change Toward the 21st Century*, National Education Association, Washington, D.C., 1977.

Toffler, Alvin, *Future Shock*, Random House, 1970.

Tomlinson-Keasey, Carol and Clark B. Keasey;, "The Mediating Role of Cognitive Development in Moral Judgment," *Child Development*, 45, 1974, pp. 291-298.

Effects of a Public Issues Program on Adolescents' Moral and Intellectual Development

Cheryl H. Keen

In longitudinal tests, a difference in moral and intellectual development for three groups of talented high school seniors resulted from a one-month summer residential program on public issues and the future in New Jersey. Keen used the Defining Issues Test based on Kohlberg's theory of moral development and the Learning Context Questionnaire based on Perry's schema of ethical and intellectual development. The Governor's School on Public Issues and the Future provides a useful model for helping students rethink their social worlds and turn their new insights into responsible civic action.

CAN A ONE-MONTH RESIDENTIAL, summer learning experience which focuses on public issues and the future significantly affect the moral and intellectual development of gifted high school seniors? Our experience at the New Jersey Governor's School on Public Issues and the Future held at Monmouth College had suggested this was so, and we decided to do research to test our hypothesis.

Three groups each of 100 rising high school seniors completed pre-, post- and nine-month follow-up Defining Issues Tests (DIT), a paper and pencil test of moral judgment designed by James Rest and based on Kohlberg's research on moral reasoning. The DIT tests one's ability to recognize preconventional and conventional staged concepts and reject them as inadequate, expressing preference for principled responses to a moral dilemma. Two meta-analyses (Schaefli, *et al.*, 1985, and Rest, 1986) have been done on longitudinal studies using the DIT to understand the effect of educational interventions on moral judgment. These studies suggest that treatments under three weeks are ineffective and that programs emphasizing dilemma discussion and personality development produce modest effects, but they do not clarify the critical conditions necessary to produce these effects (Rest, 1986, pp. 85-86). A study of several factors in the Governor's School model sheds some light on one set of educational interventions that can greatly facilitate development.

On the same schedule, participants completed the Learning Context Questionnaire (LCQ) designed by John Griffith, which is based on William Perry's interview-based research and schema on intellectual and ethical development. Perry (1968) found that Harvard College students developed through stages of understanding from dualistic thinking, to multiplistic thinking that led them to see uncertainties in some disciplines but not in others, to relativistic thinking, and finally to commitment in the face of relativism. The LCQ results suggest significant gains in development over the nine months following participation in the Governor's School in the two years for which we have complete data. With the results of the LCQ confirming the results of the DIT, we can understand better the impact this unique learning environment has on adolescents once they return home.

Studies of Moral Judgment Using the "Defining Issues Test"

Overview of Participants and Program. One hundred rising high school seniors from the state of New Jersey are chosen to attend the Governor's School on Public Issues and the Future of New Jersey each summer. To be nominated, they must be in the top 10% of their class in grades or national test scores and fit a list of criteria for gifted and talented youth, including being risktakers and being creative. The Governor's School "scholars" represent the state geographically and racially. Participation is free. During the four-week program, they live on campus with 18 faculty and counselors; take part in public issues courses on topics such as the environment, human services, conflict resolution, and international banking and world debt; are in an integrative seminar for open discussion for which they write a daily journal; and attend a daily evening series of speakers, debates, and simulations on state, national and global issues, many of which are initiated and run by the scholars. While the student/scholars do some direct service during the residential program, the focus is on preparation for public service. This program could thus be adapted as a model of pre-service preparation for responsible action.

While there are Governor's Schools in 32 states, this was the first on public issues and has since been used as a model for schools in Florida, Texas and Washington. It was initiated by New Jersey's Governor Kean, legislators, and Monmouth College in 1983 in response to the need for a more concerned and active citizenry, a need highlighted in most of the recent national reports on education (Newman, 1985). The program sought to create a one-month experience which would foster a sense of civic pride and responsibility along with skills of participation and problem solving. The goal was for promising students to engage in public debate on complex problems and then go on to devote some measure of their lives to the public good as they develop into leaders in their professions and communities.

The school offers a challenging and loving environment in which scholars report that they learn about other people and public issues and a great deal about themselves. Typical responses of former participants are: *"I never knew before that what I say mattered." "I've realized that I can make a difference." "Governor's School really made a different person of me. Now when I hear about something that affects me, I want to know 'How? Why? And what can I do about it?'"*

On our extensive final evaluations, scholars report that they learn new ways to think about complex issues and dilemmas. Extensive contacts with alumni suggest that the value of the school remains with them far beyond the frame of the summer. But longitudinal research is allowing us to understand how widespread this growth is among the scholars and how big the developmental push really is.

Instrument. I have not found a completely adequate measure to evaluate the effects of the Governor's School on participants' sense of civic responsibility. Most studies of a sense of responsibility for others have found negative trends during college education (Jacobs, 1957; Newcomb and Feldman, 1969; Astin, 1977).

Kohlberg's theory of moral development and Perry's theory of intellectual and ethical development both address underpinnings of citizenship. Perry's research (1968) reveals the late adolescent's (1) recognition of commitment in the face of relativism and (2) evolving capacity to tolerate ambiguity while wading into complex problems, which are developmental achievements tied to our curricular goals at the school. Researchers in moral development theory increasingly seek to understand the nature of the relationships between moral reasoning and moral action. Blasi (1980) found 57 of 75 studies using Kohlberg's work showed moderate relationships between reasoning and behavior. Deemer's (1987) extensive 10-year study correlating interviews over time with the DIT found that civic responsibility and political awareness are significantly associated with DIT scores. Sheehan (1980) has shown a relationship between DIT scores and clinical performance rates in doctors.

The DIT consists of seven dilemmas which require an ethical decision. The dilemmas, on issues such as nonviolent war protest, free speech, euthanasia, and illegal acts to save a life, are followed by 12 statements that are possible "ethical" responses to the dilemma. The statements represent different stages of development in Kohlberg's theory, some of which sound like higher reasoning but are meaningless to catch participants trying to sound highly mature. After rating these statements from "great importance" to "no importance," participants are asked to select and rank order the four most important statements. Rest's DIT measures not spontaneous moral reasoning, but rather recognition, comprehension and preference for moral judgments.

The only scores we reported were those that passed Rest's consistency check, which is designed to catch guesses at higher stages or lack of attention to the task. The P score indicates the ranked importance of principled statements. This score results in a continuous measure of development rather than the few distinct stages in Kohlberg's scoring scheme. Thoma (1984) found that sex is not a significant factor in DIT scores. Rest has also summarized previous research (1979a) showing that there is little testing effect from repeated use of the test. A control group was not available, so we are limited to comparing our results with the many studies of similar populations using the DIT.

Procedure. For three summers in a row I handed the DIT to participants during orientation at the beginning of the program and again during an evaluation session one month later on the next to last day, asking them to read the instructions and complete it without talking to anyone. I collected the tests as soon as they were completed. We mailed the follow-up test to the scholars at home in March or April of their senior year. A cover letter reminded them to devote some concentrated time to completing the test, and to do so without discussing it with anyone. Participants who did not return the test were reminded again by mail one month later.

Results. Average P scores before and after the month range from 40.4 to 45.98 (see Table 1). The average scores of the first two tests for those scholars who completed all three tests are between 41.3 and 50.2 (see Table 2). Nine months later, when the scholars were in the spring of their senior year in high school, the scores of all tests are between 49.0 and 49.8, with a significant difference of p<.01 and .05. Rest (1979, 1986) lists 26 studies with high school students with scores ranging from 23 to 44. The two studies he cites with above average students in special classes similar to our population showed average scores of 44 and 37. Rest's review of 61 studies of college student populations (Rest, 1979) showed scores averaging from 24 to 58. Governor's scholars' scores nine months later are similar to those of mixed groups of college students, of roughly equal numbers of freshmen, sophomores, juniors, and seniors (Dispoto, 1974). They are higher than the junior and senior psychology majors at SUNY Stony Brook (p=46.9, n=152, Leming, 1976). Scores as high as our students' were attained in only 17 of the 61 studies. Our follow-up scores are more similar to graduate school studies, excepting those of students of philosophy and theology or quite advanced students. The average score for medical students cited by Rest was 49.2. These comparisons suggest that the scholars' development after participation in the Governor's School is quite atypical for their age. Interestingly, in all three years, scholars who completed all three tests reached similar average scores on the third test of 49 to 49.8, scores not reached in any other study of gifted high schoolers.

A repeated measures test, selecting only those who completed the test all three times, shows significant change in 1983 (p<.0005), marginal significance in 1984 (n=22, p<.06) and no significance in 1985 (n=29, p<.09). Using an analysis of variance, however, the 1985 tests resulted in a significant difference of p<.05. The difference between those who chose to complete the March follow-up, and those who didn't, was insignificant for the check we made in 1983, suggesting that the group who completed the follow-up test is representative of the whole.

While Schaefli (1985) suggests longitudinal testing to determine if developmental gains hold over time, our tests generally show more significant gains after nine months than during the experience itself.

Based on Schaefli et al.'s modified method for computing effect size used in their meta-analysis of 54 longitudinal studies using the DIT (which relies on Cohen's suggestion that the cutoff for a medium effect is .50), our 1983 data on the post- and follow-up tests show an effect size of .48, greater than the average effect size of the most powreful types of studies, that is, dilemma discussions (n=23, average effect size .41, Schaefli et al., 1985). Our 1984 averages on post- and follow-up tests show an effect size of .4, typical of the most significant studies Schaefli quotes. Finally, the effect size of our 1985 data on pre- and post-test, where the follow-up test only shows

Table 1. Results of all completed DITs, using Analysis of Variance

Year	Pre-test	Post-test	Follow-up test	Significance
1983	44.18 n=111	44.08 n=108	50.05 n=50	p<.01
1984	40.4 n=98	45.98 n=98	48.3 n=23	p<.05
1985	45.12 n=33	49.13 n=31	48.83 n=34	p<.05
1985	45.86 n=100	48.99 n=100	49.8 n=34	p<.01

Table 2. Repeated measures test with those who completed all three tests

1983 n=50	41.3	41.9	49.1	p<.0005
1984 n=22	44.3	42.3	49.0	p<.06
1985 n=29	46.4	50.2	49.8	p<.09

a maintenance of the gains of the summer, is still .3, above Cohen's cutoff of .2 for small effect (Cohen, 1969). While effect size is related to Kohlberg's theory, our participants had no exposure to the theory (Rest, p. 86). The only studies in Schaefli's meta-analysis with greater effect size than our own were those with juvenile delinquents (a group of developmentally delayed teens typically makes a big gain in an intervention), semester-long programs, and programs with adults who discuss dilemmas while studying theories of moral development.

Discussion. A possible explanation of these results is that after fully experiencing the Governor's School learning environment for a month, students went home with new perspectives, new interpersonal skills, and increased self-esteem which allowed them to gain new experiences that also promoted their development. This is confirmed by a qualitative study by Hahn (1985), who analyzed the daily journals of 100 Governor's School scholars for central themes and conducted in-depth follow-up interviews with five scholars and their parents, teachers, and friends. He found that scholars gained in four main areas: emergence from the family, gaining of a voice for expressing their own ideas, openness in the affective and cognitive areas, and the growth of ideals and a sense of empowerment. These new skills and perspectives enable them to look at the "same old" family and school in new ways. The significant developmental shift may occur with the challenge of going home, as suggested by the fact that scores did not change significantly during the month of the program.

Perry discerned a position on the developmental path he calls "commitment foreseen." We observe this position in our scholars who by the end of the school are saying "I know now that I can make a difference," although most are not clear what challenge they will take on. It takes exposure back home and in the high school to know where they will try to make a difference and what will matter enough for them to make the investment. Rest says, "What seems to be involved in moral judgment development is a change in basic and fundamental ways of thinking about social worlds which education affects slowly, over long periods of time and apparently not through teaching specific doctrines" (1986, p. 25). Perhaps the Governor's School model does this — providing experiences that help students rethink their social worlds.

Studies with the "Learning Context Questionnaire"

Participants. For three years we asked the 100 Governor's Scholars to complete the Learning Context Questionnaire (LCQ). In the first two years, 1984 and 1985, the participants were the same as those who completed Rest's DIT.

Instrument and Procedure. We administered the LCQ in the same manner as we did the DIT. The LCQ was designed by Griffith and Kelton from Davidson College to collect data on intellectual development based on Perry's scheme from large groups. College faculty all over the country are using the Perry scheme to help them understand their students' developmental stages. The LCQ is one of several attempts to simplify the coding of students' intellectual reasoning, although many working with the Perry schema do not think it is possible to discern intellectual development outside a guided interview. Its designers believe the test is "descriptive of the

changing ways in which students come to construe and understand
the nature of knowledge" (Griffith, 1986). Unable to fund an interview-based study, we have found that the LCQ shows significant
results that correlate well with the DIT. Griffith and Kelton's data
on the LCQ correlates very highly (p<.0001) with academic performance, grade level, the verbal SAT and PSAT, and English
Achievement Tests, suggestive of research that Kitchener is doing
on the relationship between reflective judgment and verbal ability.
The data also correlate very well with the Math levels 1 and 2
Achievement Tests (p<.001 and .002) and the Math SAT (p<.0001),
supporting Buerk's work on the relationship between intellectual
development and ability and proficiency in mathematics (Griffith,
1986).

Results. The LCQ scores, like the DIT, show no gain during the
month of the program itself and significant gains in each of the two
years for which we have nine-month follow-up tests (see Table 3).
Griffith and his colleagues (1986) have matched test scores with
Perry's developmental stages; we will use these labels for ease of
discussion:

Stage	LCQ score
Dualism	1 -3.49
Multiplicity	3.5-4.49
Relativism	4.5-5.49
Dialectical	5.5-7

The high school seniors in their sample, all from private, highly
selective schools, are multiplists with an average score of 3.89. In
our 1984 and 1985 samples, our scholars test similarly on pre- and
post-tests as multiplists: 3.84 with n=93; and 3.86 with n=96, respectively. In March of 1985, eight months later, our scholars scored as
late multiplists: 4.34 with n=17. In 1984 the scores still suggest
multiplism at the follow-up test time: 4.06 with n=32. The highest
average score in Griffith's sample from a highly selective college or
from college seniors was 4.1466. Our 1987 follow-up tests show
scores of early relativists: 4.68 with n=50. A Spearman correlation
coefficient run on the second and third administrations of the tests
in 1984 and 1985 indicate significant differences (1984, p<.03; 1985,
p<.05). A computer search failed to show any other published
studies using this tool, so we must rely for comparison on Griffith
and Kelton's research base. Three other Governor's Schools around
the country are using this or similar tools, so we shall soon have data
for other comparisons.

Table 3. LCQ Scores for four years

Year	Pre-test	Post-test	Follow-up test	Significance*
1984	3.84 n=93 SD=.889 Min. 1.45 Max. 5.8	3.84 n=97 SD=.787 Min. 1.95 Max. 6.45	4.06 n=32 SD=.814 Min. 1.9 Max. 5.5	p<.03
1985	3.86 n=99 SD=.729 Min. 1.7 Max. 5.95	3.86 n=96 SD=.783 Min. 1.8 Max. 5.6	4.81 n=22 SD=.771 Min. 2.85 Max 5.55	p<.005
1986	4.69 n=98 SD=.9 Min. 2.65 Max. 6.92	4.64 n=90 SD=.89 Min. 2.72 Max. 6.69		
1987			4.64 n=51 SD=.75 Min. 3.17 Max. 6.4	

*Significance between post-test and follow-up.

We cannot run a repeated measures test on the smaller number who completed all three tests, as we did with the Rest data. Yet our July scores are like those of similar high schoolers, supporting the validity of the test. There are no studies, however, to show if repeated use and familiarity with the test leads to higher scores.

Discussion. If indeed moral judgment is related to moral action (Blasi, 1980; Deemer, 1987) and if the DIT and LCQ do tell us anything about our students' ability to grapple with complexity and with their roles regarding society's needs and responsibilities, then we might be right in assuming that the Governor's School experience contributes significantly to the development of a sense of social and civic responsibility.

These results suggest to high school teachers the kind of curriculum to which this population of bright and curious youth responds well. If the data is correct and a graduating class of Governor's Scholars is on average late multiplists, they are beginning to understand that knowledge is relative and contextual. Our scholars and students like them need an educational experience more like college students receive, or they may be bored and fail to engage in the educational process. Indeed if we want students to take full advantage of the kind of education college offers, which is very much in a relativist framework, we might do well to provide learning experiences like those at the Governor's School for all college-bound students.

Our research also responds to the nagging question that remains in intellectual developmental theory: Does more mature intellectual reasoning translate into more intellectually sophisticated work? One study suggests that the Governor's School experience does lead its alumni into more advanced intellectual abilities. In a 1987 study of our alumni at Princeton (n=19) each one had an above average GPA of 3.63 out of a possible 4.0, as compared with the median for the total student body of 3.22 (Popenoe, 1987). One Governor's School scholar had the highest GPA in the freshman class. One would expect our alumni to look quite like the other exceptionally gifted students matriculating at an institution like Princeton. But I would argue that the Governor's School experience prepared them to make use of the kind of education that college offers. They may see faculty as friends and resources rather than authorities. They may see content areas as problems to grapple with and relate to other problems, time and people, rather than disciplinary subjects with the right answers etched in stone. And they may see the future as something to which they can contribute. To this day, many scholars of the 1983 Governor's School remain inspired by the words of Millicent Fenwick in her speech on their opening day:

> Remember, you may never arrive at the solution, but you are never absolved from the responsibility of trying. The most wonderful saying is "Success is not the measure of a human being, effort is." What are you trying to do? How hard are you trying to do it? How much of your life, time, energy and zeal [are you committing]? And for God's sake, don't abandon enthusiasm.... You've hammered out what you believe and what you're prepared to struggle to achieve and what you believe ought to be the goal, but keep your mind open, be humble to the truth, and seek justice ....

Cheryl Hollman Keen is Co-Director of the Governor's School on Public Issues and the Future at Monmouth College in New Jersey. She organized the 1989 National Conference on Governors' Schools. She earned her docotorate at the Harvard Graduate School of Education in 1981 and is now Professor of Humanities and Social Sciences at Monmouth College.

References

Astin, Alexander, *Four Critical Years*, Jossey Bass, 1978.

_____, et al., *The American Freshman*, Higher Education Research Institute, 1987.

Belenky, Mary, Blythe Clinchy, Nancy Goldberger, and Jill Tarule, *Women's Ways of Knowing*, Basic Books, 1986.

_____, personal communication.

Blasi, A. "Bridging Moral Cognition and Moral Action: A Critical Review of the Literature," *Psychological Bulletin*, Vol. 88, 1980.

Cohen, J., *Statistical Power Analysis for the Behavioral Sciences*, Academic Press, 1969.

Deemer, D., "Moral Judgment and Life Experience," doctoral dissertation, University of Minnesota, 1987.

Dispoto, R.G., "Moral Valuing and Environmental Variables," *Journal and Research in Science Teaching*, Vol. 14, 1974.

Fenwick, Millicent, speech on opening day of 1983 Governor's School on Public Issues and the Future, Monmouth College.

Griffith, John,"Research Report: High School and College Data on Student Intellectual Development," Project Match, October, 1986.

Hahn, Andrew, "The New Jersey Governor's School and Its Impact on Adolescents," doctoral dissertation, Hahnemann University, 1985.

Jacobs, P.E., *Changing Values in College*, Harper and Row, 1957.

Keen, Cheryl, and Jim Keen, "Educating High School Students for a Vision of the Public Good," unpublished paper, 1988.

Keen, Cheryl, "Sources and Supports for a Sense of Global Responsibility in College Students and Adults," doctoral dissertation, Harvard Graduate School of Education, 1981.

Kelton, John, and John Griffith, "The Learning Context Questionnaire for Assessing Intellectual Development," unpublished paper, 1986.

Leming, J.S., "Curricular Effectiveness in Moral/Values Education: A Review of Research," *Journal of Moral Education*, Vol. 10, 1976.

Newcomb, T.M., and K.A. Feldman, *The Impact of College on Students*, Jossey Bass, 1969.

Parks, Sharon, *The Critical Years: The Young Adult's Search for a Faith to Live By*, Harper and Row, 1986.

Perry, William, *Forms of Ethical and Intellectual Development in the College Years: A Schema*, Harper and Row, 1978.

Popenoe, Catherine, personal communication, 1987.

Rest, James, *et al.*, "Age Trends in Judging Moral Issues: A Review of Cross-Sectional, Longitudinal, and Sequential Studies of the Defining Issues Test," *Child Development*, Vol. 49, 1978, pp. 263-279.

_____, "Revised Manual for the Defining Issues Test: An Objective Test of Moral Judgment Development," Minnesota Moral Research Projects, 1979.

_____, "Recent Research on an Objective Test of Moral Judgment: How the Important Issues of a Moral Dilemma are Defined" in *Moral Development: Current Theory and Research*, ed. David DePalma and Jeanne M. Foley.

_____, *Moral Development : Advances in Research and Theory*, Praeger, 1986.

Schaefli, Andre, James R. Rest, and Stephen Thoma, "Does Moral Education Improve Moral Judgment? A Meta-analysis of Intervention Studies Using the Defining Issues Test," *Review of Educational Research*, Vol. 55, No. 3, 1985, pp. 319-352.

Sheehan, T.J., S.D. Husted, D. Candee, C.D. Cook, and M. Margen, "Moral Judgment as Predictor of Clinical Performance," *Evaluation and the Health Professions*, 1980, pp. 393-404.

Thoma, S.J., "Estimating Gender Differences in the Comprehension and Preference of Moral Issues," unpublished manuscript, University of Minnesota, 1984.

Learning Morality

Robert K. Fullinwider

Reprinted with the permission of the Institute for Philosophy and Public Policy, School of Public Affairs, University of Maryland, from Robert K. Fullinwider, "Learning Morality," QQ: Report from the Institute of Philosophy and Public Policy, Vol. 8, No. 2, Spring 1988, pp. 12-14.

The "ethics crisis" is box-office boffo these days. Political corruption, insider trading, racial bigotry, Abscam, Watergate, Contragate, street crime, vandalism, divorce, teenage pregnancies, Ivan Boesky, Gary Hart, selfishness, greed, pornography, Joseph Biden's plagiarism, Jim and Tammy's fall from grace — these and countless related subjects fill our headlines and dominate our airwaves. And, as usual with a crisis in our society, our first instinct is to look to education. President Reagan and his Secretary of Education are only the most visible of the many who urge renewed teaching of morality in the schools. Derek Bok, President of Harvard University, is in the vanguard of those who urge the colleges and universities likewise to attend to the moral growth of their students. So we might ask: what is moral judgment, how does it develop, and how can the schools assist or retard it?

Start with a simple analogy: learning morality is like learning how to write. It is not like learning geography or mathematics. Learning how to write consists in learning a few elementary concepts — noun, verb — and a few simple pieces of grammar — subject and predicate should agree in number — and then *doing it*, that is, writing over and over and over, with the advice, recommendations, and corrections fo those who already do it well.

Moral education is the same. The child in his earliest experiences and interactions on the playground and at home picks up rudimentary concepts such as taking turns and simple rules such as don't hit people and don't call them names. In his interactions within this simple framework and under the tutelage of adults, the child will come to attach feelings of shame and regret to bad behavior, experience the pleasures of sharing and giving, and feel appreciative and grateful for benefits and resentful at wrongs. With this elementary foundation, moral learning is set in motion: it is simply, as Aristotle says, learning by doing. There is not a science of moral judgment any more than there is a science of writing. Instead, in both cases, we get better through increased experience and practice, which enables us to make finer and sharper discriminations. We develop the capacity to *see* a sentence or a paragraph as clumsy, graceless, plain, clear, or needed, and to *see* a moral action as ungrateful, cowardly, generous, or obligatory.

... If moral learning is essentially learning by doing, then the central and ongoing resource for moral education is experience, real or vicarious.

... Nor is this deficiency [in moral learning] adequately made up by instituting explicit courses in moral reasoning. Moral reasoning is reasoning *about* experience, not a substitute *for* it. It would not make sense to set up a course in critical reflection on good writing for students who had very little experience writing, and it is generally useless, if not counterproductive, to put students with limited moral experience in courses to talk about moral reasoning.

Part II

Rationales and Theories for Combining Service and Learning:

Career Development

A Longitudinal Study at the University of Virginia

Nancy J. Gansneder and Paul W. Kingston

Two faculty at the University of Virginia report on their longitudinal study of participants in its University Year for ACTION program. The results show that ten years after graduation over half of those who participated in the program are now in human service careers, and they devote twice as many volunteer hours to community activities than graduates who did not participate in the program. Adapted from Experiential Education, *National Society for Internships and Experiential Education, Vol. 9, No. 2, March-April 1984, pp. 5, 11.*

BECAUSE MANY INTERNSHIP PROGRAMS are relatively young, attempts to ascertain their *long-term* impact on their participants are not yet feasible. The nation-wide University Year for ACTION program of the 1970s is a potential data source for examining the long-term effects of participation in experiential learning. One such study has recently been completed at the University of Virginia.

While the original goals for University Year for ACTION project did not specify what student outcomes were expected or even desired, nonetheless, a student's decision to participate in the year-long UYA program would seem to reflect a fairly serious commitment to human service, at least during his/her college years. In considering the long-term consequences of participation in the UYA program, then, an important issue which almost naturally arises is whether this commitment persists throughout the participants' post-college lives. Among the questions this study sought to answer were: (1) To what extent did participants in UYA pursue human service careers after completing their education; and (2) How involved are they in voluntary human service activities within their community?

Procedures

Using existing UYA participant files and University alumni records, the project staff attempted to locate and interview by telephone the 65 undergraduates who served as UYA interns between the Summer of 1973 and the Summer of 1976. Alumni records were also used to select a small sample of students who graduated from the University in 1974 and 1975, but who did not participate in UYA. A printed version of the telephone survey was mailed to the comparison group. A response rate of 65 and 50 percent, respectively, was achieved.

UYA respondents differed from the comparison group students on two background characteristics. The proportion of women and minority students participating in UYA was greater than their respective proportions enrolled at the University at the time. In all other respects, however, UYA interns were very similar to their peers.

Findings

Initiators of internship programs will be heartened to know that some seven to ten years since serving as UYA interns, program participants have very strong, positive feelings about having been part of UYA. Retrospectively, they had few complaints about the program. Overwhelmingly, they cited either "the responsibility given" or "doing something that made a difference" as the thing they liked best about UYA. When asked whether they would do it again, nearly 90 percent responded with a resounding "YES, definitely."

Career Plans: There was no difference between UYA and non-UYA students with respect to their recollection of their career plans when they entered college. Upon graduation, however, a significantly greater proportion of UYA participants had a career in mind. Eight-six percent of UYA students had specific career plans compared to 67 percent of non-UYA students. Similarly, there was no difference between UYA students and their peers regarding their plans to go into human service careers when they entered college. But upon graduation over 40 percent of the UYA participants indicated a preference for human service careers versus 12 percent of the non-UYA students.

Although only 40 percent of all UYA participants had definite plans to pursue a career in human services, 65 percent found their first job in this general area. Furthermore, UYA students were more likely to have taken their first job in the human service field than non-UYA students. Two-thirds of both UYA and non-UYA participants indicated that their first job was consistent with their long-range career plans.

Eighty percent of the former UYA interns said that participation in UYA affected their career goals. Ten percent indicated that it had changed their mind about pursuing a career in human services while 70 percent said it had strengthened their commitment or directly influenced their decision to go into the human service field. Twelve percent of the UYA interns actually got their first job directly through or as a result of their UYA experience.

Today 86 percent of the UYA participants are in the labor market. Only one former UYA intern was unemployed at the time of this study. Two have returned to graduate school and 3 are homemakers. Of those employed 52 percent have remained in human service occupations and have now assumed supervisory or managerial roles in these helping professions.

Community Activities: A greater proportion, though not statistically significant, of UYA participants are now active in community organizations. Of greater importance, however, is the amount of time and type of organization in which they are involved. Former UYA interns currently devote an average of 28 hours per month to community activities. Of those participating in community activities, 85 percent are involved in one or more "service" activities. This level of involvement is remarkable when compared to their peers who devote an average of 13 hours per month to various community organizations, and only 50 percent of their involvement is with "service" activities.

Summary

The University of Virginia's University Year for ACTION program of the 1970s appears to have had long lasting effects on its student participants. It remains an important educational experience in the hearts and minds of the participants. Given an opportunity to do it again, nearly 90 percent would. Seventy percent of the former UYA interns claim that it played an important positive role in their career choice. Virtually all of the UYA placements were in the human service field. Upon entering college, only 30 percent of the UYA students with career plans intended to pursue a career in human service. After completing a UYA internship and upon graduation, only 40 percent of those students with career plans planned a career in human service. However, 65 percent of all UYA participants took their first job in a human service occupation and 52 percent of those still in the labor market are in human service occupations.

Equally important is the former UYA students' current commitment to community service. These students were no more actively involved during their college years than their peers in extra-curricular activities of any type. However, today, those involved in community activities devote twice as many hours and are far more likely to spend them in "service" activities than their non-UYA peers.

While the findings of this study cannot causally be linked to the UYA experience, these results present strong evidence to support the optimistic claims of proponents of experiential learning. Participation in a UYA human service internship appears to have affected both the career choices and the community involvement of its participants. If experiential learning programs are deliberately designed to help students make career choices or to heighten their awareness of social issues, then the effects of such programs might prove to be even more dramatic.

Nancy Gansneder directs the Undergraduate Internship Program at the University of Virginia, and Paul Kingston is a professor of sociology.

References

Gansneder, Nancy J., and Paul W. Kingston, *University Year for ACTION Interns and their Post-Graduate Career Choices,* University of Virginia, 1984.

PART III

Public Policy Issues and Guides

A Resource Guide for States

National Governors' Association

A short summary of the NGA's recommendations on the states' role as catalysts for community service; guidelines for states; and a 1989 survey of state-funded or state-supported youth and community service programs. The definition of service programs used here is "systematically organized programs providing opportunities for youth or other members of the community to work on meaningful community problems in ways other than specific job training." Reprinted with permission from Community Service: A Resource Guide for States, *National Governors' Association, 1989, pp. 7, 9-12.*

The States as Catalysts

"Through community service, we can provide assistance to people and places with needs that have defied traditional solutions."
— Governor Thomas H. Kean, New Jersey

FROM THE PERSPECTIVE of the statehouse, where complex social problems are considered every day, the long-term value of strengthening the self-esteem of both young and old and instilling an ethic of lifetime work and service is obvious. American youth, in particular, are an untapped reservoir of energy and strength. Young people often bring fresh thinking to old problems. By incorporating service into education and education into service, state officials can enrich both domains. Enthusiastic and service-motivated students, teachers, and administrators can revitalize school systems with experiential learning.

States are emerging as pivotal players in creating a new system of service programs. They are optimally situated to manage this system. They are able to bring focus to recognized problems, to offer perspective on a range of problems and possibilities, to react quickly to local needs and grassroots movements, and to mobilize and target limited resources on politically acceptable goals.

States are providing innovation in service policies, processes, and institutions. In the past several years, public officials at the state level have begun to involve persons from different jurisdictions and to develop programs that serve multiple functions. Through a careful arrangement of mutually reinforcing program elements, comprehensive approaches that benefit both the service provider and recipient are working well in many states.

State policymakers are working hard to rediscover and redirect obscure authorities and funding and to reconfigure and reinterpret the traditional missions of certain programs. Small changes in direction can have a significant overall impact. Simply setting up new lines of communication and coordination among related state programs can result in significantly enhanced service systems. In dealing with the complicated problems of alienated youth and deteriorating communities, it is advantageous to view all state functions through the prism of service and to focus on the long-term cost efficiencies that are embedded in its cumulative effects.

Guidelines for States

Given limited resources, where should a state place its emphasis? How much is it worth to bring young people back from the margins of society? Is it possible to apply hard measures to the enrichment of schooling, the development of curiosity, and the cultivation of self-discipline? While quantitative data is scarce, success stories abound. The accumulated mass of these tales, in fact, underlies most policy statements on youth and community service. This is the ground upon which the debate takes place.

The examples presented in [NGA's] report illustrate how many states have gone about putting together their programs for youth and community service. The experience of the states demonstrates that there are many doorways into the chamber of service. Each state must design the configuration that best fits its own history and culture and its own resources and ambitions.

The diversity of state experience also provides guidelines for answering the basic questions of whether service should be national or local, public or private, voluntary or mandatory, full-time or part-time, paid or free. The answer depends upon the prevailing circumstances in each state — its history, its resources, its culture. While California may choose a system that is oriented toward its

outdoor culture, that is predominantly centralized in state government, and that is partly mandatory, partly full-time, and partly
paid, another state may feel more comfortable with a different
approach. In the California Conservation Corps, attention is paid to
fighting forest fires and floods; in New York City, the focus is on
having the young help the old.

It is virtually impossible to attach a bottom-line number to
service programs. Some are quite expensive, for they attempt to
bring intensive, remedial attention to marginal and at-risk populations. Others are quite inexpensive, for they draw upon older
volunteers with highly valued skills to donate.

Most such programs return hard-to-measure value — work
done that would otherwise be left undone; a sense of teamwork,
bonding, community, patriotism, and solidarity generated; skills of
life and technical expertise mastered; processes of education enriched; and idealism rekindled.

In sorting through the variety of successful models, states will
be looking for the most efficient, effective means of achieving their
priorities. In any national program, flexibility must be paramount
so that states are able first to identify goals and then to establish a
strategy to meet these goals based on their resources and needs. A
state strategy may, for example, make fighting illiteracy and homelessness its program objectives and subsequently target as volunteers the state's college students, high school students, adults, or
senior citizens. States may compensate monetarily, with vouchers
for education, or not at all. The options are numerous. Ultimately,
there is no one approach that must be followed, and there is no need
to struggle over which is best, since good programs exist with all or
some of these characteristics.

Survey of State Youth and
Community Service Programs

At their 1988 annual meeting, the Governors called on the National Governors' Association (NGA) to develop an inventory of
state community service programs in order to begin a first-of-its-
kind, systematic collection of information on state-level activities.
Knowing of the interest at the national, state, and local levels,
Governors needed current information on the roles states are playing in creating, implementing, and expanding service opportunities
for their citizens to contribute to their communities.

At this writing, forty-two states, three territories, and the District of Columbia have responded to the survey. Twelve states

reported that they do not have a state-funded or state-supported youth and community service program, while thirty states, Guam, Puerto Rico, the Virgin Islands, and the District of Columbia reported that they have at least one program.

Highlights of the survey results are as follows:

- Information was provided for a total of 115 programs that met NGA's definition of a "youth and community service" program. [See definition at beginning of chapter.]

- These five program categories had the following number of programs reported:

Conservation/Youth Corps	17 programs
School-Based and Campus-Based	14 programs
Literacy Corps	6 programs
Senior Citizens Programs	9 programs
Programs for Youth Offenders	5 programs

- Thirteen states reported having a state policy on youth and community service.

- Seventeen states reported having a coordinating mechanism at the state level for their youth and community service programs.

- Fourteen states indicated that they collect and disseminate information about the youth and community service programs from central locations in state government.

- Twenty states reported that they currently have a Governor's initiative on youth and community service in the planning or implementation phase.

A valuable lesson gleaned from the survey was the great variance in program definition. Indeed, the findings were somewhat compromised due to a definitional problem, manifested across the states, about what constitutes a youth and community service program. Many states submitted information on programs that provide services to youth but that do not involve community service activities. Determining which programs to include in the survey findings was an important analytic task.

The survey also revealed that in many states information regarding youth and community service programs is not routinely shared within the state. As a consequence, knowledge about certain programs is limited to those operating the program, and staff at the state or local level remain in the dark regarding each other's efforts. An unanticipated but positive benefit of the survey was that some states reported it helped bring key staff in contact with each other to learn about other programs being operated in the state.

Perhaps the most important result of the survey is the wealth of information that was received from the states about youth and community service opportunities. [*Community Service: A Resource Guide for States*, available from NGA,] presents a compilation of these programs, offering a brief profile of each program and identifying a contact person when possible.

California's Human Corps Legislation

For a summary of the Human Corps legislation passed in California in 1988, see pages 457-458 of Volume II of this resource book, *Combining Service and Learning: A Resource Book for Community and Public Service*, National Society for Internships and Experiential Education, 1990.

School-Sanctioned Community Service
How State Education Agencies Can Help Local Programs

Claire Cunningham

This summary is excerpted from a paper prepared by the Council of Chief State School Officers in Washington, D.C.: "School-Sanctioned Community Service: The State Perspective" by Claire Cunningham. It also appeared in the Community Education Journal, *Vol. XV, No. 1, of the National Community Education Association.*

IN 1985-86, THE COUNCIL of Chief State School Officers (CCSSO) and the National Association of State Boards of Education (NASBE) examined and reported to the Ford Foundation on *School-Sanctioned Community Service: The State Perspective*. This study found that, while at least 30 states permit students to participate in school-sanctioned community service programs, few states actively encourage establishment of and participation in such programs. Approximately 10 states provide written guidelines or other forms of official encouragement. Only one state, Maryland, has gone so far as to require local school systems to provide community service opportunities for elective credit.

The study also identified actual and potential deterrents to community service. In some states, regulations concerning academic requirements, student jobs, transportation, and health/safety issues seem to discourage school-sanctioned community service programs. Local education agencies (LEAs) have a significant amount of latitude with respect to community service initiatives, but their discretion is clearly not unlimited. LEA efforts to implement community service programs may be unintentionally hampered by state-wide mandates and policies that do not specifically address community service issues. To some extent, therefore, the future of school-sanctioned community service may depend on educators' ability and willingness to reconcile community service initiatives with academic and other state-mandated requirements.

State education agencies (SEAs) and state boards of education may wish to take steps to encourage or assist LEAs in the development of community service programs. In doing so, state-level policy makers should try to create incentives for LEAs, and remove obstacles to effective programs. The following suggested strategies have been compiled for the benefit of education policy makers who choose to assist or encourage LEAs in their community service initiatives. The strategies are based on information collected through staff research and discussions with the advisory panelists, other community service specialists, and SEA staff.

• *Develop and disseminate written policies endorsing community service as part of the school curriculum.*

• *Demonstrate moral support for community service programs.* For example, endorse community service initiatives in SEA and state board speeches and publications.

• *Assign SEA staff to assist in organizing and coordinating local community service programs.* While program development and implementation are likely to remain local issues, SEA staff can act as liaisons among local programs, give guidance on state-level curriculum requirements, and provide other types of technical assistance and coordination of activities.

• *Highlight existing community service programs in SEA and state board newsletters.* The articles should include program descriptions as well as the names and telephone numbers of persons able to provide additional program-specific information.

• *Provide inservice training/staff development seminars on ways to incorporate community service into the curriculum.* Once introduced to the idea, local staff are likely to develop new and creative ways of addressing community needs through students' curriculum-related activities.

• *Organize and maintain a clearinghouse on community service programs, publications, and service opportunities available in the state.* This clearinghouse will be a valuable resource for LEA personnel seeking to develop or expand their community service efforts.

• *Sponsor conferences on strategies for improving school-community relationships.* Through SEA and LEA representatives, students, and community-based employers, illustrate at the conferences ways in which school-sanctioned community service programs can benefit both the student and the community.

• *Assist in developing public television "spots" highlighting the benefits of school-sanctioned community service programs.*

• *Make videotapes and other resource materials discussing examples and benefits of community service available to LEAs.* These materials could be housed at the clearinghouse described above.

• *Require LEAs to offer community service for elective academic credit.* Maryland might serve as a model for this type of initiative.

• *Assist LEAs in evaluating their community service programs.* Guidelines or instruments could be developed to assist in evaluation by LEA staff, students, and employers.

• *Offer grants to LEAs for developing community service programs.* Even small grants can provide incentives for LEAs, including those who wish to develop programs but lack sufficient local funds.

Although the development of precise regulatory language is best left to individual state and local policy makers, information derived from existing community service programs suggests that, in developing any type of service program, certain facts must be recognized and certain questions addressed to ensure the success of the program. Experience shows that programs are more readily accepted and more likely to succeed if:

1. Policy makers and program administrators ensure that the service opportunities provide worthwhile learning experiences for the students. Community service programs should not be simply out-of-class activities that may or may not have educational value, nor should they be designed solely to provide a low-cost mechanism for accomplishing tasks in the community. They should also ensure that students performing community service activities do not displace paid employees.

2. A sense of cooperation and mutual understanding is established among the student, the school officials, and the community employer. The terms of the student's service commitment should be thoroughly discussed and agreed upon prior to the student's placement.

3. Specific staff members are assigned responsibility for developing, maintaining, and evaluating the program.

4. Policy makers and program administrators develop mechanisms for periodically evaluating the program. Since the evaluation must assess the impact on the student as well as on the community, students, educators, and service employers should be involved in

the evaluation process. Among the factors to be assessed are: the educational value of the service experience, the student's attitude towards the experience, specific tasks accomplished by the student, and perhaps the financial value of the work performed for the community.

Youth community service programs play an important role in values education. As CCSSO President David Hornbeck of Maryland said in an *Education Week* interview (February 25, 1987): "We ought to be teaching students that giving to their community is better than taking from their community. All of us learn best by doing, not by reading and being told."

Thanks to Claire Cunningham and Barbara Gomez of the Council of Chief State School Officers and to John Formy-Duval, Ellen Voland, and Mary Boo of the National Community Education Association.

Minnesota Board of Education
Definitions for Youth Service Rule

Youth Service Rule: Youth service-learning must be integrated into the elementary, middle, and secondary school curriculum. School districts must provide opportunities for students to participate in youth service activities.

Youth-service activities. Youth service activities means curricula or co-curricular activities performed by elementary or secondary school students that meet the needs of others in the school or community in such areas as peer tutoring or cross-age tutoring, work with children or seniors, and environmental or other projects.

Youth service-learning. Youth service-learning means the integration into the curriculum of study and reflection on the experience of youth service activities. Youth service-learning must be designed to enhance the student in such areas as personal growth, career exploration, understanding of community and citizenship, social science skills, and communication skills.   — July 1989

Pennsylvania State Board of Education:
Resolution on Student Community Service

WHEREAS, education has long sought to instill the sense of public purpose and responsible citizenship in its graduates; and

WHEREAS, many schools and colleges have found that organized and supported student community service serves an important educational and community building role; and

WHEREAS, students are an important and often underutilized resource for solving pressing public problems such as illiteracy, school failure, underachievement and isolation of elders; now therefore be it

RESOLVED: That the State Board of Education believes that programs of community service should be an integral part of education at all levels and strongly urges schools, colleges and universities to institute or strengthen community service programs so that every student is encouraged to serve and participate in volunteer services.   — January 1989

State of Connecticut's Community Service Fellowship

Reprinted with permission from "State Level Activity on Youth Service" by Dan Liebert, in The State Board Connection: Issues in Brief, *National Association of State Boards of Education, Vol. 9, No. 9, September 1989, p. 7.*

In 1988, the State of Connecticut General Assembly passed innovative legislation to promote community service on college campuses by establishing a Community Service Fellowship to be administered by the Department of Higher Education. It mandated two full-time, one-year positions, a faculty fellow and a student fellow, and start-up funds.

The second part of the legislation mandated that a portion (5% of the annual increase) of the total State financial aid money received by a Connecticut institution of higher education be designated for paid community service work by eligible students who are Connecticut residents.

In its first year, the Community Service Fellowship developed a solid structure of student leadership to support the service efforts on many campuses around the state. It has tapped the energy of the student leadership to implement several projects. For example: (1) a demonstration mini-service award competition has begun for students and faculty to enable them to start or expand a community service project; (2) student fellows have begun pilot projects to form community service organizations at U Conn and Connecticut Central State; and (3) a state-wide community service newsletter is being published and distributed to campus administrators, students, and legislators. For more information, contact Community Service Fellowship, Department of Higher Education, 61 Woodland Street, Hartford, CT 06105.

A Vision for Minnesota, A Vision for the Nation

James C. Kielsmeier and Rich Willits

This chapter outlines the recent developments in youth service in Minnesota and suggests approaches that could be considered by other states. Publication of this article is made possible in part through a grant from the Mott Foundation to the National Youth Leadership Council.

National Service or national service

IN APRIL 1861, hours after the smoke cleared at Fort Sumpter, the first volunteer military units from the North were organized in preparation for the battle to preserve the Union. They were from Minnesota.

Over a century later the North Star State is again mobilizing, capturing some of the fresh air of the service movement sweeping the nation, and adding its own populist brand of citizen involvement. Youth service is blooming in America's heartland with community educators leading the way.

National Service has traditionally been viewed as a right-of-passage from childhood to adult and citizen responsibility. William James' (1910) essay entitled "The Moral Equivalent of War" framed the concept in military terms declaring the adversary to be the "forces of nature" rather than a human enemy. War, according to James, was an experience that built character, but with a cost far too great. Coal fields, fishing fleets in December — hard outdoor work demanding commitment and sacrifice — were the non-military contexts designed to make men out of boys. (James saw national service as a male right of passage).

A Populist Vision

The close connection with military service has, over the years, limited our vision of citizenship development through service to the time of young adulthood. Yet, the emergent Minnesota concept of youth service offers a broader vision based on the principle that service — unselfish giving to others — is a learned behavior rooted in life experience which should be taught incrementally starting at the earliest years. Presenting opportunities for service throughout the growing-up experience of Minnesota youth has been the goal.

In 1984, the National Youth Leadership Council at the Center for Youth Development and Research took on the mission of developing a comprehensive youth service model in the state of Minnesota which would offer community service opportunities to every young person growing up in the state from kindergarten through college, or for non-college young adults in a full-time service corps. The Council sought to create an ethos of service where giving of one's time and talents to meet the needs of the community would be a commonplace experience, available at every level of school and throughout the community in much the same way that athletics are available today.

With the involvement of young people, teachers, administrators, community educators, youth workers, and many others, including the Attorney General of Minnesota, the Mayors of Minneapolis and St. Paul, several state legislators, U.S. Representatives Gerry Sikorski and Bruce Vento, the Governor and Lt. Governor, we are well on our way toward achieving our mission.

Linking the Spheres of Service

Early on we identified four major "spheres of service" which could develop separately as well as overlap to provide mutual support.

School-Based Youth Service

Curricular and co-curricular opportunities to engage in service have been explored and encouraged. In 1987 Minnesota legislation authored by state Representative Ken Nelson was passed authorizing school districts to levy an added $.50 per capita for community education to be used in designing and implementing youth development plans. A Minnesota Department of Education survey of the 186 school districts which levied (out of a possible 435 in Minnesota) shows that most include proposals to develop youth service.

A more extensive phone survey conducted of 31 area school districts by the Minneapolis Area United Way in June 1988 revealed that 15 of these districts include youth service in their current Youth

Development Plans and four others will include it in the future. The youth development legislation has been heartily supported by the Minnesota Community Education Association, which has backed the legislative effort, developed in-service training for youth service teachers, and highlighted youth service in publications.

The 1987 Youth Development Legislation was the first state and community-funded school-based service effort in the nation. In 1988-89 of an estimated two million dollars levied for youth development, one million dollars was earmarked for youth service projects and programs.

This effort represents solid grass roots support statewide: from the educators, parents, youth workers, interested citizens and — most important — youth, all of whom have participated as part of the youth development planning process in their communities. With facilitation by community educators, these groups are envisioning what their communities might, at best, be like for youth, and youth service is playing a major role in their dreams, their plans and their labor.

Legislation passed in 1988 strengthened the language of the 1987 bill and spelled out how youth service should be conducted in Minnesota as part of formal education. The statute reads in part:

Programs must include:

1. Preliminary training for pupil volunteers conducted, when possible, by organizations experienced in such training.
2. Supervision of the pupil volunteers to ensure appropriate placement and adequate learning opportunity.
3. Sufficient opportunity for pupil volunteers to give genuine service to their community.
4. Integration of academic learning with the service experience.

Examples of appropriate pupil service placements include: child care, Head Start, early childhood education and extended day programs; tutoring programs involving older pupils tutoring younger pupils; environmental beautification projects; and regular visits for shut-in senior citizens.

The Legislature went further in 1989 passing an additional $.25 levy (the first year as state aid) specifically for youth service programs through youth development. Youth service has also found support at the State Board of Education. On July 11, 1989, the Board mandated that all school districts offer youth service at both the elementary and secondary levels.

Even though there is interest in developing school-based service, existing programs are few and under-recognized. Less that 15% of school districts responding to a 1988 survey conducted by the Minnesota Department of Education and the National Youth Leadership Council reported curricular or co-curricular programs. At the same time in another survey conducted by the Department of Education, over 175 districts reported a high or moderate need for assistance in youth service program development. A follow-up survey reveals a doubling in the number of youth service programs reported in the state. These surveys and high attendance levels at recent workshops indicate that Minnesota will likely experience further growth in the area of school service programs in the next few years.

Agency-Based Service

Scouts, YMCAs, YWCAs, Red Cross, 4-H, Campfire and other nonprofit youth service organizations have historically employed community service as part of their youth development curricula. In Minnesota an already high level of interest has heightened. Nonprofit professionals have not only pressed their own organizations to offer more service opportunities, but have joined in support of youth service efforts in other spheres. Currently, a task group is exploring how the formal and non-formal educational systems can link to provide enhanced service experiences for the school-age child. Recommendations include:

- Inviting organizations such as 4-H to co-sponsor service projects such as Peddle Power, a bike safety training program matching high school students with younger peers.
- Encouraging credit or recognition within school for achievements in community service outside of school. An Eagle Scout, for example, might receive some special school citation or transcript notation.
- Using school facilities for agency-based after-school programs which engage youth in public service.

Campus-Based Service

With the technical assistance of Campus Compact and COOL (Campus Outreach Opportunity League), and with initial funding from local foundations and from ACTION, the National Youth

Leadership Council has sponsored a statewide campus service effort. The Minnesota Campus Service Initiative has, in the past year, been a part of nurturing campus volunteer efforts on every four-year college in Minnesota, conducting student training, on-site consultations and pursuing policies which resulted in state legislation in 1988. The work continues with the involvement of two-year colleges having increased in 1988-89. A state faculty coalition for college-level service began in fall 1989.

In 1988 legislation called for a review of curricular service opportunities in state higher education. The Legislature appropriated $150,000 to the Minnesota Higher Education Coordinating Board for a matching grant program to fund campus service coordinators. The program is administered by the National Youth Leadership Council.

Full-Time Service

Organizing which began in 1984 focused strongly on enhancing the relatively small Minnesota Conservation Corps. A Governor's Task Force recommended in 1986 that a comprehensive, full-time service corps be established "for the purpose of giving youth unique opportunities to provide full-time necessary service to Minnesota, while enhancing their personal development, education, and future employability skills."

The bill that was proposed by Senator Mike Freeman and Representative Ken Nelson fueled the subsequent youth development legislation already mentioned — but has yet to stand on its own. Efforts continue to press forward with this creative model which was the result of hearings conducted throughout Minnesota and a year of study. The City of St. Paul is part of the Urban Corps Expansion Program of the National Association of Service and Conservation Corps and hopes to have a corps off the ground in 1990.

Pulling It Together

Campus Service	School-Based Service
Agency Service	Full-time Service

Every effort has been made to advance youth service in each of the spheres and at the same time working to link the areas for mutual support. Key to the view that youth service can be advanced in several sectors has been the involvement of Governor Rudy Perpich, who was the 1988-89 chair of the Educational Commission of the States (ECS), the educational organization of the nation's governors. Perpich made youth service a major plank of his tenure with ECS.

The formation of the Minnesota Youth Service Association has also played a key role in strengthening connections between the spheres of service. Already over 100 organizations representing diverse approaches and populations have joined and are uniting behind a Comprehensive Youth Services Plan for Minnesota. Conferences, workshops and a comprehensive curricular package are planned which will add strength to the program and legislative initiatives. A strong partnership between the Minnesota Department of Education, Minnesota Office of Volunteer Services and the National Youth Leadership Council has done much to insure a solid future for youth service in Minnesota.

A Vision for the Nation

Minnesotans were quick to respond to the needs of the nation during the Civil War. Today, people in the heartland reflect a most basic love of country, concern for children and enduring hope for the future, and see these values expressed in the process of engaging youth in acts of citizen service. Efforts to organize this movement through the Minnesota Youth Service Initiative have received solid community support. The idea of service is rooted deeply in the rich soil of the American experience and with cultivation in Minnesota has yielded a variety of program initiatives which will do much to address the need of modern youth to be needed, while addressing the well documented needs of the society for their services. With similar nurturing at the state and local levels, a vision of a comprehensive national service model for the nation has begun to take shape.

James Kielsmeier is President of the National Youth Leadership Council (NYLC) and Assistant Professor at the Center for Youth Development and Research at the University of Minnesota. Rich Willits is Associate Director of the NYLC.

References

James, William, *The Moral Equivalent of War*, International Conciliation, Vol. 27, February 1910.

Willits, Rich, Minnesota Department of Education Youth Development Survey, June 1988.

Hearing before the Subcommittee on Human Resources of the Committee on Post Office and Civil Service, House of Representatives, statement by James C. Kielsmeier, November 13, 1987, St. Paul, Minnesota.

Minnesota Task Force on Youth Service and Work, *Reclaiming a Needed Resource: Minnesota's Youth*, report and plan of action to Governor Rudy Perpich, November 21, 1986.

Summary of Minnesota Legislation Passed in 1989

After a concerted five-year effort, the Minnesota Legislature and Board of Education passed landmark legislation in 1989 providing support for schools and colleges to develop community service and learning programs:

K-12:
Omnibus Education Bill, Article 4 - Community and Adult Education
- Will generate nearly $1 million annually for schools doing youth service.
- $.25 per capita State aid through Community Education to districts with Youth Development Plans involving the community.
- Offers schools the opportunity to grant credit for learning derived from service activities.
- *Language excerpt:* "A school board may offer, as part of a community education program with a youth development program, a youth service program for pupils to promote active citizenship and to address community needs ... The school board may award up to one credit, or the equivalent, toward graduation for a pupil who completes the youth service requirements of the district."

State Board of Education Rule Change
- Complements above legislation by requiring school districts to offer youth service as a curricular option at elementary and secondary levels.

College:
Higher Education Omnibus Bill (Senate File 1625), Section 2 - Higher Education Coordinating Board, Subdivision 2(e)
- $150,000 state appropriation.
- Matching grants of approximately $10,000 each to be used to fund a staff person on several campuses to coordinate and champion service-learning involvement.
- Statewide coordination, training for campus service leaders also funded.
- *Language excerpt:* "$150,000 for the biennium is for matching grants to post-secondary institutions that submit acceptable proposals for campus community service projects emphasizing students performing as tutors and mentors to their younger peers ... To receive a grant, a recipient must match the grant amount from any resources available to the institution."

Other:
Department of Natural Resources
- authorization and $305,000 funding increase for the Minnesota Conservation Corps over the biennium.

Minnesota Office on Volunteer Services: Department of Administration
- $140,000 funding increase over the biennium will help enable this office to prepare community agencies for increase in number of student volunteers.

Not the School Alone

David W. Hornbeck

Maryland's former State Superintendent tells how his state sought to carry out its educational mission through the Community-Based Learning and Service Program. This program has now been replaced by a much broader statewide program affiliated with the Maryland Student Alliance Program. Hornbeck's analysis is still useful today for education policy makers. Reprinted from Synergist, National Center for Service-Learning, ACTION, *Vol. 10, No. 2, 1981, pp. 17-18.*

MARYLAND'S COMMUNITY-BASED Learning and Service Program (CBLS) exists for a number of reasons. In the first place, it reflects the policy that the State Board of Education adopted in "The Mission of Schooling" in 1977. The Board stated:

> We reassert that schooling is the responsibility of self, family, neighborhood, church, community and the many institutions which impact on our lives. It is not the responsibility of the school alone. Neither competency nor the personal qualities to which the schooling process contributes can result from schools alone. But schools can and should provide leadership to others.

In too many ways too many times over the past several years, responsibilities borne in part by other institutions in our society have been thrust upon our schools. At times this has been done explicitly; at other times it has been implicit. The list is extensive: teach discipline, keep the student from the labor market, cure drug and alcohol abuse and other self-destructive behavior, provide before- and after-school care. The list goes on, all in addition to the continuing responsibilities for reading, writing, arithmetic, science, literature, social studies, art, music, physical education, vocational education, career education, and the other components of a quality educational program.

As schools have struggled to bear up under the load, there has been an oft-cited erosion of confidence in the public schools by the wider community. The new responsibilities cannot be borne by the schools, nor can confidence be fully restored until or unless schools and communities renew a vigorous partnership and mutually assume responsibility for the lives of their youth. Thus, one reason for CBLS is to help provoke that partnership.

A second important reason for CBLS is the way human beings learn. It does not take a learning theorist to conclude that one of the ways we learn best is by doing. Each of us has had many experiences that underline that fact. Despite the simplicity and universality of the observation, the vast bulk of formal schooling takes place in the confines of the classroom, curtailing the depth and excellence of the learning experience that would be enhanced by involvement beyond the schoolhouse door. When most of us think of hands-on opportunities, we tend to think of the workplace. And then we quickly conclude that there are not enough employers to begin to place the scores of thousands of high school students in a state the size of Maryland. So we go back to the classroom.

But there is an option often forgotten. Service opportunities provide us with a nearly inexhaustible source of placement spots. Service placements can provide fundamentally the same generic learning opportunities that one can find in the workplace. Accepting responsibility, imposing self-discipline, following instructions, being punctual, and following through are as necessary in a tutor, hospice aid, or companion to emotionally disturbed children as they are in any workplace in any community. Thus, part of our enthusiasm for CBLS is rooted in the pragmatic fact that it opens thousands of new places where structured and supervised quality education can take place outside of the classroom.

The third reason for CBLS lies in the point of view that helping other people is a value that schools should reinforce among students in concert with the wider community. We may or may not have the responsibility to be our brother's keeper. Surely we have the responsibility to be our brother's helper. CBLS unabashedly endorses that proposition. There are many romanticized views of the good ol' days. They probably were not nearly as good as we remember. But a part of that backward glance reveals a premium placed on volunteerism in the service context that appears less pronounced today. Schools promote values. Sometimes they do so consciously; more frequently, the values transmitted just happen. CBLS affirms that the notion of rendering service is a good that schools properly encourage.

Two Approaches

Last year CBLS operated out of two high schools. One is in LaPlatta, a small town in southern Maryland. The other is in Baltimore City. We hope to have a third location this year. The objective in each is to build so that by the third year of operation, 50 percent or more of the student body in each of the high schools is engaged in some form of community-based learning and service.

The operation in each school differs. In LaPlatta (in its second year of operation) students who signed up for CBLS had one day per week free for community service. Response from students and community supervisors has been enthusiastic. About 450 students were involved (nearing the goal of 50 percent) in about 140 community sites. In contrast, at Baltimore's Northwestern Senior High School, students are not scheduled into CBLS. Instead they sign up for CBLS through school-based coordinators and, in cooperation with a teacher, develop a program that they then carry out at the site. Students spend between 5 and 15 days at a site, depending on the nature of the site and the student. During the first year, more than 400 students participated in the program.

Both schools already have underlined the importance of staff development to the success of the effort. Not surprisingly, teacher reaction has ranged from enthusiastic to hostile. As with so many other things, understanding and participation has led to enthusiasm as intensive inservice training has been offered.

The broad goals of the program are embodied in the reasons set out earlier for its existence: a renewed partnership with the community; an alternative approach to learning; a way to underline the significance of service in our society. Within these broad goals we seek many subordinate goals.

For students these goals include: taking responsibility for their actions; exploring how to be a responsible, satisfied person in the home, community, and workplace; gaining in understanding people of different ages, racial groups, and cultures; learning how public and private assistance agencies help others; organizing and managing community service experiences.

For teachers these goals include: identifying areas of their curriculum that can be taught and learned in community settings; identifying ways to individualize curriculum; becoming more familiar with the community, particularly in relation to their field expertise.

For administrators these goals include: learning how to help teachers to relate curriculum and community to students; developing skills as catalysts; becoming more sensitive to the community as helper, supporter, and contributor.

For the community these goals include: a renewed perspective of school as community cornerstone; an opportunity to share directly in helping students; actually being the recipient of the service.

Questions To Answer

Being very practical, at the conclusion of the three-year pilot effort, the State Department of Education will answer at least the following questions:

1. Who supports or opposes what parts of the program and why?
2. How can the program be scheduled so as to be part of the school rather than a source of disruption?
3. How will student transportation be managed?
4. How will staff development programs be structured?
5. How will students be awarded credit?
6. How will students be monitored and evaluated?
7. What effective mechanisms have been developed to enhance school- community-parent cooperation?
8. What are alternative methods of site development?
9. What administrative methods are effective for managing the program?
10. How cost effective is the program?

Those will not be easy questions to answer, particularly when we maintain the objective of having more than 50 percent of the students participating. And that in the final analysis is the crux of the issue. We know school and community need to strengthen their partnership. We know that one of the ways we learn best is by doing. It simply works. We also know that to help another is a good that most will affirm. What we know less well is how one does those things for large numbers of students in a comprehensive high school. We know less well how to solve logistical problems when a fundamental piece of the raison d'etre of a school and community is to relate to one another in the service mode.

And finally, we do not know whether the notion of service, of helping one another, can define the character of a high school in the way we know a football team or basketball team or a marching band or a cheerleading and pep team can. It sets one to thinking about a school where two students walking down the hall ask one another without other explanation what their service project for the semester is. Or maybe one can even imagine a lunchroom conversation where one senior says to another, "You know that autistic kid I've been working with the past couple of years? He spoke yesterday. That's the greatest thing that ever happened to him or me."

[The following is an excerpt from State Superintendent David Hornbeck's statement to the Maryland Board of Education in 1985. It is adapted from *Student Service: The New Carnegie Unit* by Charles H. Harrison, Carnegie Foundation for the Advancement of Teaching, 1987, pp. 9-10.]

"I strongly believe that each student should participate in a structured experience of community service as a prerequisite to graduation. Stringent academic graduation requirements that press students toward this potential excellence are crucial. But a successful and productive adulthood is more than academic or job-related prowess. It must also embody a sense of one's responsibility beyond one's self. The development of that sense of responsibility is as much the product of experience, learning, and practice as proving a theorem in geometry, unraveling the meaning of Chaucer or becoming a competent plumber or computer programmer."

Hornbeck offered four reasons why community service should be required:
1. The state "should make clear we believe helping to meet the needs of others is a fundamental component of being an effective adult."
2. It has been demonstrated that students engaged in community service acquire a responsible attitude toward others, gain "feelings of self-esteem and personal adequacy," and usually have a better record of attendance and behavior than they otherwise would.
3. Students learn important job skills. "Thus, while constituting a secondary objective of the service requirement, implementing elements of the work ethic could be taught effectively."
4. Community service helps fill the human need for belonging. "It has been shown that contributing to society in a meaningful way leads to a feeling of belonging."

David Hornbeck currently chairs the Task Force on Education of Young Adolescents, Carnegie Council on Adolescent Development.

Pathways To Success: Citizenship through Service

Youth and America's Future: The William T. Grant Commission on Work, Family and Citizenship presents its final recommendations in The Forgotten Half: Pathways to Success for America's Youth and Young Families. *This chapter reprints the Commission's thorough and insightful report and recommendations about service-learning opportunities (1988, pp. 79-90, 161-162). Thanks to Samuel Halperin, Study Director.*

Service as a Two-Way Street

THE TRADITION IN AMERICAN SCHOOLS — as though there was an official script — calls for students to memorize key passages from the great documents of American government and history. Their mastery of stirring and important material, such as the Preamble to the Constitution, is presumed to bond them to their country and its ideals. The study of US history and government is supposed to produce adults who value democratic traditions and shoulder responsibilities with their fellow citizens.

But the script does not always unfold that way. By one important measure — voter participation — it needs radical rewriting. Only 53.1 percent of eligible voters cared enough to vote in the 1984 presidential election, and voter turnouts decrease with level of earnings. While 76 percent of the people earning over $50,000 per year voted in 1984, only 38 percent of those earning $5,000 or less do so.[1]

Although the Commission reaffirms the obvious importance of learning the concepts and facts of American history and government, we strongly believe that *knowledge must be integrated with action in order to produce the desired outcome: a citizen participating fully in the responsibilities of community, state, and nation.*

That people need to help and care for one another is an idea as old as the first human communities and equally valid for a modern mass society. But too many Americans, especially the young, feel a debilitating sense of powerlessness in the face of large national and world issues that affect their lives but elude their control. The Commission believes this sense of futility, and the consequent pre-occupation with self, can be redirected into an ethic of service and commitment to others.[2] When young people have a chance to act on their humanitarian ideals, they build self-respect and strong attach-ments to family and community. *There is virtually no limit to what young people — with appropriate education, training, and encouragement — can do, no social need they cannot help meet. We reiterate: Young people are essential resources, and society needs their active participation as citizens.*

Every community's voluntary sector offers young people varied opportunities to work on their own or with adults to promote social good. By engaging young people in the real challenges of commu-nity life, rather than isolating them from adult concerns, much needed work gets done with both youth and the society the better for it.[4]

If all young people — whether college-bound or members of the Forgotten Half [non-college bound] — had opportunities to render

---

Generosity of spirit is thus the ability to acknowledge an interconnectedness — one's debts to society — that binds one to others whether one wants to accept it or not. It is also the ability to engage in the caring that nurtures that interconnectedness. It is a virtue that everyone should strive for ... a conception of citizenship that is still alive in America.

— *Robert Bellah et al.,*
Habits of the Heart[3]

---

needed service, they would come to understand that life is a process of both giving and getting. They would better appreciate that democracy involves a social compact in which society nurtures and cares for its young, and the young, in turn, care for the weak, the needy, the infirm, as well as the healthy and empowered members of society. They would become contributors, problem-solvers, and partners with adults in improving their communities and the larger society.[5] If the service commitment begins early enough and continues into adulthood, participatory citizenship would become what Robert Bellah and his colleagues call "habits of the heart," family and community traditions of local political participation that sustain a person, a community, and a nation.[6]

Documentary evidence supports the value of service in young people's lives. According to one longitudinal study, graduates of experimental schools established in the 1930s that featured problem-solving curricula, extensive community learning opportunities, peer teaching, and student-faculty control over governance were more successful in life than students from schools that provided only limited opportunities of these types.[7] A tracking of 79 high school students who performed semester-long internships in four New York county governments reaffirmed the virtues of a community-based rather than a solely school-grounded approach to learning about the processes of government.[8] Similar outcomes emerge from a broad range of hands-on service and volunteer activities by young people throughout the nation.

Yet, reports from the 1980s are uneven. From the 1,103 respondents among 5,000 high schools surveyed by the Carnegie Foundation for the Advancement of Teaching comes the heartening news that 70 percent had some form of student service program.[9] The nature and quality of those programs is, however, unknown, as is the state of service in the four-fifths of non-responding schools.

The same Carnegie study reported that only 20 percent or fewer of the students in those service-oriented high schools actually participated in the available service projects. According to the oft-quoted annual survey of a large sample of incoming college freshmen of the 1986-87 school year (209,627 students at 390 higher education institutions) by the American Council on Education and the University of California at Los Angeles, only 39 percent, as compared to 83 percent in 1967, held that "developing a meaningful philosophy of life" was a major goal.[10] Nevertheless, in 1985, nearly 70 percent claimed to have performed volunteer service during the previous year. In 1985, too, a Gallup survey reported that 43 percent of the 18-24 year age group had actually done volunteer work that year.[11] Of course, the same person driven by a desire "to be well-off

The youth population has been misnamed the self-centered generation. There's a strong desire to serve others. The problem we face in America today is not a lack of willingness to serve or help others but to find the appropriate outlet for this.

— George Gallup (1987)

financially" (the ACE-UCLA poll put that total at 76 percent for the 1986 freshmen) could have an equally strong wish "to help the community." Or, perhaps, self-reporting of service performed could simply be a pitch to college admissions officers to look favorably on a well-rounded high school senior's application.

Kim Grose, a Stanford University sophomore active in campus-based service, cautions against drawing hasty conclusions about today's young people from any survey data cited or by reference to the tumultuous decade of the '60s:

> Comparisons drawn between the student activism of the 1960s and the 1980s is often misleading because it gets caught up in '60s stereotypes and jargon and misses the true nature of volunteerism on campuses today. At my university, a school often looked upon as an elitist, career-oriented institution, public service is one of the strongest extra-curricular activities. Today's politically and socially active students are not only "hippie-throwbacks" or radicals; many are the same students who plan careers in engineering or business. They do not consider themselves crusaders and do not plan to spend their lives "changing the world." Students tutor, coach softball, paint playgrounds, and read to the elderly because they are interested in people, or because they want to learn a little about poverty and racism before they head out into the waiting corporate world. Or else they volunteer because they see their friends doing it, and it turns out to be fun.

Most students are very idealistic, and wish to use their youthful energy to get involved in a poor community. Most have listened to their university president's speeches, and feel some sense of obligation to repay society for the incredible opportunities open to them. Some will turn to politics, community organizing, or the Peace Corps after graduation as a way to help make the world a more just place. Many others have such enormous loan debts from high tuition costs that their career goals are aimed at law firms and investment banking firms, to satisfy their parents and creditors, not their own ideals.

None of us, no matter where our career paths take us, will ever forget the lessons we learned through volunteering in the community. We do not volunteer "to make a statement," or to use the people we work with to protest something. We try to see the homeless man, the hungry child, and the dying woman as the people they are, not the means to some political end.[12]

Whatever the motivation, opportunities for service beckon. The Commission believes strongly that closing the gap between the rhetoric and performance would greatly benefit young people and communities alike.

The Benefits of Service

Educator Jane Kendall cites a prime benefit of service — more effective learning. She cautions, however, that *the best learning occurs when the initial, concrete service experience is followed by a period of disciplined reflection on the experience.* Time for talking, writing, and thinking about what they have done and seen allows the servers to assimilate and synthesize the experience, and later to test what they have learned in new situations. Reflection amplifies not only the service experience, but also the education and work experiences in the server's life.[13]

For the young person who engages in community service, the experience, if reinforced and rewarded, can be beneficial in several ways:

- It expands personal learning and social horizons far beyond home and classroom;
- It eases the often painful passage from school to work;

- It imparts a greater sense of the individual's personal worth and capabilities for leadership and problem-solving;
- It bonds young people more securely and usefully to their communities and activates their civic knowledge in tangible ways;
- It creates genuine work and useful products of which youth and the community can be proud;
- It teaches basic life skills needed for generic employability and enhances critical thinking skills.

These are significant benefits. But they resist easy categorization and quantification beyond the obvious generality that they all have to do with learning and personal development.

Service-learning offers a partial key to unlock the door that leads from school to work. Lauren Resnick of the Center for the Study of Learning at the University of Pittsburgh points out that students in school are judged by what they do individually. Outside of school, however, work is more often a collaborative enterprise and requires a person to mesh several talents and skills.[14] The experience of a group service project provides important job-readiness skills for the contemporary work world. According to Sue Berryman, Director of the National Center on Education and Employment at Teachers College, Columbia University, the restructuring of many jobs in today's market compels workers to see a project as a whole, find creative solutions to problems, and work cooperatively with others — qualities that also accompany service-learning, but not necessarily traditional didactic schooling.[15]

The service ethic can be instilled incrementally with experiences appropriate to the developmental age of participants — voluntary activity in the community promotes adolescent development more broadly.[16] Fresh Force of Minneapolis, a junior high school service corps, is an example of an effort to respond to the characteristics of the 11-15-year-old age group. In all nine junior highs where it operates, students are organized to propose and implement community service projects. The Pillsbury Company funds recognition events and arranges media coverage for students who contribute 30+ service hours. The United Way pays for a city-wide coordina-

Everyone can be great because everyone can serve.

— Martin Luther King, Jr.

tor, affiliated with the YMCA. As early as possible — and especially by junior high school, when energetic young people can often learn better by doing than by sitting passively in classrooms — service and reflection on that service ought to be a part of the regular school curriculum. And every student can gain by participating.

Amplifying these observations, pediatrician Melvin Levine, Director of the Clinical Center for the Study of Development and Learning at the University of North Carolina, argues that schools constrict the ways in which our young people can demonstrate their abilities. At the very time when youth require varied opportunities to learn and to do, schools often confine them to demonstrations of academic, verbal, and specific memory skills that receive high profile in most schools. If the student is not successful in those restricted definitions of competence, he or she is labeled a failure.[17] *Learning through serving is one method of experiential learning that could be used well with students who learn best by doing and by working with others, rather than solely by reading and rote learning.*

Stephen Hamilton and L. Mickey Fenzel found that, for 44 youth in 12 projects, volunteer work had positive effects on their social attitudes, their sense of themselves, and the knowledge and skills they exercised in their voluntary activities.[18] In another study by Conrad and Hedin of 27 variations of experiential education programs, students showed significant increases in moral reasoning, self-esteem, and social and personal responsibility, as well as improved attitudes toward adults, more interest in career exploration, and better problem-solving skills.[19]

Individual or group service-learning projects bestow different benefits. One-to-one service experiences often encourage close relationships between adults and youth and foster intergenerational understanding. Group projects, on the other hand, are more complex because they entail planning and cooperating with others in the work group. The group experience itself can be a powerful learning experience for young people, who thereby try out the roles of leadership and followership.[20]

Growing efforts use service models with at-risk youth. If increased self-esteem and job preparedness are the fruits of service-learning, the reasoning seems to go, then who in our population could better use this leg up than at-risk youth? In Pittsburgh's Oasis program, 100 at-risk seventh graders are enrolled in an education/community service program with the hope that these youth will stay in school and gain self-esteem, as well as serve their communities. In Indianapolis' Dropouts in Touch, older teens encourage younger students to remain in school. Former dropouts who have

completed employment training draw on their personal, often negative, experiences to persuade young people to complete high school.
Youth on probation assist senior citizens with maintenance and
clean-up activities in the Fountain Square section of Indianapolis,
and young adolescents provide companionship services to the elderly.

*The Commission believes that care must be taken that service projects
are not designed primarily as devices to "rehabilitate" at-risk youth.* This
misses much of the true value of service, particularly its citizenship
dimension. And we worry that service opportunities open primarily to at-risk youth will stigmatize both these youth and the service
concept. With this note of caution, we applaud service for *all* young
people as an essential building block of citizenship.   Moreover,
because many young people need to work part-time, service should
be an integral part of the regular school curricula and the service
programs of community-based organizations, not an appendage to
their lives or "another course" tacked on to their regular load.

Youth service yields substantial economic benefits to the community: in-kind contributions of labor and talent, future social
welfare costs saved, and young people prepared for stable work and
family life.   An estimated 3.5 million full-time volunteers could
meet numerous societal needs[21] — among them, at a conservative
estimate, 500,000 nonprofessional workers in schools, 275,000 caring for severely restricted elderly and handicapped individuals,
225,000 in energy, environmental protection, and urban and rural
conservation, 165,000 for services to children, youth, and families,
and 200,000 in public safety.[22]

*Young people now contribute at least 250 million hours of service
annually* through state, federal, and local programs. The monetary
value of high school students contributing 17 million hours of
unpaid service annually is $59.5 million (at $3.50 per hour). The 192
million service hours by college students, at an hourly wage of $5,
represent a $940 million contribution. Youth corps members per-
form the remaining 41 million service hours.[23]

In short, service-learning promotes:
- increased competence, self-confidence, and self-esteem;
- experiences among people of diverse backgrounds;
- chances to learn in a different way — from doing, not from being
  told;
- experiences in problem-solving;
- empathy for others and working cooperatively with others;
- assumption of the responsibilities and obligations of life as well
  as enjoying its privileges; and
- tangible public benefits to the community.

Even so, community service still faces formidable barriers in becoming a "habit of the heart." Only strong backing from policymakers will overcome the most obvious barriers: (1) unresponsive regulations regarding liability insurance, (2) the troublesome matter of transportation to and from sites, (3) inflexible school schedules, (4) coordination with the students' part-time jobs and other responsibilities, and, most especially, (5) policymakers and educators who believe that service is "tangential," "a nice frill, not integral to sound education."

Good service programs do not just happen. Nor can service be "neatly wrapped and tied when so many hours have been donated, journals written, credit and/or grades given." The spark plug of a service program is the adult leader who motivates young people to go deeper — not merely to serve, but to understand and act on that understanding.[24] Service-learning programs with dedicated adult supervisors and committed administrators can match young people with appropriate service slots and monitor the quality of their actual experiences. Cursory exposure to service will not satisfy the goals of service. *Only programs that properly train and engage the participants and provide an atmosphere for serious reflection on the meaning and impact of the experience are ultimately worthwhile.*[25] *If it is to succeed in its noble goals, a service-learning program cannot exist without forceful public policy and careful attention to both purpose and details.*

Service: A Requirement for Everyone?

School-based voluntary service programs are gaining momentum. Slowly, but steadily, the main messages are taking hold. Local and state agencies are testing new structures and outreach methods, while communities, schools and colleges, local organizations, and governments are expanding service programs.[26] In 1986, two major national education associations, the Council of Chief State School Officers and the National Association of State Boards of Education, published comprehensive guidelines for state agencies wishing to undertake service programs. The CCSSO-NASBE guidelines, and several follow-up meetings to gain feedback on the implementation of service programs, demonstrate the growing interest and commitment of educational policymakers.

An expanding pattern of policy actions and program initiatives across the country, many strongly supported by governors such as Rudy Perpich (MN), George Deukmejian (CA), Richard Celeste (OH), Madeleine Kunin (VT), and Robert Casey (PA), provide examples such as these:

- Vermont requires all students to complete a research or citizenship project which many fulfill through service. SerVermont combines a "bottom-up" design in which student-faculty teams create service projects in their communities.
- The Governor's School in the State of Washington trains students from different socio-economic backgrounds to develop and lead service projects.
- In Atlanta, where service is considered part of an essential trio along with education and employment, students must complete 75 hours of unpaid service between grades 9 and 11, and seniors must take a course on "Duties to the Community." All students keep journals and a log of their after-school, weekend, and holiday service work.
- In Springfield, Massachusetts, under the active sponsorship of the mayor and the superintendent of schools, every student in grades K-12 is expected to perform community service integrated with the academic curriculum.
- About a quarter of the nation's independent schools require some form of service as part of the regular curriculum. Several public high schools in Minnesota require service. Banneker High School, a magnet academic school in Washington, DC, requires 270 hours and Metro High School in St. Louis 240 hours of service for graduation.
- Youth Community Service, a joint project of the Constitutional Rights Foundation and the Los Angeles Unified School District, is the largest program of all. Now in its fourth year, it operates in 22 Los Angeles high schools and involves over 5,000 students, largely minority, in service.[27]

Service is needed to allow us to have a future....our society has needs which cannot be met except through service. Service is our ticket to a viable future. It is essential and not a luxury.

— Hans Huessy, College of Medicine,
University of Vermont

- The Carnegie Foundation for the Advancement of Teaching recommended that a new Carnegie unit for service be included in the graduation requirements of all high schools.[28]
- The State of Maryland requires all high schools to offer service as an elective, while the Regents' Action Plan in New York calls for a required senior course in government participation that includes a practicum in school, community, or government service.

The Commission believes that more extensive involvement would produce the same result for more young people if the service ethic were an integral part of the educational system, beginning with kindergarten and the early grades.

The Commission recommends creation of quality opportunities for service, as central to the fundamental educational program of every public school, including (a) either a requirement that each school provide opportunities to every student for a voluntary serv-ice-learning program built on good practices which is eligible for elective credit toward graduation, or a graduation requirement of a specified amount of service; and (b) age-appropriate curricula and instruction, including both service and class-based reflection, during each year from kindergarten through the twelfth grade. Service-learning programs should include provisions for coordination and supervision in the schools, meaningful service sites in communities, and recognition award ceremonies for those involved in service. The resolve and cooperation of school boards, administrators, coordinators, and teachers can ensure that service be a part of the regular academic program of all schools. Sufficient importance should be attached to this school responsibility that local, state, and national resources be sought and secured from private and public sources to make quality service opportunities a reality.

The Commission believes that decisions about how to structure community service must remain in the hands of schools and communities. We urge, however, that local programs pay careful attention to the criteria we have set out when they begin service programs, especially regarding genuine engagement rather than mere exposure, time for reflection, and a clear mission statement backed up by committed personnel to administer and monitor these service-learning programs. *The Commission encourages states not merely to adopt youth service policies, but to provide local school boards and jurisdictions with financial and technical assistance to make them quality experiences for America's young people.*

The Case for Youth Volunteer Corps

In addition to school-based service-learning programs, youth corps membership offers a way for young adults to develop or continue the service habit. The Peace Corps, VISTA, and National Health Service Corps are the best-known national examples of such service. A growing number of voluntary youth corps in cities, counties, and states fuse the environmental and human service needs of communities with the equally important need for youth to serve. These full-time corps programs pay participants minimum wage for service, often offer educational opportunities, and perform beneficial community service.

Most state and local youth corps participants, dropouts and high school graduates alike, have traditionally been young people who need a second chance to make something of their lives. Increasingly, however, youth from all walks of life are deciding that youth corps offer valuable routes to experience that help them later in choosing work, training, service in the armed forces, or college. The Corps' main goal is preparation for life, including finding out what it means to be a caring and contributing member of the community. But they pursue other important goals as well: improving job readiness, learning to work with others, enhancing basic learning skills, and starting or continuing college study. For many, service means broadening perspectives about different racial or ethnic groups and thinking about college careers in human services. For all, "the corps programs aim to instill a sense of the value of work, a feeling of civic responsibility, and a sense of self-worth by doing environmental protection, physical development, and human service work that is clearly needed but would otherwise not be done."[29]

To meet goals of service and job readiness, several program components are key. Well-trained crew leaders, who have daily contact with corps members, are critical to corps' success. They are responsible for job supervision, individual and group counseling, and ongoing assessment and motivation.[30] Many corps offer opportunities for education — General Education Development Certificate (GED) preparation, instruction in English as a second language, or college courses. Corps in cities, counties, and states incorporate general goals in a variety of ways determined locally.

The number of youth corps is growing steadily. Currently, the 50 year-round or summer state and local corps operate with 50,000 participants annually and budgets totalling $145 million.[31] Several states have launched or expanded youth service corps, broadening them to urban areas and including human services as well as conservation work. The Congress is considering legislation to boost both conservation and human service corps.

Following a long tradition of service in American history — the Civilian Conservation Corps under Franklin Roosevelt, the Peace Corps under John Kennedy, VISTA under Lyndon Johnson, AC-TION under Richard Nixon, Youth Conservation Corps under Jimmy Carter — the California Conservation Corps started in 1976 under Governor Jerry Brown, became a permanent state agency in 1983 under Governor George Deukmejian. The CCC has had 36,000 participants, including 2,200 this year. Its current budget of $58 million provides more than three million hours of public service conservation work and emergency assistance to the state each year.

Other state corps operate in a variety of ways. The Wisconsin Corps has a two-year $4 million budget to support 65 predominantly rural projects and 750 participants. The Corps is 28 percent women, 19 percent minorities, and four percent persons with disabilities. In Maryland, the Department of Natural Resources coordinates and funds 24 county programs. The Washington State Service Corps focuses entirely on human service projects.

Cities, too, are active in the youth corps movement. San Francisco Conservation Corps (SFCC) graduates are sought-after employees because of the skills they have learned and the attitudes about work they have acquired. The Corps, which began its program with community development block grants, is partially funded by payments for the services it performs. For example, one work crew our Commission visited is learning advanced carpentry and construction skills by converting a cavernous former embarkation pier at Fort Mason into a community theater and cultural center. New corps programs, however, need start-up money before they can establish a reputation for service deserving of public and private contracts.

The Fairmont Park Urban Ranger Program, created by the William Penn Foundation of Philadelphia, combines service, employment training and college course studies. This new $13 million project serves 80 young people who have completed high school, but need additional training and job opportunities. At the end of four years, there will be 120 fully-trained Rangers who have also completed two years of coursework at Temple University. The goal of the uniformed Rangers is to restore and maintain Fairmont Park as a place of beauty, safety, and civic pride.

The City Volunteer Corps of New York City (CVC), with an annual $8 million budget from the city, has pioneered volunteer efforts in human service delivery. Conscious of the need for broad economic and ethnic participation, CVC has also started a summer program for high school youth who work full-time in the summer and part-time during the school year. In Summer 1988, CVC instituted a small program for students already in college in the city, offering summer stipends and bonuses for one and two semesters of part-time Corps work while continuing college. The 600 CVC volunteers fan out daily across the city in their uniforms sporting the CVC Big Apple logo. Their projects are located in city parks, building rehabilitation, centers for retarded adults, nursing homes, and schools. Every three months the volunteers change projects so that participants have environmental, construction, and human service work experiences during a one-year period. CVC also offers completion incentives: $2,500 for those who complete one year of service or $5,000 toward college for those who choose to resume their studies.

The New York City model spawned Youth Volunteer Corps of Greater Kansas City in which 40 percent of the first 76 volunteers were minority group members. A recent urban corps effort, Boston's 'City Year', has the added feature of adult mentors from the civic and business community who are paired with youth corps participants. Organizer Michael Brown says, "We see youth service as a way to break down barriers.... This is citizenship at the broadest level."

Public/Private Ventures, a research and evaluation institute based in Philadelphia, studied nine representative corps programs across the nation and in Canada that have similar goals but different settings and approaches. P/PV found that:[32]

- The Corps produced a large volume of quality work of considerable value to the communities in which they operate.
- The traditional rural corps model of physical work has been successfully translated in the urban environment to human service work.
- Youth corps do not include diverse populations; most are fairly homogeneous, with populations that have major educational and economic needs.
- Corps are highly successful in promoting youth development through the work process and team involvement, but less successful in improving basic skills and educational attainment.
- Programs produce in-program benefits for all corpsmembers and significant post-program economic benefits for disadvantaged corps members.
- Non-economic benefits were mixed, depending on whether or not explicit mechanisms were in place to achieve them.

- A cost/benefit analysis of the California Conservation Corps shows that the combined value of its work and impact on post-program earnings very nearly equals the cost of running the corps and that this finding is likely to be true of other corps as well.

The most serious concerns of the P/PV assessment have to do with the important relationship between education and work. Youth corps programs, particularly newer ones, are seeking solutions by variously mandating that all youth participate in a formal educational component, offering individually-based competency remediation, or awarding cash scholarships for completion of the program. In addition, a lack of diversity in most corps populations means that stimulating interaction among participants from different backgrounds is often missing.[33]

One-third of SFCC volunteers drop out in the first month despite the lure of a $100 bonus for 60 days of perfect attendance. The attrition rate of New York City's CVC, 25 percent in 1988, decreased gradually over its five-year history as different approaches to retain Corps members were successful. Local situations demand local solutions. What works for some will not work for all. *The Commission strongly supports the youth corps concept and encourages — as elsewhere in this report — the use of diverse methods to achieve the same goals: that youth learn, work, participate, and contribute.* We suggest state and local planners consult the experience of existing programs before they design their own. Briefly stated, experienced corps leaders recommend that corps:

- promote the idea that communities need young people just as youth need community support;
- provide work and life skills and continuing education for corpsmembers;
- serve a public need by producing tangible products that have lasting value and economic benefit to their communities; and
- be environmentally sound.[34]

The relationship of youth corps to community business and industry is clear. Chevron loaned a personnel specialist to the San Francisco Conservation Corps. An Oregon logging company retained the corps for after-cut environmental restoration. A New Jersey Corps branch is starting a small business with help from the private sector. Each Boston 'City Year' service team is financed by a Boston area corporation. Conservationists, the elderly, and community safety organizers — interests and constituencies served by youth — need to be enlisted to support other youth corps activities.

Based on the positive results of programs from around the country, *the Commission encourages communities to expand youth corps programs and to combine support from business, local foundations, city and state resources, and grants from organizations that are natural allies of the youth corps movement to begin or extend youth corps programs.*

Toward National Service?

The issue of national service has been simmering on the back burner for some time. The US Congress is considering several efforts to encourage local and state youth service programs. H.R. 18, the proposed Youth Service Corps Act, for example, would establish: (1) an American Conservation Service to improve, restore, maintain, and conserve public lands and resources, and (2) a National Youth Service to encourage young persons to participate in voluntary human service projects.[35] The programs would be open to young people from ages 16 to 25 throughout the year and from ages 15-21 during the summer. The proposed legislation would:

- encourage states and localities to launch their own youth corps activities;
- provide matching funds for start-up and planning of youth corps; and
- offer technical assistance to start-up projects to train successful planners and workers.

In addition, the Act calls for the creation of a 32-member Commission on Service Opportunities to examine major issues associated with national service.

The Commission on Youth and America's Future warmly supports legislation that would provide federal funding to launch youth service programs provided that states and communities would retain wide latitude in the design of programs that meet local needs and preferences. We also support a revitalization of such important national service corps as the Peace Corps and VISTA. Serious consideration should be given to proposals for a National Youth Conservation Corps to work primarily in our national parks, wilderness areas, and national forests.

In 1986, the Coalition for a Democratic Majority proposed voluntary national service that would establish a civilian service component and make federal aid to college students contingent on their "performance of civic duties — either military or civilian."[36] A 1988 report of the Democratic Leadership Council added another ingreo dient to the debate over national service. It proposes voluntary national service with accompanying incentives to persuade many high school graduates, from all economic strata, to choose one or two years of service. The plan would replace existing financial aid grants and loans with vouchers available to youth who complete national service in one of three ways: citizen corps (1-2 years), citizen soldiers (2 years), or career military (4 year minimum). Paralleling a new GI Bill, the proposal offers benefits to the individual and society, a stimulus for more young people to attend college, and long-term financial benefits to the nation in tax revenues and service performed.[37]

The Commission does not endorse a model that ties all education aid to student service. Such legislation would require the poor to serve as a condition of obtaining postsecondary education, while allowing the wealthy to study without assuming any comparable civic obligation. Nevertheless, we recognize this proposal as a possible platform from which to initiate serious discussion about how to combine the three attributes our young people strive for: (1) a sound educational background in high school and postsecondary skills training or college, (2) an economic base from which to build healthy family life, which includes affordable housing and health care, and (3) an opportunity and an obligation to serve and to practice the responsibilities of citizenship. A comprehensive debate over national service is beyond the scope of this Commission, but we support all responsible efforts to bring such a discussion to the forefront.

Service is the most concrete way to inculcate the ideal of reciprocity and civic responsibility that is at the heart of this nation's democratic traditions. It is in giving that one receives, as it is in loving that one is loved.[38] The Commission believes that youth will be better learners, workers, and citizens if they practice serving others early and regularly in their lives.

Pathways to Success:

Recommendations

At the core of citizenship is the willingness to contribute to the common good. When young people are asked to channel their idealism and energy into helping others and solving community problems, they build respect for themselves and attachments to others. Therefore, we recommend:

•   Creation of quality student service opportunities as central to the fundamental educational program of every public school including (a) *either* a requirement that each school provide opportunities to every student for a voluntary service-learning program eligible for elective credit toward graduation, *or* a graduation *requirement* of a specified amount of service; and (b) age-appropriate curricula and instruction, including both service and class-based reflection, during each year from kindergarten through twelfth grade.

•   State-level encouragement of local school jurisdiction efforts to enlist the young in serving their communities including the provision of sufficient financial and technical assistance to ensure high quality programs.

•   Financial support from business, local foundations, city and state resources, and grants from organizations whose constituencies are served by youth — the elderly, neighborhood organizations, and conservationists — to ensure that the maturing effects of service to others will be available to all youth; and the use of diverse methods to achieve the goals that youth learn, work, participate, and contribute.

•   Unification of the many existing organizations interested in expanding youth service into one nationwide service federation.

•   Support for federal financial assistance to launch youth service programs provided that states and communities retain wide latitude in the design of programs that meet local needs.

•   Revitalization of existing national service programs such as VISTA and the Peace Corps, and serious consideration to proposals for a National Youth Conservation Corps to work primarily in national parks, wilderness areas, and national forests.

Footnotes

[1] Bureau of the Census, *US Statistical Abstract: 1988*, 108th Edition, Table 419, p. 250. Curtis B. Gans, director of the Committee for the Study of the American Electorate, links the decline in voting with a general decline in civic involvement: Michael Oreskes, "An American Habit: Shunning the Ballot Box," *New York Times*, January 31, 1988, p. E5. Herbert J. Gans, "Is Voting Just for 'Upscale' People?" *Washington Post*, July 8, 1988, p. A23, argues for substitute forms of participation that might make American Democracy more representative. See also Frances F. Piven and Richard A. Cloward. *The Class Gap: Why Americans Don't Vote*. New York: Pantheon, 1988.

[2] Daniel Yankelovich, *New Rules: Searching for Self-Fulfillment in a World Turned Upside Down*, New York: Random House, 1981.

[3] Robert Bellah et al. *Habits of the Heart: Individualism and Commitment in America Life*. New York: Harper and Row, Perennial Library, 1985, pp. 194-95.

[4] Dan Conrad and Diane Hedin. *A Guidebook on Volunteer Service and Youth*. Washington, DC: Independent Sector (1828 L St., NW, Washington, DC 20036), 1987, p. 3.

[5] *The Forgotten Half: Non-College Youth in America*. Washington, DC: YAF, January, 1988, pp. 47-50.

[6] Bellah et al., p. viii.

[7] Wayne Jennings and Joe Nathan. "Startling/Disturbing Research on Program Effectiveness," *Phi Delta Kappan*, March 1977, pp. 568-72.

[8] Stephen F. Hamilton and R. Shepherd Zeldin, "Learning Civics in the Community," Toronto, Ontario, Canada: Ontario Institute for Studies in Education, John Wiley & Sons, 1987, pp. 407-20.

[9] Charles Harrison, *Student Service*, Princeton, NJ: Carnegie Foundation for the Advancement of Teaching, 1987, pp. 63-64.

[10] Deirdre Carmody, "Freshmen Found Stressing Wealth," *New York Times*, January 14, 1988, p. 14.

[11] Commission on the Future of Community Colleges. *Building Communities: A Vision for a New Century*. Washington, DC: American Association of Community and Junior Colleges, 1988, p. 49.

[12] Letter to the Commission, July 12, 1988.

[13] Jane Kendall, "Commentary" on Anne C. Lewis, *Facts and Faith: A Status Report on Youth Service*. Washington, DC: YAF, 1988. Lewis' survey is a major source of information for this chapter. See also Stuart Langton and Frederick T. Miller, "Youth Community Service: A New Era for America's Ethos of Community Service," *Equity and Choice*, Vol. 4, Spring 1988, pp. 25-34; National Society for Internships and Experiential Education, Janet Luce, ed. *Service-Learning: An Annotated Bibliography*, Raleigh, NC: National Society for Internships and Experiential Education, 1988.

[14] Lauren Resnick, "Learning In School and Out," President's Address, Washington, DC: American Educational Research Association, 1987. See also the two commentaries by Albert Shanker in *New York Times*, June 19 and 26, 1988, p. E7.

[15] Sue Berryman, "The Economy, Education, and At-Risk Children: What Do We Need and What Do They Need?" Paper presented to Education Writers Association. Racine, WI: Wingspread Conference Center, Fall 1987; Berryman, "Breaking Out of the Circle," New York: National Center on Education and Employment, Teachers College (Box 174, Columbia University, New York, NY 10027), 1988.

[16] Stephen F. Hamilton and L. Mickey Fenzel, "The Impact of Volunteer Experience on Adolescent Social Development: Evidence of Program Effects," *Journal of Adolescent Research*, Vol. 3, No. 3, Summer 1988.

[17] Melvin D. Levine, MD. *The Difference that Differences Make: Adolescent Diversity and Its Deregulation.* Washington, DC: YAF, 1988.

[18] Hamilton and Fenzel, "The Impact of Volunteer Experience on Adolescent Social Development."

[19] Dan Conrad and Diane Hedin. *Experiential Education Evaluation Project.* St. Paul, MN: University of Minnesota, 1982, as cited in Lewis. *Facts and Faith*, p. 6.

[20] Stephen F. Hamilton, "Adolescents in Community Settings: What is to Be Learned?" *Theory and Research in Social Education*, Vol. 9, No. 2, Summer 1981, pp. 23-28.

[21] Richard Danzig and Peter Szanton. *National Service: What Would It Mean?* Lexington, MA: Lexington Books, D.C. Health, 1986.

[22] Frank Slobig and Calvin George. *Blueprint for Community Service and Youth Employment.* Washington, DC: Roosevelt Centennial Youth Project, 1984.

[23] Lewis, *Facts and Faith*, p. 7.

[24] Anne C. Lewis, "Learning to Serve," *Basic Education*, Vol. 31, No. 8, April 1987, p. 8.

[25] Lee M. Levison, *Community Service Programs in Independent Schools*, Boston, MA: National Association of Independent Schools, January 1986.

[26] Lewis. *Facts and Faith*, p. 11.

[27] Constitutional Rights Foundation, 601 South Kingsley Drive, Los Angeles, CA 90005 (213)487-5590.

[28] Charles H. Harrison. *Student Service, The New Carnegie Unit;.* Lawrenceville, NJ: Princeton University Press, 1987; Ernest Boyer, *High School: A Report on Secondary Education in America.* New York: Harper and Row, 1983.

[29] Alvia Branch, Sally Leiderman, and Thomas J. Smith. *Youth Conservation and Service Corps: Findings from a National Assessment.* Philadelphia, PA: Public/Private Ventures, December 1987, p. i.

[30] Jane Lee J. Eddy, Remarks to Conference of National Association of Service and Conservation Corps, April 7, 1988.

[31] Anne Wyman, "Group Hopes Summer Vacations Create an Urban Peace Corps," *Boston Globe*, April 19, 1988, pp. 29, 43. A description of current

youth corps may be found in Lewis. *Facts and Faith*, or obtained from Human Environment Center, Suite 507, 810 18th St., NW, Washington, DC 20006 (292)393-5550.

[32] Branch, Leiderman, and Smith, pp. iv, v.

[33] Branch, Leiderman, and Smith, p. 8.

[34] National Association of Service and Conservation Corps. "Recommendations for Quality Program Development." Washington, DC: Human Environment Center, 1988.

[35] HR 18, US House of Representatives, 100th Congress, 2d Session.

[36] Coalition for a Democratic Majority. *Military Manpower: National Service and the Common Defense*. Washington, DC: October 1986.

[37] Democratic Leadership Council. *Citizenship and National Service: A Blueprint for Civic Enterprise*. Washington, DC: May 1988.

[38] St. Francis' Prayer for Peace.

Policy Statement from the National Association of State Boards of Education

State boards should encourage every school to develop community service programs as an integral part of the elementary and secondary learning process. There is now documentation that participating in structured community service provides significant benefits to both young people and their communities. Specifically, community service:

- contributes to the maturing process by placing students in situations that demonstrate and require independence of action, decisionmaking, and caring for others in the community, and by giving students a sense of belonging in the adult world. This in turn helps build identification and self-esteem.

- promotes intellectual development through reasoning skills, problem-solving, organization, and interpersonal relations. As opposed to much of the abstract, independent work done in school, service projects provide students with hands-on, experiential learning in a collaborative setting.

- develops a sense of social responsibility, an empathy for the conditions of others, and a corresponding sense of obligation to contribute to society.

- emphasizes the inherent value of performing voluntary service over approaches that offer financial incentives or government entitlement in return for voluntary service.

State boards should foster these activities through encouraging local school districts and schools to offer all students opportunities to participate; ensuring that service learning experiences are monitored and evaluated; ensuring that local districts and schools help students make connections between their service learning experiences and the rest of the educational program; encouraging local districts and schools to explore ways to develop effective community service curriculum; and exploring opportunities for community service to be offered during the school day and/or for academic credit.   — October 1989

A Voice for Reform

James Kielsmeier

The National Youth Leadership Council's President Jim Kielsmeier calls for a radical transformation of the climate and culture of education. Reprinted from Experiential Education, *National Society for Internships and Experiential Education, Vol. 14, No. 4, p. 23.*

SHINING BLACK HAIR, agile bodies and alert faces filled the baseball field at Camp Lutherhoma. One hundred yards west the Illinois River sluggishly wound its way past the camp emptying into the rugged Ozark foothills of northeastern Oklahoma. The moist, green forest canopy of late spring in the Cherokee Nation resonated with life while, for most of the 84 Native American children on the baseball field, a death ritual would soon begin. Their next school year was the first year of high school, when nearly half of Oklahoma Cherokee children drop out. Only between 30 and 40% ever graduate.

I had read these and similar statistics years before about special groups of American children, but never reflected as deeply on their significance. I have come to know and respect the Cherokee children of northeastern Oklahoma. They are bright, caring and healthy, much like any group of junior high kids, a perception which stands in stark contrast to the school failure and life of unrealized potential that most face. Born of a minority culture, with darker skin than European-Americans and often burdened by impoverished, fractured family lives, most of these children will never glimpse a flicker of the American dream, or any dream. Like the title of Johnathan Kozol's scathing book about the Boston Public Schools, *Death at an Early Age*, a kind of death descends on these children as vectors of social pathology converge in the alienating context of the American public school.

Camp Lutherhoma changed my life. I had worked with youth in Spanish Harlem, Washington, D.C., Denver and St. Louis, but never before had the tragic dissonance between many children and school been so obvious, and the need for a new path to alleviating this national tragedy so compelling. Reconstruction of the institutions of society which affect children came to dominate my thinking and command the choices I would make for my life. I also came to see my tools as an experiential educator as picks and shovels for social and educational reform.

In the hands-on, experiential setting of camp, the children of Oklahoma brightened and grew. They learned basic skills in the context of cultural tradition, they studied and played in a cooperative climate which produced good feelings, enhanced relationships with peers and adults, and strong motivation to learn. The children left camp to take on programs of service in their community — to give back, and know the genuine sense of self which comes from being authentically useful.

By 1984 it was apparent that the time had come to speak to a larger audience about what I knew and believed about experiential education/service-learning and its role in educational reform. Shortly after formation of the National Youth Leadership Council, I took the first step by crafting a goal stating that service-learning programs using well-designed experiential methods should be part of the growing up experience of every Minnesotan, and every young person in the nation. This audacious statement of purpose launched NYLC into "the policy domain" and a five-year legislative battle.

In 1987, due in part to the work of NYLC, youth development legislation was passed in Minnesota to fund Community Education to convene community members, including youth, for the purpose of creating new youth initiatives. By 1989 school districts which served 80% of the state population had initiated plans. Approximately $1 million per year was invested in these new programs. In 1989 legislation increased youth service funding to include service-learning in schools and colleges. The State Board of Education now requires all schools, K-12, to offer service opportunities to students.

Minnesota's policy strides are mirrored by similar activities underway in other states, notably Pennsylvania, California, and Ohio. President Bush joined the service bandwagon in June with his Points of Light Initiative, and this fall Congress will likely pass a National Youth Service bill. The Federal initiatives in particular are driven by a newly defined "national service" interest emphasizing citizenship and voluntarism. Laudable as these outcomes are, proponents neglect the educational reform implications of national youth service.

Service-learning in schools and colleges not only introduces active citizenship to the curriculum, it brings with it the compellingly democratic methodology of experiential education. It requires the classroom to become more participatory as students become owners and designers of their learning.

It is time for the voices of those who understand the linkages between learning and service to be amplified and heard. This country's greatest threat is not beyond our borders, it is in the disparity of development among our children. Many children are not adequately motivated nor effectively engaged in learning. Schools are frozen in tired patterns of teaching which reach a declining percentage of young people.

We must move beyond the superficial rearranging of school schedules and school years to a radical transformation of the climate and culture of education. Our tools as experiential educators have been honed through years of labor, but now it is imperative to put them to work in a larger vineyard. We must tell not only our individual stories; we must gather together and press forward with the strength of collective conviction to shape educational policy in this country! The children of Oklahoma, Minnesota, Chicago, Oakland and New York deserve nothing less!

Jim Kielsmeier is President of the National Youth Leadership Council in Minnesota.

PART IV

Institutional Policy Issues and Guides

Action Steps from a President's Perspective
The Faculty's Role in The Public Service Initiative

This manuscript was prepared by Timothy Stanton as a background paper for "Linking Service to the Curriculum: The Faculty Role," a session convened by Presidents Donald Kennedy of Stanford University and David Warren of Ohio Wesleyan University at the Campus Compact National Meeting on January 20, 1988, in Washington, D.C. To fit your local context, you may want to substitute "community and public service" or "service learning" for the term "public service" used here.

CAMPUS COMPACT HAS BEEN successful in stimulating student involvement in public and community service. Signs of change can be seen in the increased number of service projects and organizations: both are proliferating on our campuses, and they are receiving increased institutional support. At both state and federal legislatures, policies have been established to encourage students to become involved in public service and to help institutions remove financial disincentives to service involvement. At meetings of higher education administrators, there is increased discussion of the need to educate students toward an understanding of social problems and an awareness of the traditional responsibilities of democratic citizenship.

With some exceptions, however, faculty have been noticeably absent from these activities. Little attention has been given to the faculty role in supporting service efforts on the part of students, and in setting an example of civic participation and leadership through their own efforts. What institutional recognition and reward systems can we develop to provide faculty with incentives for becoming more involved?

In addition, and perhaps more importantly, we presidents have had little discussion on how faculty can enable students to integrate their civic concerns and service-based learning with their education. What curricular structures and pedagogical practices exist, or can be developed, which would provide incentives to faculty to consider this question and enable them to support our initiative in this manner? It is time to turn our attention to these matters.

The Issues

What is the faculty's role in supporting student interest and involvement in public and community service? As teachers in the formal curriculum? As advisors? As project sponsors and participants? As role models? How can institutions better recognize and reward faculty for these activities?

The answers to these questions will vary according to the institutional context and resources. What is appropriate at a residential liberal arts institution may not be possible at a commuter college, or *vice versa.* Nevertheless, we have an obligation to stimulate our faculty and staff to propose recognition and reward systems that will elicit greater faculty support for students' public service involvement.

This need for increased faculty support cuts across an active existing debate on many campuses, one that concerns faculty responsibilities for and involvement in co-curricular activities in general. This overlap provides a timely opportunity for directing attention to these questions.

How can faculty members play a stronger role in enabling students to link their public service and academic experiences, to integrate their service-based and academic learning, to connect study with service so that the disciplines illuminate and inform students' service and so that service experience lends meaning and energy to the curriculum? What structures and practices exist, or can be developed, which will enable faculty to better play this critical role?

These are more complex issues which lack simple solutions. Work and academic learning are separate activities on most of our campuses — a separation that reflects higher education's traditional distinction between theory and practice. But that separation inhibits both the effectiveness of experiential learning by students *and* the depth of their involvement. It relegates the development of young citizens who are committed to thoughtful, value-oriented participation in public life to be an accidental, secondary outcome of education instead of making it an explicit educational objective.

These difficulties must be confronted by each of the disciplines — not just by the social sciences, which often support and sponsor practica, field study, or internship courses in public service areas. Faculty in the humanities have the same responsibility for assisting students to reflect critically about their public service experiences and to relate them to broader academic and vocational purposes as do their social science colleagues. Indeed, an examination of the traditions of liberal arts education, civic education, and public service suggests that combining service and learning can strengthen both undergraduate education and student service in the community.

As Georgine Loacker and her Alverno colleagues point out in a U.S. Department of Education publication (forwarded, ironically, by William Bennett), those who are liberally educated are those with abilities to make "an action out of knowledge — using knowledge to think, judge, decide, discover, interact and create." As Richard Morrill says in *Liberal Education*, "Education for democratic citizenship ... requires more than knowledge and information; it includes the exercise of personal responsibility, active participation, and personal commitment to a set of values." Do we meet these educational goals for our students when their education and their public service interests and involvement are separate, compartmentalized parts of their college experience?

How can faculty effectively enable students to integrate the experience of public service with academic learning? Surely part of the answer is: through the development of instructional programs, courses and methods in which students are encouraged to think critically about their service experience and integrate that thinking with concepts represented in the disciplines. For example:

- academically sponsored *internship or practica courses* may require students to engage in service as a primary learning activity designed to illuminate, explain or question a set of theories, or apply a body of knowledge.

  Example: At San Diego State University, political science majors take a course that requires them to undertake training in community mediation skills and to work afterward in the city's community dispute mediation center. Through a concurrent seminar, students explore their experience for applications and testing of political science theories relating to conflict and compromise.

  Example: At institutions across the country, "practicum" courses enable psychology students to explore discipline-based theories and issues, and develop para-professional skills through service in day care centers, hospitals, work with the handicapped, etc.

- *Field study and interdisciplinary courses and programs* utilize community-sponsored research, policy analysis, or volunteer work as a means for learning about a set of intellectual questions.

  Example: Cornell University's Field and International Study program in New York City places students in service-learning internships with public and private organizations to help them learn about "the ecology of urban organizations." As part of their experience students work on a group action research project — most recently with the Essex Street Market Tenants Association.

  Example: At Duke University "The Leadership Program" provides a related series of courses, "projects aimed at the common good," and internships designed to "help students deepen and act upon their own capacities for leadership."

- *Independent and group study mechanisms* may enable students to contract with faculty for academic supervision and sponsorship of learning resulting from their public service work.

  Example: At Stanford University a group of students has been researching service needs for homeless people for a San Francisco Bay Area community organization, and they are now working with faculty to develop a seminar on homelessness.

  Example: At the University of California at Santa Cruz, the Merrill College Field Program enables students to propose independent service learning projects in both domestic and international arenas. Students participate in academic seminars both before and after their off-campus experiences.

  Example: At Worcester Polytechnic Institute, the Interactive Qualifying Project challenges students to "identify, investigate, and report on self-selected topics relating some aspect of science and technology to social needs and social issues." Many of these projects take students off campus and have direct service impact.

- Students can be encouraged to select analysis of a *community service experience* in place of a library research paper or *for additional credit* in a regular academic course.

  Example: At UCLA the Office of Field Studies Development trains graduate teaching assistants to assist faculty who agree to let students undertake field study in the community in lieu of traditional academic research papers. Faculty in history and English utilize this service as do those in sociology, psychology, etc.

Example: At Stanford an anthropology professor who instructs a course entitled "Aging: From Biology to Social Policy" encourages students to volunteer in organizations working with elderly people to explore applications of course subject matter in "the real world" for an additional credit.

Good models of effective academic programs that integrate public and community service with the curriculum exist in our member institutions. We need to examine how these programs function and recognize their accomplishments. There are additional resources for assistance to campuses seeking to address these issues within Campus Compact and through other organizations like the National Society for Internships and Experiential Education. We need to be certain that faculty and staff on our campuses who share our concern are aware of these resources and can gain easy access to them.

Action Steps

Other immediate steps can be taken by presidents. Our role as presidents is to support faculty who participate in the public service initiative now, to stimulate others to get involved, and to recognize those instructional pioneers who are developing means for students to integrate service and learning. These are the action steps you as a president can take:

- Establish on your campus a faculty committee on public service whereby prestigious faculty are charged with considering means for strengthening campus support for students' interest and involvement in public issues, and for ensuring that these activities are both challenging and educational.
- Have your faculty committee suggest means for recognizing faculty members who sponsor and supervise students' service learning through courses and independent studies — for their involvement in the development of civic-minded students, as well as for their practice of an innovative and effective teaching methodology.
- Sponsor a forum through which faculty members discuss the issue of integrating public issues and students' public service involvement within the curriculum and explore methods for

doing so. For example, do core courses related to western culture requirements explicitly address questions of civic responsibility or the relationship of the individual to the state in history? In the present? Could departments offer reflective seminars which have participation in an internship as a prerequisite?

- Offer tangible rewards and incentives such as released time, research support, and support for service learning course development for: faculty who set effective citizenship examples through their professional responsibilities and as community volunteers; faculty who support students' service efforts; and faculty who develop and teach courses which effectively link service and academic learning.
- Establish a fund to support faculty who want training and instruction in integrating learning that arises from students' public service activities into their regular course curricula.
- Consider the development of a summer public service fellowship or stipended internship program for faculty seeking direct involvement in public issues and human service organizations.

Public service advocates have tended to focus on the virtues of service and the resulting personal development of students rather than on academic learning from service activities. Administrators of public service programs, concerned with getting students into the community and based in student or religious affairs sectors of their institutions, rarely think of themselves as instructors. Faculty, while often recognizing the important values of service, have tended to remain on the sidelines — viewing service as inherently lacking in academic substance, and best pursued by students and staff people apart from the academic program. These trends tend to reinforce each other, with the result that faculty involvement in the initiative for social responsibility is less than it might be. Thus, educational issues that relate to public service and lie within the faculty's responsibility may never be addressed without some encouragement and support.

This period in which higher education is experiencing intense examination and external criticism regarding basic purposes is an appropriate one in which to engage the support of our faculty in putting education for social responsibility squarely within the mission of higher education.

Supporting Service-Learning in the Economic System of Your Institution

Jane Kendall, John Duley, Thomas Little, Jane Permaul, and Sharon Rubin

This chapter summarizes suggestions for supporting the use of experiential education — the teaching methods essential for combining community service and learning effectively — in the economic system of a college or university. Adapted with permission from Strengthening Experiential Education Within Your Institution *by Jane Kendall, John Duley, Thomas Little, Jane Permaul, and Sharon Rubin, National Society for Internships and Experiential Education, 1986, pp. 108-111, 117-119.*

No matter how good your program is, it will not last long if it does not have value in the economic system of your institution. There are many ways to consider value in an economic system. One that eventually arises in any service-learning program is that of financial value *for the institution*. How does service-learning fit into the economic system that eventually generates "student contact hours" and pays faculty salaries?

How can your school design (or re-design) community service-learning in a way that is consistent with the dominant model for allocating instructional resources? Start with the unit currency of higher education resources — the 50-minute hour of classroom instruction. Faculty work load is generally measured by the number of 50-minute units provided during a week. Allocating institutional resources by such a simple time measure may be questionable, but it is unlikely that you can change the system to secure recognition of another currency. The quantification of public higher education by state agencies, acting under a mandate to provide equitable allocation across institutions, is simply too powerful a trend to challenge successfully. While private schools have more flexibility, they have generally adopted a similar measure by time or tuition credits.

Tom Little summarizes the question of working within the institution's system:

> I am concerned that we try to support an alternative program in a traditional system. You have to make some decisions. Are you going to try to contest that system — and probably lose? Or are you going to try to develop a model that can accommodate that system? It works better for a longer time if you try to make it work within the system instead of trying to turn the system on its head so you can have a little piece of it. It's a matter of either being part of the institution or trying to exist in spite of the institution. You know which approach will probably succeed over time. If your program is not part of the culture, it won't be part of the institution's resources for long.[1]

Alternatives to classroom-based instruction — such as service-learning and other approaches using experiential education — have to seek positive accommodations within the current system for allocating resources. Programs and courses that follow the principles described below are more likely to meet this challenge successfully because they emphasize the unit currency — faculty work load in terms of credit courses taught — and make minimum claims on other types of institutional resources. The principles are:

1. **Experiential education programs and courses should usually be credit bearing.** Public institutions receive state allocations according to the number of instructional hours provided for academic credit courses. In private institutions, where student tuition provides much of the instructional budget, academic credit for experiential education is usually critical.

2. **Experiential education should provide academic credits which have real value to students.** Most students are not as attracted to — or cannot *afford* to participate in — programs which do not provide credits toward degree requirements. Programs which provide academic credits in the academic major are the most attractive because students concentrate on the major for improving their chances for employability or graduate school admission.

3. **The amount of academic credit from experiential education should accurately reflect the learning achieved.** Except in applied programs where experiential education is traditional, the tendency is to treat experience-based learning as an inefficient learn-

ing mode, deserving only minimum academic credit. Actually, theories of learning suggest that complete, effective learning requires an experiential component. Accordingly, this component should receive due recognition in terms of academic credit.

4. **The variety of learning which can be effectively pursued experientially should be recognized.** Although at least eight different types of learning that result from experiential education have been identified, most faculty consider only one or two possibilities (Kendall *et al*, 1986, p. 32). Recognition of the multiple outcomes of experiential education provides a basis for greater institutional support.

5. **Experiential education should emphasize and document student learning in areas which are seen as academically important and consistent with the institution's mission.** It is unrealistic to expect instructional resources for learning outcomes, such as student career development, which may have minimum academic standing in a particular institution.

6. **Experiential education is best recognized within the institution as a course** — i.e., at least the minimum number of students as required by the institution, learning under the supervision of an instructor, and during a specified academic term. It should be understood, however, that the work tasks of the instructor in field-based courses will differ greatly from those of a classroom lecturer. For examples of how schools and departments make these arrangements, see "Samples of Policies for Faculty Compensation" at the end of this chapter.

7. **Faculty involvement in experiential education is best recognized in terms of teaching responsibility for a course.** A course taught experientially should have the same standing in determining faculty work load as one taught in a classroom.

8. **Academic administrative support for experiential programs other than provided by faculty should be kept at a minimum.** Comparison studies of the time required of faculty for classroom-based and experience-based instruction indicate that the work load is roughly equivalent for up to twenty students. Sinclair Community College, for example, did a time-and-motion study comparing the work requirements of faculty in credited experiential courses and traditional lecture courses. While the tasks were different, the time required was the same. Requests for additional academic administrative support thus may not be well received.

9. **Support services for experiential education should come whenever possible from existing (i.e., already budgeted)**

institutional resources. Instructional resources centers, career centers, faculty development programs, counseling centers, and other existing campus units can help. Such cooperation requires an understanding of the goals of experiential education by all these actors and an institutional commitment to a carefully coordinated effort.

10. **A separate administrative support unit — such as a public service center, service-learning center, or office of experiential education — should concentrate its efforts on coordinating resources and assisting other parties, such as faculty and students, who are responsible for various aspects of service-based experiential learning.** The support unit should not assume responsibility for a program task that can be done by another unit already on campus. If one office tries to do all the tasks itself, the staffing required will be so great that the office will inevitably provide an attractive target for institutional budget cutters. Periodic institutional budget cutting is a predictable process in *any* college or university.

11. **The location of any administrative support unit for experiential education should be consistent with the school's system for managing other educational resources.** At most institutions, this means experiential education is best located within academic affairs, and at large institutions, this means within academic divisions or schools. Programs that use experiential education methods for community service can benefit from this same advice.

Financial Hurdles

The main financial hurdles to making service experiences universally available to students are of two heights. The low hurdle is the administrative one.... Eventually, administrative costs of the service curriculum would probably be built into the overall college budget; in the interim period, outside support appears necessary.

The high hurdle takes the form of economic discrimination as a determinant of who may serve. Scholarship students are often required to work during the school year and the summers in order to maintain their scholarships. If tutoring could be substituted for washing dishes, many more students would be enabled to derive the benefits of a service experience. The Work-Study program under the Higher Education Act makes this possible.... Work-Study funds are clearly a major resource for getting over the financial hurdle to a service experience.

Reprinted from "Service Experience and Educational Growth" by Donald J. Eberly, National Service Secretariat, in Educational Record, *American Council on Education, Spring 1968, p. 8.*

Examples of Policies for Faculty Compensation

Examples of ways that schools have developed equitable arrangements for compensating faculty when they supervise learning in the community rather than in the classroom

• *Most schools that have a policy for compensating faculty for supervising students in experiential learning go by a normal student/ teacher ratio* since the amount of time it takes to supervise students in community service is approximately the same as in normal classroom teaching. At Rhode Island College and Westmont College, for example, supervising students in the field is part of a faculty member's regular credit load. Often the ratio is presented in terms of average class size. The average number of upper division students might be 12-15 per course, for example, and the average number of lower division students might be 15-18. For example, the Faculty Work Load Policy at the College of Public and Community Service, University of Massachusetts, Boston, states: "Field Education: Faculty serve as liaisons for college/agency agreements. Duties include curriculum development, agency linkage, instruction. Time spent in the activity varies, but is substantial. College regulations permit the assignment of instructional load equivalent to one scheduled course for each agency agreement that includes ten or more students." At many institutions, such as the University of Maryland, faculty who sponsor a number of students may organize a seminar for all their students rather than seeing each one individually.

• *At some schools, faculty get credit "after the fact."* For example, a professor may sponsor 12 students in service-learning this spring, then get released time in the fall for the equivalent of one course. In this case 12 students form an average class size. This is the policy, for example, at George Mason University. At small colleges where it may be difficult for one department to have enough students on field experiences at one time to make up a course, there are several creative solutions possible. At Guilford College, faculty members accrue credits for sponsoring students on internships and community service-learning until they build up enough for released time from one course. In many small colleges, some departments sponsor enough students each semester to provide one course for one faculty member as the coordinator and sponsor. This is the case in the Psychology Department at Hartwick College, for example, and in several departments at Westmont College. Guilford College and Westmont are also examples of colleges that group different majors into one course as a way to offer field experiences to majors from several departments. Such groupings also pave the way for excellent interdisciplinary seminars concurrent with the students' community experiences.

- *At some schools, faculty are compensated on an overload basis for each student supervised.* This is the practice at the University of Maryland's University College, Mary Washington College, and Flint Community College. The range quoted in the mid-1980s by these and other institutions was $50-250 per student. Some schools use this overload model only for summer internships.

- *Some schools pay faculty on a per-student basis, but not as an overload.* At Sinclair Community College in Dayton, Ohio, for example, a faculty member gets .2 credit hour for each student supervised for a quarter. Because Sinclair has 15 credit hours per quarter as the average faculty load (3 credit hours = 1 course), supervision of 15 students on internships is the equivalent of teaching one course (15 x .2 credit hours = 3 credit hours). This credit is recorded on the faculty member's payroll form, and the faculty member is compensated accordingly during the same quarter. Faculty can therefore be paid proportionally for supervising fewer than 15 students on field experiences during particular quarter. Madonna College has a similar policy. Faculty supervising students in the community receive .1 - .3 semester hours per student (.1 semester hour requires one visit and evaluation; .2 semester hour requires two visits and evaluation, etc.). This is the equivalent of a regular course for 10-30 students.

- *Professional schools programs often have a smaller student/teacher ratio for supervision.* When the faculty spend more time on field supervision, such as in social work or other programs involving licensure, the policies often allow for a smaller number of students for the equivalent of one course.

If You Think a Grant is the Answer...

Many institutions approach the National Society for Internships and Experiential Education with questions like "Should we apply for soft money?" or "What foundations give grants for community service-learning?" And often the query is more like "Our grant just ended. How are we going to support our program?" Some tips —

$ Grants can be an excellent way to start something new or "prime the pump" to leverage other sources from the institution on a matching basis. Such funds can motivate people to participate.

$ Grants can be the kiss of death if you expect them to fund basic, ongoing program functions indefinitely.

$ Use grants or other special funds as seed money for the extra push needed at the start of a project or program expansion.

$ Be cautious about seeking grant funds for student or faculty stipends. Once you, the students, departments, or field supervisors get used to a model of soft money for stipends or release time, it is very hard to get the same participants to continue their involvement using their own organizational or individual resources.

$ If you do seek outside funds for program operations, get funds that can be continued for a relatively long time (at least 3-4 years). For example, the University of Virginia once had so many interns in human services that it was able to get United Way funds.

$ If you have a grant or are thinking of applying for one, plan NOW how the institution will fund the program after the grant ends. Sue Williams from rural Coker College suggests, "Do a careful market analysis before applying for a grant. Be sure the area can absorb the number of students you project."

$ If a grant pays for any faculty or staff time, pay for small portions of several persons' time rather than paying for two or three full-time salaries. It is much easier to get several departments to pick up small pieces of salaries later than to try to get new institutional funds for full-time positions.

$ Do not try to do it alone. Work with your Development Office and only approach funding sources that have demonstrated serious interest in related efforts. Each grant application or funding source you approach will require 500% more time than you expect.

Ask and Ye Shall Receive

Sharon Rubin

As experiential educators, we too often slink around the edges of our institutions. We are in some uncomfortable, never-never land between academic and student affairs. We know we are not a department, so we don't have the clout of Biology or English, but we *do* have a significant impact on the curriculum. We serve students, but we have often little connection with the co-curriculum. In short, we don't fit easily into a box on an organizational chart, and we may not feel at home with faculty, students, or administrators.

Because of our discomfort, we may see ourselves as marginal people, or perhaps more positively as educational reformers. In either case, we generally don't put ourselves forward. We don't approach the power centers on campus. We don't ask for our due.

Both at Hartwick College and the University of Virginia, some surprising things happened when the program coordinators *had* to ask for support from their Deans or Vice Presidents. In order to participate in NSIEE's project on "institutionalizing" experiential education, some agreements had to be negotiated between these coordinators and their superiors. In both cases, a monetary commitment had to be sought. And in both cases, the weight of the institution had to stand behind the coordinator's efforts. Guess what happened? They asked, and they got the kind of response they needed — cooperative, interested, and supportive. A few keys to receiving what you ask for are:

- Be able to document in what ways the increased support will lead to excellence in the program.
- Collaborate with other units on campus and other organizations.
- Arrange some funding from another source to prime the pump (surprisingly little will do).
- Indicate thoughtful planning rather than whining.
- Keep administrators well-informed and involved in the program ceremonially or actually.
- Act with confidence in your mission and its significance to the institution.

— *Reprinted from* Experiential Education, *National Society for Internships and Experiential Education (NSIEE), Vol. 10, No. 1, January-February 1985. Sharon Rubin is Dean of the School of Liberal Arts at Salisbury State University and President of NSIEE.*

The Value to the Institution of Combining Community Service with Learning

To the Faculty —
- course revision and development
- greater awareness of the field or profession
- interaction with more mature and directed students in the classroom and in research
- professional growth and development
- state-of-the-art education of faculty through students
- a network of colleagues and contacts outside academia
- possibilities for consultantships and research
- possibilities for leaves or temporary employment

To Academic Departments and Colleges —
- external recognition of students and faculty
- program recognition
- attraction and retention of students
- faculty growth and development
- curriculum development and revision
- access to new research opportunities
- state-of-the-art education
- attraction of funds from new sources
- building of alumni loyalty and faculty self-image

To the University —
- greater service to the public
- faculty growth and development
- attraction and retention of students
- raising of academic standards
- curriculum revision
- better relations with the public and with particular community and government organizations
- enhanced ability to attract funds from the private sector
- better career opportunities for students
- greater access to higher education by a more diverse population and access to research opportunities

— *Adapted from Illinois State University's statement of benefits of its Professional Practice Program directed by Marlyn Lawrentz. Reprinted with permission from* Strengthening Experiential Education Within Your Institution, *National Society for Internships and Experiential Education, 1986, p. 118.*

Footnote

[1] From the "Forum on Institutional Change" sponsored by the National Society for Internships and Experiential Education in Alexandria, Virginia, on June 10-12, 1985.

References

Kendall, Jane C., John S. Duley, Thomas C. Little, Jane S. Permaul, and Sharon G. Rubin,"Supporting Experiential Education in the Financial Structure of Your Institution, " in *Strengthening Experiential Education Within Your Institution*, National Society for Internships and Experiential Education, 1986, pp. 105-119.

MacTaggart, Terrence, and Janet Warnert, "Improving Cost Effectiveness" in *Evaluating Student Volunteer and Service-Learning Programs: A Casebook for Practitioners*, ed. by Michele Whitham, National Center for Service-Learning, ACTION, 1983, pp. 157-173 (available from National Society for Internships and Experiential Education).

Wagner, Jon, "Cost-Effective Design of Sponsored Experiential Education," in *Making Sponsored Experiential Learning Standard Practice*, ed. by Thomas C. Little, Jossey-Bass, New Directions for Experiential Learning, No. 20, 1983, pp. 83-97.

A Student's Advice on Connecting Community Service to the College Curriculum

S. Kim Grose

An undergraduate student at Stanford University offers sound advice to other students based on her own experience and her research in connecting community service to the college curriculum.

BEING EDUCATED IN THE 1980s in the United States has come to mean sitting in classrooms listening to lectures, reading non-fiction, and then writing persuasively and analytically about such readings. Students are programmed to be passive, listening to and regurgitating the knowledge dictated by professors. At the same time, however, many students on college campuses across the country are drawn by their own initiative into active roles in their communities. As volunteers, they thrive in emotionally and physically demanding situations, from homeless shelters to literacy corps. In these positions youth become teachers, for young children or illiterate adults; students work alongside adults, struggling together to understand and solve problems for which neither feels prepared. In the field they are confronted with questions, controversies, and issues that are difficult for anyone to understand.

Given this, is it surprising that many students see little connection between their classroom work and their community experiences? In most schools, community service is an extra-curricular activity, like sports or chorus; motivated students lead separate academic and community lives. Aren't there connections to be made? Wouldn't a political science student understand the nature of poverty and the political system better if he worked at a soup kitchen? Wouldn't a pre-med jock gain knowledge and experience if she also volunteered at a public clinic? While these volunteers are learning more than anyone could plan in advance, where are the academic programs to help them reflect on their experiences, and assimilate the knowledge they are gaining into the wisdom of the campuses?

College graduates who work in the field of public service look back and wish there had been classes to help them relate to different cultures and populations, understand the historical and political background to the social problems they are facing, and connect (or indeed separate) their community obligations and their personal lives. Anne, who worked in the Higher Achievement Program in Washington, D.C. the year after she graduated from Carleton College, recalls,"I was unprepared to deal with the social issues on a personal level. I had studied the philosophical theories of, and solutions to, poverty and racism, but they were not practical theories or solutions that took into account people's emotions. I felt unprepared and alone out there."

Students need the opportunity to test their classroom learning out in the real world. Such opportunities they will surely have in good time, but why not right away, when the academic perspective can still be introduced into their own activities? Students — while they are still students — need the structure and opportunity to reflect on their community experiences and to discuss the issues raised, in order to integrate their new knowledge into their classroom knowledge. Students who do make the connections between their classroom work and their volunteer work are more excited in class and more competent in the field. In class, they have hundreds of questions to ask, personal experiences to share, and a direct interest in material covered in class. In the field, they have a broader perspective of the complexities, the history, and the politics of their work.

By encouraging reflection, group discussion, and increased student-faculty interaction, colleges and universities can help to integrate their students' concerns, and promote students' deeper understanding of, and involvement in, community issues.

What Does It Mean to Integrate Community Service into the Curriculum? It means to:

• Create an atmosphere on campus where community service is not a mere extra-curricular activity, but an integral part of students' intellectual experience.

• Provide formal and informal opportunities for students to reflect on and discuss their volunteer experiences, through the community service program and through regular academic classes.

• Encourage all students to test their academic knowledge in the real world, by getting involved in the community, and to enhance their studied classroom experiences with their spontaneous community knowledge.

• Stimulate not only a student presence in the community, but a community presence on campus; mentor programs, lectures, and faculty and administrative involvement in community service programs set up subtle role models which students notice.

• Promote not only a student sense of obligation to serve his/her community, but an educational institution's commitment to serve its larger community.

What Can Be Done?

Community service directors, administrators, and faculty members all can play important roles in students' efforts to integrate academics and community service.

Community service directors and "green deans" (recent graduates who serve in one- or two-year positions to support students' community service) can integrate their own programs into the curriculum by providing reading materials for interested students, promoting informal group discussions, or holding workshops, lecture series and seminars without regard for academic credit. They can give guidance to students about classes that relate to their community work and help them develop proposals for alternative class projects involving community service.

Faculty members can themselves integrate service into their classes by encouraging students to volunteer, even if it is not part of the syllabus, or by giving students the option of doing a community project instead of a term paper or test. They can advocate that other faculty colleagues do the same, promoting the idea of service-learning and the value of reflection. Often instructors receive little recognition or support for their efforts to develop experiential classes. If their efforts are coordinated with active green deans and students, building a support network and exchanging knowledge of successes and failures, then recognition and support will follow.

Administrators can push for service-learning in their own circles. They can discuss the idea with their trustees, the faculty senate, and other deans and administrators to encourage awareness of the issue, and lay the groundwork for acceptance of the concept. They can single out faculty who provide community options in their classes. They can promote articles about integrating service into the curriculum in newsletters, annual reports, and alumni magazines, also encouraging students to write such articles for publication.

The people with the most power to generate a movement toward integrated service curriculums are the students. An inspired and excited student has more chance of influencing an instructor than a high-level administrator. Students encouraging other students to get involved are more productive than faculty preaching to students to get involved, or green deans holding workshops. Through student-faculty partnerships students can work directly with professors to develop personal alternatives to regular classwork. If there is to be change in higher education in the near future, it will have to be student-initiated.

What Can Students Do?

• The first thing that you can do as a student is realize that you hold a lot of power on campus. Administrators may have a lot of control over many parts of the institution, but when it comes to curriculum, the faculty are autonomous. But what is the role of the faculty? To teach students. What more could a professor want than an eager, active and inspired class? That is your job — to show that you can be eager, active and inspired, given the proper stimuli, which in this case could be community service.

Take an active role in what professors ask of you, and recommend to them what you want to do. Working alone or in teams, you can do a great deal to refocus existing courses by suggesting alternative papers, oral presentations, group projects and debates. With any of these options, get the faculty involved in the process. Let them feel a part of your efforts to integrate your service work and classroom experiences, whether it is with writing a personal proposal or developing an entire class. Professors will be much more receptive to your ideas if they are included from the beginning.

• Create a partnership with a professor. Why?

1) Because faculty ultimately control the curriculum.

2) Because faculty want excited, interested students in their classes.

3) Because faculty will be good advocates in their circles, if you win them over to the value of service-learning (and often they are much more interested than you may think).

4) Because if faculty have a role in the process of integration they will be more receptive to it, rather than having students or administrators decide what they want and handing it to professors.

5) Because a partnership will get faculty involved, will give them a stake in the initiative's success, and will broaden the base of the movement.

How can you create a partenership with a professor?

1) Look in your course catalog for a class that might connect to work you are doing in the community. Good departments to look into are sociology, psychology, anthropology and political science because the connections between their subject matter and community issues are very clear; however, you may know of a great biology professor or math teacher who is interested in social issues.

2) Ask around to find out what professors are sympathetic to the issue of service-learning, or are involved in the community.

3) Let your professor know that you are taking his/her class because you are doing related work in the community and you are eager to learn more about the theories behind it.

4) Let him/her know that you have actually met with a few other classmates who are volunteering and discussed his/her class and how it relates to the work that you are all doing.

5) Propose to him/her that you write your final paper not only on the readings for the class, but also on the direct experiences you have been having.

6) Request his/her help in writing a proposal that would outline exactly what your alternative work would be and how it would be evaluated by him/her.

7) Acknowledge that you are aware of the difficulties in evaluating non-traditional work, but that you will incorporate enough of the traditional reading and writing to allow for a traditional grade.

8) Keep in touch with the professor during and after the class so others can follow suit, and so that you or your community service office can involve him/her in the development of further integration efforts.

• Look into the independent study option, and see whether you and a few friends could get credit from faculty sponsors to read, write and talk about your community work. This most likely would have to be well-defined and well-structured to work. Or, do it yourself and request that you meet with your faculty sponsor on a regular basis to discuss your work. This oral reflection component is important not only for you, but also so that your professor will have a way to measure your performance and evaluate your work. The drawback to this arrangement is that you are requesting time from your professor over and above his/her normal work load, and you may find that some professors would love to do it, but do not have the time to supervise it.

• Find out whether your school has an experimental division of the curriculum where professors can design and teach a class once or twice without the hassle of proposing it to a curriculum board. If you have created a successful faculty partnership, maybe the next time around he/she would be willing to redesign the syllabus through this type of experimental division. The strength of this type of arrangement is there are less politics and pressure involved. A professor might be more willing to try something new on an experimental level, avoiding a major justification in his/her department.

• If you feel more ambitious, try to design your own class that will focus on questions raised in service work. To create a class, think about pulling together a task force of faculty, administrators, community leaders and students to get feedback on ideas and to help you write and present a proposal. Check out whether your school has a mechanism through which innovative classes can be taught. Once you have a proposal together, ask if any professors would be interested in sponsoring a group of students under independent study to take the class. Plan an evaluation of the class and a follow-up report to be used by future students and also to give the school some assurance that you will be accountable for what you propose. Recognize that your class may not be accepted the first or even the second time around, but keep pushing, redesigning and reproposing.

• If plunging into the curriculum right away is too difficult, then start to work from the outside in. Begin with your community service network/center. If you really want volunteer work to be not just an extra-curricular, then bring some academics into your own work and your volunteer center.

1) Start a casual discussion group with some of your volunteer friends.

2) Look out for interesting articles in magazines and newspapers that you could read and discuss with others. Ask your community service director to help you find some books to read.

3) Start keeping a journal on your own of your volunteer experiences, and encourage others to do it as well. This personal

reflection and group questioning will help you to understand your own work in a broader context, and it will also help you in any later attempts to get professors interested in integrating service into their classes. What professor could turn you down if you said, "I have been so interested in how the material you are teaching relates to my work with homeless families, that I have read these articles and discussed them with some of my classmates. Could you give me some further guidance and maybe read my journal to help me understand some of the issues I am confronted with?" Or go even further and ask him/her if you can do your term paper based on your experiences in the community instead of on library research.

What Can Green Deans and Other Community Service Directors Do?

• Rather than mount a huge campaign to change the curriculum, start with what is already in place.

• Encourage students to initiate this movement. Help students develop alternative classwork proposals, and encourage them to create student/faculty partnerships personally and as groups. Know the mechanics of the curriculum and the processes of change, to help students work within your institution's defined methods for change. Educate yourself as to the classes most adaptable, and the professors most agreeable to such student initiatives.

• At the same time that you are working with students to build service into regular classes, build academics into your community service program. By integrating the traditional academic skills of reading, writing and analyzing into community service, you are giving students access to many of the connections between community and classroom experiences, and community service will become less and less an extra-curricular activity. Ask community leaders to come onto campus to lecture or debate. Develop small group extra-curricular seminars and workshops focusing on questions and issues that students bring up in their service work. Suggest reading materials for volunteers and build up a community issues library.

• Create a program where community leaders are mentors for students, hosting informal dinners to discuss community issues, and acting as role models to help students determine possible career paths in public service.

• Match classes taught with community needs. Assess a community need, and arrange a meeting with community leaders involved and professors of related classes to discuss ways to fill the need with student work. For example, host a discussion of technical assistance where officials from government agencies or non-profit organizations outline the statistics they want and the data they need collected. Ask business, computer science, and math professors to decide how they can help get this work completed through their classes. This example brings in students not typically associated with public service, and gives them direct experience in their field. At the same time it provides a valuable community service. This approach also gets the college or university to begin asking the question, "What can we as an institution do to help our larger community?"

• Support faculty who are taking the initiative and developing alternative class projects or giving students community options. Request that the president or another high-level administrator write them letters of recognition and thanks. This token bit of support is a crucial step in keeping faculty involved. Most probably have never received letters from the president, and many may think they are the only ones out there going out on a limb for their students. Let them know who else is integrating the community into classes so they know they are part of a larger movement.

Pitfalls to Avoid

The Assumption that Academic Credit is for the Service Experience Itself

In the 1960s when college students were clamoring for classes that were "relevant," many colleges introduced internship programs and independent study options where a student could receive academic credit for work in the real world. Unfortunately the system was abused by some, with students taking the credit and not following through on the internship, or ultimately doing very little reading, writing, and analyzing (the skills one is supposed to acquire in college). Professors began to guard their right to grant academic credit, refusing to accept anything that was not grounded in traditional classroom work. So, today it is wise not to open up the debate again of whether credit should be granted for "relevant" work in the community. Be sensitive to professors' fears that community service waters down the standards of academic excellence.

To get around this problem, ask for academic credit for the academic work that would be done before, during and after the actual volunteer work. Ask for credit for the papers you write, the books you read, the journal you keep, or the group project that you write up and present, but be careful about asking for credit for the specific hours that you spend in the field. This way professors have a much more difficult time arguing that you are not being "academic". It is simply playing by their rules, and emphasizing the academic component of the project. *Focus on academic credit for what you can demonstrate that you learn, not for the experience itself.*

Unclear Evaluation Standards

One of the questions always asked when the issue of service-learning is brought up is, how do you grade or evaluate what students learn through service? Most internship programs like the Boston College Internship Program and the Washington Center have standard evaluation processes involving academic and field supervisors' evaluations, contracts with agencies, student assessments and a final grade. They are comprehensive in their evaluation, but they may be too time-consuming for smaller-scale alternative class projects.

Professors may be reluctant to accept an alternative class project because he/she may feel at a loss to evaluate your untraditional work. Would he/she have to supervise your field work? Meet with your field supervisor, or just grade the work you produce as a result of your field experiences? If it means any extra work or worry on his/her part you may be out of luck. In developing a proposal with your professor clearly state what form of evaluation you are expecting and based on what. For example, will you write a final paper based on an issue discussed in class with which you have had direct experience with in the community? Will you keep a journal that will be graded? How different will your work be from that of the rest of the class? Will your professor understand your work enough to be able to give you a grade? Bruce Payne, director of the Duke University Leadership Program, suggests that if professors do not have the time or resources to evaluate the field work, then they can evaluate the traditional, academic component of your work: "What is graded is not what you do, but what you write or what you say."

Transplanting Another School's Successful Program

Looking at what other schools are doing can give you ideas for programs and readings, strategies for working with students, faculty members, or administrators, and tools for pressuring your school to follow suit. However, all institutions have different histories and politics that play important roles in the development of the curriculum.

For example, Hamilton College, a small liberal arts college in upstate New York, has a very flexible academic curriculum and students there do not have a hard time creating alternative classes and class projects. Carleton College, on the other hand, a small liberal arts college in Minnesota, has a very traditional curriculum and might have a harder time introducing the notion of service-learning in academic classes where it is not already being used. On the West Coast, Stanford University has an established mechanism for accepting and offering student-designed classes, but because of this option, students may have a more difficult time getting faculty members to accept alternative class projects. Drawing on other institutions' experiments and your own knowledge of your institution, you can help design a strategy suited for your school.

Kim Grose is a senior majoring in anthropology at Stanford University. In addition to her work on her own campus, she spent a summer researching ways that students could become more actively involved in the service-learning movement. She has also been involved in the Campus Outreach Opportunity League (COOL) during her undergraduate years.

Service-Learning and Schools' Three Roles

Eliot Wigginton

Foxfire *creator Eliot Wigginton shows how service-learning can help fulfill the three responsibilities of schools. Wigginton also wrote* Sometimes A Shining Moment, *another valuable resource for those interested in dynamic combinations of service and learning. Reprinted from* Synergist, *National Center for Service-Learning, ACTION, Vol. 9, No. 2, Fall 1980, p. 91.*

THE BEST SERVICE-LEARNING PROJECTS are ideally and uniquely suited to filling all three of the roles that are part of any school's responsibility. These roles are:

- to develop the basic skills and basic academic knowledge of students;
- to develop and nourish the more esoteric appreciations and understandings — the arts, the humanities, the areas of human artistic and moral sensitivity and concern for life on this globe, and the ways to express those appreciations and concerns through action; and
- to develop and foster the qualities students must have for success in any career — curiosity, self-confidence and self-esteem, patience and persistence, vision, leadership, wisdom, and the ability to think creatively, to analyze and problem solve, to make human and wise decisions, and to act on them.

Let me use our Mountain City project as an example of what I mean. To address the first area of development (basic skills and academic knowledge), I met daily for 50 minutes with the students, sometimes also with visitors, such as mayors and architects, who could lead our class discussions onto another plane. The work we did in those classes was largely academic: developing and polishing an effective and forceful slide show script (English and public

speaking); researching the histories of Mountain City and the surrounding towns, their political structures, and their city ordinances
(history and government); charting population changes and trends
— and shifts by percentages of land ownership patterns and economic developments and per capita income — and figuring out
budgets for possible town projects (math and statistics).

Better still was the fact that, as with all activities of this sort, the
academic disciplines were linked and interrelated rather than separated and compartmentalized as in so many schools, and they took
on real life implications.

The second area of development (artistic and moral sensitivity
expressed through action) was addressed through photography
(Which of these 50 color slides took of my town tells its story best?),
through interviews with town residents (What conditions must be
present in any town in order for its residents to feel secure and
happy and comfortable and productive and useful —and thereby
committed to its future?), and through work with landscape architects and city planners (How is a town made to look physically
attractive, for example, and what types of collective action can
enhance its beauty and preserve it, and how can such collective
action lead to an increased appreciation on the part of the residents
for the various needs each of them has and for the ways those
various needs can best be met?).

The third area of development (qualities necessary for success
in any career) was addressed initially by focusing on the students'
sense of their own self-worth and self-confidence, believing that it is
only after students truly believe that they have worth and value that
they can then begin to think about extending themselves to others.
Said another way: It's hard to give unselfishly and naturally to
others until you feel you have something to give. Before the project
started none of the students involved had ever used 35mm cameras,
had ever conducted interviews, had ever spoken before in public,
had ever developed a product like a slide-tape show — had ever
done any of the sorts of things we all did together. Nor had they
ever had reason to believe that the mayor of a town might actually
sit down with them and trade ideas and solutions face to face.

All that changed during the 12 weeks we worked together. And
toward the end, as the town meetings actually began and the students worked with the residents in planning sessions — and had to
work around various political and economic realities — creative
thinking and problem solving became a vital and natural part of
their daily routine.

Over the past 14 years, it has been my experience that in service-learning projects many of the educational and personal benefits I have mentioned happen almost automatically due to the nature and the demands of many of the projects themselves. I also have found, however, that it is not enough to simply assume that they will happen and then charge blindly ahead. Leaders of the best of the projects I have observed carefully build in activities that insure that these benefits happen for all the students involved. They rely on conscious design and rigorous planning and evaluation rather than serendipitous happenstance.

When carefully put together these projects can easily turn into some of the most powerful and positive experiences in a young person's life. And those of you out there doing it deserve more credit and praise than you're probably getting, for through your efforts and energy, in the end, all of us win.

Arguments for Educators: A Rationale for High School Service-Learning Programs

Dan Conrad

Well-known thinker, researcher, writer and practitioner Dan Conrad provides a simple outline of arguments for educators, parents, and administrators. His focus is on high school programs for service-learning, but his arguments are also useful for college- and community-based programs. Adapted from Synergist, *Vol. 3, No. 3, pp. 9-13.*

"There is always the danger in a new movement that in rejecting the aims and methods of that which it would supplant, it may develop its principles negatively rather than positively and constructively. Then it takes its cue in practice from that which is rejected instead of from the constructive development of its own philosophy."

— John Dewey, *Experience and Education*

WE ARE INUNDATED with critiques of the American system, many of which focus on our schools. A good number are thoughtful and articulate, but some are merely diatribes against a system that is "doing us wrong." Some of this is crisis literature, feeding on the deep sense of concern felt in all parts of the land.

As such, it performs a service by articulating these fears, focusing attention on particular ills, and sometimes fostering creative remedies. People are looking for ready solutions, and there is a widespread conviction that any change may be a step in the right direction. Many a proposal has been supported with little more rationale than that "the old way of doing things just isn't working" and "we're not going to make the same mistakes."

We now have a climate of openness to new ideas. It is our responsibility to take advantage of it. As John Dewey reminds us, more is required than a sense of outrage at the status quo, and more is needed than a conviction about the rightness (and righteousness) of our proposed alternative.

Service-learning, if not a new idea, is one that is being developed in new ways. Those of us who support it must be able to present a clear statement of goals for our programs, we must show why and how service-learning is a practicable means to those ends.

The major arguments for service-learning come from a variety of sources — ranging from the sophisticated theories of John Dewey and Jean Piaget to common sense about kids needing experiences beyond the classroom. Advocates can be grouped into three categories according to their attitudes toward (a) general societal needs and the social needs of youth, (b) psychological development of young people, (c) more effective learning of subject matter. While these are not mutually exclusive categories, the division is useful in making the case for service-learning.

Youth's Societal and Social Needs

The objections to service-learning are familiar enough:

"We simply can't have our kids running around the community. We'll be getting irate calls by the dozens!"

"Kids need to learn some discipline, some sense of responsibility before you turn them loose."

"Without training and skills they may do more harm than good."

"There's plenty to do right within the school itself."

"The whole thing is a plot to co-opt kids into the 'system'."

"Leave social action to the churches, the Girl Scouts, and the YMCA."

"I'll be convinced that kids are ready to do something for society when I see them picking up the paper in the halls and volunteering for school committees."

"There aren't enough jobs for them to do out there. I mean, what if all our schools got into this service-learning?"

These are rather crudely-stated objections, perhaps less sophisticated than most, but it's wise to assume that behind them lie legitimate questions about the nature of schooling and concern for the welfare of youth.

Underlying those questions are at least three fundamental issues relating, first, to the relationship between the school and other
institutions in the wider community; second, to the relative role
each must play in the development of youth into adulthood; and
third, the appropriate roles of adolescents in modern society. In
addition, there is a legitimate question about the ability of untrained
youths to contribute to the well-being of society and an understandable concern for the image of the school in the community.

A positive rationale, relevant to such concerns, might be organized around the benefits that a service-learning program can bring
to maturing students, to the community, and to the school itself.

Schools originally were assigned the task of imparting general
knowledge about the world and developing basic intellectual skills,
usually symbolized by the three R's. Other aspects of education —
emotional, social, moral, vocational — were the chief responsibility
of the family, church, and work place. The school's efforts were
largely supplemental and supportive. Now, for a variety of reasons,
the other social institutions are often not able to fulfill traditional
educative responsibilities. Partly by default, the schools have been
left to play a much more comprehensive role in the total development of the young.

Much attention has recently been focused on this situation and
the problems resulting from it. Several recent reports on the status
of youth in the United States have proposed that the dominant
institutions that work for the development of young people are not
adequately preparing them for adulthood.

The argument of some of these reports runs like this:

School occupies an increasingly large portion of a young
person's life, and this has produced certain dislocations.

We are overemphasizing cognitive and intellectual skills, while
opportunities for developing independence and responsibility have
been limited.

Schools provide few opportunities for learning to manage one's
own affairs or for acquiring the ability to take decisive action.

Youth has become too insulated from adults and from the productive tasks of society.

Schools provide few opportunities for participating with other
age groups, for exploring larger sections of economic, political, and
social life, and for learning to care for others.

There is little opportunity, either in school or elsewhere, for a
young person to be a contributor or to be recognized as a contributor; to experience the satisfaction of undertaking a needed task and
completing it creditably; to feel the joy and endure the pain of

significant participation in the world; of acting and not always just preparing for action.

Community Benefits

The problem is not that youths today do not have experiences, but that the experiences open to them are too restricted in variety and quality and do not prepare them adequately for later experiences.

Some of these reports recommend encounters with people in all segments of the community. They encourage responsible work and volunteer experiences in community and public service. They look toward expanding the roles of young people in schools beyond those of tutor and teacher's aide; they encourage intense concentration on a particular activity, and allow for expanded leadership and self-management within youth organizations. Behind these specific recommendations lies an assumption of societal health. If this society is to produce adults who can function effectively as parents, workers, and citizens, new structures and processes for bringing youth into society must be created, either within the school or in cooperation with other institutions serving young people.

There is no need to rely solely on long-run, hypothesized benefits of youth participation. Communities have very immediate needs. In thousands of cities and towns across America and the world, high school students are accomplishing tasks critically needed by their communities.

In one small town their assistance has made it possible for the local school to run its own program for persons with severe physical disabilities. Elsewhere students manage and operate the only available recycling centers. In another city they have convinced a local manufacturer to install filtering devices in smokestacks that had previously enveloped a neighborhood with foul-smelling odors. In still others students are working to record and preserve the history and traditions of their area.

Home economics students provide free pre-school experiences for children; industrial arts students build and reclaim houses for sale at cost to families with low-incomes, while others design and build special equipment for children and adults with physical disabilities. Science students have advised their city government on where a bicycle trail can be laid through a marsh without disturbing the local ecology; math students have done the mapping and surveying for a team of archaeologists, most of whom were high school students themselves; physical education students are teaching swimming, canoeing, and other recreational skills to youngsters with physical and mental limitations.

These and many other examples demonstrate that many young people are willing and able to make a valued contribution toward alleviating their communities' problems.

The major contribution of youth often lies in performing tasks which, while needed and desired, are not high on the list of needs that society is willing — or feels able — to pay for. Many of these are tasks that would lead to tedious and low-paying careers but can be turned into rewarding, short-term experiences. This is not to say that any job will do, but the value of a task is not always well defined by its price tag. Its significance must finally be determined by the doer himself.

It is critical that young people have the power to define needs for themselves. They must be able to make a just claim to a unique contribution. Then young people can bring a spirit of adventure to even mundane tasks. To institutions mired in routine, they can bring a fresh perspective and a new set of skills. To the poor they can bring a sensitivity quickened by their own experience of being without status. To a community grown accustomed to its flaws, they can bring an idealism that demands perfection — and the audacity to try achieving it.

Some critics say that encouraging youth participation in small local projects diverts attention from larger social issues and burns off energy better spent on attacking the basic structural flaws that created these problems. But recent experience supports just the opposite view. Constant focus on the big issues may produce frustration, numbness, and finally withdrawal. Effective concern for "the system" requires direct acquaintance with its casualties, practical knowledge of its existing mechanisms for self-correction, and a sense of personal efficacy. It requires a confidence built not on theory but on the experience of knowing that even in a small way you can make a difference.

This is not to endorse the romantic view that suspects every 16-year old of sainthood. There is a thin line between idealism and self-righteous bull-headedness. Young people can be tactless, impatient, overly critical, and rigid. They often lack skills, knowledge, and a sense of perspective. But why should we expect anything different? Instead, this should reveal that we who believe in them, have an important role in helping them define their concerns and achieve their goals. To let them do it entirely on their own denies the value of our own experience and accepts the artificial gulf that exists between age groups.

The School as a Resource

The concept of service-learning implies a new relationship between schools and the communities they serve. One function that service-learning can perform is that of enabling schools to take the initiative in developing open and mutually supportive relations with the wider community. If schools use the resources, locations, and advice of the community to enrich the educational process, citizens will feel themselves to be a part of the process and begin to look toward the school for assistance in dealing with the community's most pressing needs. As the role of youth expands to become that of both learner and contributor, the school will become a place where students not only come to learn, but from which they go out to share their knowledge, talents, and energy.

Psychological Development of Young People

When parents first come in contact with the idea of service-learning, reactions are sometimes negative.

"The realities of life will hit them hard and soon enough as it is."

"For me, school was reading, writing, and arithmetic, and I done OK."

"The job of the school is to pass on the cultural heritage of our society and to impart the knowledge and skills to enable our youth to become productive, contributing citizens."

"Service-learning is a nice option for kids who have proven themselves capable and responsible in their academic tasks."

"Before kids can give of themselves, they must get in touch with themselves, their own feelings and values. Caring for others presupposes the ability to care for oneself."

"My child's character and personality are no business of the school."

In response to these objections, let us turn to the psychologists with their special concern for the personal needs of the individual adolescent.

Psychologist Erik Erikson, more than any other, has awakened us to the unique and critical nature of the adolescent years. He has characterized this as the period of identify formation, the turning point, the crucial moment in the individual's search for an answer to the question, "Who am I?" But an identity is forged more than found. It is forced through experimentation and risk, through trying out new competencies, through testing different selves. It is refined through reflecting on one's self in relation to a variety of real and imagined models, and is verified by assessing the reactions of others to these attempts at self definition.

The search for self is a drama of contemplation and encounter, which must be played in a real arena, with real choices and real consequences. It is not well-served by the typical school program that turns out students who are, in James Coleman's words, "information rich and action poor."

The concepts of developmental psychology offer more systematic argument for service-learning. Cognitive-developmental theory is grounded in the educational philosophy of John Dewey, and spelled out in the theories of Jean Piaget and Lawrence Kohlberg.

The key argument is that a child's cognitive and moral development occurs through the interaction between the child and his environment and requires active doing combined with active thinking. Passively absorbing knowledge while sitting in a classroom is not a sufficient condition for stimulating growth.

Neither is growth the result of the gradual piling up of knowledge like rocks onto a pile. Rather it is a hard-won movement through distinct stages. Whether or not one reaches his highest level of cognitive and social development is determined by the kind and quality of his experiences, and what is done with them. The essential is conflict. Conflict stretches the child's existing thinking and drives him to seek more adequate ways of reorganizing his experience and action.

Among the practical implications of the developmental theory of education is the need to provide new and stimulating experiences for the student, experiences involving new intellectual challenges and new social roles. These might include being a tutor, nursery school helper, legislative intern, or peer counselor.

But experience alone will not produce cognitive growth. Beyond this, the student must be encouraged to reflect on his experience and be helped to formulate new frameworks for both understanding and interacting with others.

The humanistic, as opposed to the developmental psychologist, would approach the need for non-classroom experiences from a different viewpoint. Given the chance to choose, a person will always choose to grow rather than regress. But this growth is not inevitable. It implies a healthy self-regard, and this requires a supportive social environment. Typically, the humanists argue, the school is not such an environment. With labels, grades, regimentation, and the rest, it is not a fertile ground for developing a healthy view of the self. But simply to replace these with open praise and expressions of love would not be enough.

Strong self-concepts are the result of actual positive experiences in social interaction with a variety of people. Schools must encourage this interaction. Students must have the opportunity to use their school learning in personally meaningful ways. The organization of the school must allow for self-direction, self-discipline, and creative endeavor — all within this supportive environment. The denial of opportunity for choice and for responsible action, the separation of knowing and doing, has led to alienation and an overwhelming apathy on the part of students.

Concern for self must also include a concern for others and a recognition of the interdependence of all human kind. Otherwise, it becomes just another form of self-indulgence. Drawing on this deeper meaning of humanism, educator Mario Fantini has criticized some of the techniques and emphases of his colleagues and has urged that, "Rather than feel the 'joy' of a 'blind walk', why not also feel the 'repulsion' and 'outrage' of seeing children starving? In addition to spending time in peak experience retreats, why not also spend time in state hospitals for retarded children or in despair-laden institutions for the elderly?"[1] Affective education should stress social renewal as well as self renewal. Fantini's remarks clearly convey the message of humanistic psychology. A similar spirit is reflected in Erik Erikson's moving references to an all-inclusive human identity, and in Lawrence Kohlberg's description of the developmental process as culminating in a universal sense of social justice. Viktor Frankl says, "As the boomerang comes back to the hunter who has thrown it only if it has missed its target, man, too, returns to himself and is intent upon self...only if he has missed his mission."[2]

Something in this suggests that we may have to go beyond the formulations of sociology and psychology to capture the full meaning of a student's community experiences. In watching a student working with handicapped children, or in talking with another about her visit to a nursing home, it is clear that something very deep, something perhaps mystical or religious, is occurring within the student. It's more than feeling good about oneself or moving to a new stage of development. It is finding and affirming an identity. It is transcending oneself. Frankl calls it a sense of mission, and that seems close. Is this not part of our rationale for service-learning programs?

More Effective Learning

Not only parents but teachers have objections to service learning.

"We've got too much to teach already! If you insist on service-learning, what do you suggest we take out?"

"It's not real learning."

"The job of the school is to impart academic knowledge and intellectual skills."

"It's marvelous that our young people want to help with these problems, but they shouldn't get academic credit for it. That would cheapen the experience and lower our standards."

For schools to assume that they need concern themselves only with intellectual growth is both naive and self-defeating. It is naive in the assumption that young people will spontaneously flower into mature human beings without the challenges and social interactions that a less schooled society made possible (or mandatory); self-defeating in the assumption that intellectual growth can be achieved without deliberate attention to total personal development.

Even for those educators who see the role of the school limited to the intellectual growth of students, an equally persuasive case for service-learning can be made. An experience-based learning model that requires students to pursue or apply their acquired skills through direct involvement in non-classroom settings can make academic learning more effective.

These programs have the potential of increasing students' motivation. They begin to see the connection between what they learn in school and experiences in the world. I have had students sit fascinated while I read the state regulations on nursing home standards. They listened because they were angry about treatment given to the elderly in a facility where they volunteered. Their motivation to learn the state regulations sprang from their personal involvement.

Furthermore, in these service-learning programs, students have opportunities to generalize and transfer their school learning to problems confronting them outside school. For example, a student in a psychology course can better remember and understand the concept of "individual differences" if he works in a first-grade classroom with children at various levels of physical, intellectual, and social development. The experience gives him the opportunity to gather his own data about child development and to reality-test both his own conclusions and those presented in the classroom and text. It provides an arena in which to practice what is learned, and in which to evaluate the usefulness of acquired knowledge and skills. Finally, by applying academic learning, the students will be able to recognize their successes or errors and receive help if needed.

The negative consequences of separating learning from doing are serious for both students and teachers. Without the experience of finding classroom learning useful, it is difficult to see how one can develop any faith in the value of knowledge. If interest and facility in learning are to continue beyond formal schooling, skill must be gained in learning in non-school settings where all the data is not given, the questions not delineated, the chapters not outlined, and the answers not printed in the back of the book.

And If Reason Fails...

If in presenting your case for service-learning, calm reason and practical wisdom fail, here are 10 arguments that will at least make you feel better for trying:

1. *Why can't we...* "Why is it considered educational for a student to leave school to work as a soda-jerk but not to volunteer in a nursing home or intern at city hall?"

2. *Everybody's doing it...* "In a survey by the National Association of Secondary School Principals, more than 2,000 high schools reported having some kind of action-learning program." [Recent surveys by the National Association of Independent Schools, the Council of Chief State School Officers, and the Carnegie Foundation for the Advancement of Teaching document the current widespread use of community service by K-12 schools across the country.]

3. *It's safe...* "This isn't a radical new proposal but a return to the oldest idea in education — learning by experience."

4. *Appeal to prejudice...* "Our teachers wouldn't deliberately slant the truth, but shouldn't students also be exposed to the views of business and community leaders and other responsible adults in our community?"

5. *Prestigious endorsement...* "The National Association of Secondary School Principals (October, 1974, *Bulletin*); the National Council for the Social Studies, (Curriculum Guidelines); the President's Advisory Panel on Youth (*Youth: Transition to Adulthood*); [the William T. Grant Foundation Commission on Work, Family and Citizenship, (November, 1988); the Carnegie Foundation for the Advancement of Teaching (Student Service: The New Carnegie Unit, 1987; *High School*, 1983; *College*, 1987); the Carnegie Report on Education and the Economy (*A Nation Prepared*); the National Association of Independent Schools (1986); the Council of Chief State School Officers and the National Association of State Boards of Education (1986); Independent Sector (1986); and the Education Commission of the States (*Reconnecting Youth* and *Higher Education and the American Resurgence*, 1985)] have all called for more service-learning."

6. *Semi-valid analogy...* "You can't learn about people without direct involvement any more than you can learn a language without practice or chemistry without a lab."

7. *Quote a Founding Father...* "As Thomas Jefferson said, 'Knowledge is of little use when confined to mere speculation. But when speculative truths are reduced to practice, when theories, grounded upon experiments, are applied to common purposes of life... knowledge then becomes really useful.'"

8. *Dubious consequences...* "That bond issue will never pass unless we find some way to build better relations with the community, and this is a way."

9. *Loaded terms...* "A commitment to democratic ideals requires that the school abandon futile efforts to insulate pupils from social reality, and, instead, find ways to develop the habit of participation in our future citizens and leaders."

10. *Name calling...* If even these fail and you're dragged screaming to the door, try yelling, "You wouldn't recognize a good idea if it came up and slapped you in the face!"

Dan Conrad directs the Community Involvement Programs at Hopkins High School in Minnesota. He coordinated the Student Community Involvement Project at the University of Minnesota's Center for Youth Development and Research. He has done extensive research on the impact of experiential education on students' learning and written numerous books and articles on service-learning, youth participation, and experiential education.

Footnotes

[1] Fantini, Mario, "Humanizing the Humanism Movement," *Phi Delta Kappan*, February 1974, p. 401.

[2] Frankl, Viktor E., *The Will to Meaning*, New American Library, New York, 1969, p. 38.

Rationale: Selling the Youth Service Learning Program

Dan Conrad and Diane Hedin

Reprinted with permission from Youth Service: A Guidebook for Developing and Operating Effective Programs *by Dan Conrad and Diane Hedin, Independent Sector, 1987, pp. 50-56, 61. The term "youth service" as used here includes an emphasis on combining service and learning.*

KNOWING THAT YOU WANT to organize a youth service program, having projects for young people to do, and developing a plan for incorporating service into your overall program are necessary but not sufficient conditions for actually implementing the plan. Usually someone else must be convinced — either to allow it to be tried or continued, to provide resources for it, or to become a part of it. Overcoming this hurdle is the focus of this section.

Most readers of this book already will be believers in youth service, so the arguments presented here are offered primarily as a guide for convincing others. They also may serve as a reminder to practitioners of why they do what they do and as reinforcement for the efforts they are putting forth.

The arguments are presented in terms of anticipated benefits to youth, to the community, and to the school or agency. For consistency — and because decision-makers in this realm may be the hardest to convince — the arguments are stated in reference to schools, with the understanding that all of them could be adapted to other settings as well.

Setting the Scene

It's 8:00 a.m. on a drizzly spring morning. As you stand outside the door of the program committee of ... (you pick it: school, youth agency, church, foundation, etc.) you are reviewing the arguments you have planned to give them.

It was only yesterday the chairperson notified you that some of the committee members had doubts about your proposal and wished to ask some questions. Last night you tried to anticipate their possible concerns and to formulate several concise statements that you could use as various issues arose in the conversation.

To help keep your case focused on the right issues you have sorted them out in your mind as benefits of the program to the community, to your own organization, and to youth themselves.

Benefits to the Community

It's entirely possible that this issue will not even be raised, but it is one you want to be ready for and even raise yourself if the group does not. It is of fundamental importance because the very bedrock of the program is that it is geared to meeting real needs in the community. That the young volunteers will be providing important services is what makes the program vital and real and what raises it above the level of just another activity or lesson.

Imagine, then, that a committee member opens with such a statement as: "It's hard for me to imagine exactly what they're going to do out there. Is there really enough for them to do?" Another comments: "We have enough trouble controlling these kids in our regular program. It's hard for me to see what good they're going to do running around the community like maniacs." A third adds: "We already have high unemployment here and won't this just exploit kids while taking away jobs from people who need them?"

Those questions are just what you were hoping someone would ask, and you are ready.

1. *Cite an obligation to the community.* "Our young people receive a great deal from this community — free education being only one of those benefits. I feel they have a responsibility to acknowledge this debt by returning to it some service of value — even while they are young."

That said, you might need to raise their consciousness regarding the potential contributions that young volunteers can make. The best way to do that is to tell what youth in other areas already are doing.

2. *Note that young people in other communities are making a great contribution.* "There are thousands of examples from all over the country of young people making important contributions to their communities:

- providing services to elderly people in their homes and companionship for those in nursing homes;
- collecting food for the hungry;
- teaching swimming, canoeing, and other recreational skills to handicapped children;
- running recycling centers;
- cleaning rivers and streams;
- turning vacant lots into playgrounds;
- putting out community newspapers;
- using cable TV public access channels to document and dramatize local health and safety issues;
- petitioning city hall;
- serving on civic administrative boards; and
- tutoring their peers and younger children.

"The examples are endless. Our kids are as capable as kids anywhere, and our community's needs as great as those of any other. I think we should be part of this great effort to bring together the energies of kids and the needs of society."

3. *Cite a particular local need.* "We have the highest percentage of people over 70 of any community in the state and they sit there locked up in their homes and apartments afraid that if they come out someone will mug them. We can help change that."

Or you could say: "Nobody else is going to remove that huge pile of debris from behind the playing field, though everyone knows it's a public nuisance. If we mobilize the kids we could do it ourselves in an afternoon. The place would be safer and we would show the neighborhood that we practice what we preach about the environment."

4. *Tabulate how much person-power you have.* "We have 1500 students in our high school. If we averaged one hour of service by each student each week that would add up to more than 50,000 hours of service to the community in one school year (and, figured at the minimum wage, over $200,000 worth of time contributed)."

5. *Promote the school as a center of expertise.* "One of the greatest concentrations of technical know-how and potentially available human energy in this community is right here in this school. Wouldn't it be great if our students and their teachers could go out to apply their knowledge to help their community? We could take the lead in promoting unified efforts to attack some of our most difficult community problems."

6. *Note that a service-learning program can help bring the community together.* "A meeting I propose calling early in the year will involve kids, school administrators and department heads, and representatives of youth agencies, social service agencies, service

clubs, the chamber of commerce, the mayor, and a couple of other groups. We will discuss ways we can work together to improve our community. We all face the same problems and share a stake in solving them. It's time we got together."

7. *Emphasize that volunteers do not replace paid workers.* "I'm sensitive to your concerns about jobs, but the major contribution of young volunteers is usually to perform tasks that, no matter how needed and how much desired, are not very high on the list of things society is willing to pay for.

"A lonely old woman without family or friends deserves to look forward to a visit from someone. It's important that she does. But we're not likely to pay someone to do it — and I'm not sure it would be the same if we did. Because they are young, and precisely because their commitment is voluntary and short-term, young people are able to bring a fresh energy and commitment to tasks that for others would be tedious and burdensome — and not very attractive as careers."

8. *Don't oversell the case.* "I don't mean to endorse the romantic notion that every sixteen-year-old is a candidate for sainthood. Kids also are capable of being selfish, tactless, bull-headed, and undependable. They often lack the skills, knowledge, patience, or sense of perspective a situation demands. This only reinforces the case that they need these kinds of experiences and that we, as adults, have an important role in working along with them and guiding them."

Should you manage to convince — or at least silence — your critics on those issues, you can expect someone to raise another by saying something like: "Don't get me wrong. No one is more in favor of youth doing things for others than I am. It's just that *we* are in the business of ... (whatever) ... not social service."

> *"If this society is to produce adults who can function effectively as parents, workers, and citizens, then new structures and processes for socializing youth must be created within the framework of the school itself and in cooperation with other institutions serving young people."*

It's time, then, for you to outline the organizational benefits of a youth service-learning program.

Benefits to School or Agency

1. *Emphasize the public relations value of such programs.* "Let's face it, we're in trouble on the new bond issue, particularly with that block of voters who don't have any kids in school. If we could demonstrate that our school is doing things for many segments of our community, and that it is a valuable resource for everyone, that would be just the kind of publicity we could use most right now."

2. *Stress the immediate and practical benefits to the organization.* "One aspect of the program will be to provide service to the school itself. Tutoring is one obvious example, and I'm sure we can think of many others. What a difference it could make to our whole organization if the kids shared responsibility for making it work better."

3. *Note the wide range of meaningful options offered.* "Community service is one of those rare things that really do offer something for everyone. For kids who are used to a steady diet of failure in school it provides the opportunity for success and achievement and recognition. For those who find academic work a breeze it offers a significant new challenge, demanding a new set of skills. It gives everyone an insight into social issues that they are unlikely to get from textbooks and lectures. It helps the school meet its goals of providing a wide range of options for all students."

4. *Describe the program as a source of school pride and spirit.* "Last year, when we had that food drive, it was inspiring to see how the kids responded, how the whole school got behind it with such spirit and seriousness. A community service program could make that kind of experience an integral part of our school's life. It would provide a new source of school pride and spirit.

5. *Note that community service helps fulfill a stated mission.* "We all care about building character: developing attributes such as honesty, responsibility, concern for others, and selflessness.

"But those traits, like being a good citizen, are not things to know or believe in, or even things to possess, so much as what you *do* and what you *are*. They do not become part of a student through reading or discussion, but they can through action. We've known that since Aristotle pointed out that you become just by doing just acts, brave by doing brave acts, temperate by acting with temperance, and so forth."

6. *Stress that service nurtures idealism.* "Sure there's plenty of cynicism, apathy, selfishness, prejudice, and foolishness among kids, but there's also idealism, love, and concern for justice. It ought to be an important part of our program to nurture that idealism and create ways for people to act on the very best that is in them. The point is we don't have to create good character, only allow its expression and development."

That's two arguments down. You are making progress. The committee members are more interested, less hostile. There's a moment's silence, broken finally by one person who says: "The job of the school is to impart academic knowledge and basic intellectual skills — period! We're already being asked to do too much and now you want us to become a volunteer agency for the community besides."

You're now ready to defend the program's benefits to young volunteers.

Benefits to Youth

This is exactly the issue you've been waiting for and you pause a moment before answering. In that moment, you reflect on the limited social role occupied by adolescents and the way their lives have been compartmentalized. This has long been acknowledged as a serious hindrance to the healthy development of youth, and the arguments that you'll raise all trace themselves in some way to this general problem. You may not have an opportunity to spell out the whole argument, but it will be helpful for you to have in mind the general context out of which arise the particular points you present.

A number of recent reports on the status of youth have concluded that the dominant institutions that socialize young people are not preparing them adequately for adulthood.

School occupies an increasingly large portion of a young person's life, and with that has come an overemphasis on cognitive skills and book-knowledge and restricted opportunities for developing independence and responsibility. Schools provide few opportunities for students to learn to manage their own affairs or acquire the ability to take decisive action.

Young people have become too insulated and isolated from adults and from the productive tasks of society. Schools provide few opportunities for participating with other age groups; for exploring larger sections of economic, political, and social life; or for learning to care about and for others.

There is little opportunity, either in school or elsewhere, for a young person to be a contributor or to be recognized as one. Too little opportunity is afforded young people to experience the satisfaction of undertaking and completing a needed task, to feel the joy and endure the pain of significant participation in the world — of *acting* and not always just *preparing* for action.

"A powerful function of service experiences can be to show that academic knowledge actually is useful."

If this society is to produce adults who can function effectively as parents, workers, and citizens, then new structures and processes for socializing youth must be created within the framework of the school itself and in cooperation with other institutions serving young people.

More specific arguments arising from this general issue are listed below starting with those most directly and later moving to those more indirectly related.

1. *Responsible contributors.* "Society needs what youth can contribute. Young people need the opportunity to make a contribution, to take on real responsibility, to make a difference to others, and to experience being needed. Self-centeredness, apathy, cynicism, hostility, and immature behavior are partly consequences of treating youth as incompetent, irresponsible and superfluous beings unable to decide things for themselves."

2. *Citizenship.* "In most schools, ours among them, the concept of 'good citizenship' has been trivialized to mean coming to class on time and not fooling around too much.

"Training for *real* citizenship requires a great deal more and ought to involve participating in the community now —knowing what's going on, caring about it, and doing something about it. If our kids could experience that now, and see that their participation *can* make a difference, that civic involvement is rewarding and even enjoyable, they're much more likely to continue being involved as adults."

3. *Social isolation.* "We live so much of our lives in little boxes: old people here, young people there, handicapped people someplace out of sight, blacks in one part of town, whites in another, rich communities, poor neighborhoods, and on and on.

"To understand people you have to interact with many different kinds: rich, poor, old, young, sick, healthy. To understand institutions you have to get behind their walls, hear the sobs in a shelter for runaways, feel the emptiness of living years without visitors in a drab nursing-home room, see how frustrating it is to have one's painstakingly prepared plan rejected by an administrative board whose members hardly glanced at the proposal.

"What honestly do we do that reveals such truths about life? What else do we do that makes us confront what needs to be done, that shows how difficult it is, how much more we need to know and be able to do?"

4. *Requisites of adult success.* "Numerous studies reinforce what we already sense from our own experience: that academic achievement in high school is not always a good predictor of success in adult life.

"Things that do predict adult success are personal and interpersonal characteristics such as self esteem and autonomy, independent thinking, skill in problem solving, ability to get along and to work with others, and the like. These are precisely the kinds of attributes that are called upon and developed in service experiences."

Young people's diminished social role and impoverished experience base also affect their personal and psychological development in ways that include the following:

5. *Self-esteem.* "One of the most valuable assets a person can possess is a healthy self-regard. Too many kids come to school with a damaged self image only to have it knocked down even further. Even warm and caring teachers bursting with praise are not enough to reverse the slide.

"Strong self-concepts are the result of actual positive accomplishments in social interaction with a variety of people. Community service offers young people the chance to discover, develop, and display talents and skills that are seldom called on in a school and to receive recognition that might never otherwise come to them.

"This is true for all students, the most academically able as well as the least. It's also an opportunity to discover one's limits and recognize abilities that need to be strengthened."

6. *Identity formation.* "There's not much that any young person is doing that is more important than asking 'who am I?,' and then forging an identity out of his or her experiences.

"Service broadens the range of those experiences, gives opportunities to try on new roles, and offers new levels of responsibility, and a chance to develop dormant parts of themselves.

"Young men in a day-care center can develop their caring and nurturing selves; young women in a recreation center or mayor's office can discover the assertive leader and decision-maker that is in them."

7. *Explore careers.* "We have become a heavily service-centered society, and the need to attract highly talented people into service occupations such as teaching is widely acknowledged.

"A community service program will allow young people to explore careers in these areas and to make a more informed decision about whether such a profession is for them. Some will decide it is not. Others will discover, as one gifted young woman wrote in her successful application as one of the country's 100 Presidential Scholars: ' ... after having the chance to teach kindergarten I may choose to teach at the elementary level. (But) wherever I am 10 years from now, I ... will continue to use my gifts in the service of others.'"

In addition to the personal benefits outlined above, community service offers benefits related to intellectual development and academic learning.

8. *Law of diminishing returns.* "The average student completing 12th grade has spent nearly 15,000 hours sitting in classrooms. Somewhere in there the law of diminishing returns comes into play. For instruction to remain vital, effective, and relevant, we need to vary the settings and styles in which it is delivered. What is learned needs to be applied and tested in a more demanding and realistic fashion than by words in a test booklet or marks on an electronic score sheet."

9. *Remoteness.* "Much of what we teach is so abstract, so remote. A powerful function of service experiences can be to show that academic knowledge actually is useful, and really can be applied to help a person better understand and more effectively carry out a task that matters to someone in the real world.

"A student in an English class who helps publish a youth newspaper or a math student calculating the angle for a wheelchair ramp not only will find academic skills useful, but will be faced with a stiffer test of excellence than any paper-and-pencil test can offer. They also will lay themselves open to both harsher criticism and more satisfying reinforcement than can be conveyed by any letter grade on a test booklet."

10. *Complex thinking skills.* "Data drawn from SAT tests and from studies of the National Assessment of Educational Progress demonstrate that the much-publicized drop in student achievement is not so much in basic skills as in complex thinking, problem solving, and the application of knowledge.

"A well-run service program that combines significant experience with serious reflection demands higher level thinking and learning by engaging youth in solving problems where all the data is not given, the questions not delineated, the chapters not summarized, and the answers not printed in the back of a book."

11. *Learning style.* "The workshop on learning styles we had last spring convinced many of us that we have to provide more varied instructional styles within our program. When classroom instruction is combined with real service experience we draw on the strength of those kids who learn best through active experimentation and we help develop that capacity in others."

12. *Application of knowledge.* "We try very hard in this school to make people aware of social problems and of real human needs. If we only inform and arouse concern, we may leave kids with a feeling of helplessness. Community service not only exposes students to the effects of social problems on real human beings, but also offers them a chance to be a part of the solution to those problems."

13. *My own wish to matter.* "I want to engage the kids I work with in learning experiences that matter, where they can see the consequences of learning, even *feel* them, where there is some intensity and sense of purpose, and where they engage in things that affect not only what they know but who they are and wish to be."

You might want to add a final note of caution:

"Enthusiasm for community service should not lead us to overstate this case either. While some things are best learned through community participation, others are most effectively learned through books, lectures, essays, discussions, and the like. It is through the intelligent mixture of all these forms that we can expect the most meaningful learning and development to take place."

You rest your case.

Dan Conrad directs community involvement programs at Hopkins High School in Minnesota. Diane Hedin is former Director of Community Relations at the Pillsbury Foundation and is now a professor at the Center for Youth Development and Research at the University of Minnesota. Over the past 17 years, Conrad and Hedin have co-directed several research and publications projects in experiential education, youth participation, and service-learning.

Aims and Outcomes of Community Service Programs: Benefits to Young People

The following outcomes for student participants typically are sought and often — but not inevitably — are achieved in youth service programs.

Personal Growth and Development

- Self-esteem, sense of personal worth, competence, and confidence
- Self-understanding, insight into self
- Self-direction, personal motivation
- Independence, autonomy, assertiveness
- Sense of usefulness, of doing something worthwhile
- Personal power, belief in ability to make a difference
- Conscious set of personal values and beliefs
- Openness to new experiences, ability to take risks and accept challenges
- Ability to take responsibility, acknowledge and accept consequences of actions
- Capacity to be productive, persevere even in difficult tasks
- Willingness to explore new identities, unfamiliar roles

Intellectual Development and Academic Learning

- Basic academic skills (writing, reading, math, etc.)
- Higher-level thinking skills (critical thinking, problem solving)
- Skills in learning from experience (observing, asking questions, thinking for oneself)
- Skills in particular subject matter (psychology, civics, biology, etc.) as related to experiences
- More positive attitude toward education, learning (possibly, but not necessarily, school itself)
- Communication skills (listening, being articulate in presenting ideas, etc.)
- Tacit learning skills (the nuances that can't be fully explained in a book or lecture but are often the most important things of all to know)

Social Growth and Development

- Concern for the welfare of others, a broader circle of people about whom one feels concern and responsibility

- Knowledge and understanding of others
- More positive attitude toward living and working with people of diverse backgrounds
- Skills in caring for others
- Ability to work cooperatively with and to trust others
- Increased likelihood of continuing to be active in the community
- Knowledge of and some experience with service-related career possibilities
- Realistic ideas about the world of work
- Contacts for future job possibilities

Taking Community Service Seriously

Robert Shumer

Shumer argues for the integration of community service experiences into the instructional agenda of K-12 schools. Reprinted with permission from "Community Service: A Bridge to Learning," special issue of the Community Education Journal *edited by John Formy-Duval and Ellen Voland, National Community Education Association, Alexandria, Virginia, Vol. XV, No. 1, October 1987, pp. 15-17.*

THE NOTION of American youth performing community service is popular today, but there is much debate over how the service should be rendered and whom it should benefit.

Central to the discussion of community service are two major questions: (1) what should be its purpose: are we interested in encouraging volunteerism or do we seek the broader goal of teaching young people about the personal, intellectual, and social value of community service; and (2) who should be responsible for teaching about civic and community involvement — educational institutions, or community and civic agencies, or both? Responses to these questions will influence how community service programs are developed.

Community service is currently an important topic because today's youth have been characterized as "selfish." National surveys of college freshmen have shown that students are increasingly interested in their own economic success; the value placed on "helping others" has declined (Astin, 1987). Partly in response, a "Campus Compact" has committed many college and university presidents to the encouragement of student community service. Many new programs have been started and existing programs expanded to encourage community service by college students. In California, legislation has been introduced to require community service for university graduation. Ernest Boyer's recent report on higher education recommends community service as a "vital part of the under-graduate experience" (Boyer, 1986).

Interest in high school community service has been bolstered by national reports on secondary education. In *High School*, Boyer (1983) recommends community service as a requirement for graduation. In *A Place Called School*, Goodlad (1984) suggests that students be more engaged in the community to learn about work, careers, and service. Many school districts have begun to act on the issue. Atlanta Public Schools has added a graduation requirement of 75 hours of community service, and the Los Angeles Unified School District is considering some form of service requirement.

But as colleges and high schools take steps to encourage community service, what kinds of programs are being provided? Surveys of independent secondary schools by Levison (1986) and public high schools by Harrison (1987) indicate that most programs are not required and occur outside the realm of the school's educational purpose. The same is true of colleges and universities: service is largely an add-on activity, not an integral part of the institution. Teachers often have little involvement in guiding or teaching students about subjects related to their service activities. Service is performed primarily as an extracurricular activity unrelated to educational goals. Whatever benefit is derived from the experience results primarily from student effort and community assistance.

The underlying (and perhaps unexamined) assumption of these optional, noncurricular, programs is that students will learn about the value of service and become less inward-directed simply by doing service work. This notion is supported by many anecdotes. Students describe personal and community benefits of their service experiences and claim greater understanding of human needs. There is, however, a self-selection process operating here — those who participate in voluntary programs already place some personal value on service. The vast majority of high school and college students do not perform community service activities.

Research on experiential learning programs suggests that optimistic assumptions about the benefits of voluntary programs may not be valid. In a national study of many types of secondary experiential learning programs (including community service), Conrad and Hedin (1982) found that students do not automatically make connections between their experiences and broader social issues; without opportunities to reflect on these experiences and to have dialogue with teachers and others, some of the educational potential is lost. Moore (1982) reported similar findings in a three-year study of an experience-based high school program. He suggests that "reflection rarely occurs as a natural component of experience," that it "has to be added on by educators." An earlier observer, John Dewey (1938), also suggests that experience can be miseducative. To have educational value, experiences must help people to grow — to see relationships between prior experiences and future action, to see how a single experience relates to a broader context. If students do not make these connections on their own, adults (teachers and community members) must assist in the process.

Levison (1986) discusses the notion of what constitutes quality programs in a recent survey of community service. He believes that most programs are "symbolic" in nature, existing more for service than for education. The greatest educational value occurs, he says, when programs are "instrumental" — integrally tied to the school's educational purpose. Programs that integrate service into the academic framework of the school have the greatest potential for providing educational and personal growth for students and effective service for communities.

If service that is instituted within the school curriculum is preferable to nonattached, independent efforts, why don't schools implement the more desirable program? While there are many reasons, three major factors stand out. First, schools as institutions are slow to change. Secondary schools, colleges, and universities are deeply rooted in departmental structures: they teach subject matter, not students; they transmit information about curricular content; educational processes are largely passive. Second, educational institutions are typically detached from communities, not part of them. Classrooms are the principal places of instruction, separated from businesses, parks, halfway houses, and skid rows. Third, learning gained through service is perceived as less substantive than learning that takes place in classrooms. Critics dismiss the suggestion that communities can become high-quality learning environments as reminiscent of the liberal rhetoric of the 1960s, or even the 1930s, when "life adjustment education" was in vogue.

There are other obstacles. Good programs take time and resources to develop. Issues of control and responsibility must be resolved. Human and financial resources must be allocated by both schools and communities for program start-up and operation. Teachers have to be retrained, or at least reoriented. Students, parents, teachers, and administrators must be willing to take the risk of moving from the safe environs of the classroom to engage in learning in the community.

Perhaps the greatest barrier is the narrow conception of education as schooling — the failure to focus on students as lifelong learners within a total educative society. Schools tend to function as though they were the educational center of the universe, rather than a part of the learning experiences of people as they journey through life. School programs can do much to help students understand living, but they are not life itself. The educational process should help young people make connections with the world in which they live, and help them understand how to learn from experience.

If one takes the position that education is a lifelong process and that the role of educational institutions is to foster growth and learning, the discussion of community service is refocused on the relationship between service and learning, the integration of service activities into the learning process. It is appropriate for schools, if they support or promote community service, to be responsible for ensuring that learning occurs, and that the learning contributes to the overall development of the student and meets the goals of the educational institution. Thus, it is reasonable to assume that schools should not leave the responsibility for teaching about service to other groups or agencies. Certainly, other community groups must be involved as partners in the process, but the educational institution must be responsible for developing, monitoring, and evaluating student activity.

Community service can play an important part in linking schools with their communities. Through meaningful service activities, coupled with feedback from adults (both community members and teachers), students can relate service to learning. They can come to understand that service is part of citizenship in a society that reveres participatory forms of government.

But as students venture out into communities, we must be concerned about the quality of the service they deliver as well as the quality of their learning experience. Without structures that assure supervision and monitoring, there is a strong likelihood that students will be relegated to filing, sweeping, or paper shuffling, and will miss the rich educational experience of caring for and about others. There may also be a tendency to underemphasize the strong affective impact that community work has on students. Through guided involvement, students can feel the effects of poverty, see true human need, and understand the impact of their service.

There are well-established principles of good practice in community service programs. Sound programs:

• are an integral part of the educational program, not an add-on activity that occurs only after school or during the summer; some form of academic credit is usually awarded for the learning derived from the service activities.

- have structures that give students feedback on what they do through frequent contact with faculty and community sponsors in a course, seminar, or other regular meeting.
- include a planned method for examining the service experiences in relation to changes in attitudes, skills, and knowledge.
- give students genuine responsibility through activities in which there are consequences contingent upon their performance.
- structure extensive contact between schools and community agencies to assure mutual benefit and the meeting of mutual goals.
- involve systematic monitoring and evaluation of student and client activities, involving all participants in the process so that the educational quality of the service experiences can be continually improved.

As educational institutions integrate community service into the instructional agenda, they must be careful not to view the community solely as a laboratory for use and study. It is not uncommon for educators to prescribe specific goals and objectives for programs without regard for those who are being served. Service recipients, as well as the community agencies and groups who assist with service, can best articulate their needs and how they might be met. That is why the development of programs and activities for community service must be negotiated in partnerships between schools and the community.

Boyer (1986) cites the experience-based career education program at Highland High School in Salt Lake City as an example of a truly "integrated" high school service learning program. Students in this program develop individual learning agreements with community agencies. The agreements define the kind of service to be provided and expectations of what students are to learn from the experiences. By working in a preschool, for example, students might help low-income children learn language skills, while studying child development or governmental programs designed to assist the poor. In this case, students earn credit in Child Development or in Government, both regularly taught courses in the school. Students spend time in the community doing their service work and time on campus in courses and seminars discussing their experiences and their readings on topics related to the service. Students also use their experiences as topics for written assignments in English. Thus community service is performed in the context of community needs and the regular school curriculum.

Although primarily an after-school model, the Academic Internship Program in Charlotte, North Carolina, maintains an educational tie to the school system. School staff actively supervise student work, help students develop individual learning plans, and emphasize learning as a function of service.

In a more educationally focused model, students at King/Drew High School for the Health Sciences in Los Angeles sometimes perform service as a part of their weekly field experiences. The service work is directly tied to academic subject matter, usually in a health-related area. A community-resource model, the Volunteer Clearinghouse of the District of Columbia incorporates academic purposes with volunteer experiences. Impetus for both the King/Drew and Volunteer Clearinghouse programs came from the community. Assistance from organizations like the National Society for Internships and Experiential Education is available to school districts and community agencies interested in developing community service programs like these.

Both communities and youth can be well served when young people are engaged in meaningful service activities. But encouraging community participation without regard for the learning dimension is disservice, reducing the opportunity for student growth and potentially diminishing the quality of service rendered to community members. Combining service with learning benefits everyone.

Robert Shumer is Associate Director of Field Studies Development at the University of California at Los Angeles. Several members of the National Society for Internships and Experiential Education assisted with this article.

References

Astin, Alexander, and others, *The American Freshman: National Norms of Freshmen*, Higher Education Research Institute, Graduate School of Education, University of California, 1987.

Boyer, Ernest L., *College: The Undergraduate Experience in America*, Harper and Row, 1986.

Boyer, Ernest L., *High School: A Report on Secondary Education in America*, Harper and Row, 1983.

Conrad, Dan, and Diane Hedin, "The Impact of Experiential Education on Adolescent Behavior," *Child and Youth Services*, Vol. 4, No. 3-4, 1982.

Dewey, John, *Experience and Education*, Collier Books, 1938.

Goodlad, John, *A Place Called School*, McGraw-Hill, 1984.

Harrison, Robert, *Student Service: The New Carnegie Unit*, Princeton University Press, 1987.

Levison, Lee, *Community Service Programs in Independent Schools*, National Association of Independent Schools, 1986.

Moore, David T., *Students at Work: Identifying Learning in Internship Settings*, National Society for Internships and Experiential Education, Occasional Paper No. 5, 1982.

National Study Shows Progress and Needs in Strengthening Institutional Support for Experiential Education

Sally Migliore

A longitudinal study of the process of institutional planning for increasing support for experiential education shows the progress made at almost 500 colleges and universities — and the challenges that remain. Experiential education is part of the method used by programs that combine service and learning. Reprinted with permission from Experiential Education, *National Society for Internships and Experiential Education, Vol. 14, No. 5, pp. 1, 18-19.*

FROM 1985 TO 1988, the National Society for Internships and Experiential Education (NSIEE) conducted a national project to strengthen the role of experiential education in U. S. colleges and universities. The Fund for the Improvement of Postsecondary Education (FIPSE), U. S. Department of Education, provided partial support. A pilot project, also supported by FIPSE, was conducted from 1983 to 1985. Advocates of experiential education at the participating institutions addressed critical issues in strengthening experiential education, such as integrating experiential education into their: institutional missions and values, curricula, faculty work loads and teaching skills, faculty reward systems, administrative structures, budgets, and systems for quality assurance.

NSIEE has worked with over 485 institutions through this project to date, and the organization has committed to continuation of this important service to academic institutions.

In 1988, NSIEE conducted an evaluation of the three-year project as well as a longitudinal study of the 20 pilot institutions over a five-year period. Four different models of service delivery were evaluated: on-site campus consultations, regional and thematic workshops, and national workshops with and without individual consultations. Other variables taken into account were the type of school (pilot school in 1983-1985 or non-pilot in 1985-1988) and the type of position in the institution held by the respondent (high-level administrator, faculty, or program director). Following is a summary of the evaluation results with the most frequent responses listed in descending order of frequency.

Purposes of the Evaluation
1. to assess the impact of the project
2. to assess the progress made toward strengthening experiential education
3. to identify barriers that schools need to overcome to strengthen experiential education
4. to evaluate NSIEE's interventions
5. to learn the current issues schools face in institutionalizing experiential education
6. to find out what schools see as the next steps
7. to identify further assistance needed by schools

Progress Made in Strengthening Experiential Education
Most progress made by participating institutions:
1. understanding the process of institutional change
2. recognizing experiential education as contributing to college mission and goals
Least progress made:
1. recognizing experiential education in tenure and promotion
2. recognizing experiential education in faculty compensation

Biggest Difference at School?
1. increased faculty involvement
2. greater recognition for faculty sponsors
3. progress toward faculty compensation

What Did NSIEE Do that Made the Biggest Difference?
1. held meetings on our campus with NSIEE Consultant
2. legitimized experiential education with faculty
3. helped us identify needed improvements
4. helped us clarify ambiguous issues

5. wrote consulting reports that were really useful
6. reinforced that we were on the right track
7. provided a broader context for planning institutionalization

Barriers?
1. lack of faculty support
2. limited faculty time
3. perceived lack of top-level commitment

What's Happened?
(Perceptions differed by type of position held by the respondent.)
1. most of the NSIEE Consultant's recommendations implemented
2. more recognition of departmental efforts
3. more quality controls
4. curricular changes
5. administrative and evaluation procedures improved
6. faculty advisory committees established
7. faculty workshops conducted
8. more communication among faculty, administrators, and program directors about experiential education
9. more program visibility

What is Needed Now?
1. greater faculty participation
2. more students
3. more top-level commitment for faculty compensation and program development

What Help is Needed Now?
1. faculty workshops
2. "strategy" workshops for developing the leadership skills of catalysts
3. assistance from a consultant
4. program information, referral to other experiential educators, and technical assistance
5. assistance with outside evaluations of our programs and of our institution's support of experiential education
6. publications

The results of the evaluation suggest that the project has been successful in helping schools strengthen experiential education on their campuses. Specifically: (1) progress has been made toward institutionalizing experiential education by schools participating in each of the four models of service delivery; (2) all of the project features evaluated were found to be helpful to participants in their efforts to strengthen experiential education; (3) *significantly* higher numbers of students were involved in experiential education programs at the participating institutions in 1988-89 than in 1983-84 when the project began; and (4) program directors have a greater understanding about how to initiate change in their institutions, and they have empowered themselves to take steps toward strengthening experiential education.

The findings also suggest that more faculty need to understand the value of experiential education and actively incorporate it into their teaching styles. Along with this, faculty need to be recognized for their experiential education activities.

Participants identified a strong need for support to faculty in learning more about (1) the design of experiential education courses and programs that follow principles of good practice, and (2) the process of institutional change as it relates to experiential education. These are strong messages from participants about improving the quality of teaching and learning on their campuses.

For information about how your institution can strengthen its support of service-learning and experiential education, contact NSIEE, 3509 Haworth Drive, Suite 207, Raleigh, NC 27609, (919) 787-3263. Also use the NSIEE sourcebook, *Strengthening Experiential Education within Your Institution.*

Sally Migliore is Associate Executive Director of NSIEE. Before joining the NSIEE staff in 1986, she coordinated the North Carolina State Government Internship Program, worked with the N.C. Commission on Indian Affairs, and coordinated a literacy program for VISTA.

Old and New Models of Academic Service

Neal R. Berte and Edward H. O'Neil

*The traditional model of academic service through faculty exper-
tise and consultation is being supplemented by "service-learning" that focuses on students. This chapter is useful for faculty
and administrators who are trying to redefine the "service" part
of the "teaching, research, service" mission of most academic institutions. Reprinted with permission from* Redefining Service, Research, and Teaching, *Warren B. Martin, ed., Jossey-
Bass, New Directions for Higher Education, No. 18, Summer
1977, pp. 17-21.*

THE ROLE OF SERVICE has not always been clearly defined
within the mission of American higher education. In fact, only in
the nineteenth century did educational institutions incorporate
service as a separate component of their reason for being. While
Harvard College and other early institutions were seen as performing a great community service, their mission was that of educating
young men into service to the community, not of providing other
direct service to the community. This particular role of the academy
evolved only as the need for technical knowledge grew, spawned by
the advent of the industrial age and expanded by the growth of
sciences related to agriculture and animal husbandry.

Great Potential, Limited Practice

Today, service is enshrined as one of the principal missions of
most colleges and universities and is seen as one of the nation's
greatest resources, supported as it is by millions of dollars from
federal, state, and private sources each year. But while the service
potential of higher education is vast, the delivery system for this
service has remained fairly simplistic. The system is based on a
scholarly or expertise model of aid in which clients such as federal,

state, and local governments or private groups contract with the institution or with its professors for highly technical knowledge and skills that cannot be obtained elsewhere.

In recent years, however, our society has witnessed the growth of another model of the service function of higher education: programs of "service-learning" in which students provide direct service while continuing their learning. Beginning first at the graduate level and now gaining large-scale acceptance at the undergraduate level, this service-learning model involves such activities as work-study internships, cooperative education programs, independent study, practica, and field experiences. Through it, students are able to take the technical knowledge they have gained in two or three years of undergraduate courses and apply it to the various needs of other institutions, as well as to learn from this application and these other institutions. Their interest in these types of programs is heightened by the growth of their interest in the career dimensions of their education experiences.

Although there are many ways in which this service-learning model manifests itself in practice, it almost always involves three participants as basic elements. The first and key to the model is the student. The second is the supervisor in the organization in which the student serves. The third is a faculty member or staff representative of the higher education institution in the discipline or area related to the student's interest and to the setting for the service-learning experience. This sponsor or adviser seeks to emphasize the theoretical underpinnings of the experience, provides advice and counsel to the student about the relation between the experience and the student's academic career, assists the student in defining learning objectives for the experience and the methodology to achieve those objectives, and sees to it that there is prior agreement as to how the learning experience will be evaluated for academic credit.

Contrasts

The service-learning model is radically different from the traditional expertise model of service in several ways. At the very heart of the difference is the role of the person who provides the service. In the expertise model, as the name implies, an expert or scholar consults or advises beyond the campus. While the service-learning model does not replace this approach to service, it adds an entirely different dimension to the delivery of service: Supervised learners are the instrument for information, action research, and actual change between the college or university and the community organization or agency.

A second contrast is the role that learning plays in the service process. In the expertise model, learning is not necessarily expected to take place, since it is assumed that the "expert" has the knowledge and skill to provide the service to the client. A basic principle of the service-learning model, however, is that learning is a two-way process, rather than one-way. It emphasizes learning both for the agency and the intern — and secondarily for the supervisor and the faculty sponsor as well.

A third and closely related contrast is that in comparison to the service-learning model, the expertise model provides few allowances for institutional development. For example, an individual faculty member may contract on his or her own time with an outside agency to perform a designated service, and once this service has been provided, the contract is completed. Any resulting improvement in the professor's teaching or research is desirable — but incidental. The service-learning model however, brings together the faculty sponsor, the supervisor, and the intern — three individuals who may not have had contact previously — into a relationship that can produce opportunities for growth and development for all concerned. At the completion of the service-learning experience, supervisors frequently carry back a better understanding of the educational community to their professional setting; faculty members know more about the needs of employing agencies; and students can better relate their classroom learning to their out-of-class experiences.

One last way in which the two models contrast is in the area of the transition of students from education to work. In the expertise model, there is little or no direct transition between education and work except for the opportunity gained by a student assistant in helping the professor provide the service itself. On the other hand, the service-learning model allows students to try out work roles temporarily as an aid to their career decisions. It also allows agencies to recruit, train, and evaluate potential employees without committing themselves to permanent employment.

Similarities

As important as the differences are between the expertise and service-learning models, there are also similarities between them. A first and vital similarity is that both models involve cooperation between the nonacademic and the academic worlds. Critics constantly comment on the ever-widening gulf between education and the "world of work," and both the expertise model and the service-learning model bring these two worlds into closer contact.

Another similarity is that both bring outside resources to bear on particular problems and issues facing agencies and individuals, assuring the application and testing of ideas. Thus both effectively blend theory and practice, benefiting both education and work. The "ivory-tower" atmosphere of most educational institutions is often corrected by a dose of "real-world" practicality, just as the world of work is often aided by the infusion of new ideas and new ways of thinking that break traditional patterns of thought or procedure and permit the development of new approaches and techniques.

Benefits of Service-Learning

A number of benefits accrue to students who participate in a service-learning program. First, as noted earlier, the experience provides them with the opportunity to gather firsthand data related to career choices and possibilities, often permits additional remuneration during the collegiate experience and may lead to possible fulltime employment later. Two such interns at the University of Alabama developed a campus-based volunteer organization and in one year were able to organize 700 of their fellow students into voluntary efforts on 27 social service projects that contributed over 58,000 hours of service to the local community. The two interns benefits from a valuable learning experience that directed their own future career interests, while allowing other students to test out their own interests.

Second, the problems that students face in many service-learning situations require them to broaden their perspectives beyond more than one discipline and demonstrate the need for interdisciplinary perspectives and competence. An example of this effect is the work of a senior home economics major with the economic development office of a southern state. The agency was responsible for generating economic development projects in rural communities, and the student was assigned to the agency because of her special interest in this area of work. She lived in the community for eight months, during which she assessed the skills of many local crafts people, organized them into a work cooperative, and arranged for the financing of their raw materials and the marketing of their finished products. The project not only became a center of community activity and an economic success, but it also taught the student valuable lessons in the areas of economics and community development as well as arts and crafts.

Conclusion

The service-learning model is not designed as a way to supplant the existing expertise model of college and university service. However, it is a way in which students can become actively involved in the service function of colleges and universities while at the same time enhancing their own educational experiences by broadening them beyond the walls of the academy.

Neal R. Berte is President of Birmingham Southern College in Alabama and former Vice President for Educational Development of the University of Alabama and Dean of its New College. He is the editor of Individualizing Education Through Contract Learning *as well as* Innovations in Undergraduate Education: Selected Institutional Profiles and Thoughts about Experimentation.

Edward H. O'Neil co-directs the Pew National Projects in Dentistry, Veterinary Sciences, and Medicine. A faculty member in Duke University's Institute for Policy Sciences and Public Affairs, he also serves on the Board of Directors of the National Society for Internships and Experiential Education and has worked with the Kellogg and Kettering Foundations.

Institutionalizing Experiential Learning in a State University

Robert F. Sexton and John B. Stephenson

A dean of undergraduate studies and director of experiential education describe how a large public university developed a central office to coordinate experiential learning opportunities — including service-learning in the liberal arts. Their advice from the 1970s reflects timeless principles of institutionalizing an educational innovation that will be important for service-learning educators into the 21st century. Reprinted with permission from Implementing Field Experience Education, *ed. John Duley, Jossey-Bass, New Directions for Higher Education, No. 6, Summer 1974, pp. 55-65.*

IN 1973, THE UNIVERSITY OF KENTUCKY created an Office for Experiential Education to develop and coordinate the off-campus learning activities of all university students. Because of contemporary interest in experiential education we have been asked many times to explain the causes and implications of this development: in essence, to explain how a traditional land grant university instituted a nontraditional program and what the phenomenon means.

Reflection on the development of experiential education at the University of Kentucky (UK) leads to two basic questions. First, what allowed the office for Experiential Education to happen, especially in a species of institution whose rigidity and inertia are legendary? The second question concerns the real progress we have made, and what the creation of an administrative office has actually meant in terms of the "institutionalization" of experiential education.

The first question can be approached through a straightforward narration of events between 1970 and 1973, when the Office was created. We would first abstract from the story some guiding concepts and principles to explain what happened. If such concepts and principles are valid, they might be put to use again, at the University of Kentucky and elsewhere. What happened at UK underscores the importance of the following principles, which are no news to social scientists, students of change, or practiced administrators:

1. The use of influential people is essential in the diffusion and adoption of innovations.

2. Timing is important in effecting change, from the standpoints of "client" readiness, competing demands for resources, and support from elites, to name only three aspects.

3. The management and coordination of communications to maintain a proper flow of information is another essential.

4. Innovations should be consistent with existing norms and shared objectives and should fulfill felt needs.

5. Of overriding importance is the very basic principle that success in bringing about change is always a mixture of calculated strategy and dumb luck. The mixture many contain 5 percent of the former and 95 percent of the latter!

Background Events

Leaving these generalities and moving on to the particular experience of the University of Kentucky, the developments here with experiential education have been the result of a combination of circumstances: some carefully planned over the past four years, some the result of specific institutional characteristics, and some the result of historical accident. To analyze these circumstances, we should examine the role of the Office of the Dean of Undergraduate Studies; the impact of the University Year for Action program; and the importance of a relatively small group of advocates scattered throughout the university.

Dean of Undergraduate Studies. Recognizing the impact on undergraduate programs of a greatly increased emphasis on graduate training in the early and middle sixties, the University of Kentucky created in 1967 the Office of the Dean of Undergraduate Studies to improve program effectiveness, improve instruction and advising, and generally attend to those academic concerns which were of common interest to the dozen or so colleges offering undergraduate degrees. The position was filled partly to respond to growing student demands for changes in undergraduate programs, and it quickly became on of the university's more visible symbols of "innovation."

University Year for Action. Through the auspices of the Dean of Undergraduate Studies, the university applied for a University Year for Action (UYA) planning grant in fall, 1971. Following a strategy laid jointly by the dean, a development official with the University Research Foundation, and the director of the Center for Developmental Change (an interdisciplinary campus center which had been important in developing proposals in such areas as welfare research, Peace Corps training, and Appalachian research), the so-called Committee of Forty was assembled to assist in drafting the proposal. The Committee of Forty was large, representative, supportive, and hardworking. For such a sizable and diverse group, it was surprisingly flexible. The planning director, together with the Committee of Forty, organized and submitted a proposal which became the model proposal for UYA in Washington for months — a fact which was later almost our undoing in Lexington.

Washington approved the UYA program proposal, and the university was in the experiential education business on a multi-college basis in January, 1972, less than four months after it had first conceived the possibility. Among the institutional changes necessary for getting the grant was the commitment to granting 30 hours of academic credit to students serving in the off-campus program. Some were incredulous, having already decided that the institution was congenitally incapable of rapid change.

Of course, scattered but significant off-campus learning activities already existed. In addition to programs in education, social work, and the medical fields, the department of political science had been active in developing state government internship programs which carried 15 hours of academic credit. These internships had been widely publicized, and their patron faculty member was a highly respected scholar. In one respect, then, education through field placements was not a radical innovation at the University of Kentucky. But the "take-off" for development of experiential learning from such scattered beginnings to the eventual creation of a university-wide Office for Experiential Education depended not only on carefully laid strategies, but on several fortuitous events and decisions.

Academic Credit. One of these was early resolution of the "credit problem" by two members of the Committee of Forty, the Vice President for Academic Affairs and the chair of the Senate Council. Their plan was to obtain top-level approval for a new university-wide course granting up to 15 credit hours per semester, but to make its use by any given student contingent on the approval of a department and a college. (The alternative would have been to wait for the unlikely common initiative of around 90 departments to come up with such a course.) This course, University Year for Action 396, was modified as a departmental 300-level course in a gradual, planned move toward an established, university-wide, variable-credit experiential education course.

Locating the Program. Another strategic decision was to place the UYA program under the Dean of Undergraduate Studies, who in turn reports to the Vice President for Academic Affairs. This meant that from the beginning the program benefitted from an aura of established academic credibility. This factor became more important in later stages than at the beginning. They are attempting to do this as their federal funding ends, so not only have they lost the initial financial advantage, but they are tackling at the same time an academic-political objective which is inherently difficult.

Numerous UYA programs across the nation were initially attached to student services, volunteer offices, or specific professional colleges such as social work or urban studies. To become "institutionalized," these programs must cross the bridge to the academic administration of the institution or expand to engage the broader university community. They are attempting to do this as their federal funding ends, so not only have they lost the initial financial advantage, but they are tackling at the same time an academic-political objective which is inherently difficult.

> Numerous UYA programs across the nation were initially attached to student services, volunteer offices, or specific professional colleges such as social work or urban studies. To become "institutionalized," these programs must cross the bridge to the academic administration of the institution or expand to engage the broader university community.

Core Group. Another fortuitous effect of UYA was the establishment of a core of persons on and off the campus, often from unexpected quarters, who could intelligently discuss and rationally visualize the potential of the UYA model. Among these were the

Vice President for Academic Affairs, whose support was vital to the effort. Another was a former Chair of the Psychology Department, a highly respected member of the university community and a person who had had experience as an evaluator of the Peace Corps. This person eventually played an important role in evaluating UYA and later became academic co-director of UYA. Another was the planning director, a vigorous, imaginative assistant professor who subsequently became assistant dean of the College of Arts and Sciences. And almost by accident, one of the authors of this narrative became involved as a member of the Committee of Forty in his role as director of the State Internship Program in Frankfort. Other members of this core group came from such diverse areas as law, architecture, dentistry, community medicine, and vocational education.

Outcome

Almost any way one looks at it, the early experience of the UK-UYA program was a near disaster. If there had been little time available for planning, there was even less for implementation. Staffing was completed virtually overnight. There was insufficient time to orient the staff to the complex philosophy of a new program which was to satisfy Washington that poverty was being attacked in a respectable academic fashion, to persuade faculty that learning was taking place under the banner of service, and to convince students that learning objectives could be achieved outside the classroom. Needless to say, the motives of those who participated in those early months were varied and conflicting. The conflict erupted. Surprisingly, it was not faculty who contested an academic ripoff; it was students who contested what they considered another ripoff of the poor. In addition, some agencies felt they had been seriously misled by an overzealous recruiter. Had it not been for a steadfast, mature director who kept a cool head throughout this period of travail, the university would have terminated the project within three months of its beginning.

But UYA survived its nervous launching, which is not to say that it was an unmitigated success even a year or so later. It still faced problems such as its narrow focus on poverty, its requirement of full academic credit for 12 months' full-time work for undergraduates, its apparent inflation of grades, its low rate of faculty involvement in supervision and evaluation, and its exploitation by students with questionable motivation, to name the most important. Nevertheless, UYA served the purpose of allowing experimentation with experiential learning so that these very problems could be identified and dealt with. And UYA has been a foundation, however shaky it may have been at the outset, upon which to build a more solid educational structure.

Thus, the university's experiment with UYA, although not completely successful, provided both the stimulant and the vehicle for the development of the broader concept of experiential education.

Success Factors

Several outcomes of the UYA experience, as well as other circumstances only partially related to the program, contributed to whatever success we now enjoy. At the top of this list of circumstances contributing to the maintenance of innovation was the *basic credibility of experiential education proponents*. In addition to the former chairman of psychology, these included the chair of the Political Science Department, highly respected faculty in anthropology and sociology, and the Deans of the Colleges of Education, Social Professions, and Agriculture, and the Vice President for Academic Affairs. Whatever their individual reasons for supporting the reform, these persons played quiet but decisive roles. Of crucial importance also was the breadth of the small support group — it silenced from the beginning the argument that such education was only advantageous to a small segment of the University or only to the professional colleges. We also saw that a *small nucleus of strong supporters*, located in the right places and mobilized by the Office of Undergraduate Studies, was as effective as larger numbers might have been.

Another contributing factor was the absence of organized opposition to experiential learning. In part this was due to the role of the persons above, but even more it was the result of the nonthreatening nature of the experiment and pure good luck. The internal proposal which created the Office for Experiential Education had argued not that some radical alternative to tradition was being undertaken, but instead that experiential education should be built upon existing programs. The proposal was also reviewed by the deans of all 15 colleges and many department chairs, forestalling organized opposition.

Perhaps there was more of a threat to existing experiential programs, but once more the cautious wording of the mandate was important. In other words, assurances were given that existing programs, such as those in education, would not be challenged by a development and coordination office.

Basically, the UYA experience itself made a mixed contribution to the furtherance of experiential education. On the one hand the program had demonstrated the weaknesses of innovation. There were problems with vague or absent criteria for measurement and absence of faculty control. The academic validity of some of the placements was a constant question as was the fact that many UYA students entered the program with fairly weak academic records. Fortunately, however, these problems were discussed openly if not widely throughout the program, and supporters of the concept in general continued to think positively; they felt that inadequacies surfacing in UYA pointed to concerns to be corrected or modified, and not toward elimination. And, in effect, the UYA program really affected only a small group of people. The credit mechanism, although it offered up to 30 hours of undergraduate credit, was couched in safeguards (it was pass/fail in most cases and needed departmental approval to count toward the major) and had been approved only on an experimental basis, so it too posed only a limited threat.

In sum, the UYA program's primary contribution to later developments was as a stimulant, not as a paragon of academic virtue. The process of getting the grant stimulated discussion, in a low-risk environment, of the advisability of granting large amounts of credit for what could be learned through experience. Administrators and faculty were encouraged during the program's duration to discuss experiential education, and the UYA project staff and advisory committee formed a focal point for this discussion. Students were also exposed to off-campus work and service in large doses for the first time, and the novelty of their placements resulted in more publicity in the campus media than had been the case with other programs. The availability of federal funds to underwrite a broader office was, of course, a constant advantage in working with the administration.

A major link between UYA and the Office for Experiential Education was an internal report from Dr. Jesse Harris. Based on interviews with virtually all academic deans, the report showed considerable support for the concept of a centrally coordinated office which would concern itself with the development of off-campus learning experiences. The degree of support shown in this report and its unimpeachable source made it difficult for the Vice President and the President to deny support for the new Office for Experiential Education from general fund sources. In July 1973 the new office was created.

Office for Experiential Education

We now come to the question of how far toward the institution-alization of experiential learning we have come. To begin, let's review briefly the role of the Office for Experiential Education. The office's primary purposes are to coordinate already existing field experience programs (this does not mean, by the way, granting approval for a college or department to place students in service-learning or internships), to create a general climate receptive to experiential learning among students and faculty, to develop new field learning opportunities, to facilitate research on the subject, and to disseminate information as broadly as possible. The office also directly administers programs with university-wide constituencies, such as the state and city government internship programs and the University Year for Action program.

Thus far, the focus of the office has been on working with colleges and departments, through the new Council on Experiential Education, to encourage them to build experiential education into the curriculum. At the same time, interdisciplinary subcommittees are also at work devising ways in which the off-campus placement can be utilized to encourage department cooperation. For example, a subcouncil for cultural patterns consists of representatives from anthropology, English folklore, geography, sociology, and history.

Efforts have also gone into cataloguing all the university field experience programs and all the university courses being used to grant credit for field work. Research has been conducted on income taxes, workman's compensation, and minimum wage requirements.

The Office for Experiential Education exists in an environment which is generally tolerant if not wholly enthusiastic about its mission. There remains a considerable degree of academic con-ventionalism, a fear of eroding standards, an anxiety about the theft of credit as though it were gold being burgled out of some academic Fort Knox.

Major Projects. Two current efforts may provide a better test of the office's ability to function. One of these is to steer course credit for experiential learning (up to 30 hours) through each academic department and the faculty senate. Thus far, 24 departments have endorsed the concept of the course, which was presented through a "model" course proposal and rationale. The adoption of this course by appropriate departments, and later the appointment of specific instructors for the course, will be a first tangible demonstration of success. The new course also carries with it the necessity of a written contract; the experiential education staff has developed this tool and is working with students and faculty in its use.

Secondly, a major information center is being established for students who want field placement, modeled somewhat on the C/AHED (See-Ahead) Center at Michigan State University. The information center is seen as the only feasible way of dealing with hundreds of student inquiries without spending massive amounts of staff time in personal counseling.

Student Role. Yet the major objective, perhaps equally as important as faculty support, is that of creating within the student body both the interest in exploring off-campus opportunities and the willingness to develop off-campus experiences aggressively for themselves. As one means of achieving this, learning opportunities in Kentucky are being gathered together into something like a *Whole Earth Catalogue.* Hopefully, by attractively packaging this catalogue, and including written encouragement for students to experiment, we will help students along the path working independently.

This last point deserves digression and elaboration.

> It is becoming fairly obvious that students have not been encouraged to take charge of and actively pursue their own educations; they do not ask why they are here, what their learning goals are, or how they can best achieve their goals. In other words they have been schooled to be told what and how they are to learn. Experiential education, which depends on student independence and initiative, cannot thrive in this environment. Consequently, not only must we create an environment where students will think "off campus," but we need to cooperate with others on the campus who are attempting to revitalize undergraduate education and encourage more creative student attitudes toward the learning process.

Experiential Education in Liberal Arts. A corollary need is to integrate experiential education into the general education program of the university. It is our opinion that it will be in the liberal arts fields that experiential learning can have its most significant impact. For it is here that the university continues to play its distinct role, not only as the keeper of the society's culture, but also as the place for helping develop men and women who can cope with society's complex ethical and cultural problems and who can lead personally satisfying and socially constructive lives as citizens in a participatory democracy. So by combining liberal arts values with field placements, a new breath of life might be blown into an old academic objective. If learning by doing is a concept valid for engineers, why is it not appropriate for all decision-making citizens? If understanding the internal workings of organizations like government is a desirable object for all educated persons, as well as political scientists, why not use the experiential technique to convey the message of the humanities?

Cost/Benefit Analysis. Another need, which will be more obvious to administrators at higher levels, is to cost our efforts to determine whether our efforts are worth the price. The Office for Experiential Education at the University of Kentucky obviously will not become institutionalized until its costs are known and are felt to be reasonable and affordable in view of the benefits derived. How these benefits can be measured is a question yet to be answered to everyone's satisfaction.

The creation of the Office for Experiential Education at UK does not mean that "experiential education" has been institutionalized at the university; it says only that an institution has been created with the goal of institutionalizing the concept. Only the first step has been taken; the most important goals lie ahead. Until the university, with full awareness and agreement, understands what it has done by creating this office and understands the implications of experiential learning as they relate to goals long held to be important in higher education, experiential education will not be institutionalized.

Historian Robert Sexton was Executive Director of the Office for Experiential Education at the University of Kentucky until 1980, when he became Executive Director of Kentucky's Pritchard Committee for Academic Excellence. He now serves as President of the Kentucky Center for Public Issues. He was a founder of the National Center for Public Service Internship Programs and a steering committee member for the Society for Field Experience Education, which merged in 1978 into NSIEE.

John B. Stephenson was Dean of Undergraduate Studies and Professor of Sociology at the University of Kentucky. He is now the President of Berea College, where he continues his support for experiential education in the liberal arts.

Required Versus Voluntary: The Great Debate

Lee M. Levison

As part of a national study conducted for the National Associa-tion of Independent Schools (NAIS) with support from the Ford Foundation, Lee Levison compares the pros and cons of required versus voluntary programs for community service for students in independent schools. This section is reprinted with permis-sion from Community Service Programs in Independent Schools *by Lee M. Levison, NAIS, 1986, pp. 37-45, 57. The full report is available from NAIS, 75 Federal Street, Boston, Massa-chusetts 02110.*

AT THE 1985 ANNUAL CONFERENCE of the National Associa-tion of Independent Schools (NAIS), a panel discussion focused on why schools choose either to require service or to make it voluntary. Steven Lorch, head of the Akiba Hebrew Academy in Merion Sta-tion, Pennsylvania, pointed out that "Akiba's motto is 'Study leads to action' ... [and] one means we have found for making a statement about the primacy of action over pure scholarship is to *require* of students a significant commitment to community service." More-over, he added, required service is consistent with the Hebrew concept of "Tzedakah, which means *just* social action." According to Lorch, "Tzedakah" is viewed as a " ... binding, divinely ordained commandment on a par with all other religious obligations." In the case of Akiba, community service is considered an obligation, and it is therefore perfectly appropriate to require it of students.

Not all religiously affiliated schools require community service. C. Thomas Kaesemeyer, head of the Westtown School in Westtown, Pennsylvania, a Quaker school, shared Westtown's rationale for its voluntary service program as part of the same program. The Westtown community, he said, is concerned " ... that by instituting a requirement of community service, there is the risk of depreciating service in other areas." The "other areas" include, in particular, a school-wide volunteer program that has students assist in the day-to-day running of the school (e.g., daily janitorial and kitchen work). The school was also concerned about the effect of "requir[ing] serv-ice by] an indifferent or uninterested student" and that the student's performance might " ... be a real hardship on the person being helped." Finally, required service is inconsistent with Westtown's Quaker values.

These examples suggest two major points of contention related to requiring service. Religious schools often see service as an obligation; service is something that all members of the faith must do — it is non-negotiable. Those who oppose required service argue that the client suffers when he or she is subjected to an indifferent student.

Among the nine schools visited [as in-depth case studies in NAIS' research], students in required service programs were found to support required community service unequivocally. Asked if they would advocate changing from a required to a voluntary program, the common refrain was "Keep it mandatory. It is too easy not to do it." Many students echoed that sentiment: "If it was voluntary, I would not have done it." "If you don't require it, students would never do it. They would just pass it over." Requir-ing students to serve "forces" them to do something which, given the choice, they would not do. Why do they need to be *forced* to serve?

For some students, the thought of working with the elderly, the handicapped, or the terminally ill is terribly frightening. Many students in required programs said they would have avoided doing service because they "were afraid." A mother told the story of her daughter who literally had to be dragged into the nursing home the first few visits because she was petrified of elderly people. A student told me about a classmate who cried uncontrollably before entering her placement. In some cases, then, students are reluctant to serve voluntarily because they fear the unknown.

Other students in required service programs say they lack the discipline to make time to do service. Their lives are busy, and spending time in a nursing home is neither fun nor profitable. Many students [in the schools studied] are over-achievers. They partici-pate in as many school non-academic activities as possible ranging from sports to drama. Some students and faculty believe that the motivation for this hyper-involvement is selfish. Students in independent schools want to insure that their "extra-curriculars" appear strong when placed under the microscope of a college admissions committee. One service coordinator expressed concern about "overworking kids in activities." He thinks "Kids are overly concerned about success; they are obsessively compulsive."

Some students seek economic trade-offs. They work at paying jobs after school. One teacher said he was confused by his students and their mad rush to work between 15 and 20 hours per week. They do not *need* the money, but they work nevertheless. Community service cuts into a student's time to earn money. Without a community service graduation requirement, many students would choose not to participate. Students in required programs believe that requiring service is the only way to get people to do service on a regular basis while they are in school.

Students in voluntary programs feel quite differently. "In a required program not everybody will be interested and they won't put everything into it. You should have people who want to do it." Required service "detracts from the voluntary nature of the program. It takes the heart out of it." "Mandatory service," observed one student," carries a large negative connotation because we feel like the faculty is trying to control our lives." "If you are forced to do it," declared one student, "it becomes a chore." As far as these students are concerned, required service forces people to do something they don't want to do. As a result, the client, the object of service, suffers. Required service, according to one student, "is stupid because you can't force someone to volunteer." Part of volunteering is the spirit of giving, which such students see as essential for *really* helping people. Making someone serve turns service into a job.

Students in voluntary programs seem to hold a theory of service that focuses almost exclusively on the spirit of giving freely. Forcing people to give, to serve, compromises the giving spirit. There is a sanctity that students associate with giving and volunteerism. If a person does not want to serve voluntarily, then he or she should not be forced to do it. This view is not limited to students.

Coordinators interviewed in schools with voluntary programs, like their students, did not demonstrate an interest in moving to required service. As most of them interviewed put it, they feel that forcing a student to serve "compromises the quality of the service and makes the client suffer." What makes service special is that "it comes from the heart." They say the value of service is lost if it becomes just another requirement imposed by the school. Some argue that since not all students are ready to do "altruistic" work, forcing a student into a service situation prematurely could turn the student away from service forever. For the most part, adults and students engaged in voluntary programs agree about the merits of the voluntary aspect

"The problem with a voluntary program," explained a coordinator from a required program, "is that you get kids who would do it anyway." In his view all students ought to engage in service, not just the "good" kids who would do it in any case. According to this view, voluntary service programs reach out to the people who need it least. Required programs, on the other hand, insure that all students have a service experience, that all students have the opportunity to benefit from service work. One coordinator remarked, "Requiring service is the only way we could be assured that everybody would have a service experience." "We give them certain academic requirements, and there is no equivocating on that," claimed one coordinator, "and we expose them to the benefits of team play. Through our required service program we expose them to the rewards of helping other people." These coordinators equate service with academic work. All students ought to be exposed to service. It is the school's duty to require this experience.

Coordinators in required programs are well aware of the arguments against requiring students to serve. "The most common argument against requiring service," observed one coordinator, is that you will ruin the student forever; he will always be antagonistic about service." He went on to share a story which, in his opinion, refutes the above argument. "There was a student who fought me vehemently about being required to do community service; he went to college and after graduation spent a year in Belize doing volunteer work." A school head shared a similar story: "One student took great umbrage at it because we were requiring him to do service. The student got involved, reluctantly, with handicapped kids. *He* got the commencement award for service." "The fighters are thinking more about the *value* of service, and they get more out of it," claimed one coordinator. The message in these statements is that requiring students to serve does not necessarily turn students away from service. In fact, the tension created by requiring service compels some students to reflect on service and to press school officials for reasons. Requiring students to serve can instigate a cognitive dissonance that results in a questioning of fundamental values and beliefs and, ultimately, in new learning.

Opponents of required service believe that forcing students to serve not only turns them away from service, but it is unfair to the clients who are victimized by indifferent students. As a student in a voluntary program observed, "Required service takes away from the beauty of volunteering. People whom we are serving shouldn't have to sacrifice for our growth." The director of volunteers at a nursing home was asked if she noticed a change in the quality of work by students when the sending program shifted from voluntary to required: "I am very pleased with the students' interest. I was concerned when the program became a requirement; I was concerned that they might feel differently. But I don't see much of a difference. It is a beautiful program." Other volunteer coordinators who utilize students from required programs responded similarly; there was no discernable difference between students from required and voluntary programs. If there was a slight difference, students from well-organized and highly supervised required programs were "better" volunteers than students from poorly organized voluntary programs.

Which side is right? On both sides of the required/voluntary dichotomy, untested assumptions abound. Those who advocate required service believe that service is good for *all* students regardless of their attitude toward it. Implicit in their advocacy of requiring service is that service helps all students, regardless of their maturity and whether they want to do it. On the other hand, proponents of voluntary service believe that forcing students to serve will forever "turn the student away from service."

Factors schools should consider when deciding whether to require service range from the school's philosophical objectives to subsidiary but important issues such as the school's location, the capacity of the community to absorb student volunteers, transportation, scheduling, and staffing.... Schools that require service without thinking about the implications of the decision may turn required service into a barrier.

Lee Levison is Dean of Students at Noble and Greenough School in Dedham, Massachusetts. He received his doctorate from the Harvard Graduate School of Education and did his thesis on student community service.

Should Service Be Mandatory?

Rosemarie Klie

This report and the one following it are adapted with permission from the (SPS) News Report, *Student Press Service, Youth Policy Institute, Vol. 11, No. 6, November 15, 1986.*

Should student community service be mandatory for high school graduation or voluntary? Students, their teachers and adult sponsors, and experts on education policy from 28 states discussed this question at a forum on community service held in Washington, D.C. The forum was sponsored by Independent Sector, a non-profit coalition of 650 corporate, foundation, and voluntary organizations interested in "activity related to the educational, scientific, health, welfare, culture, and religious life of the nation."

Diane Hedin, director of community relations at the Pillsbury Foundation, cited a study done last year that found "Five percent of all high schools [in the United States] require community service for graduation; four percent of all [the nation's] public schools require such. Twenty-seven percent of all schools have some kind of community service program as an elective or as a voluntary for-credit program."

Rocco M. Morano, assistant director of student activities of the National Association of Secondary School Principals, argued in favor of requiring service. "Community service should be mandatory. It is a good experience for students," he said. "Sometimes you have to force people to do things and then they find out that they like it."

Braircliff High School, located in a well-to-do suburb of West-chester County, N.Y., started a mandatory community service program three years ago with a grant from the Carnegie Foundation. However, exceptions in the rule are routinely made, meaning many students have not had to fulfill the service obligation. Scott Steinberg, a community service coordinator at Braircliff, stated that "the school is not enforcing the mandatory requirement. Students ... realize that they can graduate without doing any community service."

In New York state, the Board of Regents approved a plan in 1986 that requires all students to do community service in order to graduate.

In contrast, T.C. Williams High School in Alexandria, Virginia, does not require community service. Larry Trice, director of the Student Council Association at T.C. Williams, said, "Student community service should be voluntary. It's my impression that if it were a requirement a lot of kids would do it just to put the hours in. It's more meaningful if the student does it on his own."

Alec Dickson, the founder of Community Service Volunteers of London, England, whose pioneering work in this field inspired the founders of the Peace Corps in this country, suggested during his luncheon speech at the forum that schools combine the syllabus and community service. "There are ways of combining the two so that serving and learning do not tear us apart time-wise or fondness-wise," Dickson said. "For example, let kids do their gym exercises at a hospital ward and thereby entertain the elderly. You have not changed the syllabus."

Margaret Leipsitz, program coordinator of the JFK Foundation Library Corps, shared Dickson's idea. She said, "Community service should be integrated into the high school curriculum so that each class has a community service aspect."

Stephen F. Hamilton, associate professor of Human Development and Family Studies at Cornell University, strongly advocated community service. "The stuff learned in the classroom is left there and forgotten. For example, at Cornell, physics students can't relate the things they learn to the outside world," he said. Hamilton noted that students with out-of-the-classroom experience score better on standardized tests than those who only study in class. He described the ideal community service program as: 1) well organized, combining classroom learning with outside experience, and 2) requiring students to reflect and report on their experience.

Round Two: Required Public Service in School?

Gary Steele

The debate over required or voluntary community service by high school students was continued at the closing session of "New Directions in Community Service," a conference sponsored by the Volunteer Clearinghouse of the District of Columbia. Although all members of the panel agreed upon the value of community service for some, there was disagreement both on whether or not mandatory community service for all students would produce more positive than negative results and on who should decide whether such service should be required.

David Hornbeck, formerly president of the Council of Chief State School Officers and Maryland's top ranking public educator, began with a statement that community service provides essential and unique opportunities for personal growth. He proposed that states make community service mandatory for all high school students.

Claiming that the main threat to American society is the loss of the ability to care about others, Hornbeck presented community service as the best response to that threat. He said that with the increase in personal mobility and the decline of the extended family in our country, students not only have difficulty caring, but feel a lack of connection to a larger community.

Hornbeck also mentioned another reason for requiring community service. Young people today often go into the work force without basic job skills. Hornbeck said that employers frequently tell him that they want students to be able to take on responsibility, come to work on time with a good attitude, and be able to take directions. All these things, according to Hornbeck, would be best developed in America's youth through required community service programs.

Panelist William J. Burkholder urged that the disadvantages of mandatory programs must also be considered. Burkholder, Virginia's deputy school superintendent, supports leaving decisions about requiring community service to local school boards. Burkholder said that good programs take time to originate and maintain, and that schools are already overburdened. Further complicating this problem is a feeling among many education patrons that schools should be "getting back to basics" and not creating new, mandatory programs. Similarly, the community service agencies that students would be placed in do not always have the time to train students and redesign their operations so that the students play a meaningful role. Burkholder also cautioned against making changes without doing more research.

The third panelist added her voice to Hornbeck's call for mandatory service. Audrey Epperson, director of the Washington Urban League's Operation Rescue Tutorial Program, drew upon her experiences with volunteers to make several points in favor of mandatory programs. Students, and especially ones from disadvantaged backgrounds, benefit from serving in the community because it exposes them to different organizations, helps them explore career opportunities, and teaches them that they are valuable people who have something to offer to others — experiences unavailable to many underprivileged children.

Jonathan Schwartz, president of the District of Columbia Student Government Association, represented the student voice by saying that while most students would benefit from community service and help the community at the same time, the minority who would not could ruin the program for everyone. Schwartz is a student at Banneker High School, known for its mandatory Community Laboratory program. He said even at Banneker there are problems with uncooperative students, and one should expect more problems in a less ideal situation.

A member of the audience said that much of the value in service work comes from volunteering, making a commitment without outside pressure. Hornbeck and Epperson responded that while volunteerism is ideal, students who would not otherwise volunteer can have their eyes opened to new possibilities through mandatory programs. Burkholder said that states establish minimal, basic requirements and allow the local schools to establish electives. Hornbeck said that community service is important enough to be required statewide.

Part IV

Institutional Policy Issues and Guides:

Strategies for Institutional Change

Strategies for Institutional and Organizational Change

Jane Kendall, John Duley, Tom Little,
Jane Permaul, and Sharon Rubin

Whether you are establishing a new program or working to strengthen the support for service-learning programs across an institution, this summary of principles and strategies for organizational change can help. While this chapter is written in the language of colleges and universities, the principles outlined are also relevant for K-12 educators and for staff of non-profit or government organizations. Adapted with permission from Kendall et al., "Strategies for Institutional Change," in Strengthening Experiential Education WithinYour Institution, *National Society for Internships and Experiential Education, 1986, pp. 121-136. This chapter complements the one by Barry Heermann in this resource book.*

THE TERM "INSTITUTIONAL CHANGE" sounds sweeping, scary, and so difficult that it feels almost silly. We use the term on two levels. First is the level of systemic or structural change, which is indeed infinitely complex. This is the level wherein degree requirements or expectations of faculty are changed. Change at this level takes a long time. And it does not really happen as an identifiable, planned process in most institutions. Systemic changes result from a series of much smaller changes. Sometimes only after a few years of small adjustments do the scope and nature of larger changes become clear. This second level of change — small steps to strengthen service-learning within different arenas of the institution — is the one that will receive most of your attention. Each step contributes to the larger process of "institutionalizing" service-learning within your college or university. If you were just trying to start or improve one particular program, the process of change would be much more straightforward — not simple, just more straightforward. It is the very *nature* of the broader goal of institutionalizing service-learning to be slow and complex because it is reaching to the heart of the academic enterprise — your school's mission, style, curriculum, faculty expectations, quality, administrative structure, and purse strings. We challenge you to plan both your long-range vision and the incremental steps needed to help your school progress toward it. The results *will* be worth the effort, the time, and the patience because service-learning will in turn strengthen your institution's capacity to fulfill its multiple missions.

This chapter will draw on the experiences of 20 pilot institutions that participated in a process of planned change through a program of the National Society for Internships and Experiential Education. These colleges and universities were working to strengthen their institutional support for experiential education — the teaching approach essential for effectively combining community service with learning. By listening to some of the people who have been deeply involved in the process of planned change for two or more years, you can avoid reinventing the wheel. You can at least start with a wheel, and maybe even a wagon. (The quotes in this chapter without full references are from discussions at national seminars held for the 20 pilot institutions by NSIEE.)

Principles of Change in Institutions

Before you plunge into a campaign for institutional change, consider the *principles* about change in organizations that have been observed by researchers and by catalysts for change. Students of organization theory and individuals engaged in coaxing institutions toward change report remarkably similar conclusions about what works and what does not. This section divides these principles into four groups. In order to be an effective catalyst or supporter for constructive change, you will need to:

1. Recognize the basic principles of personal and organizational change. After reviewing the voluminous literature on the process of change, we think that the accompanying summary by Walter Sikes will give you one of the best overviews available.

2. Understand the conditions necessary for changes in educational practices to occur. First, like all organizations, colleges and universities respond to both internal and external forces to maintain a condition of homeostasis (Little, 1980). Therefore, changes in either internal or external needs can initiate change in the college. External forces will always be a strong factor for higher education because it is dependent on external resources. An internal or external perception that an institution is not performing a particular function well is enough to cause a degree of instability in the equilibrium of the college or university as a system. Some such instability or perception of need is thus the first general condition for change to occur. In the words of state legislators, "If it ain't broke, don't fix it." People have to perceive that something is broken.

Secondly, advocates for change are needed, usually from within the institution. External advocates can have tremendous power in initiating change or creating the level of instability needed for change, but internal advocates are required for the actual process of sustained change.

The third general condition necessary is that of resources for change. This probably does not mean additional funds are needed. With a change as pervasive as building experiential learning methods or a public service philosophy into the way the institution teaches students, the needed resources may come primarily from adjustments in the use of existing resources rather than from new funds.

There are also five more specific conditions necessary for colleges and universities to change their educational practices (Evans, 1968):

a. What is proposed must be more effective or efficient than current practices in meeting an accepted goal.

b. What is proposed must be consistent with existing values and with what is currently being done in pursuit of these values.

c. What is proposed cannot be perceived as too difficult to implement.

d. What is proposed must be dividable into separate components to be introduced across time rather than implemented as a total package at one time.

e. There must be both a mechanism and a language for communicating the benefits of the new practices.

As Tom Little says, "For any curricular innovation, favorable reception is problematic. Faculty do not see themselves essentially as educators concerned with means and methods. Even in institutions that stress instruction, the emphasis is on content, not process" (1983, p. 23).

This entire book offers a collection of ideas about communicating the benefits of service-learning. The language and knowledge needed in order for faculty to utilize experiential learning methods has also been developed. The publications of the National Society for Internships and Experiential Education, the Council for Adult and Experiential Learning, and the Cooperative Education Association, and the *New Directions for Experiential Learning* series of Jossey-Bass Publishers can all be used to communicate this knowledge. See the "References" at the end of each chapter of this resource book.

3.   *Respect the reasons for resistance to change.* Walter Sikes' summary suggests several of the most important and valid reasons people and organizations resist change. In addition, a person may discount the value of the proposed change because of a lack of trust in the change agent. Often this lack of trust is not personal, but rather a result of the position the initiator holds in the institution. If you are in a position that is usually held in suspicion or misunderstood by the group who must implement the change you want, then you must find other advocates for the change. In higher education, this means that administrators or other non-faculty personnel almost *must* work through others if they want to influence the faculty. Faculty as a group are often resistant to change because of their particularly long training in the habits of academe. They observed academicians for years before becoming faculty themselves and thus have especially persistent assumptions and habits (Rubin, 1983).

4.   *Expect that people will react differently to change.* Rogers (1962) outlines five types of people in terms of how they deal with innovation in their own social systems:

a.   *Innovators* — venturesome, willing to accept risk. Rogers' research suggests that innovators make up 2.5% of the population.

b.   *Early Adopters* — respected, regarded by many others in the social system as models (13.5% of the population).

c.   *Early Majority* — deliberate, willing to consider innovations only after peers have adopted them (68%).

d.   *Late Majority* — skeptical, willing to consider innovation only before adoption occurs (13.5%).

e.   *Laggards* — tradition-bound, oriented to the past (2.5%). "While most individuals in a social system are looking for the road to change ahead, the laggard has his attention fixed on the rear view mirror."

Specific Strategies You Can Use

1.   *Know where you want to go. (If you don't know where you're going, any road will get you there.)* You may have strong feelings about what changes are needed, but a clearer consensus on

Some Principles of Personal and Organizational Change

by Walter Sikes

This article presents seven principles which I consider the core of what is known about personal and organizational change. Although much more could be said about the various complex processes of change, the following points represent a good amalgam of the key concepts that persons dealing with change will find helpful.

1. You must know what something is before you try to change it. Diagnosis is the key to effecting planned change. A change agent must have a sound, internalized understanding not only of the "facts" but also the feelings important to the change process. Thus, data collection and feedback are essential to initiating either personal or organizational change. A thorough understanding of the particular dynamics of a system that is to be changed will allow one to tailor the innovation to the specific situation — and greatly increase the chances for success.

2. Because all human change takes place in systems or organic units, you cannot change just one isolated element. Everything in a system is ultimately connected, so a change in one part affects the whole system. Therefore, try to understand the total impact of the proposed change on all parts of the system so as to reduce the chances of unwanted and unpredicted side effects.

Whether the system constitutes a large, complex organization or a single individual, the person(s) involved probably like(s) stability and predictability. Kurt Lewin's concept of a field of forces operating to maintain equilibrium presents an accurate image of the tendency of systems to oppose change. When people return from a T Group to their families or work groups, they typically encounter much resistance to their applying their brand-new skills and insights, and much pressure to resume their old behaviors — even if those behaviors were dysfunctional. Partners in architectural firms find it almost impossible to change their functions without involving at least the entire group of partners — and often other members of the firm — in the change process. When designing change, assume that those involved will probably be reluctant to go along with the new ways of doing things.

3. People resist punishment. Change generally generates discomfort, requiring at the least that one use extra energy to adapt to a new situation. People tend to consider alterations in a system a form of punishment. Even changes that one considers desirable may entail some discomfort. For example, the families of alcoholics frequently become so programmed to deal with the problems of the addict that they resist making changes that would produce more functional behaviors.

We often have difficulty understanding why others consider change so punishing. A parent may wonder, "What does my teenage son consider so painful about reading an additional half hour per day?" Even the son may not be able to give a clear answer — but he knows it feels bad.

4. People are reluctant to undergo current discomfort for long-term gain. Learning a new skill, whether it is technical or behavioral, at the least causes the pain of feeling incompetent for a time. We feel more comfortable using familiar behaviors and already-mastered skills, so we prefer to polish, refine, and rely on them rather than develop new, possibly better skills. Even people and organizations taking part in programs to facilitate change tend to depend on the skills developed beforehand and avoid moving into untried areas.

Typically, people will resist changing their lives even on the chance that they will be better off for doing so. When the prospect of future benefit is uncertain, one especially tends to hang onto the current way of doing things. Therefore, people entering a change effort must be provided with support and motivation during the "painful" early stages. They will also find it helpful to experience early rewards.

5. Change generates stress. Studies of the sources of stress have shown that any kind of change induces stress, which is a reaction of a system accommodating new conditions. Changes that we feel we cannot control are the most stressful. Therefore, to reduce the stress of the change process, those affected must, as much as possible, perceive that they can influence the process.

6. Participation reduces resistance. Probably no principle of social psychology has been studied or confirmed more fully than the concept that one may increase people's acceptance of an innovation by getting them involved in setting goals and devising strategies for achieving these goals.

Such participation, however, requires such preconditions as time in which to consult with those involved, a communications system that allows the parties to reach one another, and sufficient common purposes or values to allow potentially fruitful exchanges to occur. Moreover, those involved must be willing to invest time and energy in the participative process, and those with the most power must be willing to share at least some of that power. These conditions do not always prevail, but frequently they do, and they may often be generated in circumstances in which we assume they are absent. In any event, to the extent that those involved in a changing system can become involved in establishing where the system is going and how it will get there, the movement will occur less stressfully and will likely be more enduring.

7. **Behavioral change usually comes in small steps.** Few individuals or organizations are willing or able to make dramatic, sweeping changes in a hurry. When we attempt to produce change in another — or ourselves — we usually seek to have it occur right away, especially if the one trying to induce the change has more power than the other. When a parent tells a child to stop bouncing on the bed, the parent means "stop now." The child, however, will try to maintain its self-worth and take a few more bounces before stopping. When a boss tells an employee to change her or his way of doing things, the boss usually expects this to occur immediately — but the employee will need some time to make the adjustments requested. We must realize that abrupt changes in behavior are rare — and probably even unhealthy — and that we must allow adequate time for changes to take place.

These seven points do not represent everything one must know to be an effective change agent. But in my own efforts to bring about or support innovation, I have found that I am more likely to succeed if I can design the effort to take these principles into account.

Walter W. Sikes, Ph. D., is the Executive Director of the Center for Creative Change and was formerly program director for the National Training Laboratories Institute and Dean of Students at Antioch College. Reprinted with permission from Walter Sikes, NTL Connections, NTL Institute, May 1985.

the current strengths and weaknesses is important for documenting (or altering) your instincts and developing a realistic strategy for sustained change.

2. *Get bottom-up support.* In short, start with input from the people most directly involved. Most colleges and universities have particularly "bottom heavy" power structures because of academic freedom and departmental autonomy. Thus, the general principle of building grassroots support is even more important in colleges than in more hierarchical organizations. As Edwin Potts, Assistant to the President at Westmont College, says:

> Negotiate rather than legislate change. Centralized decision making regarding experiential courses and programs will not be very effective. All affected persons and departments need to participate in the discussion and the decisions.... It is important to discuss the nature and benefits of experiential education on a faculty-wide basis. [If we were to start over again, we would] begin with a faculty committee to discuss the issues.

If you are in a large institution, you might translate "faculty-wide" to refer to the faculty within one department or division.

3. *Introduce doubt.* "Leaders may need to disrupt a comfortable environment in order to make it receptive to change. Few elements disrupt complacent, uncritical environments as much as doubt aimed at the core beliefs of the culture. Challenging these crucial underpinnings can bring old forms of action to a halt, create substantial uncertainty, and heighten receptiveness to change" (Cameron, 1984).

4. *Take advantage of changes in the society and in school leadership.* As economic shifts, higher tuitions, and questions of cultural values have helped to raise public concern about the quality of college teaching, the outcomes of a college education have received considerable attention. Experiential education and the service-learning programs that use experiential methods are in a strong position because they are premised on what is known about how people learn. Take advantage of the climate of instability (i.e., receptiveness to change) that this and other social developments create. Hefferlin (1969) found that curriculum changes are positively correlated with shifts in society. As might be expected, curriculum changes also correlate positively with faculty turnover, institutional growth, and turnover in departmental leadership.

5. *Use a consultant.* A person who is knowledgeable about experiential education *and* about institutional change can be help-

ful in clarifying your school's (or division's) needs, developing a strategy for addressing those needs, and planning specific next steps in getting started. The National Society for Internships and Experiential Education has developed a group of such consultants with this particular combination of expertise. As Sharon Rubin warns, however, "Such symbolic gestures as bringing in experts can give people the illusion of change while maintaining the status quo" (1983, p. 49). While a consultant can make observations and suggestions, the school has to make its own changes.

6. *Measure what you want to be noticed.* "What is measured almost always receives more attention than what is not measured. Hence, moving to quantify an activity can help increase its importance in the way it is regarded" (Cameron, 1984).

Every semester, a faculty member, graduate student or program coordinator should collect information on the number of student inquiries about community service-learning, the number of students enrolled in courses with service components, the number of agency requests for students. If development of a division-wide or campus-wide program is being considered, an even more comprehensive census is necessary. However, qualitative benefits must also be assessed. In addition to the formal assessments of the outcomes of service-based experiential learning, students, supervisors, and faculty must be polled regularly for anecdotal information on the success of participants. Regular collection of relevant comments from student self-evaluations and from agency and faculty evaluations can also reveal the academic quality inherent in service-learning experiences. Finally, a collection of student service projects can help to make decision makers comfortable about extending a program that has obvious academic quality.

7. *Use the views of students, alumni, and the community.* Encourage students to voice through all the channels available to them their desire for service-learning opportunities.

Like students, alumni often have strong views about the value of experiential learning. Most say they wish they had had more opportunities to apply concepts and gain experience while still in school so that they could better understand the relationship between theory and practice. Alumni often see in hindsight the value of building in community service as a regular part of campus life. The views of alumni can be influential to policy makers, especially if you make sure the relevant questions are posed to alumni and the results disseminated broadly. Involving alumni as field supervisors and mentors for current students can help to ensure their continued support, both philosophically and financially.

Sometimes even a reluctant faculty member will sponsor a student in community service-learning when the field supervisor is "one of our own." If that student demonstrates valuable learning from that experience, the faculty member is more likely to sponsor another student next semester. Also bring respected alumni back to campus to talk to faculty about the value of what they learned experientially through the curriculum of their alma mater.

Finally, the community can be an ally in your efforts. If there are potential needs for students to assist with environmental research, opinion surveys, publicity campaigns, computer adaptations, or other projects in your community, bring these to the attention of the appropriate faculty members. If you hear complaints that your school is "disorganized" because prospective sponsors have to go to a dozen departments for referrals, raise this problem through a committee or appropriate leaders.

8. Get others to speak for you. Whether you are trying to change attitudes or program structures, those whose support is needed will be more likely to participate if they are approached by their own peers. Faculty like to hear from other faculty. People in Academic Affairs are more likely to listen to others from Academic Affairs than they are to Student Affairs professionals (and vice versa). Work through opinion leaders.

9. Get top-level support. This may sound contrary to the previous advice to "get bottom-up support," but it is not. Support at different levels is needed for different purposes and at different times. To sell an idea in a college takes grassroots support among faculty. To implement the corresponding change of a policy or administrative structure, you need top-level support. Liberal arts dean Sharon Rubin says, "We have found that if you ask for help with good information, if you plan instead of whining about how you can't possibly do it, if you prime the pump a little bit (for example, through a university research council which gives funding to faculty for research, some outside money from a grant, collaboration with a couple of units on campus who all want to do the same thing), it takes very little to get an administrator interested in how to pursue excellence through service-learning or other approaches that use experiential education. It is really important to involve the highest level of administrators both ceremonially and actually. When you host a meeting, invite them to say hello. When you have an honor to bestow, have the President bestow it to a site supervisor or to a student whom you are honoring — so that your presence is felt on a continuing and active basis."

10. Plan incremental, not sweeping changes. Expect the overall process of change to be slow and ongoing. As Frederick Rudolph succinctly puts it, "Experimentation, which was the life of the university, and innovation, which was its gift to society, were seldom tried upon the colleges and universities themselves" (1962).

11. *Use other colleges and universities as models.* More than most institutions, higher education relies on precedent. While models from within the campus are especially powerful, programs and approaches used at other *peer* institutions are also good targets for emulation. When advocating for particular programmatic or policy changes, the key is to recommend good models from institutions that are perceived to be the same as or slightly better than your own in terms of status and academic reputation.

12. *"Use papier-mâché instead of concrete"* (Rubin, 1983, p. 53). Avoid the tendency to try to anticipate every possible problem in the program or policy by setting rules to address each one. A new approach can sink of its own weight if you load it down with too much structure before it even gets started. Instead, experiment with one department or for a limited time. Develop policies as they are needed rather than artificially imposing limitations at the beginning. A trial approach can be revised during and after the initial period so that the best model emerges over time — in small, incremental steps.

13. *Use outside funding to prime the pump.* Grants can stimulate change and offer opportunities for low-risk experimentation. They can also prime the pump for the commitment of institutional funds or other resources. Sometimes it takes very little from a foundation, corporation, or government agency to convince an institution to try something. This can be true for new programs as well as new policies. BEWARE, however, of the *frightfully* common pitfalls of outside funding. These are outlined in "So You Think a Grant Is the Answer" in this resource book.

14. *Expect each department or division to react differently.* The autonomous nature of most academic departments or other sub-units in colleges and universities means that each has its own culture and priorities. Anticipate that their responses to change will also differ, and respect these differences.

15. *Expect resistance.* If there were no barriers to overcome, you would not be in a process of change. When resistance comes, you have made progress in clarifying what problems need to be addressed. Consider the resistance as an invitation to negotiate. The strength of the resistance will also be a measure of just how big the proposed change is. If it proves to be too big, this is a helpful signal to slow down and break the changes down into smaller steps. If the resistance cannot be overcome and if the proposed change

cannot (or should not) be scaled back, work around the resistance. Remember there are five predictable types of responders to innovation — Innovators, Early Adopters, Early Majority, Late Majority, and Laggards (Rogers, 1962). You can expect several of each type on your own campus. It is not productive to spin your wheels trying to convince the Laggards of the need for change. Focus on the Innovators and Early Adaptors first and then on the Early Majority.

16.   *Share everything.*   Look for opportunities to give the visibility and "ownership" of the new policies or programs — and even the strategy — to the people who must implement them. With ownership comes commitment. If a strategy or a particular program remains "your baby," it will never gain the commitment needed from others in order for it to work. Like parenting, nurture it and then let it go — or at least bring others into the process — if you want vital and sustained results.

17.   *Publicize the progress.*   Keep as many people as possible aware of proposals and changes as they develop. Then the next incremental step will not seem like a giant leap. This does not mean you should burden people (or make costly political mistakes) by circulating every draft plan or set of brainstorming notes across the campus, but do look for opportunities for broad communication of key developments.

18.   *Use rituals or ceremonies.*   "When a professional sports organization has a losing season, it fires its coach. The firings don't represent substantive changes so much as symbolic affirmations of the team's commitment to a better future. Inaugurations, ceremonies, and commencements — not to mention receptions, teas, and parties — fulfill analogous symbolic functions at the departmental level and can be used to manage the meanings and interpretations which constitute the groundwork of change"(Cameron,1984). What are the usual ways that changes or special events are recognized on your campus? When you pass a milestone look for ways to recognize the progress through your school's usual rituals or ceremonies. Have a luncheon for your first group of field sponsors who participate in the newly developed advisory board for community representatives. Plan a faculty reception for the new director of a centralized coordinating office for departmentally controlled service-learning opportunities. Invite the dean to give the award to the most outstanding faculty sponsor for students doing community and public service.

19.   *Increase your personal effectiveness.*   Broaden your base in the institution. Become an academic advisor. Sit in on policy committee meetings. Talk to the people in the instructional devel-

opment center and the office of institutional research. Offer to help with committee assignments through which you could learn about a new area of the institution. Look at the enrollment projections and annual fiscal reports of the institution. In short, learn more about how things work across the campus. If you have not taken the Myers Briggs Type Indicator, you may find this a useful way to understand your own approach to leadership. And finally, learn to take risks. There is no way around it: change involves risk.

For any strategy you devise, the most important challenge will be to help faculty and administrators see the benefits of strengthening experiential education across the institution. If you understand the principles of how change occurs and develop strategies for incremental steps toward the changes needed, you will make a real contribution to the education offered by your institution. Your route will certainly be interesting even if it is a bit unpredictable. As F. G. Bailey (1977) says:

> "Scylla is the rock of principle; expediency is Charybdis. Politics being what they are, the ship seldom contrives to steer a straight course between them. Usually, if there is progress, it is achieved by bouncing from one rock to another."

Jane Kendall is Executive Director of the National Society for Internships and Experiential Education. John Duley is Professor Emeritus from Michigan State University. Tom Little, founder of the Virginia Program, now works with socially responsible technology. Jane Permaul is Director of the Office of Field Studies Development at UCLA. Sharon Rubin is Dean of the School of Liberal Arts at Salisbury State University and President of the National Society for Internships and Experiential Education.

References

Bailey, F. G., *Morality and Expediency*, Blackwell Publishers, 1977, as quoted in Becher, 1984, p. 199.

Becher, Tony, "Principles and Politics: An Interpretative Framework for University Management," *International Journal of Institutional Management in Higher Education,* November 1984, Vol. 8, No. 3, p. 198.

Cameron, Kim S., "Organizational Adaptation and Higher Education," *Journal of Higher Education,* Vol. 55, No. 2, March-April 1984, as quoted in *Academic Leader,* Vol. 1, No. 8, September 1985.

Evans, Richard I., *Resistance to Innovation in Higher Education*, Jossey-Bass, 1968, pp. 16-17.

Gross, Edward, and Paul V. Grambsch, *University Goals and Academic Power*, American Council on Education, 1968, Chapter 2.

Havelock, Ronald G., *The Change Agent's Guide to Innovation in Education*, Educational Technology Publications, 1973.

Hefferlin, J. B. Lon, *Dynamics of Academic Reform*, Jossey-Bass, 1969.

Little, Thomas C. ed., *Making Sponsored Experiential Learning Standard Practice*, New Directions for Experiential Learning, No. 20, Jossey-Bass, 1983.

Little, Thomas C., "Changing Educational Policy," unpublished paper, 1980, p. 7.

Rogers, Everett M., *Diffusion of Innovation*, Free Press, 1962, p. 155.

Rubin, Sharon, "Overcoming Obstacles to Institutionalization of Experiential Learning Programs," in Little, *op. cit.*, 1983, pp. 43-54.

Rudolph, Frederick, *The American College and University*, Random House, 1962, p. 492.

Watson, Goodwin B., and Edward M. Glaser, "What We Have Learned About Planning for Change," *Management Review*, November 1965, pp. 44-46.

Strategies for Change

Barry Heermann

A former community college dean summarizes successful ways to increase support for the use of experiential learning in a college setting. Because combining service and learning requires the use of experiential learning methods, these strategies are important for anyone in a college setting who is involved in service-learning. Reprinted with permission from "Experiential Learning in the Community College," ERIC Clearinghouse for Junior and Community Colleges, Topical Paper No. 63, University of California, Los Angeles, July 1977. This chapter complements the previous chapter of this book.

If a person is to grow up, he needs, in the first place, access to things, places, processes, events, and records. To guarantee such access is primarily a matter of unlocking the privileged storerooms to which they are presently consigned.

— Ivan Illich (1973)

ACCEPTANCE OF THE NOTION that learning may take place in locations other than college campuses is one thing, and providing opportunities for experiential learning is quite another. Bringing about a change of this kind in education can be exceedingly difficult. As experiential educator Samuel Baskin points out, the barriers to change include:

Habits and tradition (we teach the way we have been taught); the threat of change and the security of doing what one has done before (why change a good thing?); vested interests (we had better protect our own domain); bureaucracy (what better way to stifle creativity than to send the idea through channels?); the history of education itself (education "happens" when a student comes to a classroom, takes a seat, and looks up at the teacher); financial problems (contrast industry's investment in research and development with higher education's allocations for programs or offices of this sort); the reward system (what "gain" for the teacher who challenges the system?); lack of time (contrary to their public image, most professors are so busy doing what they are doing that they have little time to ask whether they might proceed differently); inertia; and a host of other factors which lead us — sometimes consciously, sometimes unconsciously — to want to (or think we must) preserve what we have. (1967, p. 1)

Thus, successful programs are not just the result of careful planning, systems design, and boundless energy and enthusiasm. They occur because at least some of these barriers have been overcome. Specifically, change hinges on the knowledge, skills, and attitudes of the faculty, counselors, administrators, and other participants in the program. Without their support, one cannot implement a program of experiential education; and winning their allegiance usually requires a deliberate change strategy.

Kurt Lewin's work (1935) is especially pertinent to this subject. According to his "field theory" of change in social settings, an equilibrium normally exists between the driving forces and the restraining forces in the force field. Change is the result of modifying or changing the restraining forces or adding to the driving forces. The former is preferred, because adding to the driving forces may only intensify the restraining forces (which are often negative attitudes). Increasing the resistance leads to a "spinning of wheels" without forward movement.

Before the restraining forces can be modified, they must obviously be identified. In the college, these forces usually emanate from the following: college policy, tradition, fear, lack of resources, and the change agent. Typically, fear of change and its consequent disequilibrium are at the crux of the resistance. Resentment, too, may develop in those who are not involved in designing and directing the alteration. The change agent, although not a restraining force in him/her self, may unintentionally cause resistance in others, who may interpret his or her best intentions and loftiest aims as fanaticism. Or perhaps the agent's personality or interpersonal style is not congruent with many campus constituents.

Local circumstances will suggest the crucial restraints and dictate the action necessary. At one college I know, the following were serious restraining forces:

- conventional views about the location and circumstances in which learning occurs
- a faculty reward system based on contact hours of classroom instruction
- fee payment arrangement linked to credit-hour enrollment
- credit-hour awards based upon classroom ritual
- preoccupation with informational (rather than interpersonal) skills.

Attitudes regarding how and where people learn was a significant barrier. Only after this restraining force was modulated, especially at administrative levels, was it possible to deal with "nitty-gritty" issues. Changing faculty attitudes about the circumstances of learning was initiated simultaneously with the presentation of a formula for reimbursing faculty. The handling of this situation illustrates how one should analyze and tackle first the primary resistance. Once that is reduced, the secondary forces can be modified more easily.

Some useful change tactics include:
- third-party consultation
- change teams
- affiliations with professional associations
- visits to exemplary colleges
- advisory committee involvement
- in-service programs (biased toward attitude change).

There are available numerous experts in experiential learning design and development who are also skillful as change strategists. Since they necessarily have been adept at bringing about acceptance of experiential learning in their colleges, their consultation can be extremely valuable.

Change teams, another effective mode, should include a range of persons representing both driving and restraining forces and all constituent groups. How the team is created depends on local circumstances. Although the team, however formed, typically recommends a course of action to a designated administrator, Sikes, Schlesinger, and Seashore (1973) recommend that the team actually devise and carry out steps to produce desired change. They describe the interpersonal dynamics of the group as "open, nonhierarchical, nonauthoritarian." Using a consultant in conjunction with the change team can sometimes increase the potency of this change tactic.

Professional associations can also contribute much to the academic integrity of experiential programs, especially by helping the participants develop the requisite knowledge and skills. Colleges in the process of augmenting sponsored experiential learning should investigate the National Society for Internships and Experiential Education and the Cooperative Education Association. Colleges offering prior experiential learning options will be interested in the Council for Adult and Experiential Learning. CAEL and NSIEE have published numerous working papers and reports which provide excellent how-to-do-it information.

Still another valuable change tactic is to encourage visits to colleges providing exemplary experiential programs. This is a superb way to "whet the appetite" and to find out how such programs are operated. These trips are useful both for those skeptical about the educational merit of experiential learning and for those who are helping to design and develop new experiential programs.

Existing program advisory committees ought to be involved from the outset in considering how to structure experiential learning. Such an educational re-orientation is typically applauded by seasoned practitioners who appreciate that competence is very much a function of experience. Program directors and faculty members should also be encouraged to participate in discussions with the advisory groups in order to focus on and develop an understanding of the learning potential of non-classroom experiences. The format of committee meetings should be carefully conceived and should include a thoughtful presentation of the rationale for experiential learning. The aim, obviously, is to inculcate positive attitudes toward off-campus learning.

In-service programs for the faculty and administration are likewise essential. Like the advisory committee, they should deal first with attitudes. Once the participants are committed to the principle of experiential learning, they can begin to acquire the additional knowledge and skills they need through other in-service workshops. Representatives from academic councils, faculty organizations, student government, and administrator cabinets should be included.

Barry Heermann is Executive Director of the Expanded Learning Institute in Yellow Springs, Ohio, a resource center for computer use in education. He has also served as Dean of Public Services at Sinclair Community College and as Vice-President of the Union for Experimenting Colleges and Universities in Ohio.

References

Baskin, Samuel, "Innovation in Higher Education: Developments, Research, and Priorities," *New Dimensions in Higher Education*, No. 19. Duke University and U.S. Office of Education, 1967.

Illich, Ivan D., *Deschooling Society*, Harper & Row, 1971.

Lewin, Kurt, *A Dynamic Theory of Personality*, McGraw-Hill, 1935.

Sikes, W. W., L. D. Schlesinger, and C. Seashore, "Developing Change Agent Teams on Campus," *Journal of Higher Education*, Vol. 44, No. 5, May 1973, pp. 399-413.

The Myth of Sisyphus Revisited

Dan Conrad

Considering the current odds against educational innovation in secondary schools, educators need the persistence of Sisyphus — and the support of school and community — to keep pushing service-learning. Veteran Dan Conrad offers good-humored, timeless advice and a case study of how one program keeps on pushing. Reprinted from Synergist, National Center for Service-Learning, ACTION, Vol. 8, No. 2, Fall 1979, pp. 29-32.*

THE EFFORT TO IMPLEMENT and institutionalize an educational idea is not the stuff of which enduring myth is born, and the modern schoolhouse is an unlikely setting for adventure. As educators we are not asked (or allowed) to be heroes.

Yet there is something in us that yearns for a grander vision of what we do, that seeks a loftier metaphor for our quotidian efforts to ply the teacher's trade. No modern paladins we; we claim no parallel between our work and the flights of Mercury or the battles of Thor. But perhaps we may be permitted the small presumption of seeing something familiar in the figure of old Sisyphus heaving and straining beneath a heavy rock on his tortured way up a lonely hillside. At least let the reader be warned that this writer dares presume some higher significance to what we all do.

But know also that this particular story is written neither by nor for some god(s) perched smugly atop a local Mt. Olympus. Rather it is a field report from down below, from a fellow Sisyphusian on his own peculiar hillside pausing only long enough to catch a breath and to draw some insight and meaning from a difficult and perhaps even ill-fated adventure.

The particular charge I was given was to contribute to the general stock-taking of this volume by describing how a service-learning program in one school has developed and matured, and to assess the impact of that program on the rest of the school and community. My first inclination was to tell the story of our "success" much as one might report back to a foundation or other funding agency to convince them of the wisdom of their investment and to imply how just one more year of support could reap benefits beyond their wildest dreams. But it is just such reports that have created a myth about how educational innovation occurs, how ideas are diffused, and (either worst or best of all) institutionalized.

The core of the myth is that any good educational idea will catch on, prosper, and grow. A teacher tries it somewhere and succeeds. Other teachers recognize its value, try it, succeed (of course), and before you know it the idea infuses one school and curricular area after another, moving like wildfire across the country until the idea has taken its predestined place in the mainstream of educational practice. And like a Calvinist identifying the redeemed, the outsider can confidently judge the merits of alternative ideas by seeing which ones prosper and which do not.

But there's distressingly little evidence that it works that way. The odds seem stacked against any good idea, and its implementation and growth is a slow and torturous process requiring extraordinary effort and luck even to survive. Thus I find the myth of Sisyphus a more compatible image than the myth of educational diffusion for framing the story of how service-learning has developed within my school and others.

Obstacles Confronting Service-Learning

I must set the stage first, and today the stage is most aptly set by describing the obstacles confronting service-learning programs in secondary schools. Perhaps even Sisyphus himself will extend us his sympathy! The following difficulties are listed in no particular order of hardship or exigency.

• Sisyphus had an enormous advantage over educational innovators. The hillside up which he pushed his stone, while hard and unyielding, was at least firm and predictable. Educators find a less consistent surface, with the school resembling a quagmire more than a mountain. This is true in both its general structure and day-to-day operations.

At Eisenhower High School, Hopkins, Minnesota, we began our program at least partly as a way to make better educational use of the blocks of time which a modular/flexible schedule made available in the students' day. About the time we'd accomplished this and more than 90 percent of the seniors were involved in community service, the school returned to a traditional schedule and our program went back to the drawing board.

The prosaic interruptions of a typical day make it difficult to link students with ongoing community activities. About the time a student sets Tuesday from 10 to noon as his involvement time, Homecoming, Winter Festival, or a pep fest throws the schedule off and he finds math and English where the courthouse used to be.

• Sisyphus had a second, though mixed, advantage. He worked alone. One of the great strengths of a service-learning program is the participation of a large and varied number of people and agencies. Unfortunately this is also its curse, with problems seeming to grow exponentially with the number of people involved.

In programs such as ours, the placement of one student in a nursing home, for example, requires communication between the program staff, classroom teacher, nursing home staff, and the student. It demands coordination (or lucky coincidence) of the student's interests, skills, and schedule with the needs and schedule of the nursing home, and often those of the student's parents or friends (say, to get a ride there). This is to say nothing about communication with school administrators, other teachers, funding agencies, community representatives, and so on *ad infinitum*. Murphy's Law is more than a humorous saying to service-learning coordinators!

• A related advantage enjoyed by Sisyphus is that his rock didn't keep crashing into others' rocks. About 10 [20] years ago, when service-learning was a rather new idea, schools, were bursting with students, money was available, and the philosophy was "let a thousand flowers bloom,"

I needn't detail how things are different now, but must at least note how declining enrollments and dollars have affected the practices and the atmosphere of schools. We are operating in a time of scarcity, and the effect goes deeper than a lack of money. Teachers and programs are struggling for survival, and winners mean losers. If your program rises, mine sinks; a successful program is more a threat than an inspiration. Scarcity can, of course, spawn cooperation as well as competition, but school structures don't encourage that result.

Our school's service-learning activities have been incorporated by some of our teachers, appreciated by most others, and tolerated by the rest. That the balance may be shifting to the worse seems not to be a result of faults in the program (though it has many), nor of petty jealousies, but of the general struggle to survive. For many teachers this means closing the classroom door and sticking to what has worked in the past and evokes no controversy. For others it elicits a more aggressive reaction — from wondering aloud whether a service-learning program merits extra support to charging it with shanghaiing students for service in an essentially frivolous *divertissement*.

- A fourth advantage of poor Sisyphus is that pushing a rock up a hill was all he had to do. No teacher needs further elaboration on this point!

- Sisyphus enjoyed at least one further advantage. Hard as his task was, it was not very complicated. He, and anyone watching (or evaluating) him, knew both what he was trying to do and how to do it — though perhaps not why. Such is not the case with service-learning. Our practice fits under the general rubric of experiential learning. This is an idea that has been around a long time but is still not blessed with much systematic thought or writing about what it really means or how it's best accomplished. There's much we need to learn about the rich and complex endeavor called service-learning.

The Growth Years

Somehow, despite it all, service-learning programs do survive and sometimes grow. They are in hundreds of schools and involve tens of thousands of students across the country. Clearly this is a tribute to the strength of the idea and to the creativity and tenacity of those who work with the programs and believe in their value. But no program is all we might want it to be, and our own at Eisenhower is a case in point. Like many others we began in the late 1960s before we had a name for what we were doing or even thought of it as a program. The assistant principal ran an almost secret operation out of his hip pocket. It involved placing eight or 10 high school students in an elementary school across the street, mostly to fill light schedules with something more challenging than study hall and more productive than roaming the halls.

In the early 1970s, however, we began to think more seriously about what we were doing. Our participation with the Student-Community Involvement Project (a project funded by the Surdna Foundation and operated through the Center for Youth Development and Research of the University of Minnesota) provided some extra resources and put us in contact with other schools where similar ideas were being tried. We also found (or were found by) NSVP [the National Student Volunteer Program, which became NCSL, the National Center for Service-Learning, in 1979. A part of the U.S. ACTION Agency, NCSL is now defunct. Its extensive literature is now available at the National Society for Internships and Experiential Education, 3509 Haworth Drive, Suite 207, Raleigh, NC

27609.] and the National Commission on Resources for Youth, Inc., a national network on youth participation programs. In addition to getting new ideas, we discovered we were part of a national movement.

We tried several approaches at first, but settled on concentrating most of our effort on employing service-learning as a lab experience within the twelfth grade social studies course. Students typically served from two to four hours per week in a social service agency, doing this in lieu of a research paper or series of book reports. To the degree possible these experiences were drawn upon for student papers and for invigorating class discussions by reports from the world outside the school.

The program continued to grow and had its heyday from 1975 to 1977 when a Youth Challenge grant from ACTION provided us with a full-time coordinator, a van, and a driver; we already had an interested social studies faculty and a supportive administration. In 1977-78 almost all seniors and many juniors and sophomores (a total of some 400) plus nearly 100 junior high students took part in service-learning activities. We expanded beyond the social studies department to include others. Art students wrote, produced and performed traveling puppet shows. Industrial arts students provided construction and repair services to community agencies. Anatomy students taught first aid skills to younger children. Home economics students ran a nursery school. Auto shop students put on free automobile pollution checks for the community. The school's swim club provided free drown-proofing training to all community youngsters. In these and many other ways students used their special skills to benefit the community. We also inaugurated a special Community Involvement course that met for two hours every day and combined a weekly seminar with six to eight hours of service a week for a full credit in social studies.

At this point the extra money ran out, and we rather limped through the following year. Instead of reducing and revising the program to something more realistic, we tried to maintain it as it was. We had to run it now on whatever time and energy was left over, or could be stolen, from regular teaching duties. We still had some 250 students involved, but by the spring of the year the new departments had pulled back their involvement, field supervision was almost nil, community requests for help were going unanswered, and we were very tired. The program was bigger than we were! Another grant was applied for — and rejected. To make matters worse, a new mood prevailed in the school leading to a decision to eliminate from student schedules those blocks of time that had been used by many for service activities. We weren't hopeful for the 1978-79 year.

Surviving by Popular Demand

Fortunately, the program had developed a base, a momentum, and a constituency that wouldn't let it die. The Community Involvement course was an integral part of the curriculum and would continue in any case. It had three sections and 90 students.

But both teachers and students wanted the lab component for the other courses to continue — and said so.

The administration and school board liked the program and what it was doing for kids — and the favorable publicity it was bringing the school.

The community was counting on student help — and some of their programs required it for survival. (Thirty service agencies participated in a recruiting fair last fall and have begun again to see the school as the place to call for help.)

For these and other reasons the school board decided, in the summer of 1978, to support the program with a half-time faculty position. This was no small commitment when the budget was otherwise being cut. We've since divided that position between a part-time director and part-time coordinator and have added student assistants. Tighter student schedules and lack of transportation (we're in a semi-suburban community) have restricted participation, but we had more than 200 students involved last year in more carefully developed and supervised activities.

The twelfth-grade social studies course began to meet five instead of four days a week, with the fifth day used largely for reflection and discussion of community activities and for mini field trips. Nearly a third (115) of the seniors register for the Community Involvement course.

While the social studies department remains the chief vehicle for involvement, it is very much a total school program. Students use their community experiences as material for speeches and personal essays in English class and as a focus for extensive research papers in several departments; the swimming program continues, as does the nursery school. School social workers look to the program as a source of activities that will engage turned off students; special education teachers involve regular students with their own with special needs. As important as these specific activities is the fact that our faculty members support it, tolerate the disruptions it invariably engenders, and teach many of the skills the students use to improve the community.

As hope springs eternal, we've applied for another grant. This time it's to extend service and other experiential learning opportunities from kindergarten to the twelfth grade, and to make service internships available to the faculty as well as to students.

Levers for the Rock

I don't know just how far up the mountain we've gotten with our rock, but at least we still seem to be inching along. Along the way we've learned a few things from our own and others' experience that may help all of us over the hard places between which, and our rocks, we tend to get stuck.

1. Don't hide your light under a bushel — publicize! A service-learning program can be the next best thing to a winning football team for building good public relations for a school. We extemporize a bit on the notion of service by placing a student skilled in photography at the local newspaper with the school (and our program) as his beat.

2. Examine thyself — evaluate! People are demanding accountability, and rightly so. If you're not into things like multivariate analysis and nonparametric statistics, at least poll students, parents, and community supervisors on the benefits they see in the program. Just the fact you're doing an evaluation is a positive statement — and you usually learn something. We have sociology students practice opinion sampling this way.

3. Serve your school. As dollars disappear, the school needs help just as the rest of the community does. A St. Paul school requires that students put back into their school a part of what they've received from it. They can tutor, teach mini-courses, assist classmates with disabilities, or even sweep the halls, but they must do something for the school.

4. Involve others. I seriously doubt that any speech or article, in itself, has ever convinced a soul that service learning is a good idea. But I've never seen a student fail, or known a firsthand observation to be ineffective. A university evaluator recently reported to me his amazement at the things he'd seen at a service-learning site. What sold him on the program were things any coordinator sees most every day!

5. Give your principal some credit. Better that the principal think of it as his or her program than praise you for yours. The next time you're asked to talk about it, send your principal instead.

6. Treasure your uniqueness. As good as it sounds for service-learning to infuse the entire curriculum, don't hold your breath until it happens. In the meantime, make sure it has at least one solid base in one curricular area, and take some solace in it being an oasis amidst more traditional fare. That may be your greatest recruiting advantage.

7. *Don't worry about the name.* A rose by any other .... One school system has maintained a strong service-learning program as citizenship training, action-learning, career education, and concentrated youth employment. Service-learning can fit into these (and many other) categories with little difficulty.

8. *Don't get isolated.* We do get in ruts, but can be refreshed by contact with other local programs, and through national journals, conferences, and newsletters.

9. *Look for outside resources.* Retrenchment is real. Even a few dollars from a local business or service club can help — and give others a stake in your survival. Often we overlook rather obvious resources. We just caught on that our district's volunteer coordinator could have handled most of our tutoring placements, that the Red Cross will train nursing home volunteers, and that the Junior League will help students process their experiences in career-oriented seminars.

10. *Try, try, again.* The most memorable and moving element of the legend of Sisyphus is not that he was pushing a rock up a mountain, and not that upon getting it to the top it rolls back down to the bottom. What catches the imagination is that he follows it down and immediately begins to push it back up again. Many of us have been pushing service-learning for the better part of the last decade. If there's another retrospective in another 10 years, my hope is not that we'll all be at the top but that we'll at least be somewhere on the mountain — and still pushing. [See the Program Profile about this program in this resource book for a view of it in 1989 after 10 more years of pushing!]

Dan Conrad directs the Community Involvement Program at Hopkins High School in Hopkins, Minnesota. He has been a well-known national writer and researcher on high school service-learning and experiential education for 20 years.

Starting Off Right With Teachers and Administrators

Cathryn Berger Kaye

*A practical checklist for a K-12 school program that combines
community service and learning and that acknowledges the importance of sustained support and participation by teachers and
administrators.   Reprinted with permission from* Network,
Constitutional Rights Foundation, *Vol. 1, No. 2, Spring 1989,
pp. 8-9.*

HOW IS A STRONG COMMUNITY service program established
and maintained within our schools? An essential ingredient is the
ongoing involvement and commitment of educators — school
administrators and teachers.

Youth Community Service (YCS), a joint program of the Constitutional Rights Foundation (CRF) and the Los Angeles Unified
School District, has enjoyed excellent relations with administrators
and teachers. CRF staff developed deliberate procedures to promote their participation and "buy-in" from the start. During the
past five years, these professionals provided valuable assistance in
securing the interest and enthusiasm of their peers, and ultimately
the success of the program.

Administrators

"The Youth Community Service program enhances the leadership skills of many students who normally operate outside the traditional student government structure. Students
learn to brainstorm, plan and implement a variety of projects. The YCS program gives its participants a sense of
power."   — *Jim Davis, Principal, Westchester High School
Los Angeles Unified School District*

Establish clear objectives that address priorities set by the administration. At the onset of developing a community service approach at each school, CRF and LAUSD high school division staff meets with a school administrator team — principal, assistant principal, and the teachers who will work directly with the students — to determine the goals of the community service program at their school site. Key topics and sample responses include:

➤ Identify the problems, issues or concerns of the school and surrounding community that this program should address, such as:
- Poor public relations
- Unemployment, transiency and ethnic changes necessitate the development of projects to bring the community together to address absenteeism, attrition and school performance.

➤ What programs exist at the school which already address these problems? How?
- Key club/student government involve small numbers of students.
- The Alumni Association has established a special committee to work on community relations.

➤ Identify any community groups affiliated with the school that could provide resources for the students and program. Examples:
- The local Chamber of Commerce
- The phone company has "adopted" the school; employees tutor on an irregular basis.

➤ Indicate any additional support the administration will provide teachers and students during the initial three years. Examples:
- Coverage in the school and community papers
- Active participation in projects
- Parents will be informed of community service options available for their children.

Involve school administration in program ownership. People who develop ownership in the program have personal and professional commitment to its success. Ways to promote ownership include:

➤ Keeping administrators informed by:
- One or two annual administrative review meetings to examine progress. Students frequently attend these meetings.
- Program documentation: newsletters, student written project proposals, occasional memorandum, copies of relevant correspondence.

➤ Defining an active role for each administrator within the scope of his/her normal job responsibilities.
➤ Asking successful administrators to inform their peers about the benefits of school-based community service.

Involve administration in the program. Encourage students to utilize school administrators as a resource for their community service involvement. Students can:
➤ Interview the administrator to find out about community needs, leadership, current issues. Inspiration for projects often spring from these meetings.
➤ Invite the administrator to work on a project.

Recognize a job well done. While administrators should generously congratulate students and teachers for their contributions, recognition can also be given to administrators. Examples:
➤ Appreciation from students, teachers, and program coordinators is always well received.
➤ Community acknowledgement builds positive public relations for the administration, school and district.

Teachers

"I have thoroughly enjoyed my participation with Youth Community Service. I have met dynamic, energetic young people who are bursting with good ideas. I have been privileged to witness acts of genuine, selfless kindness by students. Shy students have blossomed into activity through advocacy on behalf of others and built friendships with individuals they would never have met except for their involvement with community service."
— *Mark Wilkins, Lincoln High School Teacher,*
Los Angeles Unified Schools

Encourage teachers to network with each other.
➤ In kindergarten to high school situations, teachers are too frequently isolated within their departments, upper grades, or classrooms. Identify ways teachers can meet together formally with community service being the agenda through day-long conferences, after school workshops, and lunchtime rap sessions.
➤ Keep all teachers, including those not directly involved with community service, informed about the program on a consistent

basis through teacher-to-teacher interaction, newsletters, and by hearing directly from youth participants. Invite teachers to help out with projects or help identify community needs students can address through service.
➤ Provide opportunities for teachers to share their expertise, resources and contacts with their peers. Establish a district-wide assistance network.

Assist teachers in establishing community contacts.
➤ Teacher education programs as yet have not included methodologies for reaching out to the community. Assist teachers to develop a "rolodex" mentality of chronicling what goes on in the community.
➤ Provide a get-together forum for the community and teachers. Bring in speakers to department meetings, school gatherings or special events.

Recognize teacher professionalism.
➤ Provide periodic staff development seminars to increase their ability to address relevant topics and assist young people with leadership.
➤ Take teachers' academic and personal calendars into consideration when scheduling meetings and activities.

Reward teachers publicly for their hard work and contributions.
➤ Written commendation thanking the teacher with copies to the principal helps keep morale high.
➤ Encourage students, parents, community members to recognize the teacher through letters, awards, community breakfasts.

A Planning Conference on School-Based Service

The commitment of teachers is a crucial element of a successful school-based community service program. They are the ones who directly work with the students to develop the necessary skills and attitudes for effective service. They are the ones who monitor the projects, give advice and support and ultimately make a program work.

What can be done to promote teacher interest and involvement? We suggest an in-service or planning conference which:
• illustrates school district and community support
• introduces key concepts for effective programs

- assists teachers in establishing program criteria and design
- provides incentives for ongoing program development and implementation.

This model was used at a conference held for teachers from Pasadena Unified School District in Southern California from 9:00 to 4:00 on a Saturday. The district inaugurated a school-based program at each of six high schools the following month. The event was organized and presented by Cathryn Berger Kaye, Director of Youth Leadership Programs, Constitutional Rights Foundation, and Sharon Thralls, Community Service Director, Pasadena Unified Schools. This format can also be used for a teacher/student/community conference.

Before the conference. Establish a planning committee to develop and review the proposed agenda at least two months before the event. Include a school district representative, teacher, and experienced community member to help clarify the purpose for the day, and identify resource people.

In planning an agenda be sure to emphasize methodology of useful curriculum and strategies for working with students that promote interaction and small group discussions. This gives teachers "hands on" experiences that can be immediately applied back in their own school classrooms.

Program
ARRIVAL AND REFRESHMENTS

WELCOME — *15 minutes* — Invite a school board member or official to describe the district's community service history, including the rationale and school board/administration support.

GROUP DISCOVERY — *20 minutes* — This "ice breaker" introduces team-building through familiarity and trust. Ask the group what they want to know about the other people in the room. List topics on the board. Conduct interviews on these topics in pairs. Each person introduces his/her partner. In Pasadena, categories were hobbies and interest, family background, favorite books, and personal motivation for being involved in community service.

WHAT IS SCHOOL-BASED COMMUNITY SERVICE? — *20 minutes* — Combine an introduction and historical overview of school-based service and the current national movement with a video showing young people in action. The Pasadena conference included screening a five minute clip from *The Today Show,* December 31, 1988 showing Pedro Reyes, a Los Angeles high school Youth Community

Service student who quit a street gang to be an active community service volunteer.

➤ Personal reflection: Ask each person to recall an early experience with community service. One person remembered helping her mother deliver food to families in need and questioning her mother's generosity when food was not plentiful. She was pleased to find the connection with her past and present.

ASSESSMENT: WHERE ARE WE NOW? — 60 minutes — What community service programs are available in the district? Where are you starting from? Where are you going? Current programs and models can be examined in small groups with proposals for large-scale implementation. In Pasadena, the following topics were addressed since a program approach had been selected. For a group in the planning stage, participants could work in small groups, each addressing one topic and report recommendations to the larger group.

➤ *School Approach to Community Service.* School-based models available for adoption were introduced by each teacher: (1) course offering within the social studies department; (2) auxiliary period class meeting two mornings per week; (3) independent study for credit; (4) voluntary co-curricular programs.

➤ *Student Enrollment.* Student participation was looked at from numbers, demographics, skill levels, recruitment strategies, etc. Work in small groups to develop suggestions for promotion and recruitment.

➤ *Community Placements.* Will community placements be identified by adults or students? Can students develop their own projects? The more involved the students are, the greater the potential for service-learning and long-range benefits.

➤ *Visibility.* Student community service improves public relations and gives the school well-deserved recognition. Brainstorm ideas: school newspaper, faculty/parent information, posters, display case, t-shirts, ongoing documentation, and media contacts.

➤ *Procedures.* Review operations for maintaining the ongoing community service effort.

THE STUDENT COMMUNITY SERVICE TEACHER'S GUIDE — 20 minutes — Introduction and survey of any written materials available or adopted for the program.

LUNCH — If possible, provide lunch for the participants. Be sure enough time is left unscheduled for informal dialogue.

A STUDENT SPEAKS — *10 minutes* — Particularly if a large-scale community service program is new for the district, identify a youth representative to describe his/her experience, personal benefits, what she learned, and contributions made to others.

THE COMMUNITY PERSPECTIVE — *45 minutes* — One or more community resource persons can provide an overview of community needs, concerns, and what young people can do. With multiple guests, use a small group discussion format. These same resource persons can be scheduled to meet with students.

DEVELOPING THE SERVICE ETHIC — *60 minutes* — Discussion topics:
➤ *The Hierarchy of Participation.* A discussion of the levels of successively sophisticated involvement including: serving in existing agencies; raising questions from what is seen or experienced; identifying needs; developing projects to meet these needs; recruiting other participants.
➤ *Critical Points of Effective Service Programs.* See the principles of good practice in this resource book.
➤ *A Look at Reflection.* A brainstorm/discussion on issues that may arise from community service, both procedural (finding disorganization within a community agency, time management difficulties, inappropriate placements) and social concerns (environmental, racism, dissatisfied employees, neglected populations, power). Identify what a teacher can do when these topics arise from systematic or informal reflection. For example, films and simulation materials are available that address racism; Studs Terkel's *Working* can augment a dialogue on attitudes about employment.

CONCLUSION AND ASSESSMENT: WHERE DO WE GO FROM HERE? A short written assessment provides the presenters with information useful for future meetings. Close with a next step for follow-up — specific activities to bring to school, next meeting date, etc.

After the conference. Provide teachers and district personnel with feedback from the conference and with personal letters (copies to the principal) thanking the teachers for participating. Feature the event in a district publication to acknowledge the support and interest of the teachers, district and community for school-based service.

Cathryn Berger Kaye is Director of Youth Leadership Programs at the Constitutional Rights Foundation in Los Angeles.

PART V

History and Future of the Service-Learning Movement

Service-Learning in the South: A Strategy for Innovation in Undergraduate Teaching

William R. O'Connell, Jr.

A regional higher education official — now a college president — outlines how the "service-learning" concept was born and the promise it holds for undergraduate education. He describes the original service-learning internship model as one example of an approach that intentionally seeks a dynamic interplay between service and learning. Since its origins in 1964, "service-learning" has come to describe a philosophy and an epistemology as well as a wide range of program models. From his presentation on "Innovations in Undergraduate Instruction" at the 1972 National Conference on Higher Education in Chicago; reprinted from Service-Learning in the South: Higher Education and Public Service 1967-1972, *Southern Regional Education Board, 1973, pp. 4-7.*

OFF-CAMPUS, EXPERIENTIAL EDUCATION is fast becoming a major and acceptable part of undergraduate education across the country. More and various types of institutions are adding activities outside the classroom and off the campus for many students. In the past year there have been several national meetings which have included a focus on some aspect of this development. Current interest in providing non-traditional educational opportunities for students has been stimulated largely by recommendations from national bodies such as the Carnegie Commission on Higher Education and the Newman Task Force. Of course, interest on the part of educators is also stimulated by growing recognition that locations away from the institution can provide legitimate learning environments.

Field work, internships, and cooperative education of varying types have long been a part of most professional education, but the current interest is much more encompassing and attention is being turned to developing opportunities for all students, not just those in professional programs, to gain practical experience as a regular part of the undergraduate experience.

Over the past five years, a program has been operated in the Southern region to provide college students opportunities to combine social and economic development internships with their college programs. A major result of this program has been the emergence of a philosophy which can apply to the broader development of off-campus experiences for students. The unique contribution of this program to the development of innovations in undergraduate instruction is the concept of a balance between service and learning through the relationships among the various components of the internship.

The Development of Service-Learning in the South

Work to develop service-learning as a strategy for change in Southern higher education began with a community service program which started in Oak Ridge, Tennessee, and was further developed and expanded by the Oak Ridge Associated Universities (ORAU).

The internship program was based on two perspectives. First, students had been used as interns by the Clinch-Powell River Valley local development association during the summers of 1964 and 1965, under the leadership of several Oak Ridge staff members working on a volunteer basis. Second, with nineteen years of experience in administering educational programs involving many colleges and universities for the Atomic Energy Commission, ORAU was considering the possibility of utilizing this experience in areas other than nuclear science. The Tennessee Valley Authority, which had helped with the first local internships, expressed an interest in expanding that idea. ORAU agreed to develop a program and to seek support from other agencies for additional internships. Drawing on experience in administering similar programs for science students and utilizing Oak Ridge administrative and program development procedures, thirty-nine interns were placed in 1966.

To further expand and develop these ideas, the program was moved to the Southern Regional Education Board (SREB). This

move in 1967 officially expanded the program to the fifteen participating SREB states and began the concentrated effort to stimulate
college student involvement off campus.

The expansion of these internships in resource development
and their movement to SREB grew out of a concern for relating
higher education to programs of social and economic change, and
was based on a tested sample of the potential service of students as
well as a growing public acceptance of the pleas of students for more
relevant educational experiences.

Objectives

Since the formalization of this program, its objectives have
remained consistent, though some of the elements have been refined through experience. There are several dimensions to the program which appear to be somewhat distinct, though they are related
through these underlying objectives. The continuing objectives of
the program are:

1. to give immediate staff assistance, through the work of
   students, to agencies concerned with economic and social
   development;
2. to provide constructive service opportunities for students
   seeking to participate in the solution of social and economic
   problems;
3. to encourage young people to consider careers and citizen
   leadership in public service and provide a pool of trained
   personnel for recruitment in public service;
4. to allow students, agency personnel, and faculty to engage
   in a shared learning experience from which all can benefit;
5. to provide additional avenues of communication between
   institutions of higher learning and programs of social and
   economic development by making the resources of the
   universities and colleges more accessible to the community
   and providing a means for relating curriculum, teaching,
   and research to contemporary societal needs.

The dynamic relationship between the personnel goals and the
educational goals gives vitality to the experiences of all involved.
The term *service-learning* has been adopted as best describing this
combination of the performance of a useful service for society and
the disciplined interpretation of that experience for an increase in
knowledge and in understanding one's self. The coupling of action
and reflection has implications for both education and vocation and
also is seen as more than a useful technique for performing a task or

for educational enrichment. It leads to practice in the development of a lifestyle.

The concept of service, which is promoted in this program, implies an obligation to contribute to the welfare of others or to the community as a means of development and fulfillment as a human being. It recognizes the need for honest and rational interpretation of these experiences as a disciplined means of increasing understanding of human needs. These two concepts coupled as one unit suggest the possibility of a lifestyle of sensitivity, maturity, commitment, and creativity. Service-motivated action for meeting society's needs, either as a career or through citizen action, is encouraged and deliberate; self-directed learning as an unending process is promoted.

Service-learning has proven to have much to commend it to public and service agencies and to educational institutions. The contributions of students as extra manpower and the learning dimension of practical experience are obvious and are not unique to this internship program. The linking of service and learning, however, as provided in the SREB internship pattern provides experiences not usually found either in student jobs or in the traditional academic field experience programs.

Program Approach

The SREB internship structure varies somewhat with the type of student, the choice of topic, the character of the host agency, and the policies of the participating college or university. However, all follow a basic pattern which includes common ingredients that seem to maximize the potential for both effective service and effective learning. The SREB program model is not the only one that can balance service and learning. The following is offered as an example of a program design that intentionally seeks to balance the two.

Each intern is assigned to an organization carrying out programs related to social or economic development which can effectively utilize the student's ability and contribute to his learning.

Each internship begins with the definition of a project by the host organization, with assistance from program staff and university representatives. The work to be done in the project must be needed by the host organization, be of sufficient scope and level to assure motivation and growth of the student, and be feasible in terms of the limitations of time and the student's experience.

Universities and colleges usually participate in internship projects in their own geographical areas. They provide assistance in defining purposes, scope, and methods to be used in completing the chosen project as well as determining educational values. Interns are recruited through participating colleges and begin immediately to share in planning the specific project work and schedule. Faculty counselors for each internship come from the participating institutions.

Each intern has a project committee including a host agency official, a faculty counselor, and often a technical representative. The agency official gives the intern guidance, assists in gaining access to community resources, relates the project to the overall program of the organization, and aids the intern in obtaining any needed services. The university counselor is available to advise on procedures and methods and assists the intern to set and meet standards in carrying out the project and preparing a report. The counselor also assists the intern to review and interpret his or her experience for educational and personal development. The technical representative is someone who assists with projects in specialized areas. He or she assists the intern in identifying technical resources and in properly dealing with technical matters in the intern's report.

Interns are charged with performing a specified task and are given the time, financial support, organizational status, and personnel resources to accomplish the project objectives. They are primarily responsible for determining their own schedules and setting directions. They can call on committee members to assist rather than supervise them. This independence and self-direction is an important feature of the program in stimulating student response, growth, and achievement.

Seminars held for all students are designed to stress the interrelationships among various activities and problems in social and economic development. These gatherings allow interns to share experiences and gain a broader perspective on public issues.

All interns write a final report which gives them a means to organize and articulate their accomplishments, observations, and recommendations. The reports are written to the host agencies and therefore must be useful as well as meet academic standards. Project reports are normally reproduced in quantity for use by the host organization.

Interns have completed projects in such diverse areas as industrial development, tourism, recreation, conservation, reclamation, forest management, watershed development, manpower development, health, education, training, social services, and municipal management.

Program Expansion

From its informal beginnings with four interns in 1964 through the summer of 1968, the intern project had developed and administered internships for 356 students. Agency response was extremely favorable even to the point that many were willing to use their own operating funds to support interns.

SREB decided in 1969 that program decentralization across the Southern region should be the next emphasis. This move served to enlarge the administrative capacity of the program and, more importantly, to extend and further develop the service-learning concepts. Since 1969, SREB's effort has been devoted to encouraging and assisting the establishment of state-level programs. The results have been dramatic in terms of the number of students, institutions, and agencies involved. Five states — North Carolina, Georgia, Virginia, Texas, and South Carolina — have operated statewide programs, and several others are in various stages of program planning. Affiliated state-level programs have provided opportunities for more students to participate and for the development of internships with agencies and higher educational institutions in closer association. This closer relationship has brought more commitment from colleges, often including the assignment of staff and faculty at institutional expense.

Financial Support

Financial support for these internships has come largely from non-educational agencies. Until decentralization efforts began, all costs were paid by grants or contracts from federal agencies to SREB. These funds provided for the payment of all but agency participants as well as the general operating costs. Students received stipends for their work and faculty counselors were paid by the program, though currently many faculty participate as part of their regular institutional load. Other costs include student travel — if required by the project and to attend the seminar — and report reproduction.

Support has been provided through the years at varying levels by the Economic Development Administration (EDA), Office of Economic Opportunity, Coastal Plains Regional Commission, Appalachian Regional Commission, Tennessee Valley Authority, and the Department of Labor. The Office of Economic Research of EDA, however, has been the sustaining agency; this agency has provided financial and philosophical support for the refinement of the service-learning concept and is responsible for the program's survival.

Parenthetically, it should be noted that officials of this EDA office initiated efforts in 1969 to establish similar regional programs across the country in agencies comparable to SREB. These programs began by using the procedures and principles established in the SREB program, though each has now developed its own distinct characteristics.

Beginning with the 1969 efforts to decentralize program operations, principles of cost-sharing were also developed. Many agencies accepting students agreed to pay portions of the interns' stipends, sometimes the travel costs, and often the full cost of report reproduction. Some colleges have provided faculty counselors at no cost or on released time with expenses for travel paid by the program. Funds available under federal grants were supplemented through cost-sharing and program decentralization to the extent that there were 500 interns in 1969 as compared with 150 in the summer of 1968 with roughly the same amount of financial support from federal agencies.

Since that time, while operating with even fewer funds available through grants to SREB, the number of students involved has continued to expand with the addition of new sources of funds in each of the affiliated programs and through new arrangements for sharing the costs involved.

Successes and Challenges

The success of these service-learning internships has been judged largely on the basis of enthusiastic response to the idea and testimony of successful experiences. The demand from students for opportunities to participate has outstripped the ability of any program administrator to supply positions. Agencies that once host interns under this plan are anxious to have more, even when required to invest additional program funds. Some colleges have officially established service-learning internships as part of their academic offerings. One such college is Mars Hill in North Carolina, which has completely revised its curriculum and reflects earlier extensive participation in this program. Examples of such dramatic response are scarce however.

Several pilot studies have provided evidence that basic beliefs about the program are sound. A sample survey of agencies which had participated in the program showed that participants felt the interns had made definite contributions to the agencies and provided positive service to the communities. In efforts to evaluate the learning dimensions, interns have indicated an increase in understanding community problems, public needs, and the realities that affect solutions to these problems and needs. Through cross-cultural experiences students say they learned a great deal about people very different from themselves and ways they might work with these fellow members of society. Students and faculty counselors both indicate that generally interns gain new skills in identifying specific, practical problems and independently determining ways to deal with them.

As a strategy for affecting change in the undergraduate curriculum, service-learning in the South has still to provide the academic community with sufficient evidence that these concepts deserve special consideration. Like most suggested innovations, and particularly those in the area of experiential education, evaluating the learning dimensions is the most complex task. Some preliminary work has been done through the North Carolina Internship Office and may provide a design for further study of these concepts.

A very important aspect of this multi-dimensional program is the opportunity for new institutional-community relationships. With the student as the focus, the faculty member and agency personnel serve in a relationship that seems unique in this community-based educational approach. Working together as partners with the student helps them to develop new insights into the contributions that each can make to the other's work. Faculty often realize potential contributions to the curriculum while agencies may identify a new source of technical assistance. More systematic investigation of this aspect of the program is also needed.

The full potential of service-learning seems yet to be realized by most colleges and universities which have been involved. It seems inevitable that off-campus, experiential educational activities will continue to grow. Whether an institution chooses to adopt this particular approach to service-learning or some other, the concepts developed and tested in this action program offer additional alternatives to the traditional programs of field work, practicum, co-op, or work-study. The service-learning model offers another type of off-campus program that seems specifically suited for consideration by the college or university interested in expanding its opportunities for undergraduates to learn.

William O'Connell has served as Director of Special Programs at the Southern Regional Education Board and Vice President of the Association of American Colleges. He is now President of New England College in New Hampshire.

North Carolina: Early Leader in Service-Learning

Robert L. Sigmon and David N. Edwards, Jr.

Two early innovators in combining service and learning describe the first statewide center for service-learning developed in 1969. Their experiences and insights are useful for innovators in the 1990s and beyond. Reprinted from Service-Learning in the South: Higher Education and Public Service 1967-1972, *Southern Regional Education Board, 1973; first published in "Higher Education in North Carolina," North Carolina Board of Higher Education, June 14, 1972.*

SINCE 1969, the state of North Carolina has exposed service-learning through the North Carolina Internship Office (NCIO). This particular form of experiential learning is a distillation of considerable thought about three questions: what is worth knowing, what is worth doing, and how community-based learning can be maximized. To provide a sound learning context, service-learning requires of any internship that: (1) there be a task whose meaning is clear to the students; (2) the students receive careful support from their educational institutions; and (3) reciprocal learning among the students and their work directors be encouraged.

In the three-year history of NCIO (as of 1972), the interplay of the three preliminary questions and the three ingredients of a successful internship has led to the completion of ten substantial studies by NCIO and two major articles in national publications.

How It Happened

Obviously, however, these products of cerebral activity could not alone have convinced the governor, the General Assembly, the

Department of Administration, and the North Carolina State Board of Higher Education (BHE) to support service-learning as they have done. What dramatized not only the validity but also the utility of service-learning was the realization that most of the vast creative energies and talents of our 148,000 college students were not being directed to state program development, management, and advocacy. What better way to enlist student power than through service-learning? Thus, in March 1969 the Southern Regional Education Board (SREB) and the North Carolina Department of Administration agreed to establish a state internship office. A director was employed in April of that year, and SREB provided direct assistance through a student intern associate and staff consultation. The Department of Administration gave financial and administrative support to sustain the organizational responsibility vested in the Board of Higher Education.

The next 36 months saw NCIO manage or help initiate programs involving over 1,000 service-learning internships and assist in the development of 12 internship programs across the state. These programs have been supported by the raising of over $500,000 and by the cooperation of 150 public agencies. Several events helped mold the present configuration of NCIO. In September 1970, Governor Robert Scott told the Southern Governors' Conference:

> I want very much for us to provide leadership in developing constructive opportunities for college students and faculty to contribute more directly to programs of economic and governmental improvement in the South .... I would like to see the establishment of a network of programs so that we can extend the opportunities for service-learning to a much greater number of students and make more effective use of the energy and talents of these young people in helping their region achieve a higher quality of life. This is one approach to making our collegiate curricula more meaningful to students. It is also a promising way to attract more able students into public service careers.

During the 1971-72 session the General Assembly went on record supporting the ideals and programs underpinning service-learning. On July 1, 1971, through an appropriation from the General Assembly, the Board of Higher Education assumed fiscal responsibility for NCIO and has recently made the office an integral part of the new Center for the Continuing Renewal of Higher Education. On August 20, 1971, the Board of Higher Education passed a resolution expressing its support of NCIO and service-learning, recommending higher education's use of these two learning resources and suggesting expansion of the service-learning option to all students, with academic credit where warranted.

The programs and activities generated by NCIO have resulted from the coordinated focus of three aims: (1) to increase university and college student involvement with public needs and opportunities; (2) to increase the utilization of off-campus North Carolina as a learning environment; and (3) to provide options for students to be exposed to and to develop a service-learning lifestyle.

NCIO embarked on a strategy in the fall of 1969 that included: (1) development of regional service-learning programs in Appalachian North Carolina; (2) assistance with urban-university-model programs in Charlotte and Winston-Salem; (3) liaison with existing and newly created student internship programs and their managers; (4) development of issue-focused internship programs in planning, health, law, and the environment; and (5) sustained planning, advocacy, and evaluative review.

Using a service-learning internship design (an agency base, a specific project, university support, project committee support, seminars, and final report), NCIO initially gave attention to colleges and universities with limited or no off-campus learning experience and to nearby public-service agencies that demonstrated a readiness to participate in service-learning programs.

NCIO has also provided the leadership for convening project managers of internship programs in the state and providing a clearinghouse of information on programs. The network that is emerging is informal and committed to working collectively in improving and increasing off-campus service-learning opportunities for college students in North Carolina.

In addition, NCIO has provided technical assistance to a number of programs in North Carolina state government. Publications on the service-learning concept, faculty roles in it, and other training-related materials have been produced and distributed throughout North Carolina. Research and training designs have been developed and applied by the staff of NCIO in cooperation with different programs across the state. As the SREB-initiated effort with North Carolina in 1969 was to be a model from which other states could learn, the NCIO staff is providing direct assistance to state government personnel in Georgia, Pennsylvania, South Carolina, Virginia, and West Virginia.

Special-Issue Programs

Through the interest of the Department of Housing and Urban Development (HUD) in exposing minority students to governmental planning issues, through the interest of three predominantly black universities in off-campus learning opportunities for social planning, and through the NCIO commitment to arranging service-learning opportunities around special needs or issues, two sequential grants from HUD were made available for social planning to service-learning interns from Shaw University, Winston-Salem State University, and North Carolina Agricultural and Technical State University.

With the emergence of ecological concern, NCIO has coordinated and provided administrative assistance in arranging environmental internships. Student-originated projects relating to environmental issues were funded by the National Science Foundation (NSF) at the University of North Carolina at Asheville, Mars Hill College, Wake Forest University, and East Carolina University. The first three institutions received encouragement and support in proposal development from NCIO.

NCIO helped the University of North Carolina Medical School Department of Family Medicine at Chapel Hill initiate an extern program for fifty medical students in Appalachian learning settings.

With assistance from the North Carolina Central University Law School, NCIO through a law student intern-associate developed a program for law students to work with solicitors and defenders. This effort promises to provide a model for other clinical-education experiences for law students in the state.

Looking Backward and Forward

In the program and projects reviewed above, NCIO has attempted to maintain a consistent educational philosophy and long-range perspective. The questions set forth below reflect the controlling considerations:

1. Are the projects dealing with local community needs? Does the problem or task of the student internship assignment have a sense of human importance about it?

2. Are we meeting these needs in interinstitutional ways? Are university officials, agency officials, citizens, and students cooperating through the internship process?

3. Are we raising the levels of dialogue about the quality of life within the university, the communities, and public agencies? Are the questions "What is Worth Doing?" and "What is Worth Knowing?" being pursued with more vigor?

4. Are the students involved beginning to deal more competently with their own experiences as interns and to appropriate their learning for the development and application of their own values?

Looking to the future, NCIO, directing its resources to a service-learning promotional strategy, will:

1. Further increase service-learning opportunities for college students by urging the state to support and make accessible to the people a center for advocacy, program development, technical assistance, research, and clearinghouse on opportunities. NCIO, within the new Board of Governors, has this potential, and NCIO's current compilation of a "state-of-the-art inventory" on community-based, experiential learning programs should help develop a realistic plan of implementation.

2. Urge all public and private colleges and universities to endorse service-learning as legitimate education, make it eligible for academic credit, and recognize faculty involvement in service-learning with financial and status rewards. (The Board of Higher Education has set an example for this in the resolution cited above.)

3. Urge public organizations and private agencies to embrace public needs by participation in service-learning throughout the year. This implies appropriate regular budget designations and student staff provisions, especially under the position categories of staff personnel, contractual services, training, or special line items.

4. Help infuse existing experiential programs with service-learning possibilities. This would help expand youth involvement in public issues and events through current mechanisms (e.g., state agency internship programs, local government programs, legislative internships, field experience programs, special programs at colleges and universities).

5. Encourage greater student participation in planning and operating programs.

The functions of information brokerage, fund-seeking, moral support, cultivation of government involvement at all levels, research, program management, and training can thus be seen as common elements of the recorded past, the developing present, and the projected future of NCIO. The office has executive, legislative, and administrative mandates, a list of proven successes with the service-learning model, and at least the potential for a variety of vital services to education and government in North Carolina. With continued support, NCIO feels it can realize its goal of seeing that every North Carolina college student has the opportunity of at least twelve weeks in community-based experiential learning as part of his or her academic career.

Robert Sigmon served as the founding Director of the North Carolina Internship Office, and David Edwards was the Assistant Director.

Federal Antecedents of Community Service

National Governors' Association

The NGA outlines some of the government-sponsored antece-
dents to current programs for community service. Reprinted
with permission from Community Service: A Resource
Guide for States, *National Governors' Association, Committee*
on Human Resources, Center for Policy Research, 1989, pp. 2-3.

THE CURRENT NUMBER and variety of service proposals have their antecedents in the many service programs that historically have dotted the American landscape. The concept of community service was first introduced to the country, on a large scale, during the New Deal era with the Civilian Conservation Corps (CCC).

In the 1960s, a new era of activism swept the country. ACTION, Teacher Corps, National Health Service Corps, University Year for ACTION, National Center for Service-Learning, and Young Adult Conservation Corps are just a few of the numerous programs with a service orientation to appear in this and the following decade.

In fact, the major volunteer efforts of the sixties are still in existence: Peace Corps and Volunteers In Service to America (VISTA). Despite budget cuts during the Reagan years, the Peace Corps continues to be a very successful and even highly competitive program. In 1988, the Peace Corps received 18,000 applicants and accepted only 6,000 volunteers. The lives of the more than 125,000 Americans returning from the Peace Corps are the best available measures of success. Following Harvard and Yale Universities, Peace Corps alumni rank third among members of Congress.

VISTA, the "domestic Peace Corps," has an annual budget of approximately $20 million and typically enlists 2,500 volunteers per service year. Its volunteers generally work in distressed urban and rural areas in public health clinics, low-cost housing projects, and farm cooperatives. Despite their low numbers, VISTA volunteers continue to make valuable contributions to neighborhoods in need.

A 1968 ACE Study:
Institutional Support for the Service Curriculum

Early in 1968, the Commission on Academic Affairs of the American Council on Education and the National Service Secretariat conducted a postcard survey of 2,106 colleges and universities to determine the nature and the extent of their support for off-campus service activities. Service activities were defined in the survey as those "(a) which contribute to the welfare of others; (b) whose rate of compensation, if any, is facilitative only; and (c) which, unlike work experiences, are not designed basically as apprentice programs."

Survey Statement	Percent Affirmative Replies•
(A) Kind of Support	
"We give moral support to the value of service experiences."	93
"Our faculty assists with training and orientation of students for service experiences."	63
"We pay one or more persons to coordinate service activities of students."	28
"We award academic credit for qualifying service experiences."	13
"We offer financial support to permit students to undertake service experiences."	23

Affirmative Replies to Survey Statements (A)	Number of Institutions Replying
To all five	25
To any four	68
To any three	127
To any two	207
To any one	177
No statement	19
Total	**623**

	Percent Affirmative Replies•
(B) Campuses with Identifiable Person in Charge	87

Position of Person in Charge	Percent
Dean	43
Other administrator	19
Chaplain/religious affairs	9
Faculty member	9
Director of student activities	9
Service coordinator	5
President	4
Student	1
Title not given	1

• Replies received by the end of February 1968, breakdown as shown above.

Reprinted from Educational Record, *American Council on Education, Spring 1968, p. 2.*

Collegiate Community Service:

The Status of Public and Community Service at Selected Colleges and Universities

Marc J. Ventresca and Anna L. Waring
with Jeanne Wahl Halleck, Saphira M. Baker
and Melissa Auchard

Prepared for Campus Compact:
Project for Public and Community Service

*A survey of college and university activities in public service
confirms that a great deal of activity is occurring at campuses
across the country. The analysis, done by Stanford University,
shows different ways that institutions can support student involvement in public service. Reprinted with permission from
Campus Compact, Education Commission of the States, January
1987.*

PUBLIC SERVICE — voluntary and mandatory — by students is
coming to the fore in many discussions. One image of college
students of the 1980s is that they are apathetic, careerist and overly
specialized. Another is that today's college students have found
new ways to become involved with and committed to issues beyond
their own personal needs and concerns. The debate about the
commitment of college students has raised a number of important
questions: Have levels of student interest and involvement in
public service work — as volunteers, in internships, or as careers —
changed in recent years? Do students commit some part of their
days to public service activity, above and beyond time needed for
coursework, other degree requirements, employment, and family

responsibilities? What can and should institutions of higher education do to encourage and support student initiatives and participation in public service? These and similar questions led the Campus Compact in 1986 to undertake a review of the public service enterprise among its institutions.

Campus Compact: The Project for Public and Community Service is a coalition of over 120 college and university presidents committed to increasing the number of students involved in public service and the variety of public service activities and initiatives on campuses across the country. Public service encompasses a wide array of activities, including but not limited to, volunteer or unpaid work. The Compact, while supporting efforts to encourage all forms of public service, has identified the following kinds of public service as its primary focus:

- University-sponsored service projects,
- Service work compensated with financial assistance administered through colleges,
- Work sponsored by a community service agency,
- Church-sponsored service work where the goal is meeting secular needs, not proselytizing new members,
- Government-sponsored service work, including VISTA and Peace Corps, and work in the public sector,
- Independent community service or volunteer projects not sponsored by any agency.

Campus Compact presidents believed that their students were involved in public service but were convinced that more could be done. The survey[1] was a modest venture to establish some baseline understandings that would inform the discussion about the status of public service and related issues on individual campuses — financial support, service and experiential learning, and student connections with surrounding communities — and set the stage for broader, future initiatives.

Sixty-seven (66%) of the 102[2] Campus Compact members responded to the census. Briefly, the respondents in the sample are primarily small, four-year liberal arts colleges having student profiles and institutional resources substantially different from those of community colleges, large public universities, or other post-secondary institutions. About one-half (32) of the respondents are small colleges with combined undergraduate and graduate student enrollments of less than 5,000 students. Two-thirds (45) are private, four-year institutions. About one quarter of the respondents have enrollments over 10,000 (10% have over 20,000), and these include many state university campuses and several community college systems. The respondents display broad regional variation, with particularly strong representation from the eastern half of the country (19 from the Northeast; 6 from the Mid-Atlantic states; and 13 from the South).

The presidents of Compact institutions share a common commitment to fostering public service involvement on the part of their students. It is their interest in public service and their willingness to commit to the goals of Campus Compact that brought these diverse institutions into our sample. Because of this shared concern, generalization beyond this sample to all colleges and universities is not appropriate.

The report is descriptive and interpretive in nature and relies on self-reported data. Material provided by the respondents indicates certain trends in the level and type of commitment to public service, and suggests possible future courses of action on individual campuses and for the Compact.

A few words about the survey questionnaire are also in order. The questionnaire requests detailed and historical information about student participation and organizational arrangements. Much of this information was not easily obtained by the respondents. In many cases, the data simply did not exist. Very large, decentralized institutions appeared to have more difficulty in completing the questionnaire, although staff people at several institutions made extraordinary efforts to compile the requested information.

In addition, institutional definitions of public service informed responses. For some schools, service is what is done by students for the college or university, while for others it is what is done for those outside the school. These local definitions limit potential generalizations about service across all colleges and universities or even across Compact members.

The large number of non-responses for certain questions — the number of students involved in public service for academic credit, or data on continued participation — may be a result of several factors including the difficulty in synthesizing the efforts of decentralized programs and departments, the relative newness of formal public service efforts at some schools, staff turnover, lack of records, and the inevitable distance from independent or short-term student initiatives.

The questionnaire was best suited for colleges and universities with a traditional student population, ages 18-24. Many of our respondents noted the increasing diversity of their student populations — part-time and older students, students supporting families while attending college, commuters, and so forth — and stressed their belief that many of their students participate in public service activities of an incredible range in their home communities, essentially unknown to the institution. Due to the limitations of the questionnaire, the level of participation among such students was not recorded.

The local interpretation of questions and categories and the high non-response rates on certain questions, make certain reporting conventions desirable. Throughout the text, numbers of schools are reported, often with accompanying percentages. Unless otherwise noted, the percentages refer to the total sample of 67 responding institutions, even though the particular question may not have been relevant to and/or answered by some number of the schools. When the magnitude of the "not relevant" or "no answer" rates justifies mention, special note is made.

Some questions in the survey focused on faculty and staff involvement in public service. In general most schools (48 or 72%) encourage faculty and staff to become involved in service activities. These encouragements most often take the form of informal institutional policies, release time for service work, and consideration of service activities in tenure and promotion processes. It is important to note, however, that public service for faculty may be defined by the institution as serving on a university committee. It is likely that fewer schools evaluate faculty in terms of their off-campus service to the community itself. [*Editor's note: See in this resource book the 1988 Campus Compact survey results, which verify this assumption.*]

Thirty-six schools (54%) have created opportunities for service by staff and 28 (42%) have opportunities for service by faculty. There appeared to be some confusion about the intent of this question as indicated by the large number of responses in the "not relevant" category. It is likely that these figures underestimate actual campus conditions. Because the intention of the survey was to determine the status of public service activity among college students, little discussion of faculty and staff involvement in public service is included in the analysis section of this report.

General Dimensions of Public Service Activities

University Coordinated and/or Sponsored Projects. In general, all the respondents have public service programs either coordinated or sponsored by the university. Specifically, 51 schools (76%) have voluntary student groups with some institutional support that provide service in the community and/or public sector. Forty-five schools (67%) have students working in collaboration with faculty and administrators in comparable independent projects. The range, vitality, and success of these efforts are enormous, involving students in everything from traditional fraternity/sorority charity drives to campus governance activities; from Big Brother/Sister programs to highly sophisticated efforts to provide clinical legal services to a disadvantaged surrounding community. In addition, students at 22 schools (33%) provide service through projects that do not fall neatly under either the categories of independent student group efforts or student/faculty/administration collaboration such as working with agencies and political groups on short-term projects like blood drives or fasts.

Two-thirds of the schools (45) provide an information clearing-house of public service opportunities at the community or governmental level. These off-campus activities are administered through public service programs at a majority of the schools. Only three schools supported no external opportunities, and 55% (37) had at least three.

Internships. Internships provide opportunities for students to engage in independent service learning, contribute in local community agencies, or work in the public sector. Almost four-fifths (52) of the schools offer internships through academic departments, at both the community and government level. In addition, over one-half (38) of the schools have university-sponsored internships as diverse as work in science museums, centers for those with mental or physical disabilities, and the Organization of American States.

Involvement with local, state, and federal government through internships is well developed, with two-thirds of the schools reporting that their students have held internships at all levels of government. There is an impressive range of opportunities, from work with local planning commissions and school districts to summer internships on Capitol Hill. Students work, for example, in public health agencies, the Veterans Administration, the juvenile justice system and the Forest Service. Thirty-two schools, nearly half, noted still other sorts of public service internships.

Student-Initiated Public Service Efforts. On most campuses, an especially vibrant part of the public service enterprise is student involvement in community service projects independent of any campus organization or agency. These activities include such things as: organizing voter registration drives, tutoring students in local communities, and collecting food and clothing for the needy during the holiday season. In fact, roughly the same proportion of

schools report student involvement in public service through independent mechanisms as through campus-sponsored initiatives and
internships.

Students at 34 schools (51%) work through service organizations affiliated with religious groups seeking to meet secular needs.
Fifty-one schools report that students work directly with local
community agencies in various capacities, and 45 schools note that
students work in independent service projects not affiliated with an
agency — individual or small group projects of varying duration
that bring the skills and energy of these students directly into the
community. These include such activities as tutoring local school
children and assisting the elderly in raking leaves or putting up
storm windows.

Twelve schools (18%) identify independent programs with
which they are closely affiliated that house public service programs
for their students. The exemplars for this category are Dwight Hall
at Yale, Stiles Hall at the University of California, Berkeley, and
Phillips Brooks House at Harvard. Twenty-nine schools (43%) offer other types of service activities not detailed in the questionnaire.

Institutional Incentives. The Compact schools vary widely in
the incentives they use to encourage public service. Institutional
incentives include formal admissions preferences or graduation
requirements, scholarships or fellowships, honors and awards, academic credit for what students learn through service, and residence
arrangements for students involved in public service.

The vast majority of schools (61, or 91%) have no formal admissions policy giving preference to applicants with public service
experience, though many do consider service in determining the
achievement and leadership potential of prospective students.
Brown University, Radcliffe College, Hood College, and the University of Virginia formally recognize service experience in their admissions processes in various ways. For example, Brown offers the
Starr Fellowships to students with a demonstrated commitment to
public service.

Similarly, 61 schools (91%) do not have formal graduation requirements related to public service. Of the five that do, four — the
Universities of Notre Dame, Michigan, Nebraska, and Illinois at
Chicago — only require it for degrees in particular departments or
divisions. Alverno College is unique in requiring that its graduates
demonstrate service experience and "effective citizenship."

The most common institutional incentive for public service
work is the granting of academic credit for service learning. Fifty-
six schools (84%) allow students to receive academic credit for

learning demonstrated from experiential activities with a service focus. Most schools impose some restrictions on eligible types of activity and allow credits to count either in the major field or as electives. Only five schools restrict credit to elective courses. Among the 56 schools that grant credit for what is learned through service work, only 22 reported the percentage of students receiving credit. Nine of those 22 report that less than 5% of their students take advantage of the academic credit option. The low percentage of students receiving credit may point to a lack of perceived legitimacy for learning from service-related work, the possible difficulties of arranging for credit, low student interest in service work or in obtaining credit for it, or a lack of awareness about the options.

Institutional Financial Assistance for Support of Service Work. Financial assistance from the institution for service work includes College Work-Study funds, scholarships and/or fellowships awarded in anticipation or recognition of service as well as other forms of monetary or in-kind aid. Twenty-eight schools (42%) report that they make use of stipends, fellowships, or grants as an incentive for public service.

Forty schools allocate some portion of work-study funds to students doing public service work. Thirty-five schools report that work-study students have off-campus jobs, although most report relatively small numbers (60% report having fewer than 50 students) in this category. Thirty schools have students working off-campus in public service jobs, though most (19) have fewer than 50 students. Twenty schools (30%) have no students in off-campus positions.

Twenty-five schools reported committing some proportion of work-study funds to public service: 8 institutions have less than 2.5% of work-study funds allocated for public service, 7 have between 2.5 and 5%, and 11 have over 5%. Several small colleges use substantial portions of their work-study allocations for service work.

Twenty-six schools (39%) provide scholarships or fellowships recognizing public service, and 13 schools provide some other type of assistance for service work. Six schools have loan forgiveness programs for students who enter public service work after college. These programs tend to be restricted to students in graduate and professional schools, such as Stanford University Law School's loan forgiveness program. Dartmouth College offers a loan forgiveness program for graduating students working in lower-paying public service jobs, and Berea College has no-interest loans for student working in the mountain areas of Kentucky.

Regarding public service opportunities after graduation, 36 schools (54%) have specialized career advisory programs that routinely provide current information on public service employment, careers in the public sector, or opportunities for "entrepreneurs in the public interest," as one university termed it.

Presence of a Center. Nearly one-half (33) of the colleges and universities have public service centers which play key roles in supporting student public service efforts on campus. Eleven of them have been in existence for eight or more years, 10 go back 15 or more years, and a few count their tenure in multiple decades. Where there is no formal center, one office often takes a primary or coordinating responsibility, most commonly the offices of student affairs (9 schools) or career counseling (7 schools).

The focus of the public service centers tends to be on encouraging service work in the local community (17 schools) or on a combination of local community service and work in the public sector (15 schools). Most of the centers (20 schools) perform multiple functions, such as coordinating activities and projects, career advising, serving as a resource center as well as housing student-initiated efforts.

Of the 34 schools with centers, 22 have both paid directors and staff, 6 have only paid directors, 2 have only paid staff, and 2 have other personnel arrangements. Center directors most commonly report to a university officer such as a provost, dean, or vice-president for academic affairs (10 schools); to a dean or vice-president for student affairs (9 schools); to some other officer such as dean of the chapel or vice-president for community relations (7); or to the university president (5).

Of the 33 schools with a more decentralized model of administrative support for public service, most report multiple offices with some responsibility for or contribution to student opportunities for service. Even many of the schools with formal centers have other vigorous programs located throughout the university in the offices of student affairs, religious centers and career service departments. This suggests that, even on campuses where there is a center, additional service opportunities are created and used.

Overall, respondents reported a role in the public service endeavor for the career counseling center/staff (39 schools, or 58%), for academic departments or individual faculty (55%), for campus religious organizations or independent student organizations (each 49%), for student affairs (46%), for other university offices (33%) and for co-op or field study programs (30%).

Participation. Slightly more than one-third of the schools (23) estimate that over 20% of their students participate in one or more forms of public service. More than half the schools have over 10% of their students involved. Another 14 schools estimate that 10-20% of their students are involved. Therefore, 70% of the schools have a core of more than 100 students involved in service activities. In absolute numbers, 27 schools indicate that more than 500 of their students participated in some form of public service in 1985-86 while 19 schools indicate that between 100 and 500 students did so.

Changes Over the Past Five Years. In reviewing public service activity over the last five years, 29 schools report an increase in student participation, while another 23 have at least maintained the same level of student participation during that time. Only three schools reported decreases. Of the 29, all cited renewed student interest and changes in the institutional program — usually both — as factors in the shift.

In the group reporting increased activity over five years, over half had more than 20% of their students involved, and reported the overall largest number of participants. Although these are encouraging signs, more than one-quarter of the schools report that less than 10% of their students engage in some form of service work.

What has changed, at least for some schools, are the reasons why students are involved and the form that involvement takes. Over 40% of the schools cited improved student attitudes or institutional or societal change as the reason for increased public service on their campuses. Many noted, however, that students are involved for shorter periods of time because of financial constraints and increasingly rigorous academic requirements.

In addition to changes in society and students' outlook regarding community service, 26 colleges and universities (39%) have taken specific actions which coincided with an increased number of students being involved in public service on their campuses. Fourteen schools (21%) have changed formal policies to encourage public service, 20 have provided increased levels of funding or other financial support, and 14 have centralized their public service efforts.

Public Service Infrastructure

This section describes the resources that support and build commitment to public service, including incentives and deterrents, governance structures of public service projects and the degree of coordination among relevant college or university departments. Infrastructure does not necessarily imply centralization of programs. The organizational culture at each college or university, and the unique history of public service at each institution, make it impossible to generalize about the effectiveness of any model overall, yet each offers an approach for potentially building institutional commitment.

Participation and its Relation to Infrastructure. Schools reporting upturns in participation tended to have a more diversified infrastructure than those reporting no changes at all. They offer more university-coordinated or -sponsored projects and have multiple decentralized offices with service opportunities. Some programs had clear sponsorship by the institution while others had very little; some collaborated with a number of other departments while others worked independently.

Schools that reported increases in student participation were also more likely to identify a greater number of institutional disincentives to public service, such as financial considerations, lack of academic credit or information about opportunities, student career concerns, or diminished public support and esteem for service, than schools maintaining participation. The high rate of perceived institutional disincentives may reflect a number of factors, including younger, more aggressive programs, renewed interest on the part of students, or staff eager to increase the resources available to students at their schools. In this respect, it is possible that increased activity may generate awareness of institutional constraints.

The schools reporting little or no change in levels of participation account for many strong projects and levels of participation, as well. They tend to identify a less diversified program infrastructure, a wider array of types of internships, fewer changes in the character of their programs, and fewer institutional disincentives. This may be consistent with the idea that these are established programs, maintaining themselves, and further suggests that they have chosen to concentrate resources in a relatively focused way.

Presence of a Center and Levels of Participation. In general, schools with public service centers report that having a center tends to increase students' participation in public service, though a center does not guarantee increased levels of participation. Nineteen of the 29 schools reporting increased levels of participation maintain a formal public service center; 12 of the 19 have both a paid director and staff. Fifteen of the 23 schools reporting no change in participation do not have a formal center. However, all three of the schools reporting decreased participation have formal centers, two with a paid director and staff. The centers in all cases tend to have significant tenure: eight or more years in place at 11 of 19 schools reporting increased levels, 5 years at 7 schools reporting no change, and 3 years at the 3 schools with decreased levels.

Disincentives to Public Service. Almost every institution identified at least one factor that inhibited participation in public service and most (63) identified at least two. Perceived deterrents to public service were varied, but the most commonly cited (47 schools, or 70%) were financial considerations — the need for students to work as part of their financial aid package, the high cost of college, the expectation of summer earnings, etc. Indeed, 35 of these schools said they had evidence that these were real disincentives to participation.

The next most common obstacles mentioned (by 33 schools, or 49%) were career considerations — the perceived need to find a track early and stay with it. In addition, the lack of academic credit was cited by 29 schools as a key disincentive. Lack of an organized program, lack of information about service opportunities, diminished public support and esteem for public service, and other factors were cited by approximately 30 to 35% of the schools.

When asked how to overcome these obstacles, 7 of the 34 institutions that responded said financial resources were critical, 6 said centralization of the campus effort would help, and 11 said that various combinations of money, centralized efforts, increased credibility, and academic credit were necessary.

Final Thoughts: How is Public Service Doing?

Evidence from the survey is encouraging in its documentation of both a wide variety of public service activities and trends in student participation at Campus Compact institutions. As demonstrated by the magnitude and variety of service opportunities at these schools, students are willing and anxious to connect with issues and concerns beyond their personal ones. Indeed, many institutions have witnessed an increase in student participation in public service over the last five years and a corresponding change in students' attitudes toward such activities. At institutions where a conscious effort has been made to facilitate students' involvement in community service, the increase in participation is greater still.

Students at the Compact schools are participating in public service ventures and activities in substantial numbers, and about one-third of the schools report increased levels of participation in recent years. The kinds of endeavors students engage in tend to complement or enhance their classroom learning and are consistent with educational and service missions central to colleges or universities. Often, the work is directly related to academic training — "lab" work, field experiences, or clinical training.

The Compact schools show wide variation in the structures supporting student initiatives. The challenge for an institution is to provide a supportive but not intrusive infrastructure — one that coordinates and increases available resources, while building on the pockets of local talent and initiative found around the college or university. It is also clear that students are continuing to take initiative in performing community service and organizing efforts independent of the institution.

The best incentive for public service seems to be an institutional commitment to service regardless of the structural form that this commitment takes. The variety of programs and approaches to public service indicate that there is no single best way to increase commitment to service on the part of students. Some colleges and universities have centralized efforts, while others support a more decentralized approach.

The institutional commitment to service can occur in a variety of ways. Some schools have formal admissions or graduation requirements. Others have a commitment to service as a part of the school's mission. Those schools with the highest level of commitment to public and community service also report the highest levels of student participation in service. There is nothing mysterious about this. Supporting service, financially and symbolically, results in increased levels of activity.

A number of schools suggest that the creation of public service centers and centralized resources can be associated with increased levels of participation. The survey demonstrates that well-coordinated but decentralized models also work. In fact, organizational overlap may be effective in reaching diverse student constituencies.

Issues for further discussion and research include how institutional policies interfere with attempts to increase the level of student participation in public service. The issue of academic credit for what is learned through service activities and the failure to allocate substantial amounts of work-study funds to students interested in public service work may limit the number of students participating in service efforts. Also, some schools suggested that rising costs and increased academic standards may result in students limiting their involvement in public service activities.

With this survey, we have begun a process of documentation that will help us better understand the ways in which institutions can create an environment that facilitates and encourages college students' involvement in public service. In addition, as more and more of these institutions maintain records of student public service activity, we will have statistics available to measure the effects of policies over time.

Marc Ventresca is a doctoral student in sociology at Stanford University. Anna Waring is completing her dissertation in Administration at the Education School at Stanford. Jeanne Wahl Halleck coordinates the John Gardner Fellowship Program and the Stanford in Washington Program, both based at Stanford's Haas Public Service Center. Saphira Baker and Melissa Auchard worked with Campus Compact at Brown University at the time this survey was done.

Footnotes

[1]The word "survey" may connote a more formal inquiry than this project represents. In fact, the survey questionnaire asked staff contact persons on each campus to do a census of programs and participation. The questionnaire itself was not an easy document to work through for several reasons, among them matters of organization and substance for which we take some responsibility. The sample was one of "convenience," as our statistician friends say — the member institutions of the Campus Compact. Finally, we performed exploratory analyses appropriate to the impressionistic nature of data.

[2]When the survey was initiated, the presidents of 102 colleges and universities had been invited and agreed to participate in Campus Compact.

A Message from Britain:
Should Volunteerism Vanish?

Alec Dickson

The founder of Britain's equivalent of the Peace Corps and VISTA reflects on the problems inherent in "volunteerism" — paternalism and the assumption that such activity is an add-on to normal life and work. He also compares the evolution of student community service in the U.S. and Great Britain. Reprinted from Synergist, National Center for Service-Learning, ACTION, Vol. 1, No. 1, Fall 1971, p. 1.

"IF A YOUNG GIRL of negligible educational background — in fact, brought up in an orphanage — and so near-sighted that she had to wear special glasses, were to offer her service would you consider her?" When I asked this question of the headquarters staff of VISTA some two years ago, there was a pause, then: "Frankly, no."

A pity. Because this is a profile of Annie Sullivan, who brought Helen Keller out of an animal-like existence of darkness and silence — Annie Sullivan, the teacher of the century, the miracle worker.

Of course during this exchange I was exercising a visitor's privilege to tease his host. In this field of volunteerism there is no more unanimity about aims in Britain than there is in America. The young activists here deride the concept of service as "papering over the cracks" (The equivalent phrase to your "social band-aid"): for them the task must be to get to the root of things, to combat inequality, to alter the system. *The debate will continue till the end of time, since in essence it is the problem of reconciling justice with love.*

Today, it is reciprocity, the mutual need of one human being for another, that removes the sting of paternalism from voluntary action. The distinction between giver and taker, between social worker and client, may have been clear in the past (though not in classical times — because both in Latin and Greek the word for host and guest is the same). Today, however, we are all clients, in one way or another. By the same token we all can be givers, potential Annie Sullivans.

Having for years placed hundreds of student volunteers in training schools and correctional institutions, we are now beginning to get delinquents specially released from their institutions to undertake rather than receive community service. When a group of young offenders went camping with mentally retarded children on the west coast of Scotland recently, it was difficult to say who was giving and who receiving. The "subnormal" kids were delighted at the arrival of benevolent older brothers, taking them, in their uniforms, to be naval officers. The young offenders were moved, for their part, to see that their past meant nothing to these children and that it wasn't only themselves who were disadvantaged: for the first time in their lives they were valued.

Volunteerism has hitherto implied something extra and optional. It has been undertaken at the weekend, after retirement even, or — in the school and college context — after classes, during vacation, or upon graduation. In short, after serious business is completed. *I look forward to a day when volunteerism will vanish — and become an added dimension of a person's work, an extension of normal living.* Postal carriers in one area of London have said to the social workers at the city hall: "If you want to know who is in need, we will gladly tell you because we know the households who are in trouble." In effect they become volunteer outriders for the social work agencies — not as something quite separate from their normal work but rather through a new interpretation of their role.

Asked by a firm to deepen the social awareness of their managerial trainees, we attached a 20-year-old salesman to a subnormality hospital's therapy unit. After working for a week alongside patients at the desperately dull and repetitive tasks allotted to them, he then spent a day in the public library researching local manufactured products. Two weeks later he returned to the hospital, having secured a dozen really stimulating light assembly contracts, all within the patients' capacity. Now for the first time the patients are experiencing genuine therapy, a small amount of money is coming into the hospital's funds — and the young man himself is suddenly aware of the application of his commercial training to social needs and of a new meaning to after-sales service.

So, at last, to what is happening in colleges and schools. In my view, too much fund-raising by sponsored walks, too little action that reflects the intellectual potential of students. Community service in British schools has been excessively oriented towards helping the old and handicapped: yours, perhaps excessively towards help-ing the young. Could we try a transplant?

Queuing for meals at that incredible 1971 White House Confer-ence on Youth in the snow-bound Rockies, I asked the more youth-ful delegates what made them tick. One 17-year-old from Phoenix had dedicated himself to preventing the spread of drug abuse in half a dozen local schools. A young woman, only 16, from some-where in California, was chairing a group committed to finding jobs for unemployed adolescents. And there was a 17-year-old Indian from Oklahoma to whom school principals sent their Indian kids who were in danger of becoming dropouts — because he, and he alone, knew how to persuade them to stay on. I salute them in admiration and wish we could import more of your pattern of youth tutoring youth into our schools. Such a move would enrage our National Union of Teachers — and re-vitalize the whole process or teaching and learning.

The system of academic credits is unknown in Britain, but slowly the idea of relating the actual curriculum to social problems is catching on. As enthusiasts for "relevance," we are pledged to marry learning to doing and service to study. The scientists are leading the way. Students in a Lancashire school — most of whom at 15 or 16 will have to earn their living — have developed a device which sounds an alarm if an elderly person living alone collapses in his apartment. In Leicester, high school seniors have produced a machine to provide stimuli at various pitches to help with the psychological analysis of autism and have constructed complete libraries of tactile street maps for the blind.

I repeat, how about a transplant of your experience and ours?

Alec Dickson, C.B.E., LL.D., is the Founder of Voluntary Service Overseas and President of Community Service Volunteers in England (the equiva-lents of the Peace Corps and VISTA in the U.S.). He also serves as the Consultant on Community Service for the International Baccalaureate Schools.

Commenting on the Future of Service-Learning

Jim Case

A call for service-learning educators to assist those in all types of experiential learning programs to raise ethical and citizenship questions with their students. Jim Case advocates the use of a service-learning philosophy and principles of good practice across all types of experiential learning programs. Adapted in 1989 from an article in Experiential Education, NSIEE, *Vol. 8, No. 2, pp. 3, 9.*

"Service-learning can continue to be a critical ingredient in post-secondary education if it adapts; it will not if it becomes rigid."
— *Robert Sexton*

ROBERT SEXTON SOUNDED THIS WARNING in the fall of 1979 in a *Synergist* article ("New Times, New Alternatives") where he reviewed many of the changes at colleges and in the field of experiential education during the 1970s. Service-learning programs in secondary schools can easily be added as well. The trends in the society, colleges, high schools, and the field of experiential education during the intervening years reinforce the critical nature of both the expanding opportunity for service-learning to provide leadership in the 1990s and the parallel threat posed if it rigidly adheres to self-imposed limits on its arena of influence. Consider:

1. Most service-learning programs operate completely detached and often with uninformed suspicion of the private profit-making sector of the economy. Their attention

is almost exclusively focused on the not-for-profit and governmental sectors.

2. The profit sector provides a large majority of jobs in the economy, will employ most of our students in the future, and controls many of the key resources for defining and solving social problems and responding to human needs.

3. Pragmatic employability concerns are important motivators for our students, as are their needs to explore career options which allow them to achieve meaningful social contribution in a personal way.

The effect of these trends in the 1970s and 1980s was a shift away from social concern and the human services — traditionally the areas of expertise of service-learning educators. Service-learning programs must adapt so that students experience the continued relevance of social concerns to their adult lives, or they will be rejected as irrelevant to current needs.

Our response to this challenge must address the meaning of service-based experiential learning in a profit-oriented economy, and it must broaden our traditional concern for the human services. We must cease to define service-learning as only a form of experiential education and begin to articulate a philosophy of experiential learning, based on service-learning principles, with clear implications for evaluating program quality. We must develop a set of general principles that are broadly applicable to all forms of experiential education, and strongly advocate these standards as principles of effective practice in the field. By consciously applying these principles, we can resolve the false dichotomy between career and liberal education and empower our students with the skills needed to succeed *and* the vision, service orientation, and sensitivity needed to lead.

The unique contribution of the service-learning perspective to the field of experiential education is its concern for the social value of the learning experience for the responsibilities of citizenship, for the value assumptions inherent in the situation, and for the conscious resolution of ethical conflicts. The following principles of experiential learning flow from these unique contributions:

1. A high-quality learning experience should meet the following three tests:

a. Does it have educational value for the student?
b. Does it have productive value for the individual, group or organization being served?
c. Does it make a potential contribution to the larger society?

While there is general agreement on the need for learning and productive outcomes, the critical question of social contribution is seldom considered except in service-learning programs.

2. Students should consciously examine their roles as learners, professionals/workers, and citizens in relationship to their learning experiences, their productive activity and their social contribution. There has been general agreement and substantial development in the field as to the need and methodology for helping students reflect on their roles as learners and professionals/workers. Only service-learning programs have focused equal attention on the citizenship role.

3. The ethical and value conflicts which arise in a learning experience, and the related value assumptions behind all choices, should be central concerns in all programs of experiential education. Only service-learning has made this a central rather than peripheral concern.

The application of these principles requires the development of curricula and methods which are concrete, intentional, and organized. While experiential educators may often refer to the social contribution made by their professional work, many programs still do little to assess the potential social contributions of a learning experience, or help students examine citizenship and value dimensions. Service-learning educators should make their expertise in these areas available to our colleagues. A 1982 report of the National Commission for Cooperative Education, for instance, pointed to an enhanced sense of social contribution as a critical outcome of co-op and a strong rationale for the expansion and institutionalization of cooperative education programs. Despite this, few cooperative education programs reflect these concerns in the structure of their programs. Those who have pioneered numerous models of enhancing social contribution have a responsibility to point out such gaps in theory versus practice and consult with those interested in bridging the gap.

If we are to heed Sexton's warning and adapt service-learning to the needs of our students, communities, and educational institutions in the decade ahead, we must recognize that service-learning principles are broadly applicable and invest our efforts in experimentation, development, and advocacy. It is time that we apply the lessons we have learned experientially as service-learning educators to the broad field of experiential education.

Jim Case is Director of Career Services at the University of Rochester. He served as President of the National Society for Internships and Experiential Education from 1983 to 1985 and has been a national consultant in service-learning, career development, and experiential education for fifteen years.

What If?
What Needs to Be Done and Learned?

Robert L. Sigmon

A simple challenge to the creative visions of community leaders, educators, business leaders, and policy makers to harness the energy of the young to address seemingly intractable social problems through service-based learning.

WHAT NEEDS TO be done?

What must be learned in order to do what is needed?

These questions, when asked in the same breath, challenge public policy makers and educational leaders to consider an epistemology for service-based experiential education.

For example, recruiting and retaining public school teachers is a thing "to be done."

What if teacher assistants were identified in colleges and universities to serve regularly in the elementary, middle and high schools of this country? *What if* these colleges and universities built this service experience into the curriculum? *What if* the schools rewarded the master teachers who were mentors for these students, who would then be available to expand the pool of applicants for teaching jobs in this country and around the world? *What if* these students worked at the tutoring, teaching, befriending, coaching, and counseling that needs "to be done" in the public schools? *What if* for every 520 hours of service, these service learners were awarded a $1500 tuition payment? *What if* these service learners were guided into new patterns of teaching and learning experientially? *What if* these students who then became teachers and remained in the profession for five years were assisted in earning a Masters Degree in Learning and Teaching via a new experience-based curriculum mutually supported by the public schools and the institutions of higher education?

For example, the environmental pollution and breakdown worldwide threatens all life. Monitoring, cleaning up and preventing more destruction is a thing "to be done."

What if environmental teams were organized by the colleges and universities to monitor streams, polluting factories, waste treatment facilities, the air, acid rain and indoor air quality? *What if* governmental units, businesses and environmental groups provided the work "to be done" and college faculty provided the experiential learning dimensions for these students while they were serving? *What if* for every 520 hours of such service and learning, these environmental workers would be credited with a $1500 tuition payment?

For example, the staff resources to care for the chronically ill, dependent elderly are limited and scarce. Providing for the well being of the elderly is a thing "to be done."

What if nursing homes, rest homes, home care organizations, adult day care centers, churches, senior centers and continuing care facilities created minimum wage jobs for personal care aides who are college students for six- to twelve-month work periods? Turnover in these positions is now about 100% a year. By making a virtue of turnover, building it into the academic calendar and program, institutions can receive a steady, dependable manpower supply; college students can earn money; college students can learn abundantly about aging in America and their own aging; and the well being of the elderly can be served in a goodly style. Since the agencies who could pay would be paying a wage, the tuition payout at the end of a six- or twelve-month period would be $750. *What if?*

For example, illiteracy could be abolished if enough leaders in the business, governmental and educational sectors would simply help organize the young and tackle the problem through service-based experiential education programs.

Adequate housing for citizens living in substandard settings could be provided if the young were challenged to serve and learn in this context of what needs "to be done."

Nutritionally sound patterns of eating and growing food, and the equitable distribution of food could be addressed by developing service and learning programs centered in what needs "to be done."

Helping all the citizens of the world learn how to express themselves via an art form could do much to create a just and free world built on mutual development and respect. For the inner spirit of men and women and children of all cultures is an oft neglected dimension of our definitions of what needs "to be done."

National Society for Internships and Experiential Education

Can we learn from the best of the national service programs of other countries, the Peace Corps, VISTA, the Co-op and Work-Study programs, the experiential education movement, the outdoors education movement, John Dewey, apprenticeship programs of the past and present, the creative learning programs now offered in many workplaces and from our own common sense? *Can we* invent new patterns of doing and learning in our communities, in our workplaces and in our educational institutions?

Can we assume that all men, women and children in the world have a right to knowledge, skills, opportunities to serve, opportunities to understand their situations and to do something about what needs "to be done?"

Can we assume that higher education is ripe for the recharge of energy and support which could come from embracing service-based experiential education? Research could flourish. Teaching methodologies would emerge and grow. Service contributions would be recognized. Financial solvency would be enhanced. *Can we?*

What do you believe needs "to be done?"

What do you see as the learning opportunities if we are to see that it gets done?

This is not a concrete proposal, but a way of thinking about doing and learning for college students. Nothing new is proposed here. In all the examples mentioned, somewhere there is a small program responding to teacher education, the environment, and the elderly's needs in ways that students are involved, learning (and getting academic credit) and sometimes earning.

What if? A service-based experiential education opportunity for all the peoples of the world awaits our leadership. Can we begin and continue where we each live and learn?

Bob Sigmon helped to start the service-learning movement through his work at the Southern Regional Education Board in the 1960s and at the North Carolina Internship Office in the early 1970s. He currently serves as Acting Director of the Wake Area Health Education Center in Raleigh, North Carolina.

Toward a Gentler Society

Alec Dickson

The twentieth century's international ambassador of service-learning asks "Why not?" to the idea of programs for middle-aged and older people, for those with disadvantages or who are imprisoned. Why not a Peace Corps in reverse for foreign students? Reprinted with permission from Action Reflection, Partnership for Service-Learning, Spring 1989, *pp. 1-3.*

WHEN THE JESUITS were active in England 400 years ago, they worked in secret lest they be arrested as heretics. Today British Catholics are serving as Jesuit Volunteers meeting humans need in Liverpool. Postponing entry into career or further study to discover something about social problems is not revolutionary. What is radically refreshing is the way Jesuit leadership views the experience. Associated in the public mind with dedication to long intellectual preparation, Jesuits are now saying something quite different. "We used to believe that through deep thinking we would arrive at new patterns of action. Now we wonder whether it isn't the other way round — that through involvement in action we arrive at new forms of thinking."

Those committed to service-learning who have served in Peace Corps or Community Service Volunteers may be inclined to exclaim "But we have known this for years and our whole frame of action is based on this premise." Rather than reflecting on how right we have been, it may be more valuable to see how others are moving in this direction.

Medical students at Hacettepe University in Ankara are given, as they register, the name of a Turkish family living in the slums and told, "From today you will be the 'medical friend' of this family: you will be there when the grandparent dies and when a child is born and if a boy is hurt playing football you will help him." Four years later, when the aspiring graduates mount the dais to receive the coveted degree, awareness of the factors that make for community health will have been acquired not from books or lectures alone, but from real life. And they have been learning to care from Day One.

I recently addressed African students about to start on a course in Maseru, the capital of the little landlocked Kingdom of Lesotho. "I've taken great trouble recruiting village youngsters, bright ones who deserve a chance as much as the sons of ministers in the capital," said the Principal, and added, "Tell them about Community Service." I began, "Do any of you know anything about sheep?" Dead silence. If you have been herdboys, guarding cattle on the hillsides, let me salute you, for you have been giving service to the community." Hands shot up and faces beamed. Caring for community property, looking after sheep and cattle, wrapped only in a blanket, had seemed to them something you kept quiet about. At this point I put forward two propositions. They could, as their particular project of school-based service, run a tutoring campaign for younger children working as herdboys, enhancing their prospects of going beyond village schooling. The second proposition was this: "When in a few years time you apply for an overseas university, possibly an American college, write in the space allowed, 'I was a herdboy' — for the probability is that the Dean of Admissions will exclaim 'Now *that's* an interesting candidate, he's done something with his life already; let's accept him!'"

So far we have looked at variations of the Study-Service theme: the Jesuits who are beginning to wonder whether service should *precede* long years of study; the University of Hacettepe where nurturing concern for patients is inserted into courses at the very beginning; the African high school students ashamed of their past as herdboys, not realising they could have been proud of the service they had rendered; and myself, hoping that Deans of Admissions may recognise that experience of practical service will enhance the student's capacity to learn in the accepted sense of the word.

But there are other implications of an even more far-reaching kind. About a dozen years ago an oil-rig in the North Sea caught fire. I envisaged Aberdeen University the day following the first explosion: the special meeting of Department Heads as the Rector interrogated them one by one. "Professor Olgivie, Chemistry, what do we know about the latest means of extinguishing fire at sea? Professor Forbes, Mechanical Engineering, what do we know about capping liquids under high pressure? Professor MacFarlane, Marine Biology, what impact will the discharge of oil have on our fishing fields? Professor Chambers, Environmental Economics, if the beaches of Aberdeenshire become massively polluted, will this affect the region's tourist industry? Well, gentlemen, let us meet in

24 hours time to coordinate the University's efforts in this emergency ... oh, and do consult your students because they may have a lot to give." A nice picture? It is fantasy! No such meeting took place. Life on campus was as serene as always. Whose responsibility was it then? The oil companies? The Royal Navy? The Ministry of Energy? Robert Napier College (a technical institution for higher education, enjoying a great reputation — but not quite as prestigious as the University)? In the end the appeal went out to 'Red' Adair in Texas to take charge of dowsing the flames. To me it seemed the opportunity had been lost for the University to practice interdepartmental cooperation, to demonstrate how learning and service can be combined, and how a University can be a resource centre of help to the neighborhood or nation.

Now that Ernest Boyer has recommended that no students be allowed to graduate from high school unless they have engaged in some form of community service, we may hope to see a vast increase in the quantity of service undertaken. But if the quality is to be enhanced, then there has to be reflection too. Suppose students visiting a mental hospital catch sight of an attendant giving a sharp slap to a patient. Anger undoubtedly will be expressed by the students. Do we leave it at that, satisfied that students have not only visited mental patients but caught a glimpse of what can happen in any institution in real life — and are expressing the 'right' feelings of moral indignation? Surely we must go far deeper than that. For how long have we been working at the mental hospital? Five weeks? Compare that with perhaps 15 years of service engaged in by the staff, day in, day out: wouldn't our patience sometimes be strained? Has any member of our family been a staff member of a mental hospital? No? Does this tell us anything about the nature of such work? Straight away discussion at a shallow level, in reaction to an incident in a ward, is raised to consider profound issues. This suggests participation by adults. Why not? One dimension of a partnership for service and learning could be the companionship and maturity which develop when pupils and professors, scholars and students, join forces to understand a problem, if not actually to solve it.

A partnership between service and learning could lead to other consequences such as a review of our system of awards. An essay competition for students at international schools offered, as first prize, a round-the-world air ticket. The response was poor. Was it because students came from rich homes and had grown blase about trans-global travel? Afterwards seniors were asked at Washington International School — "Suppose the first prize had been instead three weeks at an Afghan Refugee Camp or working beside Mother

Teresa? Would you have entered the competition?" A roar of assent was the answer, indicating that responsibility, recognition and even an element of risk were what they valued at their age. The notion that the reward for having tackled something difficult might be the chance to respond to something even more daunting may not seem directly connected with the change in the thinking of the Jesuits. But the development in *their* theology and the development in *our* planning may require that we revise many educational tenets, many images of service.

In the appendix to 'The Forgotten Half' (a final report from *'Youth and America's Future'*) there is a summary of the major youth leadership development models around the country. To an astonishing extent they reflect the influence that Outward Bound has had on these programs — outdoor adventure and the combination of companionship and being exposed to stress. I agree with the compilers of the report that we need intellectual encounters, adventures of the mind as robust and moving as the hands-on experience.

Nor must service be looked upon as a monopoly for young mandarins embarking on daring journeys. We do not want to see a date-line marking the end of what can be achieved through the union of learning and service. Now that universities 'du troisieme age' acknowledge the ability and the right of the middle-aged and older to learn, we should be devoting more thought to what *they* can contribute to society. You are never too old for adventure, it has been said. What forms of service-learning can flourish past the twenties and thirties? Unless we give thought to this, hundreds of thousands of us will be faced by a great emptiness. 'Continuing education' has entered the vocabulary. We must now demonstrate the need for experiences that are not only on-going but on-giving. And certainly the impact of community service programs at the college level throughout the world could be magnified enormously if we reached out to the disadvantaged and said, "Come, join with us, we need your help."

The mechanics of enabling more young people to combine learning with service in far-away places that may want what we have to offer will obviously be major preoccupations at present. But part of our service should be to study future possibilities. Has a moment come when foreign students might be ready to help *us* with our problems and discover that they have something to contribute to *our* needs? The implications of a Peace Corps in reverse could be immense. Have we considered sufficiently the findings of a score of programs that have demonstrated the impact on young prisoners and juvenile offenders of discovering that there are others worse off than themselves whom they can assist — and be loved by? The evidence that you don't have to *be* good in order to *do* good reinforces the Jesuits' conclusion that it is through the doing that attitudes change.

_____

Alec Dickson, CBE, is the Founder of Voluntary Service Overseas and President of Community Service Volunteers, the British forerunners of the U.S. Peace Corps and VISTA. He has been a faithful mentor of the National Center for Service-Learning, the National Society for Internships and Experiential Education, and the Partnership for Service-Learning throughout their histories.

Acknowledgments

Collaborative efforts are both exhilarating and hard. They require lots of people who are willing to go beyond their usual organizational structures and job descriptions, having faith and giving of their time out of commitment to the ideas and goals of the joint effort. This book has been such a project. I have been touched, humbled, and frankly amazed at the willingness of so many people to go that extra kilometer and have that faith to further the movement to combine service and learning *effectively*.

First, I would like to thank the 160 authors in these three volumes. They wrote their chapters for absolutely no payment or other compensation other than the opportunity to express their ideas and make a contribution to the effective integration of service and learning. I will not list all of them here since their names are listed in the table of contents for Volume I at the front of this book and in the table of contents for Volumes II and III which appears just before the index at the back of this book.

Second, I would like to thank the leaders of all the Cooperating Organizations, who graciously agreed to participate in this project and who generously shared their best materials to further the common good. Every week, I have received calls and notes of "We'd like to share this" from these committed professionals and volunteers. Please see the list of Cooperating Organizations on the inside front cover of the book.

A project as broad as this involves the collective efforts of literally hundreds of people directly, and thousands indirectly. It is impossible to list all of the people here. Some of those whose particular effort or vision merits special mention are listed below. I apologize in advance for those whose names are inadvertently omitted.

1. **For help in the overall conceptualization of this resource book:** Barbara Baker, Howard Berry, Herman Blake, Bill Bondurant, Jim Case, Ran Coble, Debbie Cotton, John Duley, Barbara Gomez, Ellen Porter Honnet, Carole Leland, Tom Little, Janet Luce, Sally Migliore, Suzanne Morse, Ed O'Neil, Sharon Rubin, Bob Sigmon, Tim Stanton, Michele Whitham, Rich Ungerer, and Hal Woods.

2. **For reviewing materials as partners in editing:** Barb Baker, Jim Case, Ran Coble, Sally Migliore, Ed O'Neil, Sharon Rubin, Bob Sigmon, and Tim Stanton.

3. **For creating the annotated bibliography:** Janet Luce, Jenny Anderson, Jane Permaul, Rob Shumer, Tim Stanton, Sally Migliore, and Amy Butterworth. See also the acknowledgments at the front of the bibliography for the names of others who contributed to this massive effort.

4. **For creating projects to stimulate writing, reflection, and analysis that contributed to this book:** Jenny Anderson, Lyn Baird, Barb Baker, Shelley Berman, Howard Berry, Bill Bondurant, Mary Boo, Ernest Boyer, Steve Brooks, Bill Burke, Jean Burkhardt, Jack Calhoun, Jeanne Carney, Jim Case, Linda Chisholm, Jim Clark, Todd Clark, Dan Conrad, Mark Cullinane, Cesie Delve, Lynn De-Meester, Alec Dickson, Bruce Dollar, Jay Donahue, John Duley, Janice Earle, Don Eberly, Russ Edgerton, Sally Ehrle, John Esty, John Formy-Duval, Marina Gallin, John Gardner, Dan Garvey, Mike Goldstein, Barbara Gomez, Susan Green, David Hackett, Sam Halperin, Steve Hamilton, Diane Hedin, Barbara Hofer, Ellen Porter Honnet, Cathryn Berger Kaye, Cheryl and Jim Keen, Morris Keeton, Don Kennedy, Jim Kielsmeier, Joe Kilpatrick, Kathleen Kirby, Mary Conway Kohler, Tom Lambeth, Mark Langseth, Larry Lemmel, Arthur Levine, Lee Levison, Anne Lewis, Kendall Lingle, Tom Little, Janet Luce, Joan Macala, Bob MacArthur, Sheilah Mann, Warren Martin, David Mathews, Kate McPherson, Ed Meade, Wayne Meisel, Sally Migliore, Suzanne Mintz, Terry Modglin, Suzanne Morse, Ed O'Neil, Steve Minter, Frank Newman, Fred Newmann, Bill O'Connell, Brian O'Connell, Parker Palmer, John Parr, Cynie Parsons, Jane Permaul, Bill Ramsay, Peg Rosenberry, Julia Scatliff, Ivan Scheier, Bill Seretta, Bob Sexton, Rob Shumer, Bob Sigmon, Tim Stanton, John Stephenson, Greig Stewart, Susan Stroud, John Thomas, Scott Thomson, Rich Ungerer, Ellen Voland, Jon Wagner, David Warren, Val Wheeler, Urban Whitaker, Michele Whitham, Rick Williams, and Rich Willits.

5. **For submitting materials for review:** Steve Babb, Dick Couto, Stuart Davis, John Farr, Nancy Gansneder, Dwight Giles, Kim Grose, Garry Hesser, Jane Hogan, Rick Jackson, David Moore, Keith Morton, Maggie O'Neill, Sue Roark-Calnek, Sharon Rubin, Steve Schultz, Mary Jo White, Hal Woods, and many other individuals from the Cooperating Organizations, from the list of authors in the Tables of Contents, and from the list above of those who helped to create projects.

6. **For special leadership and vision in the development of the "Principles of Good Practice in Combining Service and Learning":** Barb Baker, Howard Berry, Joan Braun, Charles Bray, Cesie Delve, Debbie Genzer, Barbara Gomez, Ellen Porter Honnet, Lee Levison, Janet Luce, Sally Migliore, Susan Poulsen, Catherine Rolzinski, Sharon Rubin, Carol Schneider, Bob Sigmon, Tim Stanton, Hal Woods, Allen Wutzdorff, and the 200 people in the Cooperating Organizations and the NSIEE Special Interest Group on Service-Learning who spent time responding to the multiple drafts of the principles. The list is too long to include here.

7. **For years of work on *Synergist* and other projects of the National Center for Service-Learning:** Lyn Baird, Jeanne Carney, Carolyn Mulford, Bill Seretta, and others.

8. **For assisting with the case studies that became the program profiles:** Please see the names of all the contact persons named in the three "Program Profiles" sections of Volume II.

9. **For reprint permission:** Please see the names of all the individuals and organizations listed in the abstracts throughout Volumes I and II.

10. **For help in dissemination:** Barb Baker, Bill Bondurant, Jim Case, Mark Cullinane, Jay Donahue, Michelle Duggins, Jim Feeney, Garry Hesser, Ellen Porter Honnet, Kendall Lingle, Sally Migliore, Suzanne Morse, Annette Wofford, and each of the Cooperating Organizations listed in the front of this volume.

11. **For the leadership to see the need for such a resource, the wisdom to support its dynamic evolution, and the patience to allow time for the participation of so many groups:** the NSIEE Board of Directors during the three years this three-volume book was evolving — Jenny Anderson, Tammy Anderson, Carole Carter, Jim Case, Jo Calhoun, Dick Couto, Elaine El-Khawas, Jim Feeney, Garry Hesser, Anne Kaplan, Carole Leland, Barbara Lilly, Joan Macala, David Moore, Ed O'Neil, Marie Reilly, Sharon Rubin, Rob Shumer, Steve Schultz, Bob Sigmon, Louise Stone, Deborah Wailes, Urban Whitaker, Hal Woods, and Allen Wutzdorff.

Last and most, I would like to thank the people that did the hard work that made this book happen: Barbara Baker, Michelle Duggins, Sally Migliore, Annette Wofford, Carol Majors, Lacy Maddox, and Ann Farmer. NSIEE staffers Barb and Sally dug into the vast files and materials collected at NSIEE's National Resource Center for Service and Learning, found many of the timeless jewels there, recommended and screened materials, contacted the Cooperating Organizations, tracked down manuscripts, proofread, indexed, and helped with the overall concept for the book. Michelle and Annette entered manuscripts and indexes into the computer, proofread, communicated with the Cooperating Organizations, negotiated with printers, and put up with my strange hours. All of these colleagues went beyond the call of duty. Michelle worked on a Sunday on the index, following Annette who'd been in Saturday, following Barb who'd been in the entire previous weekend. These are not just "staff" who did this as part of their jobs; they are friends, partners, and servant leaders in the deepest sense of the term. I am humbled every day by the spirit, care, competence, and commitment of these unsung heroes.

The other colleagues who worked wonders on the production of this massive undertaking are Carol Majors, Lacy Maddox, and Ann Farmer of Publications Unlimited in Raleigh, North Carolina. All three stuck with us when the project took a year longer than any of us dreamed. Carol Majors managed to squeeze work on these three volumes between other projects for progressive nonprofit organizations — work she does with a graceful intensity and a razor-sharp sense of humor as an expression of her own sense of social responsibility. Ann entered texts, found my editorial inconsistencies (errors that remain are mine), gently helped with inclusive language, and cranked out an incredible volume of work. Lacy worked behind the scenes in electronic transfer of data and on all aspects of production.

I would like to end with deep thanks to all these individuals who gave of themselves to make these three volumes possible and to the service-learners and service-learning educators who rediscover the power and gift of service-learning every day. A final heartfelt thanks to my husband Ran Coble and to Barb Baker, Jim Case, Michelle Duggins, John Duley, Pam Kohl, Sally Migliore, Suzanne Morse, Bob Sigmon, Sharon Rubin, Tim Stanton, and Annette Wofford for their encouragement, faith, and ideas throughout this labor of their love.

—Jane Kendall
Executive Director
National Society for Internships
and Experiential Education

Services and Publications of the National Society for Experiential Education

About the
National Society for Experiential Education

THE NATIONAL SOCIETY FOR EXPERIENTIAL EDUCATION is a national resource center and professional association that supports the use of *learning through experience* for civic and social responsibility, intellectual development, cross-cultural awareness, moral/ethical development, career exploration, and personal growth.

NSEE's mission: As a community of individuals, institutions, and organizations, NSEE is committed to fostering the effective use of experience as an integral part of education, in order to empower learners and promote the common good.

NSEE's goals are:
- to advocate for the effective use of experiential learning throughout the educational system and the larger community;
- to disseminate information on principles of good practice and on innovations in the field;
- to enhance professional growth and leadership development in the field;
- to encourage the development and dissemination of related research and theory.

Experiential education includes community and public service when combined with learning, internships, field studies, intercultural programs, leadership development, cooperative education, experiential learning in the classroom, outdoor education, and all forms of active learning.

NSEE's services include conferences, workshops, publications, newsletters, the National Resource Center on Service and Learning, professional network services, and in-depth consulting for program and institutional planning. See the following pages for membership information and a publications list.

NSEE was founded in 1971 as the National Center for Public Service Internship Programs and the Society for Field Experience Education. NSEE's national office is in Raleigh, North Carolina.

What are NSEE's Services?

Experiential Education Newsletter – Current issues, new publications and programs, research results, legislation, opportunities for professional development, funding. Published bi-monthly.

National and Regional Conferences – Newcomers and advanced experiential educators gather for the exchange of ideas and materials, professional support and development, state-of-the-art discussions. Ask about dates for the next national and regional conferences.

Publications – Papers and books examining key issues and sound practices in experiential education, a three-volume resource book on service-learning, a directory of internships for learners of all ages, "how to" guides, sourcebooks for educational pacesetters. See order form on pages 648-651. NSEE members get a 30-40% discount.

Information on Programs, Practices, Research and Policies – NSEE houses the National Resource Center on Service and Learning, the comprehensive national clearinghouse for information on all aspects of combining learning with community and public service — history, rationales, policy issues, syllabi, research, design and administration of sound programs for particular fields and client groups, sample program materials and forms, and professional and faculty development.

Consulting Services – Assistance in assessing your needs and referrals to experienced consultants. Help available for program planning and evaluation, course development, institutional planning, faculty workshops, and other on-site needs.

National Talent Bank – NSEE sponsors the national talent bank of faculty, administrators, and program directors knowledgeable about the practical and conceptual aspects of effectively combining service and learning. They volunteer their expertise to help you with your planning. The *NSEE Membership Directory* also serves as a continuous source of contacts for members.

Special Interest Groups – Opportunities for professional leadership and support. These interest groups and committees provide forums for discussions about community and public service-learning, career development, cooperative education, cross-cultural learning, learning theories, arts and culture, human ecology and environmental studies, research, publications, conference planning and the special needs of faculty, internship coordinators, community colleges, high schools, and community and agency sponsors.

Services for Agencies and Community Sponsors – A special subscription service to help employers and field sponsors publicize their opportunities and recruit qualified students. Ask for details.

Who are NSEE's Members?

NSEE's membership is diverse. Members represent public and private colleges and universities, internship programs, school systems, deans' offices, community service programs, academic departments (liberal arts, professional, and technical fields), high schools, cooperative education programs, state and local governments, museums, international programs, counselors, career planning and placement offices, community-based organizations, corporations, consulting firms, and interested individuals from all fields.

What Benefits do NSEE Members Receive?

EXPERIENTIAL EDUCATION newsletter — a one-year subscription.

Discounts — 30-40% off — on NSEE publications, conference registration fees, consulting services.

Membership Directory— a complete directory with indexes by state, by individual name, by school or organization name, and by interest area. A handy reference book for your old and new professional contacts.

Opportunities for Professional Leadership and Contribution— NSEE offers its members vehicles to contribute locally and nationally through conference presentations, publications, conference planning, research, the exchange of ideas and information, and outreach to other groups.

Eligibility to participate in NSEE Committees and Special Interest Groups— publications, research, community and public service-learning, career development, secondary education, faculty, international and cross-cultural, learning theories, cooperative education, field sponsors, internship coordinators, human ecology and environmental studies, community colleges, arts and culture, conference planning, and nominations.

Full voting privileges; eligibility for the NSEE Board of Directors.

Access to other NSEE services (see list), including the NSEE staff's time to select and recommend resource materials in response to your specific needs.

Special projects and services— NSEE members are invited to participate in national and regional pilot projects and other services funded by grants to NSEE for innovative activities.

Categories of NSEE Membership

1. Institutional, Organizational, or Departmental Membership ($250) — for colleges, universities, departments, established programs, secondary schools and systems, nonprofit organizations, government agencies, and corporations. Covers full membership benefits for up to 5 individuals from one school, department, organization or agency. This is the membership category for presidents, deans, administrators, departmental coordinators, and directors of established programs. On the initial membership form, one person is designated as the primary NSEE liaison; up to 4 other people can then be added to receive the full benefits. Additional names beyond five can be added for $45 each. National recognition is given to members in category #1 throughout the year.

2. Individual Membership ($70) — for faculty, administrators, and other professionals who are involved in or interested in community and public service, internships, and experiential education.

3. Student Membership ($40) — for individuals *primarily* engaged as students and currently enrolled in educational institutions. Students join NSEE to stay abreast of developments in the field, often because of a potential career interest related to experiential education and service-learning.

4. Sustaining Membership ($500) — for corporations, institutions, individuals, and philanthropic organizations with a strong commitment to the value of learning through experience. Sustaining members receive the full benefits of membership plus special recognition if desired.

NSEE Membership Enrollment Form

Please cut along dotted line and return your completed form to NSEE at the address shown. Duplicate this form if needed.

Membership category: (for one year following enrollment)

☐ Sustaining Membership $ 500   *Please check one:*
☐ Institutional/Organizational $ 250   ☐ New Membership
   Membership (covers 5 people)   ☐ Renewal
☐ Individual Membership $ 70
☐ Student Membership $ 40
   Total Due $____

I believe the work of NSEE is valuable and warrants a special contribution. I am enclosing an additional amount of:

☐ $20   ☐ $50   ☐ $100   ☐ $500   ☐ $1000   ☐ Other ($____)

Contributions are tax-deductible to the extent allowed by law. NSEE is a nonprofit organization under Sec. 501(c)(3) of the IRS code. Thank you for your support.

Why are you joining NSEE? _____

_____

Name_____Title _____

Program/Department _____

Institution/Organization _____

Address _____

City _____State _____Zip _____

Phone (____)_____ FAX_____

Electronic mail # _____

Dues must be prepaid. Complete the credit card section or enclose check payable to NSEE. Foreign membership must be paid through U.S. bank. If outside North America, also add $15 for postage costs.

Credit Cards: _____   **Mail to:** _____

Visa _____ Mastercard _____   **National Society for**
                                     Experiential Education
Card Number _____   3509 Haworth Drive, Suite 207
                                     Raleigh, NC 27609-7229
Expiration Date _____   Phone (919) 787-3263
Signature _____   Federal ID# 52-1010211

Publications of the
National Society for Experiential Education

The National Directory of Internships

edited by Barbara E. Baker. Complete descriptions of over 28,000 internship opportunities across the country for students from high school through graduate school and beyond. Also lists opportunities for young people and adults not enrolled in school. Openings in government, nonprofit organizations, and corporate settings. Divided by type of host organization. Complete indexes by field of interest, location, and name of host organization. 350 pp., $18 NSEE members, $22 non-members.

Quantity ____

The Experienced Hand:
A Student Manual for Making the Most of an Internship

by Timothy K. Stanton and Kamil Ali. Ten steps show how to acquire a satisfactory internship for learners of all ages. Contains chapters on making the internship the most satisfying experience possible. Also useful as a text in courses with internship components. 96 pp., $8.95 NSEE members, $12.95 non-members. Quantity ____

Combining Service and Learning:
A Resource Book for Community and Public Service

edited by Jane C. Kendall. Published by NSEE with the Babcock and Kettering Foundations and 90 other national and regional organizations. For faculty, administrators, policymakers, and students in colleges and universities and K-12 schools; leaders in government, community, or corporate settings; lawmakers; foundations; and others interested in community and public service, youth service, voluntarism, leadership, civic awareness, or cross-cultural learning.

Volume I - Principles of good practice; rationales; theories, research; public policy and institutional issues plus strategies for gaining support; education for civic and social responsibility, for cross-cultural awareness, and for intellectual, moral, ethical, career, and leadership development. 693 pp., $32 NSEE members, $38 for members of Cooperating Organizations, $54 non-members.   Quantity ____

Volume II - Practical issues and ideas for programs and courses — integration into the curriculum, recruitment, orientation, supervision, evaluation, school/community relations, legal issues, moni-

To order publications, photocopy this form or cut along the dotted line and return.

toring and assessing both service and learning outcomes. 528 pp., $32 NSEE members, $38 for members of Cooperating Organizations, $54 non-members. **Quantity** ____

Volume III - An extensive annotated bibliography of the literature from the past three decades. Edited by Janet Luce with Jennifer Anderson, Jane Permaul, Rob Shumer, Timothy Stanton, Sally Migliore. 81 pp., $10 NSEE members, $13 for members of Cooperating Organizations, $15 non-members. **Quantity** ____

Research Agenda for Combining Service and Learning in the 1990s

by Dwight Giles, Ellen Porter Honnet, and Sally Migliore. Document produced as a result of a Wingspread Conference, which sets forth major questions in need of research. 27 pp. Available at no cost. **Quantity** ____

Strengthening Experiential Education within Your Institution

by Jane C. Kendall, John S. Duley, Thomas C. Little, Jane S. Permaul, and Sharon Rubin. A sourcebook for college and university faculty and administrators. Includes chapters on integrating community service or other types of experiential learning into the institution's mission, curriculum, faculty roles, evaluation system, administrative and financial structures. 154 pp., $17 NSEE members, $25 non-members. **Quantity** ____

Knowing and Doing: Learning through Experience

edited by Pat Hutchings and Allen Wutzdorff, Alverno College. Shows how several innovative programs help students integrate what they know with what they can do. From Jossey-Bass, Inc., Publishers. 81 pp., $12.95, available only for NSEE members. **Quantity** ____

Preparing Humanists for Work: A National Study of Undergraduate Internships in the Humanities

by Carren O. Kaston with James M. Heffernan, the Washington Center, sponsored by the National Endowment for the Humanities. Results and analysis of a major national study of internship programs offered by humanities departments across the country. 99 pp., $8 NSEE members, $13 non-members. **Quantity** ____

Guide to Environmental Internships: How Environmental Organizations Can Utilize Internships Effectively

by Jane C. Kendall. A concise handbook useful for any organization that hosts interns. 48 pp., $5 for NSEE members, $8 for non-members. **Quantity** ____

NSEE Occasional Papers and Resource Papers

Concise papers on major issues to consider in designing, administering, or evaluating programs for experiential learning and community service. Includes papers on theory, practice, and research. $6 each for NSEE members, $10 each for non-members.

Occasional Papers   Quantity

#1   "Toward a Comprehensive Model of Clustering Skills" by J. W. Munce _____

#2   "The Immediate Usefulness of the Liberal Arts: Variations on a Theme" by J. M. Bevan   _____

#4   "Field Experience and Stage Theories of Development" by A. Erdynast _____

#5   "Students at Work: Identifying Learning in Internship Settings" by D. T. Moore   _____

#6   "Life Developmental Tasks and Related Learning Needs and Outcomes" by J. Arin-Krupp   _____

#8   "Community Service, Civic Arts, Voluntary Action, and Service-Learning" edited by R. Sigmon   _____

#9   "Academic Excellence and Community Service: The Integrating Role of Undergraduate Internships" by J. Wagner   _____

#10 "Experiential Teaching" by S.G. Rubin   _____

#11 "Strengthening Experiential Education: Three Stories and the Lessons They Teach" by S.G. Rubin   _____

#12 "Experiential Education as a Liberating Art" by G. Hesser   _____

Resource Papers

#1   "History and Rationale for Experiential Learning" by T.C. Little   _____

#2   "Field Experience: How to Start a Program" by R.A. Davis.   _____

#3   "Legal Issues in Experiential Education" by M.G. Goldstein   _____

#4   "Prefield Preparation: What, Why, How?" by T. Stanton & M. Whitham   _____

#5   "Monitoring & Supporting Experiential Learning" by J. Permaul   _____

#6   "Learning Outcomes: Measuring & Evaluating Experiential Learning" by J. Duley   _____

#7   "Performance Appraisal Practices: A Guide to Better Supervisor Evaluation Processes" by S.G. Rubin   _____

#8   "Applications of Developmental Theory to the Design and Conduct of Quality Field Experience Programs" by M. Whitham & A. Erdynast   _____

#9   "Internships in History" by S. Hoy, R. Sexton, P. Stearns, & J. Tarr _____

#10 "Research Bibliography in Experiential Education" by J. Anderson   _____

#11 "Environmental Internships" by R. Rajagopal   _____

#12 "Experiential Learning and Cultural Models" by E.L. Cerroni-Long & S.G. Rubin   _____

#13 "Self-Directed Adult Learners and Learning" by V. R. Griffin   _____

NSEE Publications Order Form

Please photocopy the order pages or cut along the dotted lines and return this page with the previous three pages.

Total cost of publications = $ _____

Plus handling fee (required) + $ _____

Includes 4th class postage and processing costs. For orders:

Up to $25, add $2.50
Up to $50, add $4.00
Over $50, add 10%

Plus 1st class postage (optional). Because 4th class delivery takes 4-6 weeks, we suggest you add 1st class postage. Add 10% of the total of publications ordered. + $ _____

Plus 6% sales tax (NC orders only) = $ _____

Total Payment Due = $ _____

Name_____Title _____

Program/Department _____

Institution/Organization _____

Address _____

City _____State _____ Zip _____

Phone (____) _____ Fax _____

Electronic mail # _____

Are you a member of NSEE? ❑ *yes* ❑ *no*

I would like information about NSEE membership. ❑

FULL PAYMENT OR CREDIT CARD CHARGES MUST ACCOMPANY ORDER. Make checks payable to NSEE. Credit card users complete credit card section. All prices subject to change without notice.

Foreign orders: Orders from outside the U.S. must be paid through a U.S. bank. For orders from outside North America, also add $10 for additional postage costs.

Credit Cards: _____

Visa _____ Mastercard _____

Card Number _____

Expiration Date _____

Signature _____

Mail to: _____

National Society for Experiential Education
3509 Haworth Drive, Suite 207
Raleigh, NC 27609-7229
Phone (919) 787-3263
Federal ID# 52-1010211

Table of Contents for Volumes II and III

Table of Contents for Volume II

Table of Contents for Volume III
Service-Learning: An Annotated Bibliography

Index
for
Volume I

Index for Volume I